Indigenous Governance

Indigenous Governance

Clans, Constitutions, and Consent

DAVID E. WILKINS

OXFORD
UNIVERSITY PRESS

Oxford University Press is a department of the University of Oxford. It furthers
the University's objective of excellence in research, scholarship, and education
by publishing worldwide. Oxford is a registered trade mark of Oxford University
Press in the UK and certain other countries.

Published in the United States of America by Oxford University Press
198 Madison Avenue, New York, NY 10016, United States of America.

© Oxford University Press 2024

All rights reserved. No part of this publication may be reproduced, stored in
a retrieval system, or transmitted, in any form or by any means, without the
prior permission in writing of Oxford University Press, or as expressly permitted
by law, by license, or under terms agreed with the appropriate reproduction
rights organization. Inquiries concerning reproduction outside the scope of the
above should be sent to the Rights Department, Oxford University Press, at the
address above.

You must not circulate this work in any other form
and you must impose this same condition on any acquirer.

CIP data is on file at the Library of Congress

ISBN 978–0–19–009600–7 (pbk.)
ISBN 978–0–19–009599–4 (hbk.)

DOI: 10.1093/oso/9780190095994.001.0001

Contents

Tables and Figures	vii
Preface and Acknowledgments	ix
Introduction to Indigenous Governance	1
1. Three Sovereigns: A Comparison of Native Nations, the Federal and State Governments	20
2. Political Organization B.C. (Before Contact)	31
3. European Intrusions/Native Political Transitions	50
4. Another Star on the Flag: Attempts to Create an Indigenous State	81
5. Modern Native Constitutionalism	124
6. Governing Systems	152
7. The Enigmatic Nature of Leadership	189
8. Citizenship and Membership	223
9. Electoral Politics	238
10. Political Economics	255
11. International Diplomacy in the Twenty-first Century	297
12. Indian Country Justice	312
13. Governments and the Media	330
14. Peoples of Alaxsxaq and Kānaka Maoli	342
Conclusion	367
Notes	383
Bibliography	437
Index	449

Tables and Figures

Tables

Table 3.1. Business committees in 1929	80
Table 4.1. Timeline of indigenous political incorporation activity	82
Table 6.1. Customs and traditions-based Native nations	167
Table 6.2. Indigenous governing authority	172
Table 6.3. Native nations with divided powers of governance	176
Table 6.4. Multi-national Native communities	182
Table 10.1. Recent tax revenue collections	265

Figures

Figure 7.1. Tribal leadership in the twenty-first century	194
Figure 10.1. GGR trending FY00–FY20	268
Figure 10.2. FY16–FY20 gaming revenues by range	269
Figure 12.1. Integration of federal, state, and Tribal court systems in the United States	318

Preface and Acknowledgments

I have been building toward writing this book for just over forty years. In the fall of 1980, I began a hot pursuit of a master's degree in political science and federal Indian policy at the University of Arizona. At that time, this was a new and unique program created and led by Vine Deloria Jr. (Standing Rock Lakota), the leading Indigenous political and legal theoretician of his generation. It was an intense two-year crash course in Native treaties and diplomacy, federal Indian policy and law, and other topics designed to prepare students to actively engage with their own Native governments and other political bodies as well as intergovernmental affairs. That time with Deloria set me on the intellectual path on which I have been traveling ever since.

Before I returned to graduate school to pursue my PhD. in political science at the University of North Carolina-Chapel Hill in 1990, I had the good fortune to teach for three years at Navajo Community College (now Diné College)—the first Tribally controlled college within the U.S. boundaries. From 1984 to 1986, I taught in the Navajo and Indian Studies Department where I developed my first course on Native Government titled, not surprisingly, Navajo Tribal Government. The research conducted in preparing and offering that course, along with the experience of working with the (mostly) Diné students, led to the publication of my first book, *Diné Bibeehaaz'ánii: A Handbook of Navajo Government*, published in 1987 by Diné College's outstanding press, Navajo Community College Press.

I have been consumed by the study of Native governments since that time and have continued to teach and write about them at other universities that have hosted me since my time in Dinétah—the University of Arizona, the University of Minnesota, and presently the University of Richmond. Many of my lessons and insights are reflected in my previous works, such as *Tribes, Treaties, and Constitutional Tribulations* (with Vine Deloria Jr., 1999), *The Navajo Political Experience*, 4th ed. (2013), *American Indian Politics and the American Political System*, 4th ed. (with Heidi K. Stark, 2018), and my two-volume study *Documents of Native American Political Development: 1500s–1933* (2009) and *Documents of Native American Political Development: 1933 to Present* (2019).

With nearly six hundred distinctive Indigenous governments located within what is now the United States, my best hope is to produce a general, yet critical examination of the origins, evolution, and functions of a select number of Native governing and kinship systems from the pre-contact era to the present. It will, of necessity, be a comparative and illustrative analysis of the contents of these political systems. I will also review Native governing structures and distributions of power, provide examples of policy matters that are included in Tribal governing documents, and detail how and why Indigenous governing systems are continually modified, amended, or revised. I also intend to critically examine the vital role of Native court systems, where relevant—as not all Native nations have judicial systems—in interpreting a Native nation's organic documents, its statutes or ordinances, and how those legal systems address key social, economic, and, in particular, cultural issues.

The book is written with a broad set of audiences in mind. Although I am a comparative political scientist by training, I examine topics such as federalism, political development, electoral systems, and constitutionalism so that the work should have merit for Native governmental personnel, students of philosophy, anthropologists, historians, and those in the fields of Native American Studies, international Indigenous Studies, federal Indian law, and constitutional law. By the very nature of the subject matter, it is interdisciplinarity and it is my hope that it will be of interest and use to specialists and non-specialists alike.

I am deeply indebted to friends, colleagues, Tribal leaders, and experts who have contributed to this book's final form. First, and as always, to Vine Deloria Jr., my friend and mentor, who brilliantly authored numerous works that provided the concepts, strategies, and ideas on what Native nations might consider as they sought to stabilize and strengthen their governing bodies internally, and how they might improve their diplomatic relations externally. On a personal level, Vine was instrumental in guiding me through graduate school, helped me land my first teaching job, and invited me to be his co-author on two books.

I thank the following Native political leaders who were kind enough to sit down with me for interviews or respond by phone or via email—Candace Bear, Chairwoman of the Skull Valley Goshute Tribe; Jay Julius, former Chair and council member of the Lummi Nation's Business Committee; retired Washington State Senator John McCoy (Tulalip); W. Ron Allen, Chairman and CEO of the Jamestown S'Klallam Tribe; Puyallup Tribal Chairman Bill Sterud; Deron Marquez, former Chair of the Yuhaaviatam of San Manuel Nation; Harvey Godwin Jr., Chairman of the Lumbee Nation, consultant and affiliated law professor at the University of Washington; Ron J. Whitener (Squaxin Island Tribe); Erma Vizenor, former Chairwoman of the White Earth Tribal Business Committee; Chairman Joseph Hamilton of the Ramona Band of Cahuilla; and John Gomez, staff attorney for the Ramona Band.

Librarians, of course, are essential in the lives of all scholars, as they help guide us to the data needed to complete our work. I wish to thank three in particular. Lucretia McCulley recently retired from the University of Richmond library but remains actively involved and has continued to support my research even as she

PREFACE AND ACKNOWLEDGMENTS xi

and her husband, Dan Ream, explore state parks with abandon. Vicente Garces, reference librarian at the University of Minnesota law school has kindly provided me with countless resources upon request. And Nora Hickes, reference librarian for the Native American Rights Fund, has been particularly helpful in providing data on Native communities that are home to multiple Indigenous groups.

The following academics graciously fielded my questions about the specific Native nations within their areas of expertise: N. Bruce Duthu (Houma) reviewed my book proposal and made outstanding suggestions that fundamentally reconfigured the book's structure and orientation; Loretta Fowler provided useful insights to deepen my understanding of the unique political configuration of the Wind River community; Matthew L. M. Fletcher updated me on key court rulings; William Starna offered the benefit of his expertise on the Haudenosaunee (Six Nations Confederacy); Tom Biolsi, an old friend, shared insights about the Rosebud Sioux governing system; my dear friend and former colleague at the University of Minnesota, Patricia Albers, provided me with useful insights about Indigenous kinship systems; Justin B. Richland educated me about Hopi constitutional development; Daniel Littlefield provided data and insights about the efforts of the Cherokee, Creek, and several other nations to establish the state of Sequoyah in the early 1900s; and two Australian scholars, Patrick Sullivan and Martin Mowbray, shared their critical research on the Harvard Project on Economic Development.

Special thanks to Phyllis Deery Stanton, my former student at the University of Arizona, who kindly shared the copious research she completed during the writing of her MA thesis, "The Indigenous International Diplomacy of Indian Territory" (1991). In that study, she examined the complex diplomatic work of over thirty Native nations in Indian Territory in the latter part of the nineteenth century as they sought to fortify their individual and collective status with one another and with the federal government.

My friend, Gabriel Galanda, founder and partner of the Galanda Broadman law firm, is a fellow student of Native governments who consistently—and insistently—asks hard questions of Native, federal, and state lawmakers, particularly with regard to kinship and disenrollment matters. And thanks to Joshua Slane, of Mvskoke Media, and Sterling Cosper of the Native American Journalists Association, who shared research on the handful of Native nations that are providing substantive freedom of the press protections for their citizens and Native journalists.

I am grateful for the friendship and support of my Dean, Sandra Peart, who oversees affairs in the Jepson School of Leadership Studies at the University of Richmond. Jepson has a crackerjack staff who work extremely hard at their respective jobs to keep conditions running smoothly for students and faculty. I am grateful especially to Linda Trent, Michele Bedsaul, and Cassie Price for helping

xii PREFACE AND ACKNOWLEDGMENTS

me to transition to Richmond and for their always kind, expeditious, and superb work. Stephanie Trent, in particular, deserves my deepest appreciation. She's been a stalwart supporter of my research, my teaching (especially when I had to transition to remote teaching at the onset of the pandemic!), and the administrative work I do in Jepson.

This is the third book I have produced with Oxford, and I have been lucky to have James Cook as my editor for each one. His solid, professional support and availability to communicate when conditions warrant have been much appreciated.

I am also a proud grandparent of two lively lads, Kai David and Levi Sion, who live in Minnesota with their parents, Alyssa and Sion Wilkins. Kai and Levi, through Facetime, kept me laughing during our lengthy COVID-19-induced lockdown. My daughter, Niłtooli, and her wife, Samantha, are always focused on making the world a better place in their ways. And to my youngest—my son, Nazhone—who walked on far too soon. I'll see you down the road, Yaazh.

Finally, I thank my wife, Shelly Hulse Wilkins. She is a loving, funny, and patient partner, as well as an outstanding writer and editor. She made our transition from Minnesota to Virginia a smooth one and found us a home with the writing space I always dreamed of but never thought I would have. Little did we know when we moved in 2019 how important this sanctuary would be to the completion of this work. Her keen insights—often shared with colorful language—and our many conversations about governing concepts made this a better book.

Small portions of this book in earlier iterations have appeared in other works I've written and co-written, including *American Indian Politics and the American Political System*, 4th ed. (co-authored with Heidi K. Stark) (2018); "Blood Quantum: The Mathematics of Ethnocide" (co-authored with Shelly Hulse Wilkins, chapter of an edited book) (2017); *The Navajo Political Experience*, 4th ed. (2013); *Documents of Native American Political Development: 1500s–1933* (2009); "Oaths of Office in Tribal Constitutions: Swearing Allegiance, but to Whom?" (co-authored with Sheryl Lightfoot) (2008); *On the Drafting of Tribal Constitutions* (2006); and *American Indian Sovereignty and the U.S. Supreme Court: The Masking of Justice* (1997).

David E. Wilkins (Lumbee Nation)
University of Richmond

Introduction to Indigenous Governance

The early 2020s will be remembered for generations to come as a set of seasons marked by devastating climate-related problems; an explosion of race-related issues exacerbated by the public murders of many African Americans by law enforcement; an attempted coup that roiled the nation and exposed ongoing efforts to undermine the electoral system's ability to conduct free and fair elections; a severe economic depression that accompanied the pandemic; and, of course, the disasters wrought by inadequate responses to a global pandemic—COVID-19—that swept across the earth, killing more than 1.6 million people by the end of 2020. In the United States alone, 410,000 people died by the end of the year, just as the vaccinations arrived. Of the United States count, nearly 2,700 of that number (as of December 2020) were Indigenous individuals belonging to many of the 574 sovereign Native nations.

The Centers for Disease Control (CDC) estimates that Native individuals die at nearly twice the rate of white people. In a sample of fourteen states, the CDC stated that systemic inequities in areas such as undeveloped or underdeveloped infrastructure, inadequate public funding, transportation barriers, and lack of access to "health care, education, and other social determinants of health have contributed to health disparities that put Indigenous people at higher risk from COVID-19."[1] And since this early data analysis, additional research by the CDC and scholars confirm that COVID-19's impact on Native communities has been particularly debilitating and deadly, with over 10,000 deaths attributed to the disease by early 2022. Along with this large number of deaths, life expectancy for Natives fell by six and a half years, compared to a fall of three years for non-Native Americans.[2]

Comparatively, the risk for COVID-19 infections, hospitalizations, and deaths for Natives is higher than any other racial or ethnic group, according to the CDC. And two separate scientific studies[3] assert that chronic health conditions, a lack of federal data that often omit information about Native people, inadequate access to health care, and poor living conditions deriving from structural racism and inequalities that continue to pervade the federal government's policies dealing with Native people, help explain why the pandemic has disproportionately affected Indigenous communities.

Hardest hit of all the Native communities has been the Navajo Nation, home to nearly 400,000 citizens living on lands that are encompassed by the states of

Indigenous Governance. David E. Wilkins, Oxford University Press. © Oxford University Press 2024.
DOI: 10.1093/oso/9780190095994.003.0001

2 INDIGENOUS GOVERNANCE

Arizona, New Mexico, and Utah. As of February 2023, over 80,000 Diné citizens had contracted the virus and 2004 had died since the pandemic began.[4]

As the coronavirus crisis continued to spread in spring 2020, crippling the health and economic vitality of the nation, the U.S. Congress enacted legislation on March 27—Coronavirus Aid, Relief, and Economic Stimulus (CARES) Act[5] that provided $2.2 trillion to respond to the public health and economic crisis. One of the central elements in the act was a $150 billion Coronavirus Relief Fund created to help state and local governments address the severe economic shortfalls they were experiencing. Eight billion from the fund was earmarked as direct assistance to Indigenous governments[6] to be distributed between the nations. Those funds were particularly critical for Native communities whose economies had been crippled by the closure of many Native-run businesses, but especially the successful gaming operations—a $33.7 billion industry prior to COVID-19 that had helped stabilize and lift many Indigenous economies since the early 1990s. In May 2020, an estimated 700,000 Tribal gaming employees had been laid off or furloughed.[7]

Congress directed the Treasury Secretary, Steven Mnuchin, in consultation with the Secretary of the Interior and American Indian and Alaska Native Tribes, to fund the governing bodies of "Indian Tribes" as that term was defined in the Indian Self-Determination and Education Assistance Act.[8] Payments were to be made based on population and the submission of correct payment information. The most important element was whether or not the Indigenous community met the definition of "Indian tribe" as defined under the Self-Determination and Education Assistance Act. This act defined "Indian tribe" as "any Indian tribe, band, nation, or other organized group or community, including any Alaska Native village or regional or village corporation as defined in or established pursuant to the Alaska Native Claims Settlement Act (85 Stat. 688) which is recognized as eligible for the special programs and services provided by the United States to Indians because of their status as Indians."[9]

Almost immediately the question arose as to whether Alaska Native regional and village corporations (ANCs) were eligible for CARES money. ANCs are not federally recognized Tribal governments per se but are for-profit corporations established by Congress in 1971 under the Alaska Native Claims Settlement Act. The Act is also recognized under state law. Shortly after the CARES Act became law, the Treasury Department produced a form on April 13, 2020, titled "Certification for Requested Tribal Data" which included language indicating that ANCs would be eligible for a portion of the federal funds.

This language compelled eighteen Native nations, including the Confederated Tribes of the Chehalis Reservation, the Tulalip Tribes, the Cheyenne River Sioux Tribe, and six Alaska Native villages and others to file three lawsuits that were then consolidated into one case.[10] The Tribal governments argued that ANCs were not eligible for CARES Act funding for two reasons: (1) they did not meet the Self-Determination Act's definition of "Indian tribe," and (2) they were not a "'recognized governing body' of an Indian tribe, nor do they have such a body."[11] On June 26, 2020, Judge Amit P. Mehta of the District of Columbia District Court ruled against the Tribal governments and held that, under the CARES Act's language, (1) ANCs were "Indian tribes," and (2) for the limited purposes of delivery of public services to deal with COVID-19, the ANC's Board of Directors qualified as "Tribal governments."[12]

The Tribes' appealed Mehta's ruling to the U.S. Court of Appeals for the District of Columbia Circuit and on September 25, 2020, a three-judge panel reversed the lower court's ruling, finding that ANCs did not qualify as "Tribes" because they had not been recognized as eligible for special programs and services provided by the federal government for Indians and because they did not appear on the Bureau of Indian Affairs (BIA) annual list of "Indian Entities" recognized by the Bureau and the Department of the Interior.[13]

Kim Reitmeieu, Executive Director of the ANCSA Regional Association said in response to the Appeals court decision that "this ruling is a devastating blow to Alaska Native communities facing an alarming increase in COVID-19." She continued, Alaska Natives, like those in the lower 48 "suffer from a disproportionate number of infections, hospitalizations and deaths."[14] By contrast, leaders of the National Congress of American Indians (NCAI), the leading Indigenous interest group, were pleased with the ruling and looked forward to seeing the remaining $162 million in funds distributed to Tribal nations and Alaska Native villages, and urged Congress to extend the deadline for use of the funds to 2022.[15]

In October 2020, the ANCs petitioned the U.S. Supreme Court for a writ of certiorari in hopes of securing a reversal of the District of Columbia Appeals Court decision. They urged the High Court to grant certiorari "because the decision under review misreads the statutory text of CARES and the Indian Self-Determination Act (ISDA); undermines the self-determination of Alaska Natives; and threatens a host of federal programs for Alaska Natives that, like CARES, is built on the ISDA definition of 'Indian Tribe.'"[16]

On January 8, 2021, the Supreme Court granted certiorari. Even as this litigation was pending, Congress, after months of stalemate, enacted a second major economic stimulus package in late December to provide $908 billion as emergency relief for the American people and businesses. It also included much-needed funding for Native governments and communities in a number of areas: providing a one-year extension to December 31, 2021, for Tribal governments to spend funds previously allocated through the CARES Act; providing $1 billion for access to broadband for Native communities and higher education initiatives; extending $1 billion to the Indian Health Service for vaccine distribution and testing for COVID-19; and numerous other programs.[17]

4   INDIGENOUS GOVERNANCE

On June 25, 2021, the Supreme Court held in *Yellen v. Confederated Tribes of the Chehalis Reservation* that, for the purposes of COVID-19 relief funds, ANCs met the definition of "Indian Tribe" and were entitled to a share of the monies to help mitigate the conditions created by the pandemic.[18] *Yellen* is discussed in greater detail in Chapter 14.

Evolving Indigenous Governments

The devastating health and economic toll taken by the coronavirus in Indian Country brought into sharp relief several critical issues and questions that will be discussed and analyzed herein: (1) what roles do Native governments play in the lives of their citizens; (2) what kind of structural and attitudinal changes did Native communities devise to cope with centuries of persistent federal and state attempts to eliminate and/or diminish Native customary and kinship institutions; (3) why have just over 500 of the 574 Native nations opted to create constitutionally based governments rather than some other governing arrangement; (4) are constitutionally based governments viewed as more or less legitimate in the eyes of their own citizens; (5) what other types of governing arrangements are still present across Indian Country; (6) are these more or less effective than constitutionally based governments in meeting citizens' needs; (7) what is the relationship between Native governments (of all types) and the state and federal constitutional systems within which they are embedded; (8) what are the similarities and differences found across the four eras of constitutional creation, including the sixty or so Native constitutions adopted before the Indian Reorganization Act (IRA) of 1934, the approximately 130 created during the first few years after that law was passed, and those adopted by nations located within Alaska and Oklahoma after the IRA was amended to allow those peoples to create constitutions, and those generated in the contemporary era; (9) Finally, since Native nations face a myriad of complex human and civil rights issues including enrollment, law enforcement, civil liberties, sovereign immunity, rights of nonmembers, separation of powers, and secular or spiritual priorities, which form of Native governance has the better record of dealing with these and critical challenges?

As we seek to understand the history, evolution, and multi-faceted status that Native governments hold, alongside the intense conflicts between Native governments and ANCs, the coronavirus also exacerbated pre-existing tensions between numerous Native nations and state and local governments on the issue of whether or not Indigenous governments had the inherent right to lock down their reservations in order to stop the spread of COVID-19. In South Dakota, for instance, both the Oglala Lakota and the Cheyenne River Sioux Tribes set

INTRODUCTION 5

up roadside checkpoints in an effort to regulate entry into their communities. South Dakota's governor, Kristi Noem, demanded that the Tribes take down the checkpoints, claiming that they were "unlawful" and that they "interrupt the flow of traffic on these roads."[19]

Chairman Harold Frazier of Cheyenne River countered Noem by saying that "we have every legal right to do what we're doing. We're just doing preventative action." And he emphasized that the sovereign status of his nation, as affirmed in their treaties, upheld his nation's right to monitor those who entered their lands.[20] Chairman Frazier gained unlikely support when seventeen South Dakota congressional leaders joined in the fray by writing a letter on May 9 to Governor Noem. They sided with Frazier and other Native leaders by declaring that the state lacked authority to enforce a state law inside Indian Country. They further criticized the governor for her failure to work with state lawmakers whose districts include Native lands and peoples. They closed by urging that the governor meet with the Tribal leaders "to negotiate a resolution that reflects our combined goal of keeping all people healthy and safe."[21]

Predecessor Works on Native Governance

Indigenous nations, by definition, are the original peoples of the Western Hemisphere where they have lived, governed, and died since time immemorial. And as we shall see in this book's early chapters, their social, political, and economic systems varied widely depending on what part of North America they resided in. While they have had intergovernmental relations with one another for millennia, and since the latter part of the sixteenth century with European powers followed a short time later by U.S. powers, their internal social, political, and legal systems—largely based on kinship—did not consistently receive the attention of commentators and scholars until the late 1960s.[22] Even then, most of the writing was done by non-Native anthropologists, historians, and lawyers— not political scientists—who are only now beginning to turn their attention to examining Indigenous governments.[23]

In 1975, two works were produced by Native attorneys that focused on both the political and legal status of Indigenous communities: Rennard Strickland's *Fire and the Spirits: Cherokee Law from Clan to Court* and *Indian Tribes as Governments*, produced by The American Indian Lawyer Training Program (AILTP), directed by Alan Parker. Strickland's book was a wonderful chronological study tracing the evolution of the Cherokee legal system from its pre-contact status to its modern structure, a structure that fused elements of traditional customary law with Western constitutional principles. The AILTP book featured a descriptive analysis of the respective legal and political systems operating on

6 INDIGENOUS GOVERNANCE

seventeen Native reservations. The study was designed to answer questions such as (1) what are the strengths and weaknesses of Tribal Judicial Systems in relation to the Indian Civil Rights Act of 1968; (2) are Native governments prepared to oversee and regulate natural resource development; and most importantly, (3) how can Native lawyers assist Native governments to strengthen their self-governing institutions?[24]

In 1983 and 1984, Vine Deloria Jr. and Clifford M. Lytle wrote two stellar books, *American Indians, American Justice* (1983) and *The Nations Within: The Past and Future of American Indian Sovereignty* (1984). The first book critically assessed the origin and expansion of Native judicial systems; the second work was a detailed analysis and assessment of the impact of the 1934 Indian Reorganization Act on Native communities with recommendations on Tribal governmental reforms that would strengthen Native governing operations.

Sharon O'Brien was one of the first non-Native political scientists to write about Indigenous governments. Her 1989 study *American Indian Tribal Governments*, written at the behest of the *National Congress of American Indians*, provided a solid descriptive assessment of five Native governments and contained a useful overview of federal Indian policies that had severely impacted Indigenous communities.

Several case studies have focused on the governments and politics of specific Native communities: Loretta Fowler on the Arapahoe—*Arapahoe Politics, 1851–1978: Symbols in Crisis of Authority* (1982); Thomas Biolsi on the Lakota of Pine Ridge and Rosebud—*Organizing the Lakota: The Political Economy of the New Deal on Pine Ridge and Rosebud Reservations* (1992); James J. Lopach, Margery Hunter Brown, and Richmond L. Clow, *Tribal Government Today: Politics on Montana Indian Reservations*, revised ed. (1998), David E. Wilkins, *The Navajo Political Experience*, 4th ed. (2013), and Ezra Rosser's *A Nation Within: Navajo Land and Economic Development* (2021).

Constitutional development in Indian Country has inspired a surge of study over the last thirty years. Howard Meredith wrote a little-known book, *Modern American Tribal Governments and Politics* that was a detailed analysis of Tribal Councils as they operated within the framework of constitutions. Felix S. Cohen, considered to be the architect of the study of federal Indian law, wrote a memorandum in 1934 that offered advice to those Native communities that opted to craft constitutions under the auspices of the IRA. His memorandum was not widely known until it was released by his wife, Lucy Kramer Cohen, to Yale's Beinecke Library in either 1989 or 1991. It was published in 2006 under the title, *On the Drafting of Tribal Constitutions*. Other works include Eric Lemont, ed. *American Indian Constitutional Reform and the Rebuilding of Native Nations* (2006), Gerald Vizenor and Jill Doerfler's *The White Earth Nation: Ratification of a Native Democratic Constitution* (2012), Jean Dennison's *Colonial*

Entanglement: Constituting a Twenty-First Century Osage Nation (2012), Melissa L. Tatum, Miriam Jorgensen, Mary E. Guss, and Sarah Deer's *Structuring Sovereignty: Constitutions of Native Nations* (2014), and Keith Richotte Jr's *Claiming Turtle Mountain's Constitution: The History, Legacy, and Future of a Tribal Nation's Founding Document* (2017).

In recent years, several other texts have broadly examined Indigenous governments and their unique internal and external politics: Jerry D. Stubben, *Native American and Political Participation: A Reference Handbook* (2006), Miriam Jorgensen, ed. *Rebuilding Native Nations: Strategies for Governance and Development* (2007), the Harvard Project on American Indian Economic Development: *The State of the Native Nations: Conditions under U.S. Policies of Self-Determination* (2008), Steve Russell's *Sequoyah Rising: Problems in Postcolonial Tribal Governance* (2010), Laura E. Evans, *Power from Powerlessness: Tribal Governments, Institutional Niches, and American Federalism*, Raymond I. Orr's *Reservation Politics: Historical Trauma, Economic Development, and Intra-Tribal Conflict* (2017), David E. Wilkins and Heidi K. Stark, *American Indian Politics and the American Political System*, 4th ed. (2018), and Matthew L. M. Fletcher, *American Indian Tribal Law*, 2nd ed. (2020), a fine study of Tribal legal systems and the case law generated by them which includes a decent amount of data on Tribal governments.

One entity, in particular, the Project on Indigenous Governance and Development,[25] (HPAIED) and an associated organization, the Native Nations Institute (NNI) at the University of Arizona, warrants attention for the work it has produced for and about Native nations and their long-struggling economic systems. HPAIED was founded by professors Stephen Cornell and Joseph P. Kalt in 1987. As originally envisioned, the Harvard Project sought to "understand and foster the conditions under which a sustained, self-determined social and economic development is achieved among American Indian nations."[26] Broadly put, the Harvard Project and NNI personnel are concerned with the relationships between economic development, governance principles, and social well-being in Indigenous communities.

The principal findings of the Harvard Project that have generated significant levels of enthusiasm across Indian Country, some Canadian First Nations, and Aboriginal peoples of Australia are straightforward and simple—sovereignty is critical for development on Native lands, as is good governance, and culture matters.[27] Harvard personnel and their advocates frequently summarize these in three bullet points: sovereignty matters; culture matters; and institutions matter. In recent years they have added a fourth variable—leadership matters.[28]

In relatively short organizational histories, the two bodies and their catchy conceptual framework have garnered a great deal of attention within Indigenous communities because each of their four central concepts—deemed 'determinants

8 INDIGENOUS GOVERNANCE

of tribal economic success'—are readily recognized and embraced by Native peoples, especially sovereignty and culture. The cachet that the Harvard name embodies greatly enhances the effort.[29] As one critic put it, "The explanation for the attention the Harvard Project's determinants of tribal economic success command is, I suggest, to be found more in their staging or presentation than in their originality. The reasons I offer for this assertion concern the way in which the 'determinants' are cast. This is largely as an alternative to state interventions, including economic transfers. Harvard Project researchers are most emphatic that to end Indigenous poverty the answers lie within Indigenous localities . . . In other words, I suggest that the research appeals because of its match with localist policy."[30] Another factor contributing to the Harvard Project's successful inroads into Native country centers around its "dismissal of the efficacy of state intervention" which "parallels, and possibly nourished, the commonplace denunciation of government policies as failed left-wing social agendas or 'socialist experiments.'"[31]

Without question, the Harvard Project and Native Nations Institute have produced a raft of publications, educational programs, facilitations, constitutional resources, and other Tribal services that have merit. That said, a number of scholars and commentators,[32] nearly all from outside the United States, particularly Canada and Australia, have identified critical flaws and fundamental problems in the conceptual and empirical work produced by the two organizations, but especially with the Harvard Project. This extensive criticism may be attributed to two broad factors. First, the study of Indigenous methodologies as a viable alternative to Western methodological approaches to the study of Native issues is more robust in Canada, New Zealand, and Australia. Second, the Harvard brand is appealing to many Indigenous political and economic leaders and therefore is less prone to scrutiny in the United States[33] Dowling, for example, notes that "the Harvard model embraces Western-style economics, underpinned by an individualistic orientation and acceptance of authority based on self-interest."[34] Cornell and Kalt, the Harvard Project's co-founders, also, says Dowling, "tend to use uncritically concepts such as markets, enterprises, and westernized notions of economic development (their writings are littered with words such as 'progress' and 'productivity.'"[35] And she concludes by observing that the Harvard Project's "myopic view of the world that a society must take so that these conditions take hold (acceptance of the use of natural resources for economic gain, the resulting environmental degradation and stratification of society, to name but a few) is not consonant with their [Indigenous] cultures."[36]

Clifford Gordon Atleo, after reviewing the Harvard Project's urging of Tribal leaders to create fair dispute resolution processes, appropriate tax programs, and stable bureaucracies suggested that if Native communities established the kinds of economic and political systems called for by the Harvard Project "when tribal communities have supposedly freed themselves from poverty and government dependency, they then burden themselves with a new dependency: the capitalist market. In an age where efficiency is paramount and neoliberal 'comparative advantage' is dictated by the market, Indigenous Nations are likely to find themselves vulnerable to the uncaring whims of those markets. This dynamic has already played itself out around the world in countries that have officially 'decolonized' but have also retained asymmetrical neo-colonial relations."[37]

The most sophisticated and detailed critiques of the Harvard Project were written by two Australian academics. This is not surprising since both Harvard and the Native Nations Institute have invested a great deal of time in frequenting that continent in an effort to convince Aboriginal peoples that their economic and political paradigm is right for them. Patrick Sullivan, writing in 2006, took as a starting point the Harvard Project's original trifecta of prerequisites for development in Native communities: "sovereignty, good institutions (meaning, in this instance, good management), and cultural match." He opted to view these as "problems rather than solutions and asks whether they are reconcilable with Aboriginal political life."[38]

Sullivan then began by scrutinizing the empirical research that Harvard's researchers had carried out in North America; and then he turned his attention to how applicable those findings were to Aboriginal peoples. He found a lack of internal coherence in the Harvard Project's core concepts, and he had questions "about their practicality given our knowledge of Aboriginal traditional governance processes, and about their implications for justice and harmony in Aboriginal settlements."[39] In addition, Sullivan had a number of other concerns with the Harvard Project's concepts, empirical work, and methodology. The following quotes depict some of the more problematic aspects of the research:

- Cornell and Kalt (1992: 3) referred to deep analysis of data from 67 reservations, and Jorgensen and Taylor reported on the results of a survey in which more than seventy Indigenous enterprises responded to questions about their management, allowing the authors to make a 'multiple regression' analysis. However, neither demonstrates the relationship of the data analysis to the three conclusions reached other than to state that this is their conclusion.[40]

- They also draw on, they tell us, 400 man-days of research in a 'selected sample' of reservations over a decade, producing 225 research papers (Cornell and Kalt 1991: 20) as well as analysis of economic data from over 70 tribes (1991: 26). While this sounds impressive, many of the Harvard papers simply restate the findings of previous research. It is questionable, then, whether it has the power of cumulative evidence, or whether it has the status only of the original assertion.[41]

10 INDIGENOUS GOVERNANCE

- The problem is that the Harvard (and contemporary Australian) approaches blend the idea of good governance as organisational management with a different, though related series of processes, governance as political process, which is inherent in practice rather than in organisations or institutions. ....This is a consideration missing from Harvard analyses of cultural match, where blatantly authoritarian and gender-biased institutions pass without critical scrutiny (e.g., Cornell and Kalt 1995: 41–47).[42]
- There is another reason that the Harvard Project theorists tend to take a simple and instrumental interpretation of the term sovereignty. They are not concerned with political relations (although they have clear political sympathies) that tend to construct communities as largely self-referring and discrete nationalities, a multicultural perspective recently criticised by Benhabib (2020) which I address below with references to Kymlicka (1995, 2001).[43]
- It is important to understand where the Harvard Project researchers began when addressing good governance because it explains their conflation of governance as management with governance as political life. Their approach to good governance is founded in standard business management principles. To attract beneficial investment to Indian lands, risk must be controlled (Cornell and Kalt, 1992: 26). Where there is poor governance, there is high risk. Investment either is not attracted, or, where it is, then the investors will want to see a much greater return from this riskier environment . . . This is what the Harvard Project originally aimed to encourage: Reduce risk by good governance and attract investment to indigenous lands (Cornell and Kalt, 1991; 1992; 1998). The existence of commercial resources is at best secondary, and possibly irrelevant, in the Harvard conception.[44]
- The third point that the Harvard studies stress is that culture matters (Jorgensen and Taylor 2000: 2; Begay and Kalt 2002: 3). Development requires not only a measure of self-determination/control and good governance structures, but also that these good governance structures match with the culture of a community that is the development target. The concept of 'cultural match' has become the current mantra in many areas of remote Australia. The terminology is problematic. When we investigate what it is that the Harvard Project is actually suggesting, we find firstly that its researchers are not suggesting importing traditional forms of activity into modern organizations (Begay and Kalt 2002: 3). Yet this is the interpretation put upon cultural match by Australian development agencies and those community workers involved in facilitating community governance organisations. Neil Sterritt, an indigenous Canadian associated with the Harvard Project, is one such facilitator in his own country, yet his approach

to good governance is quite standard public affairs administration good practice (Sterritt 2003). The Harvard studies overall are concerned with transparency, accountability, the ability of the membership to recall the leadership, keeping good records, and similar basic matters. Similarly, the indigenous American, Manley Begay, who regularly tours with Cornell and Sterritt, explains that cultural match is not concerned with tradition so much as the principle of legitimacy (Begay and Cornell 2003). Clearly, this is why the Harvard Project is as attractive to government as it is to indigenous political interests. It offers a way to insist on standard governance practice in Aboriginal communities, and to do so in the name of culture and autonomy without, so far, addressing the contradictions inherent in this approach. Cultural match is a problematic response to every researcher's experience of indigenous voices—that development processes 'need to follow our culture.'[45]

- The Harvard Project scholars, on the other hand, avoid these difficulties in the fine print of their model where they stipulate that, far from importing traditional cultural forms, cultural match simply means having some form of culturally sanctioned legitimacy. In this way, they sidestep an important problem in their work—what to do if culture does not match; what if, indeed, as Martin and Sutton and others have argued, culture is the problem? The argument seems to be that, in traditional functional societies, culture legitimated the forms of governance, and therefore anything that legitimates can stand in for culture where culture itself is clearly maladaptive or does not exist in precolonial form. Legitimacy is the way out, so the idea of legitimacy itself needs some interrogation.[46]

The next Australian scholar to critique the Harvard Project was Martin Mowbray. While Sullivan focused on flaws in the empirical work conducted by the Harvard Project staff, Mowbray challenged the political and economic ideologies that provided the foundation for the Harvard work and the "methodological procedure that routinely conflate correlation with causality."[47] For example, in Cornell and Kalt's 2000 essay, "Where's the glue? Institutional and Cultural Foundations of American Indian Economic Development," the authors rely on public choice theory. A central feature of this theory is its reliance on the neo-classical economic assumption that "individuals are rational in the . . . utility-maximizing sense."[48] In other words, individuals constantly strive to act in their own interests. And in order for economic efficiency to be achieved, government—be it Native or non-Native—should be limited in size and constructed to maximize individual choice.[49]

Cornell and Kalt and the Harvard Project rely heavily on "rationality" as Mowbray points out, as evidenced by their "joint commitment to the

12 INDIGENOUS GOVERNANCE

fundamental value of individual choice and responsibility; faith in free market forces; commitment to economic growth; belief in capital investment as the main economic driver for development; with micro economic reform and cost or risk reduction as the means of attraction; central concern about corrupt management practice ('rent-seeking'); preference for civil society as behavioural regulator (self-regulation); and blame of the welfare state for encouraging dependency ('free-riding'). They also discount government expenditure as being a necessary factor in development."[50]

Mowbray then moved into a deep analysis of the data that Harvard practitioners gleaned from some 225 separate studies completed up to the year 2000—data thought to prove the effectiveness of the three core determinants that are the basis of the Harvard Project: sovereignty matters, institutions matter, and culture matters. Overall, Mowbray found that the empirical justification for the Harvard Project's claims "is weak," and that the limitations of their empirical data were so substantial that Cornell and Kalt should be far more hesitant to draw any firm conclusions. Below are the flaws Mowbray identified in the research Harvard completed up to the year 2000:

- [The researchers] use old data, vital sections of which are from no later than 1989, and some from 1986.
- Data on changes in income levels on reservations, a measure of success, rely on comparisons against a minimum income level established by undisclosed criteria. Increases determined this way might bear no resemblance to changes using other measures, such as mean or median incomes. Also measured in this way, economic gains on successful reservations may be out of keeping with those elsewhere. Indeed, Indians on the successful reserves might even have fallen behind non-reserve Indians.
- The Harvard Project researchers rely on a sample of just 12 reservations on which to base the conclusion about cultural match. The basis for inclusion of the selected reservations in the sample is undeclared, and their division into two contrasting groups is subjective.
- Other important information for interpretation of the data is also missing. For example, is someone counted as employed (another measure of success) as long as they are in paid work for only an hour a week, as in Australia? If so, how much does it mean simply to say someone became employed? Even more seriously, as far as the results are concerned, did the goalposts stay fixed during the period in which the data were collected? This was not the case in Australia where, in line with an international recalibration, in 1986 the number of hours Australians had to work to be counted as employed dropped from fifteen to one.

INTRODUCTION   13

- Data on high school graduation alone form a very limited basis for concluding that education is not a determinant of success. The use of college, university, or trade qualifications might be much more telling, especially when it comes to issues of leadership and management.
- Reliance on data from one adjacent geographic area (county), not necessarily Indian, is an exceedingly shaky measure of the strength of a reservation's own economy.
- The Harvard Project depends on a Tribe's written constitution as evidence of the strength of a reservation's governmental arrangements. What is in a written constitution is not necessarily related to the strength of local leadership.
- Statistical measures of association do not say anything about direction or effect, as the researchers insinuate. Correlation and causation are separate concepts, if two variables correlate this is not proof that they are causally linked.[51]

These are substantial problems and while they are derived from research that is at least twenty years old they are arguably still relevant because both the Harvard Project and NNI continue to draw upon the economic, theoretical, and conceptual data of their early work. In conclusion, Mowbray summarized his major complaints about the Harvard Project findings and recommendations thusly. First, its theoretical approach—economic rationalism—is inherently flawed because it omits four key analytic concepts—the role of the state, class, gender, and the ever-important notions of race and racism—that would make it more robust, timely, and comprehensive. These critical omissions mean that the Harvard Project "cannot take into account some of the reasons why past government interventions, many half-hearted at best, failed."[52]

Second, the Harvard Project also ignores a well-established reality as understood by criminologists, ethicists, and others operating in a capitalist economic system—that corruption is normal, encouraged, and endemic. This omission, says Mowbray, "is in favour of the conservative view that corruption contributes abnormal or deviant behavior and that this arises when natural or traditional social controls are dislocated, such as through state welfare transfers."[53]

Third, Harvard Project researchers tend to treat historic Indigenous communities as if they were idyllic and free of nepotism, selfishness, and other less than noble characteristics—writing as if these elements were all a direct result of Western imposition.[54] But a close reading of Native history shows that Indigenous peoples were not immune from greed and corruption, even if they had cultural and spiritual institutions in place that helped mitigate that kind of human behavior.

14 INDIGENOUS GOVERNANCE

Fourth, and most troubling from Mowbray's perspective, is that the Harvard Project's special appeal is fundamentally political. In other words, "It connects the principles of economic rationalism with indigenous (economic) development. Though they often ignore principles concerned with rights, Cornell and Kalt manage to do this in a way that resonates with indigenous commitment to self-governance."[55]

Finally, the issue of economic growth is also a topic, as articulated by the Harvard Project. Environmental sustainability is, of course, a critical concept for Native communities. But as Mowbray points out, "There is an important debate about the implications of economic development for Indigenous culture. The implicit assumption that growth is compatible with, if not good for, cultural preservation preempts this issue."[56] The Harvard Project's neoliberal orientation confirms that opening Indigenous lands to commercial development was the plan all along, and this explains their conflation of governance with management. The idea was to "reduce risk by good governance and attract investment to indigenous lands."[57]

And while such development, from the Harvard Project's perspective, theoretically upholds one of the essential tenets of the Project—that "culture matters"—the "culture" the Harvard researchers are talking about has less to do with Indigenous traditional values and principles and more to do with legitimacy, transparency, accountability, maintaining good records, and so forth: standard features of good public administration and management practices.[58] This partly explains why the Harvard Project "is as attractive to government as it is to indigenous political interests. It offers a way to insist on standard governance practice in Aboriginal communities, and to do so in the name of culture and autonomy without, so far, addressing the contradictions inherent in this approach."[59]

Each of the above sources is useful and has helped deepen our understanding of Indigenous governments. My study aims to shed light on how Native peoples and their governing bodies deliberately and mindfully organized themselves; examines how they came to have the governing arrangements they have today; and identifies and discusses key issues, factors, and actions that continue to influence Native self-determination. Since there are 574 federally recognized Native nations in the United States, not including the Hawaiian Native community— and 70-plus state-recognized Indigenous communities that are not included in this project—this study will, of necessity, be selective and general in nature. That said, armed with constitutional data from 500-plus Native nations, a bounty of primary and secondary data gleaned from those and other communities, and data gathered from interviews with Indigenous government officials, I am confident this work will be a thorough, reliable, and robust account of Indigenous governance across a large swathe of time and culture.

INTRODUCTION 15

Overview of the Book

Chapter 1: Three Sovereigns—A Comparison of Native Nations, the Federal, and State Governments

This short chapter highlights the distinctive political, legal, and cultural status of Native nations. I outline how these governments are broadly situated politically and how they relate constitutionally and extra-constitutionally to states and the federal government.

Chapter 2: Indigenous Political Organization B.C. (Before Contact)

This chapter draws broadly from historical and anthropological literature to show how Indigenous societies were historically organized via extensive kinship networks that utilized clans, reciprocity, and responsibility as organizing structures and principles. Key concepts of power, gender, order, rights, equality, consensus, authority, and leadership are also discussed as they were understood prior to the arrival of the Europeans. Several case studies are utilized.

Chapter 3: European Intrusions/Native Political Transitions

This chapter charts how the arrival of Europeans and African peoples, in particular, deeply impacted Native nations' population, economic, cultural, and governing systems. Case studies of the Cherokee Nation and several northeastern Native peoples describe some of the strategies these communities instituted to cope with their rapidly changing worlds. It also entails an overview of several policy and statutory enactments instituted by the federal government aimed at the forced assimilation of Native peoples, including institutions such as the Courts of Indian Offenses established by the Bureau of Indian Affairs, and the creation of Indian policy programs and business committees on reservations. Initiatives like these began in earnest in the 1870s and continued in full force until the 1920s.

Herein, I also describe and evaluate early Native attempts to construct new political systems to better address the daunting challenges presented by U.S. colonialism. Early Indigenous constitutions were devised by the Cherokee Nation in 1827, the Seneca Nation in 1848, and the Cheyenne River Sioux in the 1880s. Even as these documents were being devised, viable Native traditional structures continued. A survey instituted by the Commissioner of Indian Affairs in 1929

16   INDIGENOUS GOVERNANCE

affirmed that while Indigenous governance had changed considerably, strong evidence of traditional structures and principles remained in place across Indian Country.

Chapter 4: Another Star on the Flag—Attempts to Create an Indigenous State

This chapter describes treaty, policy, and statutory efforts started by both Native peoples and colonial—and later federal—representatives, that were intended to create a Native constituent state of the union. At least three plans were discussed—first in 1778 with the Delaware Nation, then in 1870 with several Native peoples in Indian Territory (present-day Oklahoma), and finally in 1906 when Native peoples in Indian Territory drafted a detailed constitution and pressed for admittance into the union as the State of Sequoyah.

Chapter 5: Modern Native Constitutionalism

This chapter focuses on the dynamic political, legal, educational, and economic changes that were begun during the Roosevelt Administration. John Collier, Felix Cohen, and Nathan Margold were the principal federal officials who created a series of policies and procedures—of their own accord and at the behest of Native nations—designed to revitalize Indigenous sovereignty and to generate greater cultural expression, widespread constitutional development, land restoration, and more relaxed federal oversight of internal Native affairs.

Chapter 6: Governing Systems

This chapter describes and assesses various forms of governance currently utilized by Native nations: Constitutions, Articles of Association, General Councils, Customs & Traditions, Corporations, Charters, and the like. It assesses the relative strengths and weaknesses of the various structures and examines the inherent tension between race-based and culturally and politically based governing systems. It also assesses the difficulties of governance on reservations that are the shared territories of more than one Native nation. For example, Wind River, home to the Arapahoe and Shoshone, and Ft. Peck, home to the Assiniboine and Sioux.

Chapter 7: The Enigmatic Nature of Leadership

This chapter examines the critical role that Indigenous leaders play in a nation's development, as they support the goals, desires, and aspirations of a community's members. While scholarly literature on Indigenous leadership is still relatively scant, the evidence thus far produced suggests that many Native leaders do not think and act in a manner equivalent to Western leaders. Factors such as their Tribal-specific cultural identity, an emphasis on persuasion rather than coercion, a community orientation rather than one based on individualism, and situation-specific rather than position-specific approaches distinguish many Indigenous leaders from their Western contemporaries. That said, the impacts of colonialism and capitalism have exacerbated intra-group and inter-group dynamics in many Native communities, culminating in questions about the legitimacy of some Native leaders that can hamper or derail political, economic, and cultural stability. Here is also included analysis of Native court cases where leadership conflicts caused significant societal damage.

Chapter 8: Citizenship and Membership in Indigenous Nations

What does it mean to belong to a Native community? Is there a difference between membership and citizenship? These and other questions are addressed in Chapter 8 where I look to shed light on some of the most fundamental problems associated with Native belonging, including blood quantum, disenrollment, and DNA testing.

Chapter 9: Native Electoral Politics

Chapter 9 provides a broad overview of how elections are conducted in Indian Country. It also includes discussion and analysis of efforts by states and local governments to deny or diminish Native voting power.

Chapter 10: Indigenous Political Economics

This chapter provides a general description and analysis of Native property issues, taxation programs, and Native gaming. I also analyze the relationship between Native governments and corporate interests, including those of multinationals that traffic in extractive industries.

18　INDIGENOUS GOVERNANCE

Chapter 11: International Indigenous Diplomacy in the 21st Century

Here is a discussion and analysis of recent diplomatic forays conducted between Indigenous nations in the United States (sometimes including First Nations located within Canada) and other Native peoples. While Native nations located within the boundaries of the United States were denied the power to negotiate treaties with non-Native governments during the major treaty era between 1778 and 1871, they retained the inherent political authority to negotiate treaties with other Native nations and are now increasingly exercising those diplomatic skills.

Chapter 12: Justice in Indian Country

This chapter provides an overview of how justice is administered across Indian Country. Tribal courts are featured and there is a discussion of traditional or peacemaking institutional arrangements, as well.

Chapter 13: Native Governments and the Media

The media plays a vital role in covering politics in societies. In Indian Country, the media occupies a particularly interesting niche since the U.S. Constitution's 1st Amendment freedom of the press does not directly apply to Native governments. Here we assess how the media impacts Native political systems and how these same political bodies sometimes look to control the media's activities.

Chapter 14: Alaskan Natives and Kānaka Maoli (Hawaiian Natives)

The Indigenous peoples inhabiting these two regions have fascinating histories and distinctive legal and political statuses. We examine the law and politics of these peoples and discuss current situations.

Conclusion

I close by recapping the major ideas and themes in the book and lay out some recommendations as to how Native governments might fortify their institutions

INTRODUCTION   19

to make them more just and useful. The relationship between traditionalism and cultural integrity is critical as Native governments look to more effectively represent their constituents, while at the same time exercise the capacity and political acumen necessary to deal with local, state, and federal governments, the corporate world, and the public.

1
Three Sovereigns

A Comparison of Native Nations, the Federal and State Governments

Nearly 600 distinctive Native peoples within the borders of what is now the United States continue to inhabit lands—their original territory or they had relocated either voluntarily or land by coercion in an effort to avoid constant pressures from ever-advancing whites. Retention of those lands, of course, has not been easy because there have been intense and sustained efforts of first, European powers and later the federal and state governments, to strip Indigenous peoples of their lands, institutions, identities, and, in many instances, their lives. As the original nations of North America, Indigenous peoples and their governing bodies are, by definition, the senior sovereigns by their longevity and persistence. After half a millennium of policies, laws, attitudes, and programs aimed at either their eradication or subjugation, they warrant recognition and deep respect both from their Native constituencies and from non-Native citizens, as well as from the local, state, and federal governments with which they must invariably engage.

This study aims to provide both the recognition and respect Indigenous governments deserve to be accorded, while at the same time offering a candid and fact-based critique of those aspects of Native governments meriting scrutiny. Governments, whether Indigenous or Western, are human constructions and, therefore, imperfect institutions. Thus, this will be a sober appraisal of Native governments, an endeavor to highlight history, evolution, and internal and intergovernmental problems, as well as to assess the structures and issues that complicate the efforts of Native peoples to exercise self-governance and self-determination.

Presently, there are nearly 90,000 non-Native governing units in the United States—including one national government, fifty state governments, the District of Columbia, five insular territories (American Samoa, Guam, Northern Mariana Islands, Puerto Rico, and the U.S. Virgin Islands), and over 85 thousand counties, municipalities, townships, public school districts, boroughs, and special district governments (including hospitals, airports, natural resources, fire). This figure does not include the 574 sovereign Native governments, most of which include a number of internal governing units. For example, the Navajo Nation—the largest land-based Indigenous nation—is home to the following:

Indigenous Governance. David E. Wilkins, Oxford University Press. © Oxford University Press 2024.
DOI: 10.1093/oso/9780190095994.003.0002

- 1 National Government
- 110 Chapters
- 1 Township
- 15 District Grazing Committees
- 3 Off-Reservation Land Boards/Grazing Committees
- 41 Off Reservation Grazing Communities
- 1 Eastern Navajo Land Board
- 6 Land Boards (On-Reservation)
- 5 Agency Councils

183 Navajo Governmental Units[1]

Despite their extraordinary length of tenure in North America,[2] Native governments have received little attention from political scientists. As evidence of this reality, a 2016 article in a leading political science journal was titled "Why Does Political Science Hate American Indians?"[3] That lead article and the ones written in response to it offered several explanations in an attempt to tease out the absence of works about Indigenous governments and politics in the broader field of political science. The list of factors explaining the silence included the following: the pluralist paradigm, which has great difficulty coping with Native peoples or politics because of Tribal nationalism which is rooted in communalism, treaty rights, and sovereignty; the diverse demographic dimension—574-plus distinctive Native communities, but with a cumulative population of less than 2% of the overall U.S. population; a research emphasis on states; a future-driven orientation that fails to heed important historical events crucial to understand Native political development and underdevelopment; and a focus on liberal individualism that struggles to address Native nationalism.[4]

This text is offered in the hopes that it will bring much-needed attention to the vital roles Native governments play in the lives of their diverse constituencies. Indigenous governments have always mattered, but today they arguably matter even more, given the weight and importance of many issues and developments confronting Native peoples—from the frightening and lasting health and economic impact of COVID-19 to the profound environmental and natural resource problems exacerbated by climate change and policy choices, to the enormous jurisdictional conflicts Native governments continue to have with local, state, and federal actors, to the substantial problems surrounding Native children, and the glaring and devastating issue of missing and murdered Native women, to name but a few.

In 2018, the U.S. Commission on Civil Rights (USCCR) published a detailed report titled "Broken Promises: Continuing Federal Funding Shortfall for Native Americans," which was an update of an earlier USCCR report, "A Quiet Crisis: Federal Funding and Unmet Needs in Indian Country," that had been

22 INDIGENOUS GOVERNANCE

produced in 2003. The 2003 study reported that while the federal government had tried to improve the living conditions of Native peoples, those peoples still suffered high rates of poverty, substandard housing, poor educational attainment, and high rates of disease and illness. Fifteen years later, the commissioners found that while some progress had been made, "Native Americans continue to rank near the bottom of all markers in health, education, and employment outcomes."[5]

Specifically, the Commission found that Native people "continue to face everyday challenges due to disproportionately high rates of violence and crime victimization; poor physical, mental, and behavioral health conditions; high rates of suicide; low educational achievement and attainment; poor housing conditions; high rates of poverty and unemployment; and other challenges, which are exacerbated by the shortfall of federal assistance."[6] These already depressing statistics were made worse by COVID-19's profound impact on Native peoples across the land.

Native governments, therefore, command our attention because as they have continued their recovery from decades of federal dominance and dependence and now exercise greater degrees of political, economic, and cultural power, they have become—despite COVID-19's crippling assault—critically important as the chief providers of basic services and the authors of solutions to collective problems in their societies. They are major vessels of Indigenous infused democratic politics; they are, for many communities, the largest spenders and employers; they are key players in negotiating intergovernmental arrangements that help fortify their unique political status vis-à-vis other governments; they are policy laboratories as they look to revitalize and incorporate historic institutional mechanisms (e.g., peacemaking, ecological knowledge) into their contemporary governing institutions; they are educating a new generation of political and societal leaders who can artfully guide their nations forward in a volatile political world; finally, since most Native nations are demographically small in scale this means that "the people" in a given Native community remain biologically close to the governing elite and, in many cases, because of the ongoing reality of kinship, it is possible that there is an actual genealogical linkage that makes Native politics particularly fascinating and nearly always intensely personal.

Governing Similarities and Differences

Similarities

All governments, including Indigenous ones, operate formal and informal institutions and processes which make critical decisions for the citizens they represent. Native governments, of course, have experienced enormous changes since the fateful date of 1492, many of which will be discussed in Chapters 2 through 5. And while elements of traditional values, principles, and governance persist in many Native communities, the vast majority of Indigenous nations today—slightly over 500—operate under established formal constitutions that have some resemblance to those of the states and the federal government.

Thus, Robert Williams' suggestion that "we live in a system of dual constitutionalism, as well as dual constitutional traditions in terms of constitutional design and practice"[7] is factually incorrect. This, therefore, is the first major similarity between Native nations and the two junior sovereigns inhabiting Native America. Structurally, as will be discussed in Chapter 6, within constitutionally based Native governments there is tremendous variety, with only forty-two Native nations having separation of powers arrangements—legislative, executive, and judicial—like, say, the Cherokee Nation of Oklahoma. Other arrangements include constitutions that vest governing power solely in an elected Tribal Council; others utilize a General Council arrangement which is a body that encompasses the entire adult population which meets periodically and serves as the governing body; others utilize an elected Business Committee or Business Council which is the governing body.

Second, Native governments, like the other two polities, provide a bounty of services, benefits, and protections for their citizens and other persons who live, work, or travel through Indigenous lands. Native governments tax businesses and some citizens; they provide healthcare; build and administer schools at every level—preschool through college; employ both Natives and non-Natives; deliver public safety and law enforcement through a variety of court systems; supply communication and technology for the benefit of their constituents; handle transportation and road issues; oversee Tribal lands, natural resources, agriculture, and water matters; provide housing for citizens; and, through Native leaders, engage in political, economic, and cultural interactions with other governments, corporations, and with the American public.

A third similarity—this one between Indigenous governments and states—is that many Native constitutions, like state constitutions, also seek to address "citizens' character, virtue, and even morality" because many Indigenous lawmakers believe that government "should take an active role in shaping citizen character and that this role should be constitutional."[8] The Makah Constitution, for example, states that one of the principal duties of the Tribal Council—the governing body of that nation—is "to safeguard and promote the peace, safety, morals, and general welfare of the Makah Indian Tribe by regulating the conduct of trade and the use and disposition of property upon the reservation."[9]

A fourth similarity, also between Native governments and state governments, has to do with the relative ease and frequency by which these two sovereigns

24 INDIGENOUS GOVERNANCE

amend or reform their constitutional charters. While it is extremely difficult to amend the federal Constitution, with only twenty-seven amendments having been added since 1789, most recently in 1992, the fifty state constitutions (and their earlier iterations) have been amended about 12,000 times, with most having been adjusted over one-hundred times.[10]

Native constitutions, particularly those that were not established under the auspices of the Indian Reorganization Act (IRA) in 1934, are also more easily amended than that of the federal government, although we do not have a precise count of how many amendments there have been. Tribal governments that created constitutions under the IRA, the Alaska IRA, or the Oklahoma Indian Welfare Act, until the 1980s, faced enormous procedural barriers to successfully amend their constitutions because virtually all of these documents contain language that requires the Secretary of the Interior to review and approve any such amendments. This paternalistic measure was put in place by John Collier and Felix S. Cohen in 1934, ostensibly to protect the Native community from doing something it might later regret.

As Native governments matured and as BIA policies became more supportive of Indigenous self-determination in the 1970s, Native governments pushed back against the secretarial approval requirement, and thus many Tribal nations have since amended their constitutions to have the secretarial power removed. With this accomplished, the number of amendments and amount of constitutional reform has increased greatly, and this trend promises to continue as Native nations look to update and modernize their constitutions to meet the needs of their ever-growing and diversifying population.[11]

Finally, Native governments and states share yet another, rather dubious, status. Both sovereigns suffer from the possibility of experiencing federal plenary power. That is to say, the federal Constitution and federal laws can limit the content or substance of provisions that Indigenous and state governments may adopt, whether in its constitution or some other organic document.[12] Thus, for example, states are denied the power to coin money, they cannot permit the impairment of contracts, they cannot enter into treaties, cannot grant titles of nobility, and cannot keep troops or ships of war in peacetime. Native governments are confronted by an even more smothering, potentially obliterating, form of federal plenary power that will be discussed in the ensuing section: Tribal governments can be legally terminated. Since 1831, they have been denied the power to negotiate treaties with foreign powers; they are constrained in how they can criminally prosecute most non-Natives who commit crimes on Native lands; and most Native lands are subject to the doctrine of discovery[13] which under the principles of federal Indian law denies to Tribal governments complete ownership rights to their own historic lands.

Differences

Numerous differences distinguish Native peoples and their governments from the federal and state political systems. Some of these differences are less vivid now than during the encounter era, but many remain in full force despite the passage of time and the political, economic, legal, and cultural entanglements that have ensued. The first difference centers around *time*. As they are Indigenous, they obviously predate those who arrived over the last 500–600 years from other lands. As mature sovereign nations, they retain their pre-existing political, social, economic, political, and cultural systems—that will be described and assessed in Chapter 2. These systems are built upon kinship, community cohesion, sacredness, and the moral equality of every citizen.

Second, since Native governments were pre-existing and self-governing bodies, they were not parties to the development of the U.S. Constitution or made subordinate to the American federal system of governance that was established by the creation of the federal Constitution.[14] Similarly, state constitutions have no direct jurisdictional bearing on Tribal governments or their lands or citizens. Tribal governments, in short, are not generally subject or bound by governmental constraints outlined in the federal or state constitutions. However, they are identified in the federal Constitution in three places—two dealing with their exclusion from taxation and their placement in the commerce clause—and in most Western state constitutions in disclaimer clauses where the states had to pledge never to tax or impose their jurisdiction over Natives or Indian Country unless specifically authorized by a congressional act.

Third, the citizens of Native governments hold membership or citizenry in their nation based on one or more combinations of cultural, racial, or genealogical criteria rather than birth, acquisition, or naturalization. Furthermore, in some Native communities, it is possible "for an individual to become a member and never be on the reservation at all. And it is also possible to live one's entire life on a reservation, be culturally and genetically of the local Tribe, and yet not be eligible for membership in the Tribe. These unusual aspects of Tribal citizenship are due in part to Tribal custom and in part to the pressures of federal law."[15] Tribal governments also wield the extraordinary power to denaturalize, disenroll, or legally terminate an enrolled member's status,[16] a power not accorded to the federal or state governments except under the most unusual of circumstances.[17]

Fourth, Indigenous governments, unlike the state or federal government, occupy a unique and, some say, constitutionally problematic status as both *political entities* and *racial entities*. As Ablavsky noted recently in an essay that sought to tease out the meanings of these categories at the time the U.S. Constitution was written, there is ample language and cultural history which supports this dual status: "Anglo-Americans of the time also alternated between referring to Native

26 INDIGENOUS GOVERNANCE

communities as 'nations,' which connoted equality, and 'tribes,' which conveyed Natives' purported uncivilized status. They also defined 'Indians' both in racial terms, as nonwhite, and in jurisdictional terms, as noncitizens."[18]

Both statuses coexist uneasily and cause some confusion for non-Natives on equality grounds, but Natives are used to their bifurcated status. Their racial status underscores their ethnic and cultural distinctiveness, while their sovereign political status as nations "largely take the place that states and municipalities occupy toward other citizens of the United States."[19]

Fifth, as separate and extra-constitutional sovereigns, one of the key manifestations of their inherent political authority was the massive amount of diplomatic posturing and maneuvering that transpired between Native nations and Europeans and later colonial, state, and federal governments in the form of hundreds of treaties, covenants, accords, leases, and so on, that were negotiated, dating back to 1607.[20] Here, of course, the difference in Native capacity to make treaties is most pronounced in comparison to states which are constitutionally deprived of the right to negotiate treaties. The federal government, through the executive branch, exercises its treaty power regularly. As Thomas Biolsi remarked, treaty-making affirmed both the national and international character of Native nations: "One would appear to be on firm ground in assuming that a treaty is a treaty, and that Indian tribes, like foreign nations, are not part of the United States but are rather entities with which the United States can have only international relations."[21]

Bilateral or multilateral political accords and treaties are not only important sources of federal law but are also a "significant repository of tribal law in such areas as identification of tribal boundaries, environmental regulation, and the use and control of natural resources on the reservation. As organic documents made with the federal government, treaties constitute both bargained for exchanges that are essentially contractual, and political compacts establishing relationships between sovereigns. In both capacities, treaties establish obligations binding on Indian nations and the federal government alike."[22]

Sixth, Indigenous governments continue to have a tenuous political existence that can be formally terminated by the federal government, and they are subject to a form of plenary power that is virtually absolute. As the U.S. Supreme Court said in *U.S. v. Wheeler*, "The sovereignty that the Indian tribes retain is of a unique and limited character. It exists only at the sufferance of Congress, and is subject to complete defeasance."[23] While states are occasionally subject to congressional plenary power they nevertheless have a constitutionally guaranteed right to exist which Native nations are denied.

Seventh, Native nations are owners of nearly 100 million acres of land, most held in trust by the federal government. This is a distinctive type of territorial sovereignty unlike that of the states or the national government. As the Commission on State-Tribal Relations (CSTR) aptly put it, "An Indian tribe must relate to the reservation economy both as a government and as a participant, because it is also landowner and entrepreneur. This dual role, when analyzed from a standard American governmental perspective, greatly complicates the tribe's performance of its governmental functions of regulating, taxing and delivering services."[24]

An eighth difference centers around the outsized amount of influence other governments and agencies, like the Bureau of Indian Affairs, have in relation to Native governments. As Lopach, Brown, and Clow noted in their excellent study of the seven Indigenous governments in Montana, *Tribal Governments Today* (1998), "Reservations do not exist in a governmental vacuum. Tribal governments have constant contacts with officials of local, state, and national governments, and these external relationships affect tribal operations just as do internal political relationships."[25] This can affect jurisdictional questions, law enforcement, social services delivery, regulatory issues, and educational institutions. States, cities, and counties deal with the sometimes quite intrusive federal government, but these bodies do not face the same degree of interference that Native nations have and continue to cope with.

Adding to the complexity is the fact that Native citizens are also citizens of their states of residence and are generally eligible for all the benefits that non-Natives of that state are entitled to; while non-Native residents of reservations or Native trust lands are in most cases not eligible for benefits or resources that enrolled Tribal members receive. This situation, put another way, is this: "Indians living within Indian Country are immune from state and local taxes and are largely immune from state and local laws. Yet they claim the right to vote for representatives who can levy taxes and make rules and regulations for non-Indians—taxes and rules from which reservation Indians themselves are immune."[26]

Finally, Native governments are unique from the states and federal government in the manner in which they engage with their own cultural systems that trace back to the primordial past. While non-Native governments are drawn philosophically and structurally from Euro-American culture—although there is some evidence that elements of Indigenous philosophical traditions had a measure of influence on the American political founders—Indigenous governments derive from an entirely different cultural and social paradigm. As the staff of CSTR noted:

> Ironically, because of federal Indian policy, many tribal governments are also constitutional governments patterned along similar lines, alien to the Indian societies they are expected to govern. Some observers have noted that Indian tribal governments are subject to criticism from two perspectives at once: they are too heavily influenced by non-Indian ideas of government and are not 'Indian' enough for some critics; at the same time, they are inadequately

INDIGENOUS GOVERNANCE

equipped to meet the challenges facing Indian people and societies in the modern world and, by this argument, are too 'Indian'—or insufficiently 'non-Indian'—for other critics.[27]

The Commission staff went on to state:

To date, no model Indian government has emerged which is generally considered to embody traditional Indian governmental processes and, at the same time, to be adequate to the complex modern challenges of taxation, regulation and the delivery of services, although there is no reason why it cannot be done. This kind of debate is unique to tribal government and rarely occupies the agendas or complicates the problem of state and local non-Indian governments in the United States. . . . Furthermore, tribal governments are seen by many as protectors of Indian cultures whose existence is perceived to be constantly threatened. Thus, tribal governments tend to sense that every major policy decision and every significant new direction taken could conceivably lead to irreversible damage to a threatened culture. It is a culture whose position is the more precarious because it has no ties resembling those fundamental links between American and European societies—a culture which, in fact, has no ties, no counterparts and no source of renewal anywhere on earth but on the reservation. This special relationship of tribal government to Indian culture dominates every facet of tribal policymaking and inculcates a caution and a conservatism which are marks of most tribal policy. Tribal governments cannot ignore this overriding concern. It is not only an important tribal value and hence a major expectation that tribal members have of their governments, it is also a major expectation of many non-Indians in the press and the public at large—an additional source of pressure on tribal governments. They can no more pursue public policy by ignoring cultural realities than could any other government.[28]

Conclusion

The sovereignty of the people is a hallmark element of every Indigenous nation. This is evidenced by the words, "We the people" or "We, the members," which are embedded in the preambles of many Native constitutions, Articles of Association, and other organic foundational documents, signifying that it is the Native citizens of a given community who embody the sovereignty of the nation; not the political elites who have merely been delegated a temporary amount of power and time to act on behalf of its citizens. As stated in the constitution of the Penobscot Nation of Maine: "We, the members of the Penobscot Nation, create this Constitution in order to: reaffirm our sovereignty as a Nation, author-itatively set forth our method of self-government, clarify areas of tribal law not thus far clearly defined, establish guidelines for the conduct of our governmental affairs, preserve our customs and traditions, foster justice and advance our common welfare. Now, therefore, we acknowledge and adopt this Constitution of the Penobscot Nation as the supreme law by which we will govern ourselves."

Native peoples and their governments, despite their lengthy tenure as the first sovereigns, find themselves precariously situated politically, legally, and cultur-ally. While they have been acknowledged as sovereigns via hundreds of treaties, have explicit recognition in the U.S. Constitution's commerce clause, and have been identified as nations in thousands of Native, federal, and state court cases, and in statutory law, they have never been formally incorporated as part of the American federalist system of government by historical action or constitutional amendment and have even been told by Clarence Thomas, an Associate Supreme Court justice, that unlike states, which are an integral part of the constitutional framework that allocates sovereignty between themselves and the federal gov-ernment, "tribes, by contrast, are not part of this constitutional order, and their sovereignty is not guaranteed by it."[29]

In other words, Indigenous governments, because of the powerful and on-going repercussions of the ravages of colonialism and the voracious demands of the capitalistic system, find themselves in a constantly vulnerable, if not relatively dependent, position vis-à-vis the federal government and those agencies like the Departments of the Interior, Justice, and Housing and Urban Development, that still wield a great deal of influence over Native governments, their resources, and their citizens' individual rights.

As Felmley observed: "[Tribal] governments are not just hampered in their practical effectiveness by federal constraints, they are too often rendered less ca-pable in the eyes of their members when they are unable to avoid delays or confu-sion or even reversals of policy. Tribal populations have a tendency to hold their tribal governments accountable for inaction or unpopular policies which are ac-tually for more the responsibility of the federal government."[30]

And Evans in her study, *Power from Powerlessness: Tribal Governments, Institutional Niches, and American Federalism*, raised an important question that is always lurking in studies of disempowered peoples: "What happens to governments when they are surrounded by actors holding greater social and economic power, when they sometimes face discourse treating them as implic-itly illegitimate or inferior, and when they must tend to the unhealed injuries of brutalities? We can't understand the nearly 600 American Indian tribal governments without engaging that question."[31]

The political precariousness of Native governments is exacerbated by an even greater, possibly irreconcilable, issue—the manner in which the ongoing

30   INDIGENOUS GOVERNANCE

presence of Native peoples is perceived by some U.S. and state policymakers and citizens as a direct challenge to American nationalism and sovereignty. Pauline Strong and Barrick Van Winkle say that "in asserting collective rights based on their status as members of indigenous nations ... Native Americans challenge modern nationalism's foundational premises of possessive individualism, bounded political sovereignty, and singular national identity."[32]

Notwithstanding the explicit, implicit, and profound structural and attitudinal issues they are confronted by, Indigenous governing bodies have proven themselves to be remarkably tough, creative, and strategic in forging necessary adaptations required to address the diverse and intense needs of their citizens and in their unpredictable intergovernmental relations to the other governments to which they are linked by geography, treaty, law, culture, and partial citizenship.

2

Political Organization B.C. (Before Contact)

The Confederated Tribes of the Warm Springs Tribe located within present-day Oregon have a concept—"Ne-shy-chut"—which means their people have always been rooted in the soil of their historic territory and that they have been free from external pressures that sought to affect their ways. The term "Ne-shy-chut" is linked to another phrase—"tee-cha-meengsh-meesin-wit na-me ah-wa-ta-man-wit"—which means "at the time of creation the Creator placed us in this land and He gave us the voice of this land and that is our law."[1] This language is incorporated in the Tribe's "Declaration of Sovereignty" which was adopted on June 25, 1992.

These symbiotic concepts emphasize ideas crucial to understanding how Indigenous peoples were organized socially, politically, and culturally before the European arrival. These include freedom, liberty, autonomy, a sense of territorial sovereignty and integrity, an understanding of peoplehood steeped in religious or spiritual understandings, and recognition of the importance of customary and natural law as a guiding force in individual and collective lives.

Since the vast majority of Native peoples did not document their histories or means of community organization in written form, information about these nations must be derived from the scattered and spotty oral recollections of Native people—spotty largely due to the unparalleled death and destruction unleashed upon Indigenous peoples during the colonial and postcolonial period—"anthropological studies of variable quality, and the sometimes unreliable written accounts of early non-Indian traders, missionaries, and military."[2] Notwithstanding the uneven quality of the scarce historical data, there is still sufficient material for us to glean a panoramic understanding of early Indigenous political organization.

European and early Euro-American philosophical, political, and religious traditions were dominated by two broad theoretical perspectives. The divine right of kings arose from the belief that monarchs ruled because God "intended them to."[3] Under this system, European states wielded governments that were based on the concept of legitimate authority that produced the doctrine of royal absolutism. For example, Louis XIV of seventeenth-century France described

Indigenous Governance. David E. Wilkins, Oxford University Press. © Oxford University Press 2024.
DOI: 10.1093/oso/9780190095994.003.0003

32 INDIGENOUS GOVERNANCE

royal authority as divinely ordained and the response to God-given natural instincts:

> Under God, monarchy is, of all forms of government, the most unusual and the most ancient, and therefore the most natural. It is likewise the strongest and most efficient, therefore the best. It is analogous to the rule of a family by the father, and, like that rule, should be hereditary. The hereditary monarch [has] four qualities. (1) He is sacred because he is anointed at the time of coronation by the priests of the church, and hence it is blasphemy and sacrilege to assail the person of the king or to conspire against him. (2) He is, in a very real sense, the father of his people, the paternal king. . . . (3) His power is absolute and autocratic, and for its exercise he is accountable to God alone; no man on earth may rightfully resist the royal commands, and the only recourse for subjects against an evil king is to pray God that his heart be changed. (4) Greater reason is given to a king than to anyone else; the king is an earthly image of God's majesty, and it is wrong, therefore, to look upon him as a mere man. . . . As in God are united all perfection and every virtue, so all the power of all the individuals in a community is united in the person of the king.[4]

The other key tenet is social contract theory, a critical response to the monarchical system. Social contract theory is, most simply, the idea that individual actions and obligations are predicated on a shared agreement to form a community or society. The social contract could be overseen by a monarch, but this ruler also had reciprocal responsibilities to their subjects. Advocates included John Locke, Charles de Montesquieu, Thomas Hobbes, and Jean-Jacques Rousseau who posited that "the best and most rational basis for government was the establishment of a social contract in which free individuals" in a hypothetical state of nature willingly surrendered "their right to arbitrary action to a superior in return for the guarantee of law and order."[5]

Indigenous peoples did not adhere to either of these theoretical systems of governance. While leadership was certainly evident, there were no absolute monarchs in North America nor were there contractual agreements between Native individuals opting to form governing structures. Rather, Native communities generally were formed and drew legitimacy from their origin or creation stories as noted by the Warm Springs Tribe's account at the beginning of this chapter. The Navajo Nation's sense of participatory democracy, for example, derives from "a deeper, more profound system of governance,"[6] that, like the Warm Springs Tribe, is also rooted in their emergence account that describes how they entered the current world.

Thus, according to Deloria and Lytle, "The idea of the people is primarily a religious conception," and,

POLITICAL ORGANIZATION BEFORE CONTACT   33

with most American Indian tribes it begins somewhere in the primordial mists. In that time the people were gathered together but did not yet see themselves as a distinct people. A holy man had a dream or a vision; quasi-mythological figures of cosmic importance revealed themselves, or in some other manner the people were instructed. They were given ceremonies and rituals that enabled them to find their place on the continent. Quite often they were given prophecies that informed them of the historical journey ahead. In some instances, the people were told to migrate until a special place was revealed . . . Tribal names generally reflect the basic idea that these particular people have been chosen from among the various peoples of the universe—including mammals, birds, and reptiles, as well as other humans—to hold a special relationship with the higher powers. Thus, most tribal names can be interpreted simply to mean "the people."[7]

This is because the citizens of the great variety of Native nations shared languages, lands, cultures, kinship, and political authority with one another and understood their place in the universe as one designated especially for their community.[8]

Diversity in Indigenous Political Organization

With over six hundred distinctive Native nations living in what is now the United States, it is impossible to generalize about how these communities were organized politically. But if we define political organization as the manner "in which people who live in a particular territory are integrated internally with respect to each other and to outsiders" we can at least establish several broad categories of Indigenous organization that will help group these disparate peoples into several cohorts. Harold Driver developed a useful typology for North America that described three broad categories: (1) Areas without True Political Organization (Native peoples in the Arctic, Great Basin, Northeast Mexico, and Baja California); (2) Areas with Borderline and Mixed Systems (the Sub-Arctic, Northwest Coast, Plateau, California, and the Southwest); and (3) Areas with Tribal Organization in the Historic Period (Plains, Prairies, Northeast, and Southeast). He also included a fourth category which we will not examine, "The State," which focused on the Aztecs, the Tarascans, and others inhabiting what became Mexico.[9]

For Driver, Native societies which "have no territorial organization larger than the residential kin group will be classed as lacking true political organization while those with territorial ties based on non-kinship factors will be classed as possessing it."[10] In the former, there was an absence of clans, they were nomadic, the population was meager, band organization was not formalized, and

34 INDIGENOUS GOVERNANCE

the largest fixed unit was the family. Their lack of structural political organization was attributed to the "impossibility of maintaining a permanent local group of sufficient size in the face of such adversities."[11] While those in the latter group, with evident political organization, including such peoples as the Crow, Shawnee, Cheyenne, Fox, Haudenosaunee (Iroquois), Cherokee, Choctaw, Chickasaw, Creek, and Seminole, had established blood, clan, and village organizations, more substantial populations, clear distinctions between peace and war leaders, and occupied well-defined geographical areas. [12]

Driver's typology provides us with a comprehensive way to conceptualize some of the key differences in Indigenous political organization. But other commentators have highlighted many of the shared aspects of Native political, legal, cultural, and economic experience. We have already noted the spiritual foundation of Native societies. Cohen also pointed out a few important similarities.

> Kinship groups and associated social relations, rather than individual citizens, typically served as the basic units of larger social, economic, and political structures. Power was more clearly identified with the community than with individual leaders, and leaders served only so long as they maintained the confidence and respect of the people. And the values that most often animated traditional tribal governments were those of responsibility to the community and respect for each individual's place within the sacred order. An important function of most early tribal governments was to resolve conflicts and restore harmony within the community in accordance with those values. Legislative action, so prominent in the American system was often less central than the judicial process.[13]

Cohen's last point—conflict resolution—is echoed by Deloria and Lytle who noted that historically Native communities

> were once primarily judicial in the sense that the council, whether it was that of a village, a league of tribes, or a simple hunting band, looked to custom and precedent in resolving novel and difficult social questions that arose. Tribes were homogenous units—linguistically, religiously, economically, and politically. All aspects of life were interwoven so that there were no sharp distinctions between the various aspects of life such as those we see in today's world. Everyone knew and respected the customs and beliefs of the tribal community. The task of the council, when it had a difficult question to resolve, was to appeal to that larger sense of reality shared by the people of the community and to reach a decision that people would see as consonant with the tradition.[14]

POLITICAL ORGANIZATION BEFORE CONTACT   35

This judicial orientation, with an emphasis on the primacy of conscience, dictated that Native societies wielded a "very pure form of democracy characterized by its lack of central authority . . . and in which any collective action requires the consent of everyone affected—or at least the consensus of all their families."[15]

Thus, ridicule and embarrassment, rather than harsh coercive measures, were utilized to maintain order and harmony in the community. As Radin put it, "The fear of ridicule is thus a great positive factor in the lives of primitive peoples. It is the preserver of the established order of things and more potent and tyrannous than the most restrictive and coercive appositive injunctions could be."[16] Another central notion that was pervasive in Indigenous political organization was the idea that since all community members were morally equal regardless of their differences, everyone, including the Tribal leadership, adhered to it and was entitled to what Radin called the theory of an "irreducible minimum," which is to say that every person "possessed an inalienable right to food, shelter, and clothing."[17] This was so regardless of the type of political organization or the method of food production, and "irrespective of whether society [was] socially stratified or unstratified, democratic or monarchical, or whether the food economy is that of the food gatherer, the hunter-fisher, the agriculturalist or the pastoral-nomad."[18] In sum, the three most outstanding features of Indigenous organization, according to Radin, were "respect for the individual, irrespective of age or sex; the amazing degree of social and political integration achieved by them; and the existence there of the concept of personal security which transcends all governmental forms and all tribal and group interests and conflicts."[19]

Prominent Organizational Structures: Clans and Moieties

Clans and moieties were two of the critical organizational units utilized by many Indigenous political bodies. While similar, the two concepts represent different levels of organization. Moiety, the broader of the two constructs, signifies a divided society. The Tlingit, located within what is now Alaska, utilizes clans, as well as the Raven and Wolf moieties. The customs are such that a member of the Raven moiety cannot marry another Raven. Within each moiety are clans that are sometimes described as corporate kin groups in so far as each clan has corporate rights to particular names, titles, ceremonies, and places to fish.[20] Each clan has its own origin story and traces its history to the primordial past and to the animals representing it.

The Pueblo peoples of the Southwest are similarly organized. For the Rio Grande Pueblo, the moiety has been the most important framework from

36 INDIGENOUS GOVERNANCE

both a governmental and religious perspective. Membership is divided about equally between the Winter (Kwaereh) and the Summer (Hajeb) people[21] with the two moiety groups alternating responsibilities. The Winter moiety guides governmental and ceremonial affairs from the fall to the spring equinox; the Summer moiety governs the rest of the year.[22] Moieties serve many functions, including curative, religious, and governmental. Their tasks include the following:

> The maintenance of an annual solar and lunar calendar and the announcement of dates for fixed ceremonials during the year; (2) the organization and direction of large communal dances and ceremonies; (3) the coordination of purificatory and cleansing rites for the village conducted by medicine associations; (4) the coordination of communal hunts conducted by the hunt association; (5) the coordination of warfare ceremonies conducted by the war association; (6) the organization and direction of planting and harvesting activities; (7) the supervision of the cleaning and construction of irrigation ditches; (8) the repair and construction of communal *kivas* and the cleaning of the Pueblo courtyards for communal ceremonies; (9) the appointment of officers to compel Pueblo members to participate in all communal activities, both religious and secular; (10) responsibility for maintaining the secrecy of ceremonial activities and the imposition of fines and punishment on violators; (11) the nomination and installation of officers of the civil government system imposed by Spanish colonial and Church officials.[23]

Pueblo members are required to obey the instructions of the moiety leaders. Dozier points out that violators or nonconformists can be harassed, persecuted, deprived of homes, land, and property, and even evicted from the Pueblo "for the infractions of any ceremonial and secular act interpreted to be for the welfare of the whole community."[24]

According to Upham, within the moieties clan membership is determined by birth and follows the maternal line.[25] Individuals must be initiated into their groups between the ages of six and ten. Thus, an individual has little choice regarding clan affiliation (although adoptions are possible). And, as with the Tlingit, particular clans are understood as being the "owners" of certain ceremonies.

Many other Native nations relied solely on clans as their chief organizational unit. And as Radin reminds us, "The primary fact to remember about the clan is that it was a political institution, the earliest truly cohesive governmental unit of which we have any record."[26] The Anishinaabe clan system, for instance, was a governmental mechanism that defined the division of roles and labor in a way that reinforced the principles of their shared way of life. Each of the seven original clans—represented by an animal—had a specific role in governing and structure. The Crane and Loon clans had the power of chieftainship. The Bear clan acted as a police force and protected the community from outside threats. The Fish clan was constituted of intellectuals since they focused on meditation and philosophy.[27]

Clans embodied groupings of individuals whose cohesion included not only blood-related kin but others who shared descent either from a common animal ancestor or some distant common event.[28] Frederick Hodge identified the following characteristic rights and privileges in the clan systems of the Iroquoian and Muskhogean peoples:

(1) The right to a common clan name, which is usually that of an animal, bird, reptile, or natural object that may formerly have been regarded as a guardian deity.
(2) Representation in the council of the tribe.
(3) Its share in the communal property of the tribe.
(4) The right to have its elected chief and sub chief of the clan confirmed and installed by the tribal council, among the Iroquois in later times by the League council.
(5) The right to the protection of the tribe.
(6) The right to the titles of the chiefships and subchiefships hereditary in its *ohwachiras*.
(7) The right to certain songs, chants, and religious observances.
(8) The right of its men or women, or both together, to hold councils.
(9) The right to certain personal names, to be bestowed upon its members.
(10) The right to adopt aliens through the action of the constituent *ohwachiras*.
(11) The right to a common burial ground . . . .[29]

Understanding Law and Authority

All human groups have to maintain social order if they are to have functioning societies. We have already seen how clans and moieties operated to organize and structure community relations in Aboriginal societies. If we define law as that aspect of culture "which employs the force of organized society to regulate individual and group conduct and to prevent, redress or punish deviations from prescribed social norms" then it is plain that Native nations had legal systems that were tailored to their communities.[30]

Early European explorers struggled to comprehend how Native communities operated and tended, at least early on, to treat Indigenous

38   INDIGENOUS GOVERNANCE

peoples as a "rude miniature of Europe." They gradually realized, however, that Native governments and their legal traditions were quite different from their own.[31] Thus, when Europeans—including traders, soldiers, and missionaries—became familiar with Central Algonquians (Potawatomie, Sac, Menominee, Fox, Kickapoo, and others living in present-day Wisconsin, Illinois, and Indiana) they were taken aback at how these people carried out subsistence, religious, administrative, and military activities "in the virtual absence of any sort of recognizable authority."[32]

In the European and Euro-American political and cultural tradition, authority or power is, as Miller noted, conceptually equated with height or elevation, verticality, if you will. "It is conceived as originating in some elevated locus, and as passing down to lower levels . . . In general, the structure of authority is pictured as a pyramidal, with greater authority at a relatively narrow apex, and more diffuse authority at increasingly lower levels."[33] In effect, the equation of authority with altitude is deeply embedded in European and Euro-American linguistic structures. For instance, concepts like subordinate, inferior, and superior are critical examples in this analysis. Other examples include the phrases "top position, high ranking, way up there; one with little authority is on the bottom, in a lowly position, down and out."[34] By contrast, the Central Algonquian and many other Native people emphasize the notion of horizontality in their understanding of law and authority—that essential elements are on the same plane and share a sense of universal kinship "that is continuous in time, space, and across species . . . and uniquely define each individual in relation to every other."[35]

Vaughan and Rosen point out a number of specific differences in the manner in which law was understood and practiced by Indigenous societies in contrast to those of European and Euro-Americans. Most fundamentally, Western law emphasizes culpability whereas Native law emphasized liability. That is to say, in Indigenous cultures, perpetrators were not generally perceived as deserving of blame "but rather as liable for appropriate restitution to the aggrieved individual or . . . to his/her kin group."[36] Another difference centered on the government's role. In Western law, the state—in criminal cases—was the aggrieved party. But in Native societies, there was no "state," per se, so no governing entity was involved. Typically, individuals or kinship groups were the parties who meted out punishment.[37]

Finally, there was great significance in the forms of punishment handed down. In Western law, depending on the crime, corporal punishment or incarceration could result. While corporal punishment was not unusual in Native societies, there were no jails or prisons in traditional Native cultures.[38]

Gender Roles in Governance

The status of women and those whom we would now refer to as LGBTQI and Two Spirit during pre-contact times is not easily discerned for the reasons alluded to earlier (i.e., lack of documentary data, stereotypes and misunderstandings, spotty oral recollections, and so on) and is further complicated depending on whether the group was sedentary or mobile, whether it was based on agriculture, the economic environment, the community's origin account, and the social and political organization of the community.[39] Regardless of the circumstances, it seems that gender roles, as a rule, were not rigidly defined nor punitively enforced as compared with European customs. As *Two Spirit Journal* editor Harlan Pruden (Nehiyawe/First Nations Cree) explains, the modern term Two Spirit evokes "the time before the harshness of colonization where many, not all, First Peoples had traditions and ways that were non-binary . . . and these genders were not only accepted and honored but also had distinct roles within their respective Nations."[40]

Tribes were pragmatic, concerned with bringing all talents and resources to bear in order to assure community survival. It would make little sense to judge, punish, or banish a relative who did not conform to a particular gender or binary choice. That is not to say that assigned roles did not exist, but rather that such a negative and limited focus would have been inconsistent with the organizations and structures necessary for communal success. For our purposes, it is important to keep in mind that governance was not the exclusive domain of one gender.[41]

While some Native communities followed patrilineal lines (e.g., Blackfeet), others were matrilineal, like the Pamunkey, Iroquois, and the Diné. The data suggest Native women occupied a variety of critical roles in Native societies: clan mothers, producers of art objects, warriors, beloved women, as healers—and they had many responsibilities—determining the fate of captives, deciding on whether or when to go to war, choosing leaders as intermediaries between men and power, daily care of medicine bundles, oversight and organization of the camp, to name but a few.

Klein reports that "in many aspects of the culture the role of gender identity was either a non-issue or a secondary one." "Political leadership," she noted, "was embedded in the realms of kinship and rank," which meant that while most Native 'chiefs' were men, the occasional woman could become a leader, too.[42] And Ackerman, writing about the Colville people in the Plateau region found that comments from elderly informants indicated that authority within the family unit was not "institutionally assigned to either the men or the women," but that when dominance did become evident "it was due to the presence of a strong personality, often belonging to the women."[43]

40   INDIGENOUS GOVERNANCE

Non-Native violence against Native women and girls has long been a plague throughout Indian Country, and presently the degree of gendered violence against Indigenous women is at a stunningly high record level.[44] Sarah Deer's research shows that historically this was not a social problem in Native communities. She hypothesizes that such violence was rare because of the "gendered cosmology of Native peoples." While European women were largely bereft of property and were disenfranchised, "Native women were largely free from systemic oppression because, in contrast to European women, the traditional laws of Tribal nations honored and protected the role of women in both family and government."[45]

In those Native societies where agricultural pursuits were the dominant subsistence method, women often had the primary responsibility for cultivating the land. This responsibility provided them "with a degree of autonomy unknown to their white counterparts, as they were the ones who decided what crops to plant, how the fields were to be tended, and what would be done with the foodstuffs produced."[46] This amount of critical responsibility meant that "women had substantial property rights and they had greater control over the descent of property, including the family name."[47]

For the Diné (Navajo), Changing Woman is the greatest symbol of the female essential role in Diné life as she is the creator of the present world.[48] This sacred origin account dictated a vital role for Diné women and their common law tradition reflects these values through women's property ownership and control, their superior role in determining ancestry, and married couples' practice of living with the wife's family.[49]

All this is not to suggest that Indigenous cultures were or are perfect societies or that everyone's standing was uniformly just, fair, and equal. There is clear evidence that some women experienced brutal treatment—especially when accused of adultery; that young girls were allowed less sexual freedom than boys; and that they were denied leadership opportunities in some Native societies.[50] In general, however, at least from a comparative perspective with Europeans, Indigenous women and Two Spirit people exercised a far greater amount of freedom (especially over their own bodies), had more personal autonomy, and had well-demarcated rights to property that were rooted in sacred narratives and origin accounts.

Leadership in Native Societies

Efforts to arrive at an understanding of how the concept of leadership was practiced in the distant past are also extremely difficult to discern. Still, there are some data available that allows for at least a broad view of this vital aspect of Indigenous political organization. Keith Grint offers what is arguably the simplest and certainly shortest definition of leadership: "Having followers."[51] But given what we described in the previous pages, and drawing from the work of Kracke, I would argue that a more appropriate definition is this: "Leadership is a relative thing."[52] This statement has a dual meaning, from my perspective. First, it is "relative" in the sense that it shifts, is situational, and is not an individual phenomenon. In other words, "the focus usually moves from an individual formal leader to multiple informal leaders," depending on the situation and the particular talents of the individuals. This is a collective process. Second, it has a genealogical and social component in that as Native societies were kin-based social groupings, a person was literally a relative to virtually everyone within the community. As Ella Deloria, a Dakota anthropologist put it: "Before going further, I can safely say that the ultimate aim of Dakota life, stripped of accessories, was quite simple: one must obey kinship roles; one must be a good relative."[53] The Dakota kinship system, then, "was practically all the government there was. It was what men lived by."[54] We might reformulate Grint's definition by declaratively saying that leadership in a Tribal context means "having relatives."

While Native nations historically produced noted leaders such as Sitting Bull (Lakota), Crazy Horse (Lakota), John Ross (Cherokee), Plenty Coups (Crow), Susan Laflesche, Henry Barry Lowry (Lumbee), Lozan (Apache), Tecumseh (Shawnee), Manuelito (Diné), among many others, the primacy of individual conscience throughout the Indigenous world dictated that "leadership is a burden upon the selfless, an obligation for the most capable, but never a reward for the greedy."[55] Since each Tribal member, for example, in Fox society, was directly related to the source of supernatural power, and each has his own individual deity,[56] there was no hero worship or cult of personality that would be blindly followed by the masses.

As Barsh observed,

> In the indigenous North American context a 'leader' is not a decision-maker, but a coordinator, peacemaker, teacher, example and comedian. He cannot tell others what to do, but he can persuade, cajole, tease, or inspire them into some unanimity of purpose. His influence depends on his ability to minimize differences of opinion, to remain above anger or jealousy, and to win respect and trust by helping his constituents through death, danger and hard times at his own risk and expense. He is 'good talk thrown out to the people,' as the Shoshoni say, not a rule maker—'essentially an advisor, not an executive,' on his particular area of expertise . . . There is no room in aboriginal government for men or women who aspire to power, because there is no power.[57]

42 INDIGENOUS GOVERNANCE

The topic of "power" is significant as it directly connects individual Native citizens to the grander forces of the universe. Native philosopher Vine Deloria Jr. described *power* as "spiritual power or life force" and linked it with *place* as one of the two experiential dimensions that helped Natives understand their world.[58] Native leaders were expected to share this understanding of power and to abide by its force. Deloria's comments were echoed by Miller's research on the Fox people who had this take on power:

> Power is universally available and unlimited; it does not have a unitary locus; is everywhere, and equally available to all. The possession of power is temporary and contingent; it is not a quality permanently possessed by any being, but can be gained and lost . . . Demonstrated power does not grant to its possessor the subsequent right to direct the actions of any other being. Power is not hierarchical; since its possession is temporary and contingent, fixed and varying amounts of power are not distributed among a group of beings arranged in a stable hierarchy. The control of power is dangerous; powerful beings are to be feared, not adored or admired.[59]

Fox society had a village chief who acquired the position by hereditary factors and was a permanent role, but the chief's function lacked directive authority. The Fox term for this role was "piece chief" or "kindly chief" and the chief's behavior symbolized peace and harmony, mild and un-aggressive behavior, and unity of the village community. There was also the role of "war leader" which involved a measured amount of authority. In the event of a war, this leader had the authority to ascertain the scope of the threat and could suggest action. But even this authority was constrained in two key respects. First, no one was required to accept the war leader's call to action; war party involvement was voluntary. Second, the war chief role was of limited duration, and as soon as the campaign had ended the person had to participate in a ceremony where her temporary authority was "symbolically revoked."[60]

Anthropologist Robert Lowi noted that Tribal civil leaders in the past generally lacked coercive power and shared three main attributes: (1) skills as a peacemaker; (2) a willingness to be extremely generous with whatever goods were available; and (3) possess the gift of oratory.[61] Lowi concluded by observing that in his opinion, "the most typical American chief is not a lawgiver, executive, or judge, but a pacifier, a benefactor of the poor, and a prolix Polonius."[62]

Finally, in the case of the Diné (Navajo), the people recognized—as did numerous other Indigenous nations like the Cherokee, Creek, Fox, and the Choctaw—the importance of having separate War and Peace leaders for the successful functioning of social harmony. It was unusual for a person to hold both offices. Among the Navajo, for example, to attain the position of a War

POLITICAL ORGANIZATION BEFORE CONTACT   43

Naataanii, an individual needed extensive knowledge of one or more of the War Ways. Anyone who had acquired this ritual knowledge was eligible to serve as a War leader. These were ceremonies designed to bring about successful raids or counterraids against outside forces. The Diné attitude toward War leaders, according to Hill, was equivocal. That is to say, while these individuals were respected as great fighters, they were also frequently criticized. It was believed by some Diné that War leaders were largely responsible for the defeat and imprisonment of Navajo at Bosque Redondo in the 1860s.[63]

A Peace Naataanii, by contrast, was chosen or elected if the person had knowledge of the Blessingway Ceremony, and only if he or she had excellent moral character, great oratorical abilities, and charisma. Also, the individual had to possess the ability to serve in both the sacred and day-to-day aspects of Navajo life and culture. According to Hill, the Navajo community members met to select these Naataanii. He noted that "in this the women had as much voice as the men. Usually the choice was nearly unanimous. If two men appeared to have nearly equal capabilities, they might be asked to make speeches in order to determine the selection. Once a decision had been reached the man was notified and the induction ritual performed."[64]

In effect, the selection of a Naataanii followed what could be termed a democratic process involving the adult population of a natural community.[65]

Traditional Case Studies

Reprising Harold Driver's typology which consisted of three broad categories of Indigenous political organization—(1) Areas Without True Political Organization, (2) Areas With Borderline and Mixed Systems, and (3) Areas With Tribal Organization in the Historic Period—here are short community case studies from each of those categories.

Inuit and Yupik Peoples of Alaska

The Inuit occupy a vast territory that today includes Alaska, Canada, and Greenland. They have lived in these territories for thousands of years. They always understood themselves to be self-governing peoples exercising sovereignty over defined areas domestically and externally.[66] For the vast majority of Inuit and Yupik peoples, the most important institution was the nuclear family unit, although Inuit and Yupik families normally lived in a larger settlement most of the time, especially during winter. These villages averaged less than one hundred persons. The sparsity of the population and their necessarily mobile habits in

44 INDIGENOUS GOVERNANCE

pursuit of game precluded an approach toward a more unified Tribal system. Nevertheless, the interpretation of the names of their separate groups provides insight into how they conceived of themselves as distinctive communities. Here, the suffix "miut" is used. It means "people" or "people of."[67] For example, Harvaqtôrmiut translates to "the people where rapids abound," Arviligjuarmiut means "the people of the land of the great whale," and Kitdlinermiut translates to "the frontier people."[68]

Most non-Native observers of Inuit and Yupik communities appeared struck by the apparent absence of governmental aspects of organized society and therefore assumed that they lived in a state of anarchy. "But such reasonings," according to Anderson and Eells, "is an error, failing utterly to take into account those naturally developed means of social control which serve the purposes of government and in fact are government."[69] The Inuit and Yupik's loose political structures were most likely responsible "for the success which the Eskimos attained in adapting their mode of life to their hazardous environments, thus enabling them to survive."[70]

Evidence of political organization was manifested in the rules and practices established to oversee the spatial arrangement of family possessions and the placement of igloo dwellings. In addition, fixed taboos were in place, particularly around the issue of hunting and the distribution of game. Excessive accumulation of wealth was anathema to social norms, while hoarders would be punished and ridiculed. Anderson and Eells describe an organizational structure called *Khashgii* which was a social body whose membership was limited to adult men and young hunters. When Khashgii met, village affairs such as hunting, interpersonal conflicts, and decisions about infrastructure needs were discussed.[71]

Regarding leadership, virtually all villages had a leadership position with the designee perceived as "tacitly, half-unconsciously recognized as first among equals."[72] This person was most commonly the best hunter in the village and led discussions about hunting trips. As discussed earlier, this individual had no fixed authority, was not elected, and had no formal office.[73] Baffin Islanders called their headperson *pimain*, which meant someone "who knows everything best."[74] Such individuals tended to be more economically well-off than others, but if they did not redistribute and share their wealth and lacked persuasive skills they were simply viewed as *tu-gu* or "rich man."[75]

In sum, the Inuit and Yupik are an example of Indigenous peoples "who had developed the modicum of formal government necessary for survival, while placing their dependence in social custom which had the weight of age-old and successful practice behind it. This form of organization was sufficient for their purposes prior to the coming of the white man. They had little need for formal government and made little use of it."[76]

Tohono O'odham (Desert People: formerly known as Papago)

The traditional homeland of the Tohono O'odham (T.O.) is the Sonoran Desert near the Gulf of California. The T.O. are likely descended from the ancient Hohokam Indians, also known as the "people who are gone."[77] They were mobile people and moved between summer field villages and winter mountain settlements to take advantage of the meager rainfall essential for their agricultural pursuits. Historically, the T.O. did not have a centralized government.[78] Instead, they lived in one of eleven autonomous villages in which kinship connections predominated. Unlike the Inuit and Yupik of Alaska, T.O. villages utilized clans and moieties and each village was divided into a pair of patrilineal moieties—three clans in the Buzzard moiety and two in the Coyote moiety. Their system differed from those of most other Native nations in that clan and moiety membership was not a factor in the choice of marriage partners.[79]

The T.O. maintained their village communities through ceremonies, marriage, economic cooperation, and social interaction, but with limited political association.[80] As with virtually all Native societies, consensus was the mechanism utilized to arrive at decisions.[81] T.O. cultural sovereignty and their legal system are embodied by the concept *himdag* which refers to "a way of life inclusive of terms such as culture, heritage, history, values, traditions, customs, beliefs, and language."[82] Centering around community, generosity, modesty, and family, *himdag*, a spiritual term, offered guidance for ideal behavior and appropriate social norms. When norms were violated, the parties took their grievances to the headman. The leader would then confer with the elders. After all parties had been heard they would then talk about the situation until consensus was achieved and a resolution identified.[83]

The role of the leader in T.O. village life was essential because public life focused on that person. But they were neither executives nor legislators. They led by example, oratory, and generosity. The following titles have been used for them: "Wise Speaker," "Fire Maker," "Keeper of the Smoke," "The One Above," "The One Ahead," and "The One Made Big," with each title reflecting an aspect of leadership the designee was expected to fulfill.[84] As Bahr notes, "The road to authority at the nightly council meetings was gift-giving. Those leaders ruled public life only in the sense of being in control of the agenda of the meetings and in being able to speak first and last on any issue. They could not compel agreement, and, in fact, strong argument over an issue—whether to go to war, when to work on communal irrigation ditches, when to hold a ceremony, whether sorcery was being practiced—was studiously avoided." In other words, a leader's legitimacy was a "backlog of respect earned through industry and generosity. It was essential to becoming the leader for there was no strict

46　INDIGENOUS GOVERNANCE

rule of succession. It was also the requirement for keeping the position, and the problems involved with it helped to keep groups in flux and to keep authority soft-spoken."[85]

Fox (also known as Meskwaki)

The Fox name for themselves is Meshkwakihug, or "Red Earth People," so named because of the kind of earth they were created from.[86] An Algonquian-speaking people, the Fox historically lived in northeastern Wisconsin. Today, as a result of colonization by the French and later the United States, the Fox joined with the Sauk (Sac) and gradually split into three separate nations known now as the Sac and Fox Nation of Missouri (Kansas and Nebraska), Sac and Fox Nation (Oklahoma), and the Meskwaki Nation (Sac and Fox Tribe of the Mississippi) (Iowa). For purposes of this chapter, the focus will be on the political organization of the Fox before and during the early years of colonization.

As was true of virtually every Native nation encountered by Europeans in the encounter era, the Fox, when met in 1770 by Jonathan Carver, an Englishman, were described as a people living in a near state of anarchy:

> Although [the Indians have both military and civil chiefs], yet [they] are sensible of neither civil nor military subordination. As every one of them entertains a very high opinion of his consequence, and is extremely tenacious of his liberty, all injunctions that carry with them the appearance of a command are instantly rejected with scorn. On this account it is seldom that their leaders are so indiscrete as to give out orders in a peremptory style . . . there is no visible form of government; they allow of no such distinction as [that between] magistrate and subject, everyone appearing to enjoy an independence that cannot be controlled.[87]

Such was not the case, of course, as a closer examination of their society reveals. This is another example whereby knowledge of religious traditions is essential to the understanding of political organization. The most fundamental religious concept for the Fox was *Manitu*—a kind of supernatural power that has been compared to the Maori concept of *mana*, or spiritual energy.[88] The possession of Manitu power was understood to be temporary and conditional. The only proof that a person possessed it was by the display of skill in a particular activity, whether that be success in battle or favorable hunting results.[89] Importantly, because the power was potentially dangerous it was considered perilous and immoral for one person to exercise substantial control over others.[90] Powerful beings were to be feared, not admired.

Thus, Manitu functioned as the "fundamental precept governing concrete day-to-day behavior in Fox life" and permeated the political organization of Fox society.[91] This is evident in the authority wielded by the three principal leadership positions: village chief or peace chief, war leader, and ceremonial leader. The village chieftainship was permanent, patrilineal, and based on heredity—always held by a Bear clan member. The primary role was as arbiter and peacemaker.[92] The war leader position was filled by someone who had received the call in a vision. However, the war leader's authority was limited to a single campaign, and they could not coerce anyone to join their party. Finally, the ceremonial leader could be anyone who had learned one or more of the many religious rituals of the nation. But like the other leaders, their powers were limited to ceremonial activity.[93]

Finally, there was a village council comprised of the leaders of several extended family units. The village chief was the titular head of the council but had no more influence than any other council member. Decisions were made by consensus. "Public opinion, therefore, was almost automatically followed because every family was represented on the council."[94]

Conclusion

It is clear that Indigenous peoples' political organization varied tremendously from those of non-Native peoples and included many impressive elements. First, kinship formed the basic social building block for larger social, economic, and political structures. Indigenous societies were bound together in complex, interwoven social relationships based on ties such as blood, language, clan, ceremonial practices, and land boundaries.

Yet, Native communities were not idyllic societies, and interpersonal conflicts occasionally erupted which led to deep political, social, cultural, and economic divisions that predated European arrival. This despite the fact that consensus was the predominant decision-making process in the vast majority of nations. There may be some truth to Metcalf's comment that "a strong commitment to the ideal of consensus in some societies may even have aided the emergence of factional politics by precluding the development of effective institutions to control and reduce conflict."[95]

Second, and entwined with kinship, was the idea that individual or personal autonomy was essential and to be protected and respected. But, unlike the rugged individualism of Euro-America, virtually all Tribal societies tempered personal autonomy with a sense of community obligation and responsibility.

Third, there was an emotional-spiritual-physical connection to homeland. Indigenous people, animals, plants, and virtually every other part of the

48   INDIGENOUS GOVERNANCE

landscape were integral to the balance of Creation, of which humans were but a part. Technologically, Indigenous peoples in North America required less sophisticated systems of agriculture and metallurgy—though some nations were quite advanced in both—because their mental, intellectual, creative, cognitive, and spiritual capacities were so great.[96] As a result, most Native peoples' bonds with their environments were deeply personal. As one commentator put it: "People, animals and plants could change the form in which they appeared, a transformation recorded in myths and stories and represented today by the use of animal masks in dances and rituals. In many Indigenous cultures, human beings were simply mediators of complex relationships between plants, animals and themselves, touching and consuming the spirits of those they hunted and cultivated."[97]

Fourth, traditional Indigenous cultures rarely separated the political world from the spiritual world. Political actions generally were carried out with "spiritual guidance and oriented toward spiritual as well as political fulfillment."[98]

Fifth, sovereignty, the intangible bond that binds a people together with their environment, was vested in the community—the people—not in positions of leadership. Native leaders were servants of their people, and an individual was not placed in a leadership role unless they had "demonstrated over and over again that he or she has the spiritual and physical well-being of the rest of the tribe at heart."[99]

Sixth, men tended to hold most of these types of elected or hereditary political leadership positions. Historically, women held significant influence in other areas, particularly in family networks at the center of Indigenous social life. This fact, of course, varied across Native nations and there were exceptions. Women were warriors and hunters, and the idea of gender itself is a subject with significant cultural variation among Indigenous peoples.[100]

Seventh, the primary thrust of Indigenous governments was more judicial than legislative or executive in structure and orientation. Adjudication and mediation figured more prominently in coping with the unpredictability of human interactions, particularly for resolution of conflict, than did prosecuting or legislating. This adjudicatory nature of original Indigenous societies is in distinct contrast to the predominantly legislative approach introduced to them by Europeans.[101]

Finally, definitions of leadership and the relationship between "leaders" and "followers" was strikingly different in Indigenous communities. Leaders generally lacked coercive power and were expected to rely on persuasion, generosity, and oratory in their roles. But there were important differences across nations. For example, among the Western Pueblo communities, secrecy was utilized by certain Pueblo leaders as a means to retain political power.[102]

POLITICAL ORGANIZATION BEFORE CONTACT 49

Even before Europeans arrived, Native political leaders showed they were capable of making necessary modifications to their social and political institutions as their internal and external relations unfolded. Those powers of adaptation would be stretched to new levels with the sustained and destructive European intrusions into Native lives and lands.

3

European Intrusions/Native Political Transitions

In virtually every respect imaginable—political, economic, cultural, sociological, physiological, psychological, geographical, and technological—the years from Columbus' arrival in 1492 to the 1930s Indian Reorganization Act, when over 100 Native nations adopted formal constitutions—brought massive upheaval and transformation for Indigenous peoples. Everywhere, U.S. Indian law (federal and state)—by which I mean the law that defines and regulates that nation's political and legal relationship with Indigenous nations—aided and abetted the upheaval. This comprehensive legal system has been characterized by Rockwell as "big government." He defines "big government" loosely as "the combination of (1) national, programmatic social, economic, trade, and regulatory policies touching the lives of millions; (2) the bureaucratic capacity, discretionary authority, and administrative autonomy to plan, to innovate, and to effectively implement policies and programs; and (3) an awareness, a sense of the state, seamlessly and inextricably woven into the fabric of everyday life and never far from the consciousness and activity of American society." Big government, says Rockwell, "won the West."[1]

The nature of U.S. Indian law is, of course, radically different from the various Indigenous legal and customary traditions that encompassed the social norms, values, customs, and religious views of Native nations. These fundamentally distinct legal and political cultures, and their diverse practitioners and purveyors, are thus frequently in conflict. Nonetheless, important moments of recognition did occur, particularly during the early treaty period (1600s–1800s), and later, there were infrequent spasms of U.S. judicial recognition. In Ex Parte *Crow Dog* (1883) and *Talton v. Mayes* (1896), for example, the U.S. Supreme Court acknowledged the distinctive sovereign status of Native nations by holding that the federal Constitution did not constrain the inherent rights of Indigenous nations because their sovereignty predated that of the United States.

Perhaps the period of greatest European acceptance occurred during the encounter era, when Indigenous practices of law and peace, particularly among the Native nations of the Northeast, served as the broad philosophical and cultural paradigm for intergovernmental relations between Indigenous peoples and the various European and Euro-American diplomats and policymakers with whom

Indigenous Governance. David E. Wilkins, Oxford University Press. © Oxford University Press 2024.
DOI: 10.1093/oso/9780190095994.003.0004

they interacted. Whether Tribal, based on Indigenous custom and tradition, or Western, based on English common law and tradition, law speaks to the basic humanity of individuals and societies. In both cases, it provides guidance for human behavior and embraces ideals of justice. Initially, therefore, law was a powerful tool used by for Indigenous and non-Indigenous leaders to forge well-founded diplomatic relations.

Regrettably, this state of multicultural negotiations, of treaties and mutual respect, would not be sustained. Over time, Euro-American attitudes of superiority—legal, political, religious, cultural, and technological—gained the upper hand to such a degree that Native systems of politics and law and culture came to be disrespected, displaced, and sometimes utterly destroyed. Shunted aside into the corners as colonized peoples, Native peoples who sought justice or simply to maintain their political autonomy were required to use the same Anglo-American legal system that had devastated their basic rights. They were frequently coerced to accept Western-based political and legal systems that rarely reflected their values.

Since the early 1800s, U.S. Indian law has only occasionally acknowledged the distinctive condition—inherent Native sovereignty—that is the foundation of every Indigenous community's efforts to endure in their political and legal relationship with the federal government and the constituent states. The absence of genuine bilateralism—the lack of Indigenous voice in law and politics despite the rich and lengthy diplomatic record—has plagued the political, legal, and cultural relationship between Tribal nations and the United States ever since.

The greatest absence in the study of American political and legal history and federal Indian law is the actual voice and presence of Native peoples. That daunting silence enables Western political and legal practitioners to act as if their vision and understanding of the law are all there is or ever was. Their presumption is contradicted by the ways the treaty relationship unfolded and the ways Indigenous peoples still struggle to practice their own governmental and legal traditions in the face of overwhelming pressure to ignore or belittle those very traditions. But the presumption is immensely powerful. How did U.S. law and politics come so to dominate, directly and indirectly dominating, diminishing, and sometimes dismantling the inherent sovereign status of Native nations and their equally legitimate political and legal traditions?

The short answer is an unwillingness to acknowledge or inability to address the inexorable, simultaneous assaults from extant factions of political and legal pluralism. National and state politicians, the legal establishment, business entrepreneurs, and white settlers all acted with the common goal to ensure that nothing derailed Euro-American expansion from a fledgling national polity to an internationally recognized industrial state wielding unprecedented power, domestically and abroad. Or as Rockwell aptly put it "conquest was to be had

52 INDIGENOUS GOVERNANCE

in battle only if necessary; otherwise, the path of conquest would be laid by federally controlled administrative mechanisms. States delegated policymaking and administrative primacy regarding expansion to the national government. Congress delegated power and discretionary authority to the president and the executive branch's administrative offices, such as the War Department and, later, the Department of the Interior. Agents of these departments designed and implemented Indian policies and administered Indian affairs across the continent with substantial effectiveness in the century and a half before the New Deal."[2]

The U.S. political and legal regime as defined and exercised by those in power in federal, state, and corporate offices, occasionally recognized Indigenous sovereignty, resources, and rights. Far more often it was employed to destroy or seriously diminish them. Alexis de Tocqueville, one of the first commentators to note the almost fervid concern that Americans had with law and the legal process, observed its application to Indigenous affairs. "The Americans," said de Tocqueville, in contrast to the "unparalleled atrocities" committed by the Spaniards, had succeeded in nearly exterminating the Indians and depriving them of their rights "with wonderful ease, quietly, legally, and philanthropically, without spilling blood and without violating a single one of the great principles of morality in the eyes of the world. It is impossible to destroy men with more respect to the laws of humanity."[3]

Coming to power during the bloody American Revolution and anxious to establish the legitimacy of their new state in the court of world and American settler opinion, federal policymakers, in constructing their framework for democratic society, fervently supported a social contract that theoretically recognized the rights of virtually everyone. With sufficient flexibility of interpretation, the same contract allowed the oppression of basic human rights of women and peoples of color, indeed of any non-whites who lacked the proper skin color, class, and social connections to profit from the expansion of the state.

Native nations, because of their preexistence, political and economic independence, and early military capability, won a degree of respect from colonizing European nations and later the United States that African slaves and women could not attain. However, the American public and lawmakers simultaneously stressed the allegedly inferior cultural, political, technological, and social status of Tribal nations in relation to Euro-Americans. This contradictory mindset evidenced itself in U.S. Indian politics and law in three distinctive, yet interrelated paradigms or predispositions. They are distinctive in the sense they originate from different sources, time periods, and motives. They are interrelated as underlying each is the same foundation of colonial and ethnocentric/racist assumptions. The three paradigms can be summarized by three keywords: treaties, paternalism, and federalism.[4]

The treaty paradigm deems law the most effective instrument to ensure justice and fairness for Indigenous people. Here, the federal courts and the political branches formally acknowledged Native nations as distinctive political bodies outside the scope of federal law or constitutional authority. The most basic assumption of this viewpoint was that treaty considerations (i.e., ratified treaties and agreements) were the only appropriate and legitimate instruments to engage and determine the course of diplomacy between Indigenous communities and the United States. As only nations may enter into treaties, the constituent states were reduced to the role of frustrated observers, unable to interfere in the nation-to-nation relationship without federal and Indigenous consent.

When federal lawmakers and jurists acted in accordance with the treaty paradigm, as they did in enacting the Northwest Ordinance of 1787 and in cases such as *Worcester v. Georgia* (1831), *The Kansas Indians* (1867), and Ex Parte *Crow Dog* (1883),[5] the United States was formally acknowledging that Native peoples were separate and sovereign nations and that the treaties that linked the two sovereigns, much more than being mere contracts, were the supreme law of the land under Article VI of the Constitution. Under this disposition, the federal government's actions generally left Indigenous nations free of the constitutional constraints applicable to the states and to the federal government, itself. Early interactions under the treaty paradigm granted both explicit and implicit recognition to legal pluralism, even though the language used in the various policies, laws, and cases still sometimes contained racist and ethnocentric discourse that perpetuated stereotypes about Indigenous peoples.

The other two paradigms, federalism and paternalism, were far more commonly used throughout the period under examination—and beyond—to justify federal and state laws and court decisions that had devastating consequences for Indigenous collective and individual rights. The consequences were so severe, in part, because neither of these frameworks gave any consideration whatsoever to Native governments, values, laws, or morals.

When the United States operated in accordance with the paradigm of federalism, the law was perceived as the prime mechanism for furthering the political and economic development and territorial expansion of the United States as a nation in conjunction with its constituent states. This view of the law was maintained notwithstanding the simultaneous presence on the North American continent—in fact and in law—of Native nations, each intent on maintaining its own political and economic development and historic territories. The federalism paradigm was inward looking, concentrating its gaze on the Euro-American political community. It treated Tribal nations largely as obstacles to that entity's self-realization, otherwise unseen and unheard. This paradigm was very much in evidence prior to the American Civil War.

54 INDIGENOUS GOVERNANCE

When operating in accordance with the paradigm of paternalism, the United States tended to portray itself as a deeply moralistic, civilized, and Christian nation, virtually always above reproach. This view predominated from the 1850s into the 1930s, when the federal government inaugurated the Indian reservation program, established boarding schools, imposed Western legal and political systems on Indian Country, allotted Native lands, and forcibly sought to acculturate Indigenous peoples. Deeming Native persons and nations culturally inferior, the law became an essential instrument in moving them from their so-called uncivilized or primitive status to mature civility. The United States envisioned itself as a benevolent "guardian" to its naïve Indian "wards"; their cultural transformation was considered inevitable. The only question was whether the process would be achieved gradually or rapidly.

Fundamentally, the various processes used by federal and state officials and corporate powers under the three paradigms brought about the cultural genocide, segregation, expulsion, and coercive assimilation of Native peoples. Of these, coercive assimilation—the effort to induce by force the merger of politically and culturally distinctive cultural groups (Native nations) into what had become the politically dominant cultural group (Euro-Americans)—has been the most persistent process employed by federal lawmakers. The most vigorous and unapologetic manifestations of forced assimilation commenced in the latter part of the nineteenth century and continued into the 1920s. During this period, the Supreme Court sanctioned the denial of treaty rights, the confiscation of Native lands, and a host of other coercive intrusions on Native peoples by the creation of a new and wholly non-constitutional authority, congressional plenary power. The court defined this new power as virtually boundless government authority and jurisdiction over all things Indigenous. Since that time, federal power has rarely been wielded in such an openly crass manner. Yet, today, the court appears far less concerned with consistency or fairness, let alone the appearance of either. The bottom line is that both the Supreme Court and Congress continue to insist that they retain virtually unlimited authority over Tribal nations and their lands and only seem to differ in the approach and justifications for these actions.

The three paradigms or predispositions described here—treaties, federalism, and paternalism—have successively defined the parameters of the imaginative field in which U.S. lawmakers and politicians operated from the late 1700s to the 1930s and after and, to a real extent, in which they still operate today. Indigenous nations at the beginning of the nineteenth century were generally recognized by the United States as political sovereigns and territorial powers, even though they were usually deemed to be culturally and technologically deficient peoples. Between 1790 and 1930, Indigenous nations and their citizens experienced profound shifts in their legal and political status: from parallel if unequal sovereigns to domestic dependent sovereigns; from relatively autonomous to removable and confinable entities, then to ward-like incompetents with assimilable bodies. Then, finally, to semi-sovereign nations and individuals entitled to degrees of contingent respect for their unique cultural, political, and resource rights, but only through the condition of attachment to land, which in turn meant continued subordination to an overriding federal plenary control.

These oscillations in the fundamental legal and political status of Indigenous peoples confirm federal lawmakers' and American democracy's inability or unwillingness to adopt a consistent approach to Native peoples' sovereignty and their distinctive governmental rights and resources based on treaties and constitutions. The successive changes arise from Euro-American perceptions of Native peoples—albeit perceptions with all too real consequences—rather than from the actual realities of Native peoples. They lead us to the conclusion that the United States has refused consistently to acknowledge the de facto and de jure political and legal pluralism that has always existed in North America. The federal government has still to live up even to the potential outlined in many treaties, the Constitution, and the Bill of Rights, far less the reality of what is written there.

As the discussion of the treaty paradigm has shown, Indigenous governments, law, and sovereignty occasionally have been recognized in U.S. law. They continue to play an important, if variable, role in structuring Tribal political and economic relations with the United States and the several states. A number of commentators have observed that recognition and support of the Indigenous legal and cultural traditions of Native nations are critical if a democracy of law is ever to be achieved in the United States. Despite the remarkable efforts of Native nations to retain and exercise essential components of their cultures and traditions, the political, legal, economic, and cultural forces wielded by non-Indians have made it impossible for Native peoples to act unencumbered. Yet their traditions remain "deeply held in the hearts of Indian people—so deeply held, in fact, that they retained their legal cultures in the face of U.S. legal imperialism, creating a foundation for a pluralist legal system in the United States today."[6]

Indigenous Political Adaptations

Native nations are uniquely constituted social, political, and cultural entities. As we have seen, the consistent failure to recognize that reality has meant that colonial and federal efforts to develop a coherent and consistent body of legal principles to deal with Native nations were never very successful. Still, not all Tribal nations were brought under the colonial or federal umbrella, nor were they all viewed in the same way by Western governments. Several groupings of

56 INDIGENOUS GOVERNANCE

Indigenous peoples were considered distinctive, becoming the focus of a great deal of Western law and thus meriting specific discussion: The Pueblo nations of present-day New Mexico, the Algonquian peoples of the Northeast that were organized into praying towns, and the so-called Five Civilized Tribes[7]—the Cherokee, Chickasaw, Choctaw, Creek, and Seminole.

Pueblo Peoples

The nineteen Pueblo nations are distinctive in part because of their particular political, cultural, and linguistic institutions and because of their long historical relationship with the Spanish and, later, the Mexican governments. The Pueblo communities within modern-day New Mexico organized—many say in 1598, the year they met Juan de Onate, the Spanish governor—a broad coalitional system of intertribal governance called the All Indian Pueblo Council (AIPC). The AIPC, while respecting individual Pueblo political and cultural autonomy, enabled collaborative effort when dealing intergovernmentally with the Spanish, Mexican, and later the federal and state governments. Onate, in fact, launched a sustained program of cultural change aimed at converting and civilizing Pueblo members. The Spanish imposed a civil government system early in the seventeenth century in each of the Pueblos with a set of Native officials to deal with Spanish civil and missionary authorities. Among the Tewa people, for example, the officers were governor, lieutenant governor, an *alguacil* or sheriff, a *sacristan*, two *fiscales* or church wardens, and four *capitanes de la guerra* or War Captains.

> The governor," according to Dozier, "represented the village in all important dealings with the Spanish authorities. The lieutenant governor served as assistant to the governor, represented him in his absence, and in the event of the governor's death succeeded him. The *alguacil* had the function of maintaining law and order within the Pueblo. The *sacristan* was a church assistant and a helper to the priest. The *fiscales* were responsible for mission discipline. The War Captains were responsible for maintaining adherence to Spanish civil law and for punishing infractions; as they were often selected from among the assistance of the moiety priests, they also exacted obedience to native customs.[8]

Spanish Catholic priests sought to eliminate traditional beliefs and ceremonial practices—with force, when necessary.[9] The priests' brutal and ethnocidal efforts culminated in the Pueblo Revolt in 1680 when the united peoples drove the Spanish from their homelands, although the Spanish would return near the end of the seventeenth century.[10] During the next two centuries, according to

Dozier, Spanish efforts to forcibly assimilate the Pueblos were far less brutish and, as Spanish authorities were increasingly forced to expend resources to repel Navajo and Apache attacks, the Pueblo communities were better able to maintain their cultural, political, and religious institutions. The Pueblos accommodated the Spaniards by outwardly appearing "to have accepted the imposed cultural patterns, but they continued to practice their own indigenous religion and customs behind closed doors, heavily guarded against church and civil authorities. The officers of the Spanish civil government system made a pretense of cooperating with Spanish governmental authorities, but the positions were filled by Indians chosen by native ceremonial leaders and they simply served as a buffer group for the latter."[11]

Over time, the imposed Spanish system of government became a useful tool that masked the activities of Native priests who embodied the original, organic political–religious traditions of the Pueblos.[12] Thus, despite many institutional changes in community life initiated during the Spanish era, the basic outlines of their traditional sociopolitical and ceremonial life continued to exist. In fact, according to Crandall, while Pueblo electoral practices clearly evolved over time, many aspects persisted, including: "Nomination of candidates by traditional religious leaders; approval of candidates by society leaders; absence of campaigning for office; elections taking place at the New Year; a clearly defined, typically limited, electorate; unanimity as a guiding principle; use of scripted, ceremonial language throughout the process; swearing in of officers by both traditional Pueblo and Spanish Catholic officials; and distribution of ceremonial canes to elected officers as insignias of power."[13]

Thereafter, Pueblo connections to previous Spanish and Mexican authorities, their apparently enfranchised status, and generally peaceful demeanor toward American settlers and the federal government raised the question of whether the Pueblos were to be considered "Indian tribes" within the meaning of existing federal statutes, such as the 1834 Trade and Intercourse Act, designed to protect Native lands from white encroachment. Because of the Pueblos' ambiguous legal status and less confrontational comportment, increasing numbers of Mexican–American and Anglo-American settlers became squatters on lands granted to the Pueblos by Spanish authorities. The Pueblos resented these intrusions and, with the support of their Indian agents and the federal government as their trustee, sought to have the trespassers evicted. The matter came before the U.S. Supreme Court in *United States v. Joseph* in 1877.[14] In that case, the court was asked to decide whether the Taos Pueblo constituted an Indian "tribe" under the meaning of the 1834 Intercourse Act. If they were recognized as a "tribe," federal officials could expel the white interlopers. If they were not, the federal government had no such authority, leaving the Pueblo members to deal with the squatters on their own.

58 INDIGENOUS GOVERNANCE

The court found that the Pueblos were far more "peaceful, industrious, intelligent, honest, and virtuous" than the neighboring "nomadic" and "wild" Navajo and Apache tribes. Therefore, they could not be classed with the Indian tribes for whom the intercourse acts had been passed. Being far too "civilized" to need federal guardianship, the Pueblos could decide for themselves who could live on their lands. The justices opted not to address definitively the issue of whether or not Pueblo individuals were American citizens, but they did acknowledge that the Pueblos' Spanish land grants gave them land titles superior to those issued by the United States.

In 1913, a year after New Mexico gained statehood, Pueblo status was dramatically reconfigured by the Supreme Court in *United States v. Sandoval*.[15] So long as New Mexico had only territorial status the Pueblos had been of peripheral concern to the federal government. With statehood, the subject of intergovernmental relations and Pueblo status required clarification. Congress had provided in New Mexico's Enabling Act that the terms "Indian" and "Indian Country" were to include the Pueblos and their lands. These provisions were incorporated into the state's constitution as well.

Although a sizable body of statutory and judicial law had held that the Pueblo were not to be federally recognized as Indians for purposes of Indian-related legislation, by 1913 the number of whites inhabiting Pueblo territory had increased dramatically, and federal policy was now focused on the coercive assimilation of all Natives. A general guardian–ward relationship had become the guiding policy assumption of many federal officials. All Tribal peoples were viewed as utterly dependent groups in need of constant federal tutelage to protect them from unscrupulous whites and their own vices.

In *Sandoval*, the Supreme Court found that the civilized, sober, and industrious Pueblo peoples of its 1877 decision had somehow culturally regressed, becoming "primitive" and "inferior" and completely dependent on the federal government. Relying on a legal paradigm steeped in paternalism and arbitrarily expanding upon congressional actions meant solely to protect the Pueblos from whites selling liquor, the High Court went to extraordinary lengths to show that, although the Pueblo peoples remained "industrially superior" to other Native nations, they were still "easy victims to the evils and debasing influence of intoxicants because of their Indian lineage, isolated and communal life, primitive customs and limited civilization." The Supreme Court proceeded to reconfigure Pueblo legal status, holding that their alleged cultural debasement necessitated federal trust protection of their lands from unscrupulous liquor traders.

Ultimately, while the Pueblos proved most adept at accepting and incorporating the Spanish secular offices into their communities, this transition did not fundamentally disrupt ongoing Pueblo political–religious structures. As Reginald Fisher notes, "In a single generalization, it might be said that each individual Pueblo has been [and still is] a miniature, theocratic, community-state."[16]

Algonquian Peoples of the Northeast

In the northeastern part of North America in the mid-1600s, contact with European settlers and the need for a different type of organization to cope with the increasing complexity of political, social, and religious relationships that followed these early encounters, compelled several Native nations to make substantial adaptations in their political organization.[17] The Algonquian peoples of colonial Massachusetts (including the Pawtucket, Massachusetts, Wampanoag, and Narragansett) had early and sustained political, economic, and religious involvement with white settlers, particularly those who practiced Puritanism. As more members of those Native nations converted to Christianity over time, they saw a need to reform the ways in which they were organized, resulting in profound changes in their traditional forms of government without a complete abandonment of it.

From 1646 to 1675 about fourteen praying towns were built and inhabited by Christian Indians following the political system of other municipalities in the Massachusetts Colony. Praying towns were home to converted Native citizens who dressed in English clothing, participated in the market economy, and learned to read and write in both their own language and English. Yet, the political system they adopted was unique since it was "made up of the English colonial and the traditional tribal systems; and superimposed on both of these was a biblical arrangement straight out of Moses."[18]

The first praying town was established through the efforts of a recently converted Native named Waban and Puritan missionary John Eliot, also known as the "apostle to the Indians." Waban and his followers, all survivors of a smallpox epidemic, became Christian converts as a result of Eliot's guidance and, after several meetings, the Natives informed Eliot that they wanted a piece of land so they could build a town.

A set of law laws were developed by Waban and others to guide the community's affairs. While Christian influence is certainly evident in the laws' structure and tone, the town's leaders were selected according to the customs and traditions of the Native community. In fact, the Indians had "actively searched for an alternative social order that would sustain them, even while they selectively retained and reshaped Indian cultural practices."[19]

60 INDIGENOUS GOVERNANCE

Laws of the Praying Town Indians

1. That if any man be man be idle a weeke, at most a fortnight, hee shall pay five shillings.
2. If any unmarried man shall lye with a woman unmarried, hee shall pay twenty shillings.
3. If any man shall beat his wife, his hands shall bee tied behind him and [he shall be] carried to the place of justice to bee severely punished.
4. Every young man, if not another's servant, and if unmarried, hee shall bee compelled to set up a Wigwam and plant for himselfe, and not live shifting up and downe to other Wigwams.
5. If any woman shall not have her haire tied up but hang loose or be cut as a men's [sic] haire, she shall pay two shillings.
6. If any woman shall goe with naked breasts they shall pay two shillings sixpence.
7. All those that wear long locks shall pay five shillings.
8. If any shall kill lice between their teeth they shall pay five shillings.[20]

Five Civilized Tribes

Every Indigenous nation was directly affected by a tsunami of outside forces and each group responded in ways appropriate to their cultural systems. The Cherokee, Choctaw, Creek, Chickasaw, and Seminole—the so-called Five Civilized Tribes of the Southeast—arguably engaged in the most extensive adaptations to their traditional systems of political organization, commencing in the early 1800s with the adoption of constitutions. Each of these nations has received considerable scholarly attention[21] so we need not replicate their findings in detail.

These nations adopted formal written constitutions throughout the 1800s— with the Cherokee's codification of the first formal Native constitution in 1827. Why a formal constitution? After Georgia acquired statehood and increased its assault on the lands and rights of the Cherokee people, the nation's leadership engaged in several strategic actions designed to strengthen their resistance to jurisdictional losses, land dispossession, and so on. Centralization of Cherokee governmental powers was, in large part, a public relations campaign to garner support and assert national rights—the continuation of an acculturation plan controlled by the Cherokee themselves.

The Cherokee's adoption of a secular national constitution that effectively supplanted their traditional political system based on clan structures, decentralized towns, and oral traditions was a most profound political gesture. The constitution demonstrated the Cherokee's adaptive power and fervent desire

NATIVE POLITICAL TRANSITIONS   61

to resist the threats posed by local, state, and federal policymakers. The Cherokee Constitution, the first written document adopted by an Indigenous nation, in key respects was loosely modeled after the federal and state constitutions in its stipulations of three branches of government, bicameralism, disenfranchisement of African Americans and women, and free exercise of religion, yet it also contains specific provisions (e.g., communal land ownership) that sustained a measure of traditional Cherokee values and property notions.[22]

The Cherokee people, in fact, were also the first Native nation to publish their laws,[23] beginning in 1808, create their own written language, and publish a newspaper, *The Cherokee Phoenix* in 1828. It was also evident early in their relationships with the colonial and the federal governments, that they were a people with clear political, clan, and economic differences which made uniform decision-making more difficult than it was for smaller Native nations.

Cherokee contact with Europeans dated back to 1540. More than two centuries later, Cherokee law professor, Rennard Strickland, coined the term "white ascendancy" (1786–1828) to refer to the strategies the splintered Cherokee used to effectively confront the issue of adjusting their traditional culture to meet the ever-encroaching Euro-American territorial, legal, and political demands and impositions. During this era, certain members of the Cherokee leadership set about to modify the U.S. legal system in ways that would benefit their changing needs.

Important factors influenced their shifting political, legal, and cultural systems, including an evolving economic base; their enslavement of African American peoples, fracturing of their religious system (in part because of the influence of Christian missionaries); increasing influence of mixed-blood Cherokees; federal, state, and private pressures aimed at reducing the Tribal land base; and the federal government's failed attempt to vitiate the political sovereignty of the Cherokee Nation (and others) via the Curtis Act of 1898.[24]

The other four "Civilized Tribes" would also adopt constitutions, but these were not established until some three decades later. Champagne points out that one reason the four nations adopted constitutional governments "was to protect themselves from the ever-increasing bureaucratic pressures in land expansion of the United States."[25] While the Cherokee (1827) and Chickasaw (1855) were similar in that they did not incorporate traditional elements like clans or villages into their constitutions, the Choctaw maintained some traditional structures in their governing systems. They had historically operated under a Confederated type of government consisting of three districts—Apukshunnubbee, Mushulatubbee, and Pushmataha[26] led by chiefs. These chiefs and their Tribal councils made up the national government. When the Choctaw established their first constitution in 1834 they maintained the offices of the three chiefs and provided for a "unicameral legislature consisting of ten elected representatives from each district."[27]

62   INDIGENOUS GOVERNANCE

The Muscogee (Creek) and Seminole had somewhat similar constitutional trajectories in that their "traditionally autonomous villages remained the primary local political groups and were incorporated into the central constitutional government as political districts."[28] The Muscogee, for their part, had as early as 1859 adopted a constitution that called for the election of a principal chief and an assistant principal chief in their two established political districts. This document, at least initially, did not substantially interfere with the political autonomy of the historically vital town governments.

In 1867 the Muscogee Nation adopted a new charter that was more clearly patterned after the U.S. Constitution, although the bicameral legislature was divided into a House of Warriors and a House of Kings. While some commentators have suggested that the authority of the constitution did not directly interfere with the existing village governments, others maintain that various rebellions and internal conflicts were generated by the confrontation between the newly centralized government and the pre-existing *talwa*, or town governments.

This constitution would remain in effect until the early 1900s, when, as a result of the Curtis Act,[29] the courts and laws of the Five Civilized Tribes were essentially rendered ineffectual, although they were later reconstituted. Nevertheless, a strong reform movement arose in 1893 with the aim of making additional changes to the political system and to the constitution, in particular. The plan to amend the constitution was approved in November 1893, and the new document was completed on January 17, 1894. Although adopted by the National Council, the proposed constitution was never ratified by the Muscogee people and therefore never put into effect. The constitutional government remained largely intact from 1867 to 1906 because more traditional-minded citizens were denied opportunities to modify their nation's government by a political and economic alliance among Tribal members committed to constitutional-based government and relations with U.S. officials.

While the Five Civilized Tribes were among the first Native nations to adopt formal written constitutions, they were not alone. Prior to the 1934 Indian Reorganization Act and the great surge of constitutions that would subsequently be developed under that law, over sixty additional Indigenous nations as diverse as the Absentee Shawnee, the Seneca Nation, the Sisseton-Wahpeton, the Pima, and the Red Lake Anishinaabe, also adopted constitutions and filed them with the U.S. Department of the Interior.[30]

Native Sovereignty and Western Expansion

The three decades between the Indian Removal Act (1830) and the inception of the American Civil War (1861) was a tumultuous time in American history. These were the opening years of "Manifest Destiny," when the United States acquired political control of large parts of the far West and unexpectedly encountered a new Indian frontier. The new territories included Texas (1845), Oregon (1846), more than one million square miles of the Southwest and West obtained from Mexico by the Treaty of Guadalupe Hidalgo (1848), and an additional 29,640 square miles acquired from Mexico in the Gadsden Purchase (1853). Within the span of a decade, the size of the United States increased by 73%.

These vast conquests and purchases resulted in the physical incorporation of scores of previously unknown Indigenous nations into the United States. The inevitable cultural and territorial collisions resulted in a congressional policy of containment, specifically the establishment of Indian reservations. Between the 1830s and 1850s, the reservation policy remained in an experimental stage. It would not be implemented fully until the 1860s. In fact, treaties, rather than congressional legislation, formed the basis of the law during this era of rapid expansion. That said, the broad outline of this still visible U.S. Indian policy can be found in two comprehensive laws enacted by Congress on June 30, 1834.

The first measure was the final in a series of statutes that regulated trade and intercourse with Tribal nations. The second act, enacted the same day, provided for the organization of the Department of Indian Affairs. With the adoption of these laws, Congress began to codify a set of institutions and procedures that clarified what had been a thoroughly ill-defined structural relationship between the United States and Indigenous nations.

By the late 1840s, two additional statutes had been enacted that were to have a lasting effect on Native peoples. The first amended 1834 Non-Intercourse Act that had organized the Department of Indian Affairs. The new measure made two significant changes in federal Indian policy. It stiffened and broadened preexisting Indian liquor legislation, which had long outlawed liquor in Indian country (a prohibition that would remain in effect until 1953). And it signaled a profound change in the manner and to whom the federal government would distribute monies owed to Native nations. Until that time, those funds had been distributed to Native chiefs or other leaders. Section 3 of the 1834 Act declared that moneys owed to Native nations would instead be directly distributed to the heads of individual families and others entitled to receive payments. Ostensibly designed to reduce the influence of white traders on Tribal leaders, this amendment, in effect, gave federal officials tremendous discretionary authority on the question of Tribal membership, in so far as the disposition of funds was concerned. According to legal scholar Felix S. Cohen, this was the first in a series of statutes aimed at individualizing Tribal property and funds in a way that diminished the sovereign character of Native nations.

The second act, adopted in 1849, established the Department of the Interior. It contained a provision calling for the transfer of administrative responsibility

64 INDIGENOUS GOVERNANCE

for Indian affairs from the War Department to the new department. Supporters of this move believed, prematurely, that Indian warfare was ending and that responsibility for Indian affairs should therefore be placed in civilian hands. Congress retained constitutional authority to deal with Tribal nations, but the legislature more often deferred to the president and the executive branch, especially in the sensitive area of Indian treaties, which were being negotiated by the dozens during this period.

During this era, we begin to see how disruptive colonialism was to Native nations and how federal officials sought to eliminate or control the political structures of Native peoples. Anderson, writing about the Eastern Dakota of the 1830s and 1840s, illustrates the significant political degeneration experienced by the Dakota during this time.[31] Traditionally, Tribal Council gatherings had been places where issues of importance were considered, and leaders worked by consensus to resolve problems. However, internal problems mounted largely as a result of treaty annuities (payments in goods or cash made to Natives in fulfillment of treaty obligations) that were distributed by government officials with trader involvement. Annuities made the Dakota economically dependent, and their leaders felt obligated to adhere to the officials' demands. "Consensus," says Anderson, "became more difficult to obtain, and when leaders did arrive at major decisions . . . they frequently represented the will of whites more so than Indians."[32] As one federal official noted in 1857, "The per capita system of payment directly affected the Chiefs' ability to control their young men."[33]

From the late 1860s through the early twentieth century, the United States—Congress in particular—was openly bent on the domination and paternalistic control of Native nations as identifiable cultural, sociological, and political bodies. The era of congressional unilateralism vis-à-vis Indigenous peoples began during Reconstruction; its clearest expression was a rider inserted in the Indian Appropriation Act of March 3, 1871, which provided "that hereafter no Indian nation or tribe within the territory of the United States shall be acknowledged or recognized as an independent nation, tribe, or power with whom the United States may contract by treaty." Congressional unilateralism culminated in 1906 in systematic efforts to terminate the sovereign status of the Five Civilized Tribes in Indian Territory. Throughout, Congress wielded self-assumed and virtually unrestrained powers over Natives that could never have survived constitutional muster had they been asserted against non-Indigenous citizens.

The treaty process was essentially stymied and extant treaties were subject to implicit disavowal. At the same time, white settlers and land speculators were flooding into the far reaches of the West driven by powerful economic motives and a sense of racial superiority, Federal lawmakers struggled with how best to support what they deemed the inevitable spread of capitalism and

Protestantism while still providing some degree of respect and protection for Indigenous peoples and their dwindling lands. In response, a loose coalition of individuals and institutions that would come to be called the "Friends of the American Indian," was formed. It consisted of law professors, Christian leaders, reformers, leaders of the bar, and a few members of Congress, who stood up against the powerful economic and political interests intent on destroying, or at least diminishing dramatically, the rights and resources of Indigenous peoples. This alliance of Native supporters, Petra Shattuck and Jill Norgren have written, "linked adherence to principles of rationality and morality with the pragmatic needs of manifest destiny. Their debates proved a forceful and convincing counterpoint to the popular clamor for the abrogation of the legal and moral commitments of the past."

The Friends of the American Indian may have helped ameliorate federal policy, but it did not alter its direction (nor did it wish to). Assimilation dominated federal Indian policy and law from the 1870s into the first two decades of the twentieth century. It rested on consistent adherence to six basic goals: transform Native men and women into agriculturalists or herders; educate Natives in the Western tradition; breakup the Tribal masses by means of individual allotment of Native lands and, in the process free non-allotted land for white settlement; extend U.S. citizenship to individual Tribal members; supplant Native customary law with Euro-American law; and finally, transform traditional forms of government into a more pliable version of an informal council or committee which could be relied upon by the local Indian agent when it became necessary to secure Tribal approval for some program or federal decision.

These ideas had already been well in evidence, but their implementation had been spasmodic. From the 1870s onward, with Natives essentially immobilized on reservations and weakened by wars, alcohol, diseases, and displacement, the guardian-like U.S. government and allied institutions—notably the churches—could develop a more systematic and thorough approach to the increasingly ward-like status of Indigenous peoples.

Native Governing Arrangements

Two of the most dominant political institutional structures utilized by both Native peoples and federal officials from the late 1700s to the present were General Councils and Business Committees—the latter otherwise known as Business Councils. Historically, General Councils were made up of the entire population of a given Native community that would usually assemble together during treaty negotiations or for annuities distribution. Later, Councils came to refer to the entire adult population who, depending on the context, could be

66 INDIGENOUS GOVERNANCE

called together by either Native leaders or federal officials when votes were to be cast. This latter meaning is the one that will be further discussed in Chapter 6.

One of the earliest references to a General Council in its original plenary sense is found in the 1794 Treaty of Canandaigua (or Treaty with the Six Nations), the oldest treaty that the United States is still legally bound to enforce. In the preamble we find this language: "The President of the United States having determined to hold a conference with the Six Nations of Indians, for the purpose of removing from their minds all causes of complaint, and establishing a firm and permanent friendship with them; and Timothy Pickering being appointed sole agent for that purpose; and the agent having met and conferred with the Sachems, Chiefs and Warriors of the Six Nations, in a *general council*."[34] (emphasis added)

In 1803, in a treaty with the Delaware, Shawnee, Potawatomi, and others, it was stated, "And the said United States being desirous that the Indian tribes should participate in the benefits to be derived from the said spring, hereby engage to deliver yearly and every year for the use of the said Indians, a quantity of salt not exceeding one hundred and fifty bushels, and which shall be divided among the several tribes in such manner as the *general council* of the Chiefs may determine."[35] (emphasis added)

A final example is found in a removal treaty with the Ottawa Nation in 1831. As partial payment for improvements to the land they were forced to leave in what had become the state of Ohio, they were to receive some $2,000 to be distributed by the Chiefs "with the consent of their people, in *general council* assembled, to such individuals of their band as may have made improvements on the lands ceded by the first article of this convention, and may be properly entitled to the same."[36] (emphasis added)

Frederick Jackson Turner once remarked that by the end of the Civil War, "The West would claim the president, Vice-President, Chief Justice, Speaker of the House, Secretary of the Treasury, Post-master General, Attorney-General, General of the Army, and Admiral of the Navy."[37] Turner hypothesized that this was because the West was the "region of action, and in the crisis it took the reins."[38] He described how the "free lands are gone, the continent is crossed, and all this push and energy is turning into channels of agitation."[39]

The focus of much of this "agitated" behavior was Native lands, Native souls, and Native culture. Within a stunningly brief period, 1866–1871, several critical shifts occurred that, in tandem with established federal Indian policy and law, caused major impacts on Native governments. First, those Native nations who had sided with the Confederacy in the Civil War were compelled to negotiate new treaties by which they surrendered vast amounts of land.[40] Soon thereafter, Congress authorized an Indian Peace Commission to negotiate peace treaties to end the growing hostilities between the Western Native nations and the Americans.[41] Two years later, in 1869 a ten-member Board of Indian Commissioners was authorized. Composed of prominent philanthropists, this unpaid group of influential Eastern citizens was tasked to work closely with the Secretary of the Interior in administering the political relationship between Native nations and the United States.[42] Then, President Ulysses S. Grant, partly in an effort to eliminate abuses in the Indian office, but primarily as a key step in a larger plan to assimilate Indigenous peoples, laid out his famous "Peace Policy." This policy paired the Indian agencies scattered throughout the country with various Christian denominations so that they could more efficiently convert and civilize Native peoples. According to Grant, "No matter what ought to be the relations between such settlements and the aborigines, the fact is they do not harmonize well, and one or the other has to give way in the end."[43]

According to Grant, "A system which looks to the extinction of a race is too horrible for a nation to adopt without entailing upon itself the wrath of all Christendom and engendering in the citizens a disregard for human life and the rights of others, dangerous to society."[44] It was not, however, merely the wrath of other "civilized nations" that propelled the Grant Administration to seek alternatives to warfare with Indigenous nations. Economics and the railroads also played a key role in his decisions.

In the report issued by the Senate's Committee on the Pacific Railroad, Senator William Stewart (R., Nevada) wrote that Native nations "can only be permanently conquered by railroads. The locomotive is the sole solution of the Indian question, unless the government changes its system of warfare and fights the savages the winter through as well as in summer."[45]

Furthermore, Senator Stewart noted that the previous thirty-seven years of wars with Indigenous nations had cost the United States 20,000 lives and more than $750 million. Stewart reported, "The Chairman of the House committee on Indian affairs estimated recently that the present current [expense] of our warfare with the Indians was $1,000,000 a week—$144,000 a day." [46] Grant's "Peace Policy," it was believed, could do no worse and would undoubtedly be far less expensive and more morally defensible.

The final, and arguably the most important, modification in federal Indian policy of that time centered on the subject of whether or not to continue the treaty process with Native nations.[47] The rapidity and comprehensiveness of Western expansion had forced federal officials to rethink their Indian policy approach. Treaty-making thus came under fire. However, Commissioner of Indian Affairs D. N. Cooley in his 1866 *Annual Report* noted that peace could best be maintained with Indigenous nations by "treaty arrangements" and he urged "the continuance of the policy which has met with such gratifying success during the present and last year."[48]

68   INDIGENOUS GOVERNANCE

In his *Annual Report* for 1869, Commissioner Ely S. Parker, a Seneca Indian, rekindled the treaty debate. He believed that the treaty process with Native nations should be closed, though he agreed that treaties already in force should continue to be faithfully executed. On February 11, 1871, Representative William Armstrong (R., Pennsylvania) introduced the following joint resolution: "That hereafter no Indian nation or tribe within the territory of the United States shall be acknowledged or recognized as an independent nation, tribe, or power, with whom the United States may contract by treaty; *and all treaties or agreements hereafter made by and between them, or any of them, and the United States shall be subject to the approval of Congress:* Provided, That nothing herein contained shall be considered to invalidate or impair the obligation of any treaty heretofore lawfully made and ratified with any such Indian nation or tribe."[49] (emphasis added)

This House resolution, except for the important italicized passage, which was later deleted, was attached as an amendment to the Interior Department's 1872 appropriation bill. The deleted sentence was an acknowledgment that although the ratification process was changing, the essence of the treaty relationship itself was to be preserved. The amendment underwent intense bipartisan scrutiny but was eventually approved. Representative Sargent Aaron A. (R., California) proudly noted that the adoption of this measure had three beneficial results: (1) it would end what he called an "improvident system," (2) it would say the federal government millions of dollars, and (3) it would give the House a voice in the process of negotiations with Native nations.[50]

In the midst of all this activity and as part of its efforts to economically assimilate Natives, the federal government introduced the *business committee* concept (a three-member body) to the Potawatomi Nation in 1866 via a short treaty consisting of a single provision.[51]

Interestingly, the provision extended to Potawatomi women the same rights of citizenship and shares in the capital fund of the nation that had been established in an 1861 treaty.

The Pottawatomie Business Committee, at this point, did not supplant their pre-existing political organization which consisted of chiefs and headmen, but effectively gave these leaders a new set of responsibilities—that of businessmen. This is obvious because several of the named "chiefs, braves, and headmen," including Mazhue, Mianco, Shagwe, B. H., Bertrand, J. N. Bourassa, M.B. Beaubien, and L. H. Ogee, were also identified as members of the Business Committee. This sent a message that federal officials were intent on utilizing this new body to carry out federally sanctioned policies and procedures. Such is evident in language found in a Potawatomi removal treaty signed a year later, in 1867. Although acknowledging that the Potawatomi were "represented by their chiefs, braves and headmen," Article Three declared the following:

> A register shall be made, under the direction of the agent and the *business committee* of the tribe, within two years after the ratification of this treaty . . . all existing restrictions shall be removed from the sale and alienation of lands by adults who shall have declared their intention to move to the new reservation: But, provided, That no person shall be allowed to receive to his own use the avails of the sale of his land, unless he shall have received the certificate of the agent and *business committee* that he is fully competent to manage his own affairs; nor shall any person also be allowed to sell and receive the proceeds of the sale of the lands belonging to his family, unless the certificate of the agent and business committee shall declare him competent to take the charge of their property . . . and any contracts for sales so made, if certified by the agent and business committee to be at reasonable rates, shall be confirmed by the Secretary of the Interior, and patents shall issue to the purchaser upon full payment.[52] (emphasis added)

Gradually, other Tribal nations, at the behest of their federal Indian agents, also established business committees or other newly crafted political bodies that became vital organizations. "The experience of many Western tribes," notes Deloria and Lytle, can best be characterized "as a government-sponsored transformation of traditional forms into a more workable version of an informal council, which could be called upon by the agent whenever it became impossible for him to work without some form of approval from the people concerned. This council generally reflected the tribe's pre-existing political subdivisions but it also incorporated the principles of American democracy—like formal election of leaders—the Indian agents were intent on bestowing to the tribes."[53]

On June 25, 1890, the Citizen Band of Potawatomi, now located in Indian Territory negotiated a bilateral land cession agreement with federal officials that was signed by their seven-member business committee. According to the agent it had been "authorized by law and custom and by General Council now and here present and in session." In 1891 the General Allotment Act was amended to provide for equal allotments to all Natives and for the leasing of allotments under particular situations.[54] Section Three of the act authorized business councils, in conjunction with the local agent, to lease those lands which were "not needed for farming or agricultural purposes, and are not desired for individual allotment." This provision also reappeared in an 1894 statute.[55]

In 1893 two additional Native nations established business committees at the Department of the Interior and their agent's behest: the Saginaw Chippewa of the Isabella Indian Reservation and the Arapahoe people of the Wind River Reservation. The five members of the Saginaw Chippewa business committee were tasked with addressing land issues. Several of these were younger men who had received more non-traditional education than the existing chiefs.[56]

70   INDIGENOUS GOVERNANCE

In the Arapahoe case, according to Fowler, "The government's introduction of a business council was an effort to undermine the Arapahoe's practice of discussing important matters in a tribal meeting until consensus was reached. Federal agents supposed that the individuals selected to represent the tribe would make their own decision."[57] But Fowler notes that "in actuality, the council chiefs continued to do as they had always done: they reiterated positions taken and decisions reached by all prominent men."[58] These business councilmen were elected by majority vote, a process aimed at circumventing the influence of traditionally chosen chiefs. Equally important, the new institution was expected to "relieve the government of the customary burden of meeting with and providing a feast for the entire tribe when an important decision had to be made."[59]

Of course, not all Native business committees or councils were established by federal decree or with other outside influences. The Menominee of Wisconsin, as was the case with many Native nations, experienced internal tensions as they struggled against the crushing forces of colonialism. Fortunately for the Menominee, their reduced territory still contained a vast forest of harvestable timber, and some Menominee saw logging as the best chance to gain a measure of economic independence. Tribal members who pushed for the nation's first written constitution in 1892 engaged in what Hosmer has called "purposeful modernization" in an effort to moderate the tension between the rampant individualism of non-Indian society (which typically fails to recognize the larger society) and the communal values of traditional Tribal society (which was typically viewed as inhibiting economic development).[60]

By enacting P.L. 153 on June 12, 1890, Congress acknowledged the Menominee's right to cut and market its own timber, created a mechanism for funding this Tribal enterprise—including the per capita distribution of earnings to Tribal members—and generally endorsed Native participation in logging, something most other lumber-rich Native nations had been denied. Passage of this law was a strong impetus for some Menominee political leaders, like Mitchell Oshkenaniew and Peter LaMotte, to demand a greater degree of self-determination. The proposed 1892 Constitution, written by Oshkenaniew and LaMotte, focused heavily on the construction and implementation of a business council that would have guided the nation's affairs had it become law. It was not approved, however, because of resistance generated by the local Indian agent and certain hereditary chiefs.

By 1904 the Menominee's logging industry had proved a major success, and another attempt was made—this time successfully—to adopt a constitution. Similar to the 1892 iteration, this document contained language rejecting the traditional system of hereditary chiefs, creating in its place a modern structure of governance with a fifteen-member business committee and a tribal chairman. After declaring that "the government of the Menominee Tribe of Indians is not organized according to civilized principles" the document declared in Article Two, Section 1 that "all powers and authority relating to the conduct and settlement of all tribal business, and such matters as concern the general welfare of the tribe herein granted, shall hereafter be entrusted to the general supervision, direction and management of fifteen members of the tribe, who shall be chosen biennially and be known and designated as the 'Business Committee' of the Menominee tribe of Indians."[61]

The Bureau of Indian Affairs at this time acted in a dictatorial fashion on many reservations. Increasing numbers of Native peoples were pressured to organize business committees or business councils organized by the local agents or superintendents who, in some cases, also handpicked who would serve on those bodies. Thus, the Flathead (1909), the Assiniboine Sioux of Ft. Belknap (1908–1909), Sac and Fox (1912), Crow (1922), Navajo (1922), Yankton Tribe (1924), and others had business committees installed on their behalf. As Congressman Melville Kelly stated in 1921, "Almost entirely through items on appropriation bills, and without authorization in any statute, divisions and sections have been added, until today this agency of the Government is a nation within a nation, a duplicate organism which performs almost every act undertaken by every other department of the Government. It is legislative, executive, and judicial in his functions. It acts as judge, jury, prosecutor, and executioner. It is a mammoth anomaly in American form of government."[62]

In the case of the Sac and Fox, Horace J. Johnson ignored the wishes of community members, and personally selected a three-man business committee in 1912 to replace the council and chiefs that had long served the community.[63] But in the case of the Sac and Fox, since the business committee was given no real functions to perform it was "distrusted for obvious reasons by the Indians, and in 1914 it lost what prestige it had when the salaries of its members were eliminated. By 1920 it existed in theory only."[64]

The Crow Tribe of Montana adopted a set of bylaws in 1922 and instituted a seven-member business committee. However, this committee did not supplant the general council, and its members agreed that "matters of great importance to the tribe" should be heard by the full Tribal body whenever at least five members voted for that to occur, along "with the advice and consent of the Superintendent" who had to agree to call a general council into session.[65]

There had been no Navajo national government before the 1920s, except for the brief opportunity generated by their internment at Fort Sumner in the 1860s incarceration. But when oil was discovered on the treaty portion of the reservation in 1922, the federal government established the semblance of a central national governing authority through which Washington might interact in providing leases for mineral development. Prior to this, interested energy companies had to contact the agency superintendent, who then convened a "general council" of

72   INDIGENOUS GOVERNANCE

adult Navajos in that agency to consider the companies' requests for leases. But, as Lawrence Kelly noted, "The obvious implication was that the councils were to be subordinate to the government agent," for the Navajos "were not members of any deliberative body which had been in existence prior to that time."

Oil and gas companies, anxious to exploit the mineral wealth of the reservation, pressured the Department of the Interior and agency superintendents to convene additional "general councils" in both the San Juan (Shiprock) and Southern Navajo (Fort Defiance) agencies. And although several new leases were granted by the Navajos to the companies, most were rejected. Rebuffed, the oil companies then exerted more pressure on the Department of the Interior and the Commissioner of Indian Affairs to take away the inherent leasing power of the Navajos and place it in the hands of a federal representative. The Navajos, however, refused to surrender their right to lease their lands.

Developments in the fall of 1922 signaled an end to the leasing stalemate. First, the Interior Department changed its policy to assert that oil and gas royalties, bonuses, and rentals derived from discoveries in any part of the reservation belonged to the Navajo Tribe as a whole, and not "exclusively to those Navajo residents in whose jurisdiction it was found." This policy change resulted in the Interior Department's creation of a "business council" which was initially composed of three Navajos authorized to deal with lease grants: Henry Chee Dodge, Charlie Mitchell, and Daagha'chii Bikiss. These men were apparently selected by the Secretary of the Interior. However, the legality of this nonrepresentative and nonelected body was immediately questioned because it utterly failed to meet the 1868 treaty requirement of securing the approval of three-fourths of the adult males for any transaction involving Navajo lands. A new, somewhat more representative, council was then established in 1923.[66]

Survey of Native Business and Other Organizations in 1929

In March of 1929 Charles Burke, the Commissioner of Indian Affairs, distributed a Bureau of Indian Affairs Circular, #2565, that was sent to every superintendent of Indian agencies and schools in the United States. Approximately 120 officials received the circular, which reads:

To All Superintendents: Please furnish the Office with the following information at the earliest possible date, and not later than April 10.

1. Have the Indian tribes under your jurisdiction a tribal Business Committee, or other similar elective representative body of Indians to handle matters of business for the tribe?

2. Give the names of the present membership of such committee or committees, showing office held, date of election, term of office, existing vacancies, etc.
3. Have they a form of Constitution and By-laws governing their election, authority, etc.? If filed with the Office, give date, file number, etc. and furnish a copy thereof.
4. If the tribe or tribes under your jurisdiction also have representatives to a super-organization of several branches of the same tribe, the appropriate information relative thereto.[67]

In the months that followed, seventy-eight of the 120 superintendents responded. The information provided gives a vivid eyewitness account of what political life was actually like on many reservations. As important as these records are, the reader must carefully consider the information these records convey within context. First, some of the superintendents' responses were very brief. Many reeked of racism, paternalism, and author bias, riddled with contempt for Indigenous culture and political systems. Second, Commissioner Burke had requested information only about "Business Committees," the preferred organizational form endorsed by the BIA at the time as they were a key component in its plan to stoke capitalism and exercise economic and political control over Native nations. Thus, other forms of Native governing institutions that may have been in place were sometimes ignored or openly denigrated by the superintendents.

Still, Elmer Rusco, who wrote a detailed study of the 1934 Indian Reorganization Act informs us that "the replies to Circular 2565 do provide more information in one place on important questions about Native American governance than any other source. They reveal, first, the existence and vitality of many clearly traditional governments, although the superintendents were not asked about this topic."[68]

A close analysis of the seventy-eight superintendent responses—prefaced with the important caveat that these were all written by non-Native federal employees generally intent on fulfilling the national policy aimed at the eradication or belittlement of Indigenous culture, language, government, and identity as well as the extraction of Native resources—yields a firsthand glimpse of the institutional and cultural structures in place in a number of Indigenous communities.

The data reveal a plethora of business, political, and sundry other organizations dotting Indian Country: Business Committees, Business Councils, Tribal Councils, General Councils, Constitutions, Traditional Governments, Farm Chapters, Livestock Improvement Associations, and Chapters. Not surprisingly, the most frequently identified structures were Business Committees and

74 INDIGENOUS GOVERNANCE

Business Councils. These were present, permanently or sporadically, in thirty-four Native communities.

These tended to be small organizations, consisting of Native leaders selected by the local agent or superintendent. They were often chosen because they had been deemed competent and were willing to work closely with federal officials in their efforts to inculcate the Protestant ethic value of hard work, increase economic efficiency (particularly in agricultural pursuits), expedite the dissemination of information for the entire community, and introduce rudimentary forms of electoral politics in Indian Country. In two instances, agents reported that the Business Committees on their reservations—at Crow Agency and Navajo—met "infrequently." And in three other communities—Flathead (MT), Lower Brule (SD), and Shawnee (OK)—federal officials reported that the Business Committees were "defunct."

But in the communities where the Business Committees were active, there was quite a bit of diversity both in terms of structure and functions. At Fort Berthold, located within North Dakota, for example, home of the Gros Ventre, Mandan, and Arickara, the Business Committee consisted of ten members, one of whom, Clair Everett, an Arickara, was female. The members were appointed annually, although the superintendent did not say whether he or the Tribal communities made the appointment.

The Standing Rock Sioux (SD) had a fourteen-member Business Committee, with two members elected annually from each of the reservation's seven districts. The superintendent of the agency called for the election of these individuals "at the request of the chairman of the committee." The superintendent, E. D. Mossman, stressed that the Indians preferred to hold meetings regularly, but he noted that "I advised them to not overdo the matter as it is expensive for everyone concerned and there is not a large amount of business for them to transact."[69] The Standing Rock Sioux's principal "business," according to Mossman, consisted of "claims against the government [early land claims efforts] and the adoption of new members and a few other such matters."[70] Mossman indicated that the committee members sometimes made policy recommendations to his office and the BIA.

In Oregon, the district superintendent stated that the Siletz Confederated Tribe of Oregon had established an eleven-member Business Committee in 1921 specifically to address questions of Tribal enrollment. This committee, which in 1929 also included one female member, Mrs. Alex Catfish, among its members, also understood that it was to act for the Tribe in all matters affecting the community.

Finally, in at least sixteen cases Business Committees were described as consisting of members who served for life or an indefinite period. This is evidence of retained traditional attitudes about leadership, since historically a number of Indigenous communities had leaders who enjoyed lifetime tenure once they had attained a position of prominence.

The second largest category of political structures was those nations described as having retained "Traditional" forms of governance. There were twenty-seven such nations identified. Most of these were the various Pueblo peoples—nineteen in all—of the Southwest, who for federal administrative purposes had been divided into two large agencies, northern and southern. The Northern Pueblo Agency consisted of the Picuris, Taos, San Juan, Santa Clara, San Ildefonso, Nambe, Tesuque, Santo Domingo, Cochiti, and Pojoaque. Superintendent T. F. McCormick had this to say about the Pueblos under his administrative jurisdiction:

> I wish to state that the status of the Pueblo Indians is much different from any of the Indian Tribes of the United States. The business transacted by the Pueblos is done through the Governor and his Council. No matter what proposition you have to put over, if it does not meet with the approval of the Governor and the Cacique [non-elected traditional religious and secular leaders], you can do nothing. They do not wish and will not tolerate any other council but this old tribal system that they have. . . . They have no form of constitution or laws governing their elections. In practically all cases the Cacique is the ruling man, and he chooses the Governor at his Pueblo. The Indians, in talking it over call it an election, but very few of them have what really could be called an election. Their present form of government has been in existence for hundreds of years and there is no way of introducing any other business committee as long as the old form of government exists in the pueblos.[71]

The Southern Pueblo Agency oversaw relations with the following Pueblos: Acoma, Laguna, San Felipe, Jemez, Zia, Santa Ana, Sandia, Santo Domingo [also listed with the Northern Agency], and Isleta. Laguna was unique at the time as the only Pueblo operating under a written constitution, dating back to 1908. Lem A. Towers, the Superintendent, had this to say about the traditional-minded pueblos under his charge: "The Pueblos of this jurisdiction are organized under their own form of government, consisting of a Governor, subordinate officers and council. This organization conducts the business of the Pueblo. They are elected under their tribal customs, the Governor being elected every year and having the authority to appoint his subordinate officers, the council being made up of the older men of the pueblo. The councils in most of the pueblos are closely associated with their religion and the method of appointing same is not known. However, in the Pueblo of Isleta the council is composed of twelve men selected annually, six by the Governor and six by this office."[72]

76   INDIGENOUS GOVERNANCE

The White Mountain Apache of the Fort Apache Indian Agency in Arizona also adhered to traditional governing structures, as evidenced by Superintendent William Donner's statement that "they have a Tribal Council, according to their old Indian custom, consisting of the head chief and a number of sub-chiefs. . . . This council or business committee is to some extent elective; that is, when a sub-chief dies, the band meets in conference to decide on a successor and the name is then referred to the head chief, who makes the appointment."[73] The head chief and each of the twelve sub-chiefs were "appointed for life."[74]

Many of the historic governing structures of the Puyallup Tribe, located within what is now Washington state, also remained intact, although they had changed the terms used to refer to them from "tribal committee" to "Trustees of the Puyallup Tribe" to "the Council of the Tribe." Henry Sicade, the Tribe's secretary, wrote a letter to the Indian agent in Tulalip on April 2, 1929, describing his people's current governing structure: "We have a tribal committee of the Puyallup Tribe known as the 'Trustees of the Puyallup Tribe.' In early days before the advent of the whites, it was known and called 'The Council of the Tribe.' The Council then did all the tribal business; selected and recommended who would be the chief, sub-chief; made treaties, etc., and did all affairs for the tribe. Today this committee is composed of seven men of the tribe, elected for life."[75]

Another fifteen Native communities employed Tribal Councils as their representative governing body, including Fort Hall (ID), Gila River (AZ), Klamath (OR), Maricopa (AZ), Northern Navajo (AZ), Osage (OK), Pima (AZ), Seneca (OK), Southern Navajo (AZ), Tulalip (WA), Warm Springs (OR), Western Navajo (AZ), Western Shoshone (NV), Winnebago (NE), and Yakima (WA). Two of these nations had adopted constitutions—the Pima in 1901 or 1902 and the Osage—first in 1861 and then in 1881. In the case of the Osage, their 1881 Constitution was terminated by the Department of the Interior in 1900. Interior Secretary, Ethan Hitchcock, listed the following as the principal causes for the abolition of the Osage tribal government: "(1) Acrimonious disputes between the two factions over elections; (2) entire absence of harmony between the Osage tribal officers and the Indian agent in the administration of tribal affairs; (3) the selection of ignorant men as officeholders; and (4) the profligate use of monies received from permit taxes."[76] CIA William A. Jones in his annual report for 1900 noted that the dismantling of the Osage national government had "resulted in the reduction of expenses and consequently a considerable saving to the tribe in the amounts heretofore expended for salaries of a long list of tribal officials."[77]

Circular 2565 also called for information about existing constitutions or bylaws among the Native nations. According to the responses, eleven Native communities had (or were believed to have) written constitutions. Among these were the Crow Tribe (MT), the Gros Ventre and Assiniboine Sioux (MT), the Menominee (WI), the Nez Perce (ID), the Lakota of Pine Ridge Reservation (SD), the Rosebud Sioux (SD), the Standing Rock Sioux (SD), the Winnebago (NE), the Yankton Sioux (SD), the Cheyenne River Sioux (SD), and the Confederated Salish and Kootenai (MT). Interestingly, the Choctaw, Chickasaw, Creek, Cherokee, and Seminole—the so-called Five Civilized Tribes, discussed earlier—were not included in these circular responses. They may have been excluded because their constitutional governments, while still in existence, had been effectively devitalized by congressional decree in 1898 under the Curtis Act.[78]

The list of Indigenous nations with constitutions identified by superintendents in 1929 is incomplete, however, because as previously noted at least sixty Native nations had written constitutions or constitution-like documents on record with the BIA before the 1934 Indian Reorganization Act was adopted.

The superintendents identified and, in some cases, discussed a number of other "elected" organizations that were also present in 1929, including committees, farm chapters, chapters, farm improvement associations, welfare associations, and livestock improvement associations. The organizations that dealt with farming and livestock are informative because they reveal the efforts of both federal officials and Native individuals to find viable economic outlets through modern farming and livestock management techniques that would enable Native entrepreneurs to gain a measure of self-sufficiency to compensate for what they had lost by being confined to reservations. The Native citizens of Fort Totten Agency in North Dakota, for example, had established four farm chapters, each with a president, vice president, and treasurer. These chapters followed parliamentary procedure and maintained minutes.[79]

The communities with the most sophisticated and largest number of "chapter" organizations were the Navajo located within northern Arizona, southern Utah, and western New Mexico. By 1900 the Navajo reservation had nearly quadrupled in size through several presidential executive order extensions, and it was clear that a single federal agent could no longer oversee the affairs of such a greatly expanded area with an increasing population. Thus, Navajo territory was divided into six separate agency jurisdictions, each with its own superintendent. The agencies were Leupp, San Juan, Western Navajo, Navajo Agency, Pueblo Bonito, and Hopi Agency (which included some Navajo members).

John G. Hunter, the superintendent at Leupp Agency in 1927, is credited with the development of what became the chapter system of local government in Navajo country. Hunter recognized a need to reach more Navajos in order to better understand their common problems, especially those related to livestock and agriculture. By 1929 five chapters had been established within the Leupp Agency, each with a president and vice president. According to then superintendent J. E. Balmer, the chapter officials had "authority to settle all minor disputes arising in their district and to consult with their members on everything of importance."[80] Chapter meetings were held once a month.

78 INDIGENOUS GOVERNANCE

However, in other Navajo communities, traditional structures and roles remained prominent. Superintendent Edgar Miller of the Hopi Agency (which was also home to some Navajo) replied to Burke's circular: "The Navajos of this reservation have a local Council, governed by the chief and head man, with the three Navajo judges. The women take part as well as the men. This Council meets at the agency once a month, weather permitting, and goes into session on matters pertaining to the reservation, holds trials of offenders, etc., assisting the superintendent in all local matters of importance and administration."[81]

The gender dynamics of these early twentieth-century governing entities are of particular interest. While not every superintendent identified the Native individuals then serving in governmental capacities by name or gender, most did. Sixty-four superintendents listed the names of elected members, chiefs, or sub-chiefs of Tribal business committees or other elective or nonelective councils as being all male. However, ten Native political systems identified elected or appointed leaders as having at least one female member. The ten included the Crow (eight men, two women), Fort Berthold (nine men, one woman), Fort Hall (five men, one woman), Kaw (two men, one woman), Prairie Band of Potawatomi (five men, one woman), Siletz (ten men, one woman), Snohomish (ten men, three women), and Quinaielt (three men, one woman). Comparatively, white women did not secure the right to vote in U.S. elections until the Nineteenth Amendment was ratified in 1920.

In at least fifteen cases (e.g., Choctaw of Mississippi, Indians of the Colorado River Agency (AZ), Colville and Spokane Indians (WA), Paiute and Pit River of Fort Bidwell (CA), Jicarilla Apache (AZ)) the superintendents actually declared that they could discern no evidence of a business committee or, indeed any form of Tribal organization, for that matter. It is not easy to parse those observations. Did they mean that the Tribes in question had no governing structures at all? That the Natives had some organizational units but had managed to conceal them from the superintendent? Were the political, social, and economic developments in such a state of flux that the agent could find no single term to accurately describe what was in place? Or did the Natives' silence indicate the circular's query was so narrowly focused that the superintendent simply had no reason to describe other, less formal, structures that may well have been present? Additional research is required in order to make a more informed analysis of what, if any, kinds of governing structures were, or were not, in place for those Tribal nations.

Here are a few choice comments from agents describing the apparent absence of any form of Native political organization within their respective agencies:

> *Choctaw Indian Agency* (Mississippi): "The Superintendent of this agency wishes to report that we have no tribal organizations, committees, nor finances of any kind or description at this agency."

Colorado River Agency (Arizona): "I have to respectfully advise that neither the Mohave nor the Chemeheuvi Indians have any tribal organization." The superintendent then noted, however, that "they do have several factional makeshift organizations that are of no benefit because what one faction wants another faction does not and they quarrel constantly. They are divided by religion and tribes."

Colville Indian Agency (Washington): "The Colville and Spokane Indians under the jurisdiction of this Agency do not have tribal business committees or any other elective representative body to handle matters of business for the Tribes."

Jicarilla Apache Agency (New Mexico): "The Jicarilla Apaches do not have any organized tribal council or business committee, and there seems to be no desire among sufficient of them to organize one. Under present differences between members of the tribe it would be difficult to obtain a unified sentiment, and for that reason the matter is not being pressed by them."

Lac du Flambeau Agency (Wisconsin): "None of the Indian tribes under the jurisdiction of this office maintain any tribal Business Committee. Neither is there any other representative body acting in such business capacity."

Walker River Agency (Nevada): "The Indian tribes of this jurisdiction have no tribal business committee or elective representative body of Indians. . . . Attempts have been made heretofore to formulate something along this line, but the plan did not prove to be a practicable one owing to existing conditions.[82] Such association has drawn them away from the tribal customs and has brought them more in touch with the ways and methods prevailing among white people."

This lengthy descriptive assessment of the seventy-eight superintendents' responses reveals an extensive range of governing, business, and customary institutions in Indian Country, some of which resembled pre-contact structures that had persisted. Understandably, there had of necessity been many changes because of the devastating impact of nearly six decades of federal, church, and societal pressures, policies, and personalities. In other words, by the time John Collier and the Indian New Dealers gained office in 1933—while Native nations were still reeling from ethnocidal educational policies, decrepit housing, continuing land and natural resource losses, and cultural and religious oppression—the remarkable persistence of many of their traditional, albeit modified, governing mechanisms provided them with a foundational core widely unacknowledged by many commentators.

Hence, while no Native nation was left unscathed by the forces of American expansion, capitalism, and colonialism, it is clear that many integrated or selectively adopted, and then often modified, the governmental suggestions and

80 INDIGENOUS GOVERNANCE

Table 3.1. Business committees in 1929

Absentee Shawnee (OK)	Pawnee (OK)
Apache (OK)	Pine Ridge Sioux (SD)
Caddo (OK)	Ponca (OK)
Citizen Potawatomi (OK)	Quapaw (OK)
Comanche (OK)	Quinaielt (WA)
Delaware (OK)	Sac and Fox (OK)
Fort Berthold (ND)	Snohomish (WA)
Iowa (OK)	Snoqualmie (WA)
Kaw (OK)	Standing Rock Sioux (SD)
Kickapoo (OK)	Swinomish (WA)
Kiowa (OK)	Uintah and Ouray (UT)
Menominee (WI)	Warm Springs (OR)
Mexican Kickapoo (OK)	Wichita (OK)
Nez Perce (ID)	Winnebago (WI)
Northern Cheyenne (MT)	Wyandotte (OK)
Otoe (OK)	Yankton Sioux (SD)
Ottawa (OK)	

demands pushed by federal officials. Nevertheless, the ravages of allotment, diseases, forced assimilation, and reservation confinement had wreaked havoc on all Indigenous nations, and by the 1930s Tribal complaints were joined by the complaints of white reform groups and others interested in improving the lot of Native peoples.

4

Another Star on the Flag

Attempts to Create an Indigenous State

Notwithstanding the inherent political, territorial, and cultural autonomy and sovereignty of Native nations that has been recognized by external powers from the late 1500s to the present, there have been several attempts by a variety of actors—both Native and non-Native—to establish autonomous colonies for Natives. Some envisioned independent but fully incorporated Native-run territories, while others proposed actual Native states to be admitted into the federal union. Most of these efforts occurred before 1906, but since then there have been occasional, if sporadic, discussions about the need for structural political rearrangements that would incorporate Native nations into the U.S. federalist system of governance. To date, all such attempts have failed to be enacted. This chapter describes and analyzes the previous attempts to politically incorporate Indigenous nations into the United States. See Table 4.1 for a broad timeline of these developments.

The political idea of incorporating Native nations either as a territory, zone, or colony, with or without a governing structure, or as incorporated subunits of non-Native national governments has come from three directions during the past two and a half centuries. European colonial powers, including France, Great Britain, and Spain, first envisioned a comprehensive sovereign Native nation that would effectively act as a buffer zone or neutral belt that would block the expansion of competing colonial powers. These nations' plans explicitly acknowledged Indigenous sovereignty. And, as Annie Abel noted, the only way those powers could ensure their regime's safety and advancement "was to seek their [Native] alliance, guarantee their integrity, and admit your territorial claims, even while asserting a preemptive right of its own."[1] As the fledgling United States developed into a major political and economic contender, this Native buffer zone was also meant to stymie the spread of the American population.

Americans—either on behalf of the government or as religious and private actors—also sought to create a separate Native state. With regards to governmental entities, we will discuss such documents as the 1778 Treaty of Fort Pitt with the Delaware, wherein the sixth article stipulated that friendly tribes, led by the Delaware, with congressional approval, could join the confederacy by forming a state with representation in Congress. Many other such examples of

Indigenous Governance. David E. Wilkins, Oxford University Press. © Oxford University Press 2024.
DOI: 10.1093/oso/9780190095994.003.0005

82 INDIGENOUS GOVERNANCE

Table 4.1. Timeline of indigenous political incorporation activity

1754 Thomas Pownall creates a chart outlining a plan for an Indian colony.

1761 French call for an Indian barrier colony or Indian reservation.

1763 Royal Proclamation Line is established by the British colonial government. It denies any settler the right to purchase Native land west of the boundary drawn along the crest of the Appalachian Mountains without Crown permission. This serves as official confirmation that all lands west of the line remained Indigenous territory.

1778 Treaty with the Delaware contains provision urging the Delaware to form a "state" entitled to a representative in Congress.

1783 General Haldimand proposes the idea of a Neutral Indian State.

1785 Cherokee Treaty contains a provision for the Cherokee to send a "deputy" to Congress.

1787 Alexander McGillivray calls for a separate territory for Native peoples.

1791 Lord Dudas urges the creation of a Neutral Indian State.

1799 William Augustus Bowles creates the "State of Muscogee."

1811 Tecumseh attempts to organize an international body of Indigenous nations.

1820 Jedediah Morse proposes the creation of an Indian Territory that might eventually mature into a Native State.

1824 President Monroe calls for civil governments for Native nations.

1824 Congressional resolution proposes creation of an Indian Territory.

1825 President Monroe calls for "internal government" of all Native nations.

1825 John Calhoun promotes unification of Tribes under a government similar to the states.

1826 James Barbour, Secretary of War, proposes a territorial government for Native nations.

1827 Congressional resolution outlines plan for an Indian Territory to be established.

1827 Isaac McCoy pushes for an Indian State.

1830 Choctaw Nation calls for statehood and a delegate to Congress.

1830 Choctaw Treaty contains a provision for a "delegate" to Congress.

1834 Congressional bill defines Western Territory—home to Native nations—to be "admitted as a State."

1835 Cherokee Treaty features an article giving them the right to a "delegate" in Congress.

1836 Congressional bill calls for an "Indian Territory."

1836 Secretary of War suggests creation of Native government and a delegate to Congress.

Table 4.1. Continued

1837 G. P. Kingsbury calls for a confederated Indigenous government and congressional delegates.

1841 Congress calls for "territorial government" for Native nations.

1843 Grand Council of numerous Native nations is held in Cherokee Nation. They forge an International Compact.

1845 Creation of an "Indian Territory" is proposed in a congressional bill.

1848 Rep. Abraham Robinson McIlvaine (PA) urges creation of an Indian Territory.

1848 Congressional bill for an Indian Territory that includes organizational plans for a "confederacy" of all the Native nations to be represented by a governor, national council, and a delegate to Congress.

1849 N.C. Legislature drafts a resolution calling for an Indian State.

1854 Henry Rowe Schoolcraft advocates for establishment of Indian colonies.

1854 Senator R. W. Johnson introduces a bill calling for three Indian territories— Cherokee, Creek, and Choctaw with the eventual goal of statehood. The Indigenous state was to be called Neosho.

1865 Senate bill proposes consolidation of Indian Tribes into an Indian Territory.

1866 U.S. treaties with the Five Civilized Tribes establish a General Council among the nations.

1870 Okmulgee Council is formed of several Native nations. They draft a constitution.

1872 National Commercial Convention adopts resolution urging President Grant to establish a "mixed" State/Territory—both Indigenous and white.

1878 House Report supports a bill to allow an "Indian Delegate" to the House for the Five Civilized Tribes.

1905 Indigenous nations in the Indian Territory craft a constitution and urge the federal government to support their efforts to create the State of Sequoyah.

1972 Hank Adams, prominent Native rights activist, crafts the "Twenty Point Proposal," a blueprint for improvement of Native political and legal status, that features a call for the restart of treaty-making between Native nations and the federal government.

1980 Authors Russel L. Barsh and James Youngblood Henderson in *The Road* call for a constitutional amendment to incorporate Native nations into the U.S. Constitution.

2004 Peterson Zah, former President of the Navajo Nation, calls for statehood for his nation.

2008 N. Bruce Duthu in *American Indians and the Law* proposes a return to bilateral, negotiated political arrangements between Indigenous nations and the federal government.

84 INDIGENOUS GOVERNANCE

formal Indigenous political incorporation were tendered during the next century. However, federal officials could never agree on the precise nature of such an Indigenous State. Regarding the efforts of religious and private actors, several attempts were made by such individuals who proposed, of their own accord, suggestions for Indigenous colonies, territories, or states. Isaac McCoy and the Reverend Jedediah Morse, among others, advocated such policies in an attempt to "save" Natives from collapse and presumed extinction.

Native political leaders also instituted vigorous, if futile, efforts to restructure their nations' political status through attempts to establish either an Indigenous territorial government or an Indigenous state government with a formal place within the framework of American federalism. Alexander McGillivray (Creek), William Augustus Bowles (a white who married a Creek woman), and others led sporadic efforts from the 1780s through the early 1900s to create separate Indigenous political bodies that would have had a degree of autonomy while still embedded in the U.S. political system. And Native nations in Indian Territory (later within Oklahoma) made numerous attempts to forge a Native state between the 1860s and 1906.

European Plans for an Indigenous State

Great Britain was the first colonial power to discuss the creation of a neutral Indian state in the North American interior, sometime between 1754 and 1755.[2] The idea's genesis dates to 1750 when Great Britain and France began competing for control of the Ohio River forks for commercial and military purposes. As diplomats for both powers negotiated their differences, Britain's ministers constructed plans for the Indian state idea as a means to gain the upper hand in their negotiations with the French.[3]

Thomas Pownall produced a plan of action in the form of a chart that was transmitted to Earl of Halifax sometime between late 1754 and January 1755. Governor William Shirley of Massachusetts strongly recommended Pownall's plan and said this: "I beg leave to take notice of a chart which Mr. Pownall hath transmitted to the Earl of Halifax one part of the design of which is to give a specimen of the disposition of an Indian colony in such a manner as to make the Indians inhabiting it, a good barrier against the French, and at the same time dependent upon the English. The Indians in general are certainly uneasy at any encroachments upon their lands whether by French or English: could we but persuade them by such plans of settlements in their country as the enclosed chart exhibits a specimen of, that the real design of the English was to protect them in the possession of their country, not to take it away, it would be caring all points with them."[4] Sir William Baker drafted a memorandum later in 1755 titled

"A project for Proper Separation of the British and French Dominions in North America" in which the idea of a neutral Indian barrier state was also endorsed.[5]

The imperial war that erupted in 1754 between England and France, in which a majority of Native peoples had aligned with the French, convinced the English in 1755 that a new policy direction was called for. Steps were taken to remove Indian affairs from the control of individual colonies and place them under central administration. Two departments were set up, a northern unit headed by Sir William Johnson, a man of considerable influence with the Iroquois, and a southern department to which Edmund Atkin was originally assigned only to be replaced by John Stewart in 1762. The two superintendents were given full responsibility for political relations between the British and the Indians. The northern superintendent was to have jurisdiction over the Iroquois Confederacy and its allies; while the southern superintendent would govern relations with the Native nations in the South, including the Cherokee, Muscogee (Creek), and others.[6]

The superintendents' activities included gift-giving in an effort to secure Native friendship, negotiating the boundary lines that were demanded after the adoption of the 1763 Royal Proclamation Line, the enlistment of Native warriors to fight alongside British troops, and offering protections from greedy traders and land speculators. Still, little substantive progress was made in terms of bringing trade under strict imperial control.[7] Edmund Atkin, the author of this comprehensive and lengthy master plan for imperial control of Indian affairs said it was imperative that the English support and protect Natives "since the tribesmen are the strongest barrier against French encroachment."[8]

In 1761 the French offered their new plan for a Native barrier country or Indian reservation that they said "should be formed between Louisiana and the Allegheny Mountains." This, said Frederick Jackson Turner, "exhibits an early form of her [France] desire to prevent the encroachment of English-speaking people into the valley, and the use to be made of the Indians as a means of holding this region open to the purposes of France and Spain, closely allied in the family compact of that year."[9]

Native anxieties and frustrations regarding white encroachment and land loss galvanized spirited resistance led by two key figures—Neolin, a Delaware, and Pontiac, an Ottawa. They called for a spiritual awakening and confederated response to the machinations of the colonial powers. Pontiac's allied forces successfully attacked several British posts in western Pennsylvania, Ohio, and Michigan in 1763, but they were unable to defeat the British and in 1765 he signed a peace treaty with them.[10]

Pontiac's fierce resistance to British intrusion compelled imperial authorities to devise the Royal Proclamation Line, which was officially declared on October 7, 1763, by King George III. The proclamation established three specific

86 INDIGENOUS GOVERNANCE

policies: (1) it set the boundaries and the governments for two new colonies—Florida and Nova Scotia—acquired by the Treaty of Paris; (2) it encouraged settlement in the new areas; and (3) it established a demarcated boundary line separating Native lands from those controlled by whites "for the use of the said Indians."[11] The boundary line commenced at Lake Ontario and terminated at the Gulf of Mexico. It generally followed the crest of the Appalachian Mountains.[12]

It was the creation of the boundary line that is most significant for our purposes. By this provision, the King reserved the lands west of the Appalachian Mountains to Indigenous peoples and declared that until the Crown was prepared to purchase the Native title, those lands could not be protected, and no whites were allowed to cross into that area.[13]

Interestingly, while Native ownership of all this territory was now officially recognized, with the area being denominated as "Indian Country," actual governance of the territory remained a major concern. While the authority to govern, or sovereignty, should rightly have been regarded as held by the resident Native nations, the British Board of Trade declared that "a commission for the government of the Indian Country be issued to the commander in chief of the troops in America." Thus, with one bureaucratic decision, the entire West was placed under military authority.[14]

According to Glover Gillette Hatheway, the interval between the issuance of the Board of Trade's Plan of 1764—an ambitious strategy to regulate the rules for trade—and the passage by Parliament of the Stamp Act of 1765, saw the British plan for a vast and protected Indian state in the heart of the continent coming closest to fruition.[15] But the hue and cry that erupted from colonists in the wake of the Stamp Act's enactment precluded the generation of enough support for "an Indian state in the West they considered to be their own."[16]

Between 1765 and the American Revolution the situation of Indigenous peoples and the attendant idea of a Native state was an internal problem of the British Empire. An imperial solution to Britain's Western problems, including Native affairs, was needed, but the Crown lacked the economic resources and manpower to effectuate a solution and the American colonies continued to bristle at Crown control.

At the conclusion of the Revolutionary War, Great Britain and the United States each proposed very different policies to address their relations with Native nations. Federal lawmakers insisted that, having sided with Great Britain during the war, Tribal nations had been conquered and had thus forfeited title to their lands. The British denied this and insisted that by the provisions of the Treaty of 1783, the United States had only secured the exclusive right to purchase Native land but had not gained actual ownership which had been guaranteed to the Natives by prior treaties.[17]

ANOTHER STAR ON THE FLAG   87

Here, again, British officials proposed mediation and the creation of a neutral Indian barrier state. The initial advocate of the Indian barrier state idea in 1783 was General Frederick Haldimand, commander in chief of the military forces in Canada and governor of Québec, who declared that "it would certainly be better for both nations, and the most likely means to prevent Jealousies and Quarrels that the intermediate country between the limits assigned to Canada by the Provisional Treaty and those established as formerly mentioned by that in the year 1768, should be considered as entirely belonging to the Indians, and that the subjects neither of Great Britain nor of the American States should be allowed to settle within them, but that the subjects of each should have liberty to trade where they please."[18]

After 1790, a change in British policy involving the desire for adjustment by treaty of the unsettled relations between the two countries occurred. In 1792 an effort was made to secure, through mediation between the United States and the northwestern Indians, a neutral barrier Indian state along the Canadian border. Britain's goals for such an enterprise were outlined in a letter from Lord Dundas to Lord Dorchester:

Your Lordship being already apprized of the intentions of His Majesty's Servants to endeavor to secure what may operate as an effectual & lasting Barrier, between the Territories of the American States and his Majesty's Dominions in that Quarter, I shall only refer your Lordship to my Letter of the 16 Sept. last and to the late unhappy Contests between those States and the Indians to prove the expediency of such a measure. To obtain so beneficial an end and, at the same time to heal the differences which at present exist, a plan was suggested in some late communications between Your Lordship and His Majesty's servants which Your Lordship appeared to think extremely advisable if it could be carried into Execution. The Idea suggested was, that His Majesty and the American States should *join in securing exclusively to the Indians a certain portion of Territory lying between and extending the whole length of the Lines of their respective Frontiers, within which both Parties should stipulate not to suffer their Subjects to retain or acquire any lands whatever,* and although in consequence of such a Cession the Frontier Posts now in His Majesty's Hands would be given up, Your Lordship appeared to coincide with them in the opinion that the objection to this measure would be much lessened by the Circumstance of their not being to come into the possession of the American States, but to be ceded for the express purpose of becoming part of such Territory as is to be reserved for the undisturbed and independent possession of the Indians. By placing the Indians in such a Position they will become a natural Barrier against mutual Encroachments, and at the same time hold a situation in which their

88 INDIGENOUS GOVERNANCE

attachment and friendly Disposition to His Majesty's subjects may be capable of the most serviceable because of the most extensive Operation. In ascertaining the Territory to be granted to the Indians, three points, I conceive, are principally to be attended to, One to secure, as much as possible, our Intercourse & Trade with the Indians, the second is that the interposed Country to serve as a barrier should extend along the whole Line of the Frontier of His Majesty's Dominions and that of the United States of America, and lastly to take care that their intervention, and the space to be allotted them shall be most considerable in such parts of His Majesty's Frontier as from their situation are most obvious to attack or interruption from any Quarter belonging to the American States (emphasis added).[19]

U.S. officials disagreed with this plan. Hathaway says that "the Indian barrier idea was kept alive until 1795; then two treaties, Jay's Treaty and the Treaty of Greenville, coming on top of an American acceptance of the British principle of Indian ownership dried up the sources from which the argument for an Indian barrier drew its strength."[20]

The British, for their part, revived the idea for a final time in the wake of the War of 1812, and two Shawnee brothers, Chief Tecumseh and the Prophet, played a central role in these events. The Native nations generally aligned with the British at this time, and Tecumseh's attempt at establishing a multinational Confederacy of Indigenous peoples to maintain a united front against American settler expansion led to several years of intense conflict.[21]

The Treaty of Ghent that ended the war on December 27, 1814, essentially provided for a return to conditions as they were before the war and did not directly address many of the problems that precipitated the conflict. In fact, "The crushing defeats of the Indians at the Thames and at Horseshoe Bend and the failure of the British (or the Spanish) to substantiate Indian claims against the Americans put a new complexion on the Indian problem in the West." The British had sought to include provisions in the treaty that would affirm that the territorial boundaries and land rights of their treaty partners, the Native nations, would be respected by the Americans. The neutral Indian barrier state proposed was pushed as a *sine qua non* feature by the British but John Quincy Adams representing the United States, declared on September 1, 1814, that "to condemn vast regions of territory to perpetual barrenness and solitude, that a few hundred savages might find wild beasts to hunt upon it, was a species of game law that a nation descended from Briton's would never endure. It was as incompatible with the moral as with the physical nature of things."[22] Adams and the U.S. government had their way, and the British idea of an Indian state was defeated yet again.

Private and Religious Individuals' Attempts to Create a Native State

In 1772, white settlers on the frontier in Tennessee attempted to establish their own state known as the Watauga Association or the Republic of Watauga. Recognized as the earliest effort by American colonists to form an independent democratic government, it functioned for about five years when, at the request of the settlers themselves, it came under the jurisdiction and authority of the state of North Carolina.[23] Interestingly, Lord Dunsmore of Virginia, in 1774, expressed concerns about the Wataugans' democratic experiment and noted their apparent tributary status with the Cherokee people. "In effect," said Dunsmore,

> We have an example of the very case, there being actually a set of people in the back part of the colony bordering on the Cherokee country, who finding they could not obtain titles to the land they fancied, under any of the neighboring governments, have settled upon it without, and contented themselves with becoming in a manner tributary to the Indians, and have appointed magistrates and framed laws for their present occasions and to all intents and purposes erected themselves into though an inconsiderable yet a separate state, the consequences of which may prove hereafter detrimental to the peace and security of the other colonies; it, at least, sets a dangerous example to the people of America of forming governments distinct from and independent of His Majesty's authority.[24]

A few years later, yet another attempt was made to create an autonomous territory in what is now eastern Tennessee, called the State of Franklin (also known as the State of Frankland and the Free Republic of Frankland). This was a more robust effort to establish a separate state and its people actually developed a constitution and chose a governor. While they secured the votes of seven existing states, they failed to meet the two-thirds majority threshold required under the Articles of Confederation for admittance as the fourteenth state. Interestingly, two friendship and land cession treaties were negotiated by Franklin officials with the Cherokee Nation in 1785 and 1786, which, had the state been admitted, would have been incorporated as an official part of the state and given "a representative in the new legislature."[25]

Although these white colonists were unsuccessful in establishing their own separate states, several other individuals both Native and non-Native, also made concerted efforts to create an Indigenous political body. The five most prominent were Creek Chief Alexander McGillivray, British adventurer and Marylander William Augustus Bowles, religious leaders Jedediah Morse and Isaac McCoy, and noted ethnologist Henry R. Schoolcraft.

90 INDIGENOUS GOVERNANCE

McGillivray's mother, Sehay Marchard, was half-Creek and half-French and was a member of the Creek Nation's Wind clan. Lachlan McGillivray, a well-to-do Scottish Indian trader, had acquired a large estate in Georgia. When Alexander McGillivray moved to Creek country as a young man, he became an influential chief and began to devise a political strategy that he hoped would strengthen the lot of his people.[26] McGillivray resented the incursions Georgians had made on Creek lands and looked to the federal government as an ally to help. He proposed that if Congress created a new state south of the Altamaha, he would "become its first citizen and would permit Georgia to keep the disputed Oconee lands."[27] "Presumably," says Abel, in the fall of 1789, "McGillivray had in mind an Indian state, but his suggestion proved just as futile as those that had gone before."[28]

William Augustus Bowles, a British loyalist, at the conclusion of the American Revolution in 1788, received weapons from the British in the Bahamas so he could raise a loyalist Creek Army. He soon married the daughter of a Creek leader and was adopted into the nation.[29] In an apparent effort to replicate McGillivray's career, in 1789 Bowles took two Creek and three Cherokee men to London "to petition the king to support him as 'generalissimo' of what he called the 'United Nation of Creeks and Cherokees'" in an intended invasion of Mexico and war with the United States.

When Bowles returned from England in 1791, McGillivray put a bounty on his head. He was then captured by the Spaniards and exiled to Manilla. Bowles escaped in 1797 and returned to England bearing the title "Director-General of the Muscogee Nation."[30] He returned to Florida in 1799 and rejoined the Lower Creek people. Bowles had his supporters elect him as Director-General and then declared the independent Indian "State of Muscogee." The state's territory was to be drawn from lands claimed by Spain and the United States. He proposed populating the state with Lower Creeks, Seminoles, and settlers—African Americans and whites. Subsequently, he planned to invite Cherokees, Chickasaws, and Choctaws.

The foundation for this Native state was to rest upon the understanding that the Native nation had "always been sovereign, that they had been recognized as such by Great Britain, and that the transfer of the territory involved to Spain and the United States in 1783 had in no way alienated their sovereignty."[31] Bowles secured Native support by exploiting the Natives' fear of white encroachment; and by providing them with a supply of needed trade goods and weapons. For Bowles, the State of Muscogee would have effectively been a British protectorate; would have helped keep France off the mainland; and which the United States could accept or not. He firmly believed that Britain and the Native people could control Florida and Louisiana.[32]

But his Native state did not last long. The Lower Creek resented the unrest he fomented—like the State of Muscogee's declaration of war against Spain—and

ANOTHER STAR ON THE FLAG   91

in 1803, with the assistance of Benjamin Hawkins, the American agent for the southern Indians, captured him and turned him over to Spanish officials.[33] They received a reward of 4,500 pesos. Bowles died a captive in Havana in 1805.[34]

Now we come to Jedediah Morse and Isaac McCoy, whose goals and careers overlapped as each sought to introduce reforms designed to save Natives from oblivion. Morse, a reverend and a geographer, had long been interested in both the civilization and Christianization of Indigenous peoples who were experiencing rapid physical decline. In 1819 he left the pulpit and devoted himself to the benighted situation of Native peoples. He planned to visit and inspect the nations of the Northwest and, with the federal government's help, sought to "form some general, comprehensive plan for the benefit of all our Indians."[35]

Morse went to Washington DC in 1820 where he met with and conveyed his goals to President James Monroe and Secretary of War John C. Calhoun. He subsequently received a commission from the War Department to make a comprehensive study of the condition of Indigenous peoples in the United States.

Morse was convinced that the Northwest Territory was the logical place for a separate Native territory. "Let this territory," he said, "be reserved exclusively for Indians in which to make the proposed experiment of gathering into one body as many of the scattered and other Indians as choose to settle here, to be educated, become citizens, and in due time to be admitted to all the privileges, and to other territories and states in the union."[36]

In the course of his travels through Native territories, he had occasion to interview a Wyandotte chief, Oumet-zi-ou-hou, also known as Boyer. Morse asked the chief what he thought of his plan to assemble all the Indians together so that they could be civilized and converted to Christianity. The chief emphatically said, "I will not consent—I never will."[37] Notwithstanding the Chief's stern sentiment, Morse plowed ahead with this plan.

A central focus for Morse was this concept of the model community—these were to be small communities located in prime agricultural areas under the tutelage of "education families" that would include ministers, teachers, farmers, blacksmiths, and so on.[38] Constables, sheriffs, and judges would also be provided until the communities developed their own officials. It was Morse's hope that these adjacent Native communities might eventually coalesce into a bona fide Native state.[39]

Isaac McCoy, a Baptist minister, had views on Natives that closely resembled those of Morse. Like Morse, McCoy also believed that unless something drastic was done, Indigenous peoples were doomed to extinction. For McCoy, all Natives had a single national identity. "He did not distinguish between race and nation, nor between nation and tribe."[40] And like Morse, McCoy also believed that Natives needed to have a territory set aside for them that, he hoped, might later be joined with the United States as a constituent state. He dreamed of an "Indian

92 INDIGENOUS GOVERNANCE

Canaan," an Indian state, located in the Far West that would serve Natives as a place of safety from the harsh realities of life, allow them time to develop their own nation, and as a means of salvation similar to the biblical wilderness laid out in Judeo-Christian religion.[41]

McCoy fiercely advocated for Indian colonization and by the late 1820s had secured federal legislative support for the idea. While he spent a lot of time planning how the Native state would be administered—a territory running some 600 miles north to south and 200 miles east to west—he spent very little effort trying to figure out how Natives and their nations would actually be removed to this new state.[42] McCoy worked futilely in Washington throughout the 1830s in an effort to secure congressional approval of his "Indian Canaan" concept.

Finally, Henry R. Schoolcraft, a respected geologist, ethnologist, and Indian agent produced several pioneer studies of Native peoples.[43] And while not advocating for a Native state or territory, he did call for a series of small colonies from the Rocky Mountains to the Pacific Ocean that he believed would best serve the interests of both Natives and the United States. In his words, "I think there is room for eight states inclusive of Minnesota, Oregon, and Washington Between the Mississippi and the Pacific and each of them should I think have an Indian district within it in their own latitude on which the Indians should be subject to our laws *civil and criminal*, to be administered, however, by specially appointed judges" (emphasis his).[44]

Federal Efforts to Establish a Native Territory/State

The first serious discussion of forming an Indigenous territory or state dates to 1778 in the Treaty of Fort Pitt between the Delaware Nation and the United States.[45] This discussion produced the first Native treaty with the United States written in formal diplomatic language; a treaty of peace and friendship, with the United States requesting and receiving "free passage" to travel through Delaware country. This arrangement benefited American troops and their Delaware allies who had designs on capturing Detroit, as the United States was in the throes of the Revolutionary War with England. Article Six was the crucial provision, containing language affirming Delaware territorial rights and the invitation to establish a state with congressional representation. It declared:

> Whereas the enemies of the United States have endeavored, by every artifice in their power, to possess the Indians in general with an opinion, that it is the design of the States aforesaid, to extirpate the Indians and take possession of their country: to obviate such false suggestion, the United States do engage to guarantee to the aforesaid nation of Delawares, and their heirs, all their territorial

rights in the fullest and most ample manner, as it have been bounded by former treaties, as long as they the said Delaware nation shall abide by, and hold fast the chain of friendship now entered into. *And it is further agreed on between the contracting parties should it for the future be found conducive for the mutual interest of both parties to invite any other tribes who have been friends to the interest of the United States, to join the present confederation, and to form a state where of the Delaware nation shall be the head, and have a representation in Congress:* Provided, nothing contained in this article to be considered as conclusive until it meets with the approbation of Congress (emphasis added).[46]

This language confirms the sovereign political character of the Delaware Nation and indicates they were vital actors not to be trifled with. Had that not been the case, "it would not have taken any diplomacy, let alone a formal treaty arrangement, to move through their country and attack Detroit and other British posts in Canada."[47]

Delaware statehood was subject to congressional approval, however, which was never forthcoming. Abel claims it was never acted upon "because the Indians had no adequate conception of its significance, were unprepared to take the initiative, and the white men disinclined to do so."[48] Deloria and Wilkins assert, on the contrary, that the Delaware were keenly aware of how important such an alliance with the United States was because they wished to separate from their relationship with England and desperately wanted to be "free from the bullying tactics of the Iroquois, most of whom were the staunch allies of Great Britain."[49] We do not know, however, whether the Delaware ever petitioned for statehood or how Congress might have responded if they had.

The next effort calling for some formal incorporation of Native people into the federal system occurred in 1785 with the signing and ratification of the Cherokee Treaty of Hopewell.[50] Article Twelve stated "that the Indians may have full confidence in the justice of the United States respecting their interests, they shall have the right to send a deputy of their choice, whenever they think fit, to Congress."[51] Rosser asserts that this provision "does not provide any real right to representation in Congress" because of dicta language in *Cherokee Nation v. Georgia*[52] which says that the *deputy* term was not, in fact, a representative right. While not obliging the federal government to grant the Cherokee people political representation, Chief Justice John Marshall noted that the deputy language for the Cherokee was meaningful and elevated the political status of the Cherokee over that of other Indigenous nations.[53]

The U.S. Louisiana Purchase in 1803 from France was a dramatic expansion of jurisdiction over a vast amount of territory that was home to hundreds of Native nations. This changed the complexion of defense of the Mississippi Valley and Indigenous–federal relations. President Thomas Jefferson envisioned this

94 INDIGENOUS GOVERNANCE

massive area as being a place to which many Eastern Native peoples would eventually be removed. But there is no evidence that Jefferson intended to formally establish an Indian Territory that might in time develop into a Native state.[54]

It was during President Monroe's second term (1817–1825) in office that discussion about a more formalized Indian Territory reemerged. Various departmental reports, special messages by Monroe himself, and the 1825 annual report by John C. Calhoun, Secretary of War, contain language describing a plan to lay out districts in the West and establish civil governments in each district. Although Native statehood was not expressly discussed, Calhoun broadly hinted at it:

> There ought to be the strongest and most solemn assurance that the country given them should be theirs, as a permanent home for themselves and their posterity, without being disturbed by the encroachments of our citizens. To such assurance, if there should be added a system by which the government, without destroying their independence would gradually unite the several tribes under a simple but enlightened system of government, and laws formed on the principles of our own, and to which, as their own people would partake in it, they would, under the influence of the contemplated improvement, at no distant day, become prepared, the arrangements which have been proposed would prove to the Indians and their posterity a permanent blessing. It is believed that if they could be assured that peace and friendship would be maintained among the several tribes; that the advantages of education which they now enjoy would be extended to them; that they should have permanent and solemn guaranty for their possessions, and receive the countenance and aid of the government for the gradual extension of its privileges to them, there would be among all the tribes a disposition to accord with the views of the government.[55]

It appears that Calhoun was drawing from the ideas espoused by the Reverend Jedediah Morse, according to Abel.[56]

Congress was also now keen on the idea that Indian Country should become a regular territory for Natives alone. In 1824 the House of Representatives passed a resolution instructing the Committee on Indian Affairs "to inquire into the expediency of organizing all the territory of the United States lying west of the State of Missouri and Territories of Arkansas and Michigan, into a single territory, to be occupied exclusively by the Indians."[57] Several other bills and resolutions were introduced in 1825, 1826, 1827, and 1834 to create an Indian Territory coinciding with the Indian Removal Act of 1830 and various removal treaties. All failed enactment.[58]

Three of the more interesting developments during this intense period were the Treaty of Dancing Rabbit Creek signed on September 27, 1830, between the Creek Nation and the United States;[59] House Report 474 "Regulating the Indian Department" dated May 20, 1834;[60] and the Treaty of New Echota signed December 29, 1835, between the Cherokee Nation and the United States.[61] Let us examine each of these in more detail.

The Choctaw had been the first nation to sign a removal treaty, the Treaty of Doak's Stand in 1820. But the vast majority of the Creek people had not agreed to remove to Indian Territory until the 1830 Treaty of Dancing Rabbit Creek.[62] Although the treaty would be the instrument that led to the mass migration of the Choctaw from their original homeland, it contains several provisions which showed the political acumen of the Choctaw.

Article Five, for example, stated that "the Choctaws, should this treaty be ratified, express a wish that Congress may grant to the Choctaws the right of punishing by their own laws, any white man who shall come into their nation, and infringe any of their national regulations." The Choctaw also wisely negotiated a provision which guaranteed that if there was a conflict over how to interpret the treaty's language "it shall be construed most favorably towards the Choctaws." (See Article Eighteen). Finally, and most important for our purposes, was the last article, Twenty-two, which stated, "The Chiefs of the Choctaws who have suggested that their people are in a state of rapid advancement in education and refinement, *and have expressed a solicitude that they might have the privilege of a Delegate on the floor of the House of Representatives extended to them.* The Commissioners do not feel that they can under a treaty stipulation accede to the request, but at their desire, present it in the Treaty that Congress may consider of, and decide the application" (emphasis added).

But was not just congressional representation that the Choctaw desired. A few weeks before the treaty had been negotiated, the Choctaw had more specifically declared what they expected in exchange for their agreeing to remove—money, cattle, arms, and munitions, as well as assurances of clear and perpetual title to their new lands. In Choctaw words: " . . . guaranty that country to us and our posterity forever, and lay it off into a state, and so soon as our population become great enough, allow us to send members to Congress, and be received into the union, as one of the other states in the United States."[63] Congress, however, refused to act upon the Choctaw representative or statehood requests.

The year 1834 was momentous for federal lawmakers as they sought in three separate measures to completely revamp the BIA, consolidate and permanently codify the previous iterations of the Trade and Intercourse laws, establish boundaries for Indian Territory that would set aside lands for Native nations, create a new organizational framework for the Natives, and ultimately admit the territory as a state. Three separate bills were sent simultaneously to the House Committee on Indian Affairs on May 20, 1834. Before the session ended in late June, the first two had been approved and become law on June 30: The Trade and

96 INDIGENOUS GOVERNANCE

Intercourse Act[64] and the Organization of the Department of Indian Affairs.[65] The Western Territory Bill, however, was not enacted due to "strong opposition" over the central feature of the measure—the creation of an Indigenous state. This opposition arose from both congressional members and many Native nations who preferred to remain distinctive and separate sovereigns.[66]

Several pertinent sections in the Western Territory Bill suggest that there was, at least initially, a substantial amount of interest in creating a confederated Native government under a governor appointed by the U.S. president, that would operate via a General Council with appropriate officials, congressional delegates, and culminating in a Native state. For example:

> Whatever differences of opinion may heretofore have existed, the policy of the Government in regard to the future condition of these tribes of Indians, may now be regarded as definitively settled. To induce them to remove west of the Mississippi to a territory set apart and dedicated to their use and Government forever; to secure to them their final home; to elevate their intellectual, moral, and civil condition, and to fit them for the enjoyment of the blessings of a free Government, is that policy. And a further hope is now encouraged, *that whenever their advance in civilization should warrant the measure, and they desire it, that they may be admitted as a State to become a member of the Union* (emphasis added).[67]

> For the purpose of forming this Confederacy, the Governor (so styled, for the want of a more appropriate title) is authorized to convene the tribes by their chiefs in a general council, for the purpose of defining and limiting the powers of the confederation. But no tribe can be compelled to become a member of the confederacy without its assent, formally and expressly given. Any tribe may authorize its chiefs to assent to it, or they may require that the articles shall be submitted to the tribe for its ratification. No fixed rule can now be established as to the mode of designating the delegates, or of apportioning their number in the first organization of the council; ultimately it may be by election, and in the ratio of members as far as practicable.[68]

> *The bill proposes to allow to the Confederation a delegate in Congress, with the privileges and emoluments of a territorial delegate; and a hope is encouraged of their eventual admission as a State into the Union.* Their admission into the Union must, on both sides, be voluntary; on our part, we reserve the right to judge of their fitness to be admitted; on theirs, it is to request or decline it (emphasis added).[69]

As the bill was being debated, it became clear that there was ample congressional resistance to the planned Native state. Representative Adams, for instance, challenged the very constitutionality of the notion: "What constitutional right had the United States to form a constitution and form of government for Indians? To erect a Territory to be inhabited exclusively by Indians?"[70] Ultimately, the Western Territory Bill died on the floor. It was reintroduced in the next session but never gained traction.

Finally, in 1835 the Cherokee Nation, in the Treaty of New Echota,[71] secured what is arguably the clearest and most affirmative right to a congressional delegate under Article Seven which states, "The Cherokee nation having already made great progress in civilization and deeming it important that every proper and laudable inducement should be offered to their people to improve their condition as well as to guard and secure in the most effectual manner the rights guarantied to them in this treaty, and with a view to illustrate the liberal and enlarged policy of the Government of the United States towards the Indians in their removal beyond the territorial limits of the States, *it is stipulated that they shall be entitled to a delegate in the House of Representatives of the United States whenever Congress shall make provision for the same.*"[72]

This treaty has a deeply problematic place in the annals of Indigenous treaty-making as it was pushed by a small dissident group of Cherokees led by Major Ridge and Buck Watie, who supported removal. The Cherokee signers who became known as the Treaty Party, "not only negotiated and signed the agreement without the approval of the Cherokee government, they also violated a law passed by that government in 1829 that made the selling of national land a crime punishable by death."[73] Although the Cherokee National Government, led by John Ross, refused to sanction the accord, the U.S. Senate ratified it and President Andrew Jackson proclaimed it into law on May 23, 1836.

The treaty's proclamation over the staunch objection of the Cherokee government and three-fourths of the Cherokee people—some 16,000 citizens who signed a petition protesting it—provided the impetus for Cherokee removal, culminating in the infamous Trail of Tears in which several thousand Cherokee died on a forced march to lands West of the Mississippi.[74]

The Cherokee people before and in the immediate wake of removal were bitterly divided. Nevertheless, the right to a congressional delegate provision seemingly secured political representation for the nation in Congress in a manner heretofore unknown. More importantly, this right "has not been abrogated or altered, and consequently, is an existing treaty right."[75] Rosser deftly argues that this right to a delegate was different in substance and legal import from the previous provisions discussed in the 1778 Delaware Treaty, the 1785 Cherokee Treaty, and the 1830 Choctaw Treaty as the 1835 Cherokee delegate provision "is an affirmative right subject only to minor qualification."[76] The key phrase is that the Cherokee were "entitled to a delegate;" it was not simply an offer or an invitation. Notwithstanding the legality of this provision, it has yet to be fulfilled because Congress has thus far refused to make it happen.

98 INDIGENOUS GOVERNANCE

In 2019 the Cherokee revived the effort to secure their congressional delegate and selected Kimberly Teehee to be their delegate. After Joe Biden was elected president, Chuck Hoskin Jr., Principal Chief of the Cherokee Nation, met briefly with Biden in January 2021 whereupon Hoskin reminded President Biden of his nation's treaty-supported right to a delegate.[77] In March 2022, Hoskin and Teehee returned to Washington and had meetings with several congressional representatives, including House Speaker, Nancy Pelosi, who was said to support the idea. A potential stumbling block to carrying this out is the idea of dual representation. The question has been raised whether the Cherokee delegate "would be representing citizens who are already being represented by elected members of Congress, like Markwayne Mullin," who also happens to be an enrolled Cherokee. As of this writing in August 2022, no action has yet been taken on the issue.[78]

During the next three decades, the ideas of an Indian Territory, Indian colonies, Native statehood, and congressional representation continued to be sporadically discussed and debated. The following excerpts confirm that these conversations were ongoing:

It is proposed to unite the tribes as one people, and to allow them to meet annually by delegates to enact laws for the government of the whole, without infringing the rights of the tribes severally to manage their own internal affairs. (Senate bill (S. 159), calling for an "Indian Territory." Senator Tipton's remarks, 1836.)

The bill provides for only two officers to be filled by citizens of the United States, viz: a superintendent of Indian affairs and a clerk. Their improvement will be better promoted by allowing offices of profit or honor to be filled by themselves, so far as they can find among them men possessing the requisite qualifications. As a measure calculated in no ordinary degree to promote the general design of the bill, it provides that an agent for the confederacy, to be selected under such regulations as the President of the United States shall believe will consist with harmony of feeling among the several tribes, shall remain at the seat of Government of the United States during each session of Congress. The sphere of his duties will embrace the interests of all within the confederacy. He must be an Indian, and his pay will be equal to that of a member of Congress. (U.S. Senate Report, 24th Cong., 1st Sess., 1836)

In the late treaty with the Cherokees East of the Mississippi, it is expressly stipulated, that they shall be entitled to a delegate in the House of Representatives whenever Congress shall make provision for the same. It is not to be doubted that the hopes thus held out to these tribes [Choctaws and Cherokees] had an important influence in determining them to consent to emigrate to their new homes in the West . . . And, at as early a day as circumstances will allow, the expectations authorized by the passage above quoted from the treaties with the Choctaws and Cherokees should be fulfilled. Indeed, from the facts stated by the Commissioner, it is scarcely to be doubted that the Choctaws are already in a condition to justify the measure. *The daily presence of a native delegate on the floor of the House of Representatives of the United States, presenting, as occasion may require, to that dignified assembly, the interests of his people, would, more than any other single act, attest to the world and to the Indian tribes the sincerity of our endeavors for their preservation and happiness.* In the successful issue of these endeavors, we shall find a more precious and durable accession to the glory of our country than by any triumph we can achieve in arts or in arms . . . (B. F. Butler, Secretary of War, December 3, 1836. Gales and Seaton's Register, vol. XIII, pt. 2 appendix, pp. 11–21) (emphasis added).

Having one common governor, to whom to refer all their difficulties, and who would establish the same rules and regulations overall, it would tend to produce a uniformity of views, and they would be induced to cooperate in measures to their mutual advantage, and which would tend to a gradual amelioration of their condition. Every two years there should be a general council or congress, to consist of a delegation of all the different tribes of Indians, to assemble at some central point in the Indian country . . . *In short time, if such should be the policy of the Government, they might, this general council, elect delegates to Congress, which would open a new field of ambition for them* [emphasis added]. Many other advantages will arise from this plan which will at once occur to you; and I will not, therefore, trouble you with an enumeration of them. (G. P. Kingsbury calling for a confederated Native government and a delegate to the U.S. Congress. U.S. House. Document #276 (February 18, 1838).)

This policy of collecting the Indians has proceeded on the idea of relieving them from their dependent and degrading condition when mixed with a white population, and of isolating them from the vices of a semi-civilization. Scarcely capable of self-government, they are quite incompetent to protect themselves from the frauds and from the violence of the white man. the present system of superintendents and agents is inadequate; and the time seems to have arrived when we should turn our attention to devising some form of government which may secure peace and order among themselves and protection against others . . . *The plan of something like a territorial government for the Indians has been suggested* [emphasis added]. The object is worthy of the most deliberate consideration of all who take an interest in the fate of this hapless race. (U.S. House. Message from the President. House Document #2. 27th Cong. (December 7, 1842).)

It provides for a confederation of the respective tribes inhabiting the territory, who may accede thereto, with a governor, appointed in the first place by the President, a national council, and a delegate in the House of Representatives

100 INDIGENOUS GOVERNANCE

leaving everything which can safely and profitably be committed to them to their own management and control; and contemplating a gradual withdrawal of all agency of the government in the management of their concerns as fast and as early as their condition and the interests of the government will permit; and, to satisfy the Indians that no undue advantage is intended to be taken by the government of the tribes entering into the confederacy provision is made for the recession of any of them whenever they shall desire so to do. . . . By giving them a representative in Congress, they would feel that they were no longer considered inferiors, strangers, jealous of the encroachments of power, but part and parcel of ourselves, possessing the rights and enjoying the privileges of citizens. (U.S. House. "Indian Territory West of the Mississippi" Report #736, 30th Cong., 1st Sess. (June 27, 1848), 11.)

Be it therefore resolved, that we recommend the subject to the serious consideration of the Congress of the United States, that, in the exercise of their wisdom, they may mature a plan by which the Indian tribes inhabiting our western territory may be placed more directly under the paternal care of the general government, by which a specific region of country may be set apart for their permanent abode, secured to them forever against further encroachment, and undisturbed by the great current of western emigration; by which their moral, intellectual and social condition may be improved and elevated; by which the blessings of education, civilization and Christianity may be imparted to them; by which they may all be brought together and united in one grand confederation, and thus prepared for the enjoyment of civil and religious liberty; *and if found practicable, they may be ultimately admitted into our federal Union* [emphasis added]. (N.C. State Resolution urging Congress to establish a Native State, 1849.)

In order more fully to extend the protection of the Constitution and laws of the United States over the Cherokee, Muscogee or Creek, Seminole, Choctaw, and Chickasaw nations or tribes of Indians, and to enable them to advance in civilization, and hereafter become citizens of the United States, the bill, as amended, provides for the erection (with the assent of the several nations) into Territories of the country which they own and occupy, and certain other country to be annexed thereto. The Territory of Chah-ta is to consist entirely of the lands owned by the absolute grant from the United States by the Choctaws and Chickasaws. That of Muscogee, of those owned by the Creeks and Seminoles, and that of Chelokee of those owned by the Cherokees south of the thirty-seventh parallel of north latitude . . . The object, therefore, now to be attained, is to persuade these Indians to open their country to emigration and settlement—to cease to hold their lands in common—to divide them out in severalty, giving to all their people the right of free sale and disposition—to intermingle with, and become an integral part of, the people of the United

States—to merge their useless nationalities in that of the American republic, *and to look forward with confidence to the time when they will constitute a portion of the union and add another Star to its flag* [emphasis added]. (U.S. Senate. Committee on Territories introduced a bill, S. 483, to organize the Territories of Cha-lah-kee, Muscogee, and Cha-ta which would ultimately merge to establish the Territory of Neosho, 1854, 1, 8.)

Sec. 36. And be it further enacted, that a delegate to the House of Representatives of the United States, to serve for the term of two years, who shall be a citizen of the United States, may be elected for each of said Territories, by the qualified voters thereof. (Ibid., 28.)

Sec. 48. And be it further enacted, *That whenever the people of the said three Territories shall, by acts of their respective legislatures, consent to unite together and form one people, and be included in one Territory, they shall be entitled to be erected into a Territory of the United States, to be called the Territory of Neosho, in the same manner as other Territories have been created*; and afterwards, when Congress shall be satisfied as to their capacity for self-government, and whenever they open their country to emigration and settlement, they shall be entitled to be erected into a State, by the same name, on the same footing, in all respects, as the original States. (Ibid., 30.)

The Cherokees are governed by their own laws. As a people, they are more advanced in civilization than the other Indian tribes, with the exception, perhaps, of the Choctaws . . . This organization is not only under the sanction of the general government, but it guarantees their independence, subject to the restriction that their laws shall be consistent with the Constitution of the United States, and acts of Congress which regulate trade in intercourse with the Indians. *And whenever Congress shall make provision on the subject, the Cherokee nation shall be entitled to a delegate in the national legislature.* (*United States ex rel. Mackey v. Cox*, 59 U.S. 100, 103 (1855).)

Mr. Doolittle: I move to take up Senate Bill No. 459, to provide for the consolidation of the Indian tribes and establish civil government in the Indian Territory. The motion was agreed to; and the Senate, as in Committee of the Whole proceeded to consider the bill. It proposes to create and establish within the territory of the United States, bounded as follows, to wit: on the north by the southern boundary of the State of Kansas, on the west by the eastern boundary of the Territory of New Mexico and the state of Texas, on the south by the northern boundary of the State of Texas, and on the east by the western boundary of the States of Arkansas and Mississippi, a temporary government by the name of the Indian Territory; but this government is not to be permitted to interfere with or to affect in any way the rights of any Indian tribe at peace with the United States residing and being in the Territory, secured by treaty between the United States and such Indians, without the consent of the tribe

102 INDIGENOUS GOVERNANCE

or tribes, or to affect the authority of the United States to make any regulations respecting such Indians, their lands, property, or other rights by treaty, law, or otherwise, which it would have been competent for the United States to make if this act had not taken effect. (U.S. Senate Bill No. 459 calls for the establishment of an "Indian Territory." *Congressional Globe*, "Consolidation of Indian Tribes" (February 23, 1865), 1021.)

When the American Civil War concluded in May 1865, a renewed effort on the part of federal lawmakers to establish an Indian Territory for the Native nations of the Five Civilized Tribes (FCT) ensued. This activity was driven in part because segments of the FCT had signed treaties with the Confederated States of America. For instance, the Cherokee, led by Chief John Ross, had tried to remain neutral during the war but other Cherokee, like Stand Watie, were keen on joining the Confederacy and, ultimately, the Cherokee allied with the South.[79]

At the war's end, the federal government punished those Confederate-aligned nations, claiming that their alliance had purportedly violated their treaties with the United States. Therefore, new treaties were forged in 1866.[80] These treaties included major Tribal land cessions, a requirement that the nations free their African American slaves, and that they accept territorial status under federal auspices.[81] Despite their vulnerable position, leaders of the Native nations stood in unanimous opposition to being organized into a territory. Lewis Downing, principal chief of the Cherokee Nation, on behalf of a small delegation, declared that the territorial effort and associated issues laid out in their 1866 treaty were unacceptable to the Cherokee people on multiple grounds:

First. To place us under a territorial government. Second. To abrogate our treaties. Third. To refuse to pay us our just demands. Fourth. To declare us citizens of the United States and subject to its legislative jurisdiction. Fifth. To make it appear we have no title to our lands which the government of the United States is bound to respect. Sixth. That we are civilized and wealthy, and have no need for the money the government owes us. Seventh. Then, again, that we are savages and unfit to govern ourselves. Eighth. That whether civilized or savage, wards or independents, we have no rights which the government is bound to respect; and hence, those we have should be taken from us, and those we are entitled to should be withheld. Ninth. That the tax gatherer should be sent into our country to carry off our substance for the support of a government in which we have no representation, and are entitled to none, thus compelling our people to be taxed for the support of two governments, their own and yours.[82]

Downing and his colleagues concluded by astutely observing that "we are but too fully sensible that were we even incorporated into the government of the United

States, vastly inferior in numbers and distinguished from you in color and race, we would have no power to protect ourselves or our rights, or even command decent respect. we would scarcely make a perceptible shadow on the great national political dial for an hour and then pass away forever."[83]

While the FCT were opposed to the formation of territorial government, they were willing to organize under a general council for the Indian territory. In fact, each of the 1866 treaties with the Five Nations called for a general council framework. Article Twelve of the Cherokee Treaty stated:

> The Cherokees agree that a general council, consisting of delegates elected by each nation or tribe lawfully residing within the Indian Territory, may be annually convened in said Territory, which council shall be organized in such manner and possess such powers as hereinafter prescribed.... Second. The first general council shall consist of one member from each tribe, and an additional member for each thousand Indians, or each fraction of a thousand greater than five hundred, being members of any tribe lawfully resident in said Territory, and shall be selected by said tribes respectively, who may assent to the establishment of said general council; and if none should be thus formally selected by any nation or tribe so assenting the said nation or tribe shall be represented in said general council by the chief or chiefs and headmen of said tribes, to be taken in the order of their rank as recognized in tribal usage in the same number and proportion as above indicated . . . Third. Said general council shall have power to legislate upon matters pertaining to the intercourse and relations of the Indian tribes and nations and colonies of freedmen resident in said Territory; the arrest and extradition of criminals and offenders escaping from one tribe to another, or into any community of freedmen; the administration of justice between members of different tribes of said Territory and persons other than Indians and members of said tribes are nations; and the common defence and safety of the nations of said Territory . . . No law shall be enacted inconsistent with the Constitution of the United States or laws of Congress or existing treaty stipulations with the United States. Nor shall said council legislate upon matters other than those above indicated: Provided, however, that the legislative power of such general council may be enlarged by the consent of the national council of each nation or tribe assenting to its establishment, with the approval of the President of the United States.[84]

The General Council was to elect a secretary and each council member was to receive a per diem of four dollars while attending meetings and a travel allowance as well.

While each of the Five Tribe's treaties contained provisions for a general council to represent all the nations, the Choctaw and Chickasaw treaty also

104   INDIGENOUS GOVERNANCE

called for an Indian Territorial government more along the lines of a confederation of nations rather than a U.S. territorial body. And it was this language of territoriality that would be a focal point for those who advocated for territorial government for Native peoples. Interestingly, Article Seven of the Choctaw and Chickasaw treaty also declared that although the two nations agreed to congressional legislation that might be developed for the administration of justice in their territory, that legislation would not "in anywise interfere with or annul their present tribal organization, or their respective legislatures or judiciaries or the rights, laws, privileges, or customs of the Choctaw and Chickasaw Nations respectively."[85] Similar language is found in the other 1866 treaties, as well.

The Choctaw and Chickasaw treaty contained two other unique clauses: It declared that when Congress authorized the appointment of a delegate from Indian Territory it was within the authority of the general council to elect said person from all the nations represented. And, in Article Thirteen, and at the insistence of the leadership of the two nations, it was declared that the general council should be bicameral—with an upper and lower house. The other nations were encouraged to follow suit with "the relations of the two houses to each other being such as prevail in the States of the U.S."[86]

Notwithstanding the distinctive language in the Choctaw and Chickasaw treaty, the Native leaders of the Five Tribes vehemently argued that the articles in their 1866 treaties had not authorized Congress to form a territorial government of the United States for the Natives of the Indian Territory.[87] Despite intense Indigenous opposition to the establishment of a territorial government for Indian Territory, federal officials continued to introduce legislation with that goal in mind. Meanwhile, the recently elected president, Ulysses S. Grant, also favored a territorial government for Native peoples, including the FCT.

In 1871, the same year that the United States enacted a law that ended treaty-making with Native nations, Grant called for the establishment of an Indian Territory as a "means of collecting most of the Indians now between the Missouri and the Pacific and south of the British possessions into one Territory or one State."[88] Grant believed this was necessary to not only protect Natives from the ever-increasing numbers of whites but also as an aid to economic growth for the region and for the construction of railroads.

While Grant envisioned an all-Native Territory that would eventually mature into a state, an increasing number of congressional bills called for a mixed polity, which would have included Natives and non-Natives. Native resistance to such an idea, however, was intense and Native leaders constantly memorialized Congress urging that body not to create such a bi-racial territory.[89] Abel asserts that by the late 1870s "there was practically no thought whatsoever of allowing the aborigines a separate existence as an integral part of the Union and the spasmodic efforts of 100 years had failed."[90] But this statement is only partially correct because there were ongoing, if sporadic, attempts made by federal lawmakers to politically incorporate Natives into the U.S. body politic for several more decades.

To this end, in November 1877, a bill was introduced (H.R. 7922) titled "A Bill to Provide for the Organization of the Indian Territory" which stated that "the organization of the Indian Territory is demanded equally for the best interests of the Indians themselves and of the U.S." and that "no savage ever civilized himself."[91] A year later, H.R. 2687 would have authorized the election of a single congressional delegate to Congress to represent the interests of the Five Civilized Tribes whose combined reservation landmass was "about eighteen million acres, comprising a territory somewhat larger than the State of Alabama."[92] Representative James W. Throckmorton was well aware of the 1785 Cherokee Treaty that had called for a Cherokee "deputy" to represent the interests of the Cherokee people and the 1835 treaty provision, too, which entitled them to a House delegate. "We think," he said, "that it is time that the promise made to the Cherokee forty-two years ago be fulfilled."[93]

The leaders of the FCT, however vehemently objected to this bill for the following reasons: (1) it provided inadequate representation for each Tribal nation and completely ignored the interests of the other twenty-seven Indigenous nations in the region; (2) it did not allow for the consent of the Cherokee in violation of their 1835 treaty; (3) it gave the Secretary of the Interior too much authority over Tribal affairs; and (4) it forced U.S. citizenship on the nations' members.[94]

In 1884 Representative Throckmorton tried again, introducing a bill (H.R. 3435) authorizing the appointment of a Native delegate to the House of Representatives from the "council of the Indian tribes' resident in the Indian Territory." This bill, like its predecessor, failed to be enacted.[95] Of course, there were those federal officials who did not believe that Native peoples had the necessary political acumen to form a Native state. Robert L. Owen, the agent for Union Agency in Indian Territory, writing in his annual report in 1887 after overseeing an "International Council" of Native nations from some nineteen Native peoples, declared that "it is much to be regretted that there is so little cohesive power in the Indian character and among the Indian nations. It would go far, in my opinion, to the peaceful, beneficent solution of the change of the Indian nations into a flourishing Indian State of the Union if the tribes could unite, but I do not think great interest was exhibited in this meeting, as but one chief of the five nations was present, to wit, Hon. J. M. Perryman, who lives at Eufala."[96]

A little over a decade later in 1898, Congress enacted the Curtis Act,[97] introduced by its only Native member, Charles Curtis of the Kaw Nation (who later served as U.S. vice president under Herbert Hoover). The act devastated Native governments in Indian Territory, violated treaties, opened up Tribal

106 INDIGENOUS GOVERNANCE

land for allotment, and terminated Tribal courts. This major law contained an interesting provision calling for statehood for the Indian Territory in the wake of the massive governmental upheaval that was being unleashed on the FCT. The act declared that "it is further agreed in view of the modification of legislative authority and judicial jurisdiction herein provided, and the necessity of the continuance of the tribal governments so modified, in order to carry out the requirements of this agreement, that the same shall continue for the period of eight years from the fourth day of March 1898. *This stipulation is made in the belief that the tribal governments so modified will prove so satisfactory that there will be no need or desire for further change till the lands now occupied by the Five Civilized Tribes shall in the opinion of Congress, be prepared for admission as a State to the Union.* But this provision shall not be construed to be in any respect an abdication by Congress of power at any time to make needful rules and regulations respecting said tribes"[98] (emphasis added).

William Unrau says that Curtis was less concerned with protecting the rights of the FCT and even less concerned with enforcing the treaties of the nations. His goal, according to Unrau, was statehood for the entire territory and not just Native statehood.[99] The Curtis Act presaged eventual statehood for Oklahoma in 1907, a state that, as we shall see, drew heavily upon the political work done by Native leaders in the Indian Territory who engaged in their own quest for Native statehood. Let us turn now to those efforts.

Indigenous Efforts to Form a State

As noted in the previous section, at least three Native nations negotiated treaties with the federal government in which they expressed keen interest in joining with the early U.S. government as a constituent state or with direct representation in Congress—the Delaware Nation, the Cherokee Nation, and the Choctaw Nation. As discussed, those treaty provisions were never fulfilled, although the Cherokee Nation continues to insist that their 1835 treaty provision calling for delegates is still binding on Congress.

In addition to these initiatives, Native nations engaged in other politically collaborative work in the 1800s and early 1900s during which they fortified their international diplomatic skills both to improve their individual and collective situations and, in some cases, with the express goal of linking with the United States as a separate state of the Union.[100] Much of this activity involved the FCT of the eastern part of Indian Territory and the Native nations living in the central and western areas. In the late 1830s the leaders of the FCT were also dealing with the repercussions of their coerced removals from their original homelands in the east, the internal and intratribal conflicts generated and exacerbated by their forced relocation, as well as problems with both Texas (annexed by the United States in 1845) and Mexico which fomented conflict against the Native nations and Anglo Texans. Convinced that U.S. military protection was inadequate to protect them from all the turmoil, they convened a series of international Native meetings between 1838 and 1845 that delegations from the FCT, representatives from the Kickapoo, Shawnee, Caddo, Wichita, Quapaw, Osage, Kiowa, Pawnee, and several other nations attended.[101]

The stated purposes of these international convenings were to promote better understanding between the nations, secure peace and stability, and to discourage any involvement with Mexican forays into their territories. At the 1842 Grand Council meeting, hosted by the Creek Nation under the leadership of Principal Chief, Rory McIntosh, representatives from eighteen nations gathered "for the purpose of establishing terms of friendly intercourse between the several tribes represented in the Council and for the adjustment of all existing difficulties."[102]

The following year, the Cherokee Nation, led by Chief John Ross, hosted the international gathering which met for five weeks.[103] An estimated 10,000 Natives assembled in Tahlequah, Indian Territory. The invitation had been sent, along with pipe and tobacco, to every Native nation east of the Rocky Mountains and delegates from twenty-one nations made their way to Tahlequah. Referred to as the Grand June Council of 1843, Sigourney, writing in 1932, claims it was the largest gathering of Natives ever assembled up to that time.[104] A compact was negotiated and signed by the assembled leaders that pledged peace and friendship, the foregoing of revenge, improvements in agriculture, domestic arts, the "happiness of our women," extradition of criminals, and multiple citizenship. It also recommended that alcohol be outlawed.[105]

In 1845, the Creek Nation, long viewed as the peacemakers of the FCT, called for another meeting, an event now considered the most important of the Native congresses convened in Indian Territory before the American Civil War. "Not only was a permanent peace established between the Kickapoo and the harried Choctaw and Chickasaw, and the mission of the Mexican agents completely discredited by this council, but even more significant were the genuine expressions of Indian friendship and goodwill, the concern ventured by several delegates over the erasure of Indian culture, and the earnest appeals that tribal ways be preserved in the face of the disintegrating impact of Anglo culture. And there was inherent in the speeches of various tribal delegates a proposal for pan-Indian unity, a socioeconomic fusion, based on the brotherhood of all red men, a proposition taken up by the various leaders.[106]

Although none of the international conventions held from 1838 to 1845 formally discussed or pursued admittance into the federal system as a political body, the diplomatic work set the stage for developments after the Civil War aimed at formal Native political incorporation into the U.S. political system.

108 INDIGENOUS GOVERNANCE

As discussed in the previous section, Congress in the postwar period strove mightily to compel the leaders of the FCT to accept admission as a Territory of the United States, but Tribal leaders resisted. Native leaders countered this drive with their own plan. Samuel Checote, chief of the Muscogee (Creek) Nation, invited leaders of several of the nations in the Indian Territory to an International Council on June 2, 1870. He said, "It is well known that our fathers before us often met in councils of this kind, for consultation on matters having for their object the general good of the red man. One of the good results of such meetings was, that each nation understood perfectly the relations existing between all of the brother nations, which enabled them to understand and respect each other's rights producing harmony and peace in our brotherhood."[107]

Tribal leaders of assembled in Muscogee County on September 27, 1870 (supported by federal funding) for what was to be the first of seven such General Councils authorized and backed by most of the Native nations in Indian Territory and the federal government. The international body agreed to refer to itself as the General Council of the Indian Territory and created rules for a committee governance structure. The first official resolution adopted was a memorial to the U.S. president protesting any legislative action that would "impair the obligation of any treaty provision" or any attempt by Congress to establish "any government over the Indian Territory other than that of the General Council."[108]

When the Council reconvened in a second session on December 16, 1870, they wrote and adopted an intratribal charter called the Okmulgee Constitution. The ten-member drafting committee consisted of representatives from the FCT, as well as the Ottawa, Osage, Eastern Shawnee, Quapaw, Seneca, Wyandotte, Confederated Peoria, Sac and Fox, and the Absentee Shawnee. The cumulative population of the assembled nations was about 60,000.

Although this constitution was never ratified by all of the nations whose delegates had helped draft it, it established an intertribal diplomatic precedent that continued to resonate among those nations for many years to come because it protected each member nation's right to its own territory, funds, and other property.[109] Kidwell notes that the Okmulgee Constitution unveiled serious strains in political relations—both between Native nations and between the Tribes and the federal government.[110] The 1866 treaties specified that the Superintendent of Indian Affairs would be the governor of Indian Territory with the U.S. president having the power to appoint the superintendent. The Okmulgee Constitution, on the other hand, specified that the governor had to be elected by popular vote—a declaration of Native autonomy. "Nevertheless, it was increasingly obvious that the General Council was simply a pro forma exercise, a way of dealing with the very real threat that Congress would impose a territorial government on Indian Territory. Congress had bankrolled meetings of the General Council under the assumption that Tribes would follow its agenda. Once it became obvious that this vision of unified government would not be realized, funding which made it possible for delegates to attend meetings was withdrawn. The last formal session of the General Council was held in 1876."[111]

By then, Congressional members realized that Native nations were not going to support the creation of a U.S.-recognized territorial government that might eventually develop into a Native state that would allow white settlement in the territory and federal citizenship for individual Natives.[112] From a Native perspective, the reason most often given for the failure of the proposal was that most Tribal members believed that their own international governments—under the Okmulgee Constitution—would culminate in a status of territorial governments of the United States. However, according to Applen, "These same Indians apparently realized that an Indian 'state' was their only real hope for protection from further advances by the white men. Thus, their reasons for establishing an Indian government seem to have been just as strong as their reasons for not establishing one."[113]

Federal support for the Okmulgee Constitution and the General Council of the Indian Territory was exhausted. Nonetheless, Native interest in some kind of collaborative, confederated government would continue under different guises for the next three decades. In 1888, for example, an "International Council" was convened at Fort Gibson Indian Territory with an attendance of between two to three thousand representing an estimated twenty-two Tribal nations. Leaders of the FCT urged unification with the assembled Western Native nations—including the Comanche, Kiowa, Caddo, Sac and Fox, Otoe, and others. The three dominant issues discussed included protecting existing treaty rights, fighting land allotment, and the establishment of a common government.

The following resolution was adopted on June 25, 1888:

Whereas the Indian tribes now settled in the Indian Territory have interests in common which will be better protected by closer and more helpful relations than have heretofore existed between the different tribes; and

Whereas a unification of the tribes in matters of general welfare is absolutely essential to the preservation of Indian rights, the final settlement of landed interests, and the establishment of proper safeguards for our homes in this country, which have been solemnly set apart for us; and

Whereas the welfare of the Indian people now settled in the Indian Territory will be best protected by an organization which, originating with and established by the Indians themselves, provides by a common bond of union for the good of all, and which recognizes the ability of the Indian to protect his interests and devise plans for the civilization, education, and prosperity of the Indian race; and

110 INDIGENOUS GOVERNANCE

Whereas the interest and safety of the individual is best assured when the interests and safety of the tribe or nation is secured, and the welfare of the tribe is assured when the safety and prosperity of the race is promoted, the general welfare demands that some plan of union be devised which, seeking the good of the individual, shall at the same time provide for those larger interests which attach to the Indian race as a whole; and

Whereas the United States, by its Executives, Indian Commissioner, and Congress, has repeatedly expressed approval of the unification of the various tribes, and has in many treaties endeavored to secure some form of Federal compact which would embrace the Indian nations within its scope, secure the enactment of general laws for the government of all Indians, and establish one commonwealth in the territory to control all nations; and

Whereas from time immemorial the Indian has had such forms of government, even long before the white man came to America, and has found strength in union, prosperity in justly executed laws, and security in well-planned and far-reaching measures for the public safety; and

Whereas the Indians are best able to understand and provide for the difficult problems connected with their own future, and are ready to make necessary sacrifices to secure the true welfare of the Indian race: Therefore, be it

Resolved (1), That the general welfare of all the Indians requires a stronger and more lasting bond of union between the various tribes now in the Indian Territory than at present exists.

Resolved (2), That the unification of the tribes will best secure the general welfare of the Indian race.

Resolved (3), That all the tribes should have one common government with common laws, officials and institutions, in which all the tribes should have equitable representation.

Resolved (4), That to secure such form of government for the Indian Territory as will make it an Indian commonwealth, the assent of the Indian nations and tribes here represented to such plan is hereby requested, and the councils and tribes are invited to invest their official delegates to the next international council with the authority to adopt a plan of Indian Territorial government, which will, when approved by two-thirds of the tribes and Indian nations, be the general constitution of the unified Indian tribes for the government of this Territory.

Resolved (5), That the approval of the President of the United States be requested to this plan of this Indian Territorial government and tribal unification, and that a committee of three be appointed to present the plan to him as soon as possible.

Resolved (6), finally, That the next international council be called to meet for the adoption of the plan of government provided for in the foregoing

ANOTHER STAR ON THE FLAG   111

> resolutions on the first Monday in June, 1889, and that in the meantime a
> special committee of five, to be appointed by this council, prepare a draft
> of a constitution for submission to the international council of 1889, such
> constitution to be the fundamental law of the Indian Commonwealth
> herein provided for.[114]

Railroad interests, unauthorized white settlers, cattlemen, and oil and gas corporate entities continued to expand their activities, culminating in the first major land run by 50,000 white settlers into the so-called Unassigned land or Oklahoma District on April 27, 1889.[115] A year later, on May 2, 1890, Congress passed the Organic Act for the Territory of Oklahoma, a precursor step before statehood for the Oklahoma District and for the Oklahoma Panhandle. This act authorized the U.S. president to appoint a governor, a secretary, three judges, and a marshal. Citizens were granted the power to elect members to the House of Representatives, as well as a council and an official delegate to Congress.[116]

Tribal ownership of their lands—constituting all of the eastern half of Indian Territory—was guaranteed by removal treaties. Those treaties contained language, like that of the Choctaws in 1830, declaring that "no Territory or State shall ever have a right to pass laws for the government of the Choctaw Nation of Red People and their descendants; and that no part of the land's granted them shall ever be embraced in any Territory or State."[117] Yet, these laws ultimately failed to protect the communal lands and governing bodies of the FCT from allotment and political dismemberment.[118]

Thus, as the lands of the FCT were overrun by invasive whites, homesteaders, railroads, and corporations, Tribal nations faced ever-increasing pressure to accept both the individualization of their communally held and fee-simple lands and the dissolution of their national governments. The 1898 Curtis Act, as mentioned previously, proved to be a decisive blow to the efforts of the FCT to retain their lands and functioning governments. Once Congress made it clear that the nature and status of Indigenous governments were to be transformed, the question of statehood for the entire region—both Indian Territory and Oklahoma Territory—began to receive serious consideration.

By the early 1900s, as non-native Oklahoma Territory citizens and officials continued their efforts to obtain statehood, leaders of the FCT, fearing the dissolution of their governments, separate territories, and possible absorption by Oklahoma Territory into a single state, began to aggressively pursue a new path to protect their governments and lands—separate statehood for the Indian Territory within the federal system.[119] The first serious discussion for Indian statehood began with a meeting of Tribal leaders in 1902 at Eufala, located within the Creek Nation. There the delegates made it clear that they were adamantly opposed to a political and geographic merger with Oklahoma Territory. Native

112   INDIGENOUS GOVERNANCE

resistance continued to mount, and in 1905 a major gathering, the Sequoyah Constitutional Convention, took place in Muscogee, also in Creek country. The Tribes' leaders asserted that Indian Territory met all of the requisite criteria for statehood: adequate land base (31,400 square miles), sufficient population (750,000 residents), acceptable communication and transportation infrastructure, and more than enough economic resources (e.g., coal, oil, gas, granite, and lumber). They also contended that provisions in several of their treaties with the United States, as well as the 1897 Atoka Agreement, recognized their right to be admitted as a separate state.

Convention delegates, consisting of Natives, whites, and African Americans—balanced between Democrats and Republicans—developed a detailed constitution; a lengthy document of some 35,000 words, divided into eighteen articles and 270 sections including a map illustrating proposed boundaries. It was a populist document reflecting the delegates' distrust of corporations, big government, and legislative bodies. It included support for a line-item veto and a ban on child labor. The document also contained several pro-plaintiff tort rules.[120] Interestingly, the so-called Sequoyah Movement had the support of a number of leading white politicians in Indian Territory.[121]

Once written, the Constitution was put to a territory-wide referendum, where it was overwhelmingly ratified by a vote of 57,000 to 9000. Although an impressive victory, less than half of the qualified voters actually participated in the referendum. A Memorial submitted by citizens of the Indian Territory on January 16, 1906, laid out the reasons why the State of Sequoyah should be admitted to the union:

> That we are entitled to immediate, independent statehood—First a) By area, 31,400 square miles. b) By number of our population, conservatively estimated at 750,000 souls. c) By the character of our people, being educated, industrious, thrifty, law abiding, and learned in the art of self-government. d) By actual taxable wealth, estimated at $400,000,000. e) By our developed and undeveloped resources in oil, gas, coal, granite, marble, lumber, etc., railroads, telegraphs, telephones, etc., and agricultural products, cattle, horses, etc. f) By our immense immediate respective population, our annual immigration being greater than the total population of some of the States now in the union. . . . Second, We are entitled under the treaties and laws of the United States, to wit: a) By the treaty with France of April 3, 1803. b) By the treaty with the Choctaws and Chickasaws of 1830. . . . h) By the propositions and representations made to the Five Nations by the Commission to the Five Civilized Tribes . . . Third. We are entitled under the Constitution of the United States, and its interpretation for over 100 years, and by precedent established in admitting other States into the union. Fourth. We are entitled by consideration for the welfare and true

interests of the Republic itself, in the maintenance of its honor, prestige, and power. Fifth. We are entitled under the pledges of the national Republican Party and of the national Democratic Party . . . Eighth. The Constitution herewith submitted represents the will of the people of the State of Sequoyah; the wishes of a people who have been grossly misrepresented by a propaganda advocating a union with Oklahoma, in the promotion of selfish interest, on behalf of the railroads, the liquor traffic, ambitious town promoters, and professional politicians.[122]

While bills were introduced in both houses of Congress in support of this new Indigenous state, no substantive action was ever taken. President Theodore Roosevelt and few in the Republican-led Congress wanted two additional Western states, and still fewer were willing to support a Native state.[123] Instead, Roosevelt recommended joint statehood in 1905 and, in 1906, Congress passed an enabling act that set the stage for Oklahoma's admission as a single state on November 16, 1907. When Charles N. Haskell was inaugurated as the first governor, a "symbolic marriage" was carried out in the new state capital for Miss Indian Territory and Mr. Oklahoma Territory. But as Kidwell noted, "Metaphorically, the marriage was a shotgun wedding. Miss Indian Territory had tried to say no. She was joined to the overweening Oklahoma Territory not of her own free will but by the partisan politics of the Republican Party."[124]

Rennard Strickland, a Cherokee law professor, noted that "Oklahoma may be the only state in which the Indian did have a significant and long-lasting impact on the form of state government and the nature of the constitutional legal system." In fact, "many important Oklahoma constitutional provisions, such as a prohibition of alien ownership of land and limitations on corporate buying or dealing in real estate were products of the unique Oklahoma Indian experience."[125] Cherokee humorist Will Rogers noted in hindsight that "we spoiled the best territory in the world to make a state," and sarcastically opined that "Indians were so cruel they were all killed by civilized white men for encroaching on white domain."[126]

Tom Holm, a Cherokee–Creek historian, maintains that the campaign against a Native state was also based, in part, on the notion that the wealthy mixed-blood Tribal leaders were exploiting the poor full-blood members of their nations, a racially tinged argument that had been effectively mustered during the devastating Indian Removal era in the 1830s and 1840s.[127] This argument is bolstered by the work of Craig Miner on the critical role that corporations played in Indian Territory. The evidence Miner drew upon "suggests that the degree of corporate intrusion upon a tribe's lands was inversely related to the percentage of Indian blood that flowed in the veins of its citizens."[128] "This led," says Miner, "to the mixed-blood or even white tribal citizen meant through whom the corporation

114 INDIGENOUS GOVERNANCE

gained leverage. The custom of allowing intermarriage with whites and of granting full tribal rights to white husbands of Indian women assured that the corporation never faced a united front."[129]

Twentieth-Century Attempts to Politically Incorporate Native Nations

The idea of the State of Sequoyah was arguably the most comprehensive attempt to establish a fully integrated Indigenous state within the U.S. federal system of governance. Its failure has not forestalled other attempts, particularly those arising in the halcyon days of the late 1960s and 1970s, when the notion of Native self-determination and Indigenous sovereignty was in the ascendant.

The period from the end of federal termination era of the early 1960s through the early 1980s was a crucial time in Indigenous–federal relations. It was, according to most knowledgeable commentators, an era when Native nations and Natives in general—led by concerted Indigenous activism—won a series of political, legal, and cultural victories in their epic struggle to end termination policies and regain a measure of genuine self-determination. Many of these victories arose out of activities and events like the fishing rights struggles of Native peoples in the Pacific Northwest in the 1950s–1970s such as the American Indian Chicago Conference in 1961; the birth of the American Indian Movement in 1968; the Alcatraz occupation in 1969; the Trail of Broken Treaties in 1972; the 1973 occupation of Wounded Knee in South Dakota; and an untold number of marches, demonstrations, and boycotts.

The federal government responded to this activism by enacting several laws and initiating policies that recognized the distinctive group and individual rights of Indigenous peoples. In some cases, the laws supported Tribal sovereignty; in other cases, they acted to erase or diminish it. For example, in 1968, Congress enacted the Indian Civil Rights Act (ICRA), the first piece of legislation to impose many of the provisions of the U.S. Bill of Rights on the actions of Tribal governments vis-à-vis reservation residents. Until this time, Native nations, because of their extra-constitutional status, had not been subject to such explicit constitutional restraints in their governmental capacities. The ICRA was a major intrusion of federal constitutional law upon the independence of Native nations, and it is important to understand that the ICRA does not protect Indigenous nations or their members from federal plenary power aimed at reducing Tribal sovereignty, treaty rights, or aboriginal lands.

Two years later, by contrast, President Richard Nixon explicitly called on Congress to repudiate the termination policy and declared that Native self-determination would be the goal of his administration. Congress responded by enacting a series of laws designed to improve the lot of Tribal nations and Natives in virtually every sphere; the return of Blue Lake to the Taos Pueblo, the Indian Education Act of 1972, the restoration of the Menominee Nation to recognized status in 1973, the establishment of the American Indian Policy Review Commission in 1975, the Indian Self-Determination and Education Assistance Act of 1975, the Indian Child Welfare Act of 1978, the American Indian Religious Freedom Act of 1978, and the Maine Land Claims Settlement Act of 1980.

Native peoples, of course, were divided on the best political approach to take with regard to the United States. On the one hand, there were those like Hank Adams, Vine Deloria Jr., and others who called for the resuscitation of formal treaty-making as the most viable approach by which Native nations should engage with the federal government.[130] Related to this were the efforts of the International Indian Treaty Council which had the avowed purpose of representing and supporting the interests of Native peoples at the global level by securing consultative status as a nongovernmental organization with the Economic and Social Council of the United Nations.

In contrast, the National Congress of American Indians, the largest inter-tribal interest group, pushed for a more accommodationist approach based on upholding existing treaties and enforcing the trust responsibility which calls for the federal government "to honor, enforce, preserve, protect, and guarantee, without interference, the inherent sovereign rights and powers of self-government."[131]

During this time, and as a result of the Native activism that had spread across the country, Congress, in 1975, established the American Indian Policy Review Commission, at the behest of Senator James Abourezk (D. SD). The commission, a bipartisan assemblage of eleven members, was dually tasked with investigating the rise of Indigenous activism and with proposing improvements to the Indigenous–federal relationship. To this end, the commission created eleven taskforces, each focused on a distinct topic such as the trust relationship, Tribal government, administration, jurisdictional matters, and urban and rural–non-reservation Indians. Task Force Three, led by Philip S. Deloria (Sam), examined the federal administration of Indian affairs and discussed the strengths and flaws of alternative governing arrangements on Native political and economic status.

After describing how Native nations "do not have a role as political entities, either as members of the family of Indian nations, or as political units within the federal Union that makes up the U.S.," the authors pointed out how problematic that "unique" political status was and discussed several alternative arrangements that we have previously considered, including statehood, territorial status, and colonial status. In noting that none of those structural arrangements had worked, the authors then emphasized that, after two centuries of relations, "the question of Indian political status remains unresolved. Indians, as a people, do

116 INDIGENOUS GOVERNANCE

not fully exercise the right of self-government nor do they have the right to participate as Indian nations and tribes in the decisions which affect their welfare. This state of affairs has given rise to frustration and violence in various parts of Indian Country. Indians have discussed among themselves and publicly stated alternative approaches to settling the question of Indian political status."[132]

The committee members noted that some observers still advocated for a Native state to become the fifty-first, while others called for the federal government to recognize the full sovereignty and independence of Native nations. There was no consensus but, there was general agreement that, whatever political status was agreed upon, it must "evolve from the Indian people and their respective governments and not as a result of U.S. unilateral action."[133] Finally, the Task Force members identified three possible alternatives for national Native elected bodies which they put forward for congressional and Native consideration:

Election of an Indian Congressional Delegation. This approach includes two senators and three or more representatives elected by Indians to represent Indians and the U.S. Congress. Direct election of an Indian Congressional delegation would require an amendment to the U.S. Constitution and a formal introduction of Indian Country into the Union as a state with a form of government not unlike that of the other states. The trust relationship would have to be substantially modified. This option has been considered in the past by the Delaware, Cherokee of Oklahoma, and the Navajo—as single Indian tribes and not as multiple tribes.

Union of Indian Nations. This approach would establish an Indian legislative body with tribal delegations from each Indian nation or tribe elected by popular vote among the adult population. The elected delegates would be directly accountable to the Indian constituency. Each tribal government may reserve the right to ratify actions taken by its elected delegation or actions taken by the Union of Indian Nations. The Union of Indian Nations would serve as an elected Indian voice which works directly with the Congress in the development of Indian policy. Individual tribes would naturally have unimpeded access to Congress. The Union of Indian Nations would require formal ratification by a majority of the tribes before it could be established. Financial support would be provided by the trustee, the United States.

Indian Board of Representatives or Commissioners. Through direct election by the Indian population and appointment by the president the Indian Board would define U.S. policy toward Indian nations; and oversee and coordinate the program activities of federal agencies as they relate to Indian interests.[134]

Charles Trimble would later point out that this Task Force was one of the last units to complete its work as part of the American Indian Policy Review Commission and that its final report was given only a cursory review as the life of the commission wound down and with funds having been depleted.[135]

In 1977, Theodore Wyckoff, a professor at Northern Arizona University, wrote an article titled "The Navajo Nation Tomorrow—51st State, Commonwealth, Or" in which he argued that the Navajo Nation had reached a point in its political development that a fundamental change in its political status was called for. He based his view on three factors: (1) the demographic size of the nation—approximately 150,000 citizens; (2) the impressive developments and maturation of the Navajo's self-governing capacity—including a sophisticated and multi-level court system, popularly elected chairman, and vice chairman, a seventy-seven-member Tribal Council, and active local governments known as Chapters; and (3) timing—a sense that Tribal and public sentiment were ripe for such a fundamental political change.[136]

Wyckoff suggested there were four possible alternative political arrangements to be considered: (a) statehood, (b) Commonwealth status (e.g., Puerto Rico), (c) modifying the substance of powers that Native nations might exercise, and (d) complete termination of reservation status.[137] Of course, there were constraining factors to be considered, such as the economic viability of the Navajo Nation, the impacts of profound structural change on the surrounding states of Arizona, New Mexico, and Colorado and, finally, repercussions for the Hopi Nation, whose lands were completely encircled by Navajo territory.

After assessing the relative strengths and weaknesses of each alternative and after weighing the impact on each of the entities, Wyckoff concluded that statehood for Navajo was a possibility but that this would require "that a prospective Navajo state undergo a period of apprenticeship before acceptance as a full-fledged, equal Member-of-the-Union . . . some sort of half-way status like a Commonwealth, is a prerequisite to any futuristic possibility of statehood."[138]

In 1980, Russel L. Barsh and James Youngblood Henderson, in a book titled *The Road: Indian Tribes and Political Liberty*, took the notion of Native statehood one step further by calling for an amendment to the U.S. Constitution that would establish a new type of political compact between Native nations and the federal and state governments: treaty federalism. They argued that since Native peoples were subject to inordinate federal power with treaty rights that provided a minimum amount of protection, and since they were not allowed under federal treaty or statutory law to exit their bilateral relationship with the federal government, the only viable means to stabilize Indigenous political standing was to amend the U.S. Constitution. In their words, "In a national compact, the only safety is in the architecture of its Constitution and laws."

118 INDIGENOUS GOVERNANCE

The only explicit references to Natives in the U.S. Constitution are the two archaic clauses that reference "excluding Indians not taxed," and the more important commerce clause that specifies that the only congressional power vis-à-vis Native nations is trade. While these clauses were arguably sufficient in 1789, Barsh and Henderson maintained that a more developed amendment was necessary if Native peoples were to secure their inherent rights and clarify their relationship with both states and the federal government.

As novel as this idea may have appeared at the time, it is not without precedent. In fact, several international states have amended their constitutions in recent decades to incorporate and acknowledge Indigenous peoples and their distinctive rights and autonomy. For example, the Canadian people in 1982 modified their Constitution to declare that "the existing aboriginal and treaty rights of the aboriginal peoples of Canada are hereby recognized and affirmed." In 2006 Bolivia, elected Evo Morales (Aymara) as its president, becoming one of the first international states to be headed by an Indigenous person. A new constitution was adopted in 2009 which declared in Article Two: "Given the precolonial existence of nations and rural native Indigenous peoples and their ancestral control of their territories, their predetermination, consisting of the right to autonomy, self-government, their culture, recognition of their institutions, and the consolidation of their territorial entities, is guaranteed within the framework of the unity of the State, in accordance with this Constitution and the law."

As S. James Anaya pointed out in his 2004 study, *Indigenous People in International Law*, 2nd ed., several other international states have also amended their constitutions to recognize Native sovereignty, territorial rights, and cultural autonomy. The interesting list includes Russia, Nicaragua, Guatemala, Colombia, Argentina, Mexico, Brazil, and Honduras.

Barsh and Henderson's proposed amendment was lengthy and complicated. It would, if ever enacted, transform Indigenous nations into states of the union, but they would be states with powers not identical to those of the current states. Importantly, this amendment would strip Congress of the plenary (read, absolute) power it has wielded over Native nations since the 1880s. Native governments would continue to be self-governing, but two new types of Tribal Caucus would be created to address the issue of national representation: the Senate Caucus would consist of one delegate from each Tribal nation; and the House Caucus would be apportioned on the basis of Tribal membership. The Tribal Senate Caucus would then elect two members who would represent all Native nations in the U.S. Senate. The Tribal House Caucus would choose two members who would represent all Native communities in the House of Representatives.

The Tribal citizens would control their own internal elections and elections for national seats. This would mean that the states would have no control over

Native land and, meanwhile, Tribal citizens would surrender their voting rights in state elections. Barsh and Henderson's constitutional amendment would combine a continuation of Native government, an ouster of state and most federal legal and bureaucratic constraints, and direct representation in Congress that would bring much-needed clarity and a measure of stability to Native nations' political and legal status.

There are several dimensions that complicate their proposal. First, there is the element of diversity—demographic, institutional, developmental—to name but a few. For instance, Native nations range in demographic scale from the nearly 400,000-member Navajo and Cherokee nations to the Pit River Tribe in California with fewer than a dozen citizens. And some Indigenous communities are well-developed politically, with three branches of government, substantial economic portfolios, and highly regarded educational systems while many smaller Native nations lack any of these features or resources.

Second, there is the issue of what the status of non-Natives living in, working for, or married into Native nations would be. This aspect was not elaborated on by Barsh and Henderson. Finally, nearly 60% of Native individuals no longer live within their Tribal homelands—residing now in urban or suburban areas. What would their status be if this amendment were adopted? We simply do not know.

In 1984, avowed white supremacist and Ku Klux Klan leader David Duke, made a heinous and ludicrous call for U.S. geographical segregation by race. His plan was to force various ethnic groups to relocate and remain in different regions of the country. Native peoples were to be forced into an area in the Southwest, including portions of West Texas, New Mexico, and Arizona to be called Navatona. Mexican Americans were to be contained within a region called Alto California, located along the border between Mexico and the United States. An area in southern Florida, called New Cuba, would be reserved for Cuban Americans. West Israel, located in Long Island and Manhattan, was to become the home to all Jewish Americans. And African Americans were all to be sent to a region in the southeast to be known as New Africa. The rest of the country would be open to all those determined by those in power to be white or Caucasian— who, presumably would go about their normal business as people of color were confined and constrained.

Duke and other white supremacists believed, and continue to believe, such racial colonization to be essential for the well-being of other like-minded white supremacists. "If the races are not separated," he claimed, "the Majority will have to fight for survival or go completely under."[139] Fortunately, Duke's racist and divisive ideal of separate racial enclaves was largely ignored by federal, Tribal, and state policymakers. That said, given the tense climate and dangerous actions of white Christian nationalists within the United States today, we should not be

120   INDIGENOUS GOVERNANCE

quick to dismiss such seemingly farfetched proposals. For good or ill, if human beings can imagine something, they also have the capacity to make it reality.

State of Sequoyah Revisited

In 1998 the state of Oklahoma established the Oklahoma Centennial Commemorative Commission tasked with the development of a statewide plan to commemorate Oklahoma's century of statehood. The state had been formed in 1907, so the events were to take place in 2007. Two years later, in 2000, the Cherokee Nation's principal chief, Chad Smith, was made aware of the state's plans, which included a celebration of Oklahoma's settler land runs that had occurred nearly a century earlier. The land rushes had devastated the property and sovereignty of the Cherokee Nation and the other four nations. Smith sent a letter to Governor Frank Keating urging him to reconsider that aspect of the planned festivities. Keating responded by charging Smith with holding a "historical grudge" and declared the celebration would continue as planned.[140]

Three years later Chief Smith, at the urging of Richard Allan, organized a two-day meeting called Cherokee Nation Vision Summit 2003, which brought together leading Tribal politicians, scholars, administrative officials, BIA personnel, and community members to chart out a course of action to be taken during Smith's second term as governor. A major development of the summit was the establishment of the Great State of Sequoyah Commission which was intended "to provide an alternative response to the Oklahoma Centennial events and activities." The idea was to "provide a complete historical perspective and not to create a division between the Indian nations and Oklahoma— an education rather than a fight."[141] Commission members were a Who's Who of Cherokee luminaries, including the Chief and five additional members, including Tom Holm (Cherokee–Creek Professor of History and Native Studies), Daniel Littlefield Jr. (journalist), Wilma Mankiller (former Principal Chief of the Cherokee Nation), Rennard Strickland (Cherokee Law professor), and Russell Thornton (Cherokee Professor of Sociology). The Commission was to conclude its work on December 30, 2007, with the issuance of a final report.

Over the next two years the Commission members worked to bring attention to the futile attempts by members of the FCT in 1905 to establish the State of Sequoyah, develop materials that would include this history into the current state's educational curriculum, create a traveling Museum with artistic exhibits, produce radio and television ads to inform Oklahomans about this historical era, and generate novelty items to graphically depict the Sequoyah movement.[142]

Although a "final report" was to be submitted by the end of 2007, it was never concluded. According to Daniel Littlefield Jr., a Commission member, the actual culmination of the Sequoyah Commission was a two-day conference in early September 2005 referred to as "The State of Sequoyah, 1905–2005: Yesterday, Today and Tomorrow." Topics included discussions and presentations on the Proposed State, assessments of the political and legal status of the Cherokee people before and after the statehood movement, and a set of presentations that detailed Cherokee art, literature, philosophy, and storytelling.

Steve Russell, a retired Cherokee Tribal judge, wrote a book in 2000 called *Sequoyah Rising*, that is a critical analysis of Native governments. Russell acknowledged the inherent benefits of many of the provisions laid out in the 1905 Sequoyah Constitution. "Sequoyah," said Russell, "could rise again as the all-tribal union that eluded Pontiac, Dragging Canoe, and Tecumseh, a unified vision that might someday force a U.S. president to recognize that Congress had no constitutional authority to end treaty making, a quintessentially executive function. None of this can happen while we cling to our historical role as victims, accurate as that memory may be. If we really believe we are sophisticated enough to have political ideas worth stealing by the new American republic, and if we are still the people with peaceful trading patterns that spanned the entire continent before Europeans set foot on it, then the future belongs to us."[143]

Indigenous Statehood: Implications for Native Sovereignty

The federally acknowledged Native nations continue to occupy a distinctive legal and political niche within the larger society. Their poorly understood and ambiguous status has sometimes served to protect Native nations from fatal challenges, but their existence largely outside the federal constitutional structure has also left Native individuals and their nations susceptible to exploitation, neglect, and even political termination. Other countries, such as Canada and Mexico, have enshrined Indigenous rights and recognition within their constitutions, but the Indigenous nations within those two countries' boundaries have little to show for these actions. In fact, it could be argued that with increased visibility came increased vulnerability, as their clarified status rendered them more legally susceptible targets for those seeking to erode their powers, lands, or lay claim to their remaining resources. It is no wonder that many U.S.-based Native scholars and activists are reluctant to disturb the existing precarious extra-constitutional balance that currently exists—they know that even with the best of intentions that conditions can always get worse.

While U.S.-hosted Indigenous nations have most certainly suffered from the brevity and ambiguity of their federal constitutional mentions, they have also endured, in part, because of it. Given this tenuous situation, there is great risk in relinquishing their status as *extra-constitutional* sovereigns, which constitutional

122 INDIGENOUS GOVERNANCE

statehood would entail. The very act of being incorporated as a state (or as one of several Native states) would render Native nations as *constitutional* sovereigns within the framework of U.S. federalism, a momentous change of status, were it ever to come to pass. Any proposed drive for statehood would have to take this into account. Statehood, should it ever happen, would provide definitive affirmation of residual Native sovereignty but would diminish the inherent and separate sovereignty of Native nations by stripping them of their free-standing sovereignty as incorporated bodies.

Statehood, of course, is but one of several alternative political arrangements that have been considered in an effort to fortify Native sovereignty. *Exit*, for example, was an early and obvious alternative during the first century of political interactions. When conditions deteriorated, many Indigenous nations would simply leave the region, in some cases crossing into Canada or Mexico. Then there was the multitude of *diplomatic accords* that for the first two-hundred years, were valuable and flexible arrangements wielded to adjust political relations with non-Native governments. The incorporation of Native individuals via the extension of U.S. *citizenship* was yet another approach that was aimed at the assimilation of individual Natives. Finally, the pursuit of political *independence* via international recognition has been explored by elements of some Native nations, particularly the more traditional-minded members of the Haudenosaunee (Iroquois) Confederacy and some of the leading activists affiliated with the American Indian Movement.

With the surge of Native activism in the 1960s, these and other ideas were put forth by those committed to enhancing and supporting Native sovereignty and self-determination. Vine Deloria Jr. and Hank Adams called for reviving the treaty process that had been effectively halted in 1871.[144] Others took the idea of political exit even further and called for the United Nations to fully open its doors to Native nations.

Finally, as noted earlier in our discussion of Barsh and Henderson's proposal, a *constitutional amendment* affirming inherent Native sovereignty within the confines of the federal constitution is yet another structural arrangement that has been utilized by a number of international states, including Canada, Bolivia, Russia, Nicaragua, Guatemala, Columbia, Argentina, Mexico, Brazil, and Honduras. These amendments generally contain language acknowledging a degree of Native autonomy, some territorial rights, and cultural sovereignty. They do not grant statehood or provincial status, per se.

The extra-constitutional status of Indigenous peoples within the present-day United States has always been both a blessing and a curse. From this legally obscure position and against all odds, Native nations have managed to fend off centuries of attempts at eradication and assimilation. Given this hard-fought status, any structural change—be it statehood, restoration of treaty-making, or constitutional amendment—crafted in an effort to improve the status of Indigenous peoples in the United States is a potentially destabilizing proposition. Disturbing the existing balance in pursuit of overtly recognized rights as formally integrated polities in the federalist structure is a gamble that could jeopardize the collective inherent sovereign rights and powers Native peoples have retained in themselves and for their citizens. If the scales were to be tipped in a way that was to weaken Native sovereignty, legal and moral protections could be lost, and the rights of Indigenous peoples diminished to the level of other racial, ethnic, and gendered groups.

Native sovereignty, the inherent power neither related nor beholden to the existence of the United States or any constituent state, is the shield that forestalls total overrun, absorption, and erasure. The single goal should be to clearly ground and protect inherent sovereignties for the duration of each nation's relationship with the U.S. Native peoples and these lands have always been, and will continue to be, indivisible, long after treaties and constitutions are distant memories. We have to make sure that any move to restructure this distinctly political relationship, especially if it is to be Indigenous statehood, an action that would move Indigenous nations from the safe obscurity offered by extra-constitutionality to the high visibility of over constitutional inclusion—aligns with this reality.

5

Modern Native Constitutionalism

In 1921 Congress, unrelenting in its attempt to act as a guardian for Native peoples, enacted the Snyder Act[1] which gave the Secretary of the Interior general authority to spend federal money for the "benefit, care, and assistance" of Natives throughout the United States by providing a comprehensive funding mechanism for Natives, their seemingly perpetual wards. This money was to be used for a wide variety of purposes—health and education, resource projects such as irrigation and other water developments, and so forth. This was the first generic appropriation measure designed to meet the sundry socioeconomic needs of Native peoples wherever they resided. After the Senate was reorganized in 1921, a new period of Indian policy reform began to brew.

Criticism of federal Indian policy had finally convinced federal officials that a study of the economic and social status of Natives was necessary. The Institute of Government Research in Washington, DC, received authorization from the Department of the Interior to carry out a survey. The findings of the Institute, published in 1928 under the title *The Problem of Indian Administration*, paved the way for important changes in federal Indian policy. The Preston-Engle Irrigation Report was released that year. Together, these findings compelled the Senate, in 1928, to provide for an exhaustive survey of conditions prevalent among Indigenous peoples that was to be conducted by the Senate Committee on Indian Affairs. This survey continued until 1943 and constitutes a wealth of data on the state of Indian Country and Native citizens during that period.

These changes coalesced in 1933 during the presidential election of Franklin D. Roosevelt. Roosevelt and the institution of New Deal policies ushered in dramatic changes for Indigenous nations. John Collier, Roosevelt's Commissioner of Indian Affairs, was a social scientist who understood non-Western cultures better than any of his predecessors. To assist Native nations in the stabilization and reconstitution of their political and economic bases and help revitalize their cultural traditions, Collier, with the considerable help of Felix S. Cohen, introduced the Indian Reorganization Act (IRA) in 1934,[2] also known as the Wheeler-Howard Act.

Although Congress amended and dramatically reduced the breadth of the lengthy original bill (some 48 pages) at the insistence of various forces, including "the fears of individual Indians owning allotments, the interests of non-Indian groups leasing Indian land or using Indian timber, the concerns of missionary

---

Indigenous Governance. David E. Wilkins, Oxford University Press. © Oxford University Press 2024.
DOI: 10.1093/oso/9780190095994.003.0006

groups operating on Indian reservations, and congressional beliefs about the appropriate relationship between Indians and the federal government,"[3] basic redefinitions of critical concepts produced additional changes in Indigenous status. The IRA expressed Congress's explicit rejection of the allotment policy and the harsh course of assimilation tactics that the BIA relied upon since the 1880s. The legislation was drafted by Cohen under the supervision of Collier, who had spent considerable time in New Mexico fighting for Pueblo land and water rights before becoming Commissioner of Indian Affairs.

The IRA had several objectives: to stop the loss of Tribal and individual Native lands, provide for the acquisition of new lands for Indigenous nations and landless Natives, authorize Native peoples to organize and adopt constitutions and create corporations for business purposes, and establish a system of financial credit for Native governments and individual business entrepreneurs. Most important, for our purposes, are the provisions of the IRA dealing with governmental reorganization. Under the Act, "any Indian tribe, or tribes, residing on the same reservation" had the right to organize a government and could, if they so desired, devise a constitution and bylaws to operate under that would be recognized by the federal government. In practical terms, this provision meant that tracts of land called "reservations" determined the status of political entities called "recognized tribes." Some tracts of land had been set aside for individual homeless Natives classified under extremely general characteristics. Under the IRA, these tracts, designated as reservations, made the Native inhabitants eligible for federal recognition. "Tribes," in some instances, of less than twenty people were thereby eligible to organize themselves under formal constitutions and bylaws. Also, under the provisions, two Tribal entities sharing the same reservation—although with entirely different political and cultural backgrounds, including different treaties—were melded into one organic political entity.

Collier and Cohen had realized early on during their tenure that the traumas inflicted upon Native nations by federal lawmakers and BIA policies had devastated the social, religious, cultural, and political institutions of all Indigenous communities, and that if they were serious about the concept of "self-government" flexibility in governing arrangements would have to be a part of the reorganization process. This is evident in a statement that Cohen made in March 1934 to one of ten Indian congresses that were held across Indian Country—this one in Chemawa, Oregon, when Bureau officials visited as part of a campaign to educate Native peoples about the benefits of the IRA bill that was then under consideration in Congress.

> Mr. Cohen: I should like to explain the provision of the first part of the legislation. The first part of this bill deals with self-government. I have been told by some interpreters that some of the Indian languages do not have a word for

126 INDIGENOUS GOVERNANCE

'self-government.' So, I want to explain for the benefit of the old-timers what self-government means. For one thing, self-government means that the various rules and regulations that govern your property and affairs will not be made in Washington by the Bureau of Indian Affairs and will be made by yourselves. In the second place, self-government means that you will have power to choose all your own officials instead of having them chosen for you in Washington. In the third place self-government means that you will have control over all of your own funds instead of having all the control in Washington. To sum it all up, the idea of self-government means that the Indian Bureau is to become a purely advisory Bureau to help the Indians instead of to rule them. How do we propose to achieve this end of self-government? The first part of the legislation, the whole Title One dealing with self-government is optional with the Indians concerned. This is a very peculiar law. It does not tell all the Indians what they have to do. It tells the Indian what they can do, if they want to do it. It is, in effect, a bill of rights for the Indians. Now this problem of bringing about Indian self-government is a very difficult thing and it cannot be achieved in one day. The provisions of this Title One show the various steps that will be necessary in order for any group of Indians that want self-government to get self-government.

This first part of the legislation refers to communities. I think probably some of the old-timers have not properly understood what a community means. A community is simply a group of people who have gotten together to do something. If they get together to raise cattle as the Shoshones do at Fort Hall, then they have a community for raising cattle. If they should organize a corporation as they have been trying to do up at Klamath then they would have a community for cutting and selling timber. When a number of white people who live near each other get together to form a township, well that township is a community. And a white man's county is a community. And also the old Indian tribes are communities.

When this legislation enables the Indians to form a community, it does not mean that there is one kind of community that all of the Indians must form. Some of the Indians will form one kind and some another kind. Down in the Southwest, as many of you know, some of the old tribal organizations are still in effect. Those Indians down there may want their community to be like one of these old tribal organizations. Up here in the Northwest, most of you people have had more contact with white man's organizations, and your communities can be the most modern, the most up-to-date communities that you are able to manage. There is nothing in this bill that forces you to wear blankets or to elect chiefs.

If this legislation passes, the Commissioner will come to each reservation and he will discuss with the Indians on that reservation what kind of community they want. It may be that on that reservation he will find that the mixed bloods want one kind and the full bloods want another kind. In that case, there may be two communities, and that might happen on reservations where there are two tribes which don't like each other. Now when the Secretary of the Interior and any group of Indians get together and decide what kind of organization they want, this will explain the kind of organization that is to exist in that particular reservation or on that part of a reservation.[4]

Cohen's comments were echoed by those of land expert Ward Shephard who worked alongside him. Shepard spoke at the Plains Congress held in Rapid City, South Dakota, also in March, where he said:

Now here is an extremely important point. This bill does not set up any one system of self-government. It does not seek to impose on the Indians a system of self-government of any kind. It sets up permission to the Indians to work out self-government which is appropriate to their traditions, to their history and to their social organization. We do not wish to force on the Indians the white man's system of Government. We want, on the other hand, to build on the old Indian traditions, on your old traditions of self-government, to make this legislation fit those old traditions and your own institutions. If, on the other hand, an Indian community wishes to adopt the white man's system of Government and to enter into the same kind of local Government you already have in your State, the Bill also permits that. This Bill permits traditions from the ancient tribal Pueblo in the Southwest to the most modernized communities."[5]

On July 12, 1934, less than a month after the IRA had been enacted into law, Collier, anxious to discern the political and organizational status of Tribal nations the Bureau was obligated to serve, did what his predecessor, Charles Burke, had done in 1929: he issued a circular. Circular No. 3010 was sent to all reservation superintendents asking them to provide information regarding the Tribal governments under their jurisdiction. The data, Collier noted, were essential to the Bureau's efforts to assist those Native nations who had voted to come under the auspices of the IRA and to engage in governmental reorganization.

Circular No. 3010 was titled the Questionnaire on Tribal Organization (Government). Unlike Burke's 1929 Circular No. 2565 which had called for information only about Business Committees (or other representative bodies) and three related items, Collier's was far more comprehensive. It featured nineteen questions, several with multiple subparts. Some included the following: "1. What form of tribal organization is there on your reservation? (e.g., General Tribal Council, Business Committee, or local district organization, etc.)." "3. Does your council or committee or other organization represent the entire reservation

128 INDIGENOUS GOVERNANCE

or jurisdiction or are there separate organizations for each tribe?" "6. If the meetings are called by whom? (Superintendent, Chairman of the council, or petition of a fixed number of council members by a 'chief', etc.)?" "8. Is there an approved constitution and by-laws for this organization?" "10. List the matters which such committee or council or other organization is authorized to handle, such as: Approval of tribal leases, enrollment matters, filling vacancies, selection of delegates to Washington, preparation of instructions for tribal attorneys, etc." "13. "What in your judgment are the weaknesses of the present tribal organization and what stands in the way of its exercising greater powers than it now has?" "14. What criticisms of the present organization do you hear from the Indians and what suggestions do they have for improvements?" "15. Are any of your Indians, bands or tribes, affiliated with any intertribal or super-reservational [sic] organization such as the 'Sioux Congress,' the 'Navajo Tribal Council,' the 'Confederated Bands of Utes,' etc.?" "16. Do the women of the reservation have any part in tribal business matters? Do they vote? Do they participate in the meetings? Have they the right to hold office?" And finally, "19. To what extent do hereditary chiefs, or other chiefs recognized by either the people or by the government in the past or present, play a part in tribal affairs? If possible, illustrate with concrete examples."[6] The nineteen questions raised by Collier were designed to secure as complete a picture as possible of the existing governmental and organizational structures and organic documents operating in Native communities.

A little more than half of the 120 superintendents responded to Collier's circular. The data provided offer readers a vivid eyewitness account of what political life was actually like on many reservations. As important as these accounts are, however, the reader must carefully weight the information they convey. Some of the superintendents' responses were brief, and some reeked of author bias against Indigenous culture and government. Still, like Burke's 1929 circular they provide a good amount of evidence on Native governance. A close analysis of these agent responses—prefaced with the important caveat that these were all written by non-Native federal employees who presumably, following Collier's lead, were more supportive of Native self-rule—yields a firsthand glimpse of what institutional and cultural structures were in place in a number of Indigenous communities.

In a number of instances, superintendents had more than one Native community within their jurisdiction, like, for instance, the Consolidated Chippewa Agency in Minnesota, which worked with six of the seven Chippewa communities (all except Red Lake). Question One asked about the form of organization in existence on each reservation. The data show that at least twenty-five Native communities had Business Committees or Business Councils (i.e., Blackfeet, Eastern Shawnee, Grand Ronde, Kaw); eighteen had Tribal Councils (i.e., Bad River, Bois Forte, Hualapai, Makah, Osage), while some, like the Seneca Nation of Oklahoma, had both.

Eight Native nations, including the Crow, Northern Paiute/Shoshone, and Pine Ridge, were identified as having General Councils, which meant the entire adult membership served as the governing body. The superintendents of at least four nations described traditional governing systems, including the Bad River Chippewa—which also had a Tribal Council. Peru Farver, the field agent who answered the questionnaire for the Bad River Chippewa, responded that "the pagan group opposes any change in tribal government from their original plan of chiefs and headmen. They refuse to recognize the Tribal Council . . . The pagans contend that the chiefs and head men are the proper ones to handle the claims [against the federal government] in that it was they and not the Tribal Council that signed the treaties."

Additionally, the Oneida of Wisconsin, the Seminole of Florida, and the White Mountain Apache of Arizona were described as being led by chiefs. Oneida had two separate Councils: Council No. 1 and Council No. 2. Council No. 1 was a body of thirteen chiefs, with a presiding chief, secretary, assistant secretary, and treasurer. The chiefs were elected during a general meeting of the Tribe, but they held office "indefinitely." However, in the case of misconduct, a council of elderly women known as "Condolence Matrons" could remove a Chief by unanimous vote. Council No. 2 operated as an elected Tribal Council with a chairman and vice chairman. Hereditary chiefs were also well represented on the council, "practically all being so described."

The Seminole of Florida were divided into three separate councils. As James L. Glenn reported, "The Seminole of Florida adhere to the Old Creed tribal organization of pre-Columbian days. Their tribal life centers about the annual festival—the Green Corn Dance. . . ." The communities were led by medicine men and two to three councilmen who served for life. The White Mountain Apache were led by twelve hereditary chiefs and six sub-chiefs who served as alternates. They also had life tenure.

Question Two sought information about the makeup—number of members, titles, and tenure—of the governing bodies, assuming it was a Tribal Council, Business Committee, or other representative entity. The nations with the largest number of representatives included Rosebud Sioux (74-member council), Cheyenne-Arapahoe (52 members), Pine Ridge Reservation (46 members), and the Red Lake Chippewa (42 members). Every other nation reported having thirteen or fewer representatives, with most having five to nine delegates.

With regard to titles and functions, the great majority of the nations referred to their lawmakers as councilmen. Executive positions utilized the titles president or chairman, with a few Tribal communities like Quapaw and White Mountain Apache, employing the term chief. Political leaders' functions

130 INDIGENOUS GOVERNANCE

ranged from handling all "tribal matters" (e.g., Blackfeet), to enrollment issues, reimbursements, advising the superintendent, to addressing those matters that would promote the "social, financial, and industrial welfare" of the community's members. (e.g., Mescalero Apache).

Another element of Question Two concerned how individuals attained office and how long they served once in the position. Every nation that we have discussed held popular elections for their legislators and executives, with two exceptions: the Seminole of Florida, who appointed their leaders, and the White Mountain Apache, who utilized the hereditary system. As for tenure, once in office, we see strong evidence of tradition. Seventeen nations, including the Blackfeet, Kiowa, Comanche, Apache Menominee, and Pawnee chose officers for two-year terms. Another seventeen, including the Sac and Fox (Iowa), Santa Rosa, Morongo, and Hualapai allowed leaders to serve only one-year terms.

There were, however, fourteen nations that allowed indefinite tenure in office—the Anishinaabe Tribes in the Consolidated Chippewa Agency, Fort Bidwell, Fort McDowell, Ho-Chunk, Kaw, Muckleshoot, Port Madison, Quapaw, Quileute, Red Lake, Sac and Fox, Seminole, Swinomish, and White Mountain Apache. At Fort McDermitt, office tenure was described as "until death, unless the group considers their services are no longer needed, and they are discharged by vote." Red Lake's superintendent reported that leaders served "during the pleasure of the Chiefs." And at White Mountain Apache the leaders served "until death."

Question Three on Circular No. 3010 asked if the governing body under the superintendents' jurisdiction represented the "entire reservation" or whether there were separate organizations for each Tribe: a recognition that some reservations were home to more than a single Native nation. While the overwhelming majority of Tribal governing bodies represented the entire reservation, there were exceptions. The Consolidated Chippewa Agency led by superintendent M. L. Burns, noted in his response that "there is no tribal organization of the Chippewa in Minnesota, either as a Tribal Council or a Business Committee in the sense that it is the recognized representative organization of the entire tribe." Burns did note that of the seven Ojibwe bands in the state (Bois Forte, Fond du Lac, Grand Portage, Leech Lake, Mille Lacs, Red Lake, and White Earth), the Red Lake Council, stood apart administratively and operated under its own chief system and a formal constitution. He noted that of the other six bands, the councils of the Leech Lake and Fond du Lac Reservations "might be assumed to represent their entire reservations but not the entire jurisdiction or tribe" and that the other bands only had informal councils which "spring up spasmodically." This would remain the case until the Minnesota Chippewa Tribe formally organized under the IRA in 1936—a consolidated Tribe of the six bands

MODERN NATIVE CONSTITUTIONALISM   131

that nevertheless preserved the independent self-governing authority of each individual band.

Another example is the unique political–geographical arrangement with the Hopi and Navajo peoples. The Navajo population exploded after the reservation was established by the 1868 Navajo treaty and their territory continued to expand via presidential executive orders, eventually coming to encircle the Hopi Reservation which had been set aside in 1882. Between 1901 and 1934, the Navajo Nation was gradually divided into six separate agency jurisdictions, each with its own superintendent. This included an agency for the Hopi Tribe, located at Keams Canyon which also served Navajos. The joint Hopi/Navajo agency reported in 1934 that while the Navajo operated under a General Tribal Council, the Hopis at that time had "no tribal organization" to speak of.

Circular No. 3010's sixth question asked about who called Tribal meetings when they were to be convened. The answer to this question provides evidence as to the amount of political autonomy of the nation in question. What the data reveal is that in a slim majority of instances—thirty nations—the power to convene a Tribal meeting was left solely to the judgment of the Native nations' Chairman or President, or in the case of the Seminole Nation of Florida, to a medicine man.

On twenty-one reservations, including Fort Bidwell Indian Colony, Ho-Chunk, Osage, Sac and Fox (Iowa), and Turtle Mountain, either the Chairman or President or the BIA superintendent had authority to call a meeting when necessary. In three communities, the Sac and Fox of Oklahoma, the Mescalero Apache, and the Mexican Kickapoo, a meeting required the "approval of the superintendent." And in four communities, Blackfeet, Chehalis, Skokomish, and Squaxin Island, Tribal gatherings had to be initiated by the superintendent. At Squaxin Island, for instance, the superintendent noted that "inasmuch as there are no roads on the reservation and it is necessary to contact the Indians by rowing from the mainland, from three to four miles to the island, and as the few Indians on the reservation are old and feeble group meetings have not been attempted. When information is desired from these Indians, therefore, letters have been sent to the heads of the few families on the reservation."

Question Seven focused on whether any Tribal organizations and their members were compensated for their service to the community. A majority of Tribes reported no compensation was paid to any elected government officials. However, a few nations provided compensation. At Chickasaw, the nation's governor received $3000 per year. And the Osage Nation chief was paid $900 per year; with the assistant chief receiving $750 per annum. Several other communities—Fort Hall, Hopi, Mescalero, and Sac and Fox (Oklahoma) provided small per diems during council sessions ranging from $2.50 to $5 per day.

One of the most important provisions of the IRA was that it authorized Native communities to organize and adopt a constitutional form of government. But

132 INDIGENOUS GOVERNANCE

constitutionalism was not unknown in Indian Country. The Five Civilized Tribes (FCT), as described earlier, had each adopted constitutions during the 1800s, with the Cherokee having the oldest formal constitution, dating to 1827. These documents had been effectively vitiated by Congress in 1898 under the Curtis Act,[7] although these nations eventually reasserted their sovereignty. And, in response to Commissioner Burke's Circular in 1929, which called for information about any existing Tribal constitutions, at least twelve Native communities, in addition to the FCT, were listed as operating under constitutions.[8] More importantly, in the autumn of 1934, Felix S. Cohen and a team of researchers at the BIA began collecting data on Tribal communities in the process of organizing constitutions. In a 1942 landmark legal study, the team reported that at least sixty-five Native nations had written constitutions or constitution-like documents on record with the BIA just before the IRA was enacted into law in the summer of 1934.[9]

Question Eight of Collier's Circular asked, "Is there an approved constitution and bylaws for this organization." Of the superintendents responding, seventeen Native nations were identified as having approved constitutions including Blackfeet, Cheyenne-Arapahoe, Colorado River, Hopi, Pine Ridge, Red Lake, and several others; with another forty-one communities listed having no constitution, including Chehalis, all the Ojibwe bands except for Red Lake, Eastern Shawnee, Fort Hall, Ho-Chunk, Hualapai, Kaw, Kiowa-Comanche-Apache, Seminole, Southern Paiute, and Tonkawa. Interestingly, the superintendent of both Osage and Crow claimed that those nations did not have approved constitutions, yet we know that is incorrect. Just five years earlier the Crow agent had clearly stated that "the constitution and bylaws were approved by the office June 20, 1921." And the Osage superintendent had wrongly declared that "no constitution and bylaws have ever been promulgated or adopted for guiding the functions of the Council." In fact, the Osage had two prior constitutions, the first was adopted in 1861 and another in 1881, with each document featuring three branches of government and communally held lands.[10] We may never know if those superintendents were simply ignorant or deliberately refused to acknowledge these predecessor constitutions.

The tenth question went to the very heart of governance by asking the superintendents to identify the types of issues that governing committees or councils were authorized to handle on behalf of community members. Collier took the liberty of identifying several of the matters he was aware of, including "approval of tribal leases, enrollment matters, filling vacancies, selection of delegates to Washington, preparation of instructions for tribal attorneys, etc." Many of the superintendents responded by restating several of those issues, but several others noted additional duties and responsibilities that were assumed by the Native nations governing body:

Blackfeet: ". . . Oil and gas leases, grazing leases, granting easements on tribal property, hearing complaints on various matters presented by tribal members."

Colorado River: ". . . supervision of health matters and law and order and tribal resources."

Fort Hall: ". . . appointment of Indian judges and Indian police, selection of delegates to Washington, management of tribal social and religious dances, celebrations, etc."

Grand Ronde: ". . . to promote and encourage the members in all things tending to elevate the moral standards of the people and to encourage community enterprises."

W. O. Roberts, superintendent for the Rosebud Reservation, also noted that the Tribal Council "discussed practically every sort of question which can be imagined," including leases, enrollment matters, delegate selection, and choosing tribal attorneys, but then added a note where he proceeded to suggest that the council members were not quite competent to do other things. He said:

I have been closely connected with Sioux Councils since 1921. I have attended innumerable councils, and I believe in the principle of the tribal council. There are certain matters, however, which cannot be left to a tribal council. These people are human, very human, and their experience and capacity make it difficult for them to encompass the whole program involving a reservation set up. For example, the employee who would undertake to carry out the Office policy of limiting boarding school attendance or the abolishing of Rapid City School and if such employee were left to the mercy of the tribal council in the Sioux country there is no question as to what disposition would be made of them. Similarly, employees who must handle relief are not popular. It is my personal belief that no discussion of a major sort can be entrusted to a tribal council unless responsibility goes along with the authority.[11]

Robert's attitude was fairly pervasive among the superintendents, evidencing the difficult task confronting Native leaders as they prepared to receive the reins of a greater degree of self-administration under the provisions of the IRA.

In Question Twelve, Collier called for what he deemed an "important" response: a description of the "highlights in the history of the adoption of the present form of tribal organization," including when the organization was first established. The superintendents offered a plethora of responses, some quite detailed, as they set out to chart the political history of the Indigenous nations in their charge. One of the more interesting perspectives was delivered by the Rosebud Sioux superintendent, W. O. Roberts, who had this to say:

134 INDIGENOUS GOVERNANCE

Tradition has it that when the military forces came into the Sioux country they found a rather chaotic and confusing situation with respect to the authority of chiefs and just who might be a chief. A few of the statelier personalities, like Spotted Tail, were recognized as chiefs, but it should be understood that even in those days the authority of the chiefs was undefined. No particular set rule existed. The Chief expressed himself before the group and, if given approval, his authority was considerable. The vagaries and whims of the people might have changed the whole thing overnight. Consequently, the Indians had no very definite program and no great capacity to follow a given line of endeavor.

The confusion and difficulty was so great that finally the military officers worked out a sort of designation, based on their investigation, whereby the Government would recognize a number of the Indians as Chiefs and the activities of the band under them would be presented through such chieftains.

There is some difference of opinion now as to just how many chiefs were appointed. We can find no records indicating just what was done. However, the old Indians, like Brave Bird Iron Shield, and others, remember distinctly that the military officers did appoint and designate certain men as chiefs, in both the Government officials and the Indians gave due recognition to them. Apparently, there were something like twenty of these men appointed. It is believed that the present Board of Advisors, numbering twenty, follows this general pattern. It is also true that sons and grandsons of these appointed chiefs claim some authority because of their heredity, and it is true that the Indians give them preference in meetings though their real leadership is not great nor dependable.

We are unable to find but little in the files concerning their tribal council until about 1920. It appears that a reorganization of the whole council arrangement was made, and the present system set up. The difficulty all through the years has existed in the fact that the Council is a rather loosely knit group of fellows each with his own little clientele and each man maneuvering for position and influence, not for the tribe as a whole but from the standpoint of his own little group. This situation is so definite on the Rosebud Reservation that its importance cannot be overlooked.

C. L. Ellis, the acting superintendent of the Osage Indian Agency, who had wrongly declared that the Osage had never had a constitution in question eight, now correctly noted that the nation had adopted a constitution on December 31, 1881, although his office could not track down a copy of the document. He noted further that the Osage government was separate from the Indian Agent's office and that their principal duties were the maintenance of law and order, the collecting of permit money for livestock that was grazed on their land "without authority," and to collect taxes from whites who lived on Tribal land without Tribal or Commissioner of Indian Affairs authority.

According to their Superintendent, the Crow, led by Chief Black Foot, had organized a council under provisions of the 1860 treaty. That body remained in place until 1900 when the council changed, and the positions of Chairman and Secretary were instituted.

Several Tribal nations, including the Cheyenne-Arapahoe, Fort McDermitt, Kaw, and Otoe, were led by chiefs and headmen until the 1920s–1930s. Finally, the Ottawa's superintendent declared that "there has been no change in the Ottawa Indians way of doing business for the last 200 years." They had been, and still were, led by a chief and councilmen.

Interestingly, the Grand Ronde people, according to their superintendent, established what was called the Grand Ronde Indian Legislature in 1870. Little more was said about this body save that the Grand Ronde members were "well prepared to take care of the minutes pertaining to their new government."

Finally, the Makah people of Neah Bay, located within northwest Washington, according to their superintendent, had a village government that had been formally established in 1903. At that time, the Makah also drafted their first constitution which defined community boundaries, provided for election of officers, and divided the village into wards, among other things.

Question Thirteen offered superintendents an opportunity to identify what they considered to be the major weaknesses of the Tribal organizations under their jurisdiction and to describe "what stands in the way of its exercising greater powers than it now has?" A small number—five—of the agents instead made positive remarks about the Tribal governments. For instance, the Boise Forte Ojibwe (Minnesota) superintendent said the "council is very well organized." The superintendent of the White Mountain Apache community said the "council usually displays good judgment." And at Fort McDermitt the superintendent observed that "they [the council] have done very well so far."

Major weaknesses specified by superintendents in descending order:

(1) *Tribal organization lacks legal status and clear authority* (Fort Bidwell, Makah, Menominee Otoe, Pawnee, Quileute, Sac and Fox (Iowa), Sisseton-Wahpeton, Tonkawa, and Tule River).

(2) *Tribal organization is riven with factionalism* (Fond du Lac, Fort Totten, Kiowa-Comanche-Apache, Leech Lake, Oneida (Wisconsin), Pima, Red Lake, San Carlos Apache).

(3) *Tribal organization has severe generational conflict between older and younger members* (Kaw, Mescalero Apache, Otoe, Pawnee, Tonkawa, Uintah Ouray, White Mountain Apache).

136 INDIGENOUS GOVERNANCE

(4) *Tribal organization is not representative of the entire reservation's population* (Boise Forte, Consolidated Chippewa Agency, Northern Cheyenne, Oneida (Wisconsin), Rosebud Sioux, Southern Paiute (Kaibab)).

(5) *Tribal organization has problems with jealousies and selfishness* (Fort Totten, Kaw, Otoe, Pawnee, Tonkawa).

(6) *Tribal organization members lacked sufficient education to be effective* (Fort Hall, Makah, Northern Cheyenne, Pine Ridge Sioux).

(7) *Tribal organization is too disorganized to be effective* (Hualapai, Kaw, Leech Lake, Skokomish).

(8) *Tribal organization lacks sufficient funding to be effective* (Cheyenne-Arapahoe, Pine Ridge Sioux, Seminole, Shivwits (Paiute)).

(9) *Tribal organization leaders lack sufficient political experience to be effective* (Pine Ridge Sioux, Rocky Boys, Southern Paiute (Kaibab), Turtle Mountain Ojibwe).

(10) *Several distinctive Tribal ethnic groups live within the same reservation causing serious organizational problems* (Grand Ronde, Mescalero Apache).

(11) *Life-tenure of elected officials is problematic* (Muckleshoot, Swinomish).

(12) *Tribal organization members lack confidence in their own abilities* (Cheyenne-Arapahoe, Tule River).

(13) *Tribal organization lacks strong leadership* (Fort Bidwell, Tule River).

(14) *Tribal organization deals with too many trivial and personal matters* (Hopi Tribe).

(15) *Tribal organization meets too infrequently* (Pine Ridge Sioux).

(16) *Tribal organization struggles with blood quantum issues* (Chickasaw).

(17) *Tribal organization members are appointed when they should be popularly elected* (Colorado River).

(18) *Tribal organization is too large to be efficient* (Pine Ridge Sioux).

(19) *Tribal organization members are too emotionally "volatile"* (Rosebud Sioux).

(20) *Tribal organization lacks adequate physical space to conduct affairs* (Salt River Pima).

(21) *Liquor is too pervasive and causes enormous problems* (Seminole).

(22) *Tribal organization fails to meet the needs of off-reservation members* (Yankton Sioux).

In some reports, superintendents mentioned multiple weaknesses in the nations' political organization. For example, the Sisseton-Wahpeton Sioux were said to be plagued by the following flaws:

(1) The members of the Council should receive a modest compensation, at least enough to take care of the travel expense and meals while in attendance at the meetings of the Council. (2) The powers and duties of the Council should be more fully defined. (3) The reservation should be divided into districts and members should be elected by districts instead of at a general election held at the meeting of the entire tribe. (4) Members of the Tribal Council should be given definite responsibilities and duties. Among matters which should be devolved upon them may be mentioned the following: the care of the old and indigent, cooperation in enforcement of the federal and municipal laws, cooperation in the health program, home extension work, and in the promotion of farming and stock raising. Each tribal councilman should have definite work to do all along all of these lines. Under the present faulty organization the members of the tribal committee have rendered very useful service in the administration of the affairs of their tribe."[12]

Rosebud's superintendent also suggested that their governing system had many flaws, but he had an interesting take on one particular "weakness" that he labeled "the emotional temperament of the Indians." In his words,

Tradition and popular opinion have it that the Indian is stoical; that he measures his deliberations by the slow arc of the sun, and that he thinks in terms of moons not minutes, and so on. These popular conclusions are altogether unscientific and untrue just as the 'happy hunting ground' was the invention of the white man so is this attributed psychology of the Sioux. Indians are not deliberative; they are not philosophers; they are not conservative thinkers. Rather, they form snap judgments, are exceedingly easily aroused, and will easily form a conclusion today which they will, on mature consideration, repudiate next week.[13]

The questionnaire's fourteenth question was closely linked to question thirteen and showed Collier's willingness to at least provide Natives an opportunity to be heard regarding their own political affairs. It asked, "What criticisms of the present organization do you hear from the Indians and what suggestions do they have for improvements?" A number of superintendents (i.e., Chehalis, Eastern Shawnee, Ho-Chunk, Osage, and Turtle Mountain) said they had heard no criticisms from Tribal members regarding their political organization. The Boise Forte agent noted, "As a whole there is fair satisfaction." Other superintendents related a series of criticisms including the following: "That the old tribal chiefs were not represented" in the current council (Cheyenne-Arapahoe); the council "only consists of a representative of the minority" (Crow); there is a "failure of certain Indians to recognize majority rule" (Fond du Lac); tribal members "lack

138   INDIGENOUS GOVERNANCE

confidence" in the ability of the council to get the job done (Fort Hall, Fort Totten, Hopi Tribe, Rosebud Sioux, Tule River); the Council shows favoritism and partiality to "some members of the tribe" over everyone else (Kaw, Kiowa-Comanche-Apache, and Otoe); younger Tribal members feel poorly represented and that older council delegates "are not qualified to act for the tribe because of their lack of contact with the outside world" (Mescalero Apache); council delegates "do not tell them [community members] about the business conducted at the meetings, and that their delegates did not do as they were instructed" (Northern Cheyenne); council members "are working for personal gain" and not for the interests of the community (Rosebud Sioux); and there is too much tension between the full-blooded members and those of mixed-heritage (White Mountain Apache).

There were only a few suggestions for reform offered, including that the federal government should pay the Tribal organization's expenses (Cheyenne-Arapahoe) and that more money was needed for police and healthcare (Chehalis).

The Chehalis superintendent took the opportunity to offer his own views on the subject of Tribal organization. After admitting that the Tribe could benefit from organizing at the local level, he proceeded to speculatively lament about what this might mean in terms of their expectations of the federal government, claiming that they would likely be more demanding of their trustee. "There is this danger," he said, "of formally organizing them; namely, that when they are organized and when the organization is approved by the Department they will probably feel that they are entitled to more consideration from the Department and at first, at least, will use their organization as a means of requesting certain funds and certain assistance that they have not formerly obtained from the department."

Question Fifteen was a multipart question that asked about the Tribal involvement in any intertribal or supra-tribal bodies, like the Sioux Congress, the National Council of American Indians, or other interest groups. The large majority of Native nations did not belong to such organizations, but there were many exceptions. Several nations in the Northwest—Muckleshoot, Port Madison, Skokomish, and Swinomish—were active members in the Northwest Federation of American Indians, an organization founded in 1913 to fight for the protection of treaty rights, pursue claims against the federal government, and protect Tribes from the state of Washington's persistent efforts to harm Native rights.

The Morongo and Santa Rosa Tribes of California were active members of the Mission Indian Cooperative and the Mission Indian Federation. The Mission Indian Federation, founded by a white man, Jonathan Tibbet, focused on securing land and water rights, citizenship, and legislation supportive of Native self-determination.[14] Finally, several of the Lakota nations—Rosebud and Pine

MODERN NATIVE CONSTITUTIONALISM   139

Ridge—belonged to the "Sioux Congress" which had been organized to oversee the rollout and consideration of the Wheeler-Howard bill and to study the ongoing Black Hills land claims case dating back to the federal government's illegal annexation of the Black Hills in the 1870s.

Native women were the focus of Question Seventeen which asked, "Do the women of the reservation have any part in tribal business matters? Do they vote? Do they participate in the meetings? Have they the right to hold office?" Of the sixty-four superintendents who responded, fifty-three noted that women were active in Tribal business affairs, had the right to vote, and generally participated in Tribal gatherings. However, five superintendents noted that women did not vote or were explicitly not allowed to vote, and were denied a voice in Tribal business matters. Fort Bidwell's agent, for example, said that "under the custom of most of the California tribes, the women do not appear to exercise any voice in discussions or voting. At least this is true as to the Fort Bidwell group."

The Northern Cheyenne superintendent flatly stated, "The women do not take part in tribal affairs. They do not vote, neither do they hold office. They do not participate in the meetings." The Red Lake superintendent simply said, "The Chiefs do not appoint women as members of the Council." At Tule River it was pointed out that women may "voice their sentiments, but as a rule do not vote or hold office." Finally, the Uintah Ouray agent painted a sobering picture of a Native society that openly discriminated against women: "The women of this reservation do not have any part in tribal business matters. Quite often when a woman attempts to speak in council she is told by the men-folk to sit down and keep quiet. The women are always in attendance at councils but rarely attempt to express themselves. They do not have the right to hold office. While there is nothing in the constitution or bylaws to prevent a woman from holding any office, it will, in my judgment, be many years before a woman is elected to any office."

One reservation superintendent at Colorado River hinted that, although the women could not presently participate in political or economic affairs of the community, there was an indication that, in the near future, they would receive the right to vote, although no date was specified as to when this might occur.

Although most Native communities extended the franchise to women, on the question of whether they had the right to "hold office" there was much less agreement. On twenty-one reservations, women were either explicitly denied the right or had the right but had never been elected or chosen for political office. Fort Totten's superintendent put it this way: "They have the right to hold office but have never done so due to old tribal customs." And at Mescalero Apache, while women had the franchise, they had no right to serve in office "though there is nothing in the bylaws that would prohibit a woman to hold office."

140   INDIGENOUS GOVERNANCE

Finally, of the sixty-four superintendent reports, Native women formally held elected positions in only two communities: the Potawatomi tribe of Kansas and Santa Rosa in California. This is in contrast to the data from the 1929 Circular which found that women were serving in elected or appointed positions in at least ten Native communities.

Question Seventeen dealt with the issue of absentee voting and whether the current organization's organic charter made provisions for absent tribal members to participate "on matters of great importance." Forty-eight superintendents noted that the Native governments under their charge did not allow for absentee participation of any kind. The general sentiment was best expressed by the Rosebud superintendent who said, "I do not believe that the Indians would look with favor on an absentee vote." But ten superintendents noted that the Tribes they worked with did allow absent members to have a say on relevant Tribal matters. The Cheyenne-Arapahoe, Northern Cheyenne, and Uinta Ouray, for example, permitted absent members to appoint alternates or proxies to vote in their stead. Several other communities—Chickasaw, Ho-Chunk, Morongo, Hualapai, and Santa Rosa—allowed vote by mail.

Finally, the last question of the Circular asked what role, if any, hereditary chiefs or other traditional leader positions played in contemporary Tribal affairs. Here, we see an interesting mix of views from the superintendents. Twenty-nine of them declared categorically that, from their vantage point, the days of traditional chiefs and headmen had ended. As the Chehalis official put it: "I have never heard of any of the present Indians referred to as chiefs and do not think that the chiefs, as such, have had much to do in representing these people, either in the present or in the past." The superintendent of Fond du Lac declared that "hereditary chiefs are a thing of the past. No recognition given them by the Indians. 'Chief' is in name only."

Still, some nineteen superintendents (i.e., Bois Forte, Fort Hall, Makah, Pima) noted, that chiefs continued to play a role in the community, but, from their perspective, those roles had diminished in importance over time. As the Colorado River agent put it: "Hereditary chiefs or other chiefs are recognized to a very slight extent on this reservation and have little or no influence in forming policies for handling the business of the reservation." At Fort Bidwell Indian Colony, the superintendent claimed that "they are respected, but exercise little influence. And according to the Otoe superintendent "the powers formally vested in the chiefs were displaced when the tribal committees were perfected. However, the older Indians still respect the chiefs and the tribal committees receive and act upon their suggestions many times. The Chiefs are not fully reconciled to the changes."

In at least nine reservations (Cheyenne-Arapahoe, Hopi, Havasupai, Muckleshoot, Pine Ridge, Red Lake, Seminole, Uintah Ouray, and White Mountain Apache), Chiefs retained vital positions of power and influence. At

Cheyenne-Arapahoe, for instance, the agent reported that "the hereditary chiefs are much more valuable for the knowledge of the past, such as treaties, tribal traditions, and secret ceremonies. They are most active in these matters." Loretta Fowler's research on these two politically connected Native nations confirms the essential role chiefs played, with these traditional leaders even serving on the Business Committee. After the IRA was adopted, the BIA sought to reduce the size of the Business Committee and eliminate formal positions occupied by the chiefs. The Cheyenne-Arapahoe refused to accept the Bureau's plan and "prevailed in that on the reorganized business committee each Cheyenne district would send a chief (chosen by other chiefs); the Arapahoe would elect representatives, but in practice, where chiefs were able to serve, they were elected."[15]

The Havasupai superintendent stated that "the hereditary chiefs' word is pretty much law." The superintendent at Uintah Ouray said that while hereditary chiefs were no longer recognized, headmen retained significant power. "They do not come to this by heritage but are relied upon by the common people as spokesmen, etc. These headmen play a very major part in tribal affairs."

And while the superintendents at Pine Ridge and Rosebud sought to diminish the influence of traditional chiefs by asserting that "they are recognized [more] out of courtesy" than actual influence, Tom Biolsi's research on how the IRA and the New Deal affected these two nations reveals the continuing influence of chiefs in both societies. Drawing upon the work of Scudder Mckeel, Biolsi noted the ongoing presence of the Chiefs Society on Pine Ridge in 1931, "with each of the thirty bands on the reservation having a chief, with fourteen chiefs in White Clay District alone." Biolsi further observed that the Treaty Council, made up of older, full-blooded Lakota members, considered itself the "legal and traditional Lakota body for making tribal decisions," tracing its history back to the treaty-signing days of the 1860s. Yet, by 1934, just before the Lakota had adopted the IRA, Biolsi says that "the complexity is that it's not clear how much this kind of chief was in any way an established position in a formal political structure, and how much it was more a matter of respect for older more experienced men."[16]

Organizing under the Indian Reorganization Act

Not long after Collier sent out Circular 3010 in early July 1934, he established within the BIA a Tribal Organization Committee (TOC). This committee, led by assistant solicitor Felix S. Cohen, was in charge of the Tribal constitutional development process ramping up across Indian Country. Early on, the committee members were: Walter Woehlke, Fred H. Daiker, J. R. T. Reeves, Mrs. E. Smith, and Dr. Duncan Strong. Cohen and various members of the committee traveled into Indian Country to listen to Natives and learn more about

142 INDIGENOUS GOVERNANCE

how they might proceed with structuring or restructuring their political organization if they adopted the IRA. It was during this period of study that Cohen learned of the status and utility of pre-existing Native constitutions and of the residual traditional governing systems that were still active in many communities. Nevertheless, we still see evidence of the inherent ideological and policy tension that Cohen and his colleagues faced as federal employees. On the one hand, they wanted to facilitate and encourage a degree of Native self-rule; on the other, they were operating under certain cultural and policy presuppositions that elevated their own values and governing systems over those of Indigenous nations. This produced a set of sometimes conflicting questions, policies, and views that led to contradictory constitutional results throughout Indian Country.

For example, on June 30, 1934, a little more than a month after the IRA's adoption, a memorandum was issued titled "Immediate Program for Organization of Indian Tribes." It called for about thirty Native nations to be selected on the basis of (1) "the wishes of the Indians and their intelligent understanding of the problems of self-government;" (2) their responses to an earlier circular on self-governance; (3) "the sympathy and ability of the Superintendent, in whom must be placed chief responsibility for dealing with tribal representatives in reaching a satisfactory program of self-government;" (4) the economic status of the community; and (5) the relative ease of the organization process.[17]

From this list of Indigenous nations, which, unfortunately, were not identified, the number was to be reduced to about twelve. Those twelve would then receive the concentrated attention of Cohen and the TOC as they developed constitutions, bylaws, and charters for each group by January 1, 1935. The seemingly hurried nature of the writing process for these "strategically located" nations was considered important, "since the failure to do this will subject the Indian Office to considerable criticism, and since only through actual organization can the deficiencies of the Wheeler-Howard Act and the need for amendments of this Act and the permanent implications of this Act be clarified."[18] John Collier would later observe that the pace of Native constitutional development was indeed remarkable. "These constitutions," he said, were "probably the greatest in number ever written in an equivalent length of time in the history of the world."[19]

Along with this major undertaking, the TOC was also tasked with studying the nearly forty already approved—or awaiting approval—Native constitutions. It was hoped that these documents might give committee members knowledge that would be useful in helping other Native communities gear up for the constitutional drafting process. The following specific questions were posed: (1) How was the constitution adopted? What part did Indians and/or the Indian Office play in its drafting? (2) To what extent does the constitution reflect Native traditions and political experiences? (3) Does the constitution provide for the exercise of any real powers by the Native authorities, or does it provide for a merely

MODERN NATIVE CONSTITUTIONALISM   143

advisory organization? (4) Are the provisions of the constitution clear and enforceable? (5) What incidents indicate the strength or weakness of the constitution? (6) What criticisms of our particular constitutional provisions have been voiced?[20]

After this study was completed, the TOC was to draft a comprehensive memorandum correlating and integrating the data analyzed. The memorandum was to "contain an outline of the various topics to be dealt with in a constitution and, under each heading, any extant constitutional provision which may serve as a model, any extant constitutional provisions which may serve as horrible examples, and reference to any data showing actual experience with and criticism of relevant constitutional provisions." In effect, that memorandum was intended to show "what powers may be legally entrusted to an Indian tribal organization."[21]

Along with the study of the forty already approved or pending constitutions, and the memorandum that was to result from the study, the TOC was also asked to prepare reports for each of the thirty Indigenous nations that were included in the "immediate program" of organization. These were to be comprehensive and Tribal-specific case studies that sought to ascertain (1) the persistence of social traditions, (2) the traditional legal or quasi-legal sanctions of conduct and whether these could be revived or perpetuated, (3) the political traditions of the Native nation as reflected in a centralized or decentralized structure, (4) the kind of traditional symbols (i.e., titles of office, insignia, and ceremonial inductions) used by the nation's members—and whether such symbolism could be "used to lend authority to a government set up under the Wheeler-Howard Act," (5) the extent of factional differences within the community, and, (6) the extent of the political experience of Tribal members.[22]

On the basis of these case studies, the TOC was then "to prepare draft constitutions for approximately twenty of the thirty groups studied. These draft constitutions are to be submitted to the Indians concerned and to their superintendents for discussion and criticism . . . Constitutional drafts should be submitted to the selected tribes between October 1 and November 1 [1934], allowing approximately two or three months for completing negotiations on the twelve reservations that respond most quickly to the program."[23]

According to this memorandum, we have evidence that the BIA officers did, in fact, plan not only to provide a "model" constitution for some Native communities but were going to draft the entire constitutions of a select number of nations before submitting the preliminary document to these specific Tribes for "discussion and criticism." But it is also seen, by the questions asked, that the committee, contrary to current scholarly opinion, was intent on learning and, if possible, incorporating "traditional" forms, symbols, and understandings of Indigenous governance into these newly drafted constitutions.

144   INDIGENOUS GOVERNANCE

On October 29, 1934, an important document was produced that furthered the drive toward Native self-government. Nathan Margold, the BIA solicitor, issued a detailed opinion titled "Powers of Indian Tribes." This document, which Cohen and Collier probably had a hand in developing, identified the essential powers of self-governance that were already "vested" in Native nations and could be incorporated into their new IRA constitutions and bylaws. Vine Deloria Jr. referred to this as a "revolutionary opinion" because it emphasized that Tribal powers of governance were "inherent" and not "delegated." He went so far as to say that "modern tribal government thus begins with this opinion, although it would be another generation before Indian tribes would understand the difference and begin to talk in the proper terms about their status."[24] A few weeks later, on November 19, 1934, Cohen, with an unspecified amount of assistance from his committee members, submitted to Commissioner Collier a draft of a document called the "Basic Memorandum on Drafting of Tribal Constitutions." It was an effort, from Cohen's perspective, "to outline legal possibilities in the drafting of constitutions under the Wheeler-Howard Act." This draft did not, however, include the lengthy section on bylaws, which was submitted nine days later as a supplemental memorandum.[25]

This lengthy, fascinating, and detailed memorandum on something as vital as Tribal constitutions was not widely distributed at the time it was written, and the rationale behind this decision is revealed in Cohen's cover letter to Collier: "I leave to your best judgment the question of whether this memorandum, or something closely or remotely similar to it, should be sent out to the field generally or to those reservations which have asked for advice on constitution drafting or for criticism of submitted constitutions, or whether such a memorandum should be used simply by those of us in Washington who are working on the job of organization (so far as I know, Messrs. Gordon, Woehlke, Daiker, Mrs. Welpley and myself)."[26]

In a follow-up memorandum to Collier on November 27, Cohen asked a number of questions about various aspects of the constitutional material. He wondered, for instance, "If the statements laid down in Section twelve on popular initiative and referendum [would] meet with the approval of the Indian office." His final question was most instructive: "Should this memorandum, or some other memorandum of a similar character, be sent to the ten or twenty tribes which are now preparing, or have already been submitted for approval, Wheeler-Howard constitutions? Should some such memorandum be sent out to other tribes which have voted to accept the Wheeler-Howard Act? If not, what steps should be taken to satisfy the demand of many tribes for action?"[27]

The reason this important and substantive document has received scant attention by contemporary commentators,[28] despite Cohen's obvious importance to the study of federal Indian law and governance, is partially explained by the fact

MODERN NATIVE CONSTITUTIONALISM 145

that his widow, Lucy Kramer Cohen, maintained vigilance over her husband's papers for nearly forty years after his death. She finally chose to make two separate donations to the staff at Yale's Beinecke Library in 1989 and 1991. Thus, they have been available for public review for only a relatively short period of time.

Cohen had issued an October 25, 1934, opinion, signed by solicitor Nathan Margold, acknowledging that Native nations had historically wielded complex external and internal sovereign powers. Therein, to illustrate his contention, he identified and elaborated on a host of those inherent powers that had vested in Native nations under existing law—i.e., the power to tax, to establish a government, and to regulate domestic relations, among others. In spite of his support of this opinion, a few weeks later, on December 13, 1934, Margold produced a contradictory, opinion which then attempted to situate Indigenous nations within the structure of federal constitutional law by diminishing their inherent sovereignty:

> The Indian tribes have long been recognized as vested with governmental powers, subject to limitations imposed by Federal statutes. The powers of an Indian tribe cannot be restricted or controlled by the governments of the several States. The tribe is, therefore, so far as its original absolute sovereignty has been limited, an instrumentality and agency of the federal government. Various statutes authorize the delegation of new powers of government to the Indian tribes . . . The most recent of such statutes is the Wheeler-Howard Act, which sets up as one of its primary objectives, the purpose 'to grant certain rights of home rule to Indians.' This Act contemplates the devolution to the duly organized Indian tribes of many powers over property and personal conduct which are now exercised by officials of the Interior Department. *The granting of a Federal corporate charter to an Indian tribe confirms the character of such a tribe as a Federal instrumentality and agency.*[29] (emphasis added)

This conception of Indigenous governments combined John Marshall's old idea of domestic dependent nations with the contemporary idea of chartering federal corporations such as the Tennessee Valley Authority (in 1933) to produce a new entity with aspects of federalism and elements of aboriginal Tribal status. In more abstract terms, Native governments were fully capable political entities except when they voluntarily surrendered aspects of self-government or when Congress had eliminated certain functions of self-government. Few people, however, then or now, understood which functions had been legally divested and which had lapsed through inattention and disuse.[30]

As Native constitutions began arriving in Washington for consideration by BIA and the Interior Department's officials, it became clear that there was still a great deal of uncertainty about what form these documents should take and what

146 INDIGENOUS GOVERNANCE

actual powers Native nations could legitimately wield. Cohen, in a memorandum to Collier on June 4, 1935, said, "I have, as you know, from the start, opposed the idea of sending out canned constitutions from Washington." He reminded Collier that his "Basic Memorandum" "makes it clear that constitutions must be worked out in the first place by the Indians in the field.... I think it would be very unfortunate to lay before the Sioux tribes, for instance, a model constitution prepared by a group of superintendents (with my help) in Washington."[31]

Despite this statement, in an August 19, 1935, memorandum to Jane Jennings of the TOC office, Cohen attached a "model" constitution he had drafted for office personnel to utilize as they worked with certain Native communities. Cohen did emphasize that he believed "it would be a mistake to furnish this outline to any Indian tribe, who would naturally be tempted to regard it as comprehensive rather than suggestive."[32] But he suggested it would be useful to BIA officials "to serve as an educational document" in working with Native nations that met four qualifications: (1) the Tribe was fairly small in population size; (2) the Tribe had little experience in self-government and all their ordinances were subject to secretarial review; (3) the Tribe was integrated with non-Indians to such a degree that they would not have the power to regulate their own domestic affairs; and (4) the Tribe lacked effective social controls.

In October 1935, Margold issued a memorandum to Secretary of the Interior Harold Ickes that explained Margold's response to and "approval" of the Blackfeet tribe's recently submitted constitution and bylaws. After examining the various issues and questions that had been raised by Commissioner Collier and the acting solicitor, Margold went on to say that it was "embarrassing" to question law and policy aspects of a Tribe's constitution after the BIA had already expressed support for the same document. But Margold insisted this was unavoidable until some "general understanding" was reached as to what might or might not be involved in tribal constitutions that required the Interior Department's approval.

Margold then declared that "a comprehensive memorandum on Indian constitutional provisions, passed upon by the Indian Office, the Solicitor's Office, Assistant Secretary Chapman and yourself, would eliminate many sources of delay and disappointment in the drafting of these constitutions and would permit more mature consideration of certain difficult legal questions than is permissible under the present procedure." He then mentioned the "Basic Memorandum" drafted by Cohen the previous year and "Powers of Indian Tribes," the 1934 Solicitor's Opinion that he and Cohen had worked on. Margold said these documents were "an attempt to delimit the provisions which law and sound policy permits in these Indian constitutions." Interestingly, Margold then noted that "unfortunately the memorandum first referred to is an informal document which has never been approved either by the Department, the Commissioner of Indian Affairs, or by this Office. Many constitutions presented to this Office indicate that the repeated statement, 'Reference has been had to these documents,' is a polite fiction rather than a description of fact."[33]

Nothing in the rest of Margold's memo or in any of Cohen's papers indicates why the "Basic Memorandum" remained "informal" and was apparently "never approved" by the department. A meticulous search of Margold's, Ickes', and Collier's papers might help unravel this mystery but, for now, we can only speculate. We do not know how many officials within the BIA or the Department of the Interior—or how many superintendents or Indian agents—knew of this document. We are also unable to say with any certainty how many Native leaders knew about it. Or, even if it was ever read by any Native persons. Was it not formally approved and distributed because the BIA and the Interior Department's officials simply wanted to keep it an in-house document that they could rely on for ideas on constitutional development? Or was it deemed a document too sensitive for Native eyes because it contained valuable details about traditional governance that some in the Bureau wanted to be displaced by modern constitutional language? We simply do not know. Much more research will have to be done before we can draw better conclusions about this important document's role, or non-role, in Indigenous constitutional development.

Finally, to add further ambiguity to the question of whether Native nations were presented with "model" constitutions, we have a Cohen memo dated December 14, 1935, titled "Criticisms of Wisconsin Oneida Constitution." In the opening paragraph he notes that "except for four provisions, discussed below, this constitution is identical with the 'Short Form Model Constitution which *has been presented to and adopted by various other tribes* [emphasis added]. In fact, it was apparent, said Cohen, that the Oneida had not given "any constructive thought on self-government in this constitution," meaning that it had probably been offered to them and that they had not had an opportunity to express their own views on the document, much less have had a role in its actual development.

The data reviewed confirm that while, indeed, some Indigenous communities were presented with pre-written "model" constitutions, this was not the case for all nations. The informal "Basic Memorandum" contains a wealth of information on existing Tribal constitutional provisions and a good deal of data, as well, on traditional aspects of Indigenous governance still pertinent in 1934 across Indian Country. Thus, it reveals that the concept of Native "self-governance," which had not been generally respected by federal officials for the better part of six decades, was nevertheless not an alien concept to Indigenous nations, but an idea remaining close to their hearts. This document also reveals that Felix S. Cohen acknowledged the difficulties and opportunities that accompanied the tremendous diversity evident in Indian Country and that he had respect for the importance of incorporating local Indigenous will, knowledge, and experience into the constitutional process. As he noted in the memorandum's opening pages, "model

148 INDIGENOUS GOVERNANCE

constitutions" drawn up by the Indian Office would, "for the present," not be provided to Tribes since it would then "be only an adopted child and not the natural offspring of Indian hearts and minds."

Cohen's analysis of pre-existing Native constitutions and his continuing education in local Native traditions led him to posit that IRA tribes had to carefully choose "between the older form of tribal government and the forms of government which are customary in white communities." He noted that each Tribe "must consider for itself how far it wishes to preserve its own ancient traditions of self-government." Where those traditions had been lost, Tribes could rely on modern structures. But where they adhered, he observed that "they offer a very important source of knowledge and wisdom to those who are engaged in drafting a constitution."

The document also reveals that Cohen was aware that Native court systems mattered. Yet, he also doubted that many Tribes would require three distinct branches since, in his opinion, "unified government" was the form "enjoyed by practically all Indian tribes before the coming of the white man, and it persists in the most successful self-governing Indian communities today." In his view, separation of powers was expensive and duplicative, caused friction and inefficiency, and led to uncertain responsibilities. This analysis might explain why, even today, only some Native nations operate governments that have three distinct branches of government.

In a section of the "Basic Memorandum" titled "Relation of the Indian Service to Tribal Government," Cohen asserted that there were three "levels" of self-government, the third level constituting an Indigenous government that would have "complete independence of the Interior Department." But even in this case, Cohen declared that "it must be remembered that Congress would retain the power which it now has to nullify any tribal ordinances or resolutions. No constitution or charter could take that power away. Even Congress could not deprive itself of that power." In Cohen's mind, Congress's self-assumed superior authority over Native nations ("self-assumed" since nothing in the Constitution or the many treaties authorizes such virtually absolute power over Indigenous peoples) was an unquestionable reality of Native life that they had to tolerate.

Notwithstanding that ideological point of view, the "Basic Memorandum" is replete with examples of Indigenous political, social, and cultural structures that remained viable. It also contains Cohen's own ideas on how these structures might be, and, in fact, should be, incorporated in the newly forming Tribal constitutions.

The IRA gave Native communities only one year to vote on whether to accept or reject the act's provisions. In June 1935, Congress provided Tribes an additional year in which to vote. But they could only vote once and could not revisit their decision. Within the two-year period, 258 elections were held: 181

MODERN NATIVE CONSTITUTIONALISM   149

Native communities (129,750 Natives) accepted the act's provisions, and 77 nations (86,365 Natives, including the 45,000-member Navajo Nation) rejected the act.[34]

Three controversies arose around these elections. First, "The IRA was to be considered adopted unless a majority of the adult Indians voted against its application, the vote being structured so that the majority of Indians had to vote against its application, placing the burden of action on those Indian factions that opposed the law's application."[35] This voting slant was made more controversial when the solicitor general issued an opinion that stated that all eligible Native voters who opted not to vote would be counted as being *in favor* of adopting the act. Thus, for example, on the Santa Ysabel Reservation in California, where forty-three members voted against the IRA and only nine voted for it, the nation, nevertheless, came under the act's provisions "because the sixty-two eligible tribal members who did not vote were counted as being in favor of adoption."[36]

Second, the IRA allowed for a one-time vote for entire reservations, although in a number of instances, more than one ethnic Tribal nation inhabited a single reservation, thus leading to the consolidated or confederated status of a number of reservations. Some of the reservations and Native nations affected were the Confederated Salish and Kootenai Tribes of the Flathead Reservation, the Confederated Tribes of the Colville Reservation, the Three Affiliated Tribes of the Fort Berthold Reservation (Mandan, Gros Ventre, and Arikara), the Colorado River Indian Tribes of the Colorado River Indian Reservation (Mohave, Chemeheuvi, Hopi, and Navajo), the Gros Ventre and Assiniboine Sioux of the Fort Belknap Reservation, to name but a few. In these cases, pre-existing governing structures—sometimes still extant—were collapsed into a single constitutional government, regardless of the historical relationship between the various Native political entities.

At Fort Belknap, for example, when the Gros Ventre met with Collier to discuss the IRA in bill form, they understood that "he guaranteed them that they could organize as a tribe separate from the Assiniboine . . . and determine their own membership."[37] Collier also promised them substantial fiscal aid. These assurances convinced them to vote in favor of the IRA. But when a federal official arrived to help them write their constitution, "their ideas were ignored and to their shock, he insisted that they would have to organize a joint Gros Ventre-Assiniboine business committee" as their governing body.[38]

Third, there was a question about the sequence in which the IRA elections were to be held. Under the IRA, the Interior Secretary was authorized to transfer federal surplus and sub-marginal lands to landless Indians. Upon the transference, an election could then be held by those now territorial-based Natives to adopt the IRA and establish a constitution. But the question arose whether a

150 INDIGENOUS GOVERNANCE

Tribe was required to have land before it could adopt a constitution or whether a constitution could be approved with the promise of a land transfer at a later date. Even today, this issue continues to prove a major barrier for many contemporary non-recognized Native groups, who are often informed that they cannot be recognized by the United States because they have not held onto a communal land base.

Initially, the Native peoples of Oklahoma and Alaskan Natives were excluded from most of the benefits of the IRA. But in 1936, through two separate measures, the Alaska Act and the Oklahoma Indian Welfare Act, the Indigenous groups of those two regions had an opportunity to partake of the benefits of the IRA and regain a measure of self-governance.

The IRA and its two later extensions, even though beset by severe problems, were to the Indigenous peoples in Oklahoma and Alaska, without question, the most important pieces of legislation in the first half of the twentieth century. It was a critical, if uneven, attempt by the federal government to rectify some of the damage caused by the more horrific policies and laws it had imposed on Native nations for nearly half a century. The IRA produced mixed results. It did little to clarify the inherent political status of Native nations and it failed to devise any real constraints on federal political and administrative power, vis-à-vis Tribal nations and their citizens. As Biolsi notes in his research on the Lakota of Pine Ridge and Rosebud, "Tribal self-government among the Lakota was constructed not on an indigenous model but on the model worked out by the non-Indian New Deal Indian reformers. While their intentions were humane, the product left much to be desired from the point of view of the Lakota. The constitutions were flawed for the following reasons: (1) they did not effectively transfer OIA [Office of Indian Affairs] power to the Lakota or make the OIA accountable to them, (2) they did not provide for self-correcting checks and balances in tribal government but rather imposed federal supervision, and (3) they merely added another layer of government on the reservations which violated the Lakota principle of three-fourths majority rule.[39]

Yet, for all its shortcomings, the IRA resulted in dramatic, rapid improvements. Most critical was its effectiveness in halting the rapid loss of Indigenous land. It also reminded all parties that Native peoples were substantially different from other minority groups because they continued as cultural and political nations with inherent powers of self-governance and distinctive cultural and religious identities. But the IRA's avowed goal of energizing Native self-rule was not fully realized. Some Tribal nations took the opportunity to create constitutions and establish bylaws. However, their documents were required to include clauses that reminded Indigenous leaders of the ongoing and still vast discretionary authority of the Secretary of the Interior to dictate policy to Native communities and to overrule Tribal decisions. Native nations that resisted efforts to institutionalize

MODERN NATIVE CONSTITUTIONALISM 151

their governing structures along the constitutional lines suggested by federal officials were sometimes pressured to acquiesce by Collier and his associates. Nevertheless, Native peoples regained a significant measure of self-respect and some degree of political autonomy and were better prepared to move ahead as more self-determined nations.

6
Governing Systems

For untold millennia—or, as Native people say, since time immemorial—Indigenous peoples have inhabited the region now known as the United States. By definition, these nations are the land's original sovereign political entities. Each polity, whether a fishing community in the Northwest, a Southeastern agricultural town, or a hunting nation of the Great Plains, developed and sustained particularized kinship systems, social and governmental institutions, and spiritually based values and ideologies that enabled it to function relatively well in an ever-changing physical, cultural, and intergovernmental landscape. Operating within bounded geographical territories and maintaining effective kin and clan-based relationships, Native nations perpetuated their communities and engaged in activities that would reflect favorably on their ancestors, provide relative peace and stability for living generations, and lay the moral and cultural foundation for their descendants.

Native nations have always engaged in diplomatic affairs with other Indigenous peoples, but those engagements only sometimes translated into critical and categorical changes in their demographic status, property patterns, religious orientations, economic affairs, or kinship or governmental institutions. However, the arrival, settlement patterns, and ensuing policies of European explorers and settlers—and later the federal and state governments—forever altered Native status in each of these categories, and Indigenous lands, lives, and liberties were never to be the same.

Within that harsh reality, Native nations continued despite profound poverty, horrific health and housing conditions, devastating psycho-social traumas, racism, and misogyny. They found ways to adjust to radically altered landscapes after the permanent arrival and mixture of intercultural clashes and coalitions with the newly established Euro-American entities spawned as those settlers established permanent homes in North America. Some Native communities, as we saw in the previous chapter, were able to retain essential elements of some of their traditional institutions; in many other cases they made strategic modifications to pre-existing institutions; and a number of them forged completely new institutions to cope with their radically changed environments.

In the arena of Indigenous governance, those institutional retentions, modifications, and inventions are particularly in evidence, as it is through such structures—whether kinship-based or more formally based constitutions or

Indigenous Governance. David E. Wilkins, Oxford University Press. © Oxford University Press 2024.
DOI: 10.1093/oso/9780190095994.003.0007

other charters—that Native societies have been able to function and perform the multitude of duties and services expected of them by their ever-diversifying constituencies.

Powers of Modern Native Governments

No matter who is engaged in their workings, politics is the struggle for power. And while not the only source of human strife, it is evident that in every society there are "conflicts which must somehow be reconciled if the society is not to split into separate independent parts." And, of course, "conflict and competition begin within the family, however little we care to admit it."[1] Since many, if not all, Native nations customarily rely upon kinship, that is "the relation subsisting between two or more persons whose blood is derived from common ancestors through lawful marriage", as the major definitional criterion upon which their societies are structured, then the ways and means these individuals relate to one another helps determine how politics is practiced, the structure of the governing system that is generated, and what kinds of powers that governing body—or bodies—is authorized to wield by the members of the society.[2]

Modern Native political systems are fueled by myriad inherent and delegated powers, including, but not limited to, the following powers: to establish a form of government; to define the conditions and criteria of who is entitled to membership or citizenship in the community; to protect members of the community against lawlessness within and enemies without; to administer justice; to remove or exclude persons (citizens and noncitizens) from the community; to charter businesses; to exercise sovereign immunity; to levy dues, fees, and taxes upon all individuals and businesses; to regulate the use and disposition of all property under the government's jurisdiction; to prevent the sale, lease, or encumbrance of Tribal land; to establish rules of inheritance regarding personal property within the community; to employ legal counsel and; to negotiate with other Indigenous nations, local governments, states, the federal government, and foreign businesses.

As Nathan Margold, the solicitor of the Interior Department noted in his October 25, 1934, "Powers of Indian Tribes" opinion, these and other powers do "not refer merely to those powers which have been specifically granted by the express language of treaties or statutes, but refers rather to the whole body of tribal powers which courts and Congress alike have recognized as properly wielded by Indian tribes, whether by virtue of specific statutory grants of power or by virtue of the original sovereignty of the tribe insofar as such sovereignty has not been curtailed by restrictive legislation or surrendered by treaties."[3]

154 INDIGENOUS GOVERNANCE

In other words, Native nations were complete and autonomous sovereigns historically, but in establishing intergovernmental relations with the federal government via treaty making, they, like the federal government itself, agreed to share and surrender some of their inherent sovereignty while retaining all other powers of internal and external self-governance that had not been restricted by treaty provision.[4] As the National Congress of American Indians (NCAI), the oldest and largest intertribal organization within the United States, noted in a 2020 report titled "Tribal Nations and the US: An Introduction":

> The essence of tribal sovereignty is the ability to govern and to protect and enhance the health, safety, and welfare of tribal citizens within tribal territory. Tribal governments maintain the power to determine their own governance structures and enforce laws through police departments and tribal courts. They exercise these inherent rights through the development of their distinct forms of government, determining citizenship; establishing civil and criminal laws for their nations; taxing, licensing, regulating, and maintaining and exercising the power to prosecute wrongdoers and exclude them from tribal lands. In addition, tribal governments are responsible for a broad range of governmental activities on tribal lands, including education, law enforcement, judicial systems, health care, environmental protection, natural resource management, and the development and maintenance of basic infrastructure such as housing, roads, bridges, sewers, public buildings, telecommunications, broadband and electrical services, and solid waste treatment and disposal.[5]

Indigenous societies always had the equivalent of what we term political systems and governing structures but, as we discussed in Chapter 2, the origin points and rationales for these systems differed profoundly from those of European states and later the United States. Although the federal and state governments are very different from Indigenous governments, they share some important governing features as described in Chapter 1. This chapter will describe the basic principles of government, offer working definitions of key concepts, and sketch a general overview of government structures.

The Nature of Government

Government, in its most basic sense, may be defined as the exercise of influence and control through law and coercion over a particular group of people. Many governments, of necessity, require their citizens to give up some of their freedom as part of being governed. But why do individuals surrender any autonomy to this control? The simple answer is they generally do so in order to obtain the benefits government can provide. Broadly, government serves two major purposes: maintaining order (protecting the safety of group members) and providing public goods (e.g., education, sanitation, welfare). Some governments in recent years, including the United States, have also sporadically pursued a third goal: promoting equality—based on the idea that all citizens should have equal claims to the political and economic benefits of society.

Government may also be defined as a set of institutions that makes and enforces decisions. Any group or society that endures for any length of time creates some kind of government, although the form and composition differ from place to place and group to group. A key component of any government is its authority to make binding decisions for those it governs. The important word here is authority. A government's authority is its power to make binding decisions, to direct the means by which these decisions will be carried out, to assure decisions are implemented, and, if necessary, to enforce compliance with those decisions.

As described in Chapter 2, Native peoples generally derive their distinctive means of social and political organization from their sacred creation stories and migration accounts. For the Diné (Navajo), a code of ethics generated from a set of principles expressed by the value of *Sa/a Naaghai Bik'e Hozhoo* (SNBH) has provided a broad foundation that the people and their leaders have been able to abide by. This is a spiritual system that roughly means longevity, resilience, and eternal goodness.[6]

Unlike Western models of governance which nearly always include an element of coercive authority, most Native nations did not delegate a binding or authoritative element to their leaders. Instead, persuasion rather than force, was a foundational operative principle.

The difference in power between government and its people, or "the leaders and the led," has created tension in every society. Power may be used to promote the common good, and there are many examples of these shared benefits, but it may also do serious harm. Concentrated governmental authority can send children to war, misuse public resources, or enforce racial segregation. It is not surprising, then, that people in most political systems—though not in historic Indigenous systems—are suspicious, or even fearful of government, even as they rely upon it for essential services. Individuals are weak in comparison to the collective power of a government.

Here again, there are impressive differences between traditional Indigenous societies and European–Euro-American governments. Most Western nations rely on representation and majority rule which compromise individual integrity. Majoritarianism, thus, arises from the view that society is little more than a collection of selfish and highly competitive individuals and interest groups. In such a society, consensus is virtually impossible to achieve, if it is even sought.

156 INDIGENOUS GOVERNANCE

Indigenous nations, on the other hand, relied on a sense of universal kinship—that spanned time, space, and species.

Western peoples presume that political behavior is motivated by selfishness and greed, hence, the need to have laws to protect the ruled from the rulers. In contrast, Indigenous peoples understood political leadership as a "burden upon the selfless, an obligation for the most capable, but never a reward for the greedy."[7] In the Native context, political leaders were not unattached decision-makers. Rather, they were coordinators, peacemakers, humorists, and teachers who were self-effacing, patient, and self-reliant. As Russel L. Barsh has observed, there was no room in traditional Indigenous government for individuals who sought power, because there was no power, at least no permanent coercive power.[8]

In countries striving to be democratic, the friction between the leaders and the led is especially striking. For example, the United States has struggled to create traditions, institutions, and practices that allow for peaceful change. The democratic process makes the continued tension between political leaders and American citizens a central aspect of American political life. The very structure of the government allows people to question and challenge authority. But, as a consequence, American citizens are caught between their ideal of peaceful popular control of government and the reality of disparate power.

The Role of Ideology and Politics

Political ideology as understood by political scientists refers to the more or less consistent set of values historically reflected in the political system: economic order, social goals, and moral values of a given society. It is, in other words, "the means by which the basic values held by a party, class, group, or individuals are articulated."[9] The term first arose during the French Revolution to refer to a school of thought, separate from religion, about how a government should be arranged. Today it has generally come to mean the philosophic belief of true believers, whatever their credence.

Views of how far government should go to maintain order, provide services, or pursue political and economic equality fix individuals on an ideological spectrum. At one end are those who believe that government should be actively involved in many spheres of life. At the other extreme are those who believe the government should barely exist, and if it must exist, it should have an extremely limited role in society. The two dominant political ideologies in the United States are *liberal* and *conservative*. Historically, and to a lesser extent today, small segments of the American population follow libertarianism—the political principle of persons who oppose all government action except that which is essential to protect life and property. And a small number of Americans identify themselves as supporters of socialism. Socialism, like communism (the doctrine of revolution based on the works of Karl Marx and Friedrich Engels that maintains that human history is a struggle between the exploiting and the exploited classes) centers on the government's role in the economy and is an economic system based on Marxist theory.

The scope of government from a socialistic perspective extends to the ownership or control of the basic industries (e.g., transportation, communication, etc.) that produce goods and services. Generally, Americans frown upon the symbol represented by the word *socialism*, yet they favor long-standing socialistic measures like Social Security, Medicare, Temporary Assistance for Needy Families, the Tennessee Valley Authority, and other programs, services, and agencies which help people in need.

Liberals

There is no major party that identifies as liberal, but the U.S. Constitution lays out a background of liberal principles—especially the declared protection of human and civil rights. Individuals who consider themselves liberal tend to stand mostly for job creation, universal healthcare, pacific attitudes in international relations, support for civil rights, human rights, minority rights, community politics, and policies aimed at protecting the environment. They also tend to believe that industry and commerce should be democratized.

Conservatives

Individuals who believe that a government is best that governs least, and that big government infringes on individual, personal, and economic rights are usually considered to be conservative. They support local and state action over federal action and believe fervently in free enterprise and tend not to support governmental expansion of individual rights and liberties. Conservatives by and large see government's major role as defense of the nation and its overseas enterprises. Of course, these are broad and generalized definitions, and surveys reveal that many individuals who refer to themselves as liberal also hold some conservative views on issues and vice versa. For example, some persons are liberal on social issues (i.e., education, abortion, and civil rights), but quite conservative on economic issues (i.e., wage rates and taxes). Conservatism, on the other hand, has witnessed a profound reorientation, thanks to Donald Trump's chaotic and democracy-threatening presidency that inspired a new political movement, Trumpism, that is a populist movement with fascist leanings, fueled by white

158 INDIGENOUS GOVERNANCE

Christian nationalism. Trumpism, as David Blight wrote, despises "liberalism; taxation; what it perceives as big government; nonwhite immigrants who drain the homeland's resources; government regulation imposed on individuals and businesses; foreign entanglements and wars that require America to be too generous to strange peoples in faraway places; any hint of gun control; feminism in high places; the nation's inevitable ethnic and racial pluralism; and the infinite array of practices or ideas it calls 'political correctness.' Potent ideas all in search of a history."[10]

Indigenous citizens have become much more active in electoral campaigns since the 1990s and their ideological persuasion varies quite a bit. While political data on Native voters lag far behind that of other racial and ethnic groups in 2020, *Illuminative*, a Native nonprofit initiative established to increase the visibility of Native nations, prepared a jointly sponsored report (in partnership with the Center for Native American Youth and Native Organizers Alliance) called the Indigenous Futures Project that gathered survey data about Native peoples in advance of the 2020 presidential election.

Regarding political orientation, the data showed that 60% of Natives identified as liberal, 28% as moderate, and 12% as conservative. As for party identity, 51% said they were Democrats, 26% identified as Independent, 9% said they were Democratic Socialists, and only 7% supported Republican party tenets.[11]

Ideals of Democracy

Democracy is an ancient political concept derived from the Greek word *demokratia*. The root meaning is *demos* (people) and *kratos* (rule), or "rule by the people." The question is, *who are those people*? The word democracy also describes at least three different political systems. In one system, a government is said to be democratic if its decisions serve the true interests of the people, whether or not its people are directly involved in decision-making. This definition allows various authoritarian regimes like Russia, China, Cuba, and other countries, to spuriously claim they are democratic. Democracy is also used to describe governments that closely mirror Aristotle's ideal of the "rule of the many." A government is democratic if all or most of its citizens participate directly (direct democracy) in either holding office or making policy. New England town meetings and many Native nations that have General Councils practice according to these principles.

Joseph Schumpeter describes the third definition of democracy thus: "The democratic method is that institutional arrangement for arriving at political decisions in which individuals (i.e., leaders) acquire the power to decide by means of a competitive struggle for the people's vote." This method is often referred to as representative democracy, or indirect democracy. For representative government (republicanism—a government rooted in the consent of the governed) to work there must be an opportunity for people to select their leadership by ballot. In turn, this requires that individuals and parties vie for political office, that communication be free, and that voters be given a choice in determining leadership. It is this third definition of democracy that is the one followed by most democratic nations, including the United States. Increasingly, a number of Native nations are operating in this manner, in part because, for them, direct democracy proved impractical.

The American political system is theoretically based on the idea of balance: Balance between the legislative, executive, and judicial branches; between the state and federal governments (and increasingly, Native governments); between the wants of the majority and the minority; and between the rights of the individual and the best interests of the United States as a whole. The federal government, state governments, and many Native governments feature a number of key characteristics which enable them to maintain some semblance of balance.

Popular Consent: The idea that a government must draw its powers from the consent of those it governs. This was a central tenet for traditional Native societies, as well as for the drafters of the American Declaration of Independence. A citizen's willingness to vote or actively participate represents their consent to be governed.

Political Equality: The idea that all votes should be counted and weighed equally.

Popular Sovereignty: The right of the majority to govern itself. Political authority fundamentally rests with the people who have the inherent power to create, modify, or terminate their governments. The notion that all legitimate governments draw their power from the people is found in many Indigenous communities, the Declaration of Independence, and federal and state constitutions.

Majority Rule: Even though the authority of leaders is limited, they still make decisions based upon certain criteria. In the event of disagreement, the theory of democracy provides that the will of the majority prevails. This provision is not always easy to follow nor always desirable. Still, it offers a standard against which the legitimacy of governmental decisions may be judged. Protection of minority rights is also important as recognized in some Native constitutions and the U.S. Bill of Rights.

Individualism: Americans tend to emphasize individual rights and responsibilities more than most other nations. Individualism holds that the primary function of government is to enable the individual to achieve his or her highest level of development. The American emphasis on individual

160 INDIGENOUS GOVERNANCE

responsibility is strengthened by two beliefs: (1) Many Americans are skeptical of government power and question government's competence; and 2) Many Americans believe that hard work and persistence pay off.

Personal Liberty: Liberty is freedom: freedom from government interference and freedom to pursue one's interests. Thus, this may be the most important characteristic of all. The Declaration of Independence declared that all individuals (at that time this meant only white, propertied males) were entitled to the unalienable rights of "life, liberty, and the pursuit of happiness." And the preamble to the U.S. Constitution stated that securing "the blessings of liberty to ourselves and our posterity" was one of the primary motivations for the new republic. The protection of liberty is, of course, a key concern of Indigenous governments as well.

Checks and Balances: This is the notion that constitutional devices can prevent any power within a nation from becoming absolute by being balanced against, or checked by, another source of power within that same nation. Thomas Jefferson put it best when he stated that "the powers of government should be so divided and balanced among several bodies of magistracy, as that none could transcend their legal limits, without being effectively checked and restrained by the others." This separation of powers, according to James Madison, was "essential to the preservation of liberty." A number of Tribal nations have also enshrined these concepts in their constitutions, codes, or other organic charters.

The Rule of Law: This concept affirms the idea that laws should have precedence over the arbitrary rule of persons. According to the rule of law, everyone is supposed to be equal before the law, and the law is supposed to apply equally to all.[12]

Donald Trump's unprecedented, constitution-defying bid to retain the presidency after his loss in the 2020 election, as well as persistent voter suppression efforts targeting Asian Americans, African–Americans, Native peoples, Latinx, and members of the LGBTQI community, provide unvarnished evidence that the rule of law has more validity as a theoretical construct than an actual and fully realized political reality.

Indigenous Governing Organizations

Presently, there are 574 Indigenous nations that are officially acknowledged by the federal government—345 are Native nations—whether described as Tribes, bands, Pueblos, or Rancherias in the lower 48 states; 229 are Alaskan Native Tribes or villages on a list prepared annually by the Department of the Interior.

The Indigenous people of Hawaii, who prefer to be called Kanaka Maoli, Kanaka Oiwi, or simply Native Hawaiians, while recognized as Native Americans for some legal purposes, are not currently included in the Interior Department's annual list of federally acknowledged Tribal entities. They, like Alaskan Natives, have a unique political and legal status in federal Indian law and will be treated separately in a later chapter.

A number of state governments also have established procedures that grant a form of recognition to some Indigenous communities that do not have formal federal acknowledgment. It is a means for states to acknowledge the historical and cultural status and long-standing relationship with those communities. Some Native nations have been recognized by their host states since the colonial era: the Pamunkey and Mattaponi Tribes, residing in Virginia, signed treaties as early as 1607, although others have been recognized by more recent state decrees (gubernatorial executive orders or state statutes). There are approximately four types of state recognition: *state law*, with recognition conferred by the passage of a new law; *administrative*, with recognition being bestowed by executive agencies with statutory authority; *legislative*, with the state legislature recognizing Tribal nations via statute; and *executive*, with recognition resulting from a proclamation or executive order.[13] There are currently more than sixty state-recognized Native groups in thirteen states.[14] This study will not assess the political or structural status of state-recognized Native polities.

Types of Political Organizations

Not surprisingly, there is significant diversity in the types of governing bodies operating throughout the world and within Indian Country. The following questions are helpful in determining the structure and functions of a particular government.

1. Who and how many have ultimate authority?
2. Is political power distributed into branches or consolidated into a single unit?
3. Are there subunits of government and how do they relate to the central government?
4. What is the role of government?

To better understand the distribution of governmental authority, it is useful to imagine all governments on a scale. At one end is autocracy—in which one person possesses all the power. At the other end of the spectrum is pure

162 INDIGENOUS GOVERNANCE

democracy. In a true democracy, power resides in all the people. Most contemporary governments fall somewhere between these two extremes.

Many centuries ago, Aristotle classified governments into three broad categories: government by one person (monarchical), government by the few (aristocratic), and government by the many (democratic). This remains a useful classification system and there are variants of these three basic types.

Autocracy: A kind of government in which one person—an autocrat—has supreme power (i.e., Nazi leader Adolf Hitler is the foremost example, along with Joseph Stalin of the former Soviet Union, Vladimir Putin of Russia, and Pol Pot of Cambodia).

Aristocracy: A government where a privileged minority rule. They usually inherit their wealth and social position.

Democracy: A system of rule that encourages citizens to play a significant role in government, usually through the selection of key public officials.

Theocracy: Literally, "the rule of a state by God." A government in which rulers are seen as deriving their authority directly from a creator. A theocratic government conducts its affairs according to religious doctrine (i.e., certain Hopi villages and most of the Pueblo nations of New Mexico, Iran, and Tibet).

Oligarchy: A form of government in which the ruling power belongs to a few persons who gained office by means of wealth, military power, or membership in a single dominant party.

Dictatorship: Government where political power resides entirely in one person or a group of persons. Power is wielded arbitrarily and oppressively (i.e., China, Iraq, Libya).

Monarchy: A system where supreme authority is vested in a single figure, usually hereditary.

Confederacy: A system where the constituent polities retain inherent autonomy except for those powers delegated to the central government (i.e., Haudenosaunee, America under the Articles of Confederation, the European Union)

Military Regimes: A political system where the military regime holds a preponderance of power (i.e., Pakistan and Myanmar).

Most residents of Native nations and the United States believe that democracy is the most viable form of government.

Native Nations with Formal Constitutions

Indigenous peoples employ a variety of governmental systems, though as of this writing, the vast majority—approximately 485—of Native communities have formal written constitutions. Of these, 292 are utilized by Native nations in the lower 48 states, while 193 Alaskan Native communities have such documents. These organic compacts have multiple origin points. As noted in the previous chapter, some sixty Indigenous nations had written constitutions predating the 1934 Indian Reorganization Act (IRA). But the largest number of organic charters, approximately 250, have been written under the auspices of the Interior Department. These were created pursuant to federal statutory authority conveyed by the IRA and two related measures enacted in 1936—the Oklahoma Indian Welfare Act and the Alaska Native Act. These 1936 acts extended most of the provisions of the IRA, including the adoption of constitutions and business charters, to Native peoples in those two states.

Another group of Indigenous communities adopted constitutions that were approved by the Department of the Interior outside of any specific federal statutory authority (i.e., Crow Tribe, Hoopa Valley Tribe, Lummi Tribe, and the Spirit Lake Tribe). In Alaska, several Native communities—including the Beaver Tribe, Goodnews Bay Village, Newtok Traditional Council, and Tazlina Village—have what are termed "Traditional Constitutions." These four communities are demographically small villages, with fewer than 100 members, and their constitutions contain many provisions found in other constitutions. The preamble to the Newtok community's Traditional Constitution is a clear statement of that nation's values and intent:

> We, The Newtok people, maintain our freedom as a sovereign people in historic relationship with the United States of America, in creating this Newtok Traditional Council Constitution. We adopt this Constitution to exercise the Traditional Inherent Sovereign rights, the powers in promoting the well-being and unity of this and in succeeding generations, to show our faith in fundamental Native Rights and Traditions, and in promoting our Traditional existence from the beginning of living together in Newtok Village, being a sovereign Native people, in order to organize forth common good, to govern ourselves under our own Traditional Customary Laws, and Values to maintain and foster our Traditional culture, to protect our traditional social, culture, economic, political progress, to increase the Criminal Law and Order assertions of jurisdictions. And develop its natural resources, establish and adopt the following Constitution for the government-to-government protection, relationship and common welfare of the Newtok village and its members. We adopt this

164 INDIGENOUS GOVERNANCE

Constitution and Bylaws under the inherent sovereign authority of our Newtok Traditional Council, Newtok Alaska.[15]

In Hawaii, the Kanaka Maoli developed a constitution as part of their efforts to fortify their sovereignty and autonomy. The document approved in 1993 built upon a draft written in 1987. The Constitution of Ka Lāhui Hawaii democratically formalizes the distinctive political autonomy of Native Hawaiians as a modern polity and establishes clear links with their own unique history by including provisions for traditional chiefs.[16]

Native Governments That Utilize Other Forms of Governing Documents

While most Native nations have chosen to adopt formal constitutions, the other eighty-nine communities operate under a variety of arrangements including Articles of Association or Incorporation; Tribal Codes, Charters, and Governing Resolutions; Business Committees or Councils; Village Councils; or Customs and Traditions.

Articles of Association

A number of Indigenous communities rely upon Articles of Association (AA) or Articles of Incorporation (AI) as their organic charter. These documents, typically affiliated with businesses and corporations, lay out the purpose, organizational structure, and responsibilities of the officials and procedures that guide these governments. Sixteen Native nations use AA or AI, including Barry Creek Rancheria (CA), Cabazon Band of Mission Indians (CA), Cahto Tribe of Laytonville Rancheria (CA), Cher-ae-Heights Indian Community (CA), Dry Creek Rancheria Band of Pomo (CA), Fort Independence Indian Community (CA), Mesa Grande Band of Digueno Mission (CA), Orutsararmuit Native Council (AK), Pauma Band of Mission Indians (CA), Rappahannock Tribe (VA), Rincon Band of Luiseno (CA), Shingle Springs Band of Miwok (CA), Summit Lake Paiute (NV), Sycuan Band of Mission Indians (CA), Twenty-Nine Palms Band of Mission Indians (CA), and Yavapai-Prescott Community (AZ).

These documents are most commonly found in California Native communities, many of them having been drafted in the 1960s with considerable federal involvement. For instance, the Pauma Band of Mission Indians Articles were adopted in 1966 by a vote of fifteen in favor and two against, with one undecided. The Articles are straightforward and lay out their territory, define

GOVERNING SYSTEMS   165

membership criteria, specify the General Council as the governing body, describe the election process (including procedures for vacancies and recalls), enumerate powers that may be exercised by the General Council and the Business Committee, describe the structure and functions of the Business Committee, discuss when Tribal meetings will be held, describe the duties of the political officers—Chairman, Vice-German, and Secretary-Treasurer—and conclude with a description of the approval process for the Articles and how they may be amended.

With the enormous level of socioeconomic growth that many of these communities have experienced since the early 1990s, largely due to gaming operations, some communities, like the Yuhaaviatam of San Manuel Nation (formerly the San Manuel Band of Mission Indians), have recently transitioned from the use of Articles to a formal constitution.[17]

Codes, Charters, and Governing Resolutions

Several Native nations operate under Codes (e.g., Navajo Nation), Charters (e.g., Eastern Band of Cherokee), or Governing Resolutions (e.g., Quapaw Tribe of Oklahoma). In 1986, the Eastern Band of Cherokee adopted their "Charter of Governing Document" which specifies who the officers of the Tribe will be, what powers they may exercise, how elections will be conducted, and how vacancies will be filled. It even includes the oath newly elected officers must swear before assuming their positions. Since then, the document has been expanded enormously and is now called simply "The Cherokee Code" which "constitutes a recodification of the general laws and permanent ordinances and resolutions" of the nation.[18]

The Navajo Nation has had several opportunities to establish a constitution, beginning in 1936, just after the Navajo people narrowly rejected the IRA, but all attempts have failed. In lieu of a constitution, the Secretary of the Interior in 1938 approved a limited set of "Rules for the Navajo Tribal Council," which were written by Commissioner of Indian Affairs John Collier. These original rules, with some important changes, still provide the basic framework of the Navajo Nation government. Nevertheless, over the last eight decades, many new laws have been enacted by the Tribal (later Navajo Nation) Council and signed into law by the president. These resolutions have considerably expanded the scope and form of the Navajo Government.

In 1962, all preceding Tribal resolutions and pertinent federal laws were codified—systematically arranged—into bound volumes under the title *Navajo Tribal Code*. The *Code*, now called the *Navajo Nation Code*, has expanded to six volumes. It contains the general and permanent provisions of law and resolutions

166 INDIGENOUS GOVERNANCE

of the Navajo Nation's governing bodies. It is divided into twenty-six titles (Title 25 being reserved), including an appendix which reproduces the Treaty of 1868, relevant acts of Congress, executive orders, and state disclaimer clauses.

The Quapaw also rejected the IRA, as well as the 1936 Oklahoma Indian Welfare Act. They instead created an organic document called the *Governing Resolution*, that was first adopted in 1956 to guide the activities of the Tribe's Business Committee (BC). The BC had replaced the nation's traditional leadership in 1954 after receiving an Indian Claims Commission award, worth nearly $1 million, against the federal government.[19] The Governing Resolution declares, interestingly, that "it is expensive and inconvenient for the individual members of the Quapaw Tribe to meet in general council when it is necessary to transact tribal business" . . . and "it is not the intention or desire of the individual members of the Quapaw Tribe to establish an organization for the purpose of governing the activities of the tribe." The Tribe's members opted instead to simply establish an administrative unit—the Business Council—that would act for the Tribe's members on all business matters.

Other Governing Bodies

The Arapahoe and Shoshone nations were forced to live together on the Wind River Reservation in Wyoming in 1878 and have separate non-IRA governments. These operate under Business Councils which are answerable to separate General Councils that have the authority to "overrule the Business Council, initiate policy, and even disband the Business Council and hold a new election."[20] But the nations jointly created the Wind River Inter-Tribal Council which oversees shared government functions on reservation-wide matters, like handling COVID-19 and dealing with Tribally owned trust lands.

Customs and Traditions

Approximately thirty-one Indigenous communities say that they adhere to their nation's unwritten customs and traditions as the basis for their political systems. This category includes a majority of the Pueblo peoples in New Mexico and a portion of the Hopi villages in Arizona that are sometimes characterized as theocracies—as systems where the civil leaders and Tribal officials are selected by, or are themselves, religious leaders. See Table 6.1 for a list of these communities.

The Ramona Band of Cahuilla Indians in California is a small community of about fifteen members. According to their website the Band "remains a customs and traditions Tribe and utilizes a Tribal Council for all decisions that

GOVERNING SYSTEMS 167

Table 6.1. Customs and traditions-based Native nations

Acoma Pueblo (NM)

Augustine Band of Cahuilla (CA)

Buena Vista Rancheria of Me-Wuk (CA)

Cahuilla Band of Indians (CA)

Capitan Grande Band of Digueno Mission Indians (Viejas Band of Kumeyaay and Barona Band) (CA)

Cayuga Nation (NY)[a]

Cloverdale Rancheria of Pomo (CA)

Cochiti Pueblo (NM)

Inaja and Cosmit Band of Indians (CA)

Jemez Pueblo (NM)

Kewa Pueblo (NM)

Los Coyotes Band of Cahuilla and Cupeno (CA)

Nambe Pueblo (NM)

Narragansett Tribe (RI)

Native Village of Eek (AK)

Ohkay Owingeh Pueblo (NM)

Oneida Indian Nation (NY)[b]

Onondaga Nation (NY)

Picuris Pueblo (NM)

Pojaque Pueblo (NM)

Ramona Band of Cahuilla (CA)

San Felipe Pueblo (NM)

San Ildefonso Pueblo (NM)

Sandia Pueblo (NM)

Santa Clara Pueblo (NM)

Santa Rosa Band of Pueblo (NM)

Taos Pueblo (NM)

Tesuque Pueblo (NM)

Tonawanda Band of Seneca (NY)

Tuscarora Nation (NY)

Ysleta de Sur Pueblo (TX)

Zia Pueblo (NM)

[a] This community is riven with a seemingly intractable dispute over governance.

[b] This nation purports to follow the Traditional law outlined in the Great Law of Peace, but the nation's current political leader, Ray Halbritter, was expelled from the Grand Council established under the Great Law, in part because of his decision to embark on casino development.

168 INDIGENOUS GOVERNANCE

impact Tribal interests." The Band, like virtually every other Native community, was also severely affected by COVID-19. Their long-serving Chairman, Joseph D. Hamilton, was stricken with the virus and passed away in early 2021. In keeping with their traditions, the remaining adult members convened to choose a new leader. According to John Gomez Jr., the Band's Project Manager, "Two generations of the Ramona Band, including the Chairman's sons and his nieces, agreed to elevate the Chairman's niece, Danae Hamilton Vega, to the position of Tribal Chair."[21] Her selection to Chair was formalized by a Tribal Resolution.

Ms. Vega, only twenty-two years of age, had been acting as Vice-Chair prior to the death of Chairman Hamilton. In fact, because of the small number of citizens, she was the only adult member of the Band—besides the Chairman—who was working for the Band prior to Chairman Hamilton's passing. Chair Vega attended college prior to returning to the homeland in 2018 at which time she put her talents to work for her people by serving on various boards and committees to gain experience.

Besides the Chair position, there is also a six-member council that meets irregularly as the need arises. The Ramona Reservation was established in 1893, but their small land base—only 640 acres of trust lands and 80 acres of nontrust land—was never allotted and they did not have an opportunity to vote on the IRA.[22]

Family relations, as noted above, are the essential framework that links the community's members together. As then Chairman Joseph D. Hamilton described it in a 2019 interview, the "government [has] continued on as a family." Ramona does not have a court system, although it does enact some resolutions related to land, environmental regulations, and outside parties. Project Manager Gomez Jr. noted in an interview that the community's structure of customs and traditions combined with the small size of the Band sometimes poses difficulties for outside entities like the federal government and California state agencies, which have greater familiarity working with Native nations with larger populations and that have more formalized governing systems like constitutions or Articles of Association. Gomez said the burden falls on Ramona Tribal members to educate federal and state officials about how a custom and tradition-based Tribal community operates without a formal governing document.[23]

When asked why the community continued to adhere to customs and traditions instead of adopting a more formal structure, Chairman Hamilton said simply, "We're used to it" because it's simple to operate and provides the Band with greater political and legal dexterity. Both Chairman Hamilton and Manager Gomez also emphasized that they have a strong sense of pride when they inform people that their Band adheres to customs and traditions and because their political identity is not controlled "by a piece of paper."[24]

GOVERNING SYSTEMS 169

The Capitan Grande Band of Digueno Mission Indians includes two bands—the Barona Band and the Viejas Band of Kumeyaay. When I contacted the Viejas Band to request a copy of their governing document, Diana Aguilar wrote me back and said that "the tribe relies strictly on its *customs and traditions* for guidance and does not have a constitutional-based government. Furthermore, there are no bylaws or set of codes."[25] The Tribe has both a General Council and a Tribal Council. The General Council consists of all the bands voting members and they approve land use and budget matters. They also elect the members of the Tribal Council, which include a chairperson, vice-chairperson, secretary, treasurer, and three council members at large.[26]

The Los Coyotes Band of Cahuilla and Cupeno Indians is led by a General Council, made up of all adult members. The Tribe's officers include a spokesperson and five committee members who serve one-year terms. The community's members rejected the IRA decisively in 1934 by a vote of 37–3,[27] choosing instead to retain their original system of customary law and traditions.

The largest grouping of Native nations adhering to customs and traditions are, of course, many of the Pueblos located within New Mexico and the Ysleta de Sur who reside in and near El Paso, Texas. Taos Pueblo describes itself as a theocratic government, following a "traditional system which consists of a Governor, Lieutenant Governor, Tribal Secretary, as well as a War-Chief, Lieutenant War-Chief, and War-Chief Society."[28] The leadership focuses on issues like education, community health, care for the young and old, infrastructure development, environmental health, and economic development.

Until January of 2022, Taos leaders had always served one-year terms—a custom practiced by virtually all the other Pueblos. But as a result of two major issues—a serious spike in crime and COVID-19—the leadership decided on January 4 to allow officials to serve a second year in office. A statement released by the Pueblo explained, "This is the first time as far as we know in our lifetime that an administration has been appointed to serve a consecutive term in office." Noting that this was a major change in policy, the statement continued and noted that "we understand that change is difficult for many, but it is inevitable. Many of our Councilmen and community members supported a consecutive term and others are skeptical. We understand the fear of change; all we can do is continue our efforts focusing on the best interest of our community as a whole with the hopes that reasoning and understanding will follow."[29]

The Ohkay Owingeh Pueblo political system is also based on customs and traditions. Government officials are "traditionally appointed." Selections are made "every two years for Governor, 1st Lieutenant, 2nd Lieutenant, Sheriff, and annually for all other traditional officials."[30] The Tribe also has a ten-member Tribal Council.

170   INDIGENOUS GOVERNANCE

The Pueblo of Sandia, likewise, adheres to cultural traditions regarding its political leadership. Sandia is also led by a Governor, Lieutenant Governor, War-Chief, and Lieutenant War-Chief, each appointed to annual terms. The Governor runs the community's daily operations, and the Lieutenant Governor serves as the Tribe's judge. The two War-Chiefs are responsible for religious activities. Appointees can serve consecutive terms. Upon leaving office, the Governor and War-Chief become Tribal Council members for life.[31]

Finally, the Ysleta del Surd Pueblo, also known as the Tigua Tribe, who have lived near El Paso Texas since 1882, were refugees from the Great Pueblo Revolt of 1680. They have retained their customs and traditions-based government notwithstanding the fact that their political status has only been recognized by the state of Texas since 1967 and by federal decree a year later. These recognition measures provided much-needed resources that helped the community reassert and strengthen itself.[32] The Tribal Council is the traditional governing body of the community, and it is led by a Governor, Lieutenant Governor, Sheriff, and four council members. They serve one-year terms. The Pueblo also has a Cacique and a War Captain who serve indefinitely. These individuals are the spiritual leaders of the community. They are assisted by four assistant captains. The Tribe's spiritual leader, the Cacique, has retained the walking cane that was given to Pueblo leaders during the Spanish era. The canes are symbols of political authority.

Finally, several of the Haudenosaunee, Six Nations, or Iroquois Confederacy nations, continue to draw upon the Gayanshegowa or Great Law of Peace for political guidance and inspiration—most notably the Tonawanda Band of Seneca and the Onondaga Nation. The Cayuga Nation and the Oneida Nation also purport to follow the Great Law, but Cayuga is beset by a severe and long-standing intra-tribal conflict over which political segment is the legitimate governing entity of the nation. And the Oneida Nation, which claims to follow traditional law, holds a deeply problematic position as a bona fide member of the Grand Council. The conflict originated in 1993 when their leader, Ray Halbritter, was expelled by the Council over the Oneida nation's embrace of casino gaming as an economic choice, a decision that many felt violated the norms and traditions of the Great Law.[33] Despite his ouster by the Council, the Department of the Interior continues to recognize Halbritter and the Oneida clan heads as the leaders of that nation.

Alaska is home to many small communities that continue to rely upon customs and tradition, like the Native Village of Eek. Nick Carter, the community's administrator, said, in response to a question about the governing system at Eek, that "the Eek Traditional Council does not have a written constitution or tribal ordinances. What we do have are customs and traditions passed down by our ancestors, told by our ancestors in stories, taught at home, and understood by our tribal members. As such, our tribal government is not written."[34]

Native Governing Bodies

We have just described a variety of Indigenous political systems that exist across Native America. Let us now turn to see which elements within those different governing structures are empowered to exercise "governing authority" on behalf of the community's citizenry. Not surprisingly, given the amount of political diversity evident among the 574 federally acknowledged Native nations, there are several distinct bodies recognized as having primary governing authority. See Table 6.2.

Tribal Council

Nearly half of all Indigenous communities utilize Tribal Councils as their governing body. Most of these have small councils ranging from as few as three-member councils (Augustine Band of Cahuilla) to as many as forty-two (Pueblo of San Felipe). The next two largest are those of the Navajo Nation and the Rosebud Sioux Tribe, each with a twenty-four-member council. Most councils have between seven to twelve members. Interestingly, at least five nations (e.g., Wyandotte Tribe, Comanche Nation, and Apache Tribe of Oklahoma) have Tribal Councils made up of the entire adult member population. In some cases, these bodies delegate some of their plenary power to a small Business Committee or Council to oversee the day-to-day affairs of the nation.

Regarding the inherent powers that are wielded by these nations, Article 6 of the Karuk Tribe of California's Constitution provides one example of what councils are authorized to do:

1. Negotiate and contract with federal, state, Tribal and local governments, private agencies, and consultants.
2. Purchase, lease, or otherwise acquire land, and to receive gifts for the benefit of the Tribe.
3. Prevent the sale, disposition, lease, or encumbrance of Tribal lands, interest in lands, or other Tribal assets without the consent of the Tribe.
4. Establish and manage Tribal enterprises and the economic affairs of the Karuk Tribe, including but not limited to: establishing boards, commissions, and other tribally chartered entities to regulate housing,

172 INDIGENOUS GOVERNANCE

Table 6.2. Indigenous governing authority

Tribal Councils	249 (*Native and Alaskan Native Polities*)
General Councils	73
Village Councils	54
Councils	49
Traditional Councils	47
Divided Powers of Governance[a]	42
Business Committees	19
Business Councils	19
Community Council	18
Board of Directors	5
Council of Chiefs[b]	4
Executive Councils	3
Executive Committee	3
Executive Board	2
Elected Council	1
Governing Council	1
Board of Governors	1
Tribal Assembly	1
Senate	1
Governing Board	1
Governing Committee	1
Board of Trustees	1
Tribal Chairperson	1
Nation Council	1
Council of Trustees	1
Regional Tribal Council	1
Elders Council	1

[a] This includes those communities with three distinct branches of government (e.g., Blackfeet Tribe), four separate branches (e.g., Kiowa Tribe), two separate branches (e.g., Mashpee Wampanoag), and a union of self-governing villages and a Tribal Council (e.g., Hopi Tribe).

[b] These bodies share power with Clan Mothers, including the Cayuga, Onondaga, Tonawanda Band of Seneca, and Tuscarora Nation.

employment, gaming, and other economic enterprises; approval of planning, programming, and development projects of all Tribal lands and assets; and other necessary financial and business activities.

5. Establish and oversee Tribal committees which have authority delegated by the Tribal Council for specific Tribal functions.
6. License and regulate, including assessing applicable taxes and fees, the conduct of all business activities within Tribal jurisdiction.
7. Manage, develop, protect, and regulate the use of Tribal land, wildlife, fish, plants, air, water, minerals, and all other natural and cultural resources within Tribal jurisdiction.
8. Provide for the preservation and unity of Karuk families, and the protection of Karuk Tribal children, while maintaining each child's cultural identity and relationship to the Tribe.
9. Enact laws and codes governing the conduct of individuals and prescribe disciplinary action for offenses against the Tribe; to maintain order; to protect the safety and welfare of all persons within Tribal jurisdiction; and to provide for the enforcement of the laws and codes of the Tribe.
10. Establish Tribal courts and administrative bodies, and to provide for the courts' jurisdiction, procedures, separation of the judicial branch of government, and a method for selecting judges.
11. Take all actions that are necessary and proper exercise of the powers delegated to the Tribal Council or to any person or committee under the supervision of the Tribal Council.

General Council

A little more than seventy Native communities retain General Councils as their governing body. As is stated in the Koi Nation Constitution "the General Council shall be the governing body of the Koi Nation of Northern California. The General Council consists of all enrolled members of the nation, eighteen (18) years of age older." The General Council, while having "all powers of the Nation," nevertheless exercises its powers through an elected Tribal Council. But the General Council reserves the following important powers to the people: "To encourage and foster the traditions and culture of the Nation. To elect members of the Tribal Council and other Tribal officials. To exercise the power of referendum. To recall elected members of the Tribal Council and other Tribal officials. To amend this Constitution."

The Skull Valley Band of Goshute employs a similar governing arrangement. As Candace Bear, Tribal Chair, described her nation's government: "As far as I have seen and understood, there is not a written history about the formation

174 INDIGENOUS GOVERNANCE

about the Skull Valley Band of Goshute government. Most of what we learn is through our family stories. However, there are common points that we all agree upon. There or two bodies within the Band government. The General Council which embodies all adult members. The Executive Committee, the representative body that is elected by the General Council to conduct day-to-day business and all other duties designated to it by the General Council. The governing articles of the Band are General Council Resolutions which are drafted by the Executive Committee and ultimately passed by the General Council."[35]

In several of the communities that utilize General Councils, while the General Council is recognized as the governing body, the community delegates the day-to-day operations of the nation's affairs to a smaller, elected group, usually called the Tribal Council, Business Committee, or Board of Directors. The General Council, however, reserves the broader, more fundamental powers associated with land, cultural retention and revitalization, election or recall of key leaders, and so on.

The persistence and prevalence of General Councils are a testament to the ongoing power of traditional political values and principles. As the 2005 iteration of Felix S. Cohen's *Handbook of Federal Indian Law* put it: "While the coexistence of general councils and tribal councils presents the possibility of conflict between the two, the persistence of general councils reflect traditional tribal values of consensus in the political process."[36]

Divided Powers of Governance

As noted above, separation of powers and checks and balances are considered key features in most democratic governments. Some commentators[37] have complained that many contemporary Native governments—especially IRA and IRA-related governments—are inadequate or lacking because they do not have provisions for separating power between distinct branches of government and because there is an "absence of checks and balances" in the existing governmental framework.[38]

There is a large measure of truth to this, especially with regard to those Native governments formed under the auspices of federal law. The fault here lies not with Native leaders, but with ill-informed federal policymakers like Felix S. Cohen and John Collier, who, at the time of the 1934 IRA, operated under the stereotype that Native peoples were too simple to understand the concepts of separation of powers and checks and balances and therefore needed what Cohen called "unified government, that is to say, government by a single body of representatives clothed with comprehensive powers."[39] In fact, Cohen, in his "Basic Memorandum on Drafting of Tribal Constitutions," drafted in November

1934, inaccurately declared that unified government "was enjoyed by practically all Indian tribes before the coming of the white man, and it persists in the most successful self-governing Indian communities today, with only slight modifications."[40]

While it is certainly true that Indigenous nations established unification in kinship systems, their overall spiritual worldview, and other considerations, on political terms they were far more sophisticated than Cohen[41] and Collier initially conceived. As Tatum, et al., described these nations: "A separation of powers is not a new concept nor is it a European ('Western') creation. Some American Indian governments traditionally separate responsibility for internal or domestic affairs from responsibility for external or foreign affairs. Among the Pueblos, for example, these powers lie with 'peace leaders' and 'war leaders,' while the Creek and Cherokee distributed these (and other) responsibilities across 'white towns' and 'red towns.' The Iroquois Confederacy allocates different kinds of decisions to different governmental units: broad decision-making powers rest with the Confederacy council, but clan mothers hold appointment power (they select representatives to the all-male council) as well as the power to veto declarations of war. The Lakota allocated legislative, executive, and judicial responsibilities among the *naca ominicia* ('big bellies,' or wise older men), *wicaśa it'ancan* (men chiefs), 'shirt wearers' (a type of executive leader), *wakicun* (managers of day-to-day civil and economic affairs in the camp), and *akicita it'ancan* (military society/police force)."[42]

And while many Native nations historically divided powers, at least forty-two contemporary Indigenous governments enshrine divided powers of governance in their organic documents.

But, unlike the standard tripartite system in place in the U.S. Constitution and the states, there are many examples of divided governance throughout Indian Country. The Mashpee Wampanoag, for example, have a two-tiered system. Their Constitution states in Article 5: Tribal Government Powers, that the "Tribal Council and the Tribal Judiciary shall be separate and equal branches of the Tribal Government. Each branch shall exercise only the powers vested in it and shall have no authority over the other branch except as may be granted by this Constitution."

Many Native communities employ a three-branch system. The Blackfeet Nation's Constitution states that "the government of the Blackfeet Nation shall consist of an Executive Branch, a Legislative Branch and a Judicial Branch" and that "no person or group of people charged with official duties under one of the branches . . . shall exercise any power properly vested in either of the other branches of government."

The Kiowa Tribe and the Wilton Rancheria have a four-branch system, consisting of a General Council, the Executive, Legislative, and Judicial bodies.

176   INDIGENOUS GOVERNANCE

Table 6.3. Native nations with divided powers of governance

1. Blackfeet Tribe. Three distinct branches.

2. Cherokee Nation of Oklahoma. Three separate branches.

3. Chickaloon Native Village. Two separate branches: Legislative/Executive and Judicial.

4. Chickasaw Nation. Three separate departments.

5. Choctaw Nation of Oklahoma. Three separate departments.

6. Crow Tribe. The Crow Tribe's 2001 Constitution created a three-branch government, although the General Council remains the "governing body" of the nation although it has not convened since 2001.

7. Eastern Band of Cherokee Indians. Three separate branches.

8. Eastern Shoshone of the Wind River Reservation. This reservation is also home to the Northern Arapahoe. The two Tribes have separate Business Councils but share a Joint Council for reservation-wide matters.

9. Gila River Indian Community. Three separate branches.

10. Hopi Tribe. ". . . is a union of self-governing villages sharing common interests." There are nine villages, each with relative autonomy. There is also a Tribal Council with a Chair, Vice Chair, and village representatives.

11. Jicarilla Apache Tribe. "Three distinct departments."

12. Kasigluk Traditional Elders Council. Community has a Traditional Council, Elders, and Tribal Chief.

13. Kiowa Tribe. The Kiowa Tribe has four branches of government: Kiowa Indian Council, Executive, Legislative, and Judicial.

14. Little River Band of Ottawa. Three separate branches.

15. Little Traverse Bay Bands of Odawa. Three separate branches.

16. Mashpee Wampanoag. "The Tribal Council and the Tribal Judiciary shall be separate and equal branches of the Tribal Government."

17. Menominee Tribe of Wisconsin. Tribal Legislature (executive and legislative power) works with Tribal Judiciary. Separation of powers is discussed under Article 2, section 3.

18. Mescalero Apache Tribe. "The powers of the government of the Mescalero Apache Tribe are divided into three distinct departments; the legislative, executive, and judicial."

19. Metlakatla Indian Community, Annette Island Reserve. City Council.

20. Mohegan Tribe. "The Mohegan Tribe shall be governed by the Mohegan People, and represented by a Tribal Council, consisting of nine members, and a Council of Elders, consisting of seven Tribal members."

21. Monacan Indian Nation. Three separate branches.

GOVERNING SYSTEMS 177

Table 6.3. Continued

22. Muscogee Creek. Three distinct branches: Principal Chief, House (two representatives from eight districts), and a Supreme Court.

23. Nambe Pueblo. Three separate branches that are rooted in "oral traditions."

24. Native Village of Hooper Bay. Three branches: Tribal Chief (who is also a council member); Council of seven members; and Tribal Court (Chief Judge and associate judges).

25. Native Village of Kipnuk. Two branches: Legislative/Executive and Judicial.

26. Navajo Nation. Three separate branches.

27. Osage Nation. The People are sovereign. "Governing power shall be vested in three (3) separate branches": Osage Nation Congress; Principal Chief; and Supreme and lower courts.

28. Pascua Yaqui Tribe. Three distinct branches.

29. Passamaquoddy Tribe of the Pleasant Point Reservation. Governor, Lt. Governor, and Council members.

30. Penobscot Nation. The People hold inherent power. Legislature is the General Council; Executive is the Chief, Vice-Chief, the Tribal Council, and the Council Chair; Judicial is the Justice system.

31. Pit River Tribes. Two departments: Legislative (Tribal Council) and Executive (Tribal Chair, Vice-Chair, Secretary, Recording Secretary, Treasurer, and Sargeant-at-Arms).

32. Pueblo of Cochiti. Split between the Caciques and his selections and the Pueblo Council.

33. Pueblo of Isleta. Three distinct branches.

34. Pueblo of Jemez. Tribal Council and traditional structures.

35. Pueblo of San Ildefonso. Council is the lawmaking and budgeting body; Governor and his departments are executive body.

36. Seminole Nation of Oklahoma. Executive authority is in Chief and Asst. Chief. Chief "presides over all meetings of the General Council . . . shall have general supervision over the affairs of the General Council." The legislative body . . . "shall be known as the General Council and shall consist of two (2) band representatives elected from each of the fourteen (14) Seminole bands."

37. Seneca Nation of Indians (NY). "Our government shall have a legislative, executive, and judicial department." The legislature consists of a 16-member group of councillors, a president (who presides over the Council's deliberations), and judicial department which has a Court of Appeals, a peacemaker court, and a surrogate Court.

38. St. Regis Mohawk Tribe. Three distinct branches.

39. Tohono O'odham Nation. Three distinct branches.

(continued)

178 INDIGENOUS GOVERNANCE

Table 6.3. Continued

---

40. Wilton Rancheria. "The government of Wilton Rancheria shall be composed of
a Chairperson, a Vice-chairperson, a Tribal Council, a General Council, and a
Tribal Court." "They . . . shall be separate and distinct and shall not exercise the
powers and functions delegated to any other officer or entity."

41. Yavapai-Apache Tribe. Three distinct branches.

42. Zuni Tribe. Three distinct branches.

The two respective councils are composed of all members over eighteen years
of age.

Business Committees or Councils

Some thirty-eight Native communities are governed by either Business
Committees (19 in all) or Business Councils (19). For example, the Constitution
of the Confederated Tribes of the Colville Reservation declares that the governing body of the Tribes is a fourteen-member Business Council from various districts. The council's powers, subject to limitations imposed by the Tribes
Constitution, federal statutes, and the U.S. Constitution, include the following:

(a) To confer with the Commissioner of Indian Affairs or his representatives
and recommend regarding the users and disposition of Tribal property;
to protect and preserve the Tribal property, wildlife and natural resources
of the Confederated Tribes, to cultivate Indian arts, crafts, and culture; to
administer charity, to protect the health, security, and general welfare of
the Confederated Tribes.

(b) Exclude from the restricted lands of the Reservation persons not legally
entitled to reside thereon, and ordinances which may also be subject to
review by the Secretary of the Interior.

(c) Recommend and help to regulate the inheritance of real and personal
property, other than allotted lands, within the Colville Reservation.

(d) Regulate the domestic relations of members of the Confederated Tribes.

(e) Promulgate and enforce ordinances, subject to review by the Secretary
of the Interior, which would provide for assessments or license fees upon
non-members doing business within the Reservation, or obtaining special rights or privileges, and the same may be applied to members of the

Tribes provided such ordinances have been approved by a referendum of the Confederated Tribes.

The governing body of the Ponca Tribe of Oklahoma is a seven-member Business Committee authorized during the members' four-year term of office to wield virtually plenary power over all "executive, legislative, and judicial powers of the Tribe, including such powers as may in the future be restored or granted to the Tribe by any laws of the U.S. or other authority." But the Business Committee's power cannot be inconsistent with the Ponca Constitution or applicable federal law.

Interestingly, the Kalispel Tribe's seven-member Business Committee allows at least one member of the committee to be a non-Kalispel member, though the person must have at least one-quarter Indian blood and be married to an enrolled Kalispel member or have children who are enrolled. That person must also have lived on Kalispel lands for at least ten years prior to election. While eligible to serve on the committee, they are not allowed to serve as a Tribal officer.

Miscellaneous Entities as Governing Body

The remaining Native communities field a diverse range of entities that serve as the governing body of the nations they represent. Five nations, including the Cow Creek Band of Umpqua, the Stillaguamish Tribe, and the Tulalip Tribes, have a Board of Directors. Several nations have Executive Councils, Executive Committees, or Executive Boards that govern (e.g., Bay Mills Indian Community, Nakinek Native Village, Minnesota Chippewa Tribe, the Nez Perce Tribe, and the Little Shell Tribe of Chippewa Indians).

The Modoc Tribe of Oklahoma has an Elected Council. The Sac and Fox of Oklahoma operate with a Governing Council. The Ponca of Nebraska utilize a Board of Governors. The Swinomish Tribe of Washington elect an eleven-member Senate. The Confederated Tribes of the Umatilla Indian Reservation have a Board of Trustees.

Governance and Elders

Historically, many Native peoples relied upon the knowledge and experience of elders who were the primary repository of customary law, tradition, and language. As Holm put it: "All policy-making decisions rested on the ability of these elders to recall an instance from customary practice or from the tribal sacred history that could serve as an example for a resolution and convince others in

180 INDIGENOUS GOVERNANCE

the council to accept the precedent. The idea was to gain consensus based on already established law, whether sacred or secular, because the two were blended so as to be inseparable."[43] The traditional political term for such a government is gerontocracy because leadership was lodged in an elderly group of men and women who through time and experience had acquired significant wisdom that they relied upon to make decisions for the community's welfare.[44]

Elders continue to occupy a special role in the affairs of the communities they are a part of, but their direct role in governance is far less evident than it once was. My government database of accumulated constitutions, codes, charters, and articles identifies only eleven express references to elders in over 500 organic documents. In slightly more than half the communities, the elders' role is mostly advisory. However, in a small group of nations, the elders play critical policymaking roles. Here are a few examples.

- Kasigluk Traditional Elders Council: Elders share power with the Traditional Council and Tribal Chief.
- Mentasta Traditional Council: An honorary elder has voting rights and "advises" the Council. The Elder has indefinite tenure on the Council, unlike the elected members.
- Mohegan Tribe: An elected seven-member Council of Elders serves alongside the Tribal Council.
- Pit River Tribe: The Council established an "advisory committee of elders to consult with the Council on matters pertaining to tribal lands, membership, and traditions."
- Pokagon Band of Potawatomi: An Elders Council "provides guidance and advice to the community." One member of the Council may be elected to the Tribal Council.
- Wilton Rancheria: The community created a Traditional court which is made up of elders. The Court exists to "assist the Tribal Council in the resolution of cases or controversies involving tribal members and to advise . . . on matters of custom and tradition."

The only Indigenous community in the United States that has an Elders Council serving as its governing body is the Yupik Village of Bill Moore's Slough in Alaska. It is empowered to set land policy for every member of the village, to "protect, preserve and defend the Bill Moore's Slough land, land policy and its people's traditional relationship with the land," protect the civil liberties and freedom of the community's members and perform all judicial functions. This five-member body serves three-year terms.

GOVERNING SYSTEMS   181

Multinational Native Communities

The 574 recognized Native nations live on some 326 land areas generally understood as constituting "Indian Country."[45] This term includes reservations, Pueblos, rancherias, missions, villages, and dependent communities. While a majority of Native reserved lands are owned and occupied by a single Native nation, approximately seventy-eight are communities that are home to two or more distinctive Native peoples, although in a majority of these reservations, the different ethnic groups share a common governing document. See Table 6.4 for a listing of these communities.

This table includes several of the "Confederated" peoples located within Northwest states: in Washington, Yakama Nation, Chehalis Reservation, Colville Reservation; in Oregon, Coos, Lower Umpqua, and Siuslaw, Siletz Indians, Grand Ronde Community, Umatilla Reservation, Warm Springs Reservation; and, located within Montana, the Confederated Salish and Kootenai Tribes. The Confederated Tribes of the Goshute Reservation, located in Nevada and Utah, is actually inhabited by a single Native nation, the Goshute.

Other reservations that are home to multiple ethnic groups include the Bridgeport Paiute Indian Colony of California (home to Miwok, Mono, Paiute, Shoshoni, and Washoe; the Colorado River Reservation, home to the Chemeheuvi, Mohave, Hopi, and Navajo; the Federated Indians of the Graton Reservation, home to Coast Miwok and Southern Pomo; Quinault Indian Nation, inhabited by Quinault, Quileute, Hoh, Chehalis, Chinook, and Cowlitz; and the Tulalip Tribes, where Duwamish, Snohomish, Snoqualmie, Skagit, Suiattle, Samish, and Stillaguamish peoples reside. Again, each of these multinational Native homelands operates under a single organic document, in the form of a constitution, articles, code, or charter.

There are several multinational homelands, however, where there is more than one operating government or where there is explicit recognition of the different ethnic polities inhabiting a single landmass. Arguably, the most distinctive political arrangement is that of the Northern Arapahoe and Eastern Shoshone of the Wind River Reservation. As one federal court stated, "The tribes share the Wind River Reservation. Each tribe governs itself by vote of its tribal membership at general council meetings or by vote of its elected business council.... No member of one tribe may hold office or legislate for the other tribe. The tribes have not entered into a joint constitution to consolidate their respective governments." As a result, "the tribes' joint occupation of the Wind River Reservation without a confederation agreement makes their situation unique in the nation."[46] Loretta Fowler has written extensively about these two nations[47] and she describes in great detail how in 1878 the Arapahoe urged federal officials to let them move on to the Shoshone reservation rather than be forced to relocate to Indian Territory

182   INDIGENOUS GOVERNANCE

Table 6.4. Multi-national Native communities

1. Alabama-Coushatta of Texas

2. Allegany Indian Reservation (Cayuga and Seneca)

3. Arapahoe/Shoshone (Wind River Reservation)[a]

4. Arctic Village and Native Village of Venetie

5. Assiniboine and Sioux of Fort Peck Reservation

6. Bear River Band of the Rohnerville Rancheria (Mattole, Bear River, Wiyot)

7. Big Lagoon Rancheria (Yurok and Tolowa)

8. Big Pine Paiute Tribe of the Owens Valley (Mono and Timbisha)

9. Big Valley Rancheria (Pomo and Pit River Indians)

10. Bishop Paiute Tribe (Mono and Timbisha)

11. Blue Lake Rancheria (Wiyot, Yurok, Hupa)

12. Bridgeport Paiute Indian Colony of California (Miwok, Mono, Paiute, Shoshone, Washoe)

13. Capitan Grande Reservation (Kumeyaay Res. Controlled by Barona Group of Capitan Grande Band of Mission Indians and Viejas Group of Capitan Grande Band of Mission Indians)

14. Celilo Village, Oregon (Most residents are either Yakama Nation, Confederated Tribes of Warm Springs, Confederated Tribes of the Umatilla Indian Reservation, Nez Perce.)

15. Central Council of the Tlingit and Haida Indian Tribes

16. Cher-Ae Heights Indian Community of the Trinidad Rancheria (Chetco, Hupa, Karuk, Tolowa, Wiyot, Yurok)

17. Cheyenne and Arapahoe Tribes of Oklahoma[b]

18. Chippewa-Cree Indians of the Rocky Boys Reservation (Montana)

19. Colorado River Indian Tribes (Chemehuevi, Mohave, Hopi, Navajo)

20. Confederated Salish and Kootenai Tribes of the Flathead Reservation

21. Confederated Tribes of Coos, Lower Umpqua, and Siuslaw Indians (Hanis Coos, Miluk Coos, Lower Umpqua, Siuslaw)

22. Confederated Tribes of Siletz Indians of Oregon

23. Confederated Tribes of the Chehalis Reservation (Upper/Lower Chehalis, Klallam, Muckleshoot, Nisqually, Quinault)

24. Confederated Tribes of the Colville Reservation

25. Confederated Tribes of the Grand Ronde Community of Oregon

26. Confederated Tribes of the Umatilla Indian Reservation (Walla Walla, Cayuse, and Umatilla)

Table 6.4. Continued

27. Confederated Tribes of the Warm Springs Reservation

28. Confederated Tribes and Bands of the Yakama Indian Nation (Klikitat, Palus, Walla Walla, Wanapam, Wenatchi, Wishram, Yakama)

29. Elk Valley Rancheria (Tolowa and Yurok)

30. Federated Indians of Graton Rancheria (Coast Miwok and Southern Pomo of California)

31. Flathead Indian Reservation (Bitterroot Salish, Kootenai, Pend d'Oreilles)

32. Fort Belknap (Gros Ventre, Assiniboine)[c]

33. Fort Berthold Indian Reservation (Mandan, Hidatsa, Arikara=Three Affiliated Tribes)

34. Fort Independence Indian Community of Paiute Indians (Paiute, Shoshone)

35. Grand Traverse Band of Ottawa and Chippewa

36. Grindstone Indian Rancheria of Wintun-Wailaki Indians (Wintun, Wailaki)

37. Inupiat Community of the Arctic Slope (a regional tribal council of eight villages)

38. Klamath Tribes (Klamath, Modoc, Yahooskin)

39. Lone Pine Paiute-Shoshone Tribe of California

40. Los Coyotes Band of Cahuilla and Cupeno of California

41. Middletown Rancheria of Pomo Indians of California (Pomo, Wappo, Lake Miwok)

42. Minnesota Chippewa Tribe (Six Chippewa Bands: Ojibwe or Anishinaabe)[d]

43. Mooretown Rancheria of Maidu Indians (Concow and Maidu)

44. Morongo Band of Mission Indians (Cahuilla, Serano, Cupeno, Luiseno, Chemehuevi)

45. Muckleshoot (Duwamish, Snoqualmie, Upper Puyallup, White River Valley tribes, Tkwakwamish, Yilalkoamish, Dothliuk)

46. Otoe-Missouria of Oklahoma

47. Paiute and Shoshone of Fort McDermitt

48. Paiute-Shoshone Tribe of the Fallon Reservation

49. Pyramid Lake Indian Reservation (Two Northern Paiute bands: Kuyuidokado and Tasiget tuviwarai)

50. Quartz Valley Indian Community (Klamath, Karuk, Shasta)

51. Quinault Indian Nation (Quinault, Quileute, Hoh, Chehalis, Chinook, Cowlitz)

(continued)

184 INDIGENOUS GOVERNANCE

Table 6.4. Continued

52.	Redding Rancheria (Wintu, Achomawai/Pit River, Yana)
53.	Reno-Sparks Indian Colony (Paiute, Shoshone, Washoe)
54.	Round Valley Indian Tribes (Yuki, Wailaki, Concow, Little Lake Pomo, Nomlaki, and Pit River) (Confederated under the IRA as the Covelo Indian Community.)
55.	Sac and Fox Nation of Missouri
56.	Sac and Fox Nation of Oklahoma
57.	Sac and Fox Tribe of the Mississippi in Iowa (also known as Meskwaki)
58.	Salt River Pima-Maricopa Indian Community (Pima [Akimel O'odham] and Maricopa [Piipaash]
59.	Seneca-Cayuga Nation of Oklahoma
60.	Shingle Springs Band of Miwok Indians (Maidu and Miwok)
61.	Shoshone-Bannock Tribes of the Fort Hall Reservation
62.	Shoshone-Paiute Tribes of the Duck Valley Reservation in Nevada
63.	Sisseton-Wahpeton Oyate of Lake Traverse Reservation
64.	Skokomish Indian Tribe (Skokomish, Twana, Klallam, Chimakum)
65.	Standing Rock Reservation (Hunkpapa and Sihasapa of Lakota Oyate, Ihunktuwona and Pabaska of Dakota Oyate, Hunkpatina Dakota)
66.	Susanville Indian Rancheria (Washoe, Achomawi, Mountain Maidu, Northern Paiute, Atsugewi)
67.	Swinomish Indians of the Swinomish Reservation of Washington (Swinomish, Lower Skagit, Upper Skagit, Samish)
68.	Table Mountain Rancheria (Chukchansi Band of Yokuts and Monache)
69.	Tulalip (Duwamish, Snohomish, Snoqualmie, Skagit, Suiattle, Samish, Stillaguamish)
70.	Tule River Indian Tribe of the Tule River Reservation (Yokuts, Yowlumne, Wukchumnis, Western Mono, Tubatulabal)
71.	Tunica-Biloxi Indian Tribe (Tunica, Biloxi, Choctaw)
72.	Tuolumne Band of Me-Wuk Indians (Yokut, Miwok)
73.	Ute Indian Tribe of the Uintah and Ouray Reservation, Utah[e]
74.	Wichita and Affiliated Tribes (Wichita, Keechi, Waco, Tawakonie)
75.	Winnemucca Indian Colony of Nevada (Western Shoshone, Northern Paiute)
76.	Yavapai-Apache (Arizona)

[a] Two Tribes operate separate governments but share a joint business council.

[b] Legislature is divided into four Cheyenne and four Arapahoe districts.

GOVERNING SYSTEMS 185

Table 6.4. Continued

---

[c] Tribal Council divided between Gros Ventre and Assiniboine—two for each voting district.

[d] Six bands share a confederated constitution, but each has its own Business Council.

[e] The Business Committee is comprised of two representatives from each of the three bands—Uintah, Uncompaghre, and White River.

"Joint-use" Areas: These are areas designated by the U.S. Census Department as "land administered jointly and/or claimed by two or more American Indian tribes that have a delineated OTSA (Oklahoma Tribal Statistical Areas). The designation also applies to Tribal communities outside Oklahoma.

1. Miami/Peoria

2. Creek/Seminole, https://censusreporter.org/profiles/25200US5915R-creekseminole-joint-use-otsa/

3. Kiowa/Comanche/Apache/Ft. Sill Apache/Caddo/Wichita/Delaware

4. Kaw/Ponca, https://censusreporter.org/profiles/25200US5950R-kawponca-joint-use-otsa/

5. Sac and Fox/Meskwaki

6. San Felipe Pueblo/Santa Ana Pueblo, https://censusreporter.org/profiles/25200US4930R-san-fel ipe-pueblosanta-ana-pueblo-joint-use-area/

Source: Special thanks to Nora Hickes, staff librarian at the Native American Rights Fund, who helped identify many of these communities.

---

or to Lakota lands. Black Coal, an Arapahoe leader, noted that his people had made peace with the Shoshone and that they would be "good Indians" if allowed to settle on the Shoshone Reservation.[48]

The United States reneged on Black Coal's earlier treaty commitment to the Shoshone when it placed the Arapahoe on the reservation without the consent of the Shoshone people.[49] This melding of the two peoples occurred in 1878. Since that time, the two nations have been considered equitable owners and sovereigns, in common, of the reservation. And, while they jointly contract with the BIA to provide certain services to both tribes' members, each nation is politically autonomous.[50] They have, however, created a joint body known as the Wind River Inter-Tribal Council which oversees shared government functions and matters that impact the entire reservation. For instance, when COVID-19 struck, the Council passed a resolution ordering members of both nations to remain at home, except when seeking medical help or securing needed foodstuffs.

The Fort Peck Reservation in Montana, established in 1888 by congressional act, is home to two nations—Assiniboine and Sioux. Both nations are composed of distinctive bands. The Sioux bands include the Sisseton, Wahpeton, Yanktonais, and Teton Hunkpapa. The Assiniboine bands are Canoe Paddlers and Red Bottom. Historically, the two nations engaged in frequent warfare with one another, and their political cultures were distinct, according to Lopach, Brown, and Clow.[51] The Assiniboine were more politically conservative, while the Sioux were considered more aggressive. Some of these cultural distinctions continue today and they are retained, in part, because of geographical residence

186 INDIGENOUS GOVERNANCE

patterns. The Sioux live on the eastern part of the reservation, and the Assiniboine inhabit the western part. For a number of years, up to 1911, each nation had its own court. The courts were combined when World War I ended but they were reprised in 1926.

The members of the two Tribes first adopted a constitution in 1927 that featured a General Council as the governing body. This document lasted until it was replaced in 1960 by a new constitution that established a Tribal Executive Board as the governing authority that is nevertheless "subject to the powers of the General Council." The twelve-member Board is led by a Chairman and Vice Chairman. There is no clear separation of power between the Executive Board and the chairman. While sharing a common government on Reservation wide affairs, the two nations retain separate "tribal or community governments the budgets of which come from distinct treaty claims."[52]

The Cheyenne and Arapahoe Tribe of Oklahoma have a four-branch government, led by a Tribal Council (made up of all adult members of the two Tribes), which has the power to set policy for the respective Tribes, along with legislative, executive, and judicial branches. Interestingly, for purposes of legislative districting, Cheyenne-Arapahoe lands are divided into Cheyenne and Arapahoe districts. Each nation is allotted four districts so that each community has four lawmakers serving in the legislature. These members then jointly elect a Speaker from their membership.

In Minnesota, six of the seven Anishinaabe bands, excluding the Red Lake Band,[53] are member reservations operating under an IRA-consolidated constitution, that were established in 1936 and known collectively as the Minnesota Chippewa Tribe (MCT). Each of the six bands—the Bois Forte (Nett Lake), Fond du Lac, Grand Portage, Leech Lake, Mille Lacs, and White Earth—has its own elected Business Committee and each community has representation on the consolidated Minnesota Chippewa Tribal executive committee. But in 2007, Chairwoman Erma Vizenor of White Earth declared that one of her goals was constitutional reform and political separation from the consolidated Chippewa Tribe. Issues such as the lack of separation of powers and reconfiguring citizenship away from blood quantum were of intense concern to Vizenor and many White Earth citizens.[54] Shortly thereafter, a constitutional convention was assembled, and between 2007 in 2009 four conventions were held, culminating in the writing of a new constitution for the White Earth Reservation. The constitution was largely drafted by the noted Anishinaabe author, Gerald Vizenor,[55] with ample support from Jill Doerfler, a White Earth citizen.

As Vizenor put it, "The White Earth Reservation is the largest in the Federation and there are specific treaty, charter, and constitutional issues that should be determined by the legislative and judicial powers of the individual reservations, not exclusively decided by the Tribal Executive Committee." A Tribal-wide referendum was held in 2013 and an overwhelming majority—over 80%—of White Earth citizens voted to adopt the constitution. Despite massive support, internal resistance on the part of the Tribe's Business Council has thus far prevented efforts to enable the White Earth Nation to secede and chart their own political course. Doerfler suggests that part of the leadership's resistance to secession centers on concerns over how the community will determine its citizenry, especially on the topic of lineal descent.[56] As of February 2023, the White Earth Band remains politically wedded to the federated MCT.

The Fort Belknap Reservation, located within northern Montana not far from the Canadian border, is also home to two separate Native peoples—the Gros Ventre and the Assiniboine. Both nations had been devastated by smallpox in the 1860s and 1870s and their citizens were harassed by the Lakota. An agency was established in 1882, followed by a negotiated agreement in 1887 that established the reservation.[57] Fort Belknap is well known, in part, because it was the focal point of federal litigation that culminated in the noted 1908 water law case, *Winters v. United States*,[58] which set forth the doctrine that when Indian reservations were established the Native residents were entitled to a sufficient amount of water to make their lands productive.

Fort Belknap members enjoyed separate governmental status as the IRA loomed, but federal pressure compelled the two Tribes to vote collectively on the Act. It was adopted in October 1934 by a vote of 371 to 50. A constitution was then crafted and approved in 1935. It was built upon previously used Business Committees that had representation from both Tribes. The Tribes' current constitution includes a Community Council, which is the governing body of the reservation. The council is composed of eight members—four Gros Ventre and four Assiniboine. These members serve two-year terms, and they are elected from two Gros Ventre and two Assiniboine districts. Part of the reason for this four-four ethnic split dates back to 1931 when the Gros Ventre were awaiting a land claims settlement and they "wanted to preclude the Assiniboine from using the Community Council to share in the settlement."[59] According to Lopach, et al., "Intermarriage has substantially eliminated tribal affiliation as an issue, but the custom of [ethnic] quota representation persists."[60]

Consensus or Robert's Rules?

As described in Chapter 2, historically, most Native nations relied on consensus as their decision-making process, with consensus being understood as a "group process in which the common will is determined through patient listening to all points of view."[61] This is no longer the case. According to the governing database of materials I have compiled, only two Indigenous communities—Healy

188 INDIGENOUS GOVERNANCE

Lake Village and Northway Village—both Alaskan Native groups, attempt to utilize consensus in their political deliberations. Both community's constitutions use the same language, declaring that "during meetings, the council shall make decisions by consensus when possible and by majority vote when consensus is not possible."

Many Native nations today employ the parliamentary procedures outlined in *Robert's Rules of Order* as their means of organizing meetings and conducting elections. This is understandable on a certain level. Native governments have grown increasingly sophisticated, bureaucratic, complex, and certainly much larger over time and Robert's Rules provide an efficient set of parliamentary procedures that enable diverse and sometimes contesting actors to navigate sometimes perilous interpersonal politics. But as Deloria and Lytle noted, as Native nations have become more legislative in their orientation and bureaucratic in the way they govern and do business, "the structures, the functions, the technologies, politics, and even the goals of the white community are in many ways displacing the traditional ways of the Indians."[62]

7
The Enigmatic Nature of Leadership

The lords of the Confederacy of the Five Nations shall be mentors of the people for all time. The thickness of their skin shall be seven spans—which is to say that they shall be proof against anger, offensive actions and criticism. Their hearts shall be for peace and goodwill and their minds filled with a yearning for the welfare of the people of the Confederacy. With endless patience they shall carry out their duty and their firmness shall be tempered with a tenderness for their people. Neither anger nor fury shall find lodgment in their minds and all their words and actions shall be marked by calm deliberation.[1]

My primary claim is that we do need saving, most commonly from our own political leaders.[2]

These two remarks, written generations apart, describe a deeply concerning issue at the heart of Native governance—that a wide chasm exists between the way Native leaders *historically* governed compared to the way many of them *presently* govern. The first statement is attributed to Deganawida and Hayehwatha as laid out in the ancient Great Law of Peace—an aspiration that every chosen leader of the Five (later six nations, when the Tuscarora Nation joined) Nations was expected to work toward. Leaders were chosen who exhibited the traits and characteristics laid out above—traits that the Clan mothers who had installed them had witnessed in their behavior.

The second statement, by the late Cherokee Tribal judge and commentator Steve Russell, appeared in his 2010 book, *Sequoyah Rising: Problems in Postcolonial Tribal Governance*. In it, he bemoaned what he termed a "democracy deficit" in Indian Country attributable to the endemic corruption of many Indigenous leaders. Corruption, he argued, was crippling the abilities of these leaders and thus rendering their governments incapable of fulfilling obligations to their citizens in a fair and just manner.[3]

In some respects, it is not surprising that some contemporary Native leaders lack the clarity, maturity, coherency, sense of accountability, and spiritual vigor of their ancestors. Colonialism fueled by capitalism, after all, has been and continues

Indigenous Governance. David E. Wilkins, Oxford University Press. © Oxford University Press 2024.
DOI: 10.1093/oso/9780190095994.003.0008

190 INDIGENOUS GOVERNANCE

to be a dominating, exploitative, and seductive force that has turned some Native leaders away from values and principles like kinship, spirituality, generosity, and reciprocity. And, of course, the federal government has historically meddled in the leadership selection process of numerous Native communities as it sought to install or influence those Native leaders who would be more amenable to federal goals of assimilation and integration.[4] This is because colonialism is so pervasive and saturates all that it touches. For, as Turner points out colonialism "influenced virtually every aspect of indigenous people's daily lives: language, religion, sexuality, art, philosophy, and politics" and Native leaders have clearly been affected, as well.[5]

A robust study of Indigenous political leadership would be a monumental social scientific undertaking, given that there are 574 sovereign Native polities led by several thousand leaders. This project is not the vehicle for such an endeavor. Yet, this platform is sufficient to accomplish at least four things: to broadly depict how Native leadership differs from Western political and corporate notions of leadership; share data drawn from interviews with current and former Indigenous political leaders on their particular style and approach to leadership; analyze data on oath-taking practiced in Indian Country; and, finally, to evaluate recent political developments and court cases wherein Native political and judicial systems have been tasked with sorting out internal leadership struggles. These struggles pertain to a variety of critical issues—ethics violations, interest group authority, malfeasance and misfeasance, separation of powers, judicial review, popular sovereignty, and the ongoing importance of traditional customary law.

Indigenous Leadership Perspectives

As impactful as colonialism and capitalism have been on the cultures, resources, and identities of Indigenous nations, the evidence presented previously shows elements of traditional kinship principles persist to varying degrees across Indian Country. This was evinced by the governing arrangements and provisions described in the last chapter, including General Councils, indefinite tenure of office, and the role of elders that dot the Native landscape. Such issues might explain why Vine Deloria Jr., in his 1969 watershed book, *Custer Died for Your Sins*, included a chapter titled "The Problem of Indian Leadership" which contains this seemingly incongruous passage about the tenure of elected Native officials:

> Frank Ducheneaux of the Cheyenne River Sioux, Joe Garry, six-time President of the NCAI and longtime chairman of the Coeur d'Alenes of Idaho, Marvin Mull of the San Carlos Apaches, Roger Jourdain of the Red Lake Chippewas,

and James Jackson of the Quinaults have all had many years as chairman of their respective tribes. Each man has been able to keep his chairmanship because of the progressive programs he has initiated, which have in turn created more respect in a greater following for him within the tribe. Success and respect go hand-in-hand in Indian affairs. But other tribes throw out chairmen with such regularity it's almost an annual event, anticipated with pleasure by the reservation people. In those cases, the tribe has no discernible goals except to throw the rascals out. The safest political position is always as member of the out group.[6]

Later in the chapter, Deloria made an astute observation that added support to the second half of his statement above: "Because Indian people place absolute dependence on their leaders, they exhaust more leaders every year than any other minority group. The useful life of an Indian leader today is about two and a half years. After that his ideas have been digested and the tribes are ready to move on."[7]

Deloria is generally correct on this later point. In fact, the two-and-a-half-year life expectancy is not far off the actual codified two-year term of office for many elected Tribal officials. However, some nations are modifying their governing documents to extend the term of office to three or even four years. For example, in 1996, the Northern Cheyenne amended their IRA constitution to lengthen a council person's tenure from two to four years and to stagger the council members' terms to avoid a complete turnover of members for purposes of legislative continuity.[8]

Deloria also discussed what he called the "War Chief complex,"[9] a phenomenon where too many Indigenous communities and their leaders overrely on images of powerful and spiritual leaders reminiscent of great individuals from the past, like Crazy Horse, Chief Joseph, Red Cloud, and Geronimo. "Initial spectacular success," he wrote, "creates speculation as to how a leader compares with well-known tribal heroes. If a man compares favorably, more work is placed upon him because of his capability and the people, satisfied with his performance, depend on him more and more and do less for themselves."[10]

Depending on the Native nation, there appears to be a good deal of evidence that supports Deloria's "War Chief complex." Prominent Pueblo scholar, Alfonso Ortiz admitted as much in a review of *Custer*, insofar as this complex applied to Native nations of the Plains region. Ortiz pointed out, however, that Deloria's description of strong leaders was far less fitting when applied to Pueblo communities. "The more common pattern," said Ortiz, "is for leadership to be balanced—tensely to be sure—between peace and war, spiritual and mundane, intra-tribal and intertribal considerations. In this kind of arrangement, the 'peace' chief is preeminent, with the 'war' chief or his functional equivalent in

192   INDIGENOUS GOVERNANCE

charge only of dealings with the outside world, and coming into preeminence only in times of crisis. Uniformly throughout the Pueblos, for instance, there is an attempt to achieve total consensus for all decisions, consensus still based on aboriginal religious precepts. Indeed, the Hopi have not even had a war functionary in modern times, while the Pimas have historically disavowed war and violence. Today, no Southwestern tribe but the Apaches sanction aggressive leadership to my knowledge."[11]

In fact, Ortiz and Deloria are both accurate as the descriptions they offered apply to very different groups of Native peoples. As noted in Chapter 2, Native peoples in different geographical regions organized their communities in ways designed to take advantage of the distinctive landscapes and seascapes of which they were a part. What most shared was the idea that power was never defined in authoritarian terms. "Anyone was free to follow or not, depending upon his own best judgment. The people only followed a course of action if they were convinced it was best for them. This was as close as most tribes ever got to a formal government."[12]

Keith Grint, who specializes in Public Leadership, once said that "the simplest definition of leadership was 'having followers.'"[13] But as we know from our previous assessment of Indigenous culture and political traditions, kinship remains a dominant construct upon which most Native societies still operate. If that prescription is correct, we might rework Grint's short definition this way— leadership in an Indigenous context means "having relatives." And evidence of this definition can be seen throughout the Indigenous world.

For example, Waud Kracke, an anthropologist who studied the Kakwahiv people, a Native community located within Brazil, had this to say in his intimate account of how leadership was exercised by two Kakwahiv headmen. Kracke said, "Leadership is a relative thing. It is never exercised by one person. If one looks at leadership as a set of functions necessary to keep the group going, each member of the group makes some contribution, large or small."[14] Kracke's apt description of leadership as "a relative thing" works splendidly on two different levels. First, it acknowledges both the genealogical kinship that community members tend to share; second, it recognizes that kinship is both fluid and situational. No "relative" therefore, is a mere follower, for the kinship relationship acts as the backdrop against which the actual political and cultural relationships are to be experienced.

This notion of kinship extends beyond human-to-human relationships. As Carolyn Kenney, a Professor of Human Development and Indigenous Studies at Antioch University in Canada stated, "A sense of place brings coherence to Aboriginal people and suggests an aesthetic engagement with the land—an intimate spiritual commitment to relationships with all living things . . . To maintain this sense of coherence, we can accept the earth as our first embodied concept of leadership. We follow Earth. We respond to the guidance of the processes expressed in our home place."[15] Kenney continued by echoing Kracke's comment that "at its core Indigenous leadership is relational. In healthy tribal societies, individuals acted on behalf of others in the community. Their leadership was the glue that helped to keep the nation together."[16]

Finally, Linda Sue Warner, a Comanche scholar, and Keith Grint also emphasized the communitarian, relational, and situational aspects of Indigenous leadership. These leadership traditions in Indian Country, they wrote, "tend to be more related to the requirements of the community, to be much more dispersed throughout that community, and to be rooted in situations rather than individuals. Thus, one could argue that American Indian traditions of leadership are more akin to heterarchies than hierarchies: flexible and changing patterns of authority rather than rigidly embedded in a fixed and formal bureaucracy."[17]

Native Leader Case Studies

W. Ron Allen (Jamestown S'Klallam)

Ron Allen has been the chairman of his small nation—500 citizens as of 2022—-for forty-six years. He is currently the longest-tenured Tribal Chairman of all Native nations. Allen, writing in 2004, echoed Deloria's concern about the short public life of Native leaders by bemoaning the fact that too few Native nations had experienced leaders because "regrettably, tribes tend to eliminate seasoned leaders. Too often they distrust leaders who pursue a vision for their communities or who gain the experience needed to fight for their interests in the national trenches. In many tribal governments, leaders tend to move in and out of office so frequently that they fail to become seasoned."[18]

In my conversation with Chairman Allen on May 6, 2021,[19] he emphasized that his length of tenure and success as a leader could be attributed to three principles: patience, perseverance, and balance. He noted the enormous responsibilities of Tribal leaders and how they are expected to understand a multitude of subject matters in order to be effective. Figure 7.1 is a figure that Allen developed that depicts a great many of the areas of knowledge and various constituencies Native leaders must be ready and able to engage on a consistent basis—including Congress, Tribal–State relations, media, intertribal affairs, natural resources, social service programs, education, law and order, healthcare, economic development, labor policy, tourism, and treaties.

Besides inspiration derived from those core principles, he noted that his political life has been devoted to helping his nation achieve and maintain "self-governance, self-determination, and self-reliance." An important way, he said, to

194 INDIGENOUS GOVERNANCE

Figure 7.1. Tribal leadership in the twenty-first century
Source: W. Ron Allen, Jamestown SKlallam Tribal Chair/CEO

have success in these areas is to be consistent. For Allen, "consistent leadership leads to consistent vision," and a "vision dedicated and steeped in the principles of patience, perseverance, and balance and focused on self-governance, self-determination, and self-reliance of the community will lead to positive results."

Jeremiah Jay Julius (Lummi Nation)

Jay Julius,[20] who has served as a council member, secretary, and chairman of the Lummi Nation's Business Council, is today an active fisher. He emphasized that one of his goals as a political leader was to help fortify his people's efforts to retain and regain the lands and waters—like the San Juan Islands—that are central to the Lummi's cultural identity, political, legal, and cultural sovereignty, and economic vitality. As Julius put it, "We are salmon people." Much of our conversation centered on salmon, the ecosystem that supports salmon, and other important species found in the water. We also spoke of the Treaty of 1855[21] that his ancestors negotiated with the federal government. This vital document reserved to the Lummi people (and several other nations) their right to fish at all their "usual and accustomed places."

When asked about the current state of Lummi governance, Julius said, "We are still strong," emphasizing that his community was still peopled with individuals who cared deeply about the values and traditions of the nation, including their ongoing relationship with salmon and the Salish Sea. That said, he noted that, at that time (June 2021), there were no "full-time fishermen on the Council" and this posed a leadership problem in terms of what the Business Council prioritized. "All the treaty signers had been fishers and reef net owners," he observed, and they made decisions that reflected the Lummi people's love for and dependence upon salmon and other species that then teemed in the waters.

Like Ron Allen, Julius said that one of his nation's most persistent battles was with the state of Washington which frequently engages in what he called "criminal behavior," wherein the state pushes to extract tax revenue from the Lummi Nation's various business enterprises against the sovereign will of the Lummi Nation and "encroaches on the ability of the tribe to tax as a sovereign."

When I asked him about his leadership style, he summarized it this way: "Hit hard, fight hard, never give up, but do it in a jujitsu way. Hit them with the truth. Don't sugarcoat it." He also said that when he was in office, he "was big on establishing relationships. How do we get in the same room, have a conversation, and create empathy? Trying to come up with solutions when we don't always have to be in the courtroom." He also said that relationship-building included working closely with white farmers, citizens, counties, the state, and the federal government.

196 INDIGENOUS GOVERNANCE

Another dimension to his leadership style was that he understood he had to educate the various groups and governments his nation engaged with. This was especially the case when dealing with the ratified treaties his nation had signed with the federal government. He sought to educate non-Natives about the reality that treaties are not merely "Indian treaties" but are their treaties, too. Whites, he said, should look at "their half of the treaty that was bargained for. Their end of the treaty heavily outweighs the tribes, yet what very little the Lummis reserved we find ourselves in court trying to protect." He said he always sought to remind whites that "this is your treaty too; it's not just the Indians' treaty. And when we are fighting to protect sovereignty, the other side should be fighting just as hard."

Finally, he concluded that his leadership style was heavily focused on the environment, and by that, he meant that the Lummi, unlike "the newcomers[whites]," had a kinship relationship with the natural world that acknowledged the integrity of the land, the waters, and all the species that inhabit the earth—but especially the salmon.

Erma Vizenor (White Earth Anishinaabe)

Vizenor is a citizen of the White Earth Nation in northwestern Minnesota, the largest of the seven Anishinaabe (Ojibwe) bands in Minnesota, with nearly 20,000 members. Born into a large family, she spent several years as a youth in California. When she returned to White Earth she completed high school, was married, and then she and her husband moved to Minneapolis during the Bureau of Indian Affairs relocation program that began in the 1950s. Finding it difficult to secure full-time employment, Vizenor and her family returned to the reservation. She and her husband then left again to attend school, both graduating from Minnesota State College.

After graduation, she returned to the reservation and became active in Tribal politics. She had witnessed how federally funded housing that had been built on the reservation under the auspices of the federal government's Housing and Urban Development program had caused serious problems in the community. The income-based rules and regulations associated with applying for the homes and housing construction patterns disrupted existing residential arrangements by breaking up communities.

This and other developments she witnessed and experienced—both political and socioeconomic—"everyone was poor,"[22] she said, convinced her that she needed more formal education so that she would be better prepared to enter the political fray. She secured a Bush Fellowship, and this paved the way for her to pursue a PhD from Harvard University. She finished the coursework for her PhD and returned to White Earth to write her dissertation. She was immediately

THE ENIGMATIC NATURE OF LEADERSHIP   197

drafted into service by a group of elders who asked her to be their spokesperson and to scrutinize the Tribe's electoral system because they believed "the elections were rigged." Over the five years that followed, she spearheaded a movement, called "Justice," questioning the activities of Tribal officials. During that time, she was jailed on three occasions for her efforts. Ultimately, her leadership and investigatory skills culminated in criminal indictments against three Tribal Council members, an important first step toward cleansing corruption in her nation.

Vizenor was then compelled to return to Harvard to conclude her dissertation work. She came home and was elected secretary/treasurer of the Tribe's Business Committee. During her four-year stint in that role, she saw firsthand how fundamentally flawed the Tribe's financial situation was and dedicated herself to improving the government and the quality of life for the White Earth People. She lost her reelection bid in 2002, but community members urged her to run again, this time to be the chairperson of the Business Committee, the highest position in Tribal government.

She complied, and in 2004 was elected chairwoman of the White Earth Business Committee, becoming the first female chair in her nation's history. Vizenor said that at least half of the reservation's population feared that once in office she would act dictatorially by punishing and purging all those who had opposed her election. But, she said, that was never her plan. In fact, she told me she was driven by four internal value-based goals as chair that she did not share with the public. These were to (1) stabilize the White Earth Nation politically, culturally, and economically; (2) build the White Earth Nation, particularly—homes, roads, communication, and more, (3) heal the White Earth Nation because of all the recent political scandals that had ravaged the community's spirit; and (4) always be completely honest with herself and with the community's members.

She took pride in the fact that she fired no one during her first four-year stint as chair. This stability and the quality of the people she brought in, including the Finance Director and the Executive Director, enabled her to fulfill each of the four goals she had set for herself and for her nation, culminating in a resurgence of trust being displayed by the people for those now in elected office. With her dynamic personality, she was able to convince the White Earth electorate that her policies and programs, which included strengthening schools, building a new community center, new housing and other infrastructure construction, and youth program, were worthwhile and that she was doing a fine job. She was reelected in 2008 and again in 2012.

One of the most important subjects she championed during her tenure centered around her efforts to strengthen the political autonomy of the White Earth Nation by overseeing the writing and ratification of a new constitution. By necessity, adoption of the document would have triggered plans to politically secede from the Minnesota Chippewa Tribe. This consolidated constitutional

198 INDIGENOUS GOVERNANCE

government was established in 1936 under the IRA and is comprised of representatives from six of the Anishinaabe bands. They share a single constitution that guides their operations under an executive committee, with each of the six bands' chairpersons serving as a member of the executive committee. The six bands retain local governance authority and have their own Business Committees which oversee that particular band's activities.

Vizenor sought, by having the White Earth band develop its own constitution—written by the noted literary figure and fellow Tribal citizen, Gerald Vizenor—to forge their own political independence separate and apart from the Minnesota Chippewa Tribe. After a series of meetings of the constitutional convention and the drafting of the constitution, a Tribal-wide referendum was held with nearly 80% voting in support of the new constitution. Shortly after this referendum, a new election for Business Committee positions saw three new council members elected who were opposed to the new constitution and to the idea of secession. They proceeded to stymie Vizenor's efforts to establish a separate and independent White Earth Nation.

The new council members pushed to have Vizenor censured by the Minnesota Chippewa Tribe, with the goal of having her removed from office. Seeing the futility of combating these baseless charges, Vizenor chose to resign from office in 2016. While resignation was a difficult decision, she said it was "a noble one."

When I asked about her particular leadership style, she emphasized that she always "believed in people—people making the decisions." She said she had studied community decision-making in graduate school and had been heavily influenced by Mahatma Gandhi, Martin Luther King, and other prominent civil rights leaders. So, when she became chair of the Business Committee, she organized a series of Community Councils throughout the reservation and in Minneapolis and the Iron Range to give the people an opportunity to have direct input into the kinds of policies they desired. "I believe," she said, "that whenever the people have input in a decision, their decisions are almost always right." For Vizenor, it was always about trust—trust in the people to know what was in their best interests, and acting and leading in a way that convinced the people to trust her with their individual and collective sovereignty.

Accountability of Native Leaders by Oath-Taking

Here,[23] I'd like to turn to the wording of Tribal constitutions,[24] particularly the oaths of office, as these reveal much about what nations require of their elected leaders. Are oaths of office in these documents an imposed colonial practice? Were oaths of office part of an alleged boilerplate IRA constitution that was said to have been imposed upon Native nations during the IRA era? Or, can the wording of oaths of office actually reflect a strong sense of Indigenous self-determination?

In light of these research questions, three working hypotheses pertaining to oaths of office found in Native constitutions guide this section:

1. If Native communities voted to come under the provisions of the IRA, then the oaths of office for Tribal officials would tend to reflect a higher degree of deference and loyalty to the federal, though not the state, government as a sign of relief and appreciation at the opportunity to begin the process of rebuilding their nations.

2. If communities wrote constitutions well before the IRA, then various factors (e.g., the presence of Christian missionaries, the activities of students returned from boarding schools, Native elites anxious to forge stronger governments in order to be more effective in dealing with state, corporate, and federal officials) will determine to whom Native officials swear allegiance.

3. If communities adopted constitutions during the Indian Self-Determination era of the 1970s and since the 1970s, their oaths likely reflect a burgeoning sense of self-governance, autonomy, and a purposeful distance from the federal and (especially) state governments.[25]

Before proceeding with a content analysis of oaths in Native constitutions, is important to first consider the origin of oaths of office and whether the practice of an oath is borrowed from Europeans or whether it is inherent to Native nations. After examining the history of oaths of office, I will then analyze the content of the oaths in various types of Native constitutions to test the above hypotheses on IRA and non-IRA constitutions.

The Oath of Office in Historical Perspective

Oaths and oath-type induction practices for incoming public officials have appeared in many cultures throughout the world. The modern, constitutionally articulated oath of office is primarily Western in origin, derived from Anglo-Saxon ceremonies, but there was a traditional presence of oath-type induction practices in Indigenous America, as well. A 1965 study found that, worldwide, oaths tend to appear in cultures with a particular set of characteristics, including intermediate to high political integration, higher stratification, economic complexity, and territorial sovereignty.[26] In all cases where oaths had been employed, their central purpose has been to restrain the exercise of power by appealing

200 INDIGENOUS GOVERNANCE

to morality and a sense of responsibility, especially pertaining to the duties of public office.

The oath can be traced to early human history when it was utilized as a self-curse and a magical way of guaranteeing a promise.[27] H. S. Maine argues that the oath developed in societies as they moved from association based on family and clan toward the contract stage of development.[28] While an oath might originally have been construed as a self-curse, as monotheistic religions developed, God came to be seen as the executor of human oaths.[29]

The oath in ancient Greece dates from the establishment of the Athenian government in 403 BC.[30] Although it played an important role in the life and law of the ancient Greeks, the oath had more of a legal emphasis than a religious one. A Greek oath represented a binding of one's conscience before a civil authority or other people, so it became more of a social contract than had been the case in earlier historical periods, although the Greeks still felt that the oath had a divine element. The oath of investiture was a very important type of official oath in ancient Greece. It was always necessary for public office. Incoming officials promised themselves, to the divinity, and to those that governed that they would faithfully discharge their duties. All incoming public officials were required to "swear allegiance to the laws, constitution, and guards of the state" as a type of social contract.[31] The Romans institutionalized oaths during the fourth-century rule of Emperor Constantine, who erroneously believed it to be a Christian practice and duty.[32]

The modern executive oath of office has a distinctly Anglo-Saxon character. Beginning with Edward the Confessor, there is documented use in Britain of a coronation oath that pledged the king to respect the laws of the land.[33] The American Republic followed this British tradition of placing an internal constraint on the president in the sense of a moral obligation to the duties of office. The presidential oath of office is the only oath specified in the U.S. Constitution, which underscores its importance.[34]

Although the modern constitutional oath is strongly rooted in the West, oath-type induction practices are a more generalized phenomenon. They appear in various cultures throughout the world and are generally required in an effort to restrain the exercise of power by appealing to a sense of moral and social responsibility. Traditional practices in pre-contact Indigenous America were no exception. As Cohen wrote: "The induction or inauguration of tribal chiefs, headmen, or other officers was in early days a matter of great importance. Public ceremonies made the occasion auspicious, and impressed upon the minds of the people the picture of their own leaders, and impressed upon the minds of these leaders a vision of their new responsibilities. Speeches were made by the older men or women of the tribe to instruct the new leaders in their powers and duties. Insignia of office symbolized these new powers and duties."[35]

The Great Law of Peace of the Iroquois Confederacy documents a specific use of a traditional Indigenous induction ceremony that includes a lengthy oath-like statement, which reads thus:

28) When a candidate Lord is to be installed he shall furnish four strings of shells (or wampum) one span in length bound together at one end. Such will constitute the evidence of his pledge to the Confederate Lords that he will live according to the Constitution of the Great Peace and exercise justice in all affairs.

When the pledge is furnished the Speaker of the Council must hold the shell strings in his hand and address the opposite side of the Council Fire and he shall commence his address saying: 'Now behold him. He has now become a Confederate Lord. See how splendid he looks.' An address may then follow. At the end of it he shall send a bunch of shell strings to the opposite side and they shall be received as evidence of the pledge. Then shall the opposite side say 'We now do crown you with the sacred emblem of the deer's antlers, the emblem of your Lordship. You shall now become a mentor of the people of the Five Nations. The thickness of your skin shall be seven spans—which is to say that you shall be proof against anger, offensive actions and criticism. Your heart shall be filled with peace and goodwill and your mind filled with a yearning for the welfare of the people of the Confederacy. With endless patience you shall carry out your duty and your firmness shall be tempered with tenderness for your people. Neither anger nor fury shall find lodgment in your mind and all your words and actions shall be marked with calm deliberation. In all of your deliberations in the Confederate Council, in your efforts at law making, in all your official acts, self-interest shall be cast into oblivion. Cast not over your shoulder behind you the warnings of the nephews and nieces should they chide you for any error or wrong you may do, but return to the way of the Great Law which is just and right. Look and listen for the welfare of the whole people and have always in view not only the present but also the coming generations, even those whose faces are yet beneath the surface of the ground—the unborn at the future Nation.[36]

The Oath of Office in Contemporary Native Constitutions

I conducted a content analysis of my constitution database in order to identify various oaths of office required of incoming Native governmental officials. The specific research questions included the following: Is there a substantive difference in the oaths of office between IRA Native nations and non-IRA nations? Are non-IRA nations' oaths of office always more reflective of Tribal sovereignty

202 INDIGENOUS GOVERNANCE

and self-determination than those of IRA Native nations? Are newer or revised constitutions more reflective of Indigenous self-determination than pre-IRA and IRA-era constitutions? The database was queried for all entries containing "oaths of office" for incoming Native government officials.

To gauge the extent to which an oath of office reflects Indigenous sovereignty and self-determination, the content of each oath was analyzed to determine (1) the governmental entities to which incoming Native officials pledge loyalty—their nation, the state, and/or the U.S. Constitution; and (2) the order in which the governmental entities appear in the oath provision. We assumed that the ordinal appearance of governmental entities in the oath reflects both the perceived importance of the loyalties pledged and the Tribal nation's assertion of self-determination. In other words, if an incoming Native government official must pledge loyalty to the U.S. Constitution before they pledge loyalty to their home tribal government, we assumed that the Tribe's officials are acting or at least are appearing to act deferentially to the federal government. On the other hand, if the incoming Native official is required to pledge loyalty only to the Tribal constitution and there is no mention whatsoever of loyalty to the U.S. Constitution or the state constitution, it was assumed that these individuals and the Native nation were exhibiting a higher degree of self-determination.

Oath Findings

Of the 500 Native nation constitutions in the database, nearly 150 contain specific oaths of office. Of these, a majority are IRA-type constitutions.[37] Why the other nations with constitutions (both IRA and non-IRA) do not have oaths of office specified in their constitutions is an important question that will have to be explored at a later date. Typically, a Native nation that specifies an oath of office within its constitution is located in a Western state, has a small to medium-size population and reservation, and operates under an IRA constitution drafted in the 1930s to 1940s.

The following typology of Native nation oaths of office was developed from this analysis.[38] Of those constitutions that specify oaths of office for incoming Native officials, the specifics of how those oaths appear in Tribal constitutions fall into three categories.

Oath Type I: Federal Allegiance

Under this oath type the incoming Tribal official swears to support and uphold (1) the Constitution of the United States, (2) the duties of the office, and

THE ENIGMATIC NATURE OF LEADERSHIP 203

(3) the "best interests of the tribe/community/village in accordance with this Constitution." Although there are slight variations within this type, it is the most common pattern of oath (when an oath is present), and the verbiage is nearly identical in all cases.[39] Seventy of the seventy-two nations that use this type of oath are IRA Tribes, and the vast majority of Tribal nations with this oath type adopted their constitutions during the mid-1930s and into the early 1940s.

The Constitution of the Confederated Salish and Kootenai Tribes of the Flathead Reservation in Montana, an IRA constitution ratified in 1935 (updated in 2004), contained a typical oath of this type. According to this constitution, incoming elected officials must take the following oath: "I _____, do solemnly swear (or affirm) that I will support and defend the Constitution of the United States against all enemies, to carry out faithfully and impartially the duties of my office to the best of my ability; to cooperate, promote, and protect the best interests of my Tribe, in accordance with this Constitution and Bylaws." Interestingly, this is the exact same oath found in the Flathead reservation's 1930 Constitution, with one major deletion. The clause "and will cooperate with the Superintendent" has been omitted, a firm recognition of at least a measure of increasing Flathead independence from the superintendent's paternalistic oversight.

A slight variation of the Flathead document is the Constitution of the Minnesota Chippewa Tribe, an IRA constitution ratified in 1936.[40] For this consolidated group of Anishinaabe bands, the oath of office reads as follows: "I do solemnly swear (or affirm) that I shall preserve, support and protect the Constitution of the United States and the Constitution of the Minnesota Chippewa Tribe, and execute my duties as a member of the Tribal Executive Committee to the best of my ability, so help me God." This oath clause reflects a constitution that is seemingly not very strong in terms of Indigenous self-determination. There is a nod to Native self-governance, but the prominence of the U.S. Constitution coupled with the lack of emphasis on the Tribal government in the oath implies that this set of Tribal nations' self-governing abilities operate from a deferential position to that of the federal government more than as a separate and autonomous political entity, since there is no explicitly articulated call for loyalty to the Native nations' or the Tribes' own collective organic charter. The final clause, "So help me God," which is found in several pre-IRA and a number of post-IRA constitutions, is one that also warrants additional research. Certainly, many Native individuals had adopted Christianity by the 1930s, but in other cases the reference could simply be an acknowledgment of the deep traditional values that many Indigenous communities continue to adhere to that may not necessarily be associated with Judeo-Christian thought and practice.

204   INDIGENOUS GOVERNANCE

Because oaths appear in only one-fifth of all the Native constitutions I have collected, I do not assume, contrary to popular opinion and much of the IRA literature, that these clauses or these constitutions were forced on Native elites or their communities as they prepared their constitutions. In fact, scholarship by Rusco and Wilkins debunks the view that IRA constitutions were imposed on all those nations who adopted the IRA.[41] Still, the language of this oath type, with top placement given to the U.S. Constitution, is weighted with meaning and bears further examination. The lack of specific mention of swearing allegiance to the Native nation or the nation's own constitution is striking in this oath type.

Oath Type II: Native Self-Determination

In this oath type, loyalty is pledged solely to the Native nation, or, in some cases, loyalty to the nation is placed ahead of loyalty to the U.S. Constitution. This oath type appears to represent a much stronger statement on Indigenous sovereignty and self-determination. There are four appearances of oaths in which Indigenous loyalty appears ahead of loyalty to the U.S. Constitution: the Cherokee Nation of Oklahoma, the Chickasaw Nation of Oklahoma, the Shawnee Nation of Oklahoma, and the Sisseton-Wahpeton Tribe of South Dakota. Only one of these tribes—Sisseton-Wahpeton—has an IRA constitution. The Revised Constitution of the Chickasaw Nation of Oklahoma (1990) contains a representative oath of office of this variety, placing loyalty to the nation's constitution ahead of the U.S. Constitution: "I, _____, do solemnly swear (or affirm) that I will support, obey and defend the Constitutions of the Chickasaw Nation, and the United States of America and will discharge the duties of my office with fidelity, so help me God."

The oath in the 2006 Sisseton-Wahpeton Constitution, the only IRA constitution in this group of oaths that pledges loyalty to the Tribal nation ahead of loyalty to the U.S. Constitution, differs in the more elaborate language used, but the content remains substantially similar: "I, _____, do solemnly swear (or affirm) that I will support the Revised Constitution and Bylaws of the Sisseton-Wahpeton Sioux Tribe and the Constitution of the United States, and will faithfully and impartially perform the duties of my office to the best of my ability and will work to promote and protect the best interest of the Indians of the Sisseton-Wahpeton Sioux Tribe, and will assist them in every way within my power toward better citizenship and progress."

There are an additional ten oaths in which loyalty is pledged to the Native nation alone, with no reference whatsoever to the U.S. Constitution: the Comanche Nation of Oklahoma, the Osage Nation of Oklahoma, the Hoopa Valley Tribe of California, the Menominee Tribe of Wisconsin, the Passamaquoddy Tribe of

THE ENIGMATIC NATURE OF LEADERSHIP 205

Maine, the Sac and Fox Tribe of the Mississippi in Iowa, the Shoalwater Bay Tribe of Washington, the Skokomish Tribe of Washington, the Smith River Rancheria of California, and the Central Council of the Tlingit and Haida in Alaska. Only two of these are IRA tribes—the Sac and Fox and the Skokomish Tribes. Only two constitutions with this oath type were adopted prior to 1970: the Comanche Nation and the Sac and Fox Tribe.

The constitution of the Shoalwater Bay Indian Tribe, a non-IRA 1982 constitution that replaced its 1971 document, does not specify the precise oath to be administered to incoming officials, but does state that "every person elected to the Tribal Council shall . . . assume office when he or she takes an oath or swears to uphold the Constitution and laws of the Shoalwater Bay Indian Tribe."

The 1990 Constitution of the Sipayik Members of the Passamaquoddy Tribe of Maine, a nation that gained federal recognition in 1972, also includes "a provision requiring each elected tribal official to swear an oath of office to uphold the Constitution and laws of the Passamaquoddy Tribe" but also adds "and to honor orders of the Tribal Court." This final phrase about honoring the orders of the nation's court is unique among all the Native nations' oaths of office and suggests that this Tribe is intent on building support for and maintaining the integrity and jurisdictional authority of the nation's judicial system. This is critical, since the maintenance of law and order and the administration of justice play a pivotal role in shaping and expressing a nation's values and identity.

And the 2006 Osage Constitution contained strong language affirming both Osage sovereignty and spirituality. It bears repeating: "I, _____ (name) _____ _____ do proudly swear (or affirm) to carry out the responsibilities of the office of _____ (name of office) to the best of my ability, freely acknowledging that the powers of this office flow from the Osage People and Wak-Kon-Tah. I further swear (or affirm) always to place the interest of all Osages above any special or personal interests, and to respect the right of future generations to share the rich historic and natural heritage of our Osage People. In doing so, I will always uphold and defend the Constitution of the Osage Nation, so help me God."[42]

Oath Type III: Federal/State Deference

Under the third oath type, the Native official pledging allegiance swears fealty to the U.S. Constitution first but also pledges loyalty to the state constitution. The Tribal nation is mentioned third. The 1960 Constitution of the Assiniboine and Sioux Tribes of the Fort Peck reservation in Montana (updated in 2013) contains an oath representative of this type: "I do solemnly swear that I shall faithfully execute the duties of my office, defend the Constitution of the United States of

206 INDIGENOUS GOVERNANCE

America, the State of Montana, and the Assiniboine and Sioux tribes of the Fort Peck Indian Reservation, so help me God."

The oath in the 1936 Constitution of the Makah Indian Tribe of Washington follows the same deferential pattern: "I, _____, do solemnly swear (or affirm) that I will support and uphold the constitution of the United States, the constitution and laws of the state of Washington and the constitution, bylaws and ordinances of the Makah Indian Tribe of the Makah Indian Reservation in the State of Washington."

This highly deferential oath type was a somewhat surprising finding since Indigenous nations have generally conflicted with state governments since the early days of the American Republic and since, under the U.S. Constitution's Commerce Clause, Indian affairs became federalized. The Commerce Clause, the Treaty Clause, and the Supremacy Clause in the U.S. Constitution all attest to the nation-to-nation relationship that was forged at the time the federal Constitution was adopted. This oath type, however, appears only five times in the data set (the Assiniboine and Sioux Tribes of the Fort Peck reservation in Montana, the Choctaw Nation of Oklahoma, the Makah Tribe of Washington, the Ute Tribe of the Uintah and Ouray Reservation in Utah, and the Yankton Sioux Tribe in South Dakota) and four are IRA nations.[43] Additionally, four out of five of these nations drafted their constitutions prior to 1970, although the Choctaw Nation of Oklahoma adopted its constitution in 1983 at the height of the Indian Self-Determination era. Interestingly, while the Choctaw swear loyalty to both the federal and state constitutions, there is also specific language that includes a reference to preserving the culture and heritage of the nation.

Analysis

Content analysis of these oaths of office shows general support for all three of our hypotheses. There does appear to be a substantive difference between the oath of office in IRA constitutions and those that are not IRA. There is also a marked difference between constitutions drafted between 1935 and 1970 and those drafted after 1970. In general, but not surprisingly, the oaths of office of earlier IRA constitutions are more deferential to federal and/or state authority, while non-IRA constitutions, especially those drafted after 1970, tend to contain much stronger statements of Indigenous sovereignty and self-determination. The implications of these oath patterns in terms of citizenship identities and primary and secondary affiliation are important, especially when these loyalties come into conflict.

This necessarily brief examination of several pre-IRA constitutions provides tentative support for a second hypothesis. The constitutions of Native nations known to have been written prior to the passage of the IRA, with the exception of the important Iroquois Confederacy document, the Great Law of Peace, and the constitutions of the Cherokee, Choctaw, Chickasaw, and Creek, have not all been collected or thoroughly researched.[44] But the evidence accumulated thus far for a number of these organic charters shows that various external and internal forces—Christian missionaries, Indian agents, non-Indian lawyers, Native students returned from boarding schools, and mixed-blood individuals—affected Native autonomy and played a critical role in the shape and tone of a number of these pre-IRA constitutions.

Sorting out the complicated interracial, intercultural, and intergovernmental relationship between Native nations, the United States, and the states is far more complex than many would care to admit. The coexistence of the antithetical doctrines of Native sovereignty (the inherent right to self-governance) and federal plenary power (the U.S.-alleged claim of virtually absolute power over all matters Indigenous) produces a situation of utmost uncertainty for Indigenous nations. Both the coercive and voluntary assimilation that has reciprocally taken place over the last several centuries only complicates matters further. And the treaty relationship and trust doctrine, which further links Native nations to the federal government if not the states, adds yet another layer of ambiguity to the government-to-government relationship.[45] The factor number of these constitutions contain oath clauses that profoundly connect Native political officials to polities other than their own organic nation should, therefore, not be a surprise.

The complexities and multiple allegiances exposed in analyzing these important clauses open a number of questions for further inquiry, particularly for qualitative research. Because oaths of office may place moral weight on public officials, it is conceivable that oaths of office could have a restraining effect on Tribally elected officials who may, in exercising self-determination, feel that they are violating their loyalty oath by engaging in disputes with the federal or even the state government. Future research should explore whether this has been the case and what impact the often competing and multiple allegiances in oaths of office have had on Native officials and governance in practice.

Future research should also expand exploration of historical Native constitutions, specifically how and why Native nations chose to add these particular oath types to their constitutions. What were the discussions and debates surrounding these constitutions within specific communities? Are there Indigenous nations that replaced their IRA constitutions with new constitutions that are more reflective of Native values and allegiances? If this is the case, how, when, and why did they do so? These case studies would serve as a valuable model for Native nations that are engaged in constitutional reform or in constitutional development.

208 INDIGENOUS GOVERNANCE

Finally, a more complete analysis of Native constitutions must be conducted that should include both content analysis and qualitative research. Only through dual analysis can we gain a comprehensive view of Native nation constitutions and how they either support or detract from Indigenous self-determination.

Segmentation and Factionalism in Indian Country

Like all human collectivities, Indigenous nations are fluid and dynamic polities in a perpetual, if futile, quest for long-term stability and security. Rationality or irrationality, nobility or ignobility, innate conservatism or progressivism are three of the major factors of human nature that have historically served as effective deterrents of long-term stasis and continuity in the community life of homo sapiens. Not to mention the realities imposed by limited and finite natural resources, and the uncertainties of shifting demographics. There are simply too many unknown dimensions and unknowable factors that mitigate against Indigenous or non-Indigenous communities' locating that perfect place of balance and harmony in their ever-changing interpersonal and interspecies relations.

Thus, for Indigenous peoples, no utopia existed before European invasion and settlement. Certainly, none has existed since the invasion of North America and the subsequent developments—depopulation from diseases, internecine wars, tainted leadership, genocidal and ethnocidal policies targeting Indigenous life and culture, and the ongoing problems of Tribal economic dependency and federal political dominance. Together, these developments have shattered the possibility of Native peoples to evolve comfortably on their own imperfect terms.

In fact, even for communities as verifiably "traditional" as the nineteen Pueblos, internal segmentation or factionalism has been an issue since well before the Spaniards' arrival in the late 1500s, according to anthropologist and Santa Clara Pueblo member Edward Dozier.[46] He described the following:

> Although disputes have sometimes been sparked by influences from the outside, Pueblo factionalism cannot be considered a result of acculturative factors alone. The highly conservative nature of Pueblo communities indicates that the authoritarian, totalitarian characteristics of these societies are deeply rooted. It is opposition to the compulsory dictates of the Pueblo authorities which has brought about dissatisfaction and discord in the past as well as present. Forced participation in all communal activities and the prohibition of all deviant behavior, though designed to discourage the rise of dissident groups, have often had the opposite effect and have resulted in frequent factional disputes.[47]

Marilyn Norcini has more recently written about Pueblo factionalism and describes it as "a persistent and dynamic process in the social and political relation within Pueblo society."[48] And her work corroborates Dozier's by emphasizing that sorting out the roots of factionalism is not easy. It is, in fact, "A complex mix of issues inextricably connected with a religious ideology, land and property rights, governance, membership, individual civil rights in the communal society, youth education, language preservation, kinship alliances, resource management, and a common bond to a particular Pueblo community."[49]

Interestingly, while eighteen of the nineteen Pueblos voted to adopt the 1934 IRA (Jemez rejected it), only three Pueblos—Santa Clara, Laguna, and Isleta—adopted constitutions—in part as a way of addressing persistent factionalism. Ironically, Kelly points out that the other sixteen Pueblos "refused constitutions because they believed the inflexibility of written documents would eventually weaken tribal cohesion and lead to factionalism."[50]

Factionalism was also a major force animating early American policymakers, like the authors of *The Federalist Papers*—Alexander Hamilton, James Madison, and John Jay. In fact, the very idea of a Republican form of government was necessary, said Hamilton, "as a barrier against domestic factions and insurrections."[51] Madison believed that the causes of factions were inherent in human nature, but he emphasized that in the American context, "the most common and durable source of factions has been the various and unequal distribution of property. Those who hold and those who are without property have ever formed distinct interests in society."[52] But as we have seen in the case of the Pueblos, while factions were and are active in those societies, property was rarely a dominant cause of factionalism. Furthermore, the practice of kinship, which formed the moral and ethical universe for those and other Native societies, provided a social structure that helped to mitigate disputes whenever they arose.

Thus, factionalism was not uncommon among other Native peoples and, according to Fenton, the very existence of dual divisions and moieties, which typically have ceremonial functions and serve to alleviate tension between segments of Native communities, "suggest[s] that the system of reciprocating sides may have had its origin in an effort to control factionalism."[53]

The previous discussion begs the question of the difference between factions and political parties. According to Shafritz, a political party is "an organization that seeks to achieve political power by electing members to public office so that their political philosophies can be reflected in public policies."[54] Meanwhile, Fenton describes factions as "partisan groups which are as yet unorganized and do not have their claims validated by constitutional appeal to a free democratic election."[55]

Importantly, the existence of factions, notwithstanding their seminal role in forging the U.S. Constitution and some Tribal organic charters, almost always

210 INDIGENOUS GOVERNANCE

implies dissidence and carries a pejorative connotation, while the term "polit-ical party" generally has a more favorable image and is a characteristic of a democratic state. Of course, authoritarian states also have political parties. Nancy Lurie, an anthropologist, identified an interesting absence in the development of Native constitutional governments under the IRA. "When Indian groups accepted elective, constitutional government under IRA, they were introduced only to the formal or ideal side of the arrangement but given no explicit instruction about the very real side which makes it work: political parties."[56] While acknowledging that political parties in the U.S. context emerged naturally and over a lengthy period of time—and were not given official recognition via federal legislation until the twentieth century—she pondered, "It is an open question whether political parties can or should develop in the Indian interest." "Perhaps," she suggested, "outsiders should have viewed the now entrenched divisions of 'friendlies and hostiles,' 'progressives and traditionalists,' 'mixed-bloods and full-bloods,' in positive terms as nascent political parties rather than negatively as 'factions.' Semantic usages have been known to reify actualities."[57]

Whether or not political parties are ever established in Indian Country is impossible to predict, but we can safely assume that political factionalism will almost certainly persist to the detriment of Tribal community cohesion.

Indigenous Leadership Crises: Case Studies

Rifts, factionalism, and segmentation have long been an issue in Native societies, but evidence suggests that since the 1970s, the level of intra-Tribal conflict, especially regarding the topic of leadership, has increased dramatically. Robert Porter, a Seneca lawyer, has written extensively about what he considers the key factors fueling the modern surge of governmental and leadership crises within Native nations. These include the increased wealth now prevalent in many Native communities attributed largely to casino gambling, federal funding cutbacks of Native programs, Native reliance upon Western-inspired legal and political systems, increased competition for political power, the return of many expatriate Tribal members who are oftentimes ignorant of local Tribal customs and traditions, continuing loss of Native languages and cultural systems, development of an individual–rights mentality which sometimes directly contradicts a community orientation, and what Porter calls the "reemergence of democracy" which he describes as "many people are now becoming involved in tribal government who have no idea how to govern."[58]

Raymond I. Orr, a member of the Citizen Potawatomie and a professor of Native Studies, recently offered a more nuanced political study that closely examines why some Native nations experience more or less internal conflict than others. Orr utilized comparative political tools and socio-psychological theory on intergenerational trauma to tease out how three Native communities—Isleta Pueblo, Rosebud Sioux, and Citizen Potawatomi—responded to historical trauma associated with colonization.[59] Orr began with two major assumptions about human behavior:

> . . . [T]hat the creation of wealth and experience of economic markets shifts individual and collective perspectives toward a self-interested worldview. Self-interest inclines individual and community motivation toward greater material accumulation at the expense of other values such as social harmony, the sense of togetherness or equality, and long-held communal norms. I call this the rise of self-interest. The second is that certain forms of traumatic experience, violent loss, and exploitation can alter the individual and collective perspective of a community toward a melancholic worldview. Melancholy inclines individual and community motivation toward perpetuating grievances, grieving, and reliving trauma to the detriment of material self-interest in community harmony. I call this process the rise of melancholia. The absence of rises in melancholia or self-interest is likely to allow for the continuation of communal affect, which emphasizes collectivism and social cohesion over self-interest and melancholia. When the system survives without disturbance by rises in self-interest or melancholic worldviews I call this the *persistence of communal affect*.[60] (emphasis his)

In short, Orr's thesis is that historical trauma—brought on by massacres, forced assimilation, relocation—and the imposition of capitalist economies led to the formation of dissonant worldviews that also "explains the political decisions an ideological orientation of tribes" and by extension how intra--Tribal politics is played out in a given Native community.[61] Of the three nations studied, the Citizen Potawatomi appear to suffer a deeper level of entrenched factionalism, notwithstanding that they appear to have "semi-formal political parties" that are active. The nation is divided into two hard factions. John Barrett, the Chairman (at the time of the book's publication), leads one group. He has emphasized economic development, social services, and efficiency during his tenure in office. The other faction, known as the Sacred Heart Citizen Potawatomi, rejects Barrett's economic orientation "as violating the spiritual and social nature of the tribe." Their central tenets are strengthening Potawatomi culture and religious tradition, drawing upon and exercising consensus-based politics, and looking to reconstruct the best of their past.[62]

The intra-Tribal tensions of Potawatomi society have three characteristics that render them formidable and perplexing: "(1) the lines of conflict are pronounced; (2) the division between ideologies is broad . . . and (3) the animosity

212 INDIGENOUS GOVERNANCE

is strong."[63] Such characteristics sometimes culminate in legal battles, with different Native leaders seeking to legitimize their positions of power in an effort to lay claim and wield power.

Let us now examine several Native court cases from different nations to see how Tribal judges have handled intra-Tribal leadership friction. There are, of course, numerous court cases where Native politicians or Tribal members have filed lawsuits in federal district and appellate courts seeking external judicial remedies to a variety of leadership issues that sometimes involve federal agencies, most notably the BIA. These cases will not be featured,[64] in part to highlight Indigenous legal systems and processes, but also because the vast majority of lawsuits taken to federal court by Natives against their own government or the Bureau of Indian Affairs are dismissed for one of several reasons. First, Native communities are sovereign bodies that exercise the powers of self-government over their own affairs. Second, as inherent sovereign nations, Native nations, like states and the federal government, enjoy sovereign immunity—that is, they are "immune from suit by states, individuals, and businesses in federal, state and tribal courts unless the tribe consents to suit or Congress abrogates tribal immunity for a particular statutory purpose."[65] Tribal governments are, however, subject to lawsuits by the federal government.

Third, comity (the principle that courts of one state or jurisdiction will give effect to laws and judicial decisions of another state or jurisdiction, not as a matter of obligation but out of deference and mutual respect) and exhaustion of tribal remedies (an issue must first be addressed in Tribal proceedings before it can be pursued in federal court[66]) add another layer of protection.

As was stated in *Tillett v. Lujan*,[67] "as a matter of comity, a federal court should not exercise jurisdiction over cases arising under its federal question or diversity if those cases are also subject to tribal jurisdiction, until the parties have exhausted their tribal remedies."

Coalition for Fair Government II v. Lowe

The Ho-Chunk Nation's General Council (formerly known as the Wisconsin Winnebago Nation) in 2018 became the first Native nation to formally enshrine the rights of nature in their constitution. The amendment declared that "ecosystems, natural communities, and species within the Ho-Chunk territory possess inherent, fundamental, and inalienable rights to naturally exist, flourish, regenerate, and evolve."[68] This progressive amendment was overwhelmingly approved, by nearly 90% of the electorate and it set a powerful example for other Native nations to consider.

THE ENIGMATIC NATURE OF LEADERSHIP 213

Twenty years earlier, in 1996–1997, the Ho-Chunk Nation was in the throes of a constitutional and leadership crisis that threatened the very essence of their recently approved constitution—a new document that had been approved by the Secretary of the Interior in 1994.[69] As Judge Mark Butterfield put it, "This is a case of paramount importance to the separation of powers within the Ho-Chunk government and the checks and balances built into the Ho-Chunk Constitution. On the one hand are a group of concerned Ho-Chunk citizens and the Ho-Chunk Nation Legislature and on the other are the representatives of the Ho-Chunk Nation General Council of April 27, 1996, one of whom is also the President of the Ho-Chunk Nation and the head of the Executive branch of government. Each in turn is requesting relief, or a declaration of rights from the Ho-Chunk Nation Judiciary."

The most important issue to be resolved by the court was whether the General Council Planning Committee (GCPC)—a committee of Tribal members who assist with the operation of the General Council[70] by choosing the site, arranging the meals, preparing ceremonial openings, and preparing the General Council agenda—had constitutional authority to attempt the removal of three legislators for alleged malfeasance. Judge Butterfield, after reviewing all the data, determined that the GCPC did not have legal authority from the General Council to remove the lawmakers; that the lawmakers had not received proper notice or due process; and that the General Council's meetings where the removals were discussed had not met quorum requirements.[71]

Butterfield bluntly said that the actions of the GCPC were a "naked unilateral usurpation of power possessed by the Ho-Chunk eligible voters as a whole and is without support in the Ho-Chunk Nation's Constitution."[72] Thus, their efforts to remove the three lawmakers were declared unconstitutional and were permanently enjoined.

Young v. Tribal Grievance Committee

In this case,[73] before the Sac and Fox Supreme Court, Dora S. Young, the Principal Chief of the Sac and Fox Nation of Oklahoma, and Mary McCormick, the Secretary of the Nation, faced removal from office by the governing body of the nation, which happens to be called the Governing Council, consisting of all adult members of the community. The nation, formed from a merger of two separate peoples in the eighteenth century, has operated under various iterations of a constitution since 1885. The most recent constitution was adopted in 1990. While the Governing Council is the supreme governing body, there is also a Business Committee, a Grievance Committee, and a Supreme Court (and several lesser courts).

214 INDIGENOUS GOVERNANCE

In October 1996 a petition was submitted to the Business Committee containing a long list of grievances against Chief Young, Secretary McCormick, and several other officials. One of the grievances was misfeasance ("the improper doing of an act which a person might lawfully do" in contrast to malfeasance which is "the doing of an act which a person ought not to do at all").[74] The petition requested a Governing Council meeting to address the charges. One of the signers of the petition was Oma Patrick, then a private Sac and Fox citizen, but who would later be appointed to the Grievance Committee and become a party to the current litigation. The Business Committee would later validate the petition and set a date for a special Governing Council meeting. At this meeting, Patrick was also pointed to the Grievance Committee.

The three-member Grievance Committee is an elected body and is charged with hearing complaints of misconduct in office by members of the Business Committee. If evidence is produced showing that misconduct has occurred, the committee may call a Governing Council meeting to address the complaints. As the court noted, there are no parallel institutions to the Grievance Committee in the federal government, state government, or in common or civil law. "The best analogy," said the Court, "is that the Governing Council acts similarly to the U.S. House of Representatives in determining and passing a bill of impeachment, and the Governing Council acts similarly to the U.S. Senate in sitting as an impeachment court."[75] The Grievance Committee is, in fact, a separate branch of government and "serves a function which is primarily quasi-judicial in manner."[76]

When the Governing Council held its hearing, Oma Patrick participated, and the Chief and Secretary were given the opportunity to make their case. The Committee found that probable cause existed for the removal of the two officials and then called for a Governing Council. When the Governing Council convened, a vote was held to remove the Chief and Secretary from their respective offices. After the parties were urged to address issues by the Tribe's District Court, the nation's Supreme Court assumed jurisdiction and assigned the case to a Special Master. Following that report issued in December 1997, the Supreme Court stepped in, heard oral arguments, and rendered its decision on August 20, 1998. The High Court determined that the Sac and Fox Bill of Rights and the 1968 Indian Civil Rights Act accorded Tribal officials equal protection and due process, in part, because "we must understand and know and agree that the chieftainship of the Sac and Fox Indian Tribe is a valuable right . . . It is the honor of being the chief of one of the finest and largest and oldest of the tribes of this country."[77]

In addition, the Supreme Court found that Oma Patrick, who was originally a complaining petitioner and later an elected member of the Governing Council, should have recused herself from the Governing Council hearing and ruling and said that, by not doing so, had put herself "in the role of complaining witness, judge, and jury."[78] Thus, the removal vote of the Governing Council was unconstitutional and void, and the chief and secretary were reinstated to their positions.

Citizen Potawatomi Nation Business Committee v. Barrett

As Raymond I. Orr described earlier in this chapter, the Citizen Potawatomi Nation is riven with factional conflict between two groups—a segment led by the long-time chairman, John Barrett Jr., and a group called the Sacred Heart Citizen Potawatomi. Orr's book was published in 2017 when Barrett's group was in control of all the organs of the nation's government. The lawsuit now being discussed[79] arose in 2000, when, although Barrett was Chairman of the nation's Business Committee, his ideology was seemingly not as pervasive as it is presently.

In August 2000, the nation's Business Committee filed an action in the Tribe's District Court asserting that the Business Committee had not authorized Barrett, as chairman, to also assume the day-to-day responsibilities of the role of Tribal Administrator. They informed the Tribe's Secretary/Treasurer to stop paying Barrett's annual salary and to take away his personal use of a Tribal vehicle. Barrett countersued and challenged the Business Committee's authority to exercise the power to strip him of his salary and his car.

The District Court sided with Chairman Barrett and held that the Business Committee's resolution denying Barrett's salary was unconstitutional because it violated the separation of powers between the legislative branch—i.e., the Business Committee—and the executive branch—i.e., the Tribe's officers, including the Chairman, Vice-Chairman, and the Secretary/Treasurer. This decision was appealed to the nation's Supreme Court which reversed the District Court's holding and remanded the case back to the District Court. The High Court took up the principal issue of whether the Business Committee had the constitutional power to "terminate the tribal administrator, or whether such action may occur only through a decision of the chairman."[80]

The Supreme Court declared that since the position of Tribal Administrator was not a constitutional office, it was within the power of the Business Committee to discharge a Tribal employee, including the Tribal Administrator, in the absence of legislation that provides for a different result. The Court also reasoned that while the constitution created separation of powers, it did not clearly delineate an explicit executive branch and legislative branch, as the District Court had stated. It held instead that governmental powers were divided and vested in several bodies—including the Citizen Potawatomi Indian Council, the Business Committee, the Courts, the Grievance Committee, the Election Board, and

216   INDIGENOUS GOVERNANCE

the three Executive officers. Finally, the justices declared it was not the court's role to decide this issue, since it was clearly a decision best left for lawmakers to hash out.[81]

Blind v. Wilson

This case[82] originates on the lands of the Cheyenne-Arapahoe, located within what is now northwest and north-central Oklahoma. The two culturally distinctive peoples participated in the Medicine Lodge Treaty of 1867 which established the Cheyenne-Arapahoe Reservation. They adopted and ratified a constitution in 1937 under the provisions of the Oklahoma Indian Welfare Act of 1936. That document was radically revised in 1975 creating a Tribal Council of all adult members and an eight-member (four Cheyenne and four Arapahoe) Business Committee. The 1975 Constitution was further amended in April 2006 to establish a three-branch government.[83]

In this case, the Tribe's Supreme Court was called upon in 2006 to address a profoundly dysfunctional governing arrangement wherein the eight-member Business Committee had, according to Justice Arrow, "Over the years preceding this decision, the membership of the Cheyenne-Arapahoe Business Committee collectively found itself unable or unwilling to convene with the constitutionally-requisite five-member quorum for constitutionally-required monthly Business Committee meetings."[84] Arrow did not elaborate as to why the Business Committee refused to hold monthly meetings but did note that there had been "litigation between various Business Committee members."[85]

Under the Tribe's constitution, the Chairman has a duty to convene and preside over regular Business Committee meetings. Should the Chairman refuse to fulfill this task, the Business Committee members may convene meetings of their own accord. If they do not, the Tribe's District Court is authorized to call and preside over a meeting in order to see that Tribal business is addressed.

Conditions had so deteriorated—no Business Committee meetings had occurred at all—that the BIA refused to recognize the status of several Business Committee members or even the claims of the Tribal Chairman and the Secretary. This lack of recognition culminated in a situation where Tribal employees and business partners went unpaid and an Indian Health Service contract faced non-renewal. These activities prompted the Tribe's District Court to appoint an Interim Chairman and an Interim Treasurer in the hope that Tribal business could at least be restarted. But these appointments were challenged as unlawful, compelling the Tribe's Supreme Court to take up this action.

In their ruling, the five-member court bluntly declared that when the citizens elect Business Committee members, they expect them to act "in the interests of *tribal* cohesion and prosperity. They do not, presumably, elect persons who they believe will put their own personal interests ahead of tribal interests or take actions that bring tribal government to a halt."[86] "The Constitution of the Cheyenne-Arapahoe Tribe," said the justices, "is not a suicide pact."[87] The Court held that the District Court had not abused its discretion in appointing individuals to the interim positions of Chairman and Treasurer, given the gravity of the governing crisis confronting the nation's citizens.

Shirley v. Morgan

The Navajo Nation, situated on the largest and most populous reservation in the United States, has been at the forefront of executing innovative political, cultural, and legal changes that have served as models for many other Indigenous peoples. It is also the largest nation operating without a formal written constitution. The Navajo, by the first decade of the twenty-first century, had constructed a sophisticated three-branch government. They did so after enduring many years of internal political conflict that compelled the people and some of the nation's leadership to reincorporate more traditional values and structures of governance into their organic laws. Over the years, such changes often proved difficult for the Navajo Nation to implement because their legislative and executive branches were less inclined than their judicial branch to accept that more culturally attuned direction.

By the spring of 2010, tensions were running high between the three branches and across the entire nation. In May of that year, the Navajo Nation's Supreme Court handed down two major decisions, *Nelson v. Shirley* and *Shirley v. Morgan*.[88] Not unlike John Marshall's *Marbury v. Madison* (1803), the decisions firmly served to remind the Diné legislators, the president, and the entire nation of the High Court's authority to interpret the nation's laws, especially the Fundamental Law of 2002 that incorporated unwritten Diné customs and traditions into the government's Tribal Code. They also reminded the Diné community that the people, not the elected government officials, were the true sovereigns.

In the *Nelson* case, the justices unanimously held that "the Navajo people had the inherent authority reserved to them to enact laws. The People's laws are superior to the statutory laws enacted by the Council, and the referendum/initiative processes are modern acknowledgments of this authority." The Court went on to note that "while the Council may limit itself in creating laws, it cannot limit the Diné when they are attempting to address the structure of their governing system."

The next decision, *Morgan*, issued the same day, was a powerful companion to *Nelson*. In *Morgan*, the Court went even further in elaborating on the inherent

218   INDIGENOUS GOVERNANCE

authority within the people as articulated in their traditional origin accounts, values, and traditions. This decision spawned from the Council's action in October 2009 to strip President Joe Shirley Jr. of power by placing him on administrative leave over allegations of ethical and criminal wrongdoing in several business transactions. Shirley filed for relief in the District Court in December, asserting that the Council's action violated his rights and was an affront to the separation of powers doctrine. He also claimed the legislature had violated his right to due process under statutory and Fundamental Law. The District Court ruled in Shirley's favor, declaring that the Council had exceeded its legislative authority.

The Speaker of the Council appealed the District Court's ruling to the Supreme Court. With relations at breaking point between the three branches of government, the justices took the opportunity to dramatically and emphatically issue a bold and precedent-setting opinion that affirmed the power of judicial review, recast the separation of powers doctrine, clarified that the People were the superior sovereign, and reminded everyone in the Navajo Nation that the Fundamental Law was superior to statutory law. The Court affirmed the District Court's ruling but relied on different rationales in their ruling. "This appeal," said the justices, "comes to us at a critical time of great disharmony between the Navajo Nation government that is evident to the Navajo people. The leadership of the branches have been in conflict over governmental reform, and unable to sit down with each other and talk things out for almost two years, with the Executive and Legislative Branches each claiming interference with their inner operations and the very structure of their respective authority."[89]

In the preliminary part of the decision, the justices pointed out that the principle of k'e, which fosters fairness, was the lens through which they would interpret procedural due process. More importantly, k'e was viewed as the dominant principle under the Fundamental Law or *Dine bibee hazáanii*, and this larger body of organic law would provide the philosophical and cultural paradigm by which any dispute involving the Navajo Nation's political leadership would be understood and addressed.

In invalidating the Council's resolution against President Shirley, the Court used powerful language that rebuffed the legislators' attempts to limit the Court's discretionary authority over cases, independence, and ability to rely on the Fundamental Law as the most essential source of authority. "The totality of the circumstances show that the Council passed CJA-08-10 with the purpose of controlling the type of law that is used in the courts due to the negative impact the use of traditional laws have had on the Council's partisan interests in recent court decisions. Such partisan use of legislative power is an impermissible legislative purpose that, furthermore, violates the doctrine of separation of powers."[90] "The Council," the justices emphatically declared, "may not encroach upon the independence of the Judicial Branch . . . Neither may the Council redefine the Fundamental Law of the Navajo Nation to include man-made law."[91]

And then in startlingly frank language, the justices chided the Speaker and the Council, who had surprisingly argued that the concepts of separation of powers and checks and balances were somehow foreign to the Diné people and, therefore, need not be respected:

> Appellants are the Speaker and Council of the Navajo Nation asserting, in the context of this lawsuit, that the Council is the absolute source of governance for the Navajo People, that there is nothing indigenous about the three-branch government, and that traditional laws of the Navajo People have no relevance in modern governance. Quite frankly, this Court is startled, *bik'ee dlyees*, by the propositions being advanced by our Navajo leaders; that the Speaker and Council, the elected leaders of the *Alaaji' Naataji Nahat'a* component of our government, believe that the government that they have been entrusted with really is not a Diné government, and that Diné values, principles, laws, tradition and culture have nothing to do with our government structure. It is, indeed, sad to hear from our own leaders such a belief and how they propose that such a government must be maintained. It shows disrespect for oneself and the People they represent. We hear this, we are reminded of the terrible history of colonialism and its terrible impact on all Indian Nations. Our leaders of the Legislative Branch apparently believe that colonialism has succeeded with the Diné. The Court strongly disagrees that there is nothing indigenous to our government. The Court is obligated to respond in a blunt manner to such an outrageous proposition.[92]

The justices then embarked on a detailed and culturally based explanation of the origins of the Diné understanding of participatory democracy. Acknowledging that it derived from neither U.S. law nor the Navajo Nation Council, the justices declared that instead "it comes from a deeper, more profound system of governance," the Navajo Peoples' traditional communal governance, rooted in the Diné Life Way . . . The ideal Navajo Nation government is not one that is governed by perfect individuals, but which is oriented toward the public interest and recognizes fully that the power to govern comes from the People, Hózhóoji doo Hashkeejii."[93]

To bolster their finding that the doctrines of separation of powers and checks and balances were embodied in Fundamental Law, the justices explained that the ways the laws, culture, and values of the Diné People have as their genesis pointed to the Emergence account of the Navajo People into the present world. In the story they related, the People have long understood the need to separate the functions of various leaders but that in order to survive there must be

220 INDIGENOUS GOVERNANCE

coordination and collaboration of the leaders. In other words, the Fundamental Law enshrined that no single person or political branch should have absolute or concentrated powers.

Finally, the justices closed by reminding the President and the Council that the People had the inherent power to choose and to modify their form of government. "Egalitarianism," they said, "is the fundamental principle of Navajo participatory democracy." This principle holds that the People "as a whole" have the right to determine the laws by which they will be governed."[94]

Eastern Band of Cherokee v. Lambert

The Eastern Band of Cherokee Indians is comprised of those Cherokee who had either avoided the horrific relocation process under the 1830 Indian Removal Act or returned to the Smoky Mountains after they had been physically removed. The Tribe was officially incorporated under North Carolina state law in 1889 and is today one of but a few Native nations that hold fee-simple title to their own reservation lands.

In the *Lambert*[95] case, the Principal Chief, Patrick Lambert, who was elected in 2015, faced removal and impeachment by members of the Tribal Council for allegedly having engaged in a number of unethical activities they believed justified his ouster from office. The council's members had asked the Tribe's Chief Audit Executive, Sharon Blankenship, to conduct a compliance audit of such matters as the hiring, firing, demoting, and transferal of Tribal employees, unwarranted pay raises, and certain contract approvals.[96] Lambert alleged that the Council's audit was retaliation for an audit that he, himself, had initiated, that resulted in a federal investigation of the Tribe's Qualla Housing Authority (QHA). Six of the twelve council members happened to serve on the QHA Board of Directors.

After the compliance audit was completed, the Tribal Council enacted three resolutions against the Chief: Resolution 502 called for the drafting of Articles of Impeachment, Resolution 546 laid out the seven Articles of Impeachment, and Resolution 547 suspended Chief Lambert until the impeachment process had concluded. Lambert immediately filed a complaint in the Tribe's trial court against the Tribal Council and nine of its members, urging relief from the court. He alleged that the Council was not validly constituted because the Tribe had not conducted a census in keeping with the Tribe's Charter and Governing Document. He also maintained that the Council had neither the power to suspend him nor the authority to remove him should he be impeached. In addition, he claimed that his due process rights had been violated by the Council's actions.

The Tribe's Attorney General also got involved and raised virtually all of the same issues Chief Lambert had posited. Tribal Judge Sharon Barrett determined that the Tribal Council lacked statutory authority to suspend Chief Lambert and that a Grand Council vote in favor of suspension and impeachment did not have the force of law. When the Tribe's Supreme Court heard the case on appeal, the threshold question before the justices was whether the Tribal Council could lawfully proceed to impeach and remove the Chief. After reviewing the pertinent language in the Tribe's Charter and Governing Document, the justices held that the Chief or any other Tribal officer could, in fact, be removed by a two-thirds vote of the Tribal Council.

Aaron Payment vs. the Sault Ste. Marie Tribe of Chippewa Indians

On June 4, 2022, the Board of Directors, the governing body of the 44,000-member Sault Ste. Marie Tribe of Chippewa, located within Michigan, voted 10–2 to "censure" and express "no confidence" in their four-term Chairman, Aaron Payment, on the grounds he had violated a number of Tribal laws and ordinances.[97] Payment was not only a well-respected leader of his Tribe but also an influential figure at state, regional, and national levels. At the time of his censure, he was the Secretary of the National Congress of American Indians and President of three regional and state entities, including the Midwest Alliance of Sovereign Tribes, the Inter-Tribal Council of Michigan, and the United Tribes of Michigan. Payment's censure meant that, as long as he remained Chairman, the Board of Directors could effectively revoke his authority to represent the Tribe in the other leadership positions he held, effectively stripping him of his positions on state, regional, and national bodies.

Payment decried the Board's action, declaring that "the board acted as judge, jury and executioner by imposing sanctions without a single piece of evidence."[98] And he further complained that "I never imagined when re-elected in 2020 with the greatest margin in over a quarter century that my elected career would end like this."[99]

A few days later, the Board of Directors, concerned about what they called "misinformation" that was being disseminated by local media outlets surrounding Payment's censure, released a statement that spelled out the numerous allegations against the Chairman that had necessitated their censuring and no-confidence vote of his behavior.[100] Allegations included the following:

- Violated his duty to create an environment that fosters respect and dignity;
- Violated his duty to maintain an environment free of harassment and intimidation;
- Intimidated, harassed, and publicly attacked employees;

222 INDIGENOUS GOVERNANCE

- Continuously committed malicious public attacks upon tribal members;
- Violated the Medical Privacy and Procedures of individual tribal members;
- Violated Resolution 2012-222 Privacy of Board Member Phone and Computer Records;
- Breached/Released confidential information, violating tribal law;
- Campaigned prior to the Notice of Election pursuant to Tribal Code, Chapter 10;
- Violated Tribal Resolution 93-123 Code of Professional Conduct.[101]

Board members then explained precisely what their censure and no confidence meant for Payment: his removal from all internal Tribal committees (except for those specified in the Tribe's Code) and all external committees; he was stripped of the protections offered by the Tribe's sovereign immunity making him personally liable for his actions; and the Tribe's Executive Director, with the assistance of legal counsel, was authorized to hire an external legal firm to investigate all the allegations tendered by the Board and other members.[102]

In response, the embattled Chairman began circulating a petition within the community in an effort to pressure the Board to withdraw their censure action. As of this writing, July 2022, the situation has yet to be resolved.

Leadership, along with the followership (defined as "active engagement in helping an organization or a cause succeed while exercising independent, critical judgment of goals, tasks, potential problems, and methods"[103]—which we did not explore in this chapter) has been and will remain crucial factors in Indigenous governance. To re-define "leadership"—at the beginning of the chapter—from Keith Grint's "having followers," to "having relatives," is effectively to say that Native nations historically were kin-based polities in which every citizen took seriously their responsibilities for the maintenance and fortification of their communities' identity and stability. Leadership could be exercised by virtually any citizen since it was understood as fluid and situational. Kinship remains a dominant construct across Indian Country, but today it operates alongside constitutional-based governing systems that feature formalized positions of power—Chairperson, Secretary, Council members, Judges, Justices, and so on. These roles sometimes directly conflict with the more malleable and flexible style of leadership that once predominated, sometimes leading to intense governing conflicts such as those just discussed. This promises to be an ongoing issue for many Indigenous nations as they gain a deeper understanding of how to govern and determine what works best for their citizens.

8

Citizenship and Membership

A *sine qua non* (that which is indispensable) of any sovereign nation is the right to decide who belongs—who is entitled to membership or citizenship—in that body politic. Unless this right has been expressly ceded in a treaty or restrained via federal statute, it is arguably the most essential component of Native self-government. If Native governments were to lose the inherent right to identify their own people, then it would logically follow that any government could dictate the criteria for a nation's membership.

Historically, lands, languages, kinship systems, and spiritual values and traditions provided the most recognized framework enabling each Native nation and the individuals, families, and clans constituting those nations, to generally rest assured in their collective and personal identities. They did not have to wonder—much less prove—who they were. As one commentator aptly put it, "Allegiance rather than ancestry per se [was] the deciding factor" in determining membership in a given nation.[1] The citizenship criteria varied, of course, from Indigenous nation to Indigenous nation, and as Felix Cohen noted in 1934, "It is impossible to lay down a general ruling on the subject applicable to all reservations."[2] Complicating conditions is the fact that Native nations are distinctive communities in that they have not only a racial and an ethnic character but also have sovereign political governments. This dual nature often leads to confusion in cultural identity, federal Indian policy and law, and administrative regulations.

As the federal government's power surged by the late nineteenth and early twentieth centuries, with the corresponding waning of Indigenous power, Native cultural, social, and ceremonial-based understandings of Tribal identity began to be ignored, coercively adjusted, or simply supplanted by purely Western legal and frequently race-based definitions that were articulated in congressional laws, Bureau of Indian Affairs (BIA) administrative circulars, and federal court cases.

Federal Intervention in Native Identity Decisions

In the early 1900s, both Congress and the BIA began to employ and—still rely upon—ethnological data, including varying fractions of blood quantum, most typically 3/4ths, 1/2, 1/4, and 1/8th.[3] In fact, blood quantum remains one of the

Indigenous Governance. David E. Wilkins, Oxford University Press. © Oxford University Press 2024.
DOI: 10.1093/oso/9780190095994.003.0009

224 INDIGENOUS GOVERNANCE

most important criteria used by both the federal and many Native governments to determine membership status, notwithstanding the fact that its ongoing use "poses enormous conceptual and practical problems" since blood is not the carrier of genetic material and cultural traits as was thought during the nineteenth century.[4]

Terms like "half-blood" and "mixed-blood" appear in some ratified treaties, reflecting the reality that Native individuals, like those of other ethnic groups, have always intermarried with members of other racial and ethnic groups. Yet, formal rules and regulations dealing with blood quantum criteria were never used by Native nations until the early part of the twentieth century. Federal lawmakers, looking to find ways to reduce expenditures were the ones to enshrine blood quantum formula into policy and law. They sought to cut funding associated with treaty commitments to Native peoples, seeking to justify the considerable costs of carrying out their self-imposed policy choices aimed at civilizing and Christianizing Natives and individualizing Native property. The calculations were simple and effective—if Natives of mixed heritage could be erased from the rolls, there would literally be fewer Natives in need of services, instantly resulting in lower costs.

For instance, in 1908 Congress enacted legislation declaring that the allotment of any deceased Tribal member of the Five Civilized Tribes of one-half or more Indian blood would remain protected, provided of course, that the Secretary of the Interior decided not to remove the restrictions. Section 3 of this statute acknowledged that the Tribal rolls, as approved by the secretary, were to be "conclusive evidence as to the quantum of Indian blood of any enrolled citizen or freedmen."[5] The issue, however, transcended the Five Civilized Tribes of Indian Territory. Indian education had long been considered a crucial step in the assimilative process of Natives into mainstream American society. In 1912, for the first time, Congress incorporated a one-quarter blood degree limit[6] in order to save federal dollars. Extensive hearings were held on the merits of excluding Native children of one-quarter or less Native blood "where adequate school facilities exist in their own state, thus permitting Indian children now deprived of school facilities an opportunity to secure an education under the laws of the state wherein they live."[7] The insidious message wasn't just a call for belt-tightening. Instead, so-called mixed-blood children were at fault for taking away services that rightly belonged to real Indians. The government was pitting Native against Native as they all struggled to survive with the inadequate help the government provided.

Blood quantum rules were soon embedded throughout the federal agencies dealing with Indigenous peoples, particularly within the halls of the BIA. And when the Indian Reorganization Act was adopted in 1934 it enshrined into law a definition of "Indian" as "persons of one-half or more Indian blood." "This provision," said Kirsty Gover, "provides the legislative basis for the Bureau of Indian Affairs' certification of Indian blood quanta and its issuance of Certificates of Degree of Indian Blood (CDIB)" cards that many federally recognized Tribal members must possess in order to receive services and benefits as citizens of their nations.[8]

In October 1934, an opinion by Asst. Solicitor Felix S. Cohen and signed by Solicitor Nathan Margold titled "Powers of Indian Tribes" identified and elaborated on a host of inherent powers vested in Native nations under existing law, for example, the power to tax, form a government, and regulate domestic relations, among others.[9] Two additional powers are of significant import for this study. The first was outlined thus: "To define the conditions of membership within the tribe, to prescribe rules for adoption, to classify the members of the tribe and to grant or withhold the right of tribal suffrage and to make all other necessary rules and regulations governing the membership of the tribe so far as may be consistent with existing acts of Congress governing the enrollment and property rights of members." Second: "To remove or to exclude from the limits of the reservation non-members of the tribe, excepting authorized Government officials and other persons now occupying reservation lands under lawful authority, and to prescribe appropriate rules and regulations governing such removal and exclusion, and governing the conditions under which non-members of the tribe may come upon tribal land or have dealings with tribal members, providing such acts are consistent with Federal laws governing trade with the Indian tribes."[10] These two powers provide Native government officials with considerable authority in regard to their own citizens and over non-member residents (both Natives from other nations and non-Natives).

Native Citizenship Criteria: Blood, Descent, and DNA testing

Kirsty Gover's important research on Native membership policies, as expressed in Native constitutions, reveals that approximately 70% of present-day Native governments employ blood quantum rules in their constitutions, reflecting the long-standing use of this pilloried concept by federal officials in census taking, statutes, and federal regulations.[11] Blood rules are of two types: those measuring Indian blood (from any Indigenous people) and those measuring Tribal blood (Tribe specific). Only fifteen Native constitutions specifically employ the term *blood quantum*. Fractions of blood, however, are another matter. The most frequently used quantum of Native blood found in Tribal constitutions is one-fourth. Seventy-four Native nations use this fraction, though in a variety of ways.

226 INDIGENOUS GOVERNANCE

Article II, Section I of the Laguna Pueblo Constitution of 2012 says this about membership:

> The membership of the Pueblo shall consist of the following persons; provided that they have not renounced their membership or do not hereafter renounce their membership in the manner set forth in Section 2 of this Article:...(c) Any person of one-fourth (1/4) or more Laguna Indian blood. (d) All persons who are naturalized as members pursuant to ordinances of the Pueblo. Such ordinances shall prescribe the conditions, limitations, and benefits of said naturalized membership status. Only the following persons shall be eligible for naturalization: i. Persons of at least one-half (1/2) degree of Indian blood of federally recognized tribes who possess at least one-eighth (1/8) degree of Laguna Indian blood. ii. Persons possessing at least one-half (1/2) degree Indian blood married to members of the Pueblo and who are members of a federally-recognized Indian tribe; provided, such membership is relinquished. iii. Persons of Laguna blood who have previously renounced their membership in the Pueblo of Laguna.[12]

The Native Village of Brevig Mission in Alaska also employs a one-quarter blood requirement but also incorporates other ways to secure membership. Article 3, Section 1 states that membership will consist of persons "(a) who are Natives possessing a minimum of 1/4 blood quantum Alaska Native (Eskimo, Indian or Aleut) and who have resided in the Native Village of Brevig Mission for a period of one year prior to filing an application for membership. Reasonable temporary absences shall not be used to establish that this requirement has not been set aside; or (b) who are direct lineal descendants of ancestors of the Native Village of Brevig Mission; or (c) who are adopted by the tribe."

Only eight Native nations use one-half blood quantum as their primary eligibility criterion: White Mountain Apache, Isleta Pueblo, Northern Cheyenne, Jamul Indian Village, Quileute, Lac du Flambeau, Crow Creek, and the Mississippi Band of Choctaw. Jamul Indian Village, for instance, declares the following persons eligible for membership:

(a) Persons of ½ or more degree of California Indian blood who filed as Jamul Indians and were listed on the September 21, 1968, Judgment Roll of Certain Indians of California.

(b) Persons of ½ or more degree of California Indian blood who reside in the Jamul Indian Village, Jamul California, at the time of the adoption of this constitution.

(c) Persons of ½ or more degree of total California Indian blood whose ancestors meet the requirements of Section 1(a) or 1(b) regardless of whether the ancestors are living or deceased.

(d) Persons who have been adopted by the village in accordance with an adoption ordinance approved by the Secretary of the Interior or his authorized representative, provided they are not less than ½ degree Indian blood.

Fifteen Native constitutions employ one-eighth quantum as their blood standard, like the Mandan, Hidatsa, and Arikara of the Fort Berthold Reservation in North Dakota, whose constitution succinctly states that membership consist solely of "persons of at least 1/8 degree blood of the Hidatsa, Mandan, and/or Arikara Tribes." And nine Tribal constitutions utilize one-sixteenth as the fractional marker, including the Caddo, Fort Sill Apache, Confederated Tribes of the Grand Ronde Community, Pala Band of Mission Indians, Iowa Tribe of Oklahoma, Manzanita Band of Digueno, Cowlitz, Stilliguamish, and Mesa Grande Band of Digueno.

The Chemeheuvi Tribe has two categories of membership. Enrolled members who have less than 1/16 blood are not allowed to vote and may not hold public office; but enrolled members with at least 1/16 degree of Chemeheuvi blood are entitled to exercise the franchise and may be elected to a position in the nation.

Blood quantum rules in Native constitutions have increased substantially since the 1930s, with nearly two-thirds of Native nations requiring some degree of blood that will allow recognition as a Tribal citizen. This rise is important as blood issues continue to form one of the most contested domains of Indigenous identity. Gover points out that while federal lawmakers do not distinguish between "Indian blood" and "tribal blood" they still insist that Native nations be composed of Indians. "Many tribes, however, insist that applicants show genealogical ties to the community, evidenced by blood quantum rules. This difference has important normative consequences for the theories of tribalism." "It suggests," says Gover, "that tribes in the US are evolving their own *sui generis* construction of membership that does not map onto the federal public law categories used to describe tribal membership in terms of race and ethnicity."[13] (emphasis hers)

Ironically, while federal agencies now rely less on blood quantum rules, some Native governments are invested in its continued usage, despite the inherent associated problems.[14] "Why," asks Gover, "would tribes increasingly elect to include rules, precisely at a time when the pressure on them to do so has apparently been relaxed?"[15] She answers her own query by noting that "tribes are moving away from a race-based model of tribal membership . . . but are not moving toward a classically liberal 'civic polity' model. Instead, findings show that tribes are evolving their own . . . form of 'genealogic' tribalism."[16]

228 INDIGENOUS GOVERNANCE

By this Gover means that Native governments are relying more heavily on lineal descent and blood quantum rules and less on residency or parental enrollment both because of the serious problems brought about by federal termination policy in the 1950s and 1960s and because the federal government still insists that Native nations be able to prove that they are descended from historically recognized Indigenous peoples.[17]

Alongside blood quantum rules now comes genetic information or DNA analysis to test for particular genetic markers. This is the latest tool used by upwards of 100 Native nations to address questions of both Tribal enrollment and disenrollment proceedings. DNA testing, according to Bardill, "has become an umbrella term that refers to many different kinds of genetic testing that provides information about an individual's genes."[18] Some types of DNA testing (like fingerprinting) have proven useful in documenting close biological relationships, say, between parents and children. It was useful in helping resolve the Kennewick Man—the Ancient One—controversy that ensued over how to treat the remains of a 9000-year-old Indigenous person discovered in Washington state.[19] Still, it is important to note that no DNA test "can 'prove' an individual is American Indian and/or Alaska Native, or even if they have ancestors from a specific tribe. Genetic testing can provide evidence for the biological relationship between two individuals (e.g., paternity testing), but there are no unique genes for individual tribes or American Indian/Alaska Natives (AI/AN) ancestry in general."[20]

Notwithstanding this scientific fact, increasing numbers of Tribal officials are turning to DNA testing to both enroll and disenroll individual members. As Kim TallBear's research shows, Tribes' reliance on such scientific enterprises goes against the grain of genuine cultural sovereignty because "tribes, at least rhetorically, claim to organize themselves according to their inherent sovereignty and the idea of the tribal nation. If this is the goal," TallBear writes, "then racializing the tribe (naming that entity as only a biological entity) undermines both tribal cultural and political authorities."[21]

Native governments such as the Shakopee Mdewakonton Sioux, Redding Rancheria, Catawba Nation, Ho-Chunk, Eastern Band of Cherokee, Mashpee Wampanoag, Suquamish Tribe, Habematolel Pomo of Upper Lake, and the Picayune Rancheria of Chukchansi Indians have used DNA testing in attempts to resolve their membership issues. The Ho-Chunk were one of the first nations to employ DNA, incorporating the testing by constitutional amendment in 2009. According to Sheila Corbine, the Tribe's Attorney General in 2011, "All the DNA testing is designed for, in our instance anyway, is to prove parentage. And that is to arrive at what the blood quantum is."[22]

Grounds for Loss or Denial of Native Citizenship

Native nations have the inherent power to determine the criteria for who can be formally enrolled in their communities, a right that has been upheld in countless federal decisions, including *Roff v. Burney*,[23] which held that the Chickasaw Nation had the power to disenroll whites who had previously been adopted into the nation; and *Santa Clara Pueblo v. Martinez*,[24] which affirmed a Native nation's right to be the ultimate arbiter of its own membership rules. The nations also have authority to banish, extradite, remove, expel, deny, exclude, and disenroll those who are already enrolled members.[25]

The most common phrase found in nearly 200 Native constitutions or other organic documents for each of the actions listed immediately above is *loss of membership*. Typically, the term is included as one of the enumerated powers of either the Tribal Council or the General Council. For example, in the Crow Tribe's Constitution, Article 3, Section 3, declares that "the Crow Tribal General Council shall have the power to adopt ordinances, consistent with this Constitution, governing future membership and *loss of membership* of members of the Crow Tribe of Indians."

Formal disenrollment can occur for a number of reasons:

- *Voluntary relinquishment*: Tribal members may "sever tribal relations," "withdraw from," "resign from," or choose to "remove" themselves from Tribal membership. This voluntary action may then culminate in a Tribal order from the governing body that formally revokes or disenrolls said person from the nation's membership roll.
- *Dual enrollment*: Most nations forbid simultaneous enrollment in more than one nation.
- *Deliberate fraud or error*: In rare instances some individuals falsely represented themselves; in others, Tribal officials made clerical errors that erroneously led to enrollment.
- *Failure to maintain contact with the Tribal body*: For those individuals who move away or do not actively stay in touch with their home community.
- *Lack of sufficient blood quantum (or inappropriate blood from another Tribe)*: This serves as both a justification and a mechanism for dismemberment.
- *Misconduct*: Neglect of duty or involvement in activities that may be considered injurious to the community (e.g., malfeasance, civil violations, criminal acts).

Alleging insufficient (or inappropriate) blood quantum is a favorite tool of those seeking to disenroll members. It is a simple, economical method of

230   INDIGENOUS GOVERNANCE

eliminating one person or entire families with one action. In some instances, the Tribal enrollment officer will decide that a deceased ancestor has been determined to lack the required amount of Tribal blood for membership. As a result, all those descended from that individual are automatically ineligible for membership. This could affect hundreds of members if the posthumously disenrolled person was a more distant ancestor. Often the only historical records used to make these determinations are those cataloged by the federal government. For decades, most of these records were kept for the sole purpose of erasing or incorporating Natives into the larger society. Even in cases where genetic testing has scientifically proven a targeted deceased individual's connection to a particular member, those behind the dismemberment process have sometimes continued, undeterred, to pursue termination.

Those confronted with disenrollment have countered, most with a wealth of documentation, that they do, indeed, have sufficient blood quantum and that their membership has not been fraudulently obtained. They assert that family feuds, personal and political reprisals, financial greed, and political power struggles are the real explanations behind dismemberments.

As of this writing (2023), nearly ninety Native nations are, or have been, disenrolling and or banishing both Tribal and non-Tribal members.[26] Of this figure, at least thirty of the Native communities are located in California. In a majority of these communities, the two most common reasons given by Tribal officials for disenrollment/banishment are lack of sufficient blood quantum and alleged fraud in having obtained enrollment. The remaining nations engaged in these egregious practices are spread over nineteen states, with most being located within the boundaries of Oklahoma, Minnesota, Michigan, Washington, and Alaska. A key difference between these states and California is that the number of banishing Tribal nations is nearly equal to the number of disenrolling Tribes. Most of the banishments occur because of civil violations or criminal behavior. Of those being disenrolled, nearly one-half are alleged by their governments to have insufficient blood quantum. Thorough, professional research is needed in order to determine whether these nearly ninety Native governments can verify that their rationale(s) for eviction or disenfranchisement of otherwise bona fide members are justified.

African American Freedmen and Native Nations Relations

The spread of overt and violent racism continues to gain speed and poses increasing problems for a number of Tribal nations, African Americans, Afro-Indigenous persons, and the federal government, as well. Although George Floyd's murder in 2020 resulted in a measure of social and political collaboration

CITIZENSHIP AND MEMBERSHIP 231

between urban African Americans, urban Natives, and some reservation-based Natives, many Native governments continue to struggle mightily with internal racism against Afro-Indigenous persons who, for centuries, have been fundamental components of Indigenous communities.

Historically, some members of the Five Civilized Tribes enslaved African Americans, a practice introduced by white plantation owners in the South.[27] Native enslavement of Blacks continued during and after the Tribes were forcibly relocated to what became Indian Territory in the 1830s and 1840s, and it endured until the end of the American Civil War. Several of the Five Tribes chose to sign treaties with the Confederate states and so, at the war's conclusion, as punishment, the federal government demanded that new treaties be negotiated. These 1866 treaties were, it is important to note, coercive documents forced upon the leadership of the Five Tribes by the victorious federal government, and they contained a number of punitive and detrimental provisions, for example, the loss of thousands of additional acres of reserved lands. This and other provisions wreaked havoc on the Five Nations. That said, an important provision mandated that all the people formerly enslaved by members of these nations, people now referred to as the Freemen, were not only free, but they and their descendants were to be Tribal members entitled to the same benefits as any other member of the Five Tribes.

From the Cherokee Treaty, Article 9:

> The Cherokee Nation having, voluntarily, in February, eighteen hundred and sixty-three, by an act of the national council, forever abolished slavery, hereby covenant and agree that never hereafter shall either slavery or involuntary servitude exist in their nation otherwise than in the punishment of crime, whereof the party shall have been duly convicted, in   accordance with laws applicable to all the members of said tribes alike. They further agree that all freedmen who have been liberated by voluntary act of their former owners or by law, as well as all free colored persons who were in the country at the commencement of the rebellion and are now residents therein, or who may return within six months, and their descendants, shall have all the rights of native Cherokees: Provided, That owners of   slaves so emancipated in the Cherokee Nation shall never receive any compensation or pay for the slaves so emancipated.[28]

Notwithstanding the clarity of this language, the ensuing decades found African American Freedmen and their descendants enduring constitutional and statutory exclusions, rank discrimination, and persistent efforts on the part of the leadership of the Five Tribes to deny them the political and legal rights of membership they had secured under the 1866 treaty provisions. Interestingly, in 1863, two years before the thirteenth amendment to the

232 INDIGENOUS GOVERNANCE

U.S. Constitution that abolished slavery was ratified, the Cherokee National Council, enacted a proclamation that abolished slavery and involuntary servitude in their country. But, according to Julia Coates, this measure did not grant the newly emancipated African Freedmen Cherokee citizenship. This was "because they did not conform to the familial requirements long established in Cherokee law for incorporation of outsiders: the majority of freedmen were not spouses or parents of Cherokees by blood, nor did they themselves have Cherokee parentage."[29]

The most common method used by Tribal officials to disenfranchise African Americans, as Coates's statement above exemplifies, was to simply redefine who was eligible for membership, by inserting language which declared that to be a "citizen" in one of the nations a person had to be descended from "by blood" citizens, thus disqualifying the Freedmen descendants who had been counted separately in the federal census commonly referred to as the Dawes Rolls of 1906.[30]

The African American Freedmen of each of the nations have used public opinion, lawsuits, and support from the Congressional Black Caucus in an unrelenting effort to reacquire their citizenship. The most successful group to date has been the Freedmen of the Cherokee Nation, led by the knowledgeable and dedicated Marilyn Vann, whose long-standing lawsuit culminated in a federal district court ruling in 2017, *Cherokee Nation v. Nash*,[31] written by Thomas Hogan. The ruling held that the nearly 2,900 Cherokee Freedmen were entitled to all the rights of Tribal citizens. As Hogan said, "The Court finds it confounding that the Cherokee Nation historically had no qualms about regarding Freedmen as Cherokee 'property' yet continues, even after 150 years, to balk when confronted with the legal imperative to treat them as Cherokee people."[32] Hogan's ruling was not appealed by the Cherokee Nation and the nearly 3,000 Freedmen were finally formally reinstated as Cherokee citizens. In February 2021 the Cherokee Supreme Court expunged the "by blood" language in the nation's constitution and declared unlawful any Tribal laws with similar racial language.[33] Since Hogan's 2017 ruling, another 5,600 Freedmen descendants have been added to the Cherokee Nation's membership rolls, adding to the nation's burgeoning 380,000 enrollment.[34]

The remaining four Tribal nations have not yet acted to formally and fully enfranchise Freedmen descendants, although they are coming under increasing pressure to do so from both the Secretary of the Interior, Deb Haaland (a Laguna Pueblo member), and the Congressional Black Caucus led by Congresswoman Maxine Waters, who chairs the House Committee on Financial Services, which conducted a hearing on the Freedmen issue on July 27, 2021.[35]

Two of the four nations, the Choctaw and the Muscogee (Creek), have agreed to reconsider their long-standing opposition to full citizenship for the Freedmen of their nations "but stopped short of a commitment to grant citizenship to the Black descendants."[36] The Chickasaw Nation, however, speaking through their Governor, Bill Anoatubby, was disinclined to follow the Cherokee Nation's lead in admitting the Freedmen to full citizenship, declaring to Secretary Haaland that "Chickasaw citizenship is a matter of sovereignty and is clearly defined in the Chickasaw Constitution."[37] The Chickasaw Constitution states that citizenship "consists of all Chickasaw Indians by blood" whose names are on the Dawes Roll "and their lineal descendants." Similarly, the Seminole Nation's political leadership was adamant that they would not voluntarily change their law to enfranchise Seminole Freedmen. It is clear that the situation of those individuals who consider themselves both African and Indigenous still haunts some Native communities and it clouds relations with African Americans and those of Afro-Indigenous ancestry. Shamefully, racism continues to motivate some Tribal officials who have access to political, economic, and media power that they use as a means to deny or discredit African or Afro-Indigenous individuals as they seek to claim their essential treaty rights.

Native Nations as Political and Racial–Ethnic Bodies

The two most common concepts used by Native individuals to describe their connection to their own nations is as *member* or *citizen*, although Tribal officialdom utilizes member and membership far more often than citizen or citizenship. In fact, less than a dozen Native constitutions use the term citizenship rather than membership, including, Catawba, Cherokee Nation, Chickasaw, Federated tribes of Graton, Jamestown S'Klallam, Kaw Nation, Muscogee (Creek), North Fork Rancheria, Pinoleville Pomo, Sitka Tribe, and the Wiyot Tribe.

A brief etymology of these two terms is revealing. *Member*, according to the *Oxford English Dictionary*, dates back to at least A.D. 1100. It has been used in several senses: (1) relating to a part of a living body organism (e.g., organ of the body); (2) relating to an individual or constituent element within a social or other organizational structure (e.g., an inhabitant or native of a county or city); and (3) relating to a part of an inanimate structure or immaterial thing (e.g., a load-bearing structure).

If one understands Native peoples as genealogically or organically related communities who share a common language, values, and territory, then the term *member* is certainly valid. After all, humans frequently used the expression, "I am a family member" or, "I try to be a useful member of society," to distinguish themselves from others. Of course, the word *member* is also associated with social clubs (e.g., fraternities and sororities, Kiwanis, Rotary, Elk, etc.) unions, churches, and political bodies (e.g., Republican party, member of Parliament).

234 INDIGENOUS GOVERNANCE

But given Commissioner of Indian Affairs, John Collier's deep understanding of the community structures, religious traditions, and value systems of the Native communities he was developing his ideas for, it is highly doubtful that he was using the term in the sense of social clubs.

The term *citizen* also has a long history, dating back to Aristotle, who believed humans were political animals, and Roman law, which cast humans as legal animals with a relationship to the state.[38] The *Oxford English Dictionary*'s earliest recorded mention of the term is in 1314. Two of its most common meanings are (1) "an inhabitant of a city or town, especially one possessing civic rights and privileges;" and (2) "a member of a state, an enfranchised inhabitant of the country, as opposed to an alien—in the U.S., a person, native or naturalized, who has the privilege of voting for public office, and is entitled to full protection in the exercise of private rights."

But as Tatum, Jorgensen, Guss, and Deer note:

> 'Citizenship' is different from the question of what it means to be 'Indian,' 'Native,' 'aboriginal,' 'Indigenous,' or, for example, 'Cherokee,' 'Apache,' or 'Ojibwe.' 'Citizenship' refers exclusively to a political status, to being accepted as a constituent of a recognized government. Being 'Indian' (or Indigenous, Native, Aboriginal, Cherokee, Apache, or Ojibwe, for example) usually refers to an individual's ethnicity. Of course, as in other nations, Native nations' definitions of citizenship may be closely intertwined with either identity—with culture, tradition, creation stories, a homeland, or an ancestral line. Yet in most circumstances ethnic identification is an individual act (an individual claims her identity), while acknowledgment of citizenship is a governmental act (a government recognizes its citizens).[39]

Again, within a clear majority of Tribal nations, there is a definite blending of the political (citizenship) status and the racial–ethnic (membership) status. For example, the Pinoleville Pomo state in their 2005 Constitution's citizenship requirements that "a person who has at least one-quarter (1/4) degree of Pomo Indian blood, and who is related by blood to a member of the base roll," is a citizen. This blended status, created in part because of enforced federal policies that enshrined blood quantum into Tribal membership practices, leaves Native nations with a unique standing in law, politics, and public perception.

The U.S. Constitution explicitly makes note of both the separate racial–ethnic and political status of Native peoples with the clauses "excluding Indians not taxed" (Article 1, Section 8, Cl. 3; and 14th Amendment, Section 2) and the "Congress shall have power to . . . regulate commerce . . . with the Indian tribes" (Article 1, Section 8, Cl. 3) and the several hundred treaties and agreements and thousands of statutes and court cases that affirm and attest both statuses in law

CITIZENSHIP AND MEMBERSHIP 235

and practice. And we have seen that Native governments, acting from a sovereign base, utilize a wide variety of criteria to decide who belongs—or who should be erased—on their nation's membership/citizenship rolls.

Urban Life and Native Identity

A complicating factor on the issue of belonging to Native nations is the fact that more than 70% of Native individuals now reside off-reservation or trust lands—typically in major metropolitan and suburban areas. And roughly half of all urban-based Natives are located in as few as sixteen cities (e.g., New York, Los Angeles, Phoenix, Oklahoma City, Anchorage, Tulsa, etc.), largely as a result of federal policies instituted in the 1950s and 1960s under the termination and relocation.[40] Of course, well before federal policies of removal and relocation came on line, some Natives had voluntarily migrated to urban areas. As Vizenor noted: "Natives have always been on the move, by chance, necessity, barter, reciprocal sustenance, and by trade over extensive routes; the actual motion is a natural right, and the tribal stories of transmotion are a continuous source of visionary sovereignty."[41] It is a fact, too, that "every city in a place like the U.S., Aotearoa/New Zealand, is, by definition, built on Indigenous territory, and the place stories we tell are implicated in this process."[42]

The relationship between Native governing bodies and Tribal citizens who no longer reside within their nation's reservation or trust lands varies widely— with some governments providing services and benefits to their urban-based members—assuming they are duly enrolled. Many others choose not to provide any recognition or rights to those who have moved away. To my knowledge, no comprehensive study has yet been conducted that grapples with this important demographic reality. And what of the federal government's obligations to urban-based Natives, particularly the Bureau of Indian Affairs and the Indian Health Service? An extended quote from the Harvard Project on the American Indian Economic Development's study, *The State of the Native Nations* is warranted because it captures well the difficulties that urban Natives endure in trying to secure support from federal agencies: the same agencies that had created the policies under which many Natives had moved to cities.

Federal Indian policy overwhelmingly focuses on tribal governments and reservations, rather than on Native American individuals. When an individual Indian lives off-reservation, treaty rights ostensibly still attach to the individual Indian and remain in place in the non-reservation environment. However, many Native Americans who reside in urban areas find that they are effectively cut off from support systems and social programs that are available, however modest, on their home reservations. The lack of services for Native individuals who

236 INDIGENOUS GOVERNANCE

leave the reservations for cities is a major concern, and individual American Indians have fought for such services, even to the point of litigation. The relative lack of services for off-reservation tribal citizens raises a fundamental question about the rights and treaties upon which much federal assistance to Indians is predicated: Which treaty obligations and other rights apply collectively and which apply individually? The question generates controversy since federal funding constraints effectively create a zero-sum conflict between urban Indians and Indians residing on or near the reservation and being served by tribes. The federal emphasis on the government-to-government relationship with tribes appropriately recognizes the sovereign status of Indian nations. At the same time, however, it makes the federal government ill-adapted to serve a large contingent of Indian individuals, many of whom the federal government encouraged to move to cities. Substantial numbers of urban Indians and advocates see a perverse irony in this controversy: the rapid growth of the urban Indian population that is now underserved was the deliberate objective of federal relocation policy.[43]

Health care is one area where urban Natives continue to languish from inadequate support from the leading federal institution authorized and funded to meet the health needs of Indigenous persons, the Indian Health Service (IHS). Despite the fact that Native youth in cities are at greater risk of serious mental health, substance abuse, suicide, gang activity, and teen abuse, IHS funding is woefully inadequate, according to the U.S. Commission on Civil Rights in their 2018 report, "Broken Promises: Continuing Federal Funding Shortfall for Native Americans." In fact, the Commission's members found that only one percent of the HIS budget is allocated to urban Indian Health care. The IHS has, in recent decades, entered into contracts and provides grants to approximately thirty-four non-profit urban Indian organizations[44] that provide health care and services to nearly 55,000 urban-based Natives, but recent data show that over one million urban Natives live in areas served by these urban Indian centers. As Elizabeth D'Amico, Alina Dickeson, et.al, found in their research on COVID-19's effects on urban-based Native youth, 20% of teens reported clinically significant anxiety and depression, 20% described feelings of insecurity, and 40% reported poor sleep.[45] There is a profound need, then, for greater coordination between Native governments, the IHS, the BIA, and other federal agencies that are charged with supporting the needs of Indigenous citizens, including urban-based Tribal citizens.

While the federal government generally supports the inherent right of Indigenous peoples to exercise self-determination over their membership decisions, federal policymakers still insist that they have the power—via the plenary power doctrine—to reverse Native governmental decisions regarding identity and membership choices when it suits their economic, political, or cultural interests and to provide benefits only to those it deems eligible. Although no constitutional or treaty basis exists for this unenumerated and virtually unrestricted federal power, it is a political reality for all Native governments.

9
Electoral Politics

Elections are government-administered processes by which people, either in competitive races or running unopposed, seek public office. Across Indian Country and throughout most of the world, elections are, with few exceptions, the only legitimate means by which governing officials can claim the right to legitimately wield authority. That said, some Native governments, like many of the Pueblos, still utilize selection or heredity to acquire office. Authoritarian regimes like Russia, Libya, and Uzbekistan, and military dictatorships, like Myanmar and Sudan, also use elections to give the ruling regime an aura of legitimacy. In short, "there are two basic kinds of elections: (1) *free*, where parties of competing philosophies compete for power in a fair contest; and (2) *sham*, where rulers hold cynically staged elections in order to justify their rule."[1]

First, an important caveat: Because of the distinctive nature of Native governments and politics, the study of Indigenous electoral systems is largely unexplored when compared to studies of state and federal elections. Recently, there has been an increase in scholarship that examines Indigenous voting behavior, at least in state and federal elections, but that is not our focus in this chapter.[2] Thus far, only a few political science or legal works have been prepared that explicitly deal with internal Native electoral politics.[3]

As we established earlier, Indigenous governments and the citizens of those polities, are uniquely situated—racially, politically, and culturally. In regard to electoral politics and voting behavior, there are several facts that distinguish Native governments from all other polities and these warrant a brief mention. First, one of the fundamental differences between Native, state, and federal elections is the fact that political parties do not play an obvious and integrated part in Native political life. At the state and federal levels, political parties permeate every aspect of those electoral systems. The two major American parties—Democrats and Republicans—act as "agents of political socialization, aggregating and mobilizing the interests of vast numbers of citizens, organizing the decision-making institutions of government, and enhancing voter capacities to hold public officials accountable."[4] But while 77% of Native individuals reported having voted in local, state, or national elections in 2020 and identify as Democrat, Republican, Independent, or Democrat Socialist,[5] there is little evidence that these national parties formally operate on reservations or on trust lands or that they have been institutionalized or directly impact Tribal elections.

Indigenous Governance. David E. Wilkins, Oxford University Press. © Oxford University Press 2024.
DOI: 10.1093/oso/9780190095994.003.0010

Second, there is, as Glenn A. Phelps, a political scientist, put it, an ongoing constitutional tension regarding Natives as citizens and voters acting in their own elections and those administered by the states and the federal government. Citizens of federally recognized Native polities have citizenship status in all three governments and can exercise the franchise in each of the three polities. Non-Natives, however, are generally disallowed from voting in Native elections. Phelps states this way: "Indians living within Indian Country are immune from state and local taxes and are largely immune from state and local laws. Yet they claim the right to vote for representatives who can levy taxes and make rules and regulations for non-Indians—taxes and rules from which reservation Indians themselves are immune."[6]

This treble citizenship status suits Native citizens as it is deeply rooted in the treaty and trust relationship that Indigenous peoples have with the federal government. But Native voters in non-Native elections, like African–Americans, Latinos, and other communities of color continue to face a multitude of structural barriers when they seek to register to vote, when they try to cast their ballots, and when having their ballots counted. As the Native American Rights Fund found in their comprehensive study of Native voting, Native voters face the following obstacles during the registration process: "(1) lack of traditional mailing addresses, (2) homeless and housing instability, (3) voter identification requirements (which can be hard for many Native Americans to obtain), (4) unequal access to online registration, (5) unequal access to in-person voter registration, (6) restrictions on access to voter registration forms, (7) denial of voter registration opportunities due to previous convictions, (8) rejection of voter registration applications, (9) voter purges, and (10) failure to offer registration opportunities at polling places on Election Day."[7]

In addition to this catalog of registration hurdles, if a Native voter is able to register they are then subject to a variety of additional barriers when they try to cast their ballots, including "(1) unequal funding for voting activities in Indian communities; (2) lack of pre-election information and outreach; (3) cultural and political isolation; (4) unequal access to in-person voting; (5) unequal access to early voting; (6) barriers *caused* by vote-by-mail, which are numerous; (7) barriers posed by state laws that create arbitrary population thresholds in order to establish polling places; (8) the use of the ADA [Americans with Disabilities Act] to deny polling places on reservation lands; and (9) the lack of Native American election workers."[8] (emphasis theirs)

Finally, Native voters face limits in having their ballots counted, including a shortage of valid canvassing opportunities, failure to count ballots that are cast outside of their precinct, ballot harvesting bans and comparable laws, and inadequate information about the status of their ballot—whether it was counted—and an unwillingness or inability to correct errors.[9] Our focus, however, will be on

240 INDIGENOUS GOVERNANCE

electoral politics within Native nations and not on electoral affairs at the inter-governmental level.

Conducting Native Elections

The vast majority of Indigenous nations—whether they are constitution-based or operate under Articles of Incorporation, Charters, Governing Resolutions, or Codes—utilize elections that, in theory, are free, open, honest, and straight-forward. This is because voting is the key component of democratic government. If elections are fair, free, and regular they provide Native citizens with the means of expressing their preferences; meaning that the chances for democracy to function are enhanced. Conversely, if elections are not fair and free, Tribal government is undemocratic and opportunities for greed, graft, corruption, and cronyism can emerge. As a means of conveying the will and consent of the people to their institutions of government and choosing who will hold its offices, Tribal elections are essential to the democratic process.[10]

While most Native elections are conducted without substantial problems, Native communities are certainly not immune to sometimes intense and brutal political skirmishes. In certain situations, some Native leaders and community members, in an effort to comport with Tribal law and conduct fair elections, have turned to outside organizations like the Carter Center—a nonprofit organization founded by former President Jimmy Carter and his wife Rosalynn, that works to resolve conflict, support democracy, protect human rights, among other objectives[11]—and have the Center monitor their elections.

To date, the Carter Center has been called in to observe the Cherokee Nation's elections on two separate occasions: in 1999 they were asked to monitor the Principal Chief, Deputy Chief, and fifteen-member council election; and in 2011 they were called upon to observe the nation's special election for Principal Chief. In addition, the Center has also observed the Cheyenne-Arapahoe Tribe's primary and general election in 2017, and the Muscogee (Creek) Nation's elections for Principal Chief, Second Chief, and members of the National Council.[12]

The Carter Center's involvement in the 1999 Cherokee Nation election "marked the Center's first comprehensive election observation mission within the U.S."[13] The Cherokee Nation had just endured a destabilizing constitutional crisis which had compelled the Bureau of Indian Affairs to intervene. The Nation's Election Commission took the drastic step of inviting the Carter Center because the days leading up to the Tribe's elections were "marked by a high level of suspicion and lack of confidence that the elections would be transparent."[14] The Center sent ten observers to oversee the election and the subsequent runoff on July 24, 1999. While determining that the elections were fair, they nevertheless made a number of recommendations to improve the Cherokee's electoral process, including:

- streamlining the voter registration system in order to decrease confusion among potential voters;
- creating at-large seats in the Tribal Council to better represent citizens who live outside the nation's geographical borders;
- clarifying the instructions for election watchers so that the parameters of their role were clear;
- reforming the procedure used to appoint CNEC [Cherokee Nation Election Commission] members so that a permanent council existed in between elections and so that the principal chief, upon election, could not constitute the CNEC primarily with his or her supporters; and
- considering the elimination of the use of challenged ballots altogether or at least the establishment of a more consistent method for how challenged ballots are handled.

The Cherokee Nation implemented some of the recommendations but opted not to streamline its registration process.[15]

The Muscogee (Creek) Nation, through their Principal Chief and election board, also took the opportunity to invite the Carter Center to observe their 2019 primary and general elections. After observing the elections, the Center commended the Muscogee people and election officials for having conducted a smooth electoral process. Nevertheless, since voter turnout has historically been low, with only 28% of registered voters participating (18,000 out of 89,000 registered voters), the Center made a number of recommendations to the Tribe: (1) the National Council should engage in a comprehensive review of the nation's electoral code; (2) the Election Board should strengthen election management; (3) the nation should create a comprehensive election procedures manual; (4) the nation should increase voter and civic education to heighten voter awareness and participation; and (5) voter registration should be increased.[16]

Case Studies: Election Procedures

Many Native nations have established election commissions or election boards that are empowered to oversee the conduct of all elections in the community, including for Tribal officials, referenda and initiative procedures, and recall or removal petitions. Here are excerpts from three Native documents—one from the Monacan Indian Nation, one from the Catawba Nation's constitutions, and one from the Articles of Association of the Ak Chin Indian Community. It is

242　INDIGENOUS GOVERNANCE

important to keep in mind that Native nations who established constitutions pursuant to the provisions of the Indian Reorganization Act, the Alaska Act, or the Oklahoma Indian Welfare Act are expected by BIA officials to follow certain procedures in crafting their election rules and regulations. Such procedures normally entail a section describing the first election authorized under the document, specifying qualifications of voters and candidates, filing of a nominating petition to be declared a candidate, providing detailed procedures for each election, establishment of an election board that is independent from the governing body to reduce potential conflict of interest, and so on.[17]

Monacan Nation (Constitution, 2022)

Article 9: Elections

Section 1. Voters
Any enrolled citizen of the Monacan Indian Nation (MIN) who is eighteen or older may vote in any election or special election.

Section 2. Election Commission

1. There shall be an Election Commission to conduct all elections in a fair and impartial manner in accordance with the laws of the MIN. The Election Commission shall select one of its members to serve as the Chairman of the Election Commission. The Election Commission shall have the power to set its own policies and the procedures for election in accordance with this Constitution with the approval of the General Council. The Tribal Council shall not have executive or administrative authority over the Election Commission, except in the event of malfeasance.
2. An Election Commission shall be seated by the last day of October every other year.
3. Members of the Election Commission shall not be nominees on the ballot of the current election they will be overseeing. Immediate family members of candidates may not serve on the commission.
4. The Election Commission will consist of the following: two citizens from Amherst County, two citizens from Rockbridge County, one at-large citizen, and two Monacan elders.

Section 3. Nominations
To be considered eligible to run for office, the prospective candidate must be an enrolled tribal citizen with complete and correct paperwork. Nominations must

be supported by ten signatures of verified Monacan citizens. A candidate must have been an enrolled citizen for a minimum of four years before being eligible to run for office.

Section 4. Qualifications for Nomination

In order to run for any office within the MIN you must be an enrolled citizen of 18 years or older. A candidate must have no felony convictions that fall under the category of 'Mala in-se'; 'Mala Prohibitum' convictions do not apply.

Catawba Nation Constitution (1995)

Article VII: Elections

Section 1. General and Special Elections

(a) General elections, at which the General Council votes for Executive Committee members, shall be held in odd-numbered years on a Saturday in July, as established by the Election Board. The Election Board shall establish the date of the election no less than six months before the date is scheduled.

(b) Special elections shall be held when called for by this Constitution.

Section 2. Election Board

The General Council shall appoint an Election Board to conduct, supervise, and oversee all elections, including special elections. The Election Board shall ensure the provisions of this Constitution and the Election Ordinance are faithfully administered and followed. The Election Board shall consist of members of the General Council. Members of the Election Board are not eligible to run for elected office within the Nation and cannot be an immediate family member of a candidate for elected office. The term 'immediate family' means a person's spouse, children, parents, and siblings. The Election Board may appoint clerks, poll workers, and others to assist the Election Board with conducting elections.

Section 3. Election Ordinance

The General Council shall enact an Election Ordinance to govern all elections of the Catawba Indian Nation. The ordinance shall include provisions for the time, place, and manner of voting, absentee voting, walk-in voting, ties, the settlement of election disputes, including the right to appeal the results to the Tribal Court, procedures for swearing in elected officials, a transition period between terms of elected officials, and all other voting procedures necessary for

244 INDIGENOUS GOVERNANCE

efficient administration of tribal elections, insofar as they are consistent with this Constitution. The Ethics Ordinance shall further include provisions on the appointment of the Election Board, lengths of terms, meeting procedures of the Election Board, and all other provisions necessary to determine the procedures of the Election Board.

Section 4. Qualifications of Voters
The General Council, consisting of citizens of the Catawba Indian Nation who are 18 years of age or older, shall have the right to vote in all tribal elections.

Ak Chin Indian Community Articles of Association (1961)

Article VI: Elections

Section 1. Any member of the Community twenty-one (21) years of age, or over shall be entitled to vote.

Section 2. The Council shall prescribe election regulations with respect to the dates thereof, polling places, election committees and their duties, absentee balloting, and any other requirements thereof.

Case Studies: Who Qualifies for Office?

Candidates for Tribal office—be it legislative, executive, or judicial—vary widely but typically include a residency requirement, education minimum, proof of blood quantum or lineal descendancy, appropriate age, and no criminal record. In some nations, like the Navajo, cultural requirements are also laid out. For instance, candidates for the presidency of the nation "must fluently speak and understand Navajo and read and write English."[18]

Gila River Indian Community Constitution (1960)

Article VI: Qualifications of Officers

Section 1. No person shall be elected or hold office as Governor, Lieutenant Governor, Chief Judge, Associate Judges, or Councilmen unless he (1) is a member of the Community; (2) has reached the age of twenty-five (25) years; (3) has been living in the particular district he is to represent for at least sixty (60) days immediately preceding the election; (4) has been living on the Reservation for at least one year immediately preceding the election. Additional qualifications may be prescribed by ordinance.

Section 2. No person who, within the year preceding the election, has been convicted of a crime involving moral turpitude shall be eligible to hold office in the Community.

Fort McDermitt Paiute and Shoshone Tribe Constitution (1936)

Article II: Qualifications for Office

Any person to be elected as an officer or councilman must be a member of the Fort McDermitt Paiute and Shoshone Tribe and over 25 years of age at the time of his or her election.

(a) No person who has been convicted of a felony shall be elected as an officer or councilman.

(b) The Tribal Council shall be the sole judge of the qualification of its own members.

Yavapai-Apache Tribe Constitution (1992)

Article VIII: Elections

Section 3. Qualifications for Office

(a) Any member of the Yavapai-Apache Tribe shall be eligible to run for tribal office if he:
 (1) is at least twenty-five (25) years of age, and
 (2) is a resident of the reservation for at least two (2) years or has resided within ten (10) miles of any lands within the jurisdiction of the Tribe for at least two (2) years, and
 (3) has no misdemeanor convictions within the last five (5) years or felony convictions within the last fifteen (15) years, and
 (4) has a high school degree or its equivalent, or has sufficient experience for a position on the Tribal Council.

(b) The requirement of sufficient experience shall be demonstrated to the Election Board. The Election Board shall base its decision on the experience of the prospective candidate relevant to the duties of the Tribal Council.

246 INDIGENOUS GOVERNANCE

    (c) If the Election Board decides that a prospective candidate does not have sufficient experience it shall do so in writing giving specific reasons for its decision. An adverse decision by the Election Board may be appealed to the Tribal Court.

Dry Creek Rancheria Articles of Association (1973)

Unlike constitutions, most of the Indigenous nations that operate under Articles of Association or Incorporation do not spell out in detail what a candidate's qualification for public office must entail. Documents tend to read like this provision from the Dry Creek Rancheria's set of Articles: "Any member of the Tribal Council, eighteen (18) years of age or older shall have the right to vote and if duly nominated and elected may hold office. All elections, whether for office or referendum, shall be by secret ballot. Notice of an election shall be given in writing seven (7) days prior to the election day. Nomination of officers shall be held every two years at the Tribal Council meeting in September. The date for the election is to be selected at this meeting. A member must be present at the site of the election to vote."

Case Studies: Grounds for Recall or Removal from Office

While the U.S. president and congressional members are not subject to recall, eighteen states have legal provisions to hold recall elections that allow voters to remove governors and other state officials from office before their term ends.[19] Likewise, well over 200 Indigenous governments have provisions for the expulsion and automatic forfeiture from office of elected officials. The purpose of a recall provision is to establish the grounds by which a Tribe's voters may by petition force an election to be held regarding whether an elected official should be removed from office. Expulsion enables elected and authorized Tribal officials to remove another Tribal official for various reasons, such as neglect of duty or misconduct. And automatic forfeiture provides, for example, that an official automatically forfeits office if they expire, resign, or are convicted of specific crimes or are shown to lack the required qualifications for office.[20] In some cases, Native elites are choosing to banish, expel, or formally disenroll those officials who are charged with particular offenses, such as fraud, improper conduct, or neglect of duty.

ELECTORAL POLITICS   247

White Mountain Apache Tribe Constitution (1993)

Article VII: Removal from Office

Section 1. Forfeiture or Resignation of office. If a Chairman or Vice-Chairman or any member of the Council resigns, fails or refuses to attend two regular meetings in succession unless excused due to illness or other causes for which he or she cannot be held responsible, or shall be convicted of a felony or of a misdemeanor involving moral integrity, or has been found guilty of public intoxication, or is guilty of consuming any alcoholic beverages while attending a meeting of the Council in session, or during any daytime recess period, the Council shall declare his or her position vacant.

Section 2. Vacancies. Any vacancies on the Council or any vacancy in the office of Vice-Chairman resulting from the application of the section immediately preceding shall be filled at once by a majority vote of the Council. A vacancy in the office of Chairman shall be filled by the Vice-Chairman. Persons so appointed shall serve the unexpired term of the office or member.

Alturas Indian Rancheria Constitution (1972)

Article VI: Vacancies and Removal

Section 1. If an officer shall die, or resign, the office shall be automatically vacated. Any office which is vacated shall be filled within thirty (30) days of the date it becomes vacant by a special election at a general council meeting called for this purpose by the business committee unless such vacancy occurs within sixty (60) days of the regular biannual election. Such replacement officer shall serve the unexpired term of office.

Section 2. Not more than ten (10) days after receipt of a petition requesting the removal from office of an elected official, which petition shall set forth the specific reasons for which removal is sought and shall be signed by not less than fifty-one percent (51%) of the voters, the business committee shall call a general council meeting to hear the charges against the official. It shall at the same time notify the accused in writing of the charges against him and of the date, hour and place of the general council meeting at which time he may appear and answer those charges. After the accused has had full opportunity to be heard by the general council, a secret ballot vote of guilty or not guilty will be conducted. The decision of a majority of those present and voting shall govern, providing at least fifty-one percent

248 INDIGENOUS GOVERNANCE

(51%) of those eligible to vote shall vote. If the official is found guilty by such vote, his office shall be automatically vacated and the general council shall proceed to nominate candidates and elect a replacement official who shall serve the unexpired term of office. Such general council meeting shall be held within thirty (30) days of the date that a valid petition for removal action is filed with the business committee.

Section 3. In neither of the elections provided for in this article shall absentee ballots be cast.

Confederated Tribes of the Chehalis Reservation Constitution (1973)

Section 1. Vacancies

If a member of the Chehalis Business Committee or other official shall die, resign, be removed from office, or be found guilty while in office of a felony or misdemeanor involving dishonesty in any Indian, State or Federal Court, the business committee shall declare the position vacant and shall appoint a successor to fill the unexpired term.

Section 2. Removal

The community council, by majority vote, may remove any member of the Chehalis Business Committee or other official for neglect of duty or gross misconduct. However, such member or official shall be given a written statement of the charges against him at least ten (10) days before the meeting of the community council before which he is to appear and shall be given an opportunity to answer any and all charges at the meeting before vote is taken in the matter.

Chippewa Cree Indians of the Rocky Boys Reservation Constitution (2004)

Article V: Vacancies, Removal and Recall

Section 1. If any elective official shall die, resign, permanently leave the reservation, or shall be found guilty while in office of a felony or misdemeanor involving dishonesty in any Indian, State or Federal court, the Business Committee shall declare the position vacant and direct the Election Board to call a special election to fill such vacancy. The candidate receiving the highest number of votes shall be elected. If six (6) months or less remain before the next primary election the vacated position shall remain vacant until it is filled at the general election following that primary, except as provided in Section 1 (f) of the bylaws.

Section 2. The Business Committee may by an affirmative vote of at least five (5) members expel any member for neglect of duty or gross misconduct provided that the accused member shall be given full and fair opportunity to reapply to any and all charges at a designated committee meeting. It is further stipulated that any such member shall be given a written statement of the charges against him at least five (5) days before the meeting at which he is to appear.

Section 3. A majority of those who participate in such election must favor recall in order for it to become effective provided those who vote constitute at least fifty (50) percent of the registered voters. Only one (1) recall attempt may be made for any tribal official during a given term of office. No recall petition shall be acted upon until at least six (6) months of the term has expired. No more than one (1) official at a time may be considered for recall.

Case Studies: Role of Traditional Offices in Native Elections

Official federal policy toward Native peoples from the 1860s until the adoption of the Indian Reorganization Act in 1934 entailed the destruction of Indigenous cultures, identities, religions, institutions, languages, and legal systems. Notwithstanding this ethnocidal assault, as discussed in previous chapters, a variable measure of traditional systems of governance persevered. Thus, by the time John Collier, Felix S. Cohen, and Nathan Margold arrived on the political scene in 1933 and dramatically moved to reorient federal policy away from cultural eradication to cultural renewal, Native people were in various states of governmental distress. Some nations were practically bereft of traditional institutions; whereas some had been able to retain and were still utilizing historic governing structures and official titles, like chiefs and headmen in their governments.

When Felix S. Cohen wrote his "Basic Memorandum on Drafting of Tribal Constitutions" in 1934, a report that offered advice to those nations who were preparing constitutions, that document included a section titled "Place of Chiefs in Tribal Government."[21] It began with this sentence: "The place of traditional chiefs, headmen, or other office (such as the caciques of the pueblos) in tribal government presents a very delicate problem on certain reservations."[22] Delicate indeed. The United States had tried mightily to eradicate such leadership positions during the previous six decades, and now the government was offering some support for those Native nations that had somehow been

250 INDIGENOUS GOVERNANCE

able to sustain these traditional positions. Some Tribal leaders, of course, had no desire to incorporate traditional leaders in their organic documents, but others insisted on reserving spaces for chiefs or headmen positions—typically through selection rather than election. As Cohen remarked: "Where these titles are generally recognized by members of a tribe, the Indian Office will not object to any constitutional provision assigning such individuals regular governmental powers."[23] Cohen urged that the Tribes' constitution contain explicit language recognizing traditional leadership positions. "Where the traditional methods of appointing new chiefs or removing old chiefs are still known and respected and are still practicable," Cohen said, "it should be possible to state in the tribal constitution in simple language what this method is. If this method involves secret matters, it would be enough to provide that the chiefs or caciques should be chosen or deposed according to the ancient customs of the tribe, and that any dispute that may arise over those matters should be finally settled by the tribal court, by the tribal council, or by some other designated body."[24]

At the present time, the selection or election of a chief, clan, or religious leader in some Native communities sometimes leads to considerable disagreements as to who has the right to legitimately hold such positions, for how long they will serve, and even how they are chosen. And as Tilden said, "Since it belongs to the area of core tribalism, there is usually no resort to outside forums, such as a federal court to determine who legitimately holds such position."[25]

Here are a few examples of traditional leadership offices laid out in contemporary Native governing documents.

Orutsaramuit Traditional Native Council (1983)

Section 1. Traditional Chief. There shall be one (1) Traditional Chief who shall be elected by the members of the Orutsararmuit Native Council. He shall be a lifetime Chief.

Section 2. Duties. He shall call to order all Orutsararmuit Native Council meetings and be seated at the head of all Native Council functions. He shall attend, when available and able, any potlatches, social functions, meetings, as the Traditional Chief of the Orutsararmuit Native Council.

ELECTORAL POLITICS 251

Native Village of Georgetown (1999)

Article X: Honorary Chief

Section 1. Election. There shall be one Honorary Chief who shall be elected by the majority vote of the qualified members of the village. He/She shall be a lifetime Chief, be one-fourth (1/4) or more Alaskan Native and be a member of the Georgetown Tribe. He/She must have a sincere belief and knowledge of the traditional values and he/she must have practiced those values throughout his/her life.

Section 2. Duties. He/She shall act as an advisor to the Council. He/She shall call the meeting to order. He/She shall attend, when available and able, any potlatches, social functions and meetings as an Honorary Chief of the Georgetown Tribe.

Wampanoag Tribe of Gay Head (Aquinaah) (1995)

Section 2. Lifetime Positions. There shall be two lifetime positions with the tribe. These shall consist of a Chief and a Medicine Man. Donald Malonson, Chief and Luther Madison, Madison Man, shall continue to hold these positions under this constitution.

(a) Responsibilities. The Chief and Medicine Man may attend meetings of the tribal council and may be called upon to present their advice to the council but they may not vote nor may they be counted in order to achieve a quorum at any council meeting. They may, at the request of the council, represent the tribe at social or official functions where a representative of the tribe is appropriate.

Confederated Tribe of the Warm Springs Reservation (1938)

Section 3. Term of Office. Members of the Council shall be elected for terms of three years except that the chiefs shall serve for life, and their successors shall be selected in accordance with tribal custom.

252 INDIGENOUS GOVERNANCE

Red Lake Nation (1958)

Article IV: Governing Body

Section 1. The governing body of the Red Lake Band of Chippewa Indians shall be the Tribal Council and shall consist of 8 district representatives and 3 officers.

Section 2. In addition to the governing body there shall be an Advisory Council composed of 7 Hereditary Chiefs of the Band. The 7 chiefs shall serve in an advisory capacity to the Tribal Council and shall continue in office until the office vacated by voluntary resignation or by death. Successor chiefs shall then be chosen by the governing body by majority vote in accordance with tribal tradition and in the terms of this Constitution.

Campaign Finance and Native Elections

States have for many years set at least some minimal standards and limits on campaign finance and spending activities for elections. In fact, "most states ban Election Day expenditures; all prohibit bribery and vote buying; and each imposes some form of public disclosure and reporting of campaign receipts and expenditures."[26] The Watergate scandal in the 1970s fueled a surge of campaign finance legislation—making it the most rapidly growing body of election law at the time.

Data for whether a similar movement involving Tribal elections in Indian Country is, unfortunately, simply not available at the moment. What we do have is at least a meager amount of data that centers around how gaming revenue—beginning in the 1990s—provided at least a few Native nations with opportunities to employ both talented and sometimes nefarious lobbyists, like Jack Abramoff and Michael Scanlon, and savvy public relations firms and to make ever-increasing campaign contributions to state and national candidates in an effort to wield political influence, establish political alliances, and to defeat those who held views inimical to Indigenous interests.[27] In 2017 alone, Native governments and individual Natives donated over $17 million to both Democrat and Republican office seekers.[28]

Our focus, of course, is on internal Native electoral systems and campaign financing of Tribal elections. However, while there is some publicly available data on Tribal campaign contributions to non-Native candidates, there is far less accessible data on campaign financing in Native elections. The Navajo Nation Code is available, however, and Title II, which deals with elections, has detailed information governing all aspects of elections. Before any election campaign, all candidates must file a report with the Board of Elections giving the name(s) of the individual(s) who will serve as their financial agent, or they must declare that they have not authorized anyone to serve in this capacity.

Navajo candidates are also required, within thirty days of the election's conclusion, to file a "sworn and signed itemized statement of receipts and expenses" which details the money or other things of value the candidate has received during the course of the campaign. Failure to provide this list will preclude the winning candidate from taking office and will subject that person to a fine of not less than $300 or more than $500. There are also express limitations on how much candidates may spend in both the primary and general elections. Presidential and vice-presidential candidates can spend a maximum of $1.50 per registered voter. For the offices of council delegate, chapter official, or other elected officials, candidates are allowed a maximum of $4.00 per registered voter "within the election precinct" the candidate is running from. A candidate violating these campaign expenditure limits is guilty of an offense punishable by a fine of no less than $300 but no more than $1,000, by a jail term of no more than six months, or both. The candidate is also barred from holding any Navajo Nation office for five years.

Radio and television time that is donated on an equal basis to all qualified candidates is not factored into the expenditure limitations but must still be reported. Finally, the law explicitly decrees that it is unlawful for any nonmember of the nation or any corporation "to make any contribution of money or anything of value for the purpose of campaigning or influencing a Navajo election." However, local radio or television stations may make free airtime available so long as equal time is offered to all other candidates. Non-Native individuals who break this law will be expelled from the Reservation, and corporations who violate the law will be barred from any lease, right-of-way, or franchise for at least one year but not more than five years.

More recently, in 2022 the Cherokee Nation's Rules Committee recommended a modification to the nation's election code aimed at ending the introduction of "dark money" by any outside "corporation, partnership, and/or other legal entity" to Cherokee political candidates. The measure was unanimously approved by the Council, 15–0, which adopted a new law making "any person or entity that tries to make undisclosed donations . . . subject to prison time, a $5,000 fine and civil penalties of up to $500,000."[29] This law was precipitated by the actions of a non-Native political group called "Cherokees for Change," located in Oklahoma City, which in 2019 had contributed a large sum of money to David Walkingstick, a candidate for Principal Chief of the Cherokee Nation. Walkingstick was later disqualified from running, but the campaign contribution from this outside non-Indigenous group compelled Todd Hembree, the nation's attorney general, to investigate their activity.[30]

254 INDIGENOUS GOVERNANCE

Native Elections and Accountability

The overwhelming majority of members of the Native public rely on elections as their principal form of political action. When conducted fairly, regularly, and freely, they are the most peaceful means of linking Tribal citizens with their governing elites and institutions. Unlike non-Native voters who generally rely on a given political party—Democratic, Republican, or Independent—to assist them in their voting choices, Indigenous citizens in their elections appear to make their choices based on notions of kinship, the ideological orientation of the voter, issue positions taken by the candidate, whether those in office have performed well, and the candidate's personal attributes. But until we have a great deal more research conducted on Indigenous elections, we will be unable to answer even the most basic questions on how Native electoral politics differs from or is like that of their neighboring polities.

10

Political Economics

As we have noted throughout the text, while Native governments share many structural and bureaucratic features with their state and federal counterparts, they also exhibit profound differences that mark them as truly unique polities. Philip (Sam) Deloria, in two separate works, discussed two of those crucial differences. First, in an essay in 1978, he observed that Native governments are charged with "providing services for people whose educational, health, and economic level is far below that of the general population . . . and running profitable and competitive businesses."[1] These dual, sometimes conflicting roles, compound Tribal governments' performance of their governmental functions of regulating, taxing, and delivering services.

Second, in a report written in 1984, Deloria discussed the relationship between Native governments and the cultures they are bound to protect. While noting that non-Native governments also have some responsibility in perpetuating social and cultural values in the form of compulsory education, democracy, and the market economy, Indigenous governments, by contrast, "are seen by many as protectors of Indian cultures whose existence is perceived to be constantly threatened. Thus, tribal governments tend to sense that every major policy decision and every significant new direction taken could conceivably lead to irreversible damage to a threatened culture . . . This special relationship of tribal government to Indian culture dominates every facet of tribal policymaking and inculcates a caution and a conservatism which are marks of most tribal policy."[2]

And these differences are especially pronounced when it comes to the subject of this chapter—the political economies of Indigenous governments. By political economy I mean the broad relationships of individuals to society, the economy, and their government. Unlike purely economic approaches which emphasize growth and efficiency, the political economy paradigm, as Peter A. Gourevitch put it, emphasizes a much broader range of goals:

> Arguments are made on behalf of the quality of income, opportunity, and participation in public life; over notions of social justice, health, safety, housing, security, a good society, a protective 'net' for each citizen; over the role of leisure, culture, and individual fulfillment; over gender, ethnicity, race, and other elements of social relationships; over environmental quality and preservation of resources . . . All of these goals have an economic component. At a minimum

Indigenous Governance. David E. Wilkins, Oxford University Press. © Oxford University Press 2024.
DOI: 10.1093/oso/9780190095994.003.0011

they involve resources and the allocation of resources. They involve the use of politics to interact with the economy in order to attain these goals.[3]

In other words, this approach acknowledges the role that politics plays in the economic choices a nation makes and it also examines values, culture, and the community in the context of the institutions and interests of a given nation.

Native governments, since their sustained encounters with Europeans and Euro-Americans, have always faced a seemingly intractable set of politically inspired obstacles and constraints that frustrate their efforts to become more economically self-sufficient: a profound loss of human life and staggering territorial dispossession; a daunting history of coercive assimilation and federal colonialism that has severely constrained the abilities of Native nations to be self-determined; a Congress that has never fulfilled its treaty and trust obligations to these nations; a Supreme Court that is sometimes openly antagonistic to the idea of the retention of Native nations lands, religious beliefs, and other rights; state governments that sometimes formulate racist, inconsistent, or no policies at all that lead to appropriation of Native resources and that exacerbate ever-present jurisdictional tensions; a still grossly underdeveloped physical infrastructure; and an undereducated labor force, to name but a few of the more obvious hurdles.

These interrelated and overlapping factors paint a deeply unflattering economic picture for a majority of the 574 recognized Native nations. As the U.S. Commission on Civil Rights detailed in its powerful and damning report in 2018, "Broken Promises: Continuing Federal Funding Shortfalls for Native Americans," a follow-up to their 2003 report, "A Quiet Crisis: Federal Funding and Unmet Needs in Indian Country," over "25 percent of Native Americans live in poverty, which is higher than the poverty rate of any other racial group in the U.S."[4] In addition, for Natives living on one of the 326 reservations (this broad term includes Pueblos and Rancherias) the unemployment rate, in 2018, was about 50%, "and for certain reservations, the average unemployment rate [was] much higher, hovering around 80% or higher."[5]

These figures, as daunting as they are, pale in comparison to the employment landscape on reservations during the early months of 2020 when the COVID-19 pandemic first appeared. Every Native casino, typically the largest revenue producer for most of the nations that have them—generating over $32 billion in 2017—was shuttered for several weeks, some even longer, causing a devastating economic collapse for many of the 273 Native nations operating a little over 500 gaming facilities across twenty-nine states. More on gaming later in this chapter.

Besides a high poverty rate and an exceptionally high unemployment rate, there is also a substantial wage gap—the median household income for Natives was only $39,718 in 2016, one-third less than that of white Americans.[6] Furthermore, according to the National Congress of American Indians, additional economic

POLITICAL ECONOMICS   257

challenges include a shortage of employment opportunities, lack of access to essential utilities and clean water, constraints in accessing natural resources, complex regulatory burdens, problems generated because of climate change, limited access to capital, and so on.[7]

A Central Governmental Purpose: Economic Vitality

Native peoples historically relied on their extensive kinship system and intimate and sustainable relationship with the flora and fauna of the natural world to maintain stable and cohesive societies in which every member of the community was valued. In Paul Radin's assessment on Native communities, he remarked that "irrespective of the type of political organization and the method of food production, irrespective of whether society is socially stratified or unstratified, democratic or monarchical, or whether the food economy is that of the food-gatherer, the hunter-fisher, the agriculturist or the pastoral-nomad, all aboriginal peoples accept the theory that every human being has the inalienable right to an irreducible minimum, consisting of adequate food, shelter and clothing. This irreducible minimum is an attribute of life on a par with the biological attributes of life."[8]

This moral mandate continues to flow through the collective memories of Native political elites in many nations today. It was this communal ethic that federal policymakers sought to eradicate in earnest, beginning in the 1870s. The next several decades, as Frankie Wilmer showed, included policies that aimed at "replacing the traditional communal economic base with a system of private property; intensified education, primarily through boarding schools; the regulation of every aspect of Indian social life, including marriage, dispute settlement, and religious practice; the granting of citizenship; . . . and finally allowing the Indian tribes to become self-governing by adopting constitutions ultimately subject to the approval of the U.S. government."[9]

Thus, as the Indian Reorganization Act (IRA) neared adoption in 1934, John Collier, the Commissioner of Indian Affairs, issued a circular letter on January 20 in which he laid out the two broad purposes for those Native nations that were preparing to adopt the IRA and write constitutions. "1. To establish Indian self-government and to promote a healthy and satisfactory community life. 2. To preserve and develop Indian lands in Indian ownership and to provide the opportunity of economic livelihood for all who choose to remain within the Indian community."[10]

A close examination of the preambles—introductory statements that explain the purpose for which a constitution is devoted—of a number of Native constitutions and Articles of Association bear out that economic development

258 INDIGENOUS GOVERNANCE

was a central reason the government was being organized, at least from the federal government's perspective.

Case Studies of Tribal Preambular Statements on Economic Orientation

Confederated Tribes of the Chehalis Reservation Constitution and Bylaws (1939)

We, the Indians of the Chehalis Reservation in the State of Washington, in order to continue the formal community organization established in 1939 by the adoption and approval of our original Constitution and bylaws, do hereby establish this version of a Constitution and bylaws to handle our reservation affairs and improve the *economic condition of ourselves and our posterity*. (emphasis added)

Constitution of the Native Village of Brevig Mission (1963)

We, a group of Alaska Natives, having the common bond of living together in Brevig Mission, Alaska, by this declaration assert our freedom as a sovereign people within boundaries of the United States of America, in order to . . . 4) help our members achieve their highest potentials in education, physical and mental health, and *economic development*. (emphasis added)

Cahto Tribe of the Laytonville Rancheria, Articles of Association (2006)

We the people of the Cahto Tribe of the Laytonville Rancheria, a federally recognized Indian Tribe, do hereby adopt this updated Articles of Association of the Laytonville Rancheria in order to: promote the common good and well-being of the Tribe; protect and preserve our culture and traditions including our language, arts and crafts, and archaeological sites; protect our land, water and natural resources; promote and protect the health and welfare of our people; encourage and promote educational opportunities for members of the Tribe; *foster economic development*; protect the individual rights of our members; acquire additional lands for the benefit of the Tribe; promote self-government and ensure the political integrity of the Tribe; preserve, secure and exercise all the inherent sovereign rights and powers of an Indian tribe. (emphasis added)

Other nations incorporate language regarding economic development in those sections of their organic documents that lay out the powers of the governing body of the nation—be it a Tribal Council, a General Council, or some other entity. For example, the constitution of the Federated Indians of Graton Rancheria (2012), in Article III, Section I, declares that the seven-member Tribal Council, elected from the General Council (all adult members), shall be the governing body of the Tribe. Of the fourteen enumerated powers, #5 states:

> To manage the economic affairs of the Tribe including the power to: borrow money and provide for the repayment thereof, manage all economic affairs and enterprises, create tribally-owned and/or chartered corporations, create or license tribal not-for-profit, or other business entities, charter and license tribal or citizen owned corporations organized under any relevant provision of Title 25 of the United States Code, employ and discharge tribal of the Tribe, administer any funds or property within the control of the Tribe for the benefit of the Tribe and its citizens, officers or employees, allocate tribal funds as loans or grants, transfer tribal property and other assets to tribal organizations for such use as the Tribal Council may determine to be appropriate, invest tribal funds, and exercise such other bodies, except as may be limited by this Constitution.[11]

And the Constitution of the Burns Paiute Tribe of Oregon (updated in 1997) says simply that one of the powers of the Business Committee is "to manage all economic affairs and enterprises of the community."[12] Finally, the Articles of Incorporation of the Rappahannock Tribe of Virginia (adopted in 1921) declares that "the purpose of the Tribe is to meet the educational, social, cultural, religious, and economic needs of the Rappahannock Indian people. It is the goal of the Tribe to maintain the Rappahannock bloodline and culture for the perpetuation of its people."[13]

Political–Economic Opportunities and Challenges across Native America

Before the 1970s, a majority of Native nations, with important exceptions, were in an economically depressed and fragile position because their governing bodies, inherent powers, and economic choices were subject to the overarching dominance of the Bureau of Indian Affairs and the Department of the Interior. Those two offices wielded the power to review and veto all major Tribal decisions. Meanwhile, most Native governments had no significant sources of revenue to support themselves save for the few energy-rich nations with lands laced with coal, gas, and oil. But even those energy resources provided only precious few

260 INDIGENOUS GOVERNANCE

dollars because of the federally sanctioned leasing structures that had been in place for many decades.[14] This dire situation changed dramatically in the 1970s because of three important developments, best expressed by Tom Biolsi:

> First, a new cadre of younger tribal members came on the scene who had gained experience at both politics and public administration (and who had imbibed the idea of community self-determination) from their employment in the federally sponsored Community Action Programs on the reservations in the late 1960s and early 1970s . . . Second, new sources of tribal revenue began to appear with the opening up of federal grants to tribes under the Johnson Administration's Office of Economic Opportunity, and with the enactment of the Indian Self-Determination Act . . . by which tribes became eligible to assume the management of local BIA service delivery on reservations, along with federal funding for those services . . . Third, a new political ideology was spreading rapidly in Indian Country: the notion of recovering tribal sovereignty. The sources of this ideology were complex. A key source was the political alliance between urban, activist Indian people and 'traditionalists' or 'full-bloods' on the reservations who had always insisted upon the centrality of treaty rights in defining the political status of Indian people."[15]

Native America has not looked back since. The advent and the subsequent explosion of legally sanctioned gambling operations across Indian Country, beginning in the late 1980s, dramatically expanded the revenue streams of a number of Native nations and despite COVID-19's shocking physical and socioeconomic impact on Native communities, federal infusion of much-needed dollars to Tribal nations helped them weather the difficult early months of the pandemic, and gaming operations have now carefully reopened. Let us now turn our attention to some of the ways Indigenous governments are looking to increase revenue to pay for administrative costs and to provide the services and benefits community members need and expect.

Taxation

Taxes are a prime source of revenue for virtually all governments, including the federal and state governments, with taxing power being an essential governmental attribute. The federal government relies on tariffs (a tax on imported goods), income taxes, and excise taxes levied on specific products like tobacco, alcohol, and others. State governments also depend upon revenue gleaned from taxes—including personal income taxes, real property taxes, excise taxes, sales taxes, motor fuel taxes, corporate income taxes, and estate and inheritance taxes, among others.

Native nations did not tax within their communities historically, and there were no treaty provisions dealing with an Indigenous taxing authority.[16] But several federal court opinions,[17] as early as 1893, affirmed that Native nations retained the power to tax or impose fees on both Tribal members and non-Native persons and their business operations. Importantly, as Tribes' taxation powers are inherent, "it would seem," says Felix S. Cohen, "that the tribal taxing power is not subject to limitations imposed upon state or federal legislation by the Federal Constitution."[18]

Additionally, Native nations with trust lands enjoy at least one advantaged position with regard to tax policies that other racial and ethnic groups do not share. Indigenous trust lands and the income from those lands are not subject to taxation; nor are the businesses conducted on reservations that are owned by Natives.[19] Of course, Natives also face political, legal, and constitutional constraints not suffered by other minority groups, as described above, but the non-taxability dimension is important to keep in mind.

After the IRA was enacted in 1934, Felix S. Cohen, the assistant solicitor, and Nathan Margold, the solicitor general, authored an important opinion titled "Powers of Indian Tribes," that enumerated and described the inherent political powers of federally recognized Tribal nations, including their taxing authority: "Chief among the powers of sovereignty recognized as pertaining to an Indian tribe is the power of taxation. Except where Congress has provided otherwise, this power may be exercised over members of the tribe and over nonmembers, so far as such nonmembers may accept privileges of trade, residence, etc., to which taxes may be attached as conditions."[20]

This was deemed critical since Collier, Cohen, and Margold all understood that while the federal government was still expected to fulfill its treaty and trust-based obligations to Tribal nations in the areas of law enforcement, land records, and the like, there would be some functions a Native nation might wish to support for which federal appropriations might not be available. In these cases, they would need to resort to taxes, and the most popular taxes, if they can ever be termed popular, would be those imposed on non-Natives or non-members living on or doing business within the community.[21]

It is important to note, however, that the fact that Native governments have until recently only sporadically used taxes to support their government operations does not mean that they have not secured revenue from Tribal members. As the American Indian Policy Review Commission found in their 1977 final report to Congress: "Tribal governments often take their operating costs out of the common fund derived from tribal revenues from resources held in common by the tribe. Rather than distribute the money, assess a tax, and re-collect revenues,

262 INDIGENOUS GOVERNANCE

they simply appropriate the needed revenues in the first instance. Revenues from resources controlled by the State and Federal governments are treated in much the same way."[22]

A search of the constitutional database reveals that nearly 170 Native nations in the lower 48 states and Alaska contain explicit taxation authority in their governing documents. There is an interesting range of tax clauses in these documents. Many of the constitutions established pursuant to the IRA read like the following provision found in the Cheyenne River Sioux Constitution of 1935. It states that the Tribal Council has the power "to create and maintain a tribal treasury; to accept donations from any person, state or the United States; to raise revenue through taxation, *subject to the review of the Secretary of the Interior*; and to regulate commerce. Any money collected hereunder shall be expended as provided for in Article IV, Section 1(g) of this constitution." (emphasis added) The clause, "subject to the review of the Secretary of the Interior" served as a reminder that the Cheyenne River Sioux and similarly situated Indigenous nations were legally embedded in an unequal power position vis-à-vis the federal government.

A more general clause regarding taxation authority is found in Article 3 of the Wyandotte Nation of Oklahoma's constitution which says that "an essential governmental function is considered to be any activity, including but not limited to taxation, conducted by the Wyandotte Nation, which is designed to raise revenue for the Nation, to provide governmental services for its membership and/or enhance the economic base of the Nation for the benefit of the Nation."

Other nations' taxation clauses contain language stressing that certain limitations apply. Take, for instance, the Constitution of the Big Lagoon Rancheria (amended 1985) of California which notes that one of the powers of the Business Council is "to impose taxes on all persons, property and any business activities located or conducted within tribal jurisdiction; provided no tax shall be imposed on real property in trust by the United States of America." More interesting are those Tribal nations, like the Hopi Tribe of Arizona and the Native Village of Egegik, whose constitutions prohibit the imposition of taxes without the explicit approval of the people via a referendum. The Egegik Constitution states, "No taxes or assessments may be levied without a referendum of the eligible voters of the village." The Hopi Constitution, adopted in 1936, is more emphatic and expressly declares via a contested amendment in December 1993—278 voted yes, 213 voted no—not only that there must be a referendum before any taxes were levied, but also that "the Tribal Council shall not have the power to impose a personal income tax."

While the doctrine of inherent sovereignty as expressed in Tribal organic documents, ratified treaties, and ample Native and federal case law confirms Native nations' power to tax since the late nineteenth century, Native governments have not been on the same economic footing with states or the federal government and face persistent constraints in their efforts to tax persons or businesses within their borders who are not members or citizens of their nations. Susan M. Williams identifies some of those obstacles: "First, military action against Indian people has created Indian communities with tremendous economic needs and few financial resources. For this reason, Indian tribal governments typically are faced with a tax base that is much weaker than the tax base drawn on by state and federal governments. In addition, the problems posed by a fundamentally weak tax base are exacerbated by overly aggressive state taxation policies that seek to implement double-taxation within Indian Country." Williams goes on to note that "federal law now allows states to collect certain taxes on non-Indians on Indian reservations. But the non-Indians typically comprise the bulk of the reservation's economy, so states leave little room for tribal taxation. Finally, as mentioned above, non-Indian businesses often seek to exploit loopholes in federal law that allow them to take the benefit of governmental services in Indian communities without paying their fair share of taxes to tribal governments."[23]

Most damning for Indigenous efforts to tax non-Native businesses was the U.S. Supreme Court's 2001 decision, *Atkinson Trading Company v. Shirley*,[24] which held that the Navajo Nation lacked the authority to require a non-Native hotel owner, whose establishment was situated on privately held land located within the boundaries of the Navajo Reservation, to collect from hotel guests an occupancy tax that the Tribe had instituted in 1992. This ruling meant that Native nations' authority over non-Natives living on fee-simple land, even while nestled within a reservation and receiving services, benefits, and protections from a Tribal government, was "sharply circumscribed."[25]

Notwithstanding the uneven nature of the taxation situation, Native governments are forging ahead with increasingly more robust tax programs to raise vital revenue. Many Native governments[26] have established tax commissions, tax codes, and other arrangements to oversee this important aspect of governance. Take, for example, the Navajo Nation, which in 1974 was one of the first Indigenous governments to establish a Tax Commission to study the viability of imposing taxes to generate revenue. The first two taxes were established in 1978—the Possessory Interest Tax (PIT), a type of ad valorem tax; and the Business Activity Tax (BAT), a type of modified gross receipts tax. Since then, seven additional taxes have been created: (a) oil and gas severance tax (1985); (b) hotel occupancy tax (1992); (c) tobacco products tax (1995); (d) fuel excise tax (1999); (e) sales tax (2002); (f) liquor tax (2015); and (g) junk food tax (2015). The sales tax effectively replaced the BAT tax for most sales. The tax rate, as of 2021, was 6% of the gross receipts. This important tax is imposed on all sales of goods and services throughout the Navajo Nation. It is the responsibility of the seller to collect the tax which is usually imposed on the consumer.

These taxes did not go unchallenged by non-Native individuals and businesses who questioned the Navajo Nation's authority to tax. While the nation's authority to tax corporations without securing the approval of the Secretary of the Interior had been upheld in *Kerr McGee Corporation v. The Navajo Tribe* in 1985,[27] its authority to tax non-Natives on non-Native fee land located within the Reservation's boundaries was denied in the U.S. Supreme Court's 2001 ruling, *Atkinson Trading Company v. Shirley*.[28] Taxes have become the largest internal source of revenue for the Diné Nation. In 2019 and 2020 alone they generated over $220 million. See Table 10.1 which charts the revenue generated by the nation's taxation program for those two years.

The Swinomish Indian Tribal Community in Washington state, in 2003, created its Utility Business Activity Tax Code as a way for the community to raise additional revenue that would help support essential services like public sewage collection systems, water systems, roads, social services and education programs, Tribal police, and so on, for the entire reservation population—both Natives and non-Natives. As part of its strategy to raise revenue, Swinomish officials declared that "there shall be collected from each utility doing business within the Reservation a business privilege tax equal to three percent (3%) of the utility's gross receipts generated from retail sales within the Reservation."[29]

Even as increasing numbers of Native governments move ahead with taxation programs, they can never relax because some states continue to seek to impose taxes on Tribal business operations even in the face of legal constraints and the reality of Tribal Sovereignty. For instance, in a legal conflict dating back to 2014, the state of South Dakota, led by Governor Kristi Noem, sought to impose a use tax on non-member purchases of food and other items at the Royal River Casino owned by the Flandreau Santee Sioux Tribe in South Dakota. The state had lost in the federal district court in 2017 and the Eighth Circuit in *Noem v. Flandreau Santee Sioux Tribe* held that the state was not assessing taxes in return for governmental functions performed for those paying the tax, which meant the state could not impose the tax.[30] The state appealed to the U.S. Supreme Court which denied the state's petition without comment on May 26, 2020.

Fortunately, not all states mimic South Dakota's contentious relationship with Native governments. In fact, one method that is being increasingly used by Indigenous governments to raise money is Tribal–State compacts, contracts, or agreements that are negotiated between Native governments and state officials. These are binding documents on specific issues—whether dealing with water, gaming, cross deputization of police, or for our immediate purposes, taxation arrangements dealing with motor fuels, and cigarettes, among other items.

Table 10.1. Recent tax revenue collections

FY 2019	1st Quarter	2nd Quarter	3rd Quarter	4th Quarter	TOTAL
Possessory Interest	15,022,679	311,586	14,203,767	211,499	29,749,531
Business Activity	2,642,157	2,638,574	1,348,348	1,156,484	7,785,563
Oil and Gas Severance	1,757,729	1,860,491	2,011,976	1,880,163	7,510,359
Hotel Occupancy	429,616	348,705	245,667	489,361	1,513,349
Tobacco Products	5,174	53,952	50,459	34,924	144,509
Fuel Excise	3,454,686	2,967,257	3,345,046	3,596,392	13,363,381
Sales: Non-Retail	5,750,424	5,268,647	5,729,934	4,721,341	21,470,346
Sales: Retail	1,894,203	1,825,959	1,817,220	2,049,793	7,587,175
Total	30,956,668.00	15,275,171.00	28,752,417.00	14,139,957.00	89,124,213.00

FY 2020	1st Quarter	2nd Quarter	3rd Quarter	4th Quarter	TOTAL
Possessory Interest	16,309,330.00	217,115.00	15,769,060.00		32,295,508.00
Business Activity	3,150,372.00	2,080,982.00	2,390,726.00		7,622,080.00
Oil and Gas Severance	1,997,599.00	2,531,056.00	2,660,191.00		7,188,846.00
Hotel Occupancy	498,959.00	337,894.00	345,571.00		1,182,424.00
Tobacco Products	89,851.00	42,957.00	25,237.00		158,045.00
Fuel Excise	4,097,332.00	3,041,198.00	3,824,995.00		10,963,525.00
Sales: Non-Retail	5,840,604.00	7,262,624.00	5,207,339.00		18,310,567.00
Sales: Retail	1,927,507.00	1,932,341.00	2,070,768.00		5,930,616.00
Total	33,991,557.00	17,446,167.00	32,293,887.00		83,651,611.00

Source: https://www.tax.navajo-nsn.gov/

266 INDIGENOUS GOVERNANCE

Tribal–State relations are fraught with difficulty, including the corrosive issue of jurisdictional ambiguity. As one commentator put it:

> Excise taxes on sales between Indians in Indian country are not taxable by the state. On the other hand, Indian sales to non-Indians in Indian country are subject to state excise taxation. But states have no legal authority to require tribes to collect taxes on Indian sales to non-Indians in Indian country, so states regard such taxes as evaded and lost. While the Supreme Court has found that tribes are supposed to collect and remit state excise taxes on sales to non-Indians in Indian country, the sovereign status of tribes makes it very difficult for states to force them to remit state tax revenue.[31]

To avoid costly and uncertain lawsuits, Native governments and state officials have found it in their best interests to forge tax agreements that allow both governments to administer their overlapping territories more easily, while recognizing their parallel sovereignties. Altogether, more than 200 Indigenous governments in at least eighteen states have crafted compacts involving taxes.[32] In Oklahoma, by 2001, Native governments and the state had negotiated thirty-two tobacco tax compacts and twenty-nine motor fuel agreements with many of the thirty-one recognized Native nations.[33] As of 2019, Oklahoma is one of fourteen states that has negotiated formal motor-fuel tax agreements with Tribal governments.[34]

Some of these tax agreements deal with competition—with states looking to ensure that product prices on items sold on Tribal land are approximately equal to the prices of comparable items sold outside Indian Country—while others focus on means of maximizing revenue.[35] A variety of approaches appear in these cooperative agreements, including "dividing or sharing tax revenue, levying only tribal taxes, tax collection at the wholesale level, state refunds to tribal members, or exemptions for certain entities or individuals."[36]

As one example, in Nebraska, the Winnebago Tribe ended a long gas tax battle with the state by negotiating a compact that specifies that the Tribe and the state agreed to a revenue sharing process, "with the tribe collecting 75% of taxes from reservation-based gas sales. It then sends a quarterly check to the state for the state's 25 percent share."[37]

The National Congress of American Indians website provides examples of a number of other Tribal–State Tax Agreements between multiple states—Washington, South Dakota, Montana, South Carolina, New Mexico, Michigan, and others—and at least thirty-six Native nations sharing territory with those states. In Michigan alone, ten Native governments—the Grand Traverse Band of Ottawa and Chippewa, Bay Mills Indian Community, Hannahville Indian Community, Little River Band of Ottawa, Little Traverse Bay Bands of Odawa,

Match-E-Be-Nash-She-Wish Band of Pottawatomi, Nottawaseppi Huron Band of Potawatomi, Pokagon Band of Potawatomi, Saginaw Chippewa Indian Tribe, and the Sault-Ste. Marie Tribe of Chippewa—have forged compacts with these states in recent years.

Gaming

When the Commission on the Review of the National Policy Toward Gambling issued its final report in 1976, legalized gambling was still relatively scarce. Only thirteen states had lotteries. Nevada and New York were the only two states that had approved off-track wagering, and there were no casinos outside Nevada. A great deal has changed since that time. Legal gambling, euphemistically known as *gaming*, is now ubiquitous and is an accepted part of the social and economic landscape throughout the United States and in many countries around the world.

In the United States, in 2023, a person could make a legal wager in every state except Utah and Hawaii. Forty-five states operate lotteries, forty-four have casinos, and twenty-nine have racetrack betting. State lotteries generated $80.55 billion, commercial gaming produced $41.2 billion, pari-mutuel wagering generated $295 million, and charitable games and bingo produced $2.15 billion. All told, the American Gaming Association estimates a $261 billion annual economic impact from legal gambling across the country.[38]

Indian Country has likewise seen an exponential increase in gaming since Native governments were encouraged to enter the field during President Reagan's administrations as a means to offset the president's devastating budget cuts.[39] In 2019, 248 Native nations were operating over 500 gaming facilities across twenty-nine states. In that year, gaming revenue reached a high of $34.6 billion. Less than a year later, in a letter written by Randall Akee, Miriam Jorgensen, Eric C. Henson, and Joseph P. Kalt, all affiliated with the Harvard Project on American Indian Economic Development, to then-Treasury Secretary Steve Mnuchin on April 10, 2020, regarding allocation of COVID-19 response funds, the writers laid out in broad strokes how important gaming had been for Indigenous governments in the last thirty years and why the complete shutdown of all gaming operations, effective in mid-March 2020, because of the pandemic was having such a devastating impact on Tribal governments and their economies. Revenues for the fiscal year 2020 were reduced by nearly 20% to $27.8 billion.

According to the authors:

- As tribal enterprise and government operations are choked off, the states and regions in which tribes are embedded face the loss of more than $127

billion in annual spending on goods and services, more than 1,100,000 jobs, and more than $49.5 billion in wages and benefits for workers.
- The *largest* share of lost jobs and lost income would be borne by non-Indians. Our estimates indicate that approximately 70% of the impact—915,000 jobs, with wages and benefits totaling $40.2 billion—would be suffered by non-Indian workers. These 915,000 jobs are a larger total than the entire civilian labor forces that were employed in thirteen of the fifty states immediately prior to the onset of the COVID-19 crisis.
- The spending and jobs supported by tribal economies have been generating more than $9.4 billion in tax revenues for state and local governments. The companion figure for the federal government is estimated to be almost $16 billion.
- Prior to the total shutdown of their casinos, tribes' gaming enterprises alone were channeling more than $12.5 billion per year into tribal government programs.[40]

Figure 10.1 depicts the expansion and contraction of gross gaming revenue (ggr) from Native gaming operations from 2000 to 2020.

And see Figure 10.2 which shows the revenue range across Native nations between 2016 and 2020.

Native gaming revenue, prior to COVID-19, provided a number of Indigenous nations with a steady source of revenue that improved healthcare, education, cultural renewal, and public safety services. This revenue has also been used to improve long-neglected development of physical infrastructure, such as the construction of hospitals, schools, government buildings, water projects, and roads.

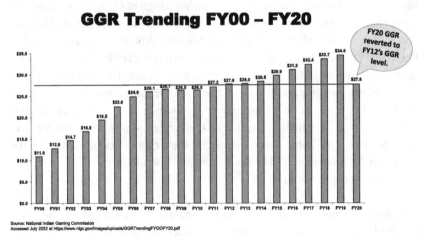

Figure 10.1. GGR Trending FY00–FY20

FY16-FY20 Gaming Revenues by Range

NIGC Tribal Gaming Revenues

Gaming Revenue Range	Number of Submissions	Revenues (in thousands)	Percentage of Submissions	Percentage of Revenues	Mean (in thousands)	Median (in thousands)
Submissions with fiscal years ending in 2020						
$250 million and over	22	$10,250,430	4.2%	36.8%	$465,929	$419,028
$100 million to $250 million	58	$9,667,030	11.1%	34.7%	$166,673	$162,040
$50 million to $100 million	43	$3,179,021	8.2%	11.4%	$73,931	$73,656
$25 million to $50 million	65	$2,396,995	12.4%	8.6%	$36,877	$36,114
$10 million to $25 million	101	$1,646,696	19.3%	5.9%	$16,304	$15,721
$3 million to $10 million	94	$566,973	17.9%	2.0%	$6,032	$5,714
Under $3 million	141	$125,271	26.9%	0.5%	$888	$551
Total	524	$27,832,416				
Submissions with fiscal years ending in 2019						
$250 million and over	33	$15,829,916	6.3%	45.2%	$473,634	$386,361
$100 million to $250 million	62	$10,444,602	11.9%	30.2%	$168,461	$165,864
$50 million to $100 million	54	$3,798,391	10.3%	11.0%	$70,341	$66,958
$25 million to $50 million	67	$2,360,435	12.8%	6.8%	$35,230	$34,292
$10 million to $25 million	97	$1,630,332	18.6%	4.7%	$16,808	$16,186
$3 million to $10 million	90	$594,918	17.2%	1.7%	$6,610	$6,824
Under $3 million	119	$119,948	22.6%	0.3%	$1,008	$721
Total	522	$34,578,542				
Submissions with fiscal years ending in 2018						
$250 million and over	34	$15,702,390	6.8%	46.6%	$461,835	$381,315
$100 million to $100 million	59	$9,658,287	11.8%	28.6%	$163,700	$163,221
$50 million to $100 million	52	$3,668,802	10.4%	10.9%	$70,554	$68,739
$25 million to $50 million	69	$2,439,840	13.8%	7.2%	$35,360	$33,559
$10 million to $25 million	94	$1,554,036	18.8%	4.6%	$16,532	$16,277
$3 million to $10 million	91	$500,180	18.2%	1.8%	$6,485	$6,675
Under $3 million	102	$106,033	20.4%	0.3%	$1,040	$910
Total	501	$33,719,569				
Submissions with fiscal years ending in 2017						
$250 million and over	33	$15,016,824	6.7%	46.3%	$455,058	$383,066
$100 million to $250 million	56	$9,058,782	11.3%	28.0%	$161,764	$164,374
$50 million to $100 million	54	$3,767,470	10.9%	11.6%	$69,768	$69,893
$25 million to $50 million	68	$2,382,602	13.8%	7.4%	$35,038	$32,287
$10 million to $25 million	91	$1,494,558	18.4%	4.6%	$16,424	$15,748
$3 million to $10 million	89	$575,005	18.0%	1.8%	$6,461	$6,754
Under $3 million	103	$108,586	20.9%	0.3%	$1,054	$883
Total	494	$32,403,927				
Submissions with fiscal years ending in 2016						
$250 million and over	33	$14,429,246	6.8%	46.3%	$437,250	$363,632
$100 million to $250 million	51	$8,286,641	10.5%	26.6%	$162,483	$166,810
$50 million to $100 million	57	$4,011,478	11.8%	12.9%	$70,377	$67,928
$25 million to $50 million	67	$2,290,160	13.6%	7.3%	$34,182	$32,673
$10 million to $25 million	96	$1,561,863	19.8%	5.0%	$16,269	$15,826
$3 million to $10 million	85	$521,096	17.6%	1.7%	$6,131	$6,420
Under $3 million	95	$95,055	19.6%	0.3%	$1,001	$723
Total	494	$31,195,549				

Source: National Indian Gaming Commission
Accessed July 2022
https://www.nigc.gov/images/uploads/reports/2020GGRChartsFY16FY20GamingRevsByRange.pdf

Figure 10.2. FY16–FY20 gaming revenues by range

Native interest in gaming has been primarily driven by job creation, generating a large employment source on many reservations.

In fact, it is gaming and the sometimes-impressive revenues gaming generates that have had the largest positive impact on the economic situation of a number of Native nations. Gaming's impact has not been uniform, of course, across Indian Country. But overall, and notwithstanding COVID-19's dark impact in shuttering Native casinos for several months in 2020, the impact has been profound. Why has this been the case? Randall K. Q. Akee, Katherine Spilde, and Jonathan Taylor discuss several of the more important factors. First, Native nations entered gaming early in the industry's growth cycle. Second, while some areas of the country saw several Tribes begin gaming, in many other cases a single Native nation might be the only operator. Third, Native nations worked tirelessly and were smart in setting their gaming operations up. They started conservatively, "sometimes with temporary buildings, to avoid overcapitalizing their businesses while assessing what was, in the early 1990s, a poorly understood opportunity."[41] Fourth, Tribal leaders wisely went to capital markets, hired established law firms, brought in management consultants, and used their own economic savvy to take advantage of available opportunities. While noting that not every Native gaming operation succeeded, unlike many of the federally proposed economic choices,

270   INDIGENOUS GOVERNANCE

"gaming development was self-determined and grew with internal consistency checks and market feedback."[42]

By the end of March 2020, the pandemic had forced Native gaming operations to close their doors in an attempt to slow the spread of the virus. These closures hit the vast majority of Native governments and their citizens hard since many governments have come to rely heavily on gaming-generated revenue to fund government operations, provide money for infrastructure, and to support social, cultural, and economic progress for their citizens and other residents. One commentator estimated that within just the first two weeks of shuttering their gaming doors in March and June 2020, the following impacts were projected on the U.S. economy: $4.4 billion in lost economic activity; 728,000 people out of work; $969 million in lost wages; and $631 million in lost taxes and revenue sharing received by federal, state, and local governments.[43] The direct impacts on Native governments and community members were estimated to be $1.5 billion in lost economic activity (gaming and non-gaming revenue to casinos); 296,000 people without work; $332 million in lost wages; and $240 million in lost taxes and revenue sharing received by federal, state, and local governments.[44]

COVID-19 devastated the entire United States and quickly spread across the globe. Congress responded in March 2020 by enacting the Coronavirus, Relief, and Economic Security Act (CARES Act)[45] which provided desperately needed economic relief to much of the country. The Trump Administration initially fought against providing any direct aid to the 574 recognized Native nations. But Senate Democrats and the Congressional Native American Caucus successfully pushed back and ensured that $8 billion of the funding was set aside for Native governments, although even after they were slated to receive those funds the Treasury Department held up distribution of the monies for over a month, as Elizabeth Warren and Deb Haaland frustratingly described in an op-ed to the *Washington Post* on May 26, 2020. As they interpreted the situation: "The federal response to covid-19 in Indian country is unacceptable—and the American people strongly agree. New surveys from Data for Progress found a bipartisan majority of Americans support increasing funding for the Indian Health Service, holding the federal government legally responsible for upholding its treaty obligations, including health care, and allowing Native nations to interact directly with the federal government to receive aid instead of going through states. The same goes for prioritizing federal aid for hospitals and other essential services needed by communities of color and Native communities that are disproportionately exposed to air pollution and covid-19."[46]

Besides the sheer difficulty in securing the $8 billion, there was the added conflict that erupted within the Indigenous community as to whether Alaska Native Corporations (ANC) were "governments" entitled to a share of the $8 billion or whether the money could only be dispensed to Native governments. This became a major legal battle that ultimately found its way to the U.S. Supreme Court. In *Yellen v. Confederated Tribes of the Chehalis Reservation*,[47] Associate Justice Sonia Sotomayor, writing for a 6–3 majority, held that for purposes of the CARES Act, ANCs were indeed "Indian tribes" as defined under the Indian Self- Determination Act of 1975. ANCs were established under the authority of the Alaska Native Claims Settlement Act (ANCSA) of 1971,[48] and since ANSCA was the only statute the Indian Self-Determination Act "Indian Tribe" definition mentioned by name, Sotomayor and the majority declared that this was satisfactory proof that they had been "recognized" as "Tribes" for purposes of the CARES Act.

The Confederated Tribes of the Chehalis Reservation, the Ute Indian Tribe of the Uintah and Ouray Reservation, and many other Native nations had argued that the ANCs did not qualify as "Indian Tribes" because they had never been formally recognized by a governmental entity or Congress as a sovereign Tribe. In other words, they did not have a "recognized governing body."[49] Furthermore, they asserted that according "Tribal" status to the ANCs would increase competition for governmental funding and would jeopardize the authority of bona fide Tribal governments. Many ANCs, they argued, were already financially well off and they suggested that the ANCs would use Tribal status to advance their commercial interests.

Sotomayor, a staunch liberal, was joined in her opinion by several hard conservatives—including Chief Justice John G. Roberts, Brett M. Kavanaugh, Amy Coney Barrett, and Samuel A. Alito—while the dissent was an interesting coalition of left-leaning Elena Kagan and two stark conservatives, Clarence Thomas and Neil Gorsuch. Sotomayor, in rebutting the Tribes' arguments said that "federal recognition is usually discussed in relation to tribes, not their governing bodies." In addition, she said that the ANC's Board of Directors was equivalent to a governing body as a matter of corporate law. "Indeed," said Sotomayor, respondents do not dispute that the plain meaning of 'recognized governing body' covers an ANC's Board of Directors."[50]

Although Native gaming operations slowly began to reopen by mid-2020 the economic, health, social, and educational impact of COVID-19 continued to cause profound harm to Indigenous communities. After Joe Biden's contested election to the presidency, he worked with Congress to secure additional economic relief for the American people and Native governments. Thus, when Biden signed into law the American Rescue Plan Act (H.R. 1319) on March 11, 2021, $350 billion in emergency funding for state, local, territorial, and Tribal governments was made available to help those governments deal with the ongoing ravages brought on by COVID-19. States were allocated $195 billion, local governments were to receive $130 billion, territories secured $4.5 billion, and Native nations were set to receive $32 billion—with $20 billion of that

272   INDIGENOUS GOVERNANCE

amount dedicated to helping Tribal governments recover and stabilize their communities. For Native nations, this was the largest amount of federal funding ever appropriated in a single congressional measure.

Tribal governments may only use the $20 million in four specific ways and the funds must be spent by December 31, 2024:

(a) to respond to the public health emergency with respect to the Coronavirus Disease 2019 (COVID-19) or its negative economic impacts, including assistance to households, small businesses, and nonprofits, or aid to impacted industries such as tourism, travel, and hospitality;

(b) to respond to workers performing essential work during the COVID-19 public health emergency by providing premium pay to eligible workers of the State, territory, or Tribal government that are performing such essential work, or by providing grants to eligible employers that have eligible workers who perform essential work;

(c) for the provision of government services to the extent of the reduction in revenue of such State, territory, or Tribal government due to the COVID-19 public health emergency relative to revenues collected in the most recent full fiscal year of the State, territory, or Tribal government prior to the emergency; or

(d) to make necessary investments in water, sewer, or broadband infrastructure.[51]

Governmental recipients, including Native governments, also learned that if they failed to comply with the provisions of subsection (c) they would be required "to repay to the Secretary an amount equal to the amount of funds used in violation of such subsection."[52]

The federal government's $32 billion investment of COVID-19 funds to Native communities will help enormously, especially for those nations that were traumatized by the shutdown of their casinos and affiliated businesses and by the devastating health toll the coronavirus wreaked. A few Native communities, however, fared better than many others. For example, the San Manuel Nation, at the urging of a former Chairman, Deron Marquez, in 2015 had decided to prepare for the possibility of a situation where a catastrophic event might occur that could force his nation's government to completely close down its hugely successful gaming operation. Marquez referred to it in 2015 as the "Doom's Day Scenario." The nation already had established two distinctive accounts—the Operating Fund and the Resource Fund, both of which were meant to provide sufficient resources to meet the fiscal obligations of the nation "in a timely manner independent of revenue produced by the gaming operation . . . protect the Tribe from a short-term business interruption . . . [and] short-term unexpected decline in free cash flow due to a decline in revenue from the casino."[53]

But Marquez implored his nation's leaders to think even deeper about the possible ramifications to the community if and, in his opinion, when, a truly calamitous event like COVID-19 occurred. That conversation propelled the San Manuel Nation's Business Committee to modify their preparations for the unforeseen but possible future event, to continue to diversify their economic operations, and consider expanding their land base as a possible hedge against some future development. The nation's subsequent economic decisions in preparation for this Doom's Day Scenario paid off and when COVID-19 landed with full force, even though the casino and some of their businesses were closed for a time, no employee lost their job, and the nation was able to weather the economic difficulties in relatively good form.

Similarly, the Nottawaseppi Huron Band of Potawatomi also planned well ahead and like San Manuel had made the strategic decision to diversify their economy so that it would not be over-reliant on gaming. The Band owns the Fire Keeper Casino located in Battle Creek, Michigan. Well before the pandemic struck the Band had established a non-gaming body known as Waséyabek Development Co., LLC, which focused on three sectors: commercial real estate (30%), commercial operating businesses (40%), and federal contracting (30%). As Deidra Mitchell, President and CEO of Waséyabek Development put it at the height of the pandemic: "Our commercial real estate has remained largely unaffected. It has built us a nice asset base that we've been able to count on and a steady revenue stream. We've been very, very lucky, but it was because we decided to diversify completely away from gaming associated companies."[54]

By most accounts, Native casino operations have reopened, and according to Kate Spilde, who specializes in gaming, many Native gaming operations are doing remarkably well considering the overall state of the U.S. economy. She noted that many Tribal governments had cut their marketing, created leaner casino operations, and reduced their payroll and, as a result, were seeing higher profit margins.[55] One area of concern is a labor shortage that is affecting Native gaming and many other sectors of the larger economy. Many individuals have opted to leave the hospitality industry, making it difficult to staff hotels, restaurants, and casino operations.[56]

Indigenous Lands: The Foundation of Sovereignty

For Native peoples the world over, including North America, lands and waters and the species and resources appurtenant to those lands and waters constitute the heart of their identities, their livelihoods, and serve as the foundation of their

274 INDIGENOUS GOVERNANCE

kinship relations to one another and the natural world. As the original peoples of the Americas, the nearly 600 Native communities had intimate contact, knowledge, and kin-based relations with virtually every corner of the continent. As European powers arrived, however, later supplanted by the newly formed United States, the intimate relations between Native nations and their lands, waters, and resources would be fundamentally disrupted and transformed.

Under persistent pressure, Native peoples gradually and grudgingly lost title to most of their lands via several hundred treaties and agreements (valid and fraudulent), outright federal land confiscations via statutes, policies, executive orders and court rulings, and other activities that slowly but inexorably overwhelmed them. By the late nineteenth century, and in part because of the 1887 General Allotment Act[57] and its amendments—which authorized the president to negotiate with many nations for a division of their reservations into farm-sized plots that were then issued to individual Tribal members, with the remainder of unallotted land being declared "surplus," then purchased by the government for a pittance of their actual value, and finally thrown open to white settlers for homesteading—Native lands were dramatically reduced even further.

By 1900 Indigenous nations had cumulatively lost title to more than 2 billion acres, with most of the loss occurring between the 1850s and 1900. The United States had purchased about half that amount via treaties or agreements, while another 32.5 million acres, according to Russel L. Barsh, had been "confiscated unilaterally by Act of Congress or executive order without compensation."[58] Finally, another 725 million acres in the lower 48 states and Alaska were taken by the federal government "without agreement or the pretense of a unilateral action extinguishing native title."[59] In fact, by the time the Indian Reorganization Act (IRA) was enacted in 1934, Native landholdings had dwindled even further to a meager 47 million acres. The non-Natives' voracious quest for Native land had finally been satiated but at the expense of Indigenous peoples.

This staggering amount of land loss by Native nations was one of the dominant reasons compelling John Collier to pursue the Commissionership of the Bureau of Indian Affairs as he sought an office that would enable him to initiate policy changes that might save the remainder of Native lands and possibly begin to rebuild that grossly shrunken landmass. Thus, the first section of the IRA categorically declared "that hereafter no land of any Indian reservation, created or set apart by treaty or agreement with the Indians, Act of Congress, Executive order, purchase, or otherwise, shall be allotted in severalty to any Indian."[60] Relatedly, Section 2 restored perpetual federal trust protection on remaining Native lands—those held in common and individual trust allotments—so those lands could not be taxed by the state and therefore not be foreclosed upon for nonpayment of taxes. Section 3 authorized the Secretary of the Interior to "restore to tribal ownership the remaining surplus lands of any Indian reservation" and

Section 4 gave the Secretary the power to make "voluntary exchanges of lands of equal value" in an attempt to consolidate Native lands. Finally, Section 7 gave the Secretary authority to establish new reservations and to "add such lands to existing reservations."[61]

As many Tribal nations voted to adopt the IRA and to establish constitutions and charters of incorporation under the Act, their organic documents generally included clauses describing their lands. The first IRA Tribal constitution, approved on October 28, 1935, was that of the Confederated Salish and Kootenai Tribes of the Flathead Reservation. Article I—Territory, states: "The jurisdiction of the Confederated Salish and Kootenai Tribes of Indians shall extend to the territory within the original confines of the Flathead Reservation as defined in the Treaty of July 16, 1855, and to such other lands without such boundaries, as may hereafter be added thereto under any law of the United States, except as otherwise provided by law."

Other Native nations have adopted more expansively defined understandings of what constitutes their territorial homeland and where their jurisdiction extends to. Take, for instance, this statement from the Articles of Association of the Ak-Chin Community in Arizona which declares that

> the territory of the Ak-Chin Indian Community shall include all lands within the exterior boundaries of the Ak-Chin Indian Reservation, all lands held by the Community, any person, or the United States for the benefit of the Community, and any additional lands acquired by the Community or by the United States for the benefit of the Community, including, but not limited to, all lands, both subsurface, water, air space, natural resources, and any interest therein, notwithstanding the issuance of any patent or right-of-way in fee or otherwise, or any other instrument in land, by the government of the United States or the Community, existing or in the future."[62]

Some nations emphasize that their territorial rights can and often do extend beyond the confines of their reservation, especially when treaties have confirmed reserved rights on lands ceded during treaty negotiations. For example, the Confederated Tribes of the Chehalis Reservation were careful to delineate their treaty-confirmed hunting and fishing rights in areas outside their reservation boundaries: "The jurisdiction of the Confederated Tribes of the Chehalis Reservation shall extend to the territory within the present boundaries of the Chehalis Indian Reservation as established by Executive Order of July 8, 1864, and to such other lands without such boundaries as may hereafter be added thereto under any law of the United States, except as otherwise provided by law. However, nothing in this article shall be construed as restricting the hunting and

276 INDIGENOUS GOVERNANCE

fishing rights of members, including the right to take fish in usual and accustomed places as provided by treaty or executive order."

Finally, the small and recently recognized (1990) San Juan Southern Paiute Tribe, nestled within the exterior boundaries of the expansive Navajo Nation Reservation, explicitly describes their territory and the trust-shared resources they have in tandem with the United States: "Section 1. Territory. The territory of the San Juan Southern Paiute Tribe shall include, to the fullest extent possible consistent with federal law, all lands, water, property, airspace, surface rights, subsurface rights and other natural resources in which the Tribe now or in the future by the United States for the exclusive or non-exclusive benefit of the Tribe or for individual tribal members, or which are located within the boundaries of a reservation which may be established for the Tribe, notwithstanding the issuance of any right-of-way."

More recently, in 2020, the Muscogee (Creek) Nation, which coexists alongside the state of Oklahoma, had their territory's reservation status acknowledged and reaffirmed in a dramatic Supreme Court decision, *McGirt v. Oklahoma*. In this case, the High Court had to answer two essential questions: (1) whether the land the Muscogee secured in several nineteenth-century treaties constitutes an Indian reservation for purposes of federal Indian law; and (2) whether Jimcy McGirt, a Seminole, who had committed heinous crimes against a four-year-old girl, had committed those crimes in Indian Country. Associate Justice, Neil Gorsuch, writing for a 5–4 court, answered both questions in the affirmative. Thus, the state of Oklahoma had no right to prosecute McGirt, or any Native, for crimes committed within the boundaries of the 3 million-acre Muscogee Reservation.

Tribal governments are the single largest landowner on most reservations. They were able to retain some of their original landholdings throughout the treaty and allotment eras, and the IRA provided resources for some nations to recover other lands both within and without the reservation through land purchases and consolidation programs. Today, Native reservations and trust lands amount to about 56 million acres. Alaska Native Corporations and its villages control another 44 million acres under provisions of the Alaska Native Claims Settlement Act of 1971.[63] Increasingly, largely as a result of the 2009 *Cobell* class action lawsuit and settlement act,[64] which provided an opportunity to pursue measures for addressing the problem of fractionated lands and heirship rights, the Land Buy Back program for Native nations, which implements the land consolidation component of the *Cobell* settlement, as of 2019, had expended $1.6 billion of the settlement act and had consolidated over 893,000 fractionated land interests—equaling another 2.6 million acres of land—and returned them to Tribal trust status. Furthermore, "Tribal ownership now exceeds 50% in 17,700 more tracts of land as a result of the Buy Back Program; this represents an increase of more than 144% for the locations where implementation has occurred."[65]

While *Cobell* was being settled, the Secretary of the Interior drew upon Section 5 of the IRA to place more land under trust status for Native governments. During the Obama era, "the Interior Department took over 500,000 acres of land into trust for more than 100 Indian tribes."[66] Of course, other nations have used portions of their gaming revenue to purchase additional acreage, both within and outside their existing territorial borders to benefit their growing populations and business ventures.

While some Native governments now have the economic wherewithal to purchase new lands, once accomplished, they then face the daunting task of having those lands placed under trust status by the Department of the Interior. The concept of *trust* is multifaceted and complex, encompassing in one commonly understood definition, a notion of federal responsibility to assist Indigenous peoples in the protection of their lands, resources, and cultural heritage through policy decisions and management actions that affirm the distinctive political, legal, and moral relationship between the federal government and Native nations as set forth in the U.S. Constitution, diplomatic arrangements (i.e., treaties), statutes, executive orders, and court decisions. The trust doctrine, along with treaties and congressional plenary power, is a foundational concept underlying the relationship between Native nations and the federal government. But despite its foundational quality, there is no universally agreed-upon definition of what the trust relationship entails. In fact, there are many questions about this important concept that remain largely unanswered. Consequently, uncertainty and ambiguity reign supreme when an effort is made to gain a clear understanding of what the trust doctrine actually entails.

A majority of political and legal commentators, jurists, and federal policymakers posit that the trust doctrine is an ancient and entrenched, if ambiguous, presence overarching the Indigenous–federal relationship. The trust doctrine has been delineated in three different ways. First, it is found in the international law doctrine of trusteeship, initially broached in papal bulls (policy statements issued by the Pope) and related documents dating to European nations' first encounters with Indigenous peoples in the fifteenth and sixteenth centuries when European secular and religious officials assumed a theoretical, if not actual, protectorate position vis-à-vis Indigenous peoples based on their alleged physical, cultural, technological, and religious inferiority.

Second, there is an implied notion of trust evident in the many treaties and other diplomatic arrangements negotiated between Native nations, European states, and later the United States. In many of these contractual compacts, Tribal nations sold varying amounts of land to purchasing states. These negotiations formally recognized the sovereign status of the Indigenous parties, and, in addition,

278 INDIGENOUS GOVERNANCE

the Native peoples received various goods, exemptions, and protections. Hence, Native nations had the legal expectation and moral assurance that the federal government would fulfill the pledges and provisions it had made in exchange for the lands and other resources received from Native nations.

Third, a number of Supreme Court decisions have held that the federal government has a general trust relationship with Indigenous peoples and that the United States is the trustee of Native lands and resources, meaning that the federal government is supposed to act in good faith, with extreme loyalty, and in the best interests of the Native nations and individual Natives. The Supreme Court case typically cited as initiating the trust doctrine is *Cherokee Nation v. Georgia.*[67] In that decision, Chief Justice John Marshall observed in dictum that the relationship between Native nations and the federal government "resembles that of a ward to his guardian." Although this was merely an analogy, it is considered by many commentators to be the basis of the trust doctrine.

In addition, Congress, through major policies (e.g., the Snyder Act of 1921) and specific acts (Civilization Act of 1819), and the president, via specific policy pronouncements and executive orders, have underscored the unique legal and moral relationship between the federal government and Native nations. With so many sources contributing to an understanding of the trust doctrine, it is not surprising that there is significant uncertainty and ambiguity surrounding the concept. This is not an insignificant issue, given the symbolic and substantive importance of trust to the Indigenous–non-Indigenous political relationship.

Ironically, while the federal government has a generalized duty to act in good faith toward Native peoples, specific tasks are not necessarily required. In other words, while the trust obligation sometimes includes implied rights (e.g., a Native nation has a right to water even though the treaty/agreement makes no direct mention of a water entitlement), Native nations and individual members cannot insist that the United States carry out a specific activity unless the treaty, agreement, or statute expressly states what the obligation or commitment is.

And contemporary Supreme Court cases like *Lyng v. Northwest Indian Cemetery Protective Association,*[68] *Jicarilla Apache v. U.S.,*[69] and *Carcieri v. Salazar*[70] have, in some respects, dramatically constrained the meaning of trust as a term that benefits Native governments. *Lyng* held that because the trust doctrine was not constitutional-based, it was not enforceable against Congress or, in the case at hand, the U.S. Forest Service, and since the federal government "owned" the lands and National Forest, it had the inherent right to do what it wanted with those lands.

Jicarilla Apache invoked the doctrine of virtually absolute congressional plenary power—that the Congress has nearly untrammeled authority over all Indian affairs—and opined that the trust relationship actually spawned from the idea of legislative plenary power, leaving Native nations with little recourse. Associate

POLITICAL ECONOMICS 279

Justice Samuel A. Alito, writing for the court, harshly noted that "while one purpose of the Indian trust relationship is to benefit the tribes, the Government has its own independent interest in the implementation of federal Indian policy."[71]

Carcieri, handed down in 2009, is the decision that has proven most damning for Native nations looking to have newly acquired lands placed under federal trust status. Prior to this ruling, the process of having lands placed under federal trust was a fairly standard procedure tracing back to when a permanent trust was reinstated under the Indian Reorganization Act of 1934. Native trust lands are actually owned by the federal government in fee status but are held in trust for a Native nation or Native allottee who is considered the holder of a beneficial interest in their territory. Once the trust is established, federal law prohibits the Tribal nation or Native allottee from selling, leasing, mortgaging, or disposing of any part of the trust land without official approval from the Department of the Interior.[72]

Native trust lands are thus subject to concurrent jurisdiction by both the federal government and the Native government, and these lands constitute "Indian Country." State law, including the power to tax and regulate, does not apply in Indian Country unless Congress has enacted specific legislation authorizing the state to step in, as it did in enacting Public Law 280 in 1953.[73] Exemption from state jurisdiction is a principal reason motivating Native governments to have newly acquired land placed under permanent trust status. And this is what led to the *Carcieri* decision. In this case, the Narragansett Tribe of Rhode Island, who attained federal recognition in 1983, sought to have some lands they had secured placed under trust by the Interior Secretary. Instead, in an opinion by Associate Justice Clarence Thomas, the court created a bizarre distinction between Tribes that had been recognized prior to the 1934 Indian Reorganization Act, which lays out the procedures for placing lands into trust on behalf of Native nations, and Tribes that had more recently received federal acknowledgment. The High Court ruled that the Narragansett Tribe was not eligible to have its land placed in trust because it was not under federal jurisdiction in 1934 when the IRA was enacted. This destabilizing decision effectively created two categories of Native nations: those with lands under trust as of 1934, and those with lands not eligible for trust who became recognized after 1934. A vigorous campaign was launched in Congress that came to be referred to as the *Carcieri fix*, and numerous bills have been introduced over the years in an attempt to remedy this bifurcation of Indigenous lands by putting all federally recognized nations, no matter the date of their acknowledgment, on an equal footing. Thus far, none have been enacted.

Native nations can still have lands placed under trust, but the process has become extremely complicated, tedious, and time consuming. The Secretary of the Interior is now required to contact and consider the opinions of the state and even local governments before making their determination, especially as to how

280 INDIGENOUS GOVERNANCE

the removal of the lands in question from the state tax rolls will impact those polities. These governments have the right to appeal a decision that they believe goes against their interests. And if the land parcels in question have been designated by a Native government for use as a site for gaming, there are more restrictive burdens applied by the Secretary of the Interior before trust status can be obtained.[74]

Thus, there remains substantial tension between how the federal government articulates and exercises its trust relationship with Indigenous peoples— particularly when it is conducted in a paternalistic manner over Tribal and individual Native lands and resources—and how it supports Indigenous self-determination and self-governance, which presumably means that Native nations and individual citizens should be positioned to make major decisions on their own accord.

Ever present in the consciousness of some federal and state policymakers, members of the public, and even some Native individuals, is the view that capitalism, which presupposes a free market economy in Indian Country, in which distribution and exchange lie outside the control of the Native government and which can only occur when privatization of property is the norm, and the division of labor is present, is the best way for Native nations to move ahead economically speaking.[75] Individuals with such a mindset were responsible for many of the exploitative statutes and policies that left Native nations with little of their remaining lands or resources: the General Allotment Act of 1887, the imposition of Business Committees as the governing units of many Native communities in the late nineteenth and early twentieth century (many of which continue to function to this day), the Indian Reorganization Act of 1934, exploitation of the lands and resources of the Osage Nation and the Five Civilized Tribes in Indian Territory during the late nineteenth and early twentieth centuries, the federal termination and urban relocation programs in the 1950s and 1960s, the Alaska Native Claims Settlement Act of 1971, Indian gaming operations, and the list goes on.

For our purposes, it is the issue of privatization of lands within Indian Country that warrants the most attention. The Trump Administration strenuously tried to end federal trust protections and to privatize native trust lands in an effort to make those lands easier to exploit. For example, in March 2020 the BIA sought to rescind the trust status of the Mashpee Wampanoag Tribe's small reservation in Massachusetts. A federal court stepped in, however, and stopped this action, declaring that the Interior Department's actions were "arbitrary, capricious, an abuse of discretion, and contrary to law."[76] Trump officials continued their privatization efforts, claiming that trust status was a handicap to the economic interests of Native nations and individuals: "It is difficult, if not impossible, to use trust land as collateral for securing a loan. Legally, federal trust obligations create a very high threshold for lands to be alienated from tribes through repossession upon nonperformance of loans. Additionally, the experience of individual tribal landowners under the Allotment Act has led to a widely shared unwillingness to put additional Indian lands at risk. As a result, Native nations and their citizens have faced high hurdles in accessing capital through securitized lending, one of the basic drivers of economic and community development elsewhere in the United States."[77] These observers stress that privately held Native land would be better for collateralization, development, and alienation on the real estate market, toward wealth maximization.[78]

But as Carpenter and Riley note, while Native lands would benefit from a less arcane federal regulatory system, "recent federal interventions have sought to achieve economic efficiency in reservation development without full-scale dismantling of the trust relationship."[79] And the U.S. Commission on Civil Rights concurred, stating that "there is concern among advocates that privatization of lands can undermine cultural preservation of tribal lands, and protecting the tribal lands can contribute to greater prosperity in Indian Country."[80]

The value of Native land ownership, in terms of the amount of land in question (which is slowly expanding); efforts to consolidate it—propelled by the ravages of the Allotment Act and the fractionated heirship afterbirth of that dreaded policy; and the choices many Native governments are making in their struggle to protect their lands and waters from abuse and exploitation by extractive industries such as coal, natural gas, tar sands, and oil pipelines are viewed by many Indigenous leaders as one of the most profoundly important cultural, legal, and economic issues that have confronted them.

Indigenous cultural identity, values, and languages are the most evident factors distinguishing Natives from non-Natives. But it is the land, the waters, and the flora and fauna connected to those bodies that provide the foundation upon which these cultural expressions can manifest. As Deloria and Lytle put it, "The fundamental question of economic stability on the reservation revolves about the dilemma of whether the land is to be exploited, and therefore simply another corporate form of property, or to be a homeland, in which case it assumes a mystical focal point for other activities that supports the economic stability of the reservation society."[81]

Evidence of this more intimate and respectful approach to the natural world is beginning to appear across Indian Country in two forms: international diplomacy and extending rights to the natural world. Regarding international diplomacy, in the past fifteen years, several treaties have been forged between Indigenous nations—both within the United States and from other regions of the world—that are focused on affirming positive diplomatic relationships, protecting lands, air, and water from environmental degradation, restoring Buffalo and acknowledging their vital role in many Tribes' lives and livelihoods, prohibiting the use of their lands and waters for the production or transportation

282 INDIGENOUS GOVERNANCE

of tar sands, and honoring and protecting the grizzly bear and wolf populations. These treaties will be discussed in a later chapter.

And following the lead of Bolivia's former president, Evo Morales, an Indigenous citizen, who in 2010 helped rewrite that state's constitution and granted rights to the natural world, the Ho-Chunk Nation General Council approved a constitutional amendment in 2018 that recognizes the inherent rights of nature.[82] The Ponca Nation in October 2017 also acted to officially recognize the rights of nature after years of enduring pollution and earthquakes caused by fracking processes in Oklahoma. A year later the White Earth Band of Anishinaabe adopted a measure granting rights to their most cherished plant, Manoomin (wild rice), declaring that Manoomin had the "right to exist, flourish, regenerate, and evolve, as well as inherent rights to restoration, recovery, and preservation."[83]

In August 2021 Manoomin, along with the White Earth Band and several other Tribal citizens, brought suit in the Tribal court of the White Earth Band in an effort to prevent the state of Minnesota from granting the Enbridge Corporation the use of 5 billion gallons of water for the construction of an oil pipeline popularly known as "Line 3." This is "the first case brought in a Tribal court to enforce the rights of nature, and the first rights of nature case brought to enforce treaty guarantees."[84]

Three additional Indigenous governments have also recently acted to extend rights to elements in the natural world, in this case, rivers. The Yurok Tribe began efforts to grant legal rights to the Klamath River; the Menominee Nation declared that the Menominee River was entitled to rights; and the Nez Perce Tribe affirmed that the Snake River was a living being entitled to essential rights.[85] These developments are arriving at a pivotal ecological moment, given the grave conditions that global warming has already generated for the earth and particularly for Indian Country. In December 2022, for example, the Biden Administration pledged to give three Indigenous nations—Newtok Village and the Village of Napakiak, in Alaska, and the Quinault Indian Nation in Washington—$25 million per community to facilitate their relocation to higher ground because of rising water levels directly attributed to climate change.[86]

Energy Development—Climate Change Consequences

There are numerous natural resources that warrant thorough discussion— agriculture, timber, water (and fisheries)—each of vital importance to a number of Indigenous nations. For our purposes, we shall focus on energy-related resources—coal, gas, oil, and uranium—not only because they are critical for economic purposes, assuming Tribes support their extraction, but also because of their role in causing and exacerbating climate change, which inarguably poses the greatest threat to life as we know it and is having a disproportionate impact on many Indigenous nations' lives, lands, resources, and cultural traditions.[87]

It is estimated that Native trust land contains an estimated $1.5 trillion in untapped oil, gas, and other energy resources.[88] This figure, of course, does not reflect the amount earned from those same resources that have already been tapped by the many corporate, state, federal, and private interests that have been extracting these resources for decades; activities that were flagrantly aided and abetted by federal lawmakers and Interior Department policymakers.

In fact, long before the oil embargo of the Organization of the Petroleum Exporting Countries (OPEC) in 1973, and before the rise of high-stakes gaming, energy-related mineral deposits on native lands dominated the economic spectrum for those nations whose resource endowments contained such deposits. Tribes received only a pittance from these extracted resources in the form of leasing payments, arranged and distributed to them by their trustee, the Secretary of the Interior. Currently, a few Native nations own very large amounts of these energy resources: 30% of the strippable low-sulfur coal west of the Mississippi River, 50 to 60% of the uranium resources in the United States, and 20% of the country's oil and gas reserves. Tribal lands have the potential to produce 37.7 trillion cubic feet of natural gas, 5.35 billion barrels of oil, and 53 billion tons of coal. And it is estimated that Native lands have the potential to generate 3.4% of the total amount of electricity for wind energy and 5.1% of the country's total solar energy generation potential.[89]

These resources are not evenly distributed among the nations, however. Of the 326 Native land areas in the lower 48 states, only about forty contain these resources in sufficient amounts to be profitable. Moreover, natural resources, particularly minerals, have historically been subject to strong cyclical price fluctuations. So just as their dependency on federal dollars has left many Native nations subject to vacillating political tides, dependency on natural resource revenues leaves them vulnerable to the changing trends in commodity prices. And just as those resources are unevenly spread throughout Indian Country, there is the more vital question of whether those resources should continue to be extracted, given their disastrous impact on the environment as the chief source of global warming gases. Some Native nations, like the Crow, Navajo, and Southern Ute, view their extractive activities as necessary to produce needed jobs and alleviate poverty. Other Native governments, like the Northern Cheyenne and Lummi Nation, see such development as a profound threat to the lands, waters, and cultural traditions of their peoples and their ways of life.[90]

Since the allotment era of the late nineteenth and early twentieth centuries, the development of these resources has been largely out of the control of Indigenous governments or individual allottees, as the Secretary of the Interior, exercising

284 INDIGENOUS GOVERNANCE

the tremendous discretionary power vested in that office, leased out Native lands to various oil, coal, and gas companies. The exportation of these nonrenewable resources had a profound political–economic impact on the nations. The Navajo Nation's first Tribal Council was formed in 1922 as a direct result of pressure exerted by oil companies on the Interior Department. The oil companies were required by law to secure the Navajo's consent before drilling. The Navajo agent and Commissioner of Indian Affairs, Charles Burke, convinced the Navajo to create a Business Council, the forerunner of the Navajo Nation Council, in 1922.

Oil and gas were discovered in great quantities on Osage Native land in Oklahoma even earlier, around 1896, and this discovery created the perception by 1906 that the Osage people, per capita, were "the richest people on earth."[91] Osage wealth, however, was viewed with great envy by many, and the Interior Department arranged a blanket lease that encompassed the entire reservation for exportation of Osage resources. This leasing arrangement "caused problems that haunted Indian people for years to come—for example, lack of surface owner and environmental protection; lack of competition; speculation; and bribery of both Interior and tribal officials."[92]

In the 1950s and 1960s, coal and uranium began to be mined in great quantities on the Crow and Northern Cheyenne reservations in Montana and on Navajo and Hopi lands in Arizona and New Mexico, although the nature and extent of reservation mineral deposits had been known and actually mapped twenty to forty years before they were leased and developed. Economics and politics, rather than geological discourse, determined the rate and extent of Native mining.[93]

Moreover, the vast majority of these leases were inequitable arrangements which ensured that revenues generated from these nonrenewable resources were only a fraction of what they should have been. A major deficiency in the leases negotiated by the Department of the Interior on behalf of the Tribal nations was that "royalty rates [were] usually too low and fixed in dollars per unit of production of the resources which, of course, ignores increases in value rather than percentage of value, which increases income as minerals increase in value."[94] As an example, in four of the five Navajo coal leases negotiated between 1957 and 1968, Diné royalties were fixed between $0.15 and $0.375 a ton. But the average value per ton of coal rose from $4.67 in 1968 to $18.75 in 1975.

Low royalty rates were just a small part of the problem Indigenous governments faced regarding their natural resources. By the late 1960s, it was clear that the entire decision-making process employed by the BIA and the Interior Department regarding the authority and manner in which the leases occurred was deeply flawed, that Native nations had rarely been informed of the true value of their mineral endowments, that they lacked any control or self-determination over their resources, and that environmental degradation was becoming a major concern of all Native people. Even as Native nations were struggling to gain greater control over these resources, the 1973 oil embargo imposed by OPEC, an international cartel of oil-producing states, led to an energy crisis and an escalation in prices in the United States, which brought the focus on Tribal nations who owned large amounts of mineral resources. Because the federal government felt compelled to develop the country's own natural resources as a hedge against future embargoes, it approached Native governing officials to discuss the need to further exploit their energy reserves. While these natural resource discussions were taking place, twenty-six Tribal governments of the northern plains formed the Native American Natural Resource Development Federation as a way to protect their mineral, water, and agricultural resources by collecting and sharing information regarding those endowments.[95]

A year later twenty-five energy-resource-rich Native nations, with federal and public interest group financial support, organized the Council of Energy Resource Tribes (CERT). These nations told federal officials that they had organized because they wanted "resource-related education; a clearinghouse for exchanging information; help arranging finances for development; expertise on alternative contractual arrangements; studies on using resources on the reservations rather than continuing the tribes' role as colonies exporting energy; impartial environmental studies; and a means for advising the federal government about Indian energy development."[96]

The fact that CERT received ample funding from both the Department of Energy and the BIA undercut its claim to be a "domestic OPEC"; also, some Tribes questioned CERT's merits, since the BIA would sometimes refuse funding to Native nations on the grounds that it had already sent money to CERT. Nevertheless, CERT continues to play an important role for its member nations by, among other things, helping them monitor and negotiate energy contracts. In 2012 CERT entered into a $3 billion biofuels and bioenergy agreement. The "Thunderbird Project" focuses on the development of feedstocks over a ten to fifteen-year period with the aim "to develop sources of energy while adhering to tenets of sustainability."[97] CERT oversees 30% of the coal west of the Mississippi River; 40% of known national uranium reserves; 9% of known national oil and gas reserves and renewable sources from some 56 million acres in the U.S., according to David Lester, executive director of CERT.[98]

There are now fifty-four member nations and four First Nations (Native communities located in Canada) in the organization. One member, the Southern Ute, after struggling for many years to gain control of its natural resources from large energy companies, now controls roughly 1% of the nation's natural gas supply, worth approximately $4 billion. The Crow, who negotiated a 2004 agreement with the Westmoreland Coal Company allowing a commercial coal mine to operate, have found that the revenue provides two-thirds of the Crow nation's

286 INDIGENOUS GOVERNANCE

non-federal budget, totaling more than $20 million in 2010. More recently, the Crow have been trying to open a second mine that could potentially produce 1.4 billion tons of coal, bringing in approximately $10 million in five years. Thus far, they have been denied the power to open the mine because of existing federal environmental standards.[99]

The year 1982 was important for energy-owning Native nations. Congress enacted the Indian Mineral Development Act, which authorized Tribal nations to join with industry as mineral developers and to choose which development ventures to pursue. And the U.S. Supreme Court handed down *Merrion v. Jicarilla Apache Indian Tribe*,[100] which recognized the right of Native nations to impose severance taxes on energy companies engaged in mining on Tribal lands. The *Merrion* case was somewhat muted by a 1989 ruling, *Cotton Petroleum Corporation v. New Mexico*,[101] which held that the state of New Mexico could impose its own severance tax on oil and gas produced on Native land by a company already paying a similar Tribal tax. This "double-taxation" of business entities in Indian Country has caused severe problems for a number of Native governments. The High Court upheld the state tax even as it admitted that double taxation would likely discourage mineral producers from doing business on Native land; a move that would have adverse effects on Tribal government income.[102]

Oil production in Indian Country, while generating important if uneven revenue, has also generated many consistently negative consequences. The boom and bust in oil production and prices have been matched with a rise in crime, especially against Native women who are sex trafficked and physically abused, traffic deaths, and massive environmental pollution. Ray Cross, a member of the Mandan, Hidatsa, and Arikara of Forth Berthold (MHA), has found the costs are significant, including the damage to the Tribes' land and an oil-tax agreement with North Dakota that he believes compromises Tribal sovereignty.[103] Despite these problems, the MHA Tribal government, as of 2018, secures 90% of its annual budget from energy-related sources—and that figure has surged over the past fifteen years from $20 million to $330 million.[104]

As the *New York Times* reported in 2018 in a detailed review of the dangers to the environment (including Indian Country) created during Donald Trump's presidency, which included efforts to eliminate or scale back federal rules and regulations dealing with environmental protection, such changes (totaling seventy-eight in all) "could lead to at least 80,000 extra deaths per decade and cause respiratory problems for more than 1 million people."[105] These crippling environmental modifications, those already completed and those still being instituted at the time of the article's publication, included air pollution and emissions, drilling and extraction, infrastructure and planning, and toxic substances and safety. Impacts on Indian Country included the rescinding of water pollution regulations for fracking on Tribal and federal lands, approval of the Dakota

Access Pipeline (DAPL) oil pipeline, and expediting the environmental review process to clear the way for drilling in the Arctic National Wildlife Refuge.[106]

The environmental impacts of fracking are impossible to deny. In 2015 alone, a North Dakota incident report from the Department of Health found there were 901 spills that included oil among the contaminants. "Between January 1, 2008, and March 11, 2016, companies operating in North Dakota's portion of the Bakken reported 9,837 spills of some kind. Of those, 5,017 breached the well pad and contaminated the surrounding landscape."[107] The MHA Nation experienced 767 incidents during this time on the reservation. On August 9, 2021, the U.S. Department of Justice filed criminal charges against Summit Midstream Partners, LLC, a North Dakota pipeline company that discharged 29 million gallons of produced water—a waste product of hydraulic fracking—from its pipeline near Williamston, ND, over a five-month period in 2014–2015. This massive discharge "contaminated lands, groundwater, and over 30 miles of tributaries of the Missouri River. The spill, believed to be the largest inland spill in history, was visible in photographs taken by satellites orbiting the earth."[108]

Two of the most prominent cases dealing with oil centers on pipelines that transport crude oil that threaten the lands and waters of Native peoples—the Dakota Access Pipeline (DAPL), built by Energy Transfer Partners, that poses a severe threat to the Standing Rock Sioux Tribe; and the Line 3 Pipeline that threatens several Anishinaabe nations, including the White Earth Band, Mille Lacs Band, and the Red Lake Band. Let's look briefly at these two cases.

Standing Rock Sioux and the DAPL

The Standing Rock Sioux Tribe, then led by Dave Archambault II, first learned of the proposed 1,172-mile pipeline in 2014. Although the original plan had called for the line to pass near Bismarck, ND, a majority-white city, the route was changed to avoid potential conflict with that constituency. The revision called for the pipeline to burrow under the Missouri River very near the present-day boundaries of the Standing Rock Sioux Reservation, which straddles the border between North Dakota and South Dakota. The pipeline would therefore be situated on land the Lakota view as "unceded Indian territory" under the tenets of two treaties: the 1851 Fort Laramie Treaty and an 1868 treaty of the same name.

A majority of the pipeline, most of it under state or private land, had already been completed, but 3% of the route was slated to cross under the river, defined as a navigable waterway per the Clean Water Act, the Rivers and Harbors Act, and the National Environmental Policy Act. Because of this designation, the Missouri River section of the pipeline required a federal permit from the Army Corps of Engineers before construction could be completed. The Corps claimed initially that the Standing Rock Sioux government had been properly "consulted" before initial authorization for the pipeline's completion was granted. Standing

288 INDIGENOUS GOVERNANCE

Rock disagreed and sued in federal court. They also sent out a call for support from others opposed to DAPL. This put in motion a series of back and forth events, culminating in a massive gathering of allies—some 10,000 strong by late 2016—opposed to the project. Supporters from around the world answered the Standing Rock call for help and descended upon their lands in solidarity. This was arguably the greatest demonstration of support for a Native nation in U.S. history.[109]

With President Barack Obama's prodding, the Corps reversed its policy course on December 4, 2016, and postponed approval of the easement. This was hailed as a major victory by Standing Rock and their thousands of supporters. But when Donald Trump assumed the presidency in January 2017 one of his first acts was to issue a presidential memorandum directing the Corps to reverse course and issue the easements. The Corps complied and granted the easement, but Standing Rock sued again. Then, in June 2017, a federal judge determined that the Corps permits that had authorized the pipeline violated federal law in certain respects, although the court allowed the oil to begin flowing.

A subsequent federal district court ruling in December placed additional constraints on the DAPL but did not shut down construction of the project.[110] In August 2018 the Corps concluded a study ordered by the court in December 2017 and maintained its earlier finding that the chances of an oil spill were low and that any impacts to Native hunting and fishing would be minimal. Standing Rock, along with three other Native nations, filed another suit against the Corps, urging the court to reject the Corps' findings.[111]

In July 2020 the Tribal nations' persistence was rewarded when federal judge James E. Boasberg of the U.S. District Court for the District of Columbia ordered that the pipeline be shut down and emptied of oil by August 5, 2020, pending a complete environmental review. Boasberg was aware of the disruption such a shutdown would cause, but he said the "potential harm each day the pipeline operates" was more compelling.[112] Within a month, a federal appeals court reversed Boasberg's ruling, finding that the lower court lacked the findings necessary for his decision. The Court, however, did not exempt the Corps from having to conduct the comprehensive environmental assessment that had previously been called for. An attorney for Standing Rock said that the Court's split decision effectively left the pipeline "operating illegally" since the permit for it had been vacated but oil was still being transported. Mike Faith, Standing Rock's Chairman said, "We've been in this legal battle for four years, and we aren't giving up this fight."[113]

In May 2021, Boasberg issued a thirty-one-page memorandum of opinion that rejected the Tribes' request to shut down the 570,000 barrel-a-day pipeline, saying that "they had failed to prove that the pipeline's continued operation would cause irreparable harm." This opinion was followed by a ruling in June that effectively dismissed the Standing Rock Tribe's request to halt the pipeline. But in February 2022, the U.S. Supreme Court denied a petition in *Dakota Access v. Standing Rock Sioux Tribe* which confirmed that the final portion of the $3.8 billion oil pipeline has been operating without a federal permit for nearly five years. This action also means that the Corps must now complete a long-delayed environmental review of the project. As of May 2023 the environmental review had still not been completed.[114]

Enbridge Line 3 and the Anishinaabe

Several Anishinaabe bands in Minnesota have been battling the State of Minnesota's Departments of Commerce and Transportation and the private firm, Enbridge Energy, for several years over a proposed oil pipeline. Enbridge Energy has designs on constructing a new $12.9 billion, 340-mile-long pipeline (known simply as Line 3), that would carry 760,000 barrels of Canadian oil to Enbridge's station in Superior, Wisconsin, and then through Minnesota across territory deemed vital by the Anishinaabe bands of Fond du Lac, Mille Lacs, Leech Lake, White Earth, and Red Lake. While the proposed route would not go through existing Native reservation lands, it would run through treaty-recognized territory that includes sacred lands, lakes, watersheds, and important cultural sites. In addition to these substantial environmental and cultural impacts, the influx of temporary workers necessary to build such a pipeline would pose a danger to vulnerable Indigenous populations, as spikes in criminal activity, particularly instances of violence against women and sex trafficking, are well-documented dark consequences of such construction projects.[115]

As Louise Erdrich wrote in an op-ed to the *New York Times*: "This is not just another pipeline. It is a tar sands climate bomb; if completed, it will facilitate the production of crude oil for decades to come." She continued, citing Jim Doyle, a physicist, who explained that "the state's environmental impact assessment of the project found the pipeline's carbon output could be 193 million tons per year. That's the equivalent of fifty coal-fired power plants or 38 million vehicles on our roads."[116]

By December 2020 Minnesota and federal officials had authorized construction of the last segment of the pipeline through Minnesota and construction began, despite significant protest from the Anishinaabe bands, environmental groups, and other concerned persons. Several of the bands, their environmental allies, and the Minnesota Department of Commerce in 2021 asked the Minnesota Supreme Court to overturn a lower court decision on Line 3 which affirmed the approvals by state regulators that allowed construction to begin. Appeals to President Biden, who had pledged action to address climate change and had already canceled the Keystone XL pipeline, have thus far proved fruitless as his administration has defended Line 3 in a court brief before the U.S. District

290 INDIGENOUS GOVERNANCE

Court for the District of Columbia urging that the Anishinaabe bands and the environmental group challenges be thrown out.

The Justice Department maintained that the Army Corps of Engineers had considered a range of alternatives, including protections for wild rice, cultural resources, and wetlands. However, it argued that the court should reject the Band's challenge.[117] On June 17, 2021, several of the lead protesters, including Tara Houska and Winona LaDuke, sent a letter to Deb Haaland, the Secretary of the Interior, inviting her to visit Anishinaabe territory so she could learn about treaty rights, how, from their perspective, the doctrine of consent was being violated, about the importance of wild rice to the Native folk of the region, and about the impact that Line 3 would have on all those nations, other species, and fragile prairie lands. Haaland, a Laguna Tribal member and the first Indigenous Secretary of the Interior, had, in her previous position as a U.S. congressional representative, been a strong advocate of the environment, as evidenced by her having been an original co-sponsor of the Green New Deal, which calls for the federal government to eradicate fossil fuel pollution within a decade. She had also joined the protesters at Standing Rock in 2016 in opposition to the DAPL. And in her early tenure as Interior Secretary, she quickly reinstated wildlife conservation rules and expanded wind and solar power on public lands and waters. Haaland never took a position on Line 3 and the oil began to flow in May 2022.[118] And her department also approved the enormous Willow oil project in Alaska that has deeply troubled many environmentalists; a project she opposed when she served in Congress.

Natural Economics

Vine Deloria Jr. and Clifford Lytle, in describing what they considered more realistic and holistic forms of economic development, said that "the critical factor in achieving economic stability seems to be in encouraging tribal officials to develop programs that are perceived by the people as natural extensions of things they are already doing." They went on to say that "a natural economy maximizes the use of the land in as constructive a manner as possible, almost becoming a modern version of hunting and gathering in the sense that people have the assurance that this kind of activity will always be available to them."[119]

Interestingly, they pointed out that even some forms of industrial and wage work—like the high steel work that some members of the Haudenosaunee have long worked at in New York City and other major urban areas, is one type of labor that has taken on the spirit of a natural economy. The Lumbee Tribe in North Carolina have established a similar relationship to Sheetrock work as well. Other types of economic development, more directly in line with their notion of a natural economy, would include the well-established shellfish hatchery of the Lummi Nation in Washington state that began in 1969.[120] The hatchery relates directly to that nation's historic traditions and close relationship to the salmon, oysters, crab, herring, halibut, and other lifeforms in the local rivers and in the Pacific Ocean. Twenty western Washington treaty tribes—(both individually and collectively through the Northwest Indian Fisheries Commission), also actively work to protect their relationship with salmon, other aquatic species, and the ecosystem that supports those species.[121]

Another natural economic venture is buffalo[122] ranching. For millennia, many Native nations had an intimate relationship with buffalo. The massive animals were viewed as relatives, not merely as resources, and they played a crucial role in many origin accounts and in the subsistence economies of the peoples. They significantly shaped the ecosystem that linked various species, including humans, to the land. The deliberate and systematic slaughter of nearly all buffalo in the nineteenth century by whites had devastating consequences for all those nations, other species, and the fragile prairie lands that depended upon the herds. Fortunately, buffalo survived and by the 1970s some Native nations began efforts to establish and manage their own buffalo herds.

The InterTribal Bison Cooperative (ITBC), with a current membership of fifty-six Native nations, was founded in 1992 with the mission to promote buffalo restoration in a manner that would support "spiritual revitalization, ecological restoration, and economic development."[123] In the ensuing years, it became evident that a broader vision was required, thus, on September 23, 2014, an international agreement, the Northern Tribes Buffalo Treaty was signed in Blackfeet territory, Montana. We will discuss this treaty and other diplomatic accords in a later chapter.

The cultivation and sale of marijuana and hemp are a potential source of revenue for those Native nations so inclined to venture into this turgid and still jurisdictionally ambiguous area. I say potential because while increasing numbers of state governments have legalized marijuana for both medicinal (thirty-six states) and recreational (eighteen states and the District of Columbia) purposes, it is still illegal under federal law and is classified as a Schedule I drug. And since Indian Country, with the exception of the Public Law 280 states, is not subject to state jurisdiction, Native governments must cope with the reality that their federal treaty and trust partner—which is also the partner that claims superior political and legal authority via plenary power—establishes the parameters for what is legal or illegal on Native lands.

Although marijuana remains illegal under federal law, President Obama's administration outlined, in 2014, its stance on marijuana-related crimes and Indian Country in a Department of Justice memorandum.[124] Referred to as the Cole Memorandum it was written to provide guidance to U.S. attorneys on the way

292 INDIGENOUS GOVERNANCE

to prioritize marijuana enforcement in their districts, including Indian Country. Specifically, it listed eight priorities that the Department would focus its resources on, including preventing marijuana's distribution to minors, preventing revenue from the sale of marijuana going to gangs and cartels, preventing violence and firearm use in the cultivation and distribution of marijuana.[125]

Although a few Native nations had already ventured into hemp and marijuana production and sales, after this memo's release, the number of Native governments desiring to take part in this business increased dramatically, despite the fact that some Native leaders and community members raised concerns that the growth and sales of these two products could negatively impact public safety since their communities suffer disproportionately from juvenile and adult substance abuse and gang and organized criminal activity linked to drug use and abuse.[126]

Labeled the "green rush," as of 2022 some ninety Native nations had developed or were in the process of developing legal cannabis, hemp operations, or both. In California alone, thirty-five of the 109 federally-recognized Indigenous nations were operating marijuana businesses or had plans to do so.[127] A partial list of the Native governments engaging with cannabis production and sale includes the Iipay Nation of Santa Ysabel, Sac and Fox of the Mississippi, the Red Lake Nation, the Winnemucca Indian Colony, the Tulalip Tribes, and the Shinnecock Nation.[128] Tribal nations with U.S. Department of Agriculture-approved hemp production plans (some fifty-two Tribes), include the Colorado River Tribes, Fort Belknap Indian Community, Cheyenne and Arapahoe Tribes, La Jolla Band of Luiseno Indians, White Earth Band of Anishinaabe, and the Yurok Tribes.[129]

These nations have found that the marijuana and hemp industries create jobs and tax revenue that benefit the government and the community. As Laurie Thom, enforcement Director of the Inter-Tribal Marijuana Enforcement Commission of Nevada put it: "Not only does it allow tribes to thrive, but it allows individual tribal members to spread their wings and their skill sets."[130]

The route forward, however, is fraught with uncertainty because of the ongoing contradiction in marijuana policy at the federal and state level, and with some Native governments remaining conflicted about marijuana's benefits and costs. In fact, on January 4, 2018, the Department of Justice, under Attorney General Jeffrey Sessions, rescinded the Obama era's Cole Memorandum from 2014 which had loosened the rules governing the Justice Department's enforcement policy on marijuana in the country. Sessions declared that the memorandum had "undermined the rule of law and the ability of our local, state, tribal, and federal law enforcement partners to carry out the work of tackling the growing drug crisis and thwarting violent crime."[131]

Sessions's attitude on marijuana is reflected in what was occurring in the Osage Nation at the time. In 2018, Oklahomans, and many Osage, voted yes on a referendum legalizing the medicinal use of marijuana throughout the state. Not long after, the Osage Nation's Police Department (ONPD) issued the following statement: "Indian Country may be located within Oklahoma State borders, but it is a different jurisdiction than the State of Oklahoma. Passage of SQ 788 does not legalize marijuana in Indian Country jurisdiction. ONPD will abide by guidance from the U.S. Attorney's Office, which is until the Department of Justice reclassifies marijuana, it will remain a Schedule I narcotic and treated accordingly—meaning marijuana is not legal to possess for any reason in Indian Country jurisdiction. Please do not bring your drugs to the Osage casinos, hotels, or any other tribal properties or you will be subject to arrest and tribal prosecution."[132]

And the Pueblo of San Ildefonso state in their Civil and Criminal Code that "any person who shall plant, grow, cultivate, keep for sale, sell, barter, give, have possession of or use marijuana or other narcotic drugs or any controlled substance, determined by the Court to be harmful to the physical and mental health of the user, shall be guilty of the offense and, upon conviction thereof, shall be sentenced to confinement for a period not to exceed six (6) months or to pay a fine not to exceed $500 or both, with costs."[133]

Conversely, it is clear that an ever-increasing number of Indigenous governments, and states, feel confident that the positives of marijuana and hemp, for example, jobs, revenue, sustainability, and so on, outweigh the negatives that have historically been associated with these plants.

Renewable Energy—Wind and Solar Power in Indian Country

Solar power and wind are potentially the two most important renewable energy sources for Indigenous governments as they look to move away from ecologically destructive coal, natural gas, and oil industry processes. It is estimated that Native lands had the potential to generate 6.5% of all the U.S. power. "Specifically, tribal land holds the potential for 891 gigawatts (GW) of wind energy, or 7.8% of the national generative potential."[134] And the Department of Energy says that over 14 billion megawatt hours (MWh) of solar resources are available in Indian Country.[135]

Notwithstanding this enormous "potential" of renewable energy, as of 2022, there is only a single utility-scale wind farm that operates on Native lands—a 50-megawatt (MW) wind farm owned by the Campo Kumeyaay Nation who reside near San Diego, California. The farm has twenty-five turbines which generate electricity for 30,000 homes. It is estimated that 110,000 tons of greenhouse emissions are saved by the wind energy generated by this farm.[136]

294 INDIGENOUS GOVERNANCE

Other Native nations, of course, have in the past attempted to cultivate wind energy, including the Navajo Nation and the Rosebud Sioux Tribe. Both of their efforts collapsed, in large part because of the failure of the federal government to fulfill its trust obligations.[137] As of 2022 thirteen Native governments have proposed wind projects that they are trying to establish in collaboration with the Department of Energy's Office of Indian Energy.[138]

Native governments have had more success with solar projects, including those established by the Blue Lake Rancheria in Northern California, the Standing Rock Sioux Tribe in North Dakota, and the Winnebago Tribe in Nebraska. The Blue Lake community, according to Sandra Begay-Campbell, "have their own microgrid, so it's solar panels plus battery storage. They also have sustainability design practices for their construction and they know how to partner with academics, institutions" and other entities.[139]

And the Navajo Nation, in 2021, already operating two solar plants, put in motion plans for two more—the Cameron Solar Generation Plant and the Red Mesa Tapaha Solar Generation Plant—that together are expected to produce 700 jobs and millions of dollars' worth of energy transmission payments, lease payments, and tax revenue.[140] In addition, these plants are expected to eventually provide power to 36,000 homes and generate $18 million over the life of the projects.

Renewable energy sources like wind and solar are enticing to Indigenous governments for both philosophical and practical reasons. Philosophically, these sustainable sources implicitly and explicitly comport with Native values that are entwined with the moral kinship relationship Native peoples report to take seriously. Pragmatically, since renewable energy must be sold at the point of generation, "the tribe has greater control over the resource production, and may receive a greater immediate benefit from renewable resource generation since the energy produced there from can be consumed on the reservation."[141]

The Tohono O'odham's 1986 Constitution contains an environmental policy—Article 18, which embraces both the philosophical and practical dimensions mentioned above. Section 1 of the Article declares that

it shall be the policy of the Tohono O'odham Nation to encourage productive and enjoyable harmony between members of the nation and their environment; to promote efforts which will preserve and protect the natural and cultural environment of the Tohono O'odham Nation, including its lands, air, water, flora and fauna, its ecological systems, and natural resources, and its historic and cultural artifacts and archaeological sites; and to create and maintain conditions under which members of the nation and nature can exist in productive harmony and fulfill the social, economic, and other requirements of present and future generations of members of the Tohono O'odham nation.[142]

Section 2 (e) states that the Nation may "enhance the quality of renewable resources and approach the maximum attainable recycling of depletable resources."[143]

Federal policy regarding renewable energy and the trust relationship to Native nations across Indian Country continues to be inconsistent, but laws like the Helping Expedite and Advance Responsible Tribal Home Ownership (HEARTH) Act of 2012,[144] when properly interpreted by federal officials, authorizes Indigenous governments to enter into business, residential, and wind and solar leases on their trust land without having to secure BIA approval, although they must still submit HEARTH applications to the BIA for initial approval. This law provides Native governments with a greater measure of economic autonomy regarding wind and solar leases, among other benefits.

Conclusion

The political economies of Native governments are wrapped in a number of internal and external uncertainties, stemming from the political and legal constraints rooted in historic policies, laws, and judicial precedent that have been imposed on their governments by federal lawmakers, the skittish nature of the American public which holds ambivalent views about Indigenous peoples, and Native electorates that are more segmented than at any other time in history. That said, inherent Native sovereignty, ratified treaties and agreements, and the trust relationship—when it is defined as supportive and not paternalistic—provide Indigenous governments a status as bona fide governments that extend to them opportunities and powers not available to other ethnic groups.

And while Native communities exist as distinctive economic sovereigns, their economic choices sometimes have substantial impacts on the local, state, and regional communities they are nested in. For example, a 2022 study by the Oklahoma Tribal Finance Consortium, found that the thirty-nine Native governments in the region were an economic driver and reliable partner to sister governments in their area. In 2019 alone, the nations had a $15.6 billion impact on the state, employed more than 54,000 people, and supported 113,442 jobs for both Native and non-Native citizens across the region. Those jobs produced some $5.4 million in wages and benefits to the overall workforce.[145]

With climate change bearing down ever harder on the peoples, lands, waters, and species of the earth, Native governments, like all governments, must ask how appropriate the free-market paradigm and unbridled capitalism are to their particular political economies and the production or sharing of income. Reservation-based economies, says Kathleen Pickering, "must explicitly consider whether they share the assumptions of the dominant society about

296 INDIGENOUS GOVERNANCE

factors that are considered external to the costs of production, such as environmental quality, community well-being, and resources for future generations."[146] And Carol Anne Hilton, a Hesquiaht woman of Nuuchah descent, and founder of the Indigenomics Institute, takes it a step further, coining a new term, "Indigenomics" to describe the manner in which Natives engage with their world; a manner that needs to be emulated by the rest of world. "Indigenomics," Hilton writes, "Is the economy behind the economy—the values that spin the relationship between nature and human kind—the life force of intention. Indigenomics is the seventh-generation economy. It is the spiritual reality behind the modern economy. It is the spiritual dimension that connects our humanity and worldview as Indigenous Peoples across time."[147]

Native economies, when drawing upon their own historic values and principles that understood the interconnectedness of all life forms, are well-positioned to serve as models of how to govern in a way that is respectful of the natural world. This is evidenced in the several international Indigenous treaties that have been forged since 2007, several of which acknowledge human relations and responsibilities to and for the ecosystem and key species—like wolves and grizzly bears—that have long played essential cultural, philosophical, and economic roles for Native peoples. We turn now to assess these important international documents.

11
International Diplomacy in the Twenty-first Century

A fair amount of attention and scholarship has been made of the 400-plus years of diplomatic and intergovernmental relations between Native nations, European states, and the United States. Unfortunately, we know far less about the structures or dynamics of diplomatic affairs that occurred between Native nations themselves. There are two notable exceptions. Vine Deloria Jr., the leading scholar on treaty-making, partnered with Raymond J. DeMallie to produce a brilliant two-volume collection on Native diplomacy that was published in 1999. The culmination of several decades of global research, it was titled, *Documents of American Indian Diplomacy: Treaties, Agreements, and Conventions, 1775–1979.*[1] This collection covered virtually every aspect of Indigenous diplomacy, including analyses and descriptions of the grand diversity of treaties and compacts, interpretation of what constitutes a valid treaty, how and why Native treaty-making with the federal government was terminated in 1871, and listings and descriptions of modern settlement acts—the contemporary equivalent of treaties.

The volumes also contained the first descriptions, analyses, and listings of international treaty-making between Native nations; from the mechanisms of pre-contact diplomacy to a chapter titled "Treaties Between Indian Nations" that lists some forty treaties, compacts, including one armistice. The last multilateral agreement was negotiated in 1900 in Sabinas, Mexico between the Caddo, Kickapoo, Shawnee, and Delaware.

The second work, written by David H. DeJong, a former student of Deloria, is titled *American Indian Treaties: A Guide to Ratified and Un-Ratified, U.S., State, Foreign, and Intertribal Treaties and Agreements: 1607–1911.*[2] This, too, is a fine work, and both draws from and builds upon the pathbreaking Deloria and DeMallie study. It includes a brief but cogent chapter on "Intertribal Treaties and Diplomatic Relations" that further examines how and why Indigenous nations engaged in diplomacy with one another before European arrival. It also recounts how the nations continued to sign accords with one another until 1902. DeJong includes a table with information about sixty-three international treaties that covers names of participants, type of accord, date, location, purpose, and resources for the document.

Indigenous Governance. David E. Wilkins, Oxford University Press. © Oxford University Press 2024.
DOI: 10.1093/oso/9780190095994.003.0012

298 INDIGENOUS GOVERNANCE

Both works are very useful and vividly demonstrate that diplomacy has been artfully practiced by Native peoples long before Europeans arrived on their shores. But both studies have little to say about inter-Tribal diplomacy post-1902. This chapter draws upon data that is not widely known to show that Indigenous nations and their political and spiritual leaders have continued to forge diplomatic compacts with one another, even if the level of diplomatic activity has not matched that of earlier eras.

National Federal Contexts

In negotiating their diplomatic affairs with the United States during the major treaty era of 1778–1868, Native nations agreed to treaty provisions requiring relinquishment of their powers to negotiate treaties with foreign nations other than the United States. Great Britain, Spain, Mexico, and France were specifically mentioned, as Native nations had forged a multitude of agreements with these polities. Each had been viewed at various points across that time as either a threat to U.S. national security or an obstacle to its expansionist goals.

Interestingly, in all the treaties between the United States and Native nations, there is found no restriction on the power of Indigenous leaders to forge diplomatic accords with other *Native* nations. As pre-existing sovereign entities, Indigenous governments reserve any powers that they did not explicitly surrender, thus, they retained the ability to enter into agreements with other Native nations. Intergovernmental coalitions, alliances, and confederacies were common among Native peoples and since time immemorial they have built international institutional arrangements in pursuit of common political, economic, or military goals.

Examples include the Great Law of Peace, the founding constitution of the Gayanashagowa member nations, Mohawk, Oneida, Cayuga, Seneca, Onondaga, and Tuscarora which constitute the Haudenosaunee or Six Nations Confederacy in what is now New York State. Established sometime between A.D. 1000 and A.D. 1525, this founding account serves both ceremonial and political purposes by providing a framework for the establishment and maintenance of peace and the resolution of disputes, a governing council of fifty sachems (chiefs), a consensus-based decision-making process, and a set of protocols steeped in the kinship traditions of the respective nations.

Other examples are the coalition formed by Pueblo nations in 1680 to drive out the Spanish invaders and efforts of Pontiac in the 1760s to create an inter-Tribal league to fend off the English invaders. A fourth instance came in the early nineteenth century, when Tecumseh and the Shawnee Prophet, Tenskwatawa, formed an alliance with a number of northeastern and midwestern Native nations in an effort to halt and reverse the flow of Euro-Americans into their territories. The Menominee utilized use agreements with other nations; they called these *apēkon ahkīhih*, meaning to "sit down upon," which allowed neighboring nations, with permission, to use Menominee lands when needed. This was reciprocated when Menominee needed to venture onto the lands of their neighbors to hunt, fish, or gather resources.[3] Finally, we have the attempts by the Five Civilized Tribes from 1846 to 1886 to compel the federal government to provide their nations with recognized status within the American constitutional framework. This ended in 1906 with the failed attempt (discussed in Chapter 4) to organize a constitutionally incorporated Native state, the state of Sequoyah.

However, in the late eighteenth and early nineteenth centuries, as the United States focused on solidifying its claims to territories held or sought by other foreign nations, there was little concern about inter-Tribal alliances. As the new country expanded, colonizing more Native territory and undermining Indigenous peoples' abilities to sustain themselves, the United States became more confident in its ability to quell resistance. The specificity of treaty limitation language is an indication that the federal government did not perceive inter-Tribal alliances as a threat to its ambitions.

Given that these centuries of treaty-making were marked by invasion, ethnocide, abuse, and exploitation, it is not surprising that Native leaders were reticent or simply unable to engage in overt international diplomacy with one another. With one important exception, a 1947 Treaty of Peace, Friendship and Mutual Assistance between various Native leaders,[4] some of whom helped establish the National Congress of American Indians in 1944, another several decades would pass before Indigenous leaders of the 1970s would begin to flex these political muscles via memoranda of agreements, sovereignty accords, and Tribal–state compacts.[5] With the rise of social movements for human and civil rights across the country, a new generation of Natives raised with an understanding of the concepts of sovereignty and self-determination came of age. They saw the potential power of inter-Tribal government-to-government relations and called for a renewal of the process of negotiating international treaties with other Native nations.

We will examine these diplomatic accords, assessing the reasons Indigenous leaders chose to convene at the bargaining table with other Native leaders, describe their respective goals, and the ramifications of these accords as they sought to enhance Indigenous sovereignty and self-determination, protect territory and relatives, and affect relations with neighboring state and local governments. No matter the subject of negotiations, each treaty is based upon a simple and profound understanding: we are all related.

300 INDIGENOUS GOVERNANCE

Creator gave us many gifts and teachings to survive this world. One of those teachings is everything is interrelated. In the Indian practice, the interrelated world is realized ... through Treaty-making with all my relations.[6]

Traditional Diplomatic Relations Prior to European Contact

As noted earlier, according to oral histories and traditions, the nearly 600 Native nations located within the boundaries of what is now called the United States engaged in diplomatic relations with one another since time immemorial. Evidence of these agreements and the relations they defined was not documented by written word, rather these societies kept records of major historical events through carefully shared oral histories, illustrations such as petroglyphs and hide paintings, mnemonic devices like wampum belts, and reenactment within extant ceremonies.

Analysis of early colonial treaties signed with various European leaders provides substantial proof in the form of recalled metaphors, symbols, rituals, and methods that diplomacy was artfully practiced between Native nations and sometimes with many parties.[7] Thus, while pen and paper were unknown, the substance and form of these diplomatic ventures were continually remembered, reconstructed, and reenacted to maintain an accurate record of events. In this regard, a treaty was not a document, but a living promise, an ever-present shared reality. Arguably, the communal construction, witnessing, and maintenance of diplomacy made it more immediate, accessible, and accurate than inked words in an unknown language on paper held by a few.

Black Elk (1863-1950), a holy man of the Lakota people, described a Hunkapi ceremony between the Lakota and the Arikara to Joseph Epes Brown who later published the account in *The Sacred Pipe* (1953).[8] According to Black Elk, the Lakota had stolen corn considered sacred by the Arikara (also known as Ree) setting off a war between the two nations. In an effort to restore peace, leaders of the two peoples agreed to partake of the Hunkapi ceremony, also known as the Making of Relatives Ceremony. During the long and complex observances, the sacred pipe was used to create a kinship bond between the two peoples.

This pursuit of peace illustrates transformational attitudes and mechanisms that profoundly differ from those that were used and continue to be utilized by Western diplomats. The Making of Relatives Ceremony was not simply the means to end a single conflict and move on as before with a clean slate. For the Lakota and Arikara, the attainment and perpetuation of peace was only possible when both parties embraced the moral duties required with the establishment of kinship relations. This was a sacred obligation and the ceremonial activities were imbued with profound spiritual significance. Once a former adversary has been

INTERNATIONAL DIPLOMACY IN THE 21ST CENTURY   301

transformed into a family member, betrayal becomes unthinkable and any strife
that might undermine community strength is avoided or dealt with peaceably.

Contemporary Indigenous Diplomacy

European and later Euro-American colonization brought profound harm, dispossession, and dislocation to Indigenous peoples but, contrary to the popular American romantic narrative, Natives were not noble savages who briefly
struggled and ultimately surrendered to the inevitable power of Manifest
Destiny. Indigenous leaders consistently engaged in diplomacy with colonizers
beginning with the 1607 Powhatan Confederacy treaty with the English until
the last formal treaty between the Nez Perce and the United States in 1868.
Although Congress officially stymied treaty-making with Native nations in 1871,
via an Appropriation Act rider,[9] more than a dozen de facto treaties (deemed
"agreements" in a semantic runaround of the new law) were codified from 1872
to 1911.[10]

In the decades that followed, although no legal obstacles precluded them
from negotiating such accords, very few Native nations took the opportunity
to forge formal alliances with one another, with the exception of the aforementioned and little-known 1947 Treaty of Peace, Friendship and Mutual Assistance,
where signers representing several nations agreed at a gathering in Santa Fe, New
Mexico, to put aside old grievances and focus collectively on conflicts with their
non-Native enemies. For the most part, Indigenous nations were not so much focused on publicly wielding sovereignty and self-determination during this time
as they were on fending off concerted federal efforts to formally terminate the
sovereign status of Native nations and dismantle the trust relationship.

Declaration of Peace between the Comanche Nation and the Ute Nation (1976–1977)

According to oral tradition, the Ute Nation (including the Southern Ute,
Northern Ute, and Ute Mountain Ute) and the Comanche Nation set about to
negotiate peace sometime during the 1700s in an effort to deal with the ever-
increasing numbers of white immigrants who were moving into their territories
from New Mexico and Eastern Colorado. The peace talks faltered, however, and
a half-century of conflict erupted between the Nations.[11]

On September 5, 1976, leaders of the respective nations gathered in Lawton,
Oklahoma to finally put an end to their conflict by negotiating "A Declaration
of Peace Between the Ute and Comanche Nations." The treaty, signed by the

302 INDIGENOUS GOVERNANCE

Chairmen of the Ute Nation and the Comanche Nation "sought to reestablish the historic friendship between the two nations which had been terminated" long ago.[12] According to Wallace Coffey, the Treaty was written on a deerskin hide in keeping with the traditions of the Nations. The Treaty was then transported to Colorado the following year where it was signed by the leaders at Ignacio on July 24, 1977.

Intertribal Reciprocal Agreement Regarding Hunting Fishing and Gathering on the Tribes' Reservations (1997)

Three Great Lakes Tribes were the next parties to utilize treaties in the modern era. In 1997, the Grand Traverse Band of Ottawa and Chippewa Indians, the Little River Band of Ottawa Indians, and the Little Traverse Bay Bands of Odawa Indians agreed to formally open their territories to one another for subsistence and cultural purposes.[13] The three Chairmen who signed on behalf of their nations agreed to allow the members of one another's nations to hunt, fish, and gather within their reserved lands in accordance with the terms of this agreement, including following the conservation laws and policies of that nation's jurisdiction. Those wishing to hunt or fish on the lands or waters of another signatory nation had to secure an appropriate permit from the host nation. This simple document[14] was important in setting the tone and expectations for future diplomatic agreements.

Anishinaabe Akii Protocol (1998)

In 1998 negotiations commenced over the Anishinaabe (also known as Ojibwe or Chippewa) Akii Protocol and it became the first international treaty negotiated across international borders by Native nations in the twentieth century.[15] The agreement was reached between the eleven Anishinaabe member nations of the Great Lakes Indian Fish and Wildlife Service Commission, located within the United States, and the Canadian-based First Nations represented by the Kabapikotawangag Resources Council, an Aboriginal non-profit organization, which provides advisory and technical services to its member nations. The U.S.-based Native nations made clear their intention to wield their authority to hunt, fish, and gather in their reserved and ceded territories, rights retained in their 1836, 1837, 1842, and 1854 treaties with the United States.

The protocol was intended to reflect the shared history, respect, and urgency of the relationship between this broad-based, yet culturally aligned set of peoples and their sacred lands, waterways, and resources. The leaders agreed, in essence, to work jointly toward the "conservation, control, and prudent use of the land, air, water, and all resources including rocks, soil, minerals, fish, flora, fauna and all other life within our traditional territory."

San Juan Southern Paiute and Navajo Nation Settlement Treaty (1999)

The San Juan Southern Paiute are the easternmost of the several bands of the former Southern Paiute Nation. Their lands historically were in southern Utah and northern Arizona. Always a relatively small band—even today there are less than 300 enrolled members—and not officially recognized by the federal government until 1989, having lived remotely from most of the other bands, their aboriginal territory was eventually swallowed by the ever-expanding Navajo Nation Reservation via presidential executive orders in the late nineteenth and early twentieth centuries.[16]

When the Navajo Nation and Hopi Tribe land conflict erupted in the 1960s, Congress stepped in and in 1974 set out to clarify which Nation owned what lands. The Paiutes were left out of this discussion because the federal government was largely unaware of their existence and because the Navajo Nation claimed that the Paiute members were actually Navajo. But when the Paiutes were made aware that their historic territory was being claimed by both Navajo and Hopi governments, they enlisted the legal help of the Native American Rights Fund (NARF), a leading legal interest law firm.[17] With NARF's assistance in 1989, the band secured federal recognition, even though their land base remained uncertain.

As the three Native nations battled to have their respective lands claims affirmed by the federal courts throughout the 1990s and early 2000s,[18] the leader of the Navajo Nation, President Kelsey A. Begaye, and the San Juan Band President, Johnny Lehi, negotiated an historic treaty in 1999 that sought to resolve the longstanding land claims between the two Nations. The Navajo Nation, for its part, agreed to "grant" to the San Juan Band some 5,400 acres of land—creating two small reservations in Utah and Arizona—land long claimed by the Band but also by the Navajo Nation. The San Juan Southern Paiute Tribal Council ratified the treaty in January 1999; the Navajo Nation Council ratified it in July 1999. Both nations joined together on March 18, 2000, and approved the treaty[19] but unlike all the other inter-Tribal accords being discussed in this chapter, this one requires congressional approval as it would involve a change in ownership of lands that are held in trust by the federal government.

This is also the most detailed inter-Tribal treaty of those being discussed. It contains twenty-two articles and is eleven pages in length. Besides the land

304 INDIGENOUS GOVERNANCE

conveyance to establish designated lands for the San Juan's own reservations, it also addresses topics such as surveys and fencing, jurisdiction, access (the right to cross the lands of the other Nation), plant gathering, protection and access to burial and sacred sites, easements for utilities, and water rights. An Addendum to the treaty was made on May 7, 2004, which added an additional parcel of land, the Bellemont Parcel, that was designated for "purposes of economic development, including gaming" for the San Juan people.

As of this writing (2022), the treaty has not yet been officially submitted to Congress, in part because the San Juan Tribal Council has vacillated in their support for the accord—with some members of the leadership calling for additional lands to be made available to them by the Navajo Nation before agreeing to its submission. But there is hope that the two Nations are nearing agreement on the need to submit the treaty, in part because the Little Colorado River water rights adjudication is being held up because of the uncertainty surrounding the ownership of lands and waters that the treaty's provisions would impact and because of litigation involving the ongoing land conflict springing from the decades-old Navajo–Hopi land dispute.

Water Protection Treaties (2004–2006)

In 2004, several nations from the Great Lakes region worked with their First Nations neighbors in Canada to craft the Tribal and First Nations Great Lakes Water Accord.[20] Eight American states, two Canadian provinces, and the Great Lakes Basin had previously begun to negotiate plans for the protection and utilization of the region's lakes and rivers but had failed to include Indigenous nations in those discussions. The thirty-nine Native nations met to claim their governmental responsibilities in any such plan going forward. "We understand that the whole earth is an interconnected ecosystem. The health of any one part affects the health and well-being of the whole. It is our spiritual and cultural responsibility to protect our local lands and Waters in order to help protect the whole of Mother Earth." The signatory nations boldly informed the U.S. state and provincial government officials that their rights and sovereignty were to be respected and that any governmental effort to protect and preserve the waters of the Great Lakes Basin required the full participation of the Tribes and First Nations. Furthermore, the Native leaders pledged that "we share the interests and concerns about the future of the Great Lakes Waters" and that they would "work together with each other and with the other governments in the Great Lakes Basin to secure a healthy future for the Great Lakes."[21]

In 2006, a similar water protection treaty addressing the waters of the St. Mary's River ecosystem was signed across international borders between the

INTERNATIONAL DIPLOMACY IN THE 21ST CENTURY   305

Sault Ste. Marie Tribe of Chippewa Indians, Garden River First Nation, Bay Mills Indian Community, and the Batchewana First Nation. This treaty had six primary objectives designed to protect the health and integrity of the river:

1. Substances that settle to form objectionable sludge deposits or adversely affect aquatic life or waterfowl;
2. Floating materials such as debris, oil, or scum in amounts that are unsightly or deleterious;
3. Thermal pollutants that produce color, odor, or taste that interferes with beneficial uses;
4. Materials and thermal pollutants that produce harmful or toxic conditions to human, animal, or aquatic life and which interfere with beneficial uses;
5. Nutrients in amounts that create growths of aquatic life, which interferes with beneficial uses; and
6. Alien aquatic invasive species that are harmful to naturally occurring aquatic life or interfere with beneficial uses.[22]

The Native parties agreed to form a Tribal and First Nation Joint Commission comprised of one representative from each nation and to meet twice a year, to develop specific objectives and joint strategies, and to investigate issues that might damage the integrity of the river.

These documents foreshadowed the work that would be done twenty years later on the lands of the Standing Rock Sioux Nation to protect their waters from the DAPL fossil fuel pipeline.

United League of Indigenous Nations Treaty (2007)

Acting explicitly from Indigenous customary law, Native leaders from nations located within several international states—U.S., Australia, and New Zealand—convened on the lands of the Lummi Nation within Washington state in 2007 to craft a more broad-based treaty aimed at strengthening their unity, protecting their respective homelands, and fortifying cultural sovereignty. The conversations culminating in this treaty actually began in 2002 during a joint meeting of the NCAI and the Assembly of First Nations in Canada.[23] Titled the United League of Indigenous Nations Treaty (ULIN),[24] the original eleven signatory nations—Lummi Nation, Confederated Tribes of the Chehalis Reservation, Akak Native Community, Makah Tribe, Hoh Indian Tribe, and the Douglas Native Village of the Tlingit Nation located within the U.S.; three First Nations—Sucker Creek, We Wai Kai Nation, and Songhees Nation; the Ngarrindjeri Nation within Australia, and the Te Runanga O Ngati Qwa Tribe of Aotearoa

306 INDIGENOUS GOVERNANCE

(New Zealand)—agreed to provide mutual aid and assistance to one another and to base their decisions and activities on Native laws, customs, and traditions.

The four principal areas of concern were cultural properties (including sacred objects and traditional knowledge), climate change, trade and commerce, and border crossings. Unlike the Anishinaabe Akii Protocol, this treaty had to be formally ratified before coming into full force and effect. Additionally, any other Native nations could join so long as none of the original eleven nations raised an objection.

Since its inception, more than eighty Native peoples have signed on and it serves as a mandate for the "implementation of political, cultural, and trade rights and protects the exercise of sovereignty of indigenous peoples." Although Native treaties do not have the same status under international law as a treaty signed by member states of the United Nations, they certainly have a moral force that binds the signers in other ways. And, according to Frank Ettawageshik, the ULIN Treaty has been successfully used by the Lummi Nation to block the construction of a coal terminal that would have endangered their lands and waters.[25]

Buffalo Treaty (2014)

Another seven years would pass before the next international Indigenous treaty was forged. This one focused on restoring and enhancing relations between Buffalo and eleven northern plains nations and First Nations from Canada. The treaty negotiators convened their talks on the lands of the Blackfeet people within Montana. For millennia, Native peoples throughout much of North America had an intimate relationship with Buffalo. The massive creatures significantly shaped the ecosystem that linked various species—including humans—to the land. Although essential to Native subsistence economies, they were viewed not as resources but as relatives and as such they played a crucial role in many Tribal origin accounts. The deliberate and systematic slaughter of nearly all Buffalo in the nineteenth century by whites had devastating spiritual, economic, and cultural consequences for all those Nations, not to mention the other species and the fragile prairie lands that depended upon the herds. Fortunately, Buffalo survived and by the 1970s some efforts were begun to re-establish and manage the repopulation.

The InterTribal Bison Cooperative (ITBC), with a current membership of fifty-six Native nations, was founded in 1992 with the mission to promote Buffalo restoration in a manner that would support spiritual revitalization, ecological restoration, and economic development. In the ensuing years, it became evident that a broader vision was required. Thus, on September 23, 2014, the Northern Tribes Buffalo Treaty was signed.[26] These nations, exercising ownership and jurisdiction over 6.3 million acres of prairie grassland, collectively agreed to help restore Buffalo within their territories and to renew and strengthen international relations with one another. After they acknowledged that "Buffalo is the essence of our holistic eco-cultural lifeways," the signatory nations invited other Native peoples with similar affinities with the animals to join their alliance. They also invited states, provinces, and allied individuals to sign, and they asked non-governmental organizations, environmental groups, and corporations to form partnerships with the signatory nations in order to facilitate fulfillment of the treaty's intent. With these additions, by 2019 the number of treaty signers had increased to more than thirty.

Declaration on the Exercise of Inherent Sovereignty and Cooperation (2014)

This accord, also negotiated in 2014, was developed on the traditional lands of the Tohono O'odham of Arizona, at Arizona State University. This gathering brought together delegates from a number of federally recognized, state-recognized, and several non-recognized groups and individuals, as well as a committed number of allies who collectively agreed to work together for the protection of their languages, sacred sites, and cultural practices. The signatories also acknowledged that they needed to put their minds together to address the effects of climate change as they had "become place-based nations unable to move with these climate changes as we have moved in the past, causing greater threats to maintaining our relationship with the plants and animals of cultural significance." Finally, they recognized the ongoing threat that legal fictions such as the *doctrine of discovery* continued to pose for all Native nations and their efforts to fortify their legal rights to their lands and resources.[27]

Treaty Alliance Against Tar Sands Expansion (2016)

After experiencing and attempting to address the well-documented disproportionate impact of climate change within their respective communities, a number of Native political and environmental leaders located in the western regions of the United States and Canada began holding meetings in 2015 to discuss collective action. They centered their attention on blocking the expansion of Tar Sands, also known as oil sands: a mixture of sand, clay, water, and bitumen. Bitumen, composed of hydrocarbons, is used to produce gasoline and other petroleum-based products and its extraction is a costly and dirty process called fracking that

308   INDIGENOUS GOVERNANCE

requires deep drilling, monumental displacement of earth, and mind-boggling amounts of fresh water that is mixed with toxic chemicals.

Fighting the Tar Sands was a strategic decision to combine forces against one of the most dangerous collective threats to their communities. Not only was this poisonous process destroying their lands, fouling waters, and killing wildlife at extraction points, but the transportation of the fracked crude oil to ports and refineries involved threading pipelines through Native lands and waterways across the entire region. Destruction of land and devastating leaks were already well known. Companies removed and transported the oil—and the profits— leaving Indigenous communities to deal with the aftermath.

The issue was also one of community safety. Labor camps built and run by the fossil fuel companies, commonly known as "man-camps," were populated by workers brought in solely to work on the Tar Sands. The massive influx of people from outside the community concentrated in rural areas lacking adequate infra-structure or law enforcement resulted in spiking crime rates and became a major factor in increasing numbers of missing and murdered Indigenous women.[28]

The leaders of fifty Native nations convened on Musqueam lands in Vancouver, BC in September 2016. There, they hammered out a strongly worded document[29] in which the nations categorically rejected expansion of the production of the Alberta Tar Sands, including the transportation of that resource via railroads, tankers, and pipelines. Five major projects were targeted: Kinder Morgan's Trans Mountain, TransCanada's Energy East, TransCanada's Keystone XL, Enbridge's Northern Gateway, and Enbridge's Line 3. The nations were deeply concerned about the environmental and community damage that had already occurred and knew that their peoples would suffer further if the Tar Sands expansion was allowed to go forward with the installation of those proposed projects.

Scholars have pointed out that this treaty establishes three principles that are rooted in Indigenous self-determination.[30] First, like its predecessor agreements, it draws from Native customary law and diplomatic values and principles. Second, it evinces the intimate relationship Native peoples have with the lands and waters "and provides Indigenous leadership for what might otherwise be framed as a non-Indigenous led environmental movement."[31] Finally, the treaty embraces a shared decision-making spirit between Natives and non-Natives, as any hope for success would require a combined and determined effort. By 2018 the number of Native signatories had grown to 150, with representation from First Nations located within British Columbia, Québec, Ontario, New Brunswick, Manitoba, Saskatchewan, Yukon, and Native nations within the states of Minnesota, Montana, Nebraska, North and South Dakota, Oklahoma, and Washington.

The Grizzly: A Treaty of Cooperation, Cultural Revitalization and Restoration (2016)

Also, in 2016, Native leaders negotiated the terms of the Grizzly Treaty,[32] pledging to work together to maintain their relationship and obligations with their relatives, the Grizzly Bear. With more than 200 signatories, it is regarded as the largest multilateral treaty in Indigenous history. Decades of threats to weaken protections for the grizzly population prompted treaty negotiations which took place initially between more than fifty federally recognized Native nations and the Assembly of First Nations, which advocates for over 900,000 Natives in Canada. The treaty united the Nations around their shared understanding of the sacredness of the bear and its integral role in their cultural and spiritual lifeways. Alliances with prominent environmental groups were critical in strengthening the effort.

Federal policymakers have long positioned themselves as the sole decision-makers empowered to determine whether or not the bears have a right to exist. Although Grizzlies were placed on the federal endangered and threatened species list in 1975, the U.S. Fish and Wildlife Service, the agency authorized to oversee these matters, had attempted many times to remove their protections. Delisting was first proposed in 2005, but federal court rulings halted that attempt. Nonetheless, the agency persisted, arguing with little scientific support that protections were not necessary as the bear population had sufficiently recovered.

Although the treaty Nations faced a formidable, well-funded coalition of hunters and ranchers, Fish and Wildlife personnel, and state game officials, their efforts, which included an appeal to President Obama for intervention, held the delisting process at bay. However, when Donald Trump became president in January 2017, pressure intensified for the Grizzlies' removal from the endangered species list.

On June 22, 2017, Secretary of the Interior Ryan Zinke announced that as the Grizzly population was no longer considered imperiled, protections provided by the Endangered Species Act were no longer warranted. Zinke's cited measure of success was an increase in the number of bears from 138 in 1975 to 700 in 2017. But a concerted campaign by the treaty signers and their many allies in the environmental movement culminated in a federal 9th U.S. Circuit Court of Appeals opinion in July 2020 that upheld endangered species protections for Yellowstone Grizzly bears, declaring that the U.S. Fish and Wildlife Service had improperly attempted to isolate and delist the animal.[33]

310 INDIGENOUS GOVERNANCE

The Wolf: A Treaty of Cultural and Environmental Survival (2021)

The wolf has influenced indigenous societal structures through the pack, imparting the communal responsibility to sustain life. The wolf taught many to survive by the hunt and to live in a spiritual compact of reciprocity. The wolf provided guidance for environmental stewardship and ecological balance. The wolf is a teacher, a guardian, a clan guide—a relative.[34]

The Wolf Treaty shares goals, sentiments, and alliances similar to those of the Grizzly Bear Treaty. It contains language describing the kinship between all living things and outlines the obligations of human beings as protectors and conservators. Interestingly, the agreement also commits the parties to study the viability of implementation of a Native American Endangered Species Act:

> It has become the norm that federal agencies place a far greater emphasis upon the input of energy companies—with considerable influence being accorded extractive industry executives—in Endangered Species Act (ESA) listing and delisting decisions than is accorded Tribal/First Nations. That disregard of the federal-Indian trust relationship has prompted Native nations to explore the formulation of a Native American Endangered Species Act (NA-ESA). Sovereign Tribal lands hold several T&E [threatened and endangered] species and vital habitat, and it is time for tribal people to have a greater input into the management and protection of these species that hold great cultural significance. In the present political climate, for some species an NA-ESA may be the only viable path to survival.[35]

The attack on wolves is finally relenting, as of this writing. In the waning days of the Trump administration, gray wolves were delisted from the Endangered Species Act by the U.S. Fish and Wildlife Service in spite of scientific evidence that the species was still vulnerable. Shortly thereafter, reacting to pressure from farmers and hunters, the Wisconsin state legislature expanded hunting permits for the wolves. The result was a shockingly rapid loss of one-third of that state's estimated 1,126 wolf population. More than 200 were killed in just three days prompting an early closure of the wolf-hunting season. The lawmakers also authorized a fall 2021 hunt of another 300 wolves, more than twice the number recommended by the state's Natural Resources Board. But on February 10, 2022, U.S. District Judge Jeffrey White vacated Trump's delisting of gray wolves, saying that Fish and Wildlife had illegally removed them from the Endangered Species Act by having conducted a flawed analysis of the wolves' viability.[36]

Indigenous Diplomacy as a Model for the Future

These modern treaties and others that were under consideration[37] exemplify the importance of collective and international Indigenous leadership—leadership that enhances not only the self-determination and autonomy of each of the individual Native nations referenced but also acknowledges the inherent self-determination and autonomy of non-human animals and entities such as rivers and forests—the natural world that nurtures all living beings. As Carolyn Kenny, a First Nation citizen said in "Liberating Leadership Theory," when describing Native leadership: "We can accept the Earth as our first embodied concept of leadership. We follow Earth. We respond to the guidance of the processes expressed in our own place. Many say we listen and respond to our Mother. Everything begins here."[38]

Indigenous political leadership as exercised within the realm of twenty-first century international diplomacy builds upon structures, norms, values, and cultural traditions embedded in Native cultures since time immemorial. At its core, this approach is an affirmation of relationships, an acknowledgment of interdependence. Coalitions built through diplomacy grounded in this understanding are no less than formalized kinship bonds committing humans to respectfully engage not only with one another but also with the Earth and the great diversity of species that live upon and within her.[39]

12

Indian Country Justice

There are approximately 400 court systems functioning on Native lands today, and they are called upon to deal with an ever-increasing number of difficult issues including contracts, child welfare and family law, zoning, natural resources, elections, traffic, ethical matters, criminal misfeasance, membership, gaming, and others.[1] Native courts, for the nations that have them, play a vital role in protecting the sovereignty of the people because they are the prime mechanism by which nations and their citizens resolve conflicts and they theoretically provide balance to the other elements constituting Native governance.[2]

Larry Nesper has pointed out that the term "Tribal court" is an inherently paradoxical concept because "Tribes are fundamentally organized by kinship, and so they traditionally and typically resolve internal disputes in largely egalitarian councils using mediation. Courts, by contrast, are characteristic of more hierarchical sociopolitical formations—with their ultimate origins in chiefdoms and kingdoms—and typically empower impartial third-party decision-makers who authoritatively adjudicate. As a result, assimilating and tailoring this institutional form to the local tribal polity has been complicated for those American Indian tribes that have done so."[3]

Many Native judicial systems are coming to resemble structurally and procedurally their state and federal counterparts; but at the same time some Native jurists—as will be discussed later in the chapter—are intent on reestablishing or establishing peacemaking and restorative justice systems that draw directly from their Nations' ancestral traditions which emphasized peace, restoration of harmony, responsibility, and restitution rather than an adversarial process steeped in a crude, retaliatory, "eye-for-an-eye" system of justice.[4]

Traditional Justice: Philosophy and Practice

Historically, there was no uniform method by which Indigenous communities resolved the occasional disputes that might lead, for example, to a killing that occurred among their members. Some nations, like the Cherokee, prior to their adoption of constitutional government in the early 1800s, had an ancient matrilineal clan system that provided an unwritten code of blood vengeance which discouraged and punished criminals and meted out revenge for their victims'

Indigenous Governance. David E. Wilkins, Oxford University Press. © Oxford University Press 2024.
DOI: 10.1093/oso/9780190095994.003.0013

kin. But central Prairie and Woodland Native peoples generally disapproved of blood vengeance. Rather, these nations "tried to redress the murder victim's kin with gifts rather than demand that the killer's life be taken."[5] Finally, Native nations of the Great Plains maintained community order and cohesion by relying on Warrior Societies which responded to, addressed, and then punished those who committed serious offenses.[6]

Regardless of the social mechanism used by the Nation, the Indigenous adjudicatory function was different from that of Western polities. "The primary goal," noted Deloria and Lytle, "was simply to mediate the case to everyone's satisfaction. It was not to ascertain guilt and then bestow punishment upon the offender."[7] The adjudicatory function of Native communities that were bound by a complex kinship system operated so well that Native nations "were able to govern themselves without any recourse to codes, rules, regulations, cases or statutes."[8]

And this was so because unlike John Locke and John Rawls, two leading Western political theorists writing several centuries apart, who sought to provide a mechanism for distributing justice within a social contract grounded in fairness and who saw human beings as other phenomena of nature "subject to the manipulations of the coercive power of institutions," Native peoples in the past established a social contract based on very different assumptions.[9]

> "Recognizing that blood and friendship were," in Deloria's words, "more influential than reasoned thought, they established rules whereby people had responsibilities toward family members and the means of including nonfamily members and even strangers within the network of concern. Foremost in the society was the necessity of calling family members by their genetic relationship—that is, mother, brother, cousin, grandmother, and so forth. While people had names that were used in social discourse in the larger society, one had to call relatives by the kinship term. This practice was to remind people of their responsibility to each other."[10]

Such societies, rooted in reciprocal responsibilities and not individual rights, meant that the two most important virtues required for communal cohesion were generosity and integrity. If most people most of the time were generous with their time and energy, practiced civility, and acted with integrity, then there was no need for a formal, coercive, and bureaucratized set of laws, rules, and policies.[11] These traditional systems were scorned by whites from the earliest days of European and later Euro-American colonialism, but beginning in the late 1860s federal lawmakers moved beyond disdain and instituted coercive policies aimed at the eradication of traditional cultural practices, the individualization of Native communal lands, the imposition of the Christian faith, the coercive education of Native youth, and the supplanting of Indigenous customary law rooted

314 INDIGENOUS GOVERNANCE

in kinship, reciprocity, and responsibility with Western law, rooted in a rights-based adversarial process.

Federal Coercion Begins: CFR Courts

Ely Parker, a Seneca, was the Commissioner of Indian Affairs (CIA) in 1869. It is interesting to imagine him sharing instructions he had received from President Grant with the newly appointed Board of Indian Commissioners, an unpaid group of ten white philanthropists charged with assisting the Secretary of the Interior in the "humanization, civilization, and Christianization of the Indians." They might as well have added "legalization" to the trifecta of goals the Board was tasked with instilling in Native communities.[12] The "legalization" element, that is, the imposition of Western legal values and institutions, was expedited in 1883 when the Interior Secretary, Henry M. Teller, working closely with CIA Hiram Price, established what they called the Courts of Indian Offenses for the reservations.[13]

Teller was intent on eliminating what he called "the savage and barbarous practices that are calculated to continue them in savagery, no matter what exterior influences one brought to bear on them."[14] Such "practices" included the stoppage of the Sun Dance, the Scalp Dance, feasts, and ceremonial dances, prohibiting the practices and activities of medicine people, ending polygamy, and so on. In April 1883 Teller approved rules establishing the Courts. Thereafter, they became known as CFR courts, as they operated under rules laid out in the Code of Federal Regulations. It is fairly evident that these were not actual "courts" in the traditional jurisprudential sense because their primary purpose early on was cultural oppression and obliteration. Most of the alleged "offenses" dealt with the cultural and religious practices of Native peoples, had little to do with law and order, and had nothing to do with anything resembling justice.[15]

The CFR courts were staffed by three Native judges who were handpicked by the local Indian agent and served at his pleasure. The judges were to be "men of intelligence, integrity, and good moral character, and preference [was to] be given to Indians who read and write English readily, wear citizens' dress, and engage in civilized pursuits."[16] The primary task of the courts, as described in *United States v. Clapox* in 1888,[17] was to serve as "mere educational and disciplinary instrumentalities by which the Government of the United States is endeavoring to improve and elevate the condition of these dependent tribes to whom it sustains the relation of guardian."

As tools of colonialism, the CFR courts were focused on imposing Western law and order on Native communities. At their apex around 1900, CFR courts were operating on nearly two-thirds of all reservations. However, a number of Tribal nations—the Five Civilized Tribes, several nations located within New York State, the Osage. The Pueblos, and the Eastern Band of Cherokee—did not have to endure a CFR court system because they had pre-existing judicial systems the federal government chose not to supplant. The already complicated tasks of the courts became even more entangled as a result of the allotment policy, which led to the individualization of Native property rights and a dramatic increase in the number of whites living in Indian Country. This, of course, led to conflicts over jurisdictional authority, greater interracial tension, and, in turn, an increase in the workload of the courts.

By the early twentieth century, a progressive mood emerged in the United States, out of which flowed developments that would produce the IRA and the modern Tribal constitutions authorized under that act. Around this time, the CFR courts began to be replaced. Many Natives had negative views of the CFR courts, as exemplified by members from the Morongo Reservation in California who wrote a letter to the chairman of the Subcommittee on Indian Affairs on February 8, 1926, testifying against a bill that would have authorized CFR courts to exercise jurisdiction and hear cases on reservations where no federal law was operative. The Morongo citizens gave several reasons why the courts should not be granted that authority:

> First. We are quite familiar with courts of Indian offenses having only in re-
> cent years escaped from their unsatisfactory operations. In our opinion to
> restore courts of Indian offenses would be a long step backward, and we
> beg you not to subject us again to their wrongs.
> Second. To preside over these courts of Indian offenses, the judges were ap-
> pointed by the superintendents. In such cases the judges were merely the
> puppets of the superintendent, and as a result we frequently swelter under
> the arbitrary rule of an unjust superintendent. Please save us from a repeti-
> tion of such experiences.
> Third. In other cases, the judges were elected by the Indians. Were only the
> educated of our people to have the right to vote for judges, there would be
> some chance of electing intelligent Indians who have some idea of law and
> justice, but under existing circumstances Indian politics have all too often
> given us judges to whom the office meant an opportunity to punish their
> enemies, to make laws out of their warped ideas of right and wrong, and
> to fill their pockets by imposing fines, whether such fines were deserved
> or not.[18]

Many CFR courts were phased out altogether, while others were folded into the constitutional-based Native courts that were being established. However, some CFR courts continued because some Nations lacked sufficient resources

316   INDIGENOUS GOVERNANCE

to establish modern courts. Today there remain five regional CFR courts across Indian Country—the Albuquerque, Southern Plains, Western Region, Eastern Oklahoma region, and Southwest Region CFR courts. These regions collectively serve sixteen Native nations, the Santa Fe Indian School Property, and the Albuquerque Indian School Property.[19]

In June 2022, CFR courts were at the center of a U.S. Supreme Court case, *Denezpi v. United States*,[20] involving a Navajo Nation man, Merle Denezpi, who had committed several serious sexual crimes on the Ute Mountain Ute Reservation. The Ute Tribe relies on a CFR court as it does not have a Tribal court of its own. In *Denezpi* the court ruled 6–3 that a Navajo citizen was not subjected to double jeopardy when he was convicted on sexual assault charges in a federal court following a prosecution in a federally funded CFR court. The court, speaking through Associate Justice Amy Coney Barrett, said that the U.S. Constitution did not block the successive prosecutions even if the federal government was behind both.

Contemporary Native Judicial Systems

The Native constitutions organized under the IRA and the court systems that ensued on many reservations were a vast improvement over the CFR courts. Judges under the IRA constitutions were directly responsible to their Nation and not to the BIA as were the CFR courts. On the other hand, Tribal constitutions contained language, ideas, and structures that did not always comport with a given Nation's historical methods of self-governance. Thus, the role of the BIA in the development of these constitutions cannot be overlooked, although the agency acted differently with each nation, depending on the state of their relations. Far more research is needed before any definitive conclusions can be drawn about the relationship between the Bureau and Native nations on this critical question.

For example, some have contended that the IRA constitutions "did not provide for any separation of powers and did not specifically create any court system."[21] This is inaccurate and oversimplifies a complex reality. It is true that Felix S. Cohen, the principal author of the IRA, and leader of the constitutional development project in the Bureau, would have preferred that Natives organizing their constitutions avoid incorporating the concept of separation of powers or two distinct legislative bodies (e.g., the two-chambered legislatures of the Cherokee, Muscogee (Creek), Chickasaw, and Choctaw) because he believed such structured arrangements were bound to cause "friction, delay, and uncertain responsibility."[22]

Cohen was aware, however, that a number of Nations already had courts in place and he also offered suggestions to Natives if they chose to create judicial systems: "The judicial affairs of the tribe, if the tribe has independent judicial officers, may be designated as judges, justices, or justices of the peace ... Courts may be designated as tribal courts, reservation courts, or Indian courts."[23] In fact, he emphatically noted that Native communities adopting the IRA were "free to decide for itself whether it wants to adopt a judicial system patterned after that of the surrounding white communities, or to adopt the general Law and Order Regulations of the Interior Department without change, or to use these Law and Order Regulations as a model and make such changes as seem desirable, or to establish or perpetuate an entirely different judicial system."[24]

In spite of the difficulties Native nations had recovering from the previous decades of intense colonialism and the inherent flaws built into the IRA system of Native self-rule, Tribal courts have grown and diversified tremendously over the last century. Although most Native courts resemble their state or federal counterparts in structure and function, their jurisdiction has broadened from primarily criminal to include civil suits of increasing complexity. "Traditional non-judicial dispute resolution mechanisms continue to function in some tribes along with Peacemaker courts, courts of specialized jurisdiction, such as administrative commissions, gaming, small claims courts, and courts of general jurisdiction. These differences are a sign of creativity as tribal councils and courts balance variances among the tribes' traditions and present needs against the traditions and requirements of the dominant society's law."[25] See Figure 12.1 which depicts the structural arrangement of the three court systems today.

The Indian Civil Rights Act of 1968 (ICRA) statutorily imposed qualified portions of the U.S. Bill of Rights on Native court proceedings for the first time. ICRA pushed Native judges in a direction resembling non-Native courts and provided a mechanism—the writ of habeas corpus—by which litigants could challenge Tribal court decisions in federal courts. Several important U.S. constitutional provisions, however, were not incorporated under the act. For instance, the establishment of a religion clause, indictment by a grand jury, and the restriction against quartering troops in homes are absent. Native governments may also discriminate in voting on account of citizenship/membership criteria and since non-Natives, in most cases, are not citizens/members of Native communities they may be barred from voting in Tribal elections even if they reside within the boundaries of a reservation. Nor are Native courts required to convene a jury in civil trials or, in criminal cases, to issue grand jury indictments or appoint counsel for poor defendants.

Nonetheless, a significant portion of federal constitutional law was made applicable to Tribal court affairs by the ICRA. This is one of the few federal laws that directly limits the powers of Natives to govern their internal affairs. Additional limits apply in cases where Indigenous nations exercise criminal jurisdiction over non-Natives, an area that has been particularly problematic since the Supreme

318 INDIGENOUS GOVERNANCE

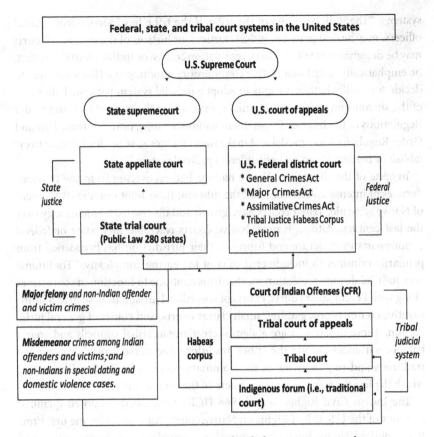

Figure 12.1. Integration of federal, state, and Tribal court systems in the United States

Original Source: Vine Deloria, Jr. and Clifford M. Lytle's *American Indians, American Justice* (Austin, TX: University of Texas Press, 1983). Updated by Steven W. Perry, Michael B. Field, and Amy D. Lauger, "Tribal Courts in the U.S., 2014—Statistical Tables," *Bureau of Justice Statistics* (Washington, DC: Department of Justice, July 2021), 4. https://bjs.ojp.gov/sites/g/files/xyckuh236/files/media/document/tcus14st_0pdf

Court's *Oliphant* ruling in 1978. The decision effectively stripped Native courts of the power to criminally prosecute non-Natives who committed crimes, particularly sexually violent crimes, against Native women, children, and men on Tribal land. The U.S. Congress restored a limited measure of jurisdictional authority to Native courts—limited to domestic and dating violence—under the Violence Against Native Women Act Reauthorization in 2013.[26] But, that law lapsed in 2019. In March 2022, President Biden, at the urging of Native women, court officials, and political leaders, signed into law the Violence Against Women Act Reauthorization as part of the Consolidated Appropriation Act. This five-year extension expands special criminal jurisdiction of Tribal courts to include non-Native perpetrators of sexual assault, child abuse, stalking, sex trafficking, and assaults on Tribal law enforcement officers on Native lands and also supports the development of a pilot project to enhance access to safety for survivors in Alaska Native villages.[27]

Native Judiciaries: Structures and Jurisdiction

As previously discussed, diversity is a hallmark of Indigenous governments. Tribal judiciaries are no exception. What follows are a few examples of Native judiciaries—their structures and jurisdictional parameters.

Timbisha Shoshone Tribe

Article XIII: Judiciary

Section 1. When the Tribal Council determines that the Tribe has sufficient resources and cause, the Tribal Council may establish a Tribal Judiciary. The Tribal Judiciary shall consist of a Supreme Court and such other inferior courts as the Tribal Council may from time to time establish. Once established, the Tribal Judiciary shall exercise jurisdiction over all cases and controversies within the Tribe's jurisdiction, in law and equity, whether civil or criminal in nature, that arise under this document, the laws of the Tribe, or which is vested in the Tribal courts by federal law.

Section 2. The Supreme Court shall consist of a chief judge, appointed by the Tribal Council.

Section 3. The duties and procedures of the court shall be determined by the Tribal Council and set forth by ordinance. To the extent that the Tribal Council authorizes the Tribal Judiciary to exercise criminal jurisdiction, the ordinance shall set forth provisions ensuring that such exercise is consistent with the Indian Civil Rights Act, 25 USC § 1301 et seq., as amended.

Pascua Yaqui Tribe

Article VIII: The Judiciary

Section 1. The judicial powers of the Pascua Yaqui Tribe shall be vested in such tribal courts as the tribal council may establish but shall include a trial and appellate court.

320   INDIGENOUS GOVERNANCE

Section 2. The jurisdiction of the courts shall extend to all cases in law and equity arising under this constitution and the laws, traditions, customs or enactments of the Pascua Yaqui Tribe consistent with the provisions of this constitution. The tribal courts shall exercise jurisdiction over all civil and criminal matters wherein members or non-members of the Pascua Yaqui Tribe are parties, unless otherwise expressly prohibited by Federal or tribal laws.

Section 3. The duties and procedures of the tribal courts shall be established by ordinance of the tribal council.

Fort McDermitt Paiute and Shoshone Tribe

Article V: Tribal Court (Judicial Code)

Section 1.

(a) It shall be the duty of the Council to provide through the necessary bylaws or ordinances, for the establishment of a Tribal Court upon the reservation.

(b) This court shall have jurisdiction over all such offenses as may be provided in the ordinances of the Council unless they fall within the exclusive jurisdiction of Federal or State Courts.

(c) This court shall have jurisdiction over all Indians upon the reservation and over such disputes or lawsuits as shall occur between Indians on the reservation or between Indians and non-Indians where such cases are brought before it by stipulation of both parties.

(d) The duties and jurisdiction of this court shall be more fully prescribed by appropriate bylaws or ordinances.

Mescalero Apache Tribe

Article XXV, Part III: The Judiciary

Section 1. The judicial powers of the Mescalero Apache Tribe shall be vested in the Tribal Courts, including a Trial and Appellate Court. The jurisdiction of the Tribal Courts shall extend to all matters, criminal and civil, except where prohibited by the Constitution, laws or treaties of the United States of America, and except as such jurisdiction may be otherwise limited from time to time by ordinance of the Tribal Council. [As amended March 4, 1977]

Section 2. The criminal offenses over which the Courts of the Mescalero Apache Tribe have jurisdiction may be embodied in a Code of Laws, adopted by ordinance of the Tribal Council, and subject to review by the Secretary of the Interior.

Section 3. The duties and procedures of the courts shall be determined by ordinance of the Tribal Council.

Judicial Review

One of the most important powers wielded by the U.S. Supreme Court is that of judicial review. This is the power of the court to render the final decision when there is a conflict over the interpretation of a clause or amendment of the U.S. Constitution, a federal or state statute, a treaty provision, or an administrative rule or regulation. Although the U.S. Constitution does not explicitly grant this power to the court, scholars, and certainly the Chief Justice who first articulated the power—John Marshall—in *Marbury v. Madison*,[28] believe that the authority to review the Constitution's provisions and federal and state statutes is implicit in the written constitution in the power granted to the federal courts over "all cases . . . arising under this Constitution, the Laws of the U.S., and Treaties made, or which shall be made under their Authority."[29]

Not surprisingly, Native courts have varying interpretations of this essential power. Most of the Nations that include it in their constitution explicitly declare that their courts have the power to judicially review and interpret the constitution and Tribal laws. For example, the Constitution of the Little Traverse Bay Bands of Odawa succinctly states that "the Tribal Court shall have the power to interpret the Constitution and laws of the Little Traverse Bay Bands of Odawa Indians."

But a few nations limit their courts' review power. The Northern Cheyenne, in addressing the status of elections when candidates die, withdraw, or are disqualified, state that after the Tribal court has made its decision their action "shall be final and *not subject to judicial review* in any court." Membership decisions are another area where some Tribal Courts have limited judicial power to review legislative or executive decisions. The Quinault Nation, in determining the status of adopted members, declares that "the decision of the General Council on the question of disenrollment of an adopted member shall be final and shall *not be subject to judicial review*" (emphasis added).

Appointment Procedures of Judges

In some Nations, Tribal judges are popularly elected, while in most they are appointed by the Tribal Council or chairperson. Native judges usually are Tribal members, though in some cases they are non-Natives or are members of other Indigenous nations.

Because of the doctrine of Native sovereignty, each Nation establishes its own qualifications for judges, which may or may not include a requirement that they be state-licensed attorneys. However, nearly all Native judges receive some measure of training in federal Indian law, sponsored by organizations like the Native American Indian Court Judges Association or the National Indian Justice Center. Judges typically serve a fixed term, usually two or four years. The Navajo Nation is the only one to grant life tenure to their justices after completing a probationary period.

Here are a few examples of constitutional provisions outlining the qualifications required to be a Tribal judge, as well as procedures for selection:

Mescalero Apache Tribe

Article XXVI: Composition of the Tribal Courts

> Section 1. The trial court shall consist of a chief judge and two associate judges, appointed by the President of the Mescalero Apache Tribe, with the concurrence of not less than a three-fourths majority vote of the whole membership of the tribal council.

Pascua Yaqui Tribe

> Section 4. The judges of the Pascua Yaqui Tribe shall be nominated by the chairman subject to the approval of a two-thirds majority vote of the tribal council. The number, salary, qualifications of tribal judges and a system of staggered three-year terms shall be fixed by ordinance of the tribal council and no person appointed to the office of tribal judge shall hold at the same time any other tribal office or position. The chairman shall nominate, subject to approval of a two-thirds majority vote of the tribal council, a chief judge who shall be responsible for the administration of judicial business and for providing assistance to the tribal council in establishing the duties of tribal judges and in formulating Rules of

Court and Rules of Procedure for adoption by ordinance as provided in Section 3 of this article.

Section 7. The Chief Judge of the Pascua Yaqui Tribal Court shall be an enrolled member of the Pascua Yaqui Tribe as defined in Article III; however, it shall not be a qualification that any other judge be an enrolled member of the Pascua Yaqui Tribe so long as he or she is a properly enrolled member of any recognized Indian tribe and (1) has had at least five (5) years experience as a tribal court judge, or (2) is a graduate of an accredited law school and has had at least one year of experience as either a tribal court advocate or tribal judge.

Chickasaw Nation

Section 3. The Supreme Court shall consist of three Justices elected by popular vote by qualified voters of the Chickasaw Nation, and shall be qualified electors and citizens of the Chickasaw Nation at least 30 years of age, and residents of the Chickasaw Nation during their tenure of office. No person who has been convicted of a felony by any court of competent jurisdiction shall be eligible to be a Supreme Court Justice. They shall be elected for terms of three (3) years and shall serve until their successors are duly elected and installed. The Justices shall select a Chief Justice from among their number on an annual basis.

Grounds for Removing a Judge

The rationale used by Native governments to remove sitting judges or justices is comparable to that employed by state and federal lawmakers. Take the following examples:

Coquille Indian Tribe

"The Chief Judge may only be removed for conviction of a felony or misdemeanor involving moral turpitude in a court of competent jurisdiction. The process for removal of the Chief Judge is the same for the removal of a member of the Tribal Council as set forth in Article VI Section 6 of this constitution provided that a two-thirds majority of the Tribal Council must vote for removal."

324 INDIGENOUS GOVERNANCE

Pueblo of San Ildefonso

Section 3.2. Removal of Judges of the Pueblo of San Ildefonso Judiciary.

(1) Tribal Judges of the Pueblo of San Ildefonso Judiciary may be removed
upon the grounds of gross misconduct involving moral turpitude or neglect of duty by the following procedures:

    A. Notice of charges served personally on the tribal judge;
    B. A public hearing before the Council ten (10) days after service of
notice;
    C. An opportunity for the Tribal Judge to appear at the hearing and to
answer all charges and to present evidence in defense;
    D. A vote for removal by an affirmative majority vote of the full Council.

Fort McDowell Yavapai Nation

Section 11. Removal of Judges.

    A. The Tribal Council may suspend, dismiss or remove any Judge of the
Trial or Supreme Court by unanimous vote of all five members of the
Tribal Council. The presiding officer of the Tribal Council shall cast a
vote relative to the suspension, dismissal or removal. A judge shall be
removed for any of the following reasons:

        1. Conviction of a felony in any Federal, state or tribal court;
        2. Conviction in any court of bribery, embezzlement, extortion, fraud,
forgery, perjury, theft, any alcohol-related or drug-related driving offense, contributing to the delinquency or dependency of a minor, or
any other crime of moral turpitude;
        3. Substantial and documented nonfeasance, misfeasance, or malfea-
sance with regard to official duties.

    B. A Judge shall be given notice of the charges and fair opportunity to reply
to any and all charges for which he may be suspended, dismissed or
removed from judicial office.

    C. A judge suspended, dismissed or removed under Article VII, Section 11
(A) may appeal directly to the Supreme Court which shall have jurisdiction over such matters. The Supreme Court decision shall be final.

Restoring Traditional Justice Practice Systems

While the United States has the highest imprisonment rate in the world, crime in Indian Country is also quite high and is only increasing, according to data generated by the Bureau of Justice Statistics (BJS) in the Department of Justice. In 2018 there were eighty-four jails in Indian Country holding an estimated 2,870 inmates, a 2% increase from the previous year. This marked an increase of nearly 1,100 inmates since 2000. From 2000 to 2018, the overall rated capacity of jails in Indian Country increased by 107%, while the inmate population increased by 62%.[30]

Most persons held in Tribal jails were convicted inmates. Approximately 30% of inmates were held for violent offenses. Domestic violence offenders accounted for 15% of the jailed population, and aggravated or simple assault (9%) for nearly a quarter of the Tribal jail population in 2018. Rape and sexual assault perpetrators were 1% and other violent offenses (4%) an additional 5%. The percentage of female inmates also rose—from 23% of all inmates in 2010 to 25% in 2018. One bit of good news was that juvenile inmates seventeen years of age and under constituted 7% of inmates in 2018 "continuing a decline in juvenile incarceration since the Survey of Jails in Indian Country began collecting data in 1998."[31]

These numbers, of course, do not reflect what is arguably the most damning subject that is finally receiving the attention it has long needed—sexual crimes against Native women and girls—frequently described as missing and murdered Indigenous women (MMIW). As the Department of Justice reported, more than four in five Native and Alaskan Native women (84.3%) have experienced violence in their lifetime. This figure includes 56.1% who have experienced sexual violence; 55.5% who have experienced physical violence by an intimate partner; and 66.4% who have endured psychological aggression by an intimate partner. Overall, more than 1.5 million Indigenous women have experienced violence. Relative to non-Hispanic white only women, Native women are 1.2 times as likely to have experienced violence and are 1.7 times as likely to have experienced violence in the past year.[32]

A 2020 report produced for the Minnesota State Legislature found that although Native women were only 1% of the state's population, from 2010 to 2018, "8% of all murdered women and girls in Minnesota were American Indian."[33] In, addition, twenty-seven to fifty-four Native women were missing in any given month from 2017 to 2020.[34] Reauthorization of the Violence Against Women Act (VAWA) in 2022 finally restored to Tribal courts the authority they have lacked since 1978; the power to punish those non-Indians who engage in violent assaults against Native women.

326 INDIGENOUS GOVERNANCE

Even before the enormous surge of crime on Native lands, some Native jurists were experimenting with how to marry traditional customs and traditions with the dictates of contemporary jurisprudence, understanding that such attempts can be a useful way to maintain and fortify cultural cohesion and utilize social institutions that historically worked well to maintain community harmony.[35] James Zion, a lawyer, has pointed out that the leading traditional Indigenous justice movements are taking place on Native lands in the United States and Canada, with New Zealand and Bolivia also being active in this effort.[36]

Restorative justice, reparative justice, or peacemaking are related terms that describe processes whereby Indigenous judicial systems draw upon inherent sovereignty and self-determination to craft community-based justice systems that are grounded in trust and support rather than punishment.[37] A number of scholars have written about Native traditional law and non-adversarial resolution methods, including Llewellyn and Hoebel (1941), Rennard Strickland (1975), Nielsen and Zion (2005), Justin Richland (2008), Raymond Austin (2009), and Gregory Bibler (2018). However, as Austin, a former Navajo Supreme Court justice observed: "Although many tribal codes authorize use of customary law (or Indian common-law), few federally recognized Indian nations in the U.S. actually use it, and even fewer have a functioning traditional justice institution to complement their courts."[38]

The courts and jurists of the Navajo Nation have been at the forefront of restorative justice. While the Navajo judiciary is the youngest of the three branches of Diné government, like the federal court system of the United States, it is, without a doubt, the most respected institution in the Navajo Nation government. This is because the traditional form of Navajo Tribal organization, like that of most Indigenous nations, functioned primarily as an adjudicatory (judicial) body, resolving disputes within the community. It is also because the Navajo courts have more explicitly folded traditional and customary Diné legal and political values and institutions, as articulated in the Fundamental Law, into the structures and functions of the courts. In addition, they have a well-respected, fully developed system—the Peacemaking process—that is based entirely on Diné traditional values and principles.[39] As described in the *Navajo Nation Code*, "The courts shall utilize Dine bibee haz'aanii (Navajo Traditional, Customary, Natural or Common Law) to guide the interpretation of Navajo Nation statutory laws and regulations."[40]

Three of the most essential concepts in Navajo philosophy are *ke*, *kei*, and *hozho*. Ke, broadly defined, entails one's duty and responsibility for all others. K'ei encompasses kinship or the clan system, while hozho centers on the idea of harmony, balance, and peace. These core values have been incorporated into the Navajo Nation's judicial system and in governance in general, via the Fundamental Law.[41] For Navajo peacemakers, "The overall goal of traditional dispute resolution (i.e., peacemaking) is restoring positive relationships so all individuals affected by the dispute can return to a life of peace, balance, and harmony."[42]

An ever-increasing number of Indigenous governments are embracing traditional justice practices as a more flexible and just way to address the myriad problems that continue to bedevil their communities—extreme rates of violence, substance abuse, widespread poverty, unemployment, and the like. The Prairie Band Potawatomi Nation, for example, as part of their Dispute Resolution System (which includes a District Court, a Court of Appeals, and an Employment Dispute Tribunal) established a mediating branch known as the Peacemakers Circle. Peacemakers are selected by the citizens during a General Council meeting. They are charged with "mediating disputes voluntarily submitted to them by the parties."[43] Other nations that have instituted Peacemaking include the Chickasaw Nation, the Mississippi Band of Choctaw, the Lower Brule Sioux Tribe, the Organized Village of Kake, the Leech Lake Band of Anishinaabe, and the Stockbridge-Munsee Tribe.[44]

Closely related are the more than ninety Wellness courts that are now spread across Indian Country. Loosely modeled after drug courts, they strive to blend Indigenous culture with rehabilitation and restorative justice as an alternative to imprisonment. These courts generally deal with alcohol and drug-related offenses.[45] In the Penobscot Tribe's Wellness Court, recovery follows four stages: "Tobacco (introduction to the program), cedar (taking responsibility for the substance use disorder), sage (treatment), and sweet grass ("making a difference for yourself, your family, your community, and the Penobscot Nation"). The participants are met by a team of individuals that includes a substance abuse counselor, cultural advisor, housing and education specialists, but also a judge, prosecutor, public defender, and police officers.

In a few instances, Native courts have reached agreements with county courts and are sharing jurisdiction over certain criminal and civil matters. For example, in 2006 the Leech Lake Band Tribal Court and the Cass County District Court, with the concurrence of the Cass County Probation Department and the Minnesota Department of Corrections, negotiated a Memorandum of Understanding[46] in which the parties agreed to share jurisdiction. Tribal Judge, Korey Wahwassuck, of the Leech Lake Tribal Court, said that "the mission of the Wellness Court is to reduce the number of repeat substance dependent and driving while intoxicated (DWI) offenders by using a coordinated team approach with the Tribal Court Judge, the County District Judge, prosecutor, defense attorney, law enforcement personnel, social services workers, probation and treatment specialists, to quickly identify and intervene with selected nonviolent substance abusing offenders to break the cycle of substance abuse, addiction, and crime."[47]

328 INDIGENOUS GOVERNANCE

As Zion and Yazzie note, efforts to use court systems modeled after those of the West to practice traditional justice in written form "are frustrated by rejection of customary law and decisions by federal courts . . . interference with the exercise of criminal or civil jurisdiction over non-Indians, and dependence on federal funding that will not come."[48]

Notwithstanding this harsh reality, it is probably unrealistic to expect Native nations to completely substitute their current judicial systems, many of which are tailored to the Western-based justice system, with customary law and the processes that use it given the dramatic changes in the social order over the past two centuries. As Jarrat-Snider and Nielsen relate:

Interpersonal violence such as family violence and sexual assault were rare in traditional times, as were post-traumatic stress and anger management issues. Incarceration of some offenders may still be necessary, and the involvement of medical personnel to help some offenders (e.g., sex offenders) may be necessary. Legal pluralism already exists within some colonial countries such as Canada where Quebec law is based on the French Napoleonic Code, and the same with Louisiana in the United States. Alvarado also gives several examples from Latin America. The point is that the development of Indigenous justice systems with full authority to practice traditional law is simple legal pluralism, for which there are precedents.[49]

Native judicial systems are becoming more effective in their assorted and diversified tasks and are gaining legitimacy in the eyes of some federal and state courts. For example, on July 28, 2005, Tribal court judges from five Wisconsin Native nations ceremonially signed into law the "Teague Protocol," with judges from the state's Ninth Judicial Circuit. The purpose of this protocol was to "effectively and efficiently allocate judicial resources by providing a legal mechanism which clearly outlines the path a legal dispute will follow when both a Tribal court and a Circuit Court have each determined it has jurisdiction over a matter." While not altering or expanding the jurisdiction of either polity, this cooperative measure establishes an institutional judicial framework that helps to ease tensions between those Native nations and the state judges.

Congressional legislation such as the Tribal Law and Order Act of 2010, which enhanced Tribal sentencing authority, and the 2022 VAWA reauthorization, which restored to Native courts their jurisdiction over non-Indian criminal offenses under particular conditions, have expanded the recognized powers of Native courts. Recent U.S. Supreme Court decisions have affirmed these powers. In 2016, the High Court in *Dollar General v. Mississippi Band of Choctaw*, upheld Tribal court authority to adjudicate civil tort claims against non-Indians in contractual relationships with the Tribe. In that same year, in *U.S. v. Bryant*, the

Supreme Court affirmed that Tribal court convictions that comply with the Indian Civil Rights Act, a measure that extended a number of constitutional protections to persons in Indian Country, can apply toward demonstrating the defendant is a habitual offender in federal convictions of domestic violence.

While these two cases appear to be a greater affirmation of the recognized authority and respect accorded to Native courts, many question the limits of this recognition. For example, the court was split 4–4 in *Dollar General* despite the clear-cut legal precedent affirming Tribal court jurisdiction. And while *Bryant* was a unanimous decision, the case specifically dealt with a statute that only applies to Native offenders, a population already grossly overrepresented when it comes to incarceration, further stripping them of constitutional protections and federal prosecution while ignoring the role of federal and state policy and law in creating the problems the statute sought to address.

Still, Native judicial systems more so than Tribal executive and legislative bodies, seem to be more willing and are structurally and normatively capable of synthesizing traditional norms and culture with Western traditions where appropriate. In fact, "The ability of the Tribal court to interpret law to the Indian people and to interpret Indian culture to other legal institutions may be the most important of all assets flowing from the tribal court system."[50]

13
Governments and the Media

The communications media are among the most powerful forces operating in the marketplace of ideas. This was evident in the spring of 2022 when Russia's military invaded Ukraine, instigating a deadly war that has killed thousands and displaced millions more. Russia's state-run television and social media have engaged in a wide propaganda campaign to cast blame on everyone except Russia's dictator, Vladimir Putin. A similar spectacle occurred in the fall of 2021 when the Taliban of Afghanistan roared back to power after the Biden administration clumsily evacuated personnel and allies from that tortured land. Since their previous short-lived reign of totalitarian terror over their own people from 1996 to 2001, which included massacres, starvation of citizens, destruction of lands and homes, discrimination and abuse of women and girls, and banning the Internet, the Taliban, like the Russians, use the power of social media in an attempt to weaken the opposition and broadcast their message.

According to the *New York Times*, the Taliban "are using thousands of Twitter accounts—some official and others anonymous—to placate Afghanistan's terrified but increasingly tech savvy urban base."[1] Of course, those opposed to Taliban domination will also have access to the same outlets and will use those to expose Taliban atrocities in an effort to secure domestic and international support for the resistance to Taliban rule. Likewise, Ukraine's president, Volodymyr Zelenskyy, has deftly utilized all forms of social media to inspire his people, seek international support, and try to blunt the Russian media campaign.

Contemporary Native governments and their key political actors are not as oppressive or cruel as the Russian state or the Taliban, but this does not mean that they are not prone to actions aimed at controlling, interfering, or at times eliminating the free flow of information to journalists or their constituencies. They do this not just through attempts to manage the release of information and manipulation of messaging but often by owning and maintaining total control of the major media enterprises on Tribal lands to a degree not witnessed in the larger society.[2]

In 2015 the Muscogee National Council enacted a law that, for the first time, guaranteed freedom of the press to their print and broadcast outlets, Mvskoke Media. Over the following three years, Mvskoke Media reported on a number of topics important to the community, including alleged sexual harassment by the Council Speaker, the arrest of a Council member for driving under the influence,

Indigenous Governance. David E. Wilkins, Oxford University Press. © Oxford University Press 2024.
DOI: 10.1093/oso/9780190095994.003.0014

GOVERNMENTS AND THE MEDIA   331

layoffs in the Health Department, and mismanagement of Housing and Urban Development funds.[3]

Tribal government officials grew increasingly irritated by the coverage, and in November 2018, enacted a law repealing the 2015 measure that had established the independent editorial board protecting the Mvskoke Media Outlet (MMO) from political influence. The Mvskoke Media Outlet then became answerable to the Nation's Commerce Secretary who reports directly to the Principal Chief of the Nation. Chief James Floyd claimed MMO was still "independent" despite being under his control. Sterling Cosper, the Outlet's manager, who resigned in protest over the Nation's decision, said that Chief Floyd's assertion of continuing press independence was inaccurate: "To say that it's independent news when the managing editor sits under Tourism and Recreation which sits under the Secretary of the Nation and Commerce—all of these people answer to the Chief."[4] Equally frustrating to Cosper was the fact that neither he, his staff, nor the Editorial Board had been consulted beforehand about the Nation's decision to strip their office of its journalistic freedom.

Council members and the Principal Chief who supported the change claimed that the Mvskoke Media Outlet had been too focused on negative news and had not provided enough positive coverage of issues emanating from the Nation's political headquarters.[5] Two years later, and after new elections, the Council, by a vote of 15–0, acted to restore free press protection for the MMO and included a mechanism for guaranteed funding, an essential support that is rare for chronically underfunded Native news outlets.[6]

The Russian, Taliban, and Muscogee (Creek) stories illustrate the critical importance of communication media, its susceptibility to political machinations, and the extent to which such manipulation can damage public trust by outright elimination of news sources or the deliberate hobbling of news providers.

Media as an Institution

Throughout history, Indigenous peoples' primary means of communication has been oral transmission. And while the oral tradition retains potency in Native societies, Indigenous peoples, since as early as the 1820s, but particularly since the 1970s, have actively developed and utilized other communication tools. Natives have formed their own professional association for journalists, the Native American Journalists Association (NAJA), established independent newspapers, and been active in filmmaking. Several Indigenous governments have established their own radio and television stations and become much more involved in telecommunications technology. Tribal governments and individual

332 INDIGENOUS GOVERNANCE

citizens have incorporated these and other tools to advance the needs of their communities and to educate and enlighten their non-Native neighbors.

Print Media

The earliest Native-owned newspaper was the *Cherokee Phoenix*, begun in 1827 at New Echota, in the heart of the Cherokee Nation in what is now Georgia. As the first editor, Elias Boudinot, stated, "[T]o attain a correct and complete knowledge of these people, there must be a vehicle of Indian intelligence. [T]he columns of the *Cherokee Phoenix* will be filled, partly with English, and partly with Cherokee print; and all matter which is of common interest will be given in both languages in parallel columns."[7] The newspaper was destroyed by the Cherokee's white Georgian neighbors when the state, with federal support, forcibly evicted the majority of the Cherokee from their original homelands as part of the Indian removal campaign.

Cherokees John Rollin Ridge, Charles Watie, and Colonel Elias Cornelius Boudinot (the son of Elias Boudinot) were active writers for various newspapers in the 1840s and 1850s. But publishing by Native governments and individual Natives was a rarity until the end of the nineteenth century, which saw a resurgence of Native journalism. This resurgence occurred mostly in Indian Territory (present-day Oklahoma), as the Cherokee, Choctaw, Creek, and Osage Nations each established their own newspaper. But the federal government's coercive assimilation plan, focused on the allotment and Christianization of Natives, weakened these efforts, and Native publishing declined and did not begin to recover until the end of World War II.[8]

After the war, federal policies of termination and relocation of Native peoples led to a new surge of periodical activity, fueled in part by the urbanization and interTribal collaborations that emerged as a result of these policies. In 1947, the National Congress of American Indians (NCAI) began publishing the *Bulletin*, and urban Natives followed with their own newsletters: the *Chicago Warrior* in 1955 and the Seattle-based *Indian Center News* in 1960. More importantly, from a sovereignty perspective, Native governments, themselves, began publishing newspapers: the *Ute Bulletin* (1950), the *Char-Kooska News* (1956), and the *Navajo Times* (1959).

The greatest proliferation of Native news media originated from Lyndon Johnson's Great Society and War on Poverty programs which provided the federal funds enterprising Natives used to start newspapers and newsletters. The continuing urbanization of Indigenous peoples, the increasing number of Native college graduates securing journalism degrees, and the strengthening of Native self-determination fueled this increase in publications. *Akwesasne Notes* was established in 1969 on the Mohawk Reservation and quickly gained both a national and hemispheric reputation as an activist paper supporting the efforts of Native peoples to reassert their sovereignty, strengthen their cultural identity, and demand the enforcement of treaty rights. *Wassaja*, published by the American Indian Historical Society beginning in 1972, also had a national focus.

The two largest Native-owned newspapers are the *Lakota Times* which started publication in 1981, continued as a weekly national Native newspaper renamed *Indian Country Today* (ICT) in 1992, and the monthly *News from Indian Country* (NFIC), established in 1987 and published monthly.[9] NFIC was founded and edited by journalist Paul DeMain (Ojibwe/Oneida) in 1986. Until it ceased publication in 2019, it claimed to be the oldest, continually run, and nationally distributed publication not owned by a Tribal government.

ICT has gone through multiple iterations since Tim Giago (Oglala Lakota) began publishing the *Lakota Times* on the Pine Ridge Reservation in 1981. Current managing editor and respected journalist, Mark Trahant (Shoshone-Bannock) wrote, "Three themes emerged in the early years of Lakota Times and Indian Country Today: An honest accounting of the boarding school experience (so relevant now); an exploration of the mascot issue and its impact on Native people; and a strident challenge to the work of the American Indian Movement."

The outlet has changed locations and ownership, owned for a time by the Oneida Nation of New York and later the NCAI. It is currently an independent enterprise. Under Trahant's leadership, ICT has evolved from a weekly printed newspaper to its current form as an online multimedia platform. It is now classified as an independent, non-profit news enterprise overseen by a Native board of directors under the name IndiJ Public Media.[10]

As of 2018, Native print media, like non-Native media, has experienced a significant decline in the number of newspapers and magazines. According to journalist Jodi Rave, in 1998 there were approximately 700 print media sources serving Native peoples across Indian Country. That number fell to about 200 by 2018, including Native government-owned newspapers and individually owned enterprises, in large part because online competition has dramatically reduced newspaper revenues from traditional print media advertising such as retail, personal ads, and help-wanted postings.[11]

For those with ready access to broadband services, such a shift may seem like progress. For many across Indian Country who lack digital access, the loss of printed newspapers, often the only reliable source of information, has been a hardship. It is very difficult to act as a responsible, involved citizen of a nation without accurate news and information.

Significantly, Native governments own 72% of all Native print and radio operations across Indian Country.[12] This is a radically different situation from that of non-Native media, which is privately owned; and while subject to some

334 INDIGENOUS GOVERNANCE

government regulation the U.S. Constitution's 1st Amendment freedom of the press clause allows the media great sway. Such is generally not the situation on Tribal lands since the U.S. Constitution's 1st Amendment does not apply to operations and activities on Native reservations or trust lands. More on this momentarily.

Broadcast Media (Radio and Television)

Radio and, to a lesser extent, television appear to be natural media for Indigenous peoples, since they involve the oral and visual transmission of knowledge, and since Native peoples rely on storytelling to carry on tradition, to educate, and to entertain. Gordon Regguinti, formerly the Executive Director of the NAJA, said that Native radio was "an electronic smoke signal, a modern version of the smoke signals that allowed Indians to communicate over long distances in times past." Regguinti, who enthusiastically supports Natives' use of radio said it "is one of the least expensive ways to reach [Indigenous] people and to set up a dialogue so those people will have a voice."[13] Given the lack of digital access, it is understandable that radio continues to be of great importance in Indian Country.

John Collier, the Commissioner of Indian Affairs in the 1930s and 1940s, was well aware of Native oral traditions, and he had funds set aside for radio broadcasts in Alaska villages and supported a national program designed to enlighten and inform Americans about Indigenous peoples, their unique histories, and Tribal affairs.[14] As mentioned, Native nations lag far behind other regions of the larger society with regard to broadband and telecommunication services. Poverty and the remoteness of many Native territories are two of the factors that explain the lack of access. According to the Congressional Research Service, as of December 2017, "Approximately 32% of Natives living on Tribal land lacked access to broadband at speeds of at least 25 Mbps download/3 Mbps upload. This compares unfavorably to about 6% of all Americans lacking access to broadband at these speeds. Tribal areas that are most lacking in broadband service or rural Alaskan villages or rural Native lands in the lower 48 states."[15]

Despite the obstacles, a few Native governments have established their own broadband providers. In 2018, the Fond du Lac Band of Lake Superior Chippewa created a corporation, Aaniin, to build and provide fiber-optic service to the 1,800 residents of the reservation.[16] The $1.2 trillion Infrastructure Investment and Jobs Act adopted in 2021 by Congress includes funds to expand broadband infrastructure throughout Indian Country.[17]

Native nations, however, did not become involved in the use or ownership of radio or television until the 1970s. The first radio stations began in Alaska in the wake of the Alaska Native Claims Settlement Act (ANCSA) of 1971. One of the major developments under the ANCSA involved the creation of thirteen regional Native corporations to manage the cash and lands conveyed under the act. Three public radio stations, two Native and one non-Native, were started to keep Alaskan Natives informed about the political, legal, economic, and cultural issues affecting their lands and rights. The stations employed a reporter to keep track of the state legislature's activities.

Other Native nations followed suit and by the mid-1990s twenty-six Tribal public radio stations (e.g., KNNB, White Mountain Apache; WYDH, Poarch Band of Creek; KSUT, Southern Ute; and KCIE, Jicarilla Apache) and one Tribal-controlled commercial radio station were serving Indigenous peoples across the country and Canada.[18] The number of Indigenous governments establishing radio stations also continues to climb. In 2018 the Cheyenne River Sioux Tribe established a commercial station, KIPI 93.5 FM, with 100,000 watts of power. According to Native Public Media, as of 2021, there were some sixty-seven radio stations owned or operating across Indian Country. There are nine television stations operating on Native lands. The Sycuan Band of Kumeyaay, the Navajo Nation, the Passamaquoddy, the Chickasaw, and the Tulalip Tribes provide programming to their members and residents on and near Tribal lands.[19]

Enter the Internet

As we well know, the Internet has totally transformed the way people deliver and receive information and Native nations are no exception. We often hear of the disinformation spread through these networks, yet, for Indian Country, those lucky enough to have digital access have been able to utilize them to help their communities. Social media platforms like Facebook, Instagram, Twitter, YouTube, and TikTok have contributed to political mobilization by generating virtual social networks where individuals, organizations, corporations, and governments can quickly share information. For many, these venues are essential for information sharing and organizing, whether about a Tribal election, distribution of COVID-19 relief funds, or the oil pipeline conflicts involving the Anishinaabe nations and Enbridge's Line 3 or the Standing Rock Sioux's struggles with the Dakota Access Pipeline.

Let's look briefly at how the Standing Rock Sioux government and their thousands of allies engaged social media in their effort to stop the construction of the Dakota Access Pipeline (DAPL), a $3.8 billion, 1,172-mile-long pipeline that carries oil across four states—North Dakota, South Dakota, Iowa, and Illinois—and under two major rivers, the Mississippi and the Missouri.[20] Even

336 INDIGENOUS GOVERNANCE

as the Standing Rock Tribe sued in federal court in 2016 to stop construction of the line, Chairman Dave Archambault, sent out a call for support. Within a short period of time, Native youth organizers, using the Internet, had collected more than 450,000 signatures by April 2016 of those opposed to the pipeline and some 360 Native nations enacted formal resolutions pledging their support to the Standing Rock community.

At its height, some 10,000 people had made their way to Standing Rock by late 2016. This was the greatest demonstration of support for a Native nation in Indigenous history. As Dallas Goldtooth (Mdewakanton Dakota/Diné) of the Indigenous Environmental Network put it, "The Movement's success came through social media and citizen journalism. Just people, regular people, live streaming, posting, updating. It was regular people who were talking about ongoing caravans from Cincinnati, from San Francisco, from Denver, from Santa Fe. It was regular common people using social media to connect with other people."[21]

As the researchers who produced Reclaiming Native Truth: A Project to Dispel America's Myths and Misconceptions found in their final report, "Research Findings: Compilation of All Research,"[22] social media plays a major role in how Native content is distributed in Indian Country and online services are the place where a majority of non-Native Americans say they get much of their news. In November 2009, the Native Public Media (NPM) gathered data on technology use, access, and adoption in Indian Country. NPM, whose mission is "to promote healthy, engaged, independent Native communities by strengthening and expanding Native American media capacity and by empowering a strong, proud Native American voice," found that Native peoples were increasingly utilizing technology to interact, communicate, and gain knowledge and skills. They concluded that "despite a lack of access, higher prices for broadband and often non-existent infrastructure, leaders in these communities have developed a vision and built self-sufficient networks and community technology centers to connect and strengthen their Native communities."[23] The NPM report stated that the success of Tribal projects focused on technology required strong leadership, planning commitment from Native leaders, and community participation.

Noting the barriers Native nations face in accessing technology, the NPM report made eight policy recommendations: (1) implement a strategic initiative targeting Tribal communications development, (2) create a Tribal broadband plan, (3) establish effectual consultation and coordination with Tribal governments, (4) reform the Universal Service Fund and their delivery of broadband support, (5) increase Internet access in Indian Country, (6) remove funding barriers facing Native applications for technology support available through the American Reinvestment and Recovery Act, (7) increase federal funding and education, and (8) increase research and analysis of Native access to and use of technology.[24]

Of course, Native and non-Native individuals, organizations, and Tribal governments have established many websites and Facebook pages that seek to address the informational needs of Natives and the public, but a critical shortage of broadband infrastructure across Indian Country continues to plague the efforts of Native governments and their citizens to be more fully connected to the opportunities made available through the Internet.

Free Press Struggles in Indian Country

Across a majority of Native nations, similar to many international states around the globe, the government owns media outlets and controls the content that is presented for public consumption. This is to be expected in communist or totalitarian regimes like China, Russia, and North Korea, but Indigenous governments are neither communistic nor totalitarian regimes. Nevertheless, there is ample data which confirms that freedom of the press in Native lands is not consistently enjoyed by journalists.

As noted earlier, in the United States, neither the federal nor state governments own or control the communication networks, although the constitutions of those polities allow for some regulation of content. In the U.S. Constitution, the 1st Amendment declares that "Congress shall make no law . . . abridging the freedom of speech, or of the press, or the right of the people peaceably to assemble." And all fifty states contain their own versions of the U.S. Bill of Rights, which include freedom of the press as one of the essential rights. Virginia's Declaration of Rights is more elaborate than that of the U.S. Constitution and states in Section 12 "that the freedoms of speech and of the press are among the great bulwarks of liberty, and can never be restrained except by despotic governments; that any citizen may freely speak, write, and publish his sentiments on all subjects, being responsible for the abuse of that right; that the General Assembly shall not pass any law abridging the freedom of speech or of the press, nor the right of the people peaceably to assemble, and to petition the government for the redress of grievances."

The federal and state constitutional amendments are inapplicable and thus unavailable to Native or non-Native journalists working for Native news organs because Natives stand in an entirely different constitutional position with regard to their Tribal governments than they do with regard to the federal or state governments. The differences arise because of the existence, meaning, and legal force of Native sovereignty and because of the extra-constitutional character of Indigenous governments. As a result, it is unclear whether censorship of Native

338 INDIGENOUS GOVERNANCE

media by Tribal politicians, who are in a sense the publishers, violates federal or Tribal law.

Native governments are exempt from compliance with such laws as the Freedom of Information Act of 1967, which gives U.S. citizens the right to inspect unprotected government documents. One act that appears to extend a measure of freedom to Native journalists is the 1968 Indian Civil Rights Act (ICRA) which imposed on Native governments certain modified versions of most of the U.S. Bill of Rights. The pertinent section for this discussion is the following: "No Indian Tribe in exercising powers of self-government shall (1) make or enforce any law prohibiting the free exercise of religion, or abridging the freedom of speech, or of the press, or the right of the people peaceably to assemble and to petition for a redress of grievances."[25]

At least ninety Native constitutions, Articles of Association, and governing resolutions explicitly mention Free Press and the ICRA. For example, the Osage Nation's 2006 Constitution declares that the government shall not "make or enforce any law prohibiting the free exercise of religion, or abridging the freedom of speech or the press, or the right of the people peaceably to assemble and to petition for redress of grievances."[26] And the Wichita Tribe's Governing Resolution (2016) in Article X—Bill of Rights states that "all members of the Tribe shall enjoy without hindrance, freedom of worship, conscience, speech, assembly, and association." Notwithstanding the explicit language of the ICRA which theoretically provides comprehensive protection for fundamental civil liberties like freedom of the press to all residents, that is Natives and non-Natives, the experiences of some journalists working for Native government-owned media is that "Free Press guarantees provide little or no protection because tribal governments view their newspaper staffs as employees wholly answerable to tribal governments."[27] The many free press problems encountered by Native newspaper editors and journalists include politically motivated firings before or shortly after elections, cutting off or selective reduction of publication funds, being forced to hire unqualified editors or reporters who are political supporters of government officials, firings as a result of the publication of unflattering news stories or editorials, the banning of journalists from Tribal government meetings, restriction of press access to particular Tribal government documents, and occasional death threats over published stories.[28]

The Native American Journalist Association (NAJA) conducted a press freedom survey in 2018 and found that 83% of respondents said that stories about Native government affairs "sometimes, frequently, or always go unreported due to governmental censorship."[29] And Steve Russell, a retired Native judge and newspaper columnist, concurred with the gist of NAJA's findings, noting that "reporters for tribal media often have to risk their jobs to bring home the bacon for the people they serve. You can't have a functioning democracy," Russell continued, "when people are not allowed to know what is going on."[30]

Besides censorship, Native news outlets also suffer from meager budgets. As Rave reported, while there are philanthropic resources available to support independent journalism, there is little funding made available to Native media personnel. As Peggy Berryhill, the station manager at KGUA in California noted, it is a struggle for a noncommercial radio station to secure funds from philanthropic organizations because they normally "do not fund general operating expenditures and also tend to fund larger nonprofits."[31]

As of 2023, a mere handful of Native governments have formally enacted laws or constitutional amendments that extend real protection and autonomy for those looking to exercise freedom of the press. The Cherokee Nation of Oklahoma was the first Indigenous government to provide legal protections for its media. In 2000, in the wake of a constitutional free press crisis fueled by the actions of former chief, Joe Byrd, a unanimous Tribal Council enacted the Independent Press Act of 2000.[32]

Three years later, the Navajo Nation Council, emerging from its own brutal intra-Tribal conflict, precipitated by the nefarious activities of their former Chairman, Peter MacDonald, also acted to allow its newspaper, *The Navajo Times*, to become independent and a for-profit publishing company. This decision was a direct result of the events leading up to and after MacDonald's reelection in 1987. Under editor Mark Trahant's courageous leadership, *The Navajo Times* endorsed Peterson Zah and ran headlines and editorials questioning MacDonald's politics and policies. A month after the election, which MacDonald won by a slim margin, and with *The Navajo Times* continuing to challenge MacDonald's administrative activities, MacDonald sent Tribal police to shut the paper down. The staff was promptly fired. MacDonald claimed that the paper was closed because it was losing too much money. The employees, however, saw their firing as politically motivated. Trahant, put it this way: "If the paper had indeed been shut down for financial reasons then why was no audit conducted before its closure, why were there no negotiations, and more importantly, why was the entire staff terminated?"[33] The newspaper's doors remain shuttered for nearly four months. When it began publishing again, it had been dramatically reformatted and was now a weekly publication of local governmental and other events. *The Navajo Times*, which had been pushing for a greater measure of journalistic independence had, for the time being, been stifled.

This tenuous situation persisted until October 23, 2003, when Tom Arviso Jr., the paper's Chief Executive Officer, went before the Council with a resolution seeking approval to incorporate the paper and become the *Navajo Times Publishing Company*. If approved, "this would allow it to become an independent

340 INDIGENOUS GOVERNANCE

newspaper and a for-profit publishing company."[34] The Council voted unanimously in favor of the resolution. This was a pathbreaking decision, similar to the Cherokee Nation's earlier actions.

Thus far, only four other Native governments have acted to amend their constitutions or other governing documents to enact free press legislation: The Osage Nation, the Muscogee (Creek) Nation, the Confederated Tribes of the Grand Ronde, and the Eastern Band of Cherokee Indians. The Eastern Band of Cherokee had first enacted an ordinance in 2006 but decided to amend and strengthen it in 2018. The new law declares that "the Eastern Band of Cherokee Indians Free Press shall be independent from any influence and free of any particular political interest. It is the duty of the press to report without bias the activities of the Tribe, the tribal government, and any and all news of interest to have informed citizens. Any incident of political pressure or influence that threatens a staff member of the *Cherokee One Feather* shall be turned over to the EBCI Office of Internal Audit & Ethics for an ethics violation investigation, review and recommendation."[35]

The rapid spread of digital media since the 1990s has dramatically changed the news media landscape across Indian Country, the United States, and the world. While digital media is less available in Indian Country, due to the lack of technological infrastructure, that gap is slowly narrowing. As discussed earlier, print media has declined dramatically throughout Native America and the country in the last two decades, while television audiences have remained more stable "but are increasingly made up of older people."[36] Younger individuals, Native and non-Native, generally receive their news online or through smartphones.

The media, regardless of how information is dispensed, occupy a crucial role in any society. And as NAJA has stated, "An independent tribal media is an essential part of a thriving, transparent tribal government. As tribal governments grow, it becomes more important that tribal media grow to inform tribal citizens how these rapid changes affect their families and communities. Tribal governments must foster an environment where tribal media can develop policies, journalistic excellence, editorial freedom and independence from undue governmental influence."

But as noted above, Native governments' ownership of a majority of Indigenous media outlets continues to pose substantial problems for many Native journalists who seek to exercise free speech and freedom of the press by reporting on issues that do not always portray the governing elites in a positive light. The media promise to remain in a position of significant influence regarding how Americans perceive Native people nationally and how Native nations perceive themselves vis-à-vis their own local issues. While gaming Nations have become increasingly adept at using their resources to influence the public and policymakers at all levels of government, especially on issues that might directly impinge on gaming revenues, they are also channeling some of their monies toward the purchase, production, and control of various forms of media. There will likely remain ongoing tension, however, between Native ownership of media and the freedom of Native and non-Native media to report on Indigenous governmental activity.

14
Peoples of Alaxsxaq and Kānaka Maoli

Indigenous peoples commonly referred to as "Alaska Natives" are more accurately identified and divided into five broad cultural groupings: Inupiaq, Yupik, Athabascan, Alutiiq, and Tlingit. These five—speaking over twenty different languages and more than fifty dialects—are organized into more than 200 communities across what the Unangan (sometimes referred to as Aleut) call *Alaxsxaq*, their name for Alaska.[1] *Alaxsxaq* means "place the sea moves toward."[2] Indigenous peoples of this region utilize several types of governing bodies, including IRA governments, traditional governing councils, cities, corporations, municipalities, and traditional villages. Some are chartered under state law and others under federal law. These communities have never signed formal treaties with either Russian or U.S. representatives, nor have they been militarily conquered or forced to relocate. Still, "the combined ideologies of racial superiority and religion worked with capitalist expansion to contribute to the early ambiguity of Alaska Native political status under American rule."[3]

Kānaka Maoli are not as culturally or organizationally diverse as Native peoples within Alaska, but their political and legal status is as complex and arguably more contested than that of Alaska Native communities or the Native nations located within the lower 48 states. They are not ethnically related to Native peoples on the mainland. Although they signed several treaties with European colonial powers and the United States, they do not have the same legal status as Native nations in the other states. The relative geographical remoteness of their Hawaiian Island homelands further distinguishes them.[4]

There remains a fair amount of confusion and uncertainty about the actual political and legal status of both peoples. The U.S. Supreme Court ruling in 2021, *Yellen v. Confederated Tribes of the Chehalis Reservation*,[5] has brought a measure of clarity to at least one element of the governing units in Alaska, but uncertainty remains regarding the overall governing status of Alaska Natives and Kānaka Maoli among state officials, federal officials, the public, and Native nations in the lower 48 states. We will begin here by describing and evaluating the political status of Alaska Natives, before turning attention to Kānaka Maoli.

Indigenous Governance. David E. Wilkins, Oxford University Press. © Oxford University Press 2024.
DOI: 10.1093/oso/9780190095994.003.0015

Alaska Natives: A Brief History

The land mass now known as Alaska has been inhabited by Indigenous peoples for at least 30,000 years.[6] Communities were composed of social units like families and clans that performed multiple functions, including addressing subsistence economic concerns, political affairs, and religious issues. Community participation "created a flexible social structure characterized by situational leadership and the fluid alignment of family lines."[7] Villages, ranging in population from less than fifty to over 1,000 inhabitants, were historically the most common type of organization, and they were loosely linked to other villages by language, biological association, and shared cultural practices.[8]

And, so they lived until Russian hunter-traders, known as *promyshleniki*, arrived, in search of sea otter pelts, "after Vitus Bering, a Dane in the czar's service who gave his name to the straits, reached the Aleutian Islands in 1741."[9] The Russians' arrival opened the door for more than a century of harsh exploitation of Aleuts who were enslaved and forced to hunt sea otters and fur seals for Russian colonists. The harsh conditions of Russian colonialism and the introduction of novel diseases that accompanied the colonists were devastating, and the Aleut population declined precipitously—by at least 80%—between 1740 and 1867.[10]

Since there were likely never more than 550 Russians in Alaska at any point, their presence had a variable impact on the Indigenous groups in the region. Their only permanent settlements were at Sitka and Kodiak.[11] The Aleuts were the most heavily impacted group—enduring slavery and diseases. More remote groups like the Inupiaq, Yupik, and Athabascans had little substantial contact with the Russians. Trade rather than land possession and permanent colonization were the dominant concerns of the Russians, so once the sea otter population was nearly wiped out by the 1860s due to over-exploitation, most left the region.

The ensuing Treaty of 1867, negotiated between U.S. Secretary of State, William H Seward and minister for the Russian Czar, Edward de Stoeckl, effectively transferred the territory of so-called Russian America to the United States for $7,200,000 in gold.[12] Not surprisingly, Indigenous peoples in Alaska were never consulted, let alone asked for their consent, to this treaty. The arrogance and hubris exhibited by the leaders of both invading countries precluded even the contemplation of the fact that Natives were the actual owners of their own lands. Their actions reflected the mindset defined by the doctrine of discovery, which purports to give Western states a self-described superior title to all lands they claim. As Fae L. Korsmo put it: "To this day, some Alaska Natives refer to 1867 as the year that 'the occupation rights' to Alaska were transferred; Russia

344   INDIGENOUS GOVERNANCE

never had legitimate possession of Alaska, so how could Russia sell something it did not own?"[13]

While Native peoples were not direct parties to the treaty involving their territories, the U.S. and Russian negotiators included in Article III a statement that directly considered their status. Therein, inhabitants of Alaska were divided into three broad categories: "(1) Russian subjects who preferred to retain their allegiance and were permitted to return to Russia within three years; (2) Russian subjects who preferred to remain in Alaska and enjoy the rights and immunities of U.S. citizens; and (3) the uncivilized tribes who would be "subject to such laws and regulations as the United States may, from time to time, adopt in regard to aboriginal tribes of that country."[14]

According to Case and Voluck, the third clause dealing with the "uncivilized tribes" acknowledges that the existing body of U.S. federal Indian law and policy was now applicable to all Indigenous peoples in Alaska.[15] They continue that if this is the case, then logically, federal law should also serve to protect their aboriginal land titles. However, this has not consistently proven to be the case for Alaskan Natives, as over the years, federal case law has vacillated on this important point.[16]

Immediately after the 1867 Treaty of Cession, the United States sent its military to assume control of the region. In 1884 Congress enacted the Organic Act which, among other things, ended military rule for the District of Alaska and made Alaska a customs district governed by federal officials.[17] That act also contained a clear statement that appeared to affirm the aboriginal rights of Alaska Natives: "The Indians or other persons in said district shall not be disturbed in the possession of any lands actually in their use or occupation or now claimed by them but the terms under which such persons may acquire title to such lands is reserved for future legislation by Congress."[18] A second organic act in 1912 renamed the District of Alaska as the Territory of Alaska. The territory was provided with congressional representation and a legislature but denied the power to manage land or hunting and fishing. Alaska Natives were denied voting rights in the measure.[19]

Interestingly, during the first few decades of U.S. colonial rule, there were debates about how these Indigenous peoples were to be dealt with from a racial perspective. Francis Walker, the Commissioner of Indian Affairs from 1871 to 1873, believed that Alaskan Natives should not be classified as "Indians" but were more likely of "Asiatic origin," and thus federal law should not be "extended unnecessarily to races of a questionable ethnical type, and occupying a position practically distinct and apart from the range of the undoubted Indian tribes of the continent."[20]

Initially, the Office of Indian Affairs refused to accept trust responsibility for Alaska Natives; instead, Congress situated them under the Bureau of Education "which became the sole federal agency charged with Alaska Native Service."[21] They would remain under the Bureau of Education until 1931 when the Bureau of Indian Affairs (BIA) stepped in and began providing them with educational services.[22]

While early federal programs focused largely on education, other developments were occurring. Native business operations, including a reindeer industry, sawmills, and salmon operations were created. Also, approximately 150 reservations were established throughout the region, ranging from a few to thousands of acres.[23] Several years later, in 1923 before the BIA took control of the federal government's relations with Alaska Natives, the Solicitor for the Department of the Interior stated that the political, legal, and cultural status of Alaska Natives was comparable to that of Native nations in the lower 48 states: "The relations existing between [the Alaska Natives] and the government are very similar and, in many respects, identical with those which have long existed between the government and the aboriginal people residing within the territorial limits of the United States."[24]

Collier, Congress, and the Alaskan Natives

Two years prior to the enactment of the 1934 Indian Reorganization Act (IRA), the Solicitor issued an even more detailed opinion elaborating on how and why the political and legal status of Alaska Natives was similar to that of other Indigenous peoples: "From the foregoing it is clear that no distinction has been or can be made between the Indians and other Natives of Alaska so far as the laws and relations of the United States are concerned whether the Eskimos and other natives are of Indian origin or not as they are all wards of the Nation, and their status is in material respects similar to that of the Indians of the United States. It follows that the natives of Alaska, as referred to in the treaty of March 30, 1867, between the United States and Russia are entitled to the benefits of and are subject to the general laws and regulations governing the Indians of the United States."[25]

Notwithstanding the force of this opinion, when the IRA was adopted in 1934,[26] Alaskan Natives were eligible for only a few of the law's benefits and programs, even though the Act had declared that "for the purposes of this Act, Eskimos and other aboriginal people of Alaska shall be considered Indians."[27] A separate act in 1936,[28] an amendment to the IRA, was necessary to extend the rest of the Act's provisions to them.

Between 1938 and 1950, some sixty-nine Native villages adopted constitutions that were then approved by the Secretary of the Interior.[29] Native property and affairs also came under trust protection. Federal and state policy encouraging the

346   INDIGENOUS GOVERNANCE

incorporation of Alaska Native communities under state law began in 1963, and approximately 127 Native communities were organized under Alaska's state municipal incorporation statutes. These state-chartered entities continue to coexist alongside the federal IRA-chartered entities.

Despite this seeming comparability, "the distinctions between Alaska Natives as governments and as landowners, however, have remained clouded." This is evidenced in a 1955 Supreme Court ruling, *Tee-Hit-Ton v. United States*, in which the Court held that Alaska Natives lacked recognized title to their aboriginal territory and that the federal government could take "unrecognized" Native lands without having to pay just compensation under the Fifth Amendment to the Constitution.

Along with this ruling came the Alaska Statehood Act of 1958,[30] which authorized the state to select 108 million acres of public land, including prime Native hunting and fishing territory, as its proprietary land based on Alaska's admission as a state. Interestingly, Alaska's Statehood Act also contains a disclaimer clause[31] that speaks to the relationship between the federal government, the state, and Alaska Natives. The disclaimer declares in Section 4:

> As a compact with the United States said State and its people do agree and declare that they forever disclaim all right and title to any lands or other property not granted or confirmed to the State or its political subdivisions by or under the authority of this Act, the right or title to which is held by the United States or subject to disposition by the United States, and to any lands or other property (including fishing rights), the right or title to which may be held by any Indians, Eskimos, or Aleuts (hereinafter called natives) or is held by the United States in trust for such natives; that all such lands or other property (including fishing rights), the right or title to which may be held by said natives or is held by the United States in trust for said natives, shall be and remain under the absolute jurisdiction and control of the United States until disposed of under its authority, except to such extent as the Congress has prescribed or may hereafter prescribe, and except when held by individual natives in fee without restriction on alienation.[32]

The state was essentially affirming that Alaskan Natives and their lands, waters, and resources would be let alone by the state because of the distinctive political relationship that existed between the federal government and Native communities. State involvement could only enter the equation when individual Natives gained fee-simple title to property. The state also had to confirm that it lacked the power to tax any lands or property held by Natives unless Congress expressly authorized the taxes. The taxation clause reads thus: "*And provided further*, That no taxes shall be imposed by said State upon any lands or other property now owned or hereafter acquired by the U.S. or which, as hereinabove set forth may belong to said natives, except to such extent as the Congress has prescribed or may hereafter prescribe, and except when held by individual natives in fee without restrictions on alienation."[33] (emphasis theirs) The state's enabling act language on Natives was reiterated almost verbatim in the 1959 state constitution.

The *Tee-Hit-Ton* ruling and Alaska's Statehood Act prompted the formation of the Alaska Federation of Natives, an interest group whose primary goal was the eventual settlement of aboriginal claims.[34] Oil discoveries on the North Slope of Alaska in 1968 only intensified Indigenous determination to secure control of their remaining territory. Energy corporations, the state, and other interested parties were also excited about the possibility of a final settlement of the Natives' land claims.

In 1971 Congress responded with a passage of the Alaska Native Claims Settlement Act[35] (ANCSA), a comprehensive law regarding the land rights of Alaska's 80,000 Indigenous inhabitants. This law significantly modified the nature of the federal government's relationship with these Native nations. Unlike most Indigenous reservations, which are held "in trust" by the federal government on behalf of the nations and their citizens, Native land in Alaska under the act was granted in fee-simple title. The act required the establishment of both regional and village business corporations organized under state law to receive and manage the money and land conveyed by the act. In addition, forty-four million acres were conveyed to these corporations, along with $962.5 million in compensation for the extinguishment of all other Native claims to the rest of Alaska. The ANSCA also extinguished aboriginal hunting and fishing rights to "public lands." However, a subsequent amendment restored the protection of subsistence hunting and fishing rights for rural Natives.

Between 1972 and 1974, twelve regional corporations (later a thirteenth corporation was formed for Alaska Native non-residents) and nearly 200 village corporations were established as "profit-making business corporations under the laws of the State of Alaska."[36] All Alaska Natives were enrolled as individual shareholders of the ANCSA corporations. The corporations were required to distribute 10% of the funds to all stockholders and 45% (after five years it increased to 50%) to village corporations and to stockholders who did not live in a village. As of December 18, 1971, all living Native persons possessing at least one-fourth or more Native blood were issued 100 shares of corporate stock in their regional corporation. There were some 74,300 initial shareholders.[37] The act required each regional corporation to use its land and resources for the profit of its shareholders.

Congressional intent in this legislation was clear: "Congress intended to promote economic development and the economic assimilation of Alaska Natives

348 INDIGENOUS GOVERNANCE

to the American mold. The results of this decision have been mixed. Some corporations became financially successful, while others remained inactive and a few faced bankruptcy."[38] But Donald C. Mitchell also points out that "more than a quarter century after its enactment, the ANCSA remains the most generous aboriginal claims settlement in United States history."[39] And while conceding that economic assimilation was a principal ANCSA objective, it was the Alaska Federation of Natives that first recommended the idea of using chartered business corporations of Alaska state to implement the Settlement Act—it was not a congressional imposition.[40]

That said, Evon Peter has voiced a concern that is shared by many Alaska Natives:[41]

> Although a few Native people participated in the debates surrounding the passage of ANCSA, it was not a legitimately negotiated treaty or settlement between the United States and Alaska Native Tribes. ANCSA was void of direct negotiation with Alaska Native Tribes and was not put to a vote of the Indigenous peoples. Furthermore, ANCSA extinguished previously recognized Indian reservations in Alaska (with the exception of Metlakatla), extinguished Indigenous hunting and fishing rights, and paved the way for the oil industry and state governments to access and transport oil from northern Alaska. This act was essentially a social and political experiment on Alaska Native peoples. ANSCA was a way of dealing with the "Indian problem" through assimilation, exploitation, corporatization, and extinguishment of Indigenous rights. It was a politically correct illusion that perpetuated colonization in contemporary times.

As originally enacted, the ANCSA prevented shareholders from selling their shares for twenty years, or until 1991. Thereafter, these shares could be sold to any person. And corporate-owned lands were to be exempt from state and local taxation for this same period. Alaska Natives became concerned about the potential long-term impact of these measures, and they successfully lobbied Congress in 1988 to amend the act and extend the restrictions on the sale of stock and on state taxation "indefinitely." But Congress also allowed each corporation to issue and sell stock to non-Natives and rejected the Natives' request to allow these corporations to transfer their land to Tribal governments in order to give this acreage additional protection.[42]

In the late 1990s, Alaska Natives and their villages and corporations fought to make their organizations more profitable and gain greater political autonomy, while preventing non-Natives and the state from gaining any additional power over them. In 1998, their efforts received a significant blow from the U.S. Supreme Court. In *Alaska v. Native Village of Venetie Tribal Government*, the Court held that Venetie's 1.8 million acres of fee-simple land did not qualify as "Indian country," and therefore, the Tribal government lacked authority to impose a 5% business tax on a non-Native contractor building a school in the village.

Notwithstanding this major judicial loss, many Alaska Natives have continued their push for a clearer recognition of their status as Indigenous governments, sensing that neither the ANCSA nor other laws are sufficient to protect their traditions and rights.[43] Encouragingly, in 1993, the Department of the Interior acknowledged that the over 200 Alaska Native entities were federally recognized governmental bodies.[44] But what governing powers these bodies have in the wake of the *Venetie* ruling is still unclear. Alaskan Native communities will continue to wield sovereignty as well as they can, given the lack of clarity. In a number of cases, they "have therefore acted independently to establish tribal courts, to dissolve city governments, to restrict outside interference, to claim jurisdiction over their lands and resources, to pursue relief in international forums, and to form regional and inter-village compacts."[45]

Alaska Native peoples have continued to push for greater protections of their lands. The Akaichak Native Community, organized under the IRA, has fought to persuade the Interior Department to take land into trust, asserting the Alaska exemptions from land under trust regulations are discriminatory. As Willie Kasayulie, the President and CEO of Akiachak Limited, stated in 2004, his community and all other Alaska Native communities are hobbled because ANCSA "does not address the rights of our tribal governments."[46] "Under the IRA," Kasayulie said, "We have a tribal government; we also have a corporate charter. The ANCSA corporations took over the responsibilities that we have the right to exercise under our tribal corporate charter. At the time of the land claims debates, the tribal governments were ignored and set aside. This is my complaint with ANCSA: the tribes were not invited to the table to be involved in the discussion of the land claims."[47]

In December 2014, the Department of the Interior announced final rules for placing lands into trust for Alaska Native Tribes. "This marks a major step forward in federal policy in Alaska. Our aim is to make it possible to secure Tribal homelands, which in turn advances Tribal sovereignty and economic development, promotes the health and welfare of Tribal communities, and protects Tribal culture and traditional ways of life," said Assistant Secretary Kevin Washburn.[48] Alaska challenged Native efforts to place land in trust, but their challenge was dismissed by the U.S. Court of Appeals in *Akaichak Native Community* et al. *v. Department of Interior* and Sally Jewell, in July 2016.[49]

After the *Akaichak* decision, state officials temporarily relented in their efforts to challenge and deny the sovereign character of Native Tribes within Alaska and the land into trust process. As evidence, the state Attorney General, Jahna Lindemuth, issued a legal opinion on October 19, 2017, in response to

350 INDIGENOUS GOVERNANCE

a query from Governor Bill Walker who wanted to learn about the political status of Alaskan Native peoples and to understand their relationship with the state. Lindemuth's lengthy (sixteen pages) opinion addressed three broad elements: (1) Tribes do exist in Alaska; (2) Tribes within Alaska retain their inherent sovereignty; and (3) Areas where the scope of sovereignty is clear are abundant. While acknowledging that Natives had inhabited the territory now known as Alaska for thousands of years, Lindemuth noted that as recently as 1993, the state had taken the contorted legal position that Tribes did not exist in Alaska. Alaska's Supreme Court in 1988 had also erroneously ruled that "there are not now and never have been tribes of Indians in Alaska as that term is used in federal Indian law."[50]

The state changed its legal stance gradually after the BIA, in 1993, issued its list of federally recognized Native polities that for the first time included Alaska Tribes. As Lindemuth noted: "The current state of the law is clear—there *are* 229 sovereign tribes within Alaska." (emphasis hers) And given the diversity of governing arrangements among Alaska's Indigenous peoples, Lindemuth also noted that this would not affect the inherent sovereignty of the groups. "Alaska Tribes," she said, "have several types of governments including traditional councils and IRA governing councils. Additionally, tribes may choose to form a governmental entity, such as the Central Council of Tlingit and Haida Indian Tribes of Alaska, which received federal recognition, in addition to the constituent Tribes, which are also recognized. All of these entities, however, are governments of Alaska Tribes."[51]

Despite recent improvements in relations between the state and Alaska Natives, on January 17, 2023, the state sued the Department of the Interior for having placed a small piece of land—a 787 square feet parcel—in Juneau in trust and declared it a reservation for the Central Council of the Tlingit and Haida Tribes. The state claims that such an act limits the sovereign jurisdiction of the state and undercuts key terms of the ANCSA.[52]

ANCSA: The Corporate and the Tribal

There was a presumption on the part of many that ANCSA extinguished all aspects of the distinctive political and legal status of Indigenous peoples in Alaska. That presumption is true in so far as aboriginal hunting, fishing, and land rights are concerned. It is not accurate, however, regarding the Indigenous right of inherent self-government and self-determination.[53] Nonetheless, the workings of the non-profit regional and village corporations and the relationships between them and the 229 federally recognized non-profit Tribal governments that have been in existence for thousands of years, have proven difficult to describe and understand.

As noted earlier, the large regional Alaska Native corporations, as organized under state law, share fundamental characteristics while also relying on a variety of distinctly governmental practices. As with other Alaska corporations, these Native bodies are subject to the state's corporate laws (with some exceptions) and are led by elected Boards of Directors.[54] While the Native corporations, by law, are subject to some financial reporting requirements, there is relatively little oversight of this reporting. Further, ANCSA exempts the corporations from complying with federal securities laws while mandating that they provide an annual report to their shareholders.

These regional corporations, the General Accounting Office (GAO) reported, "provide a wide variety of monetary and nonmonetary benefits to their shareholders and other Alaska Natives. Monetary benefits include shareholder dividends, elder benefits, scholarships, memorial benefits, shareholders' equity, and charitable donations. Nonmonetary benefits—often offered in partnership with village corporations, tribal organizations, and nonprofit organizations within the region—include employment opportunities, cultural preservation, land management, economic development, and advocacy on behalf of Alaska Natives and their communities."[55]

Alaska Native governments, while having a much longer de facto lineage, have faced a welter of conflicting federal and state laws and policies that have sometimes affirmed their existence and at other times denied it. As Thomas Swenson has observed, the tension and confusion between how Alaska Natives function within the two very different organizational paradigms of the corporate world and the Indigenous world make it difficult to understand this fluctuating situation.[56] Swenson posed these two questions which warrant more attention than we can dedicate in this study: "Does either the tribe or the corporation allow Alaska Natives to assert themselves more effectively in the political world? To what extent do the corporations serve the same population as the tribe?"[57]

A key distinction between the Native corporations and Native governments centers around the critical issue of subsistence; with subsistence defined as "customary and traditional uses by rural Alaska residents of wild, renewable resources for direct personal or family consumption."[58] Corporate ownership reduces Tribal control over ancestral lands, "while pressures for profitable development can undermine community uses of land for cultural and inheritance purposes."[59] Examples of these kinds of conflicts include timber harvesting in the Tongass National Forest and intense and recurring debates over oil extraction in the Arctic National Wildlife Refuge. Many Inupiat members support oil drilling for the economic benefits it provides, while many Gwich'in Athabascans oppose oil extraction because of its irreparable harm to the lands that Caribou and other species depend upon.[60]

Regional corporations have a more complicated relationship with those who rely on subsistence activities than the preceding examples suggest. As Huhndorf and Huhndorf stated:

> Not only have Native corporations exerted significant political pressure for subsistence protections, but they also support subsistence activities through payment of dividends that fund expensive subsistence provisions. Few villages have self-sustaining economies, and dividends subsidize household incomes so that many residents can avoid relocation to urban centers for full-time wage labor. Finally, village corporations provide local employment opportunities that allow many Natives to remain in their home communities. Although ANCSA corporations have usually also supported sovereignty endeavors, this issue, too, creates conflicts within the Native community because many corporations fear that sovereignty would enable tribes to impose taxes on corporations and to re-strict access to resources necessary for profits.[61]

On June 25, 2021, during one of the several peaks of COVID-19, the U.S. Supreme Court ruled in *Yellen v. Confederated Tribes of the Chehalis Reservation* that Alaska Native corporations were entitled to hundreds of millions of dollars in COVID-19 relief funds because they met the definition of "Indian tribe" laid out in both the 1975 Indian Self-Determination and Education Assistance Act and the CARES Act. The ANCs' (Alaska Native Corporations) boards of directors, said Associate Justice Sonia Sotomayor, were, in effect, a "regional governing body" and thus eligible to receive and dispense funding under Title V of the CARES Act.[62] While dealing a political and economic blow to the 574 federally recognized Indigenous nations, any broader efforts to treat the two as comparable "may be constrained by the justices' insistence that the companies [ANCs] are distinct from sovereign governments, as well as a desire to keep treating Alaska as a special case."[63]

Current Native Governing Structures in Alaska

According to 2020 U.S. Census data, Alaska is home to some 270,185 Native individuals, an increase of 26,112 from 2010. Of this figure, 26.9% identify as American Indian/Alaska Native (AI/AN) alone; 6.6% identify as AI/AN in combination with another race; and the remaining 66.5% identify as non-AI/AN. While 270,185 is a relatively small number, considering that there are 229

PEOPLES OF ALAXSXAQ AND KĀNAKA MAOLI   353

federally recognized Native polities in the state, it positively reflects that Alaska Natives constitute 21.9% of the overall population in the entire state—the largest Native population by percentage of any state.[64] Collectively, the 229 recognized Alaska native communities comprise nearly 40% of the 574 federally recognized polities in the United States.

This is not an insignificant percentage, but this figure pales in comparison to the tremendous amount of political and organizational diversity in evidence throughout Alaska Native country. Case and Voluck offered this description:

> Even a casual observer will be impressed by the number of both unrelated and interrelated Native governments, corporations, and associations representing modern Alaska Native interests. There are federally recognized traditional and Indian Reorganization Act (IRA) governments, state-organized municipal governments, IRA and Alaska Native Claims Settlement Act (ANCSA) corporations, nonprofit development corporations, and regional Native associations, as well as fish and game advisory boards and Regional Educational Attendance Area (REAA) school boards, to name only a few. These entities chartered under State law are frequently "Native" only because the resident populations, memberships, or shareholders happen to be Native. Some of those chartered by the federal government, such as the IRA governments and corporations, are exclusively Native under federal laws; as a consequence, they enjoy a special relationship with the United States government. Other organizations, particularly the ANCSA village and regional corporations and regional associations, occupy a conceptual space someplace between state-chartered and federally recognized Native entities.[65]

This surprising and often baffling aggregation of varied governmental, quasi-governmental, and business institutions has been smartly organized into five distinguishable types of entities: (1) governments, (2) economic profit corporations, (3) non-profit development and service corporations, (4) multi-regional political organizations, and (5) international organizations.[66] For our purposes, attention will center on the *governments*—both state-recognized and federally recognized—that currently exist within these Native communities.

Since its inception, the Territory and, later, the state of Alaska, has seen a number of Native communities organize as municipalities. The earliest was under the Municipal Incorporation Law of Alaska and the 1915 Indian Village Act that permitted Native villages to organize as local governments. Under the Municipal Incorporation Law, the Native communities of Klawock and Hydaburg were organized as first and second-class cities, respectively.[67] A number of Native communities were also organized under the Indian Territory Act, including Angoon and Hannah. The 1915 Indian Village Act was repealed just a few years

354 INDIGENOUS GOVERNANCE

later in 1929. Felix S. Cohen also reported that some Native villages continued to function informally under council-based governments that held annual elections.[68]

According to Case and Voluck, by the late 1990s, over 100 largely Native communities had organized under Title 29 of the Alaska Statutes which deal with municipal incorporation.[69] These communities have gained regulatory power and "it has been suggested that these powers are sufficient to permit predominantly Native communities to govern themselves by traditional means within broad due process limits."[70] Many of these state-recognized Native municipal governments would later be "layered over IRA and traditional Council governments," adding additional complexity to the already byzantine political status of Alaska Native communities.[71]

Let us now look at the types of Alaska Native governments recognized by the federal government: Traditional Governing Councils, IRA governments, the Metlakatla Indian Community, and the Tlingit and Haida Central Council.

Traditional Governing Councils

There are currently approximately 150 Traditional Governing Councils (TGCs), in Alaska. These are communities where customs and traditions predominate in lieu of a federally recognized governing arrangement or a state municipal system. Interestingly, some TGCs operate under constitutions that bear some resemblance to IRA constitutions, including outlining the purpose of the government, identifying the powers that can be wielded by the Council, and specifying other provisions.

The Village of Platinum operates under what it calls a "Traditional Constitution and Bylaws." It is a short document, only six pages long, but it contains many provisions similar to those of other IRA constitutions: a preamble, definition of territory, membership criteria, description of the Council, specific duties of Council officers, and meeting dates. It also contains a short "rights of members" article that identifies three essential rights: "Section 1: All numbers of the village eighteen (18) years of age or over shall have the right to vote in the village meetings and elections. Section 2: Members of the village shall have the right to speak and meet freely in a peaceable way. Section 3: Members of the village shall have equal chance to share in the benefits of the village." This constitution was adopted on February 2, 1982, by a vote of 11–0 with at least 30% of those entitled to vote casting ballots. Other communities operate under a simple set of bylaws that identify the purpose of the Council, specifies the Council's membership, and identifies the duties and powers of Council members.[72]

In contrast, Nick Carter, the Tribal Administrator for the Native Village of Eek, when asked if his village had a constitution or ordinance said simply, "The Eek Traditional Council does not have a written constitution or tribal ordinances. What we do have are customs and traditions passed down by our ancestors, told to our elders in stories, taught at home, and understood by our tribal members. As such, our tribal governance is not written."[73]

Indian Reorganization Act (IRA) Governments

Approximately seventy-five Native communities within Alaska organized under the provisions of the 1934 IRA. According to Felix S. Cohen, there were three types of organizations possible under both the 1934 IRA and the 1936 Act that extended additional benefits to those communities in Alaska that opted to organize under the IRA:

(1) A group consisting of all the native residents of a locality may organize to carry on municipal and public activities as well as economic enterprises. This type of organization would be suitable for exclusively native villages. Authority for municipal activities is based on the provision of section 16 of the Act of June 18, 1934, providing that the constitutions may contain all powers of an Indian group recognized under existing law. The best example of this type of organization is the organization of the Eskimo villages.

(2) Groups comprising all the native residents of a locality may organize solely for business purposes without contemplating municipal activities. This type of organization is specially suitable in the case of Indian groups residing in white communities, which communities already provide for municipal activities. Examples of such an organization are the organizations at Craig and Sitka.

(3) A group not comprising all the residents of a locality but comprising persons having a common bond of occupation or association may organize to carry on economic activities. In the case of such organizations, cooperative and democratic features in the method of organization are encouraged and as wide a base among the natives is sought as is possible in the circumstances of the case. An example of such an organization is the Hydaburg Cooperative Association, composed of resident Native fishermen of Hydaburg who have a 'common bond of occupation in the fish industry, including the catching, processing and selling of fish and the building of fishing boats and equipment.'[74]

356 INDIGENOUS GOVERNANCE

Central Council of the Tlingit & Haida Indian Tribes

The unique Native government called the Central Council of the Tlingit & Haida Indian Tribes had its beginnings in the formation of two interest groups—the Alaska Native Brotherhood (ANB) established in 1912, and the Alaska Native Sisterhood (ANS) established in 1915. These interdisciplinary, political, and social organizations were established to advocate for equality and human rights for Alaska Natives. Although the leadership of the ANB was closely connected to the Presbyterian mission in southeast Alaska, it was a predominantly Native organization devoted to improving the living conditions of Natives. While both groups aspired to gain territory-wide influence, according to Stephen Haycox, their membership was generally limited to the Tlingit and Haida peoples.

In 1929, Tlingit and Haida members sued the federal government for what they saw as the illegal taking of some twenty million acres held under aboriginal title. Congress consented to the lawsuit in 1935.[75] It was later determined that since the ANB allowed non-Natives to be members, there was a legal question as to whether the case could be continued. The ANB then decided to create a separate body, the Central Council, in order to move the case ahead. The two Tribes subsequently drafted and ratified a constitution with a preamble declaring, "The Tlingit and Haida Indian Tribes of Alaska, in order to form a single regional tribal entity, preserve their identity as Indian Tribes and the identity and culture of their tribal member citizens and descendants as Indian people, provide for the exercise of their tribal sovereignty and the government of the property and affairs of the Tribes, and promote the dignity and welfare of the tribal member citizens, do ordain and establish this Constitution of the Central Council of Tlingit and Haida Indian Tribes of Alaska."

In 1935 the Central Council established itself as a non-profit organization under Alaska law[76] and continued its claim against the federal government. In 1965 Congress recognized the Central Council as a regional Alaska Native IRA Tribal government entitled to exercise the full powers of other federally acknowledged Native nations. Three years later a federal Court of Claims ruling, *Tlingit and Haida Indians v. U.S.*,[77] determined that the Central Council was entitled to a $7.5 million judgment award. But it was not until 1994 that uncertainty about the Council's status as a federally recognized Tribal entity was finally resolved with the passage of the Tlingit and Haida Status Clarification Act.[78] Although this Act affirmed the Central Council's status, it also made clear that other recognized Alaska Native communities would have "precedence over the Central Council . . . in the award of federal compacts, contracts, or grants to the extent that their service population overlaps."[79]

Metlakatla Indian Community

Finally, a brief note about yet another unique community of Alaska Natives—the Metlakatla Indian Community, Annette Island Reserve—the only officially designated "reservation" in Alaska. Metlakatla[80] is a federally recognized Tsimshian Native community first established in British Columbia in 1862 by some Tsimshian Natives at the urging of their non-Native leader, Anglican missionary William Duncan. Duncan had spent a number of years among the Tsimshian dedicating himself to the assimilation and Christian conversion of their members. In service to those goals, he had drafted a set of "Rules of Metlakatla," aimed at both fostering collective responsibility and reshaping Tsimshian behavior according to Anglo-Western sensibilities. All Tsimshian who wanted to live within the colony were required to subscribe to Duncan's regulations, including no gambling, no alcohol, and mandatory attendance for religious instruction.[81]

The colony grew but it was beset by religious factionalism. Indeed, even Duncan, himself, was accused of heresy by his own bishop. In 1887, these incidents compelled Duncan and more than 800 Tsimshian to relocate to Annette Island just south of Ketchikan. This land had been set aside for Duncan and the Tsimshian by President Grover Cleveland, whom the charismatic missionary had lobbied directly. This area became known as New Metlakatla.

On March 3, 1891, the U.S. Congress formally established Annette Island as a reservation for Duncan, the Tsimshian, and others.[82] Duncan dominated virtually every sphere of life within the colony. However, in 1898 Edward Marsden, a Tsimshian and ordained minister, settled close by and began challenging Duncan's leadership through a group of Tsimshian who demanded greater autonomy.

Still, Duncan's influence was heavy, particularly in connection with economic pursuits. As evidence, in 1907 Congress enacted a law that conferred specific civil rights on the Metlakatlan people, including the right "to receive and obtain licenses as masters, pilots, and engineers, as the case may be, of any and all steamboats and other craft." The conflict between Marsden and Duncan continued to fester, and in 1915 Marsden convinced Secretary of the Interior Franklin Lane to adopt a new set of rules and regulations that essentially established a city-council type of government to regulate the Metlakatlan community's activities. This set of regulations effectively replaced the 1887 "Declaration of Rights" while maintaining a strong commitment to economic self-sufficiency.

Case and Voluck suggest that the Annette Island Reservation is unique because the Secretary of the Interior continues to play a "specified and continuing regulatory role," over the activities of the community. Thus, even when ANCSA

358 INDIGENOUS GOVERNANCE

was enacted and all other reservations were abolished in Alaska, Metlakatla endured. While the state has, for years, sought to extend its jurisdiction over the reservation, it has been consistently stymied because of the distinctive set of processes that led to its creation, including the fact that the 1891 congressional statute establishing the reservation declares that the lands are to be used "under such rules and regulations, and subject to such restrictions, as may be prescribed from time to time by the Secretary of the Interior.[83] The U.S. Supreme Court in *Metlakatla v. Egan* held that this provision denied the state any jurisdictional authority over fishing within the reservation.[84]

Judicial Systems

Among the four broad types of governing units evident within Alaska Native communities, more than half of the 229 recognized Indigenous polities in the state have or are in the process of developing court systems. That number continues to trend upward because as Robert Starbard, a Hoonah Indian Association Tribal administrator put it, "I think for us, the primary importance of a tribal court is that it gives additional legitimacy and eligibility to our sovereignty. You cannot be sovereign if you cannot exercise control over what happens with your ordinances and laws. Tribal court is a mechanism that allows us to do that."[85]

These courts differ from many of those in the lower 48 states as they are designed as befitting the small-scale, rural, and more traditional systems of governance in place across their region. "Alaska tribal courts focus more on healing than punishment. For example, informal hearing styles and justice circles are common in Alaska's tribal courts."[86] And while all Alaska Native governments are keenly interested in properly wielding their judicial capacity to protect community members' rights and resources, "very few are interested in incarceration." In fact, they are far more committed to "protecting people and healing through treatment programs and cultural activities and mending relationships."[87]

Alaska's Native courts hear a wide range of cases, including environmental regulations, juvenile delinquency, cultural protection, property damage, child custody, and domestic violence, among others.[88] However, the state has concurrent jurisdiction. Tribal court structures also vary, but many use a panel of judges rather than one judge. In some cases, the Tribal Council "may serve as the court, or a pool of judges created that may include some Tribal Council members."[89] Judges tend to be well-respected community elders or council members; not trained attorneys.

Kānaka Maoli (Hawaiian Natives)

Kānaka Maoli—meaning real people or human being—are the Indigenous people of lands they call *aina*, or our homelands. Of Polynesian ancestry, they migrated to their current homelands from the Marquesas Islands sometime between A.D. 300 and 600.[90] Like other Indigenous peoples, Kānaka Maoli shared deep kinship relations with all the entities of the universe and their cosmology includes the land, waters, celestial beings, plants, and animals. As Jonathan Goldberg-Hiller and Noenoe K. Silva stated, "The distinction between animal and human is clearly drawn nowhere in this cosmology. Humans descend from landforms, *Kalo*, animals, and humans."[91]

There are important ways in which the political and legal status of Kānaka Maoli differ substantially from that of Alaska Natives and Native nations in the lower 48 states, although none of these distinctions adequately explain "the federal government's failure to assume comparable responsibilities for the protection of Hawaiian native people, their land, and their political status. Indeed, the history of the United States' conduct in Hawaii makes a particularly compelling case for redress of claims, yet Native Hawaiians remain the only major group of Native Americans with whom the U.S. has not reconciled historic claims."[92]

Let's look at some of these differences. First, Kānaka Maoli are of Polynesian ancestry. Second, is the geographic remoteness of the Hawaiian archipelago, located in the Pacific Ocean. Third, Kānaka Maoli had developed a complicated socio-political system divided into multiple chiefdoms, which, in 1810, were consolidated into a single, governing kingdom under King Kamehameha I. This new political arrangement became known as "Hawai'i," after the lands from which Kamehameha I ruled.[93] Fourth, during the nineteenth century, the Hawaiian Kingdom negotiated a greater number of internationally binding treaties with more European powers than any other Native nation. These bilateral negotiations officially document and confirm the Hawaiian Kingdom's standing as a sovereign state.[94]

Kānaka Maoli negotiated treaties with Denmark (1846), Sweden (1852), Belgium (1862), the Netherlands (1862), Italy (1863), Spain (1863), Switzerland (1864), Russia (1869), Japan (1870), Austria-Hungary (1875), and Portugal (1882).[95] Simultaneously, the United States, between 1826 and 1893 "recognized the independence of the Kingdom of Hawaii, extended full and complete diplomatic recognition to the Hawaiian Government, and entered into treaties and conventions with the Hawaiian monarchs to govern commerce and navigation in 1826, 1842, 1849, 1875, and 1887."[96]

Fifth, the federal government has enacted over 100 laws since Hawaiian statehood in 1959 that acknowledge the shared Indigenous status of Kānaka Maoli with that of Native nations in the lower 48 and Indigenous peoples within

360 INDIGENOUS GOVERNANCE

Alaska. These include the Native Hawaiian Study Commission Act,[97] the Anti-Drug Abuse Act of 1986,[98] Native Hawaiian Health Care Act of 1988,[99] and the Native Hawaiian Education Act.[100] In spite of these laws, the United States simultaneously continues to treat Kānaka Maoli primarily as a racial minority group, a standing which confers none of the legal rights, benefits, or political standing that accrue to other federally acknowledged Native peoples.[101]

Sixth, while most Indigenous nations in the United States exercise a variable amount of inherent plenary power over their own citizens and wield jurisdiction and sovereignty over their remaining lands, Kānaka Maoli, at the present time, are denied these same powers over their members and their ancient homelands. Finally, and most important from an intergovernmental perspective, Hawaiian Natives are the largest Indigenous community with whom the federal government has yet to establish a contemporary and formal government-to-government relationship.

Current Demographic Data about Kānaka Maoli

The 2020 census data released in 2021 show that Hawaii's overall population was 1,406,430, a 5.2% increase from 2010. The Kānaka Maoli and "other Pacific Islander" population was listed at 142,997, constituting a little more than 10% of the state's population. The largest racial–ethnic group in Hawaii are Asians and Asian-Americans, at 37.79%; followed by whites at 24.95%; and persons with two or more races, at 23.89%.

While Hawaii's overall poverty rate was 9.44%, the group experiencing the most poverty in Hawaii is Kānaka Maoli, with 27.95% living below the poverty level.[102] Along with an elevated poverty rate, unemployment is also highest in the Indigenous Hawaiian community. They also comprise nearly 40% of the adult prison population, and their life expectancy is the lowest of all racial–ethnic groups.[103]

Political Dynamics among Kānaka Maoli

Indigenous political scientist Noelani Goodyear-Kaōpua has noted that since the 1970s,

[T]wo parallel streams emerged in Hawaiian movements of *ea* (sovereignty, breath, and life): one pursuing domestic dependent self-governance for Native Hawaiian people within the U.S., and the other asserting Hawaiian national independence. When the contemporary Hawaiian sovereignty movement began

PEOPLES OF ALAXSXAQ AND KĀNAKA MAOLI   361

to receive the attention of U.S. lawmakers and international audiences in the 1990s, those elements supporting federal recognition overshadowed calls for independence. But by the 2010s, the balance shifted. Grassroots Hawaiian movements refusing U.S. federal recognition frameworks and asserting the independence of the Hawaiian Kingdom have expanded substantially.[104]

Thus, the processes and paths to Kānaka Maoli nationhood have been entangled for over two decades. In 1993, on the 100th anniversary of the U.S. occupation and annexation of Hawaii, Congress "apologized to Native Hawaiians on behalf of the people of the United States for the overthrow of the Kingdom of Hawaii on January 17, 1893 with the participation of agents and citizens of the United States, and the deprivation of the rights of Native Hawaiians to self-determination."[105] The departments of the Interior and Justice issued a report on necessary steps for achieving a just relationship with Native Hawaiians following the 1993 apology and recommended that Congress "enact further legislation to clarify Native Hawaiians' political status and to create a framework for recognizing a government-to-government relationship with a representative Native Hawaiian governing body."[106]

In 2000, at the same time, the legislative and executive branches of the federal government sought to affirm their political relationship with the Hawaiian Natives, and the U.S. Supreme Court issued a ruling that called into question the status of the more than one-hundred federal statutes recognizing that Kānaka Maoli do, in fact, have a sovereign based legal status. In *Rice v. Cayetano*,[107] the High Court struck down restrictions that had allowed only persons with Native Hawaiian blood to vote for the trustees of the Office of Hawaiian Affairs, a state agency created to better the lives of Hawaii's Indigenous people. While *Cayetano* did not specifically address the political relationship of Native Hawaiians to the federal government, this decision and subsequent conservative-led legal challenges to Native Hawaiian programs and benefits generated a greater push for formal recognition from the federal government.

Five months after the Supreme Court's *Cayetano* decision, Senator Daniel K. Akaka (D-HI), later joined by his Senate colleague Daniel K. Inouye (D-HI), began introducing legislation, commonly referred to as the Akaka bill, that would have provided Native Hawaiians with a legal status and political relationship with the federal government similar to that of federally recognized Native nations. It would also have created a governing body that would have decision-making authority on behalf of the estimated 500,000 Native Hawaiians throughout the state. While the original bill, S.2899, was drafted with substantial consultation and input from Kānaka Maoli and received extensive grassroots support, it failed to be enacted. Legislation was then introduced in almost every session of the U.S. Congress between 2000 and 2012. However, these bills failed

362 INDIGENOUS GOVERNANCE

to garner sufficient Native Hawaiian support, with changes to the various bills largely reflecting concerns raised by the Bush Jr. Administration about such issues as land claims, gaming, jurisdiction, and how such recognition might impact U.S. military activities on the islands.[108]

Although the recognition bill in its various iterations continued to garner some support, the number of detractors grew, as well. Many conservative Republicans argued that the bill promoted racial balkanization and would "provide a new vehicle for Hawaiian secessionists groups and spawn endless litigation by people seeking redress against the federal government."[109] More importantly, such a measure was rejected by a number of Hawaiian sovereignty groups who argued that the bill, as well-intentioned as it was, would be a diminution of their original sovereignty. J. Kehaulani Kauanui, a Kānaka scholar, summarized the positions of many of those in opposition to the bill: "[T]he proposal for federal recognition is extremely controversial for several reasons. For one, it was initiated by a U.S. federal representative, not the Native Hawaiian people, as a remedy against new political developments in the courts that threaten current U.S. federal funding and programs for Native Hawaiians. Second, numerous Hawaiian political organizations oppose what they see as an effort to contain Hawaii's independence claim under international law. Third, there is local opposition, on the part of non-Hawaiian residents of Hawai'i, to this form of recognition. And fourth, there is rampant opposition in the U.S. Senate from Republicans who condemn this proposal because it would extend to Native Hawaiians distinct rights."[110]

The final version of the Akaka bill was not voted on by either House and, thus, died when the 112th Congress adjourned in January 2013. Senator Akaka then retired, and shortly thereafter, Senator Inouye unexpectedly passed away, leaving Hawaii without its two senior senators and Kānaka Maoli lands and programs at risk. The apology and subsequent reconciliation efforts had done little to "acknowledge the ramifications of the overthrow of the Kingdom of Hawaii, in order to provide a proper foundation for reconciliation between the United States and the Native Hawaiian people."[111] This was made clear when the Supreme Court, in *Hawai'i v. Office of Hawaiian Affairs* (2009), refused to block the development of Section 5 (b) lands until land claims could be resolved. The Court held that the 1993 apology did not cloud the state of Hawaii's title to lands or impose additional trust obligations that would prevent the state from alienating those lands. This decision, coupled with the state's sovereign immunity, left Hawaiian Native land claims largely unprotected.[112]

Following more than a decade of failed legislative attempts to establish a formal political relationship with Kānaka Maoli, the U.S. Department of the Interior in October 2016 established written procedures that encouraged Hawaiian Natives to establish a government-to-government relationship with the federal government.[113] Interior Secretary Sally Jewell noted that "throughout this two-year rulemaking process, thousands of voices from the Native Hawaiian community and the public testified passionately about the proposal. Today is a major step forward in the reconciliation process between Native Hawaiians and the United States that began over twenty years ago. We are proud to announce this final rule that respects and supports self-governance for Native Hawaiians, one of our nation's largest indigenous communities." The Interior Department had disagreed with the way the Supreme Court in *Cayetano* had racially categorized Kānaka Maoli, and instead affirmed that Native Hawaiians were Indigenous people, had retained inherent sovereignty, and were in a trust relationship with the federal government.[114]

Despite Jewell's words, the Bureau of Indian Affairs's own regulations did not reflect or support the inherent sovereignty of the Hawaiian Natives. A newly recognized Native Hawaiian government could not secure a land base, be able to exercise territorial jurisdiction, or even be allowed to have land placed under trust status.[115] While the BIA process was being worked out, two other issues also surged: efforts to craft and ratify a new Kānaka Maoli Constitution, and a fevered attempt by Native Hawaiians to prevent construction of yet another large telescope (there were already thirteen in place throughout Hawaii) on their holy lands. The University of Hawaii had plans to construct what it was calling the Thirty Meter Telescope on Mauna Kea, a dormant volcano that is one of the most sacred sites for Kanaka Maoli.[116]

Constitution-making

In February 2016 by a vote of 88–30, the "Constitution of the Native Hawaiian Nation" was approved. A four-week-long convention had worked hard to assemble the nineteen-page document. The preamble declared: "We, the indigenous peoples of Hawai'i, descendants of our ancestral lands from time immemorial, share a common national identity, culture, language, traditions, history, and ancestry . . . We reaffirm the National Sovereignty of the Nation. We reserve all rights to Sovereignty and Self-determination, including the pursuit of independence."

The government was to be composed of a forty-three-member legislature, an executive branch, led by a president and vice president, and a judicial branch whose primary focus was to be "restorative justice." Before the constitution could go into effect, it needed to be ratified. However, on March 16, 2016, the Na'i Aukpuni announced they would not be conducting a ratification vote on the proposed constitution. President Kuhio Asam stated, "Na'i Aupuni believes that it is the participants, those who prepared and voted on the document, that are

364 INDIGENOUS GOVERNANCE

best able to lead efforts in effectively sharing the proposed constitution with the community and ultimately arranging for a ratification process."

Those opposed to the constitution pointed to the failure of the Na'i Aupuni to address concerns regarding "principles of good governance: Inclusiveness, transparency, and education"[117] as well as the use of the Native Hawaiian Rolls that were established by the State of Hawaii in Act 195, 2011, following the state's expression of recognition of Native Hawaiians. The governor-appointed Native Hawaiian Roll Commission was created in 2012 and provided with approximately $2.6 million in state funds in order to establish a base roll for Native Hawaiians. The Kana'olowalu process secured registrations from 40,000 Kānaka Maloli. Constituting roughly 8% of the approximately 500,000 Native Hawaiians, this was a major shortfall from their objective of securing 200,000 registrations. The commission then added over 100,000 names to this base roll from three previously existing lists of Native Hawaiians without those individuals' consent.[118] Many Hawaiian Natives opposed this inclusion because a condition for registration involved an expression of consent to participate in the organization of a Native Hawaiian governing entity, and it falsely implied community-wide support for this process.

Donald Trump's election in the fall of 2016 compelled those who actively supported ratification of the constitution to rethink going forward. As John Wahee put it in 2020: "If somebody else, anybody else frankly, had gotten elected, it would make sense to go to the next step. But there is no practical step now."[119]

Mauna Kea and the Stars

As this latest attempt to forge a constitution unfolded, protests against the construction of the Thirty Meter Telescope on Mauna Kea on Oahu ramped up and inspired allied support from across Indian Country and beyond. As one commentator stated: "Mauna Kea is also a symptom of a much deeper problem, the latest manifestation of the unaddressed frustrations with the century-old overthrow of the Hawaiian Kingdom. It's clear the protest is about more than just the telescope—they highlight the broader unresolved historic injustice against the Hawaiian people. And they raise questions about how exactly those grievances can be resolved."[120]

While not every Hawaiian Native is opposed to the telescope's construction, many are. Additionally, the impact of such a project on a site considered sacred by Hawaiian Natives has brought even more attention to the struggles facing Kānaka Maoli. As Dennis 'Bumpy' Kanahole, leader of the Nation of Hawaii on Oahu said: "I think Mauna Kea has basically educated more people in regard to political, economic and cultural rights of Native Hawaiians. It's got a lot more attention than we've had in a long time."[121]

The vehement protests successfully stalled construction of the telescope and forced the state to generate legislation in June 2022 that will transfer to a new stewardship authority called the Mauna Kea Stewardship and Oversight Authority—an eleven-member panel including university officials, scientists, and for the first time, two seats for Kanaka Maoli. The Authority will begin to oversee the mountain jointly with the University of Hawaii in 2023. The Authority assumes full control in 2028.[122]

It remains unclear what political solution Kānaka Maoli will secure. What is clear is that they will forge a direction based on their own understanding of sovereignty and nationhood.

As Kauanui aptly put it:

> Kānaka Maoli need not rely on the U.S. state and its subsidiary or the resurrection of the Hawaiian Kingdom. Given the complex political realities that Kānaka Maoli face in the form of aggressive attacks on the Hawaiian nation and its lands, pursuing ea [life or sovereignty] is critical. Increasingly, Kānaka are laboring to revive and strengthen Hawaiian cultural practices, including the work of lo'i restoration and kalo cultivation, ahupua'a and watershed replenishment, traditional voyaging, *kākau* (tattoo), *lā'au, lapa'au* (traditional medicine), *lomi* (Hawaiian marriage), 'ōlelo Hawai'I (language), *hula* (reverence for specific people, deities, and natural elements), *mele* (song), *oli* (chant), makahiki and other spiritual ceremonies, and much more. All of this is part of the decolonial process, which refuses the 'logic of the elimination of the Native.' Such activities can also heal the internalized racism that self-degrades the 'primitive.'[123]

Conclusion

The previous chapters have taken on several interrelated tasks: (1) to provide a necessarily broad overview of the origins, evolution, and structures of Indigenous governments; (2) assess the central functions and roles that these governments perform for their citizens and other residents; (3) describe the key differences and similarities between Native governments and the federal and state governments; (4) discuss some of the critical issues confronting these governments, both internally and intergovernmentally; and (5) assess how leadership is understood and exercised in Indian Country.

This concluding chapter will address some of the positive features of governance that are evident in many Native nations and explain why they are so vitally important. It will then describe some of the more daunting challenges Native governments continue to face and examine why some Native governments are more effective than others in providing the services and protections their constituencies need and expect. Finally, it will outline recommendations that have been offered to strengthen and improve governance by Native governments.

Native Governments Matter

Since the advent of the Indian Self-Determination period in the late 1960s, Indigenous governments have slowly regained and expanded essential governing powers that had previously been handicapped or completely denied by federal and state lawmakers. Over those decades, they have made significant strides. Native governments are important for many reasons and these nations have shown how effective they can be when armed with sufficient resources and freed from overwhelming and stultifying federal bureaucratic and legal constriction. They are important, first, because many significant policy decisions are handed down at the Tribal level. They are important because Native leaders pushed back against federal dominance and regained local governing authority so that elements of federal policy (e.g., healthcare, education, social services) are now often administered through Native agencies. They are important because Native governments have proven to be innovative policymakers in areas such as water quality, fish and wildlife management, and alternative dispute resolution. They are important because they provide a significant role for their citizens to

Indigenous Governance. David E. Wilkins, Oxford University Press. © Oxford University Press 2024.
DOI: 10.1093/oso/9780190095994.003.0016

368   INDIGENOUS GOVERNANCE

participate in familiar forms of governance. And, they are important because as they generate and spend increasing sums, both generated by the Tribal government and received from the federal government, they now make most of their own decisions about how to devise, run, and modify their own institutions of governance.

It is to be expected that diversity is a central factor, given that 574 federally recognized Native nations live within their retained lands in the lower forty-eight states and Alaska, along with the Kānaka Maoli and their impressive achievements in recent decades, notwithstanding their unclear political status vis-à-vis the state of Hawaii and the federal government.

Some nations, like the Shakopee Mdewakanton and the Yuhaaviatam of San Manuel Nation, are wealthy due to their well-run and well-placed gaming operations and other business ventures. Subsequently, they have made great political and economic strides over the last three decades. Yet, as Laura E. Evans notes in her book, *Power from Powerlessness* (2011), even those Native nations lacking successful gaming operations have found ways to strengthen their political, social, and economic position by drawing upon outside support; what Evans called "institutional niches," that she defines as "source(s) of outside support that can provide small but meaningful subsidies for the cultivation of expertise."[1] These "niches" enable Native political leaders to cultivate expertise in specific policy or program areas. Gradually this accumulated expertise helps the Tribal officials craft smarter agendas, improve networking, and make more efficient and effective policy decisions. It is plausible that a majority of Native governing elites would likely fit within the "institutional niches" framework that Evans has mapped.

Challenges Facing Native Governments

Chapter 1 outlined some of the ways that Indigenous governments resemble those of the states and federal government—provision of basic services (e.g., education, public safety, housing, communication technology, etc.)—and explored the more critical differences between these governing bodies. Two of those deserve further emphasis here: the fact that Native governments enjoy both a historically recognized *racial–ethnic status* and that they are also *politically sovereign* nations; and that *custom* and *culture* occupy a particularly distinctive role in Native societies and in the way Indigenous governments operate.

The joint racial–ethnic and politically sovereign status is generally accepted and understood by Native policymakers. It is also recognized and affirmed, not only by explicit language in treaties, but within official U.S. documents like the U.S. Constitution, policies, records of proceedings, and laws that have all served to reinforce and acknowledge this bifurcated identity. Yet, Native nations' reliance on and manipulation of these two separate statuses has left them vulnerable to charges of racism and ethnocentrism by white nationalist conservatives and Republican policymakers and sometimes by elements of the Democratic establishment in areas such as employment hiring preferences and the hunting and harvesting of certain animal species like whales. It can also sometimes generate internal conflict and self-destructive Tribal policies like disenrollment, whereby Native governments oust bona fide members for personal or political reasons or refuse to enroll individuals judged to lack Native "blood," as in the case of African American freedmen within the Creek, Choctaw, Seminole, and other nations.

Despite language in the U.S. Constitution ("excluding Indians not taxed," and "commerce with the Indian tribes") and most treaties that acknowledge both the ethnic and sovereign status of Indigenous peoples, states and federal lawmakers have struggled throughout the last three and a half centuries to completely grasp the full impact of this distinctive dual status. Today, some non-Native lawmakers believe the racial–ethnic status of Native peoples is racially discriminatory because they say that status does not comport with the U.S. Constitution's allegedly color-blind framework. This spurious argument is of increasing concern as the hateful influence of white Christian nationalism grows across the US.

Kānaka Maoli have been explicitly hampered by this color-conscious mindset (see, e.g., *Rice v. Cayetano*)[2] and Tribal governments and Native beneficiaries of the Indian Child Welfare Act (ICWA) have in recent years faced a series of attacks from conservative Republicans who argue that ICWA is a race-based law because it allegedly acknowledges the racial–ethnic element of Tribes, parents, and children in adoption proceedings.[3] But the majority of Native governments defend their unique dual racial–ethnic/politically sovereign status as it fundamentally sets them apart from other ethnic groups in the United States and they are loath to jettison either position.

Second, Indigenous cultures and the customs that give expression to them constitute a profoundly complicated, overarching dimension that suffuses many decisions made by Native policymakers. Noted anthropologist, Paul Radin, summarized the differences in the ways in which Native people understood and practiced customs within their cultures compared to Euro-American society:

> A custom is, in no sense, a part of our properly functioning culture. It belongs definitely to the past. At best, it is moribund. But customs are an integral part of the life of primitive peoples. There is no compulsive submission to them. They are not followed because the weight of tradition overwhelms a man. That takes place in our culture, not in that of aboriginal man. A custom is obeyed there because it is intimately intertwined with a vast living network of interrelations,

370 INDIGENOUS GOVERNANCE

arranged in a meticulous and ordered manner. They are tied up with all the mechanisms used in government.[4]

Philip S. Deloria (Sam), is the major author of several important studies of Native governments, much of that work done in the mid-1980s with the Commission on State-Tribal Relations. Elaborating on the intense and powerful role that culture occupies in the minds and behavior of Native political elites and their constituencies he said, "Tribal governments are seen by many as protectors of Indian culture whose existence is perceived to be constantly threatened … This special relationship of tribal government to Indian culture dominates every facet of tribal policymaking and inculcates a caution and a conservatism which are marks of most tribal policy."[5]

Deloria also there noted that a variation of this "cultural expectation" is also held by the American public, the news media, and governing officials, too. This places additional pressure on Native governments to conform to a cultural standard that non-Natives themselves are not expected to meet. In Deloria's words, "Indian governments are thus subjected to a different status than other governments. There are not constant reviews of the demographic status of all the little countries in Europe that are frequently compared in size and population with Indian tribes. No one asks whether Monaco and Liechtenstein are sufficiently culturally distinct from neighboring countries to justify their continued existence. Unlike that of Indian tribes, their political status is taken for granted."[6]

Aside from these two major—possibly intractable—challenges, other issues confound many Native governing elites in their capacity to serve their constituencies. Violence is a systemic problem throughout Indian Country. Indigenous women, girls, LGBTQI and Two Spirit people, and those with disabilities struggle to remain safe and to have their inherent dignity and rights fully respected. Human trafficking is rampant in some areas and attacks by non-Native men are difficult to prevent and prosecute. The situation is fueled by the presence of so-called "man camps", temporary housing provided by the fossil fuel industry for its non-local employees—some of these sprawling structures can accommodate up to 500 men. Thousands of these workers are situated in remote areas adjacent to Tribal lands. Secretary of the Interior Deb Haaland (Laguna Pueblo) has pledged to address this horrific problem—so ubiquitous that it has its own acronym—MMIW—Missing and Murdered Indigenous Women. Congress responded by restoring some jurisdictional power to Tribal courts that allows them to prosecute those who commit these crimes. Activists and relatives are battling to protect their communities and locate the missing. Still, so much more needs to be done. The U.S. Supreme Court's recent *Dobbs v. Jackson Women's Health Organization*[7] ruling that dramatically overturned the constitutional right to abortion established in *Roe v. Wade*[8] in 1973 will only

CONCLUSION 371

exacerbate these problems, as now, that all those who can potentially give birth will face a gauntlet of restrictive laws, policies, and rules undermining their personal rights to bodily autonomy.

While most Native governments are focused on safety and justice, some continue to engage in lateral violence and discriminatory practices. One such example is retribution against Native women who marry non-Natives. For example, the Cachil Dehe Band of Wintun of California have a policy that severely punishes female members who marry non-Indians. The policy is embedded in their 1941 Constitution: "If a female member marries a non-Indian, she will automatically lose her membership and will be required to leave the community within ninety days after written notice has been served on her by the Business Committee."[9] Interestingly, female members who had married non-Indians "prior to" adoption of the constitution were not affected by this clause. The Pamunkey operated under a similar law until 2012. Their code also contained restrictions according to race that were finally expunged after a severe backlash and criticism from many quarters including the Congressional Black Caucus.

Aside from the aforementioned Freedmen of the FCT, systemic discrimination and mistreatment of Afro-Indigenous people throughout Indian Country is not uncommon. In general, it can be argued that all so-called "mixed bloods" are in some way diminished by the non-traditional hierarchies inherent in blood quantum systems, but those with African American heritage have it worse. The bifurcated nature of Native governments addressed earlier in this chapter, whereby Tribal identity is simultaneously defined by both race–ethnicity and political status, compounds this situation, as those obsessed with blood quantum feel compelled to exclude anyone they perceive as literally diluting all Tribal identities.

Another issue of concern for many Native governments is the status and rights of non-Natives in the community. This is also, by its nature, interlocked with the bifurcated racial–political nature of Native governments; and is directly related to definitions of belonging in the community—are they "members" of the Nation or "citizens" of the Nation? Historically, non-Native adoptees and spouses were frequently recognized as full-fledged members of the community. Still today within some Tribes, there have been adoptions of non-members (Johnny Depp is now Comanche) though in modern times this status tends to be largely ceremonial. Intermarriages with non-Natives in the past also might have included citizenship but that, too, is rare today. The practices of non-Native incorporation were not uncommon within the Five Civilized Tribal nations and the constitutional republics they organized throughout the nineteenth century.

Over time, however, Native governments have moved away from the more open and inclusive polities that once welcomed outsiders regardless of race, ethnicity, or religious persuasion. That said, Native courts have amassed a solid record of meting out equal justice to both Tribal members and non-members. Furthermore, this data refutes the groundless perception that Tribal courts are racially biased against non-members or non-Indians and thus incapable of protecting their rights. Several former and present U.S. Supreme Court justices, carry this prejudice, including the late Chief Justice William Rehnquist and his successor, John G. Roberts, as well as current associate justices Samuel A. Alito, Brett M. Kavanaugh, Clarence Thomas, and Amy Coney Barrett. The High Court's 2022 decision, *Oklahoma v. Castro-Huerta*, which reduced the scope of its earlier *McGirt v. Oklahoma* (2020), contains language by Kavanaugh where he implicitly and baselessly suggests that Tribal courts do not adequately protect the rights of non-Indians, asserting that "the State has a strong sovereign interest in ensuring public safety and criminal justice within its territory, and in protecting all crime victims."[10]

Bethany Berger's research on the Navajo nation's court system found that despite the fact that their courts purposefully draw upon Diné customary law, "the court is both numerically balanced in its decisions regarding nonmembers—47.4% of nonmembers win when they appear before the court, and 52.6% lose—and qualitatively balanced even in areas such as child custody, employment, and contract disputes, that might seem particularly prone to bias."[11] And Berger went on to show that other Native court systems "reveals a similar effort to decide issues fairly, even where it requires ruling against tribal members or the tribe itself."[12]

Joseph Thomas Flies Away (Hualapai Tribe), former Chief Judge of his Tribe's Tribal Court, has argued that Native governments must reconsider the boundaries of Tribal membership and they must ask whether membership is equal to citizenship. From this perspective, "tribal constitutional limitation of nonmember participation in tribal government provides anti-Indian interests with arguments for further circumscribing the scope of the sovereignty exercised by tribes."[13] Flies Away emphasized that Tribal officials should consider making some accommodations for non-members, especially those who have married into the community or have lived there for many years. Tribes, he suggested, "can be creative in developing ways to involve all residents in government without giving up [their] culture or giving up control to outsiders."[14]

Yet another major challenge confronting many Indigenous governments is that of segmentation, factionalism, or internal divisions that are present in some nations. These segments can be based on financial status, religious differences, population size, political ideology, gender, educational attainment, blood quantum, or cultural orientation (inclined toward retention and practice of traditional values and institutions or more supportive of modernist approaches to politics, law, business, etc.), to name but a few. Regardless of the basis of the

CONCLUSION   373

cleavage(s), if the divide becomes too sharp it can lead to governmental paralysis, societal tensions, and sometimes outright violence.

Robert Porter (Seneca)[15] and Douglas George-Kanentiio (Mohawk)[16] have both written about the severe segmentation that has long been present on the Mohawk Reservation at Akwesasne, driven by both economic and philosophical differences. Porter notes that three different groups purport to wield official governmental authority at Akwesasne—the Saint Regis Mohawk Tribal Council (the body currently recognized by the Bureau of Indian Affairs), those Mohawk aligned with the Haudenosaunee Confederacy who assert authority as the "traditional Mohawk Nation Council of Chiefs," and the Tribal government established under Canadian law to govern the geographical part of Akwesasne that is located within Canada—the Mohawk Band Council of Akwesasne. [17] The situation at Akwesasne is extreme, but there are many other examples of cleavages that are equally as deep and intense.

In the past, simple dichotomies like "full-blood," "mixed-blood," "progressive," or "traditionalist" predominated. But as Native communities have expanded and become more integrated into the social, economic, and institutional fabric of the larger society, diversification has increased opportunities for estrangement. Of course, within many Native communities, there is very little evidence of intense divides or factionalism. Professor and state-Tribal political expert Ron Whitener, suggests that his people, the Squaxin Island Tribe located on the southern inlets of the Salish Sea within Washington State, have retained a relative cohesiveness due to the fact that community members have always made sure their major families had continuous representation in political affairs.[18]

Last, despite the improved economic outlook for many Native nations in recent decades, it is a fact that more than 70% of all Natives do not live on trust or reserved lands. They typically reside in major urban areas. This raises several thorny questions, including the most basic: *is a reservation-based Native government responsible for those citizens who reside away from their reservation homeland?* This issue bedevils many Tribal government officials and perplexes federal officials, too. Some Native governments offer a modicum of support for citizens who live outside the nation's homeland, including financial assistance to return to the reservation should the need arise, and posting information and procedures in urban areas when Tribal elections are slated.[19]

Other nations insist they are only obligated to serve the needs of members who continuously reside on or near the reservation. No comprehensive study has yet been conducted to ascertain how many Indigenous governments acknowledge and provide services and benefits to urban-based citizens. But, the available data suggest that urban Natives endure serious neglectful conditions "such as lack of access to health care and education, and the harmful effects of welfare reform and census undercounting."[20]

374 INDIGENOUS GOVERNANCE

Effective Indigenous Governance

Angela Riley, in describing the characteristics she believed necessary for a Native government to be considered as exercising "good (Native) governance," identified the following as essential traits: "Good Native governance requires, first and foremost, that citizens are ensured the freedoms of exit (or opt-out rights) and dissent (or voice). In addition, tribal governments should be based on and guided by their own foundational governing principles and must also provide both members and outsiders with a fair forum for the resolution of disputes. Finally, good Native governance requires that every facet of tribal governance constitute a cultural match to the structure, religion, and value system of the particular tribe."[21]

Riley then proceeded to give numerous examples of Native nations that, she argued, were exercising high-quality and effective governments across Indian Country. While acknowledging that "extensive empirical studies would have to be conducted" to definitively draw the conclusion that, for instance, "the right of voice or dissent is commonly available within tribal communities," Riley seemed confident that a majority of Native nations function relatively well and generally meet the needs of their citizens.

A 2001 study by Jennifer Felmley[22] focused firmly on a central question: Why do some Native governments seem to work better than others? She closely examined four Indigenous communities—the Chickasaw Nation, Laguna Pueblo, Kaibab Paiute, and Fort McDermitt Paiute-Shoshone—and set out to determine which of the nations had the most effective governing system. She critically examined four community variables: the degree of local control exercised by members of the nation historically; the nation's present degree of relative autonomy from the federal government; the extent of internal divisions within the community; and the amount of natural and economic resources available. While she found each to be important, Felmley argued that the degree of local control or self-determination was most vital because it provides governments with the power to be "structurally and procedurally responsive to their political cultures" and aligns comfortably with the traditions and values of the community.[23]

After examining the political, economic, and cultural histories of all four nations, she concluded that the Laguna Pueblo had the most effective government. Why? Because it was stable, had a positive sense of identification, a close connection to its own history, culture, land, and religion, a "sophisticated understanding of the principles of responsibility to the community and the requirements of democratic governments," and a dynamic government that was steeped in tradition but flexible enough to adapt to contemporary conditions thus giving it cultural legitimacy.[24]

CONCLUSION 375

Recommendations for Consideration: Plenary Power, Consent, and More

Many commentators have offered proposals to strengthen and improve the governing capabilities of Indigenous governments. Not all of these would prove equally effective with all governments. This is not surprising, given the enormous governmental diversity across Native lands. But before proceeding with what I consider the most valuable suggested reforms, it is necessary to restate that every Native governing official must be ever cognizant of this reality: The federal government, since the 1880s, has authorized itself to wield virtually unconstrained power vis-à-vis Indigenous governments—power that is referred to as being *plenary*. This is a self-assumed power without a constitutional or treaty basis, but since *U.S. v. Kagama* (1886) and *Lone Wolf v. Hitchcock* (1903), Congress has maintained the view that its own inherent political power is somehow superior to that of Indigenous political power. Until and unless this extra-constitutional claim to superiority is renounced, Native political sovereignty and proprietary land rights will remain subject to cancellation or severe diminishment by its treaty and trust partners.

Along with abandonment of its purported plenary power, the federal government, if genuinely serious about improving its political relationship with Native nations, must adopt and rigidly adhere to the political concept of seeking Native *consent* rather than simply engaging in *consultation* before engaging in activities that directly or indirectly impinge on the sovereignty, lands, peoples, or resources of Native nations. These two seemingly simple concepts—consent and consultation—have received a lot of attention in recent years. Consultation has gained the upper hand in the parlance of intergovernmental relations. However, consent has the more storied history as a vital political doctrine, tracing back to the origins of Native nations and the earliest days of Indigenous–Euro-American interactions. While we all think we know what it means to be consulted or to give consent, these familiar ideas are being reworked and sometimes used as weapons by those who seek to weaken and destroy Native sovereignty and self-determination.

Although the terms are often used interchangeably, they are far from equivalent. Consultation is a formal process rooted in communication. It is about sharing information and listening to differing perspectives—an exchange that is one of the required mileposts on the road to meaningful consent. Consent, according to the *Oxford English Dictionary*, is the act of giving approval or coming to agreement in opinion or sentiment. Treaties are good examples of mutual consent between an Indigenous nation and the federal government. Consent has foundational heft as arguably the essential tenet on which Indigenous social and political systems were based. It is also the bedrock for American democracy

376 INDIGENOUS GOVERNANCE

which is premised on the notion of the consent of the governed—by the people and for the people.

Consent, unlike consultation, involves taking responsibility for an outcome which, in effect, becomes "the doing" of the consenter, even though they may not have initiated the action. According to Roger Scruton, you could give consent without first going through the process of consultation, but consultation, in and of itself, is not a complete act, it is just a tool. [25] We have seen many examples of state, local, and federal governments, as well as corporations claiming consultation fulfills their obligation to Tribes. That somehow sending an email to a Tribal leader, whether a response is received or not, is the equivalent of consultation. Even more frustrating is that such activity is often used as a substitute, not just for the process of consultation, but for the act of consent. As one commentator noted many of those agencies "have often turned consultation into a *pro forma* box to check, rendering tribal consultation inconsequential."[26]

In the context of Indigenous–State relations, consent is a fundamental political principle and is generally understood as constituting the core legitimacy of a political body. The idea is that the institutions and actions of government officials must be rooted in the free will of those engaging in political activity.

The principle of Indigenous consent was plainly visible in diplomatic relations between Native nations and European powers, and later the federal government, dating back to 1608 and continuing through the early 1900s. For the nearly 400 treaties that were ratified by the United States government, the central element of consent remains a binding obligation on both parties. Consent is also embedded in the 1787 Northwest Ordinance which established the Northwest Territory and created a process whereby new territories could be incorporated into the United States. There it was infamously declared, "The utmost good faith shall always be observed towards the Indians, their lands and property shall never be taken from them without their consent."[27]

Historically, consent was theoretically supposed to work to the benefit of all parties. Article 1 of the Kansas Treaty of 1825 declares that the "Chiefs and Headmen of the Kansas Nation . . . for themselves and their nation, do consent and agree that the Commissioner of the United States shall, and may survey and mark out a road," thus granting access to the fledging U.S. government. A decade later, the United States in the removal treaty of 1834 promised the Chickasaw, "the Government of the United States, hereby consents to protect and defend them against the inroads of any other tribe of Indians, and from the whites." In 1898, twenty-seven years after treaty-making ostensibly ended in 1871, the Lakota people of Rosebud signed an agreement with James McLaughlin, the U.S. Indian Inspector, in which they gave "permission and consent" for members of the Lower Brule community to reside on Rosebud land.

Consent is also manifest in several articles of the 2007 United Nations Declaration on the Rights of Indigenous Peoples. For example, Article 19 outlines the more appropriate relationship and progression between consultation and consent when it declares the following: "States shall consult and co-operate in good faith with the indigenous peoples concerned through their own representative institutions in order to obtain their free, prior and informed consent before adopting and implementing legislative or administrative measures that may affect them."[28]

Consent, for all its power, is not flawless. In the context of Indigenous–State relations, this principle and its promises have also been twisted and violated time and again by federal policymakers whenever it was deemed politically, economically, or culturally expedient. Hundreds of treaty provisions, for example, have been nullified by federal lawmakers. And Congress has enacted many laws in direct contradiction of this principle. Public Law 83-280 is one of the best examples. Enacted on August 15, 1953, this unprecedented measure gave five states criminal jurisdiction over Natives and non-Natives on reservations—with a few exceptions—and allowed every other state to wield similar jurisdiction if *they* chose to do so.

This profound violation of Tribal sovereignty and territorial integrity was authorized by Congress and gifted to the states without Native consent, despite the fact that President Dwight Eisenhower, when signing it into law, said he had "grave doubts as to the wisdom of certain provisions" because the law did not require Native consent. Eisenhower deemed that flaw "unfortunate," and expressed hope that in their next session, Congress would adopt an amendment to the law requiring Native consent before subjecting them to state jurisdiction.[29] Fifteen years later, such a consent provision was finally added with the adoption of the Indian Civil Rights Act in 1968.

Notwithstanding the inadequacies of consent's protective cloak over Indigenous rights, it remains a fundamentally important principle and serves to remind federal and state officials that a nation's democratic character requires permission from the people. Today, however, consent seems to have been relegated to the margins in favor of consultation. It is the preferred practice of local, state, and federal actors as they practice intergovernmental relations. For these, mostly non-Native, bureaucrats and officials, consultation has been stripped of its original meaning; it has now become synonymous with the process of informing, of checking a box. They seem under no obligation to engage in meaningful discussions and genuine exchanges of ideas. Worse still, this truncated, passive interpretation of consultation has, by and large, come to replace the powerful action of consent. This causes great harm, not just to the practice of intergovernmental diplomacy, but to the very essence of Native sovereignty and self-determination.

378 INDIGENOUS GOVERNANCE

Consultation is a far more modern concept initially used to define a respectful process of meaningful engagement between Tribes and other governments. Federal officials first implicitly endorsed consultation in 1968 when President Lyndon Johnson announced his administration's intent to abandon the pursuit of the termination of Native nations and replace the despised policy with approaches promoting Native self-help, self-development, and self-determination. He reasoned that "Indians must have a voice" in programs and decisions that mattered to them.[30]

In 1989, more than a decade after the federal *Boldt* Decision's affirmation of treaty rights ended the violent Fish Wars of the 1960s and 1970s, leaders in Washington state, chose a new path that emphasized consultation rather than litigation or coercion. In 1989, one hundred years after Washington was admitted to the union, Governor Booth Gardner worked with the leaders of the twenty-six Native federally recognized nations located within the state's borders to craft and ratify the Centennial Accord. This document institutionalized a commitment to government-to-government relations rooted in cooperation, negotiation, and arbitration.[31] Washington's accord transformed, and continues to guide, the dealings between twenty-eight of the twenty-nine federally recognized Tribes and the state. Although their leaders attend and participate in Accord-related meetings, the Yakama Nation has yet to sign the document, as it views the federal government as its primary diplomatic partner. With the signing of the 2004 Out-of-State Accord, Governor Gary Locke and leaders of federally recognized tribes located within Oregon and Idaho with treaty-reserved rights in Washington came to a similar arrangement. These Nations are the Nez Perce Tribe, the Confederated Tribes of Warm Springs, and the Confederated Tribes of the Umatilla Indian Reservation. Like the Yakama Nation, the Kalispel Tribe, whose traditional lands stretch from northeastern Washington state, across Idaho, and into western Montana, declined to sign, although they, too, have since attended and participated in related events. The success of these accords has provided a model for Indigenous–State relations in other states, including Oregon, New Mexico, Arizona, California, Minnesota, and Wisconsin.

While the process of consultation was obviously understood and practiced in these situations, it was not explicitly defined and codified in federal Indian policy until President Bill Clinton's 1994, "Memorandum on Government-to-Government Relations with Native American Tribal Governments."[32] That document declared, "Each executive department and agency shall consult, to the greatest extent practicable and to the extent permitted by law, tribal governments prior to taking actions that affect federally recognized tribal governments. All such consultations are to be open and candid so that all interested parties may evaluate for themselves the potential impact of relevant proposals."[33] It appeared to be a positive step toward establishing and improving communications in a bureaucratic world where Tribes were often excluded, either deliberately or through negligence, from decision-making. However, some legal scholars, such as Jason Searle in *Exploring Alternatives to the "Consultation or Consent" Paradigm*, see the origins of the elevation of consultation over consent in this memorandum and its 2000 revision.[34]

Unfortunately, genuine engagement is becoming rare, and what has emerged to take its place in recent years is an empty, distorted version of consultation, whereby outside governments, corporations, and other entities claim to have consulted with Tribal governments when, in actuality, they have done little more than inform them of an intent to act without input or notice from Tribes. Obviously, telling someone that you plan to do something is not the same as consulting them in the creation of that plan. Yet, those who seek to extract resources or obtain access through Tribal lands with little regard for treaty rights or respect for the integrity of Tribal nations' inherent sovereignty are using the term in just this way. They disingenuously claim to have consulted with Native peoples while diminishing the entire process.

Those Tribal leaders who attempt to engage in a true process of consultation are often penalized. Those seeking to exploit them can claim to have accepted Native input and then proceed to ignore it, merely checking a box in the event of legal action. This is a far cry from the original intent of meaningful inclusion and respectful partnership. Native nations have often been deceived and abused by those working under the cover of this bad-faith definition.

Consultation that is not wedded explicitly to securing meaningful and informed Native consent is inherently flawed and inadequate as a tool that can truly benefit the complicated nature of Indigenous–State relations. As Native nations have learned since the Clinton years, consultation is inconsistently administered by both federal and state officials. It also tends to be a process confined in many instances to the executive branches of both the federal and state governments and thus lacks comprehensive scope. Finally, and most importantly, consultation, as it is practiced, is more procedural than substantive. This means it is inadequate and ill-equipped to acknowledge the emotional, historical, political, and legal concerns, rights, and understandings of Indigenous peoples.

Indigenous leaders would be well advised to remember their ancestors' deep understanding and commitment to diplomacy and to remind federal, state, municipal, and corporate figures that their consent cannot be forcibly secured or "consulted" away. It can only be given freely, openly, and before any alteration or reduction of their lands, inherent rights, or political status.

Despite this ominous institutional backdrop, Native governments, like governments around the world, can and must be improved. What follows are some additional reform suggestions. Steve Russell (Cherokee), in his excellent book, *Sequoyah Rising: Problems in Postcolonial Tribal Governance* (2010),

380 INDIGENOUS GOVERNANCE

offered a number of ideas on how to fortify Native governments, both internally and intergovernmentally. Here are a few of Russell's ideas:

> Tribes have unlimited powers, seldom used, to make agreements among themselves. They also have authority to issue tax exempt bonds, to create corporations and trade stocks, to protect intellectual property with trademarks, copyrights, and patents. (p.148)
>
> Sequoyah [Tribal governments] could rise as interlocked court systems or joint economic enterprises. Why should many if not most tribes ever need to purchase electricity when they have the authority to issue revenue bonds and some of the finest potential sites for broad solar arrays, photovoltaic generation, windfarms, geothermal and hydropower? (p. 148)
>
> ... Sequoyah could rise again as interlocking tribal think tanks, technology incubators, or an intratribal stock market that would allow us to trade shares of our own enterprises. (p. 149)
>
> There is no persuasive reason why the tribes could not, by agreement among themselves, link their respective judiciaries into an appellate process that would function to protect both the rights of individual Indians to be political actors within their tribal traditions and the sovereign rights of tribal governments to settle disputes from within. That is, a *real* Supreme Court of the American Indian Nations. Somewhat more difficult but theoretically possible would be an agreement to submit disputes *between* tribes to such an intratribal tribunal. (p. 97)

Robert Bee, an anthropologist, offered another suggestion that might be suitable for some Native nations to consider, depending on the population, history, and degree of internal cleavages. Bee proposed that a dual system of governance, "where the imposed, constitutional-bureaucratic form of government is maintained as a kind of palisade, an outside-oriented situation periodically adjusted to preserve an effective equality of opportunity for tribal members, coexisting with heterogeneous internal political ideologies whose differences become continually negotiable as justification for action and further structural reform."[35] Bee opined that this outside–inside structural arrangement might be important for those nations where internal conflicts arise over scarcity and equitable distribution of resources.

Indigenous peoples and their governments are the senior sovereigns of the Western Hemisphere. And while there is significant diversity in the manner by which Native nations govern themselves, we can say with a measure of certainty that many of them understand the meaning of liberty, equality, respect, and justice. Native nations have endured, despite nearly half a millennium of engagement with foreign powers who intruded onto Native lands and, over time, gradually and systematically sought to eradicate Indigenous difference, secure title to most Native lands, erase languages and cultures, and dominate and transform governments. Ironically, it is now the United States which appears to be regressing democratically, culturally, and socially. Native nations, the more mature sovereigns, remain, despite institutional, racial, and constitutional constraints. They have the capacity and, it seems, the desire to educate their junior sovereign partners—the states and the federal governments—about how to govern responsibly. Respect for those who came before, sustainable and mutually beneficial relations for the present, and preparation for those to come. Governance for the health of the entire world community.

Notes

Introduction

1. https://www.usnews.com/news/healthiest-communities/articles/2020-10-07/how-native-americans-in-minnesota-beat-back-covid-19.
2. Simon Romero, Roni Caryn Rabin, and Mark Walker, "Life Expectancy Plunge Puts Number to Misery in Native Communities," *New York Times* (September 1, 2022), A14.
3. Teshia G. Arambula Solomon, Rachel Rose Bobelu, Agnes Attakai, Fatima Molina, Felina Cordova-Marks, Michelle Kahn-John, Chester L. Antone, Miguel Flores Jr., and Francisco Garcia, "The Generational Impact of Racism on Health: Voices from American Indian Communities," *Health Affairs* 41, no. 2 (February 2022): 281–288; and Aggie J. Yellow Horse, Nicholet A. Deschine Parkhurst, and Kimberly R. Huyser, "COVID-19 in New Mexico Tribal Lands: Understanding the Role of Social Vulnerabilities and Historical Racisms," *Frontiers in Sociology* 5 (December 2020): 1–11.
4. Navajo Department of Health, January 12, 2023, www.ndoh.navajo-nsn.gov/COVID-19.
5. 134 Stat. 281.
6. In addition to Tribal government funding, smaller amounts were directed to Tribal small businesses, Bureau of Indian Affairs funding for the operation of Indian programs, Indian Health Service support, and funding for the Bureau of Indian Education.
7. Simon Romano and Jack Healy, "Outbreak Spells Disaster for U.S. Tribal Nations," *New York Times* (May 12, 2020).
8. 88 Stat. 2203.
9. Ibid., 2204.
10. See *Confederated Tribes of the Chehalis Reservation v. Steven Mnuchin*, Case No. 20-cv-01002 (APM), *Cheyenne River Sioux Tribe v. Steven Mnuchin*, Case No. 20-cv-01059 (APM), and *Ute Tribe of the Uintah and Ouray Reservation v. Steven Mnuchin*, Case No. 20-cv-01070 (APM) (April 23, 24, 2020). U.S. District Court for the District of Columbia.
11. Ibid., 11.
12. Ibid., 31–32.
13. See the list of 574 Tribal entities in the 48 states and the separate list of Alaska Native entities that does not include Alaska Native corporations. *Federal Register*, vol. 85, no. 20, Thursday, January 30, 2020.

384　NOTES

14. *Native News Online*, "Appeals Court Rules Alaska's Native Corporations Ineligible for CARES Act Relief Funds," December 13, 2020. https://nativenewsonline.net/sovereignty/alaska-native-corporations-not-eligible-for-cares-act-relief-funds.

15. Ibid.

16. Amicus Curiae Brief of *Alaska Federation of Natives in Mnuchin v. Confederated Tribes of Chehalis Reservation*, and *Alaska Native Village Corporation Association v. Confederated Tribes of the Chehalis Reservation*, Nos. 20-543, 20-544 (November 23, 2020), 3.

17. Https://nativenewsonline.net/currents/trump-signs-stimulus-package.

18. 594 U.S. ___ (2021).

19. David K. Li, "South Dakota Tribes Define Governor and Maintain Checkpoints in Coronavirus Fight," *NBC News* (May 11, 2020), https://www.nbcnews.com/news/us-news/south-dakota-tribes-defy-governor-maintain-checkpoints-coronavirus-fight-n1204496.

20. Ibid.

21. Alaina Beautiful Bald Eagle, *Todd County Tribune* (May 13, 2020), 1.

22. Of course, a few anthropologists and historians wrote several important works that featured detailed treatments of the kinship and governing systems of some Indigenous nations. See, for example, Lewis Henry Morgan's *League of the Iroquois* (1851, *League of the Ho-de-no-sau-nee, or Iroquois*; reprint, New York: Corinth Books, 1962)); Arthur C. Parker's *The Constitution of the Five Nations*, no. 184 (New York State Museum Bulletin, 1916); John R. Swanton's *Social Organization and Social Usages of the Indians of the Creek Confederacy*, Bureau of American Ethology, 42nd Annual Report (Washington, DC: Government Printing Office, 1928); and Angie Debo's *The Road to Disappearance: A History of the Creek Indians* (Norman: University of Nebraska Press, 1941).

23. See Kennan Ferguson, "Why Does Political Science Hate American Indians?" *Perspectives on Politics* 14, no. 4 (December 2016): 1029–1038.

24. American Indian Law Training Program, *Indian Tribes as Governments* (New York: John Hay Whitney Foundation, 1975): iii.

25. https://indigenousgov.hks.harvard.edu/home.

26. See The Harvard Project on American Indian Economic Development, "The State of the Native Nations: Conditions under U.S. Policies of Self-Determination" (New York: Oxford University Press, 2008): Jacket cover. Note 27. https://indigenousgov.hks.harvard.edu/about.

27. Ibid.

28. Ibid.

29. Patrick Sullivan, "Indigenous Governance: The Harvard Project on Native American Economic Development and Appropriate Principles of Governance for Aboriginal Australians," Research Discussion Paper No. 17, American Institute of Aboriginal and Torres Strait Islander Studies (February 2006): 4.

30. Martin Mowbray, "Localising Responsibility: The Application of the Harvard Project on American Indian Economic Development to Australia,' *Australian Journal of Social Issues* 41, no. 1 (Autumn, 2006): 10.

31. Mowbray, "'What matters," 11.

32. See, Shalene Jobin, "Cree Economic Relationships, Governance, and Critical Indigenous Political Economy in Resistance to Settler—Colonial Logics" (PhD diss., University of Alberta, 2014); Clifford Gordon Atleo, "Aboriginal Capitalism: Is Resistance Futile or Fertile," *Journal of Aboriginal Economic Development* 9, no. 2 (2015): 41–51; Christina Dowling, "The Applied Theory of First Nations Economic Development: A Critique," *Journal of Aboriginal Economic Development* 4, no. 2 (2005): 20, 28; Mowbray, "Localising Responsibility," 87–103; and Patrick Sullivan, "Indigenous Governance: The Harvard Project, Australian Aboriginal Organizations and Cultural Subsidiarity," in *Against the Grain: Advances in Postcolonial Organization Studies*, ed. A. Prasad (Copenhagen: Copenhagen Business School Press, 2012).

33. Thanks to one of my reviewers for making note of the different methodological orientations of scholars outside the United States.

34. Dowling, "The Applied Theory," 120.

35. Ibid.

36. Ibid., 125.

37. Atleo, "Aboriginal Capitalism," 44.

38. Sullivan, "Indigenous Governance," 3.

39. Ibid., 4.

40. Ibid., 5.

41. Ibid., 6.

42. Ibid., 7.

43. Ibid., 9–10.

44. Ibid., 10.

45. Ibid., 11.

46. Ibid., 12.

47. Mowbray, "'What matters," 5.

48. Ibid., 14.

49. Ibid.

50. Ibid., 17.

51. Ibid., 24–25.

52. Martin Mowbray, "What matters? Policy Driven Evidence, Indigenous Government and the Harvard Project" (Paper presented at the Australian Social Policy Conference University of New South Wales, July 20–22, 2005).

53. Ibid.

54. Ibid., 27.

55. Ibid., 29.

56. Ibid., 28.

57. Ibid.

58. Sullivan, "Indigenous Governance," 11.

59. Ibid.

386 NOTES

Chapter 1

1. David E. Wilkins, *The Navajo Political Experience*, 4th ed. (Lanham, MD: Rowman & Littlefield, 2013), 150.
2. See, Paulette F. C. Steeve's *The Indigenous Paleolithic of the Western Hemisphere* (Lincoln: University of Nebraska Press, 2021), which shows that the evidence of human habitation of North America traces back well past 10,000 years—quite possibly as far back as 60–100,000 years. These findings confirm what most Native peoples have always maintained about their length of tenure here.
3. Kennan Ferguson, *Perspectives on Politics* 14, no. 4 (December 2016): 1029–1038.
4. See the "Reflections Symposium" section of the special issue in the *Perspectives on Politics* issue which contained Ferguson's lead article and responses from several commentators, with a final comment from Ferguson.
5. U.S. Commission on Civil Rights, "Broken Promises: Continuing Federal Funding Shortfall for Native Americans," Briefing Report (Washington, DC: Government Printing Office, 2018).
6. Ibid., 16–17.
7. Robert F. Williams, *The Law of American State Constitutions* (New York: Oxford University Press, 2009), 2.
8. Ibid., 31.
9. Makah Tribal Constitution, Article 6, section J (1936).
10. Frank P. Grad and Robert F. Williams, *State Constitutions for the Twenty-First Century: Drafting State Constitutions, Revisions, and Amendments*, vol. 2 (Albany: State University of New York Press, 2006), xi; and www.Ballotpedia.org/Amending_state.constitutions.
11. Melissa L. Tatum, Miriam Jorgensen, Mary E. Guss, and Sarah Deer, *Structuring Sovereignty: Constitutions of Native Nations* (Los Angeles, CA: American Indian Studies Center, 2014), 183–186.
12. Williams, *The Law of American State Constitutions*, 3.
13. As the Indian Law Resource Center noted in their study, *Native Land Law: General Principles of Law Relating to Native Lands and Natural Resources: 2013 Lawyers Edition* (St. Paul, MN: Thomson Reuters, 2013), the concept of "discovery" is rife with misinformation and assumptions that have elevated federal power over Native land rights. But in reality, "The idea," notes the editors, "that discovery gave the 'discovering' nation rights to Native lands is inconsistent with international law," and "although United States courts have repeatedly asserted in dicta that the doctrine of discovery gave the United States title to Native lands and resources, no court has ever held, that is, made a formal decision, that the United States validly acquired ownership of Native lands under the doctrine of discovery" (p.18, 21). That said, federal policy, particularly as it emerges from the Department of the Interior, is that the doctrine of discovery operates in a way that grants the federal government a superior title to Native land title, notwithstanding the historical and treaty record which does not support that view.
14. See, *Talton v. Mayes*, 163 U.S. 376 (1896).

NOTES 387

15. Commission on State-Tribal Relations, *Handbook: State-Tribal Relations* (Albuquerque, NM: American Indian Law Center, 1984), 31–32.

16. See David E. Wilkins and Shelly H. Wilkins, *Dismembered: Native Disenrollment in the Battle for Human Rights* (Seattle: University of Washington Press, 2017).

17. See *Afroyim v. Rusk*, 387 U.S. 253 (1967).

18. Ablavsky, " 'With the Indian Tribes,'" 1025.

19. Felix S. Cohen, "Spanish Origin of Indian Rights in the Law of the United States," in *The Legal Conscience: Selected Papers of Felix S. Cohen*, ed. Lucy Cohen (New Haven: Yale University Press, 1960), 233.

20. See Vine Deloria Jr. and Raymond J. DeMallie, eds., *Documents of American Indian Diplomacy: Treaties, Agreements, and Conventions, 1775–1979* (Norman: University of Oklahoma Press, 1999).

21. Thomas Biolsi, "Political and Legal Status ('Lower 48' States)," in *A Companion to the Anthropology of American Indians*, ed. Thomas Biolsi (Malden, MA: Blackwell Publishing, 2004), 232.

22. Nell Jessup Newton, ed., *Cohen's Handbook of Federal Indian Law* (Newark, NJ: LexisNexis Matthew Bender, 2005), 276.

23. *U.S. v. Wheeler*, 435 U.S. 313 (1978).

24. Commission on State-Tribal Relations, *Handbook*, 30.

25. James J. Lopach, Margery Hunter Brown, and Richmond Clow, *Tribal Government Today: Politics on Montana Indian Reservations*, revised ed. (Niwot: University Press of Colorado, 1998), 6.

26. Glenn A. Phelps, "Mr. Gerry Goes to Arizona: Electoral Geography and Voting Rights," *American Indian Culture and Research Journal* 15, no. 2 (1991): 70.

27. Commission on State-Tribal Relations, *Handbook*, 34.

28. Ibid., 36.

29. *U.S. v. Lara*, 541 U.S. 193 (2004), 5.

30. Jennifer Weldon Felmley, "All Good Things Come from Below: The Origins of Effective Tribal Government" (PhD diss., University of California at Berkeley, 2001), 14.

31. Laura E. Evans, *Power from Powerlessness: Tribal Governments, Institutional Niches, and American Federalism* (New York: Oxford University Press, 2011), 23.

32. Pauline Turner Strong and Barrik Van Winkle, "Tribe and Native American Indians and American Nationalism," *Social Analysis* 33 (September 1993): 10.

Chapter 2

1. The "Declaration of Sovereignty" can be viewed on the Tribes' website at warmsprings-nsn.gov.

2. Nell Jessup Newton, ed., *Cohen's Handbook of Federal Indian Law* (Newark, NJ: LexisNexis Matthew Bender, 2005), 249, note 344.

388 NOTES

3. Vine Deloria Jr. and Clifford M. Lytle, *American Indians, American Justice* (Austin: University of Texas Press, 1983), 81.

4. Walter B. Miller, "Two Concepts of Authority," *American Anthropologist* 57, no. 2 (April 1955): 271–289. Quoting from Carleton J. H. Hayes, *A Political and Cultural History of Modern Europe*, vol. 1 (Madison, WI: The Macmillan Co., 1944), 291.

5. Deloria and Lytle, *American Indians, American Justice*, 81.

6. *Shirley v. Morgan*, SC-CV-02-10 (May 28, 2010), 19.

7. Vine Deloria Jr. and Clifford M. Lytle, *The Nations Within: The Past and Future of American Indian Sovereignty* (New York: Pantheon Books, 1984), 8.

8. Sharon O'Brien, *American Indian Tribal Governments* (Norman: University of Oklahoma Press, 1989), 14.

9. Harold Driver, *Indians of North America*, 2nd ed. (Chicago: University of Chicago Press, 1969). See especially chapter 17.

10. Ibid., 287.

11. Ibid., 288.

12. Ibid.

13. Newton, *Cohen's Handbook*, 250.

14. Deloria and Lytle, *American Indians, American Justice*, xi.

15. Russel L. Barsh, "The Nature and Spirit of North American Political Systems," *American Indian Quarterly* 10, no. 3 (Summer 1986): 186.

16. Paul Radin, *Primitive Man as Philosopher* (New York: Dover Publications, 1957), 51.

17. Paul Radin, *The World of Primitive Man* (New York: Grove Press, 1960), 14–15.

18. Ibid., 106.

19. Ibid., 11.

20. Patricia Albers, email message to author, December 29, 2020.

21. Edward P. Dozier, "The Pueblos of the Southwestern United States," *The Journal of the Royal Anthropological Institute* 90 (1960): 152.

22. Ibid., 153.

23. Ibid., 152–153.

24. Ibid., 153.

25. Steadman Upham, *Politics and Power: An Economic and Political History of the Western Pueblo* (New York: Academic Press, 1982), 21.

26. Radin, *The World of Primitive Man*, 153.

27. Grahn, J. L., D. X. Swenson, and R. O'Leary, "A Comparative Analysis between American Indian and Anglo American Leadership," *Cross Cultural Management: An International Journal* 8, no. 1 (2001): 4.

28. Radin, *The World of Primitive Man*, 193.

29. Frederick Webb Hodge, ed., *Handbook of American Indians North of Mexico*, Pt. 1. Bureau of American Ethnology. Bulletin 30 (Washington, DC: Government Printing Office, 1907), 303.

30. E. Adamson Hoebel, *The Law of Primitive Man: A Study in Comparative Legal Dynamics* (1954; reprint, New York: Atheneum, 1968), 4.

31. Russel Barsh, "'Indian Law,' Indians' Law, and Legalism in American Indian Policy: An Essay on Historical Origins," in *American Indians: Social Justice and Public Policy*,

ed. Donald E. Green and Thomas V. Tonneson (Madison, WI: Institute on Race and Ethnicity, 1991), 9–10.

32. Miller, "Two Concepts of Authority," 271.

33. Ibid., 276.

34. Ibid.

35. Barsh, "The Nature and Spirit," 186. And see Christine Gish Hill's *Web of Kinship: Family in Northern Cheyenne Nationhood* (Norman: University of Oklahoma Press, 2017) who describes the comprehensive kinship system of the Northern Cheyenne people.

36. Alden T. Vaughan and Deborah Rosen, eds., *Early American Indian Documents: Carolina and Georgia Laws*, vol. 16 (Washington, DC: University Publications of America, 1998), xx–xxi.

37. Ibid. And see William W. Warren's classic account of the Anishinaabe, *History of the Ojibway Nation*, Collection of the Minnesota Historical Society, vol. 5 (St. Paul: Minnesota Historical Society, 1885) for a vivid account of how transgressions were dealt with by the Anishinaabe.

38. Ibid, xiv.

39. See Patricia Albers and Bea Medicine, eds., *The Hidden Half: Studies of Plains Indian Women* (Lanham, MD: University Press of America, 1983); and Mary Jo Fox, Eileen M. Luna-Firebaugh, and Caroline Williams, "American Indian Female Leadership," *Wicazo Sa Review* 30, no. 1 (Spring 2015).

40. Harlan Pruden, "'TWO-SPIRIT' Turns 30!!," *Two Spirit Journal* (August 4, 2020). Accessed July 2022 at https://twospiritjournal.com/?p=973.

41. A great deal of recent research offers insight into traditional Indigenous gender concepts. See Sandra Slater and Fay A. Yarbrough, eds., *Gender and Sexuality in Indigenous North America, 1400–1850* (Columbia: University of South Carolina Press, 2022); Mark Rifkin, *When Did Indians Become Straight?: Kinship, the History of Sexuality, and Native Sovereignty* (New York: Oxford University Press, 2011); Gregory Smithers, *Reclaiming Two-Spirits: Sexuality, Spiritual Renewal & Sovereignty in Native America* (Boston, MA: Beacon Press, 2022); Scott L. Morgensen, *Spaces between Us: Queer Settler Colonialism and Indigenous Decolonization* (Minneapolis: University of Minnesota Press, 2011); Mona M. Smith and Nan Toskey, *Honored by the Moon*, Minnesota American Indian AIDS Task Force DVD (New York: Women Make Movies, 2012).

42. Laura F. Klein, "Mother as Clanswoman: Rank and Gender in Tlingit Society," in *Women and Power in Native North America*, ed. Laura F. Klein and Lillian A. Ackerman (Norman: University of Oklahoma Press, 1995), 35.

43. Lillian A. Ackerman, "Complementary but Equal: Gender Status in the Plateau," in *Women and Power in Native North America*, ed. Laura F. Klein and Lillian A. Ackerman (Norman: University of Oklahoma Press, 1995), 85.

44. See the 2020 "Report to the President: Activities and Accomplishments of the First Year of Operation Lady Justice," produced by the Presidential Task Force on Missing and Murdered American Indians and Alaska Natives, a collaborative unit formed by the Departments of Justice, the Interior and Health and Human Services via

390 NOTES

President Trump's Executive Order 13898 in 2019. That order directs the Task Force to seek answers regarding the "extraordinary public safety challenges facing Native Americans across the country" particularly missing and murdered women and girls.

45. Sarah Deer and Mary Kathryn Nagle, "Return to *Worcester: Dollar General* and the Restoration of Tribal Jurisdiction to Protect Native Women and Children," *Harvard Journal of Law and Gender* 41 (2018): 190–191.

46. Bethany Ruth Berger, "After Pocahontas: Indian Women and the Law, 1830–1934," *American Indian Law Review* 21 (1997): 17.

47. Ibid., 18.

48. James W. Zion and Elsie B. Zion, "Hozho's Sokee'—Stay Together Nicely: Domestic Violence under Navajo Common Law," *Arizona State Law Journal* 25 (Summer 1993): 413.

49. Ibid., 412.

50. See Zion and Zion, "Hozho's Sokee'," 412; Berger, "After Pocahontas," 19; and Michael Lerma, *Guided by the Mountains: Navajo Political Philosophy and Governance* (New York: Oxford University Press, 2017), 112.

51. Keith Grint, *Leadership: A Very Short Introduction* (New York: Oxford University Press, 2010), 2.

52. Waude H. Kracke, *Force and Persuasion: Leadership in an Amazonian Society* (Chicago: University of Chicago Press, 1975), 114.

53. Ella C. Deloria, *Speaking of Indians* (Vermillion: University of South Dakota, 1944), 25.

54. Ibid., 32.

55. Barsh, "The Nature and Spirit," 191.

56. Miller, "Two Concepts of Authority," 280.

57. Barsh, "The Nature and Spirit," 192.

58. Vine Deloria Jr. and Daniel Wildcat, *Power and Place: Indian Education in America* (Golden, CO: Fulcrum Publishing, 2001), 2.

59. Miller, "Two Concepts of Authority," 282–283.

60. Ibid., 284.

61. Robert H. Lowi, "Some Aspects of Political Organization among the American Aborigines," *Journal of the Royal Aboriginal Institute of Great Britain and Ireland* 78 (February 1948): 16.

62. Ibid.

63. See, W. W. Hill, "Some Aspects of Navajo Political Structure," *Plateau* 13, no. 2 (October 1940): 24.

64. Ibid., 25.

65. David E. Wilkins, *The Navajo Political Experience* (Lanham, MD: Rowman & Littlefield, 2013), 6.

66. Jessica M. Shalian, *The Politics of Arctic Sovereignty: Oil, Ice, and Inuit Governance* (London: Routledge, 2014), 25.

67. E. M. Weyer, "The Structure of Social Organization among the Eskimos," in *Comparative Political Systems: Studies in the Politics of Preindustrial Societies*, ed.

Ronald Cohen and John M. Middleton (Garden City, NJ: Natural History Press, 1967), 1.

68. Ibid., 1–2.

69. H. Dewey Anderson and Walter Crosby Eells, *Alaska Natives: A Survey of Their Sociolegal and Educational Status* (Palo Alto, CA: Stanford University Press, 1935), 48.

70. Ibid.

71. Ibid., 49.

72. Hoebel, *The Law of Primitive Man*, 82.

73. Weyer, "The Structure of Social Organization," 9.

74. Hoebel, *The Law of Primitive Man*, 82.

75. Ibid.

76. Anderson and Eells, *Alaska Natives*, 49.

77. Barry M. Pritzker, *A Native American Encyclopedia: History, Culture, and Peoples* (New York: Oxford University Press, 2000), 99.

78. Kyle B. Fields, "Tohono O'odham Legal Systems" (unpublished paper, August 2018), 3.

79. Donald M. Bohr, "Pima and Papago Social Organization," in *Handbook of North American Indians*, vol. 10, ed. Alfonso Ortiz (Washington, DC: Smithsonian Institution, 1983), 187.

80. Peter MacMillan Booth, "Tohono O'odham (Papago)," in *Encyclopedia of North American Indians*, ed. Fred Hoxie (New York: Houghton Mifflin Co., 1996), 636.

81. Vivian Juan, "Tohono O'odham," in *Native America in the Twentieth Century: An Encyclopedia*, ed. Mary B. Davis (New York: Garland Publishing Co., 1996), 637.

82. Teri Knutsen Woods, Karen Blaine, and Lauri Francisco, "O'odham Himdag as a Source of Strength and Wellness among the Tohono O'odham of Southern Arizona and Northern Sonora, Mexico," *Journal of Sociology and Social Welfare* 29, no. 1 (March 2002): 41; and Fields, "Tohono O'odham Legal Systems," 3.

83. Fields, "Tohono O'odham Legal Systems," 4.

84. Ruth M. Underhill, "Social Organization of the Papago Indians," *Columbia University Contributions to Anthropology* 30 (1939): 72.

85. Bohr, "Pima and Papago Social Organization," 185.

86. Hodge, *Handbook of American Indians North of Mexico*, 472.

87. Miller, "Two Concepts of Authority," 272.

88. Chellie Spiller, Hoturoa Barclay-Kerr, and John Panoho, *Wayfinding Leadership: Groundbreaking Wisdom for Developing Leaders* (Wellington, NZ: Huia Publishers, 2015), 22.

89. Driver, *Indians of North America*, 342–343.

90. Ibid., 343.

91. Miller, "Two Concepts of Authority," 283.

92. Driver, *Indians of North America*, 343.

93. Miller, "Two Concepts of Authority," 284.

94. Driver, *Indians of North America*, 343.

95. Richard P. Metcalf, "'Who Shall Rule at Home?' Native American Politics and Indian-White Relations," *Journal of American History* 6, no. 3 (December 1974): 665.

392   NOTES

96. See, for example, Jack Weatherford's *Indian Givers: How the Indians of the Americas Transformed the World* (New York: Fawcett Columbine, 1988); and see Vine Deloria Jr. *Indian Education in America* (Boulder, CO: American Indian Science & Engineering Society, 1991).

97. Phillip Wearne, *Return of the Indian: Conquest and Revival in the Americas* (Philadelphia, PA: Temple University Press, 1996), 52.

98. O'Brien, *American Indian Tribal Governments*, 14.

99. Tom Holm, "Indian Concepts of Authority and the Crisis in Tribal Government," *Social Science Journal* 19, no. 3 (July 1982): 60.

100. See Laura F. Klein and Lillian A. Ackerman, eds. *Women and Power in Native North America* (Norman: University of Oklahoma Press, 1995); Albers and Medicine, The Hidden Half; M. Annette Jaimes and Theresa Halsey, "American Indian Women: At the Center of Indigenous Resistance in North America," in *The State of Native America*, ed. M. Annette Jaimes (Boston, MA: South End Press, 1992), 311–344; and Carolyn Kenny and Tina Ngaroimata Fraser, eds., *Living Indigenous Leadership: Native Narratives on Building Strong Communities* (Vancouver: UBC Press, 2012).

101. Deloria and Lytle, *American Indians, American Justice*, 89.

102. Upham, *Politics and Power*, 93.

Chapter 3

1. Stephen J. Rockwell, *Indian Affairs and the Administrative State in the Nineteenth Century* (New York: Cambridge University Press, 2010), 303.

2. Ibid., 7.

3. Alexis de Tocqueville, *Democracy in America*, vol. 1, ed. J. P. Mayer (Garden City, NJ, 1969), 339.

4. For a fuller discussion of these paradigms see David E. Wilkins, *American Indian Sovereignty and the U.S. Supreme Court: The Masking of Justice* (Austin: University of Texas Press, 1997).

5. 31 U.S. (6 Pet.) 515; 72 U.S. (5 Wall.) 737; 109 U.S. 556.

6. Sidney L. Harring, *Crow Dog's Case: American Indian Sovereignty, Tribal Law, and United States Law in the Nineteenth Century* (New York: Cambridge University Press, 1994), 24.

7. The phrase "civilized" became part of the Five Tribes after their forced removal to present-day Oklahoma. Once they resettled, the members of these nations made tremendous social and political changes within their societies and were soon labeled "civilized" to distinguish them from the so-called "wild" tribes of the Western Plains region.

8. Edward P. Dozier, "Factionalism at Santa Clara Pueblo," *Ethnology* 15, no. 2 (1966): 174.

9. Edward P. Dozier, "The Pueblo Indians of the Southwest: A Survey of the Anthropological Literature and a Review of Theory, Method, and Results" *Current Anthropology* 5, no. 2 (April 1964): 90.
10. Ibid.
11. Ibid.
12. Dozier, "Factionalism," 174.
13. Maurice Crandall, *These People Have Always Been a Republic: Indigenous Electorates in the U.S.–Mexico Borderlands, 1598–1912* (Chapel Hill: University of North Carolina Press, 2019), 15.
14. 94 U.S. 614.
15. 231 U.S. 28.
16. Reginald G. Fisher, "An Outline of Pueblo Government," in *So Live the Works of Man*, ed. Donald D. Brand and Fred Harvey (Albuquerque, NM: 1939), 156.
17. Vine Deloria Jr. and Clifford M. Lytle, *American Indians, American Justice* (Austin: University of Texas Press, 1983), 89.
18. Susan L. MacCulloch, "A Tripartite Political System among Christian Indians of Early Massachusetts," *Kroeber Anthropological Society Papers* 34 (1966): 63.
19. Jean M. O'Brien, *Dispossession by Degrees: Indian Land and Identity in Natick, Massachusetts, 1650–1790* (New York: Cambridge University Press, 1997), 48.
20. See David E. Wilkins, ed. *Documents of Native American Political Development: 1500s–1933* (New York: Oxford University Press, 2009), 39 for a copy of these laws.
21. See, e.g., Duane Champagne, *Social Order and Political Change: Constitutional Governments Among the Cherokee, the Choctaw, the Chickasaw, and the Creek* (Stanford, CA: Stanford University Press, 1992; William G. McLoughlin, *Cherokee Renascence in the New Republic* (Princeton, NJ: 1986); and Angie Debo, *The Road to Disappearance: A History of the Creek Indians* (Norman: University of Oklahoma Press, 1941).
22. Rennard Strickland, *Fire and the Spirits: Cherokee Law from Clan to Court* (Norman: University of Oklahoma Press 1975), 65.
23. Cherokee Nation, *Laws of the Cherokee Nation* (Tahlequah, Cherokee Nation: Cherokee Advocate Office, 1852).
24. Ibid., 41.
25. Duane Champagne, *Social Change and Cultural Continuity Among Native Nations* (Lanham, MD: Alta Mira Press, 2007), 85.
26. Clara Sue Kidwell, *The Choctaws in Oklahoma: From Tribe to Nation, 1855–1970* (Norman: University of Oklahoma Press, 2007), 5–6.
27. Champagne, *Social Change and Cultural Continuity*, 89.
28. Ibid., 74.
29. 28 Stat. 693.
30. Felix S. Cohen, *Handbook of Federal Indian Law* (1942; reprint, Albuquerque: University of New Mexico Press, 1972), 129, note 59.
31. Gary Clayton Anderson, *Kinsmen of Another Kind: Dakota-White Relations in the Upper Mississippi Valley, 1650–1862* (Lincoln: University of Nebraska Press, 1984), 174–175.

394 NOTES

32. Ibid., 175.
33. Ibid., 223.
34. 7 Stat. 44.
35. 7 Stat. 74.
36. 7 Stat. 359.
37. Frederick Jackson Turner, "The Problems of the West," *The Atlantic Monthly* 78 (September 1896): 295.
38. Ibid.
39. Ibid., 296.
40. A large number of Tribes inhabiting Indian Territory had signed treaties with the Confederate States of America. See James M. Matthews, ed., *The Statutes at Large of the Provisional Government of the Confederate States of America* (Indian Rocks Beach, FL: D & S Publishers, Inc., 1970), 289–411, which contains copies of these interesting accords.
41. 15 Stat. 17, 18.
42. 16 Stat. 13, 40.
43. See Fred L. Israel, ed., *The State of the Union Messages of the Presidents, 1790–1966*, 3 vols. (New York: Chelsea House, 1966), especially vol. 2, 1199.
44. Ibid., 1199–2000.
45. U.S. Senate, Committee on the Pacific Railroad, Report on the Pacific Railroad, Report No. 219, 40th Cong., 3rd sess. (1869), 15.
46. Ibid.
47. A good contemporary discussion on the history and legal ramifications of the effort to stop Indian treaty-making is found in George William Rice's "Indian Rights: 25 U.S.C. Sec. 71: The End of Indian Sovereignty or a Self-Limitation of Contractual Ability," *American Indian Law Review* 5 (1977): 239–253. Rice supports Felix Cohen's well-reasoned argument that the 1871 stoppage of treaty-making did not destroy or weaken Native political status, per se. The essence of treaty-making, in Cohen's words "was destined . . . to be continued for many decades" in the form of agreements (1972 ed. 67).
48. U.S. Commissioner of Indian Affairs, *Annual Report* (Washington, DC: Government Printing Office, 1866), 15.
49. U.S. Commissioner of Indian Affairs, *Annual Report* (1871), 1154.
50. U.S. *Congressional Globe* (March 1, 1871), 1811.
51. 14 Stat. 763.
52. 15 Stat. 531.
53. Deloria and Lytle, *American Indians, American Justice*, 93–94.
54. 26 Stat. 794.
55. 28 Stat. 286.
56. Todd Adams, Gary Clayton Anderson, and R. David Edmunds, "The Saginaw Chippewa Sovereignty Case: A Case Study in Indian Law," (unpublished and undated report), 128–129.
57. Loretta Fowler, *Arapahoe Politics, 1851–1978: Symbols in Crises of Authority* (Lincoln: University of Nebraska Press, 1982), 102–103.

NOTES 395

58. Ibid., 103.

59. Ibid., 98.

60. See Brian C. Hosmer, *American Indians in the Marketplace: Persistence and Innovation Among the Menominees and Metlakatlans, 1870–1920* (Lawrence: University Press of Kansas, 1999); and David Beck, *The Struggle for Self-Determination: History of the Menominee Indians since 1854* (Lincoln: University of Nebraska Press, 2005) for good overviews of the Menominee.

61. See Wilkins, Documents of Native American Political Development: 1500s–1933, 294 for a copy of this constitution.

62. U.S. Congressional Record. House. Vol. 61, Pt. 5, 67th Cong., 1st Sess. (August 24, 1921), 4661.

63. William T. Hagan, *The Sac and Fox Indians* (Norman: University of Oklahoma Press, 1958), 259–260.

64. Ibid., 260.

65. See, Wilkins, *Documents of Native American Political Development: 1500s–1933*, 423–425 for a copy of these bylaws.

66. David E. Wilkins, *The Navajo Political Experience*, 4th ed. (Lanham, MD: Rowman & Littlefield, 2013), 18–20.

67. Circular 2565, "Tribal Business Committees," March 14, 1929, U.S. National Archives, Record Group 75, "Circulars, 1904–1934." The replies are located in Record Group 75, Entry 133, Replies to Circulars, 1907–1935; Reply to Circular 2565.

68. Elmer R. Rusco, *A Fateful Time: The Background and Legislative History of the Indian Reorganization Act* (Reno: University of Nevada Press, 2000), 36.

69. Circular Responses, March 29, 1929.

70. Ibid.

71. Ibid., April 12, 1929.

72. Ibid., March 29, 1929.

73. Ibid., April 5, 1929.

74. Ibid.

75. Ibid., April 2, 1929.

76. U.S. Commissioner of Indian Affairs, *Annual Report* (1900), 173.

77. Ibid., 174.

78. 30 Stat. 495.

79. See Rosalyn R. LaPier, *Invisible Reality: Storytellers, Storytakers, and the Supernatural World of the Blackfeet* (Lincoln: University of Nebraska Press, 2017), which contains good data about the Blackfeet's well-organized agricultural contests organized by the Piegan Farming & Livestock Association during the 1920s.

80. Circular Responses, May 25, 1929.

81. Ibid., April 3, 1929.

82. The "existing conditions" referred to include the allotting of reservation lands and the fact that, according to the superintendent, the Natives had already been economically and educationally incorporated into the neighboring white community.

396 NOTES

Chapter 4

1. Annie H. Abel, "Proposals for an Indian State, 1778–1878," in *Annual Report of the American Historical Association*, vol. 1 (Washington, DC: Government Printing Office, 1907), 90.
2. Glover Gillette Hatheway, "The Neutral Indian Barrier State: A Project in British North American Policy, 1754–1815" (PhD diss., University of Minnesota, 1957), i.
3. Ibid, ii.
4. Ibid., 9.
5. Ibid., 89.
6. Michael Paul Patrick Simon, "Indigenous Peoples in Developed Fragment Societies: A Comparative Analysis of Internal Colonialism in the U.S., CA, and Northern Ireland" (PhD diss., University of Arizona 1986), 177.
7. Francis P. Prucha, *The Great Father: The United States Government and the American Indians*, vol. 1 (Lincoln: University of Nebraska Press, 1984), 21–22.
8. Wilbur Jacobs, "Edmund Atkin's Plan for Imperial Indian Control," *Journal of Southern History* 19 (August 1953): 315.
9. Frederick Jackson Turner, "The Policy of France toward the Mississippi Valley in the Period of Washington and Adams," *American Historical Review* 10, no. 2 (January 1905): 250.
10. Bonnie Juettner, *100 Native Americans Who Shaped American History* (San Mateo, CA: Blueword Books, 2003), 15.
11. Prucha, *The Great Father*, 24.
12. Anthony F. C. Wallace, *Jefferson and the Indians: The Tragic Fate of the First Americans* (Cambridge, MA: Harvard University Press, 1979), 34.
13. Turner, "The Policy of France," 250.
14. Francis P. Prucha, *American Indian Policy in the Formative Years: The Indian Trade and Intercourse Acts, 1790–1834* (Lincoln: University of Nebraska Press, 1962), 20.
15. Hatheway, "The Neutral Indian Barrier State," 210.
16. Ibid., 21.
17. Ibid., iii.
18. Haldimand to North, November 27, 1783. As quoted in Orpha E. Leavitt, "British Policy on the Canadian Frontier, 1782–92: Mediation and an Indian Barrier State," in *Proceedings of the State Historical Society, 63rd Annual Meeting* (1916), 175, note 71.
19. Leavitt, "British Policy on the Canadian Frontier," 175, and see Joseph D. Ibbitson, "Samuel Kirland, The Treaty of 1792, and the Indian Barrier State," *New York History* 19 (October 1938): 374–375.
20. Hatheway, "The Neutral Indian Barrier State," iii.
21. Prucha, *The Great Father*, 78.
22. Hatheway, "The Neutral Indian Barrier State," 445.
23. George Henry Alden, "The State of Franklin," *American Historical Review* 8, no. 2 (1903): 271.
24. Philip M. Hamer, "The Wataugans and the Cherokee Indians in 1776," *East Tennessee Historical Society's Publications* 1, no. 3 (January 1931): 112–113.

25. Alden, "The State of Franklin," 283; Vine Deloria Jr. and Raymond J. DeMallie, *Documents of American Indian Diplomacy: Treaties, Agreements, and Conventions, 1775-1979*, vol. 2 (Norman: University of Oklahoma Press, 1999), 1434, 1479-1483.
26. Abel, "Proposals for an Indian State," 89.
27. Thomas D. Watson, "Strivings for Sovereignty: Alexander McGillivray, Creek Warfare, and Diplomacy, 1783-1790," *Florida Historical Quarterly* 58 (1980): 406.
28. Abel, "Proposals for an Indian State," 90; Watson, "Strivings for Sovereignty," 410.
29. Willard B. Walker, "Creek Confederacy Before Removal," in *Handbook of North American Indians: Southeast*, vol. 14, ed. Raymond D. Fogelson (Washington, DC: Smithsonian Institution, 2004), 388.
30. Ibid.
31. Lyle N. McAlister, "William Augustus Bowles and the State of Muskogee," *Florida Historical Quarterly* 40 (April 1962): 319-320.
32. J. Leitch Wright, Jr., *Creeks and Seminoles: The Destruction and Regeneration of the Muscogulge People* (Lincoln: University of Nebraska Press, 1986), 120.
33. McAlister, "William Augustus Bowles," 326.
34. David H. White, "The Spaniards and William Augustus Bowles in Florida, 1799-1803," *Florida Historical Quarterly* 84 (October 1975): 155; Walker, "Creek Confederacy Before Removal," 388.
35. Joseph W. Phillips, *Jedediah Morse and New England Congregationalism* (New Brunswick, NJ: Rutgers University Press, 1983), 208.
36. Abel, "Proposals for an Indian State," 92.
37. Jedediah Morse, "Report to the Secretary of War of the United States on Indian Affairs, Comprising a Narrative of a Tour Performed in the Summer of 1820, under a Commission from the President of the United States, for the Purpose of Ascertaining for the Use of the Government, the Actual State of the Indian Tribes in Our Country" (New Haven, CT: Davis and Force, 1822), 16.
38. Ibid., 61.
39. George Schultz, *An Indian Canaan: Isaac McCoy and the Vision of an Indian State* (Norman: University of Oklahoma Press, 1972), 61.
40. Ibid., 96.
41. Ibid., x.
42. Ibid., 116.
43. See Schoolcraft's *Historical and Statistical Information, Respecting the History, Condition and Prospects of the Indian Tribes of the United States*, Pts. 1-5 (Philadelphia, PA, 1851-1857); and *Personal Memoir of a Residence of Thirty Years with the Indian Tribes in the North American Frontiers, A. D. 1812-1842* (Philadelphia, PA, 1851).
44. As quoted in Abel, "Proposals for an Indian State," 100.
45. 7 Stat. 13.
46. Ibid., 14.
47. Vine Deloria Jr. and David E. Wilkins, *Tribes, Treaties, and Constitutional Tribulations* (Austin: University of Texas Press, 1999), 9.
48. Abel, "Proposals for an Indian State," 89.
49. Deloria and Wilkins, *Tribes, Treaties*, 9.

398   NOTES

50. 7 Stat. 18.
51. Ibid.
52. 30 U.S. (5 Pet) 1, 17 (1831).
53. Ezra Rosser, "The Nature of Representation: The Cherokee Right to a Congressional Delegate," *Public Interest Law Journal* 15, no. 1 (Fall 2005): 121–122.
54. Abel, "Proposals for an Indian State," 90–91.
55. John C. Calhoun, *Secretary of War, Annual Message: "Location and Improvement of Indians"* (Washington, DC: Gales & Seaton Register I, Appendix, 1825), 59.
56. Abel, "Proposals for an Indian State," 90–91.
57. Prucha, *American Indian Policy*, 270.
58. J. Ruth Hegwood, Amanda Page, and Daniel F. Littlefield Jr., "The State of Sequoyah Movement" (Unpublished essay from the Sequoyah Research Center at the University of Arkansas at Little Rock, 2005), 1; Abel, "Proposals for an Indian State," 92–93; and Prucha, *American Indian Policy*, 270–272.
59. 7 Stat. 333.
60. House Committee on Indian Affairs, *Regulating the Indian Department*, 23rd Cong., 1st Sess. (1834), H. Rept. 474.
61. 7 Stat. 478.
62. Prucha, *The Great Father*, 276.
63. Niles' Weekly Register, Foreign Articles, "The Indians," 39, no. 990 (Baltimore, MD: September 4, 1830), 19.
64. 4 Stat. 729.
65. 4 Stat. 735.
66. Prucha, *The Great Father*, abridged ed. (1986), 105.
67. House Committee on Indian Affairs, *Regulating the Indian Department*, 23rd Cong., 1st Sess. (1834), H. Rept. 474, 14.
68. Ibid., 19.
69. *Western Territory of 1834*, HR 490 (May 30, 1834). Retrieved from the Library of Congress, https://www.loc.gov/item/rbpe.23100400 And see Prucha, *The Great Father: The United States Government and the American Indians*. ed. Abridged. (Lincoln, NE: University of Nebraska Press, 1986), 105.
70. Gales & Seaton Register, "Indian Bills," June 25, 1834, 4763.
71. 7 Stat. 478.
72. Ibid.
73. Rowen McClinton, "New Echota (1835), Treaty of," in *Encyclopedia of U.S. Indian Policy and Law*, ed. Paul Finkelman and Tim Alan Garrison (Washington, DC: Congressional Quarterly Press, 2009), 591.
74. Rosser, "The Nature of Representation," 91–92.
75. Ibid., 107.
76. Ibid., 124.
77. https://www.cherokeephoenix.org/news/hoskin-meets-with-president-undersco res-push-for-delegate/article_1c2084c8-c88e-11eb-99c2-ebaac5f668d3.html
78. https://www.news9.com/story/6222ae635a904f072ff80bfb/oklahoma-could-soon-have-a-tribal-representative-in-congress

NOTES 399

79. Robert J. the *Nation: A History* (Albuquerque: University of New Mexico Press, 2005), 173–177.

80. Treaty with the Seminole, March 4, 1866 (14 Stat. 755); Treaty with the Choctaw and Chickasaw, April 28, 1866 (14 Stat. 769); Treaty with the Creeks, June 14, 1866 (14 Stat. 785); and Treaty with the Cherokee, July 19, 1866 (14 Stat. 799.).

81. Abel, "Proposals for an Indian State," 100.

82. Senate Committee on Indian Affairs, *Memorial of the Principal Chief and Delegate of the Cherokee Nation of Indians*, 41st Cong., 2nd Sess. (1870), Misc. Document No. 83, 2.

83. Ibid., 5.

84. 14 Stat. 799, 945.

85. 14 Stat. 769, 921.

86. Ibid, 923.

87. Abel, "Proposals for an Indian State," 101.

88. Ibid., 101.

89. Ibid., 102.

90. Ibid.

91. House Committee on Indian Affairs, *Organization of the Indian Territory*, 45th Cong., 1st Sess. (1877), H. Rept. 7922, 1.

92. House Committee on Indian Affairs, *Election of Delegate*, HR 2687 (1878), 1.

93. Ibid., 8.

94. House Committee on Indian Affairs, *Objections of the Indian Delegation: Delegate in Congress*, 45th Cong., 2nd sess. (1878), 1–4.

95. House Committee on Indian Affairs, *Indian Delegate in Congress*, 48th Cong., 1st Sess. (1884), 394.

96. Commissioner of Indian Affairs, *Annual Report* (1887), 118.

97. 30 Stat. 497.

98. Ibid., 512.

99. William E. Unrau, *Mixed Blood and Tribal Dissolution: Charles Curtis and the Quest for Indian Identity* (Norman: University of Oklahoma Press, 1989), 122.

100. I am grateful to Phyllis Deery Stanton, who kindly shared with me the thorough research on international diplomacy among the Native nations in the Indian Territory that she gathered in the course of writing her MA thesis at the University of Arizona. Her research and analysis were most useful in the construction of this section of this chapter.

101. Arrell Gibson, "An Indian Territory United Nations: The Creek Council of 1845," *Chronicles of Oklahoma* 39 (Winter 1961–1962): 400.

102. Letter from James Logan, Creek Agent, to Sam Houston, President of Texas, June 1, 1842. Author has a copy of this letter.

103. James Mooney, "Myths of the Cherokee," in *Bureau of American Ethnology, 19th Annual Report*, Pt. 1 (Washington, DC: Government Printing Office, 1900), 485.

104. Lydia Huntley Sigourney, "The Grand June Council," *Chronicles of Oklahoma* 10 (1932): 558.

400 NOTES

105. "Compact Between the Several Tribes of Indians," in Works Progress Administration: Historic Sites and Federal Writers Project Collection, WPA4, Western History Collections, Norman: University of Oklahoma Library.

106. Gibson, "An Indian Territory United Nations," 400.

107. "Address of Samuel Checote," in Samuel Checote Collection, Western History Collections, SC1, Norman, University of Oklahoma Library, 1870, 1.

108. Clara Sue Kidwell, *The Choctaws in Oklahoma: From Tribe to Nation, 1855–1970* (Norman: University of Oklahoma Press, 2007), 83.

109. *Message of the president of the United States communicating a copy of the proceedings of the Council of Indian Tribes held at Okmulgee in December 1870*, 41st Cong., 3rd Sess., Senate Exec. Doc. 26 (Washington, DC: January 30, 1871).

110. Kidwell, *The Choctaws in Oklahoma*, 84.

111. Ibid., 85.

112. Debo, *The Rise and Fall of the Choctaw* Republic (Norman: University of Oklahoma Press, 1961), 216.

113. Allen G. Applen, "An Attempted Indian State Government: the Okmulgee Constitution in Indian Territory, 1870–1876," *Kansas Quarterly* 3 (1971): 97.

114. Commissioner of Indian Affairs, *Annual Report* (1888), 126.

115. Prucha, *The Great* Father," abridged ed. (1986), 744.

116. Kenny L. Brown, "Oklahoma Territory," *The Encyclopedia of Oklahoma History and Culture*, (2007) https://www.okhistory.org/publications/enc/entry.php?entry=OK085.

117. 7 Stat. 333.

118. See Tom Holm, "Indian Lobbyists: Cherokee Opposition to the Allotment of Tribal Lands," *American Indian Quarterly* 5, no. 2 (May 1979): 115–134; Craig H. Miner, *The Corporation and the Indian: Tribal Sovereignty and Industrial Civilization in Indian Territory, 1865–1907* (Norman: University of Oklahoma Press, 1989); and Kent Carter, *The Dawes Commission and the Allotment of the Five Civilized Tribes: 1893–1914* (Ancestry Publishing, 1999).

119. Daniel Littlefield argues that not all the Tribal leaders were opposed to joint statehood with Oklahoma Territory. In fact, the Chickasaw governor, Douglas Johnson, supported a merger with Oklahoma. The most detailed analysis of the efforts to create the State of Sequoyah is found in Amos D. Maxwell's book, *The Sequoyah Constitutional Convention* (Boston: Meador Publishing Co., 1953).

120. Steve Russell, *Sequoyah Rising: Problems in Postcolonial Tribal Governance* (Durhan, NC: Carolina Academic Press, 2010), 143.

121. Hegwood, et al., "The State of Sequoyah Movement," 59th Cong., 1st Sess. (1906), 6.

122. Senate, *Proposed State of Sequoyah*, 59th Cong., 1st Sess. (1906), 1–2.

123. Maxwell, *The Sequoyah Constitutional Convention*, 118.

124. Kidwell, *The Choctaws in Oklahoma*, 183.

125. Rennard Strickland, *The Indians of Oklahoma* (Norman: University of Oklahoma Press, 1980), 50. And see Robert F. Williams, *The Law of American State Constitutions* (New York: Oxford University Press, 2009), 95.

126. Quote in Strickland, *The Indians of Oklahoma*, 53.

NOTES 401

127. Tom Holm, e-mail message to author, February 18, 2021.

128. Miner, *The Corporation and the Indian*, 211.

129. Ibid.

130. See, e.g., Vine Deloria Jr.'s unpublished essay "On Restoration of Constitutional Treaty-Making Authority" in Wilkins, *Documents of Native American Political Development: 1933 to Present*, 172–178.

131. Quoted from the "Declaration of Sovereignty" approved by the National Congress of American Indians on October 24, 1974. Document is in Wilkins, *Documents of Native American Political Development: 1933 to Present*, 178–180.

132. Wilkins, *Documents of Native American Political Development: 1933 to Present*, 196.

133. Ibid., 197.

134. Ibid., 198.

135. Charles Trimble, "Indian Country: The 51st State?," *Indian Life* 29, no. 5 (March–April 2009): 1–3.

136. Theodore Wyckoff, "The Navajo Nation Tomorrow—51st State, Commonwealth, Or . . .?," *American Indian Law Review* 5, no. 2 (1977): 272.

137. Ibid., 280.

138. Ibid., 292.

139. See, e.g., Louisiana Coalition Against Racism and Nazism, "The Politics and Background of David Duke: Resource Packet," 5th ed. (December 1991), 46; James H. Evans Jr. "Eschatology, White Supremacy, and the Beloved Community," in *Reconstructing Christian Theology*, ed. Rebecca S. Chopp and Mark Lewis Taylor (Minneapolis, MN: Fortress Press, 1994), 365; and Daniel Radash and Timothy Long, "Yikes! Are We the Next Bosnia-Herzegovina," *Spy* 7, no. 6 (1993): 56–60.

140. Cherokee Nation Vision Summit, 2003. Copy on file with author.

141. Ibid.

142. Julie Hubbard, "Sequoyah Panel Reflects on 1905 Proposal," *Muscogee Daily Phoenix* (April 17, 2004), 1, 2a.

143. Russell, *Sequoyah Rising*, 149.

144. See, e.g., Vine Deloria Jr. *Behind the Trail of Broken Treaties: An Indian Declaration of Independence* (New York: Delacorte Press, 1974), and David E. Wilkins, ed., *The Hank Adams Reader: An Exemplary Native Activist and the Unleashing of Indigenous Sovereignty* (Golden, CO: Fulcrum Publishing, 2011).

Chapter 5

1. 42 Stat. 208.

2. 48 Stat. 984.

3. Dalia Tsuk Mitchell, *Architect of Justice: Felix S. Cohen and the Founding of American Legal Pluralism* (Ithaca, NY: Cornell University Press, 2007), 99.

4. Vine Deloria Jr., ed., *The Indian Reorganization Act: Congresses and Bills* (Norman: University of Oklahoma Press, 2002), 115.

402   NOTES

5. Ibid., 38.

6. Tribal Organizations, Circular No. 3010. Replies to Circular 3010, July 12, 1934. Record Group 75, National Archives, Washington, DC. The following section of this chapter is a descriptive analysis of these agent and superintendent replies to Collier. Author has copies of virtually all of the available responses, since some agents did not reply, and the author could not locate a few documents.

7. 30 Stat. 495.

8. David E. Wilkins, ed., *Documents of Native American Political Development: 1500s to 1933* (New York: Oxford University Press, 2009), 5.

9. Felix S. Cohen, *Handbook of Federal Indian Law* (1942; reprint, Albuquerque: University of New Mexico Press, 1972), 129.

10. See these two constitutions in Wilkins, *Documents of Native American Political Development*, 168–178.

11. W. O. Roberts, "Response to Circular No. 3010," August 14, 1934, p. 5, 5a. Tribal Organizations, Circular No. 3010. Replies to Circular 3010, July 12, 1934. Record Group 75, National Archives, Washington, DC.

12. The Sisseton Agency Superintendent, Fred A. Baker made these observations in his response to Collier's Circular on January 7, 1935.

13. In the superintendent's report there was a hand-drawn question mark in the margin next to this paragraph. One wonders what that meant, but there is no way of determining its meaning.

14. Edward D. Castillo, "Mission Indian Federation," in *Native America in the Twentieth Century: An Encyclopedia*, ed. Mary B. Davis (New York: Garland Publishing, 1996), 345–346.

15. Loretta Fowler, *The Columbia Guide to American Indians of the Great Plains* (New York: Columbia University Press, 2003), 120.

16. Tom Biolsi, e-mail message to author, March 21, 2021.

17. Felix S. Cohen's Papers (hereafter FCP), Beinecke Rare Book and Manuscript Library, Yale University, Box 8, Folder 117, no date.

18. Ibid.

19. John Collier, *From Every Zenith: John Collier, A Memoir* (Denver: Sage Books, 1963), 177.

20. FCP, Box 8, Folder 117.

21. Ibid.

22. Ibid., 3.

23. Ibid.

24. Vine Deloria Jr. and Clifford M. Lytle, *The Nations Within: The Past and Future of American Indian Sovereignty* (New York: Pantheon Books, 1984), 159–160.

25. FCP, Box 7, Folder 100.

26. Ibid.

27. Ibid., 2

28. I have seen only two explicit references to this important document. The first person to mention it was Elmer Rusco, who discussed it briefly in his book on the IRA that was published in 2000. In fact, when I met Rusco in 2002 and asked him about the

document, he was kind enough to share excerpts of it with me, and he was the person who encouraged me to pursue its publication. The only other work that mentions the memo is Robert Clinton, Carole Goldberg, and Rebecca Tsosie's federal Indian law casebook, *American Indian Law: Native Nations and the Federal System: Cases and Materials*, rev. 4th ed. (Charlottesville, VA: LexisNexis, 2003).

29. Solicitor's Opinion, M. 27810, December 13, 1934. See *Opinions of the Solicitor of the Department of the Interior Relating to Indian Affairs, 1917–1974*, vol. 1 (Washington, DC: Government Printing Office, 1974), 484–494.

30. Vine Deloria Jr. and David E. Wilkins, *The Legal Universe: Observations on the Foundations of American Law* (Golden, CO: Fulcrum Publishing, 2011), 175.

31. FCP Box 7, Folder 100.

32. FCP Box 8, Folder 106.

33. FCP Box 7, Folder 100, 3.

34. Deloria and Lytle, *American Indians, American Justice*, 100. See Chapter 3, note 17.

35. Deloria and Lytle, *American Indian Sovereignty*, 171.

36. Ibid., 172.

37. Fowler, *The Columbia Guide*, 118.

38. Ibid.

39. Thomas Biolsi, *Organizing the Lakota: The Political Economy of the New Deal on the Pine Ridge and Rosebud Reservation* (Tucson: University of Arizona Press, 1992), 108.

Chapter 6

1. Lucy Mair, *Primitive Government* (Baltimore, MD: Penguin Books, 1962), 9–10.

2. Frederick Webb Hodge, ed. *Handbook of American Indians North of Mexico*, Pt. 1. Bureau of American Ethnology, Bulleting 30 (Washington, DC: Government Printing Office, 1907), 692.

3. Solicitor's Opinion, "Powers of Indian Tribes," 55 I.D. 14, October 25, 1934. George A. Warren, ed., *Decisions of the Department of the Interior* (Washington, DC: Government Printing Office, 1938), 18.

4. The federal government, of course, has also empowered itself with self-described plenary power to wield virtually absolute power over Native lands and governments; a power Native nations have never attempted to wield over the federal or state governments.

5. ncai.org/tribalnations/introduction/Indian_Country_101_updated_February.2019. pdf

6. David E. Wilkins, *The Navajo Political Experience*, 4th ed. (Lanham, MD: Rowman & Littlefield, 2013), 78.

7. Russel L. Barsh, "The Nature and Spirit of North American Political Systems," *American Indian Quarterly* 10, no. 3 (Summer 1986): 191.

8. Ibid.

404 NOTES

9. Karen O'Connor and Larry J. Sabato, *The Essentials of American Government: Continuity and Change*, 3rd ed. (Boston: Allyn & Bacon, 1998), 19.

10. David W. Blight, "Will the Myth of Trumpism Endure?," *New York Times* (January 10, 2021).

11. http://indigenousfutures.illuminatives.org/

12. Paula McClain and Steven C. Tawber, *American Government in Black and White: Diversity and Democracy*, 4th ed. (New York: Oxford University Press, 2020), 8.

13. See, K. Alexa Koenig and Jonathan Stein, "State Recognition of Native American Tribes: A Survey of State-Recognized Tribes and State Recognition Processes," in *Recognition, Sovereignty Struggles, and Indigenous Rights in the United States: A Sourcebook*, ed. Amy E. Den Ouden and Jean M. O'Brien (Chapel Hill: University of North Carolina Press, 2013), 127–135.

14. David E. Wilkins and Heidi Kiiwetinepinesiik Stark, *American Indian Politics and the American Political System*, 4th ed. (Lanham, MD: Rowman & Littlefield, 2018), 31–32.

15. Traditional Constitution of the Newtok Traditional Council, (Newtok, Alaska).

16. This document is reproduced in David E. Wilkins, ed., *Documents of Native American Political Development: 1933 to Present* (New York: Oxford University Press, 2019), 275–306.

17. The San Manuel Nation ratified their new constitution in December 2021.

18. The Cherokee Code is maintained online by the Municipal Code Corporation at https://library.municode.com/tribes_and_tribal_nations/eastern_band_of_chero kee_indians/codes/code_of_ordinances?nodeld=PTICHGODOEABACHIN.

19. W. David Baird, "Quapaw," in *Native America in the Twentieth Century: An Encyclopedia*, ed. Mary B. Davis (New York: Garland Publishing, Inc., 1996), 523.

20. Daniel M. Cobb and Loretta Fowler, eds., *Beyond Red Power: American Indian Politics and Activism since 1900* (Santa Fe, NM: School for Advanced Research, 2007), 220–221. And see Loretta Fowler, *Arapahoe Politics, 1851–1978: Symbols in Crises of Authority* (Lincoln: University of Nebraska Press, 1982).

21. John Gomez Jr., e-mail message to author, May 3, 2022. Special thanks to John for contacting me in April 2022 to inform me of Chairman Hamilton's untimely passing and to update me on the important changes in the Band's governing elites because of the Chairman's death.

22. Joseph D. Hamilton interview with the author on April 24, 2019.

23. John Gomez Jr. interview with the author on April 24, 2019.

24. Hamilton interview, April 24, 2019.

25. Diana Aguilar, personal correspondence with the author on March 3, 2005. I visited the Tribe's website to see if anything had changed in the intervening years and learned that the community still relies on customs and traditions and has not developed any formal structures of governance.

26. http://viejasbandofkumeyaay.org/modern-government/

27. Theodore H. Haas, *Ten Years of Tribal Government under the I.R.A.* (Washington, DC: U.S. Department of the Interior, 1947), 14.

28. "Taos Pueblo Tribal Court," *Tribal Law Journal*, University of New Mexico, Tribal Court Handbook (Spring 2008): 3.

29. Rick Romancito, "Taos Pueblo Officials to Serve Two-Year Terms," *Taos News* (January 4, 2022): 1.

30. "Ohkay Owingeh Pueblo," *Tribal Law Journal*, University of New Mexico, Tribal Court Handbook (Spring 2011): 3.

31. http://www.sandiapueblo.NSN.us/administration/.

32. Barry M. Pritzker, *A Native American Encyclopedia: History, Culture, and Peoples* (New York: Oxford University Press, 2000), 97–98.

33. William Starna, e-mail message to author, on May 12, 2020.

34. Nick Carter, personal letter to author, on April 24, 2013.

35. Candace Bear, e-mail message to author, on May 11, 2020.

36. Nell Jessup Newton, ed., *Cohen's Handbook of Federal Indian Law*, (Newark, NJ: LexisNexis Matthew Bender, 2005), 276.

37. See, e.g., Eric Lemont ed., *American Indian Constitutional Reform and the Rebuilding of Native Nations* (Austin: University of Texas Press, 2006); and Duane Champagne, *Social Change and Cultural Continuity among Native Nations* (Lanham, MD: AltaMira Press, 2006).

38. Champagne, *Social Change and Cultural Continuity*, 20.

39. Felix S. Cohen, *On the Drafting of Tribal Constitutions*, ed. David E. Wilkins (Norman: University of Oklahoma Press, 2006), 28.

40. Ibid.

41. Cohen would later admit that some Indigenous nations, most notably the member nations of the Haudenosaunee (Iroquois) Confederacy, created and operated political systems that explicitly demonstrated checks and balances and separation of powers.

42. Melissa L. Tatum, Miriam Jorgensen, Mary E. Guss, and Sarah Deer, *Structuring Sovereignty: Constitutions of Native Nations* (Los Angeles, CA: American Indian Studies Center, 2014), 102.

43. Tom Holm, "Decolonizing Native American Leaders: Vine's Call for Traditional Leadership," in *Destroying Dogma: Vine Deloria Jr. and His Influence on American Society*, ed. Steve Pavlik and Daniel R. Wildcat (Golden, CO: Fulcrum Publishing 2006), 55.

44. Ibid.

45. Special thanks to Nora Hicks, staff librarian at the Native American Rights Fund, who helped identify many of these unique political communities.

46. See *Northern Arapaho v. Darryl LaCounte*, et al., Case No. 17-35662, 9th Cir. Ct. of Appeals (2017); and *Northern Arapaho Tribe v. LaCounte*, CV-16-11-BLGS-BMM (D. Mont. March 7, 2017).

47. See, e.g., Loretta Fowler's *Arapahoe Politics*, 1982 and *Tribal Sovereignty and the Historical Imagination: Cheyenne-Arapahoe Politics* (Lincoln: University of Nebraska Press, 2002).

48. Ibid., 64–65.

49. *Eastern Shoshone Tribe v. Northern Arapahoe Tribe*, 926 F. Supp. 1027 (1996).

50. *Northern Arapahoe Tribe v. Hodel*, 808 F.2d 741, 744 (10th Circ. 1987).

406   NOTES

51. James J. Lopach, Margery Hunter Brown, and Richmond Clow, *Tribal Government Today: Politics on Montana Indian Reservations*, revised. ed. (Niwot: University Press of Colorado, 1998), 106.
52. Loretta Fowler, e-mail message to author, January 4, 2020.
53. Red Lake members established their own constitution in 1918 and continue to be autonomous and self-governing.
54. Jill Doerfler, "We Aren't Like Dogs: Battling Blood Quantum," *Wasafiri* 32, no. 2 (June 2017): 43.
55. See Gerald Vizenor and Jill Doerfler's *White Earth Nation: Ratification of a Native Democratic Constitution* (Lincoln: University of Nebraska Press, 2012).
56. Doerfler, "We Aren't Like Dogs," 44.
57. Lopach, Brown, and Clow, *Tribal Government Today*, 124.
58. 207 U.S. 564.
59. Lopach, Brown, and Clow, *Tribal Government Today*, 129.
60. Ibid.
61. Taiaike Alfred, *Peace, Power, Righteousness: An Indigenous Manifesto*, 2nd ed. (New York: Oxford University Press, 2009), 117.
62. Deloria and Lytle, *American Indians, American Justice*, 109. See Chapter 3, note 17.

Chapter 7

1. Great Law of Peace, Gayanashagowa, Section 24, in David E. Wilkins, *Documents of Native American Political Development: 1500s–1933* (New York: Oxford University Press, 2009), 20.
2. Steve Russell, *Sequoyah Rising: Problems in Postcolonial Tribal Governance* (Durham, NC: Carolina Academic Press, 2010), 88.
3. Ibid., 3.
4. Evidence of this interference is found in various treaties where the U.S. treaty negotiators would create conditions that would lead to the selection of the kinds of Tribal leaders they wanted for their own policy reasons. For example, in the 1864 Treaty with the Chippewa, Mississippi, and several other nations, Article 8 declared that "no person shall be recognized as a chief whose band numbers less than fifty persons; and to encourage and aid the said chiefs in preserving order, and inducing by their example and advice, the members of their respective bands to adopt the pursuits of civilized life, there shall be paid to each of said chiefs annually out of the annuities of said bands, a sum not exceeding one hundred and fifty dollars, ($150) to be determined by their agent according to their respective merits." (13 Stat. 6930).
5. Dale Turner, *This Is Not a Peace Pipe: Towards a Critical Indigenous Philosophy* (Toronto: University of Toronto Press, 2006), 109.
6. Vine Deloria Jr., *Custer Died for Your Sins: An Indian Manifesto* (1970; reprint, Norman: University of Oklahoma Press, 1988), 206.
7. Ibid., 216.

8. Stephen Chestnut, "Firsthand Accounts," in *American Indian Constitutional Reform and the Rebuilding of Native Nations*, ed. Eric Lemont (Austin: University of Texas Press, 2006), 223.

9. Deloria, *Custer Died for Your Sins*, 215.

10. Ibid., 216.

11. Alfonso Ortiz, "Review of *Custer Died for Your Sins*," *American Anthropologist* 73 (1971): 954.

12. Deloria, *Custer Died for Your Sins*, 205.

13. Keith Grint, *Leadership: A Short Introduction* (New York: Oxford University Press, 2010), 2.

14. Waud H. Kracke, *Force and Persuasion: Leadership in an Amazonian Society* (Chicago: University of Chicago Press, 1978), 114.

15. Carolyn Kenny, "Liberating Leadership Theory," in *Living Indigenous Leadership: Native Narratives on Building Strong Communities*, ed. Carolyn Kenny and Tina Ngaroimata Fraser (Vancouver: UBC Press, 2012), 3.

16. Ibid., 7.

17. Linda Sue Warner and Keith Grint, "American Indian Ways of Leading and Knowing," *Leadership* 2, no. 2 (2006): 227.

18. W. Ron Allen, "We Are a Sovereign Government," in *The State of Native Nations: Conditions Under U.S. Policies of Self-Determination*, ed. The Harvard Project on American Indian Economic Development (New York: Oxford University Press, 2008), 31.

19. W. Ron Allen, personal interview with the author, May 6, 2021.

20. Jeremiah Jay Julius, telephone interview with the author, June 6, 2021.

21. Treaty with the Duwamish, Suquamish, etc., also known as the Point Elliott Treaty, signed on January 22, 1855. 12 Stat. 927.

22. Erma Vizenor, telephone interview with the author, September 12, 2021.

23. This section derives from an article I co-authored with Sheryl Lightfoot titled "Oaths of Office in Tribal Constitutions: Swearing Allegiance, But to Whom?," *American Indian Quarterly* 32, no. 4 (Fall 2008): 389–411.

24. I say constitutions because a search of Tribal nations with non-constitutional-based governments, like most of the sixteen that have Articles of Association or Incorporation, tend not to include oaths in their documents. The Summit Lake Paiute Tribe of Nevada is an exception. In their Articles, all elected officers must take an oath to perform their duties, although the oath is not included in the document. The Navajo Nation, which operates under a voluminous Tribal Code, also requires elected officials to take an oath that requires the individual to "swear to uphold and abide by the laws of the Navajo Nation and Treaty of 1868 between the Navajo Nation and the United States."

25. The Self-Determination era of federal Indian policy means the time period after the passage of the Indian Self-Determination Act of 1975, an act that was intended to give Native nations a greater degree of control over their own financial affairs. For more information on the trend toward constitutional reform by Native nations, see Eric Lemont, "Developing Effective Processes of American Indian Constitutional

408 NOTES

Reform: Lessons from the Cherokee Nation of Oklahoma, Hualapai Nation, Navajo Nation, and Northern Cheyenne Tribe," *American Indian Law Review* 26 (2001): 147–176; Lemont ed., *American Indian Constitutional Reform* (2006); Melissa Tatum, et al., *Structuring Sovereignty: Constitutions of Native Nations* (2014); Miriam Jorgensen, ed. *Rebuilding Native Nations: Strategies for Governance and Development* (Tucson: University of Arizona Press, 2007); and Jean Dennison, *Colonial Entanglement: Constituting a Twenty-First Century Osage Nation* (2012).

26. J. M. Roberts, "Oaths, Automatic Ordeals, and Power," *American Anthropologist* 67 (1965): 186–212.

27. L. S. Goodman, "The Historical Role of the Oath of Admission," *American Journal of Legal History* 11 (1967): 404–411; Law Reform Commission, *Report on Oaths and Affirmations* (Dublin: Law Reform Commission, 1990); Helen Silving, "The Oath I," *Yale Law Journal* 68 (1959): 1329–1390; Helen Silving, "The Oath II," *Yale Law Journal* 68 (1959): 1527–1577.

28. H. S. Maine, *Ancient Law: Its Connections with the Early History of Society and Its Relation to Modern Ideas* (London: Oxford University Press, 1931).

29. Silving, "The Oath I."

30. J. Plescia, *The Oath in Perjury in Ancient Greece* (Tallahassee: Florida State University Press, 1970).

31. Ibid., 15.

32. Law Reform Commission, *Report on Oaths*; and Silving, "The Oath I."

33. D. M. Jones, *Conscience and Allegiance in Seventeenth Century England: The Political Significance of Oaths and Engagements* (Rochester: University of Rochester Press, 1999); H. G. Richardson, "The English Coronation Oath," *Speculum* 24 (1949): 44–75; and Law Reform Commission, *Report on Oaths*.

34. M. A. Pauley, *I Do Solemnly Swear: The President's Constitutional Oath—Its Meaning and Importance in the History of Oaths* (Lanham, MD: University Press of America, 1999).

35. Felix S. Cohen, *On the Drafting of Tribal Constitutions*, ed. David E. Wilkins (Norman: University of Oklahoma Press, 2006), 95.

36. Great Law of Peace, Gayanashagowa, Section 28, in Wilkins, Documents of Native American Political Development, 2009, 21.

37. Because there is no widely available breakdown of IRA and non-IRA constitutions, we examined each constitution individually to determine whether or not it was an IRA constitution.

38. Credit here goes to my co-author of the article, Sheryl Lightfoot, who came up with this framework for analysis.

39. In some cases, loyalty to the Native nation/Native constitution is placed ahead of the duties-of-office phrase, but loyalty to the U.S. Constitution appears first in all instances of this oath type.

40. The Minnesota Chippewa Tribe is the name used for federal purposes. Tribal members usually refer to themselves as "Anishinaabe" or "Ojibwe." The Minnesota Chippewa Tribe is a consolidation of six distinct Ojibwe bands: Bois Forte, Fond du Lac, Grand Portage, Leech Lake, Mille Lacs, and White Earth. These bands consolidated some of

NOTES 409

their governmental authority under a single constitution, the Minnesota Chippewa Tribe, while some governmental functions remain vested in each individual band and each band fields its own Business Committee to oversee day-to-day affairs.

41. See, e.g., Elmer R. Rusco, *A Fateful Time: The Background and Legislative History of the Indian Reorganization Act* (Reno: University of Nevada Press, 2000); and Cohen, *On the Drafting of Tribal Constitutions* (2006).

42. See Jean Dennison's study *Colonial Entanglement* (2012) for a good account of the process employed by the Osage people as they moved to develop and ratify their new constitution in 2006.

43. The Assiniboine and Sioux tribes of the Fort Peck Reservation do not have an IRA constitution.

44. See L. Hargrett, ed., *A Bibliography of the Constitutions and Laws of the American Indians* (Cambridge, MA: Harvard University Press, 1947) for a partial listing of several of these early Native constitutions with special emphasis on those of the Five Civilized Tribes.

45. The treaty relationship between the federal government and Native nations, from a federal perspective, emanates from Article 6 of the U.S. Constitution, which gives the federal government the sole authority to negotiate treaties and makes treaties the "supreme law of the land." Under the authority of this section of the U.S. Constitution, the federal government entered into hundreds of treaties with Native nations over the past several centuries. The treaty relationship, therefore, defines the relationship between the federal government and Native nations as a government-to-government relationship. Since Indigenous nations are sovereigns that have treaty-making authority, Indigenous rights are neither based on nor subject to U.S. constitutional law. See Vine Deloria Jr. and Clifford M. Lytle, *The Nations Within: The Past and Future of American Indian Sovereignty* (New York: Pantheon Books, 1984) and Vine Deloria Jr. and David E. Wilkins, *Tribes, Treaties, and Constitutional Tribulations* (Austin: University of Texas Press, 1999) for two accounts that explore this turgid field. The trust doctrine, another pillar on which the Indigenous–federal relationship is founded, according to the Supreme Court in *Seminole Nation v. United States* (316 U.S. 286, 297 (1942), means that the federal government "has charged itself with moral obligations of the highest responsibility and trust. Its conduct, as disclosed in the acts of those who represent it in dealings with the Indians, should therefore be judged by the most exacting fiduciary standards."

46. Edward P. Dozier, "Factionalism at Santa Clara Pueblo," *Ethnology* 15, no. 2 (1966): 172–185.

47. Ibid., 175.

48. Marilyn Norcini, "The Political Process of Factionalism and Self-Governance at Santa Clara Pueblo, New Mexico," *Proceedings of the American Philosophical Society* 149, no. 4 (December 2005): 544.

49. Ibid.

50. Lawrence Kelly, "The Indian Reorganization Act: The Dream and the Reality," in *Constitutionalism and Native America, 1903–1968*, ed. John R. Wunder (New York: Garland Publishing, Inc., 1996), 144.

410   NOTES

51. Alexander Hamilton, James Madison, and John Jay, *The Federalist Papers*, ed. Clinton Rossiter (1961; reprint, New York: Mentor Publishing, 1999), see Federalist No. 9, Hamilton, 39.

52. Ibid., Federalist No. 10, Madison, 47.

53. William N. Fenton, "Factionalism at Taos Pueblo, New Mexico," *Bureau of American Ethnology Bulletin*, vol. 164, Smithsonian Institution (Washington, DC: Government Printing Office, 1957), 331.

54. Jay M. Shafritz, *The Dorsey Dictionary of American Government and Politics* (Chicago: The Dorsey Press, 1988), 417.

55. Fenton, "Factionalism at Taos," 332.

56. Nancy Lurie, "The Will-o-the-Wisp of Indian Unity," in *Currents in Anthropology: Essays in Honor of Sol Tax*, ed. Robert Hinshaw (New York: Moulton Publishers, 1979), 8.

57. Ibid., 9.

58. Robert B. Porter, "Strengthening Tribal Sovereignty Through Government Reform: What Are the Issues?," *Kansas Journal of Law and Public Policy* 7 (1997): 78–80.

59. Raymond I. Orr, *Reservation Politics: Historical Trauma, Economic Development, and Intratribal Conflict* (Norman: University of Oklahoma Press, 2017).

60. Ibid., 49–50.

61. Ibid., 18.

62. Ibid., 87.

63. Ibid., 96.

64. See, for example, *Newtok Village v. Patrick*, Case No. 4:15-CV-00009 RRB (2021, WL 1105722) (March 26, 2021); *Anderson v. Duran*, 70 F. Supp. 3d 1143 (2014); *California v. Picayune Rancheria of Chukchansi Indians of California*, 725 Fed. Appx. 591 (2018); *Nooksack Indian Tribe v. Zinke*, 2017 U.S. Dist. LEXIS 72364 (2017); *John S. v. Garcia*, 2018 WL 1569760 (2018); *Timbisha Shoshone Tribe v. Kennedy*, 687 F. Supp. 2d 1171 (2009); *Winnemucca Indian Colony v. U.S.*, 2012 WL 4472144 (2012); *Goodface v. Grassrope*, 708 F.2d 335 (1983); *U.S. Bancorp v. Ike*, 171 F. Supp. 1122 (2001); *Sac & Fox Tribe of the Mississippi in Iowa, Election Board v. BIA*, 438 F.3d 832 (2006); *California Valley Miwok Tribe v. Salazar*, 967 F. Supp. 2d 84 (2013); *Caddo Nation of Oklahoma v. Court of Indian Offenses for the Anadarko Agency*, 2014 WL 3880464 (2014); and *Cayuga Nation v. Bernhardt*, 374 F. Supp. 3d 1 (2019).

65. Matthew Fletcher, *Principles of Federal Indian Law* (St. Paul, MN: West Academic Publishing, 2017), 176.

66. See *National Farmers Union Insurance Co. v. Crow Tribe of Indians*, 471 U.S. 845 (1985).

67. 931 F.2d 636, 640 (10th Circ. 1191).

68. See the Resolution and Article in David E. Wilkins, ed. *Documents of Native American Political Development: 1933–Present* (New York: Oxford University Press, 2019), 458–460.

69. *Coalition for Fair Government II v. Lowe*, 1 American Tribal Law, 145, 1 (1997).

70. The General Council consists of all eligible voters who are entitled to participate in General Council meetings and is recognized as embodying the ultimate sovereignty of the nation with the power to set policy and with verse actions of the legislature.

71. 1 American Tribal Law, 145 (1997).

72. Ibid., 26.

73. *Young v. Tribal Grievance Committee*, 5 Oklahoma Tribe, 470 (1998).

74. *Black's Law Dictionary*, 5th ed. (St. Paul, MN: West Publishing Co., 1979), 902.

75. 5 Oklahoma Tribe, 470 (1998).

76. Ibid.

77. Ibid., 9.

78. Ibid., 10.

79. 7 Oklahoma Tribe, 310 (2001).

80. *Citizen Potawatomi Nation Business Committee v. Barrett*, 7 Oklahoma Tribe, 310 (2001).

81. Ibid., 9.

82. *Blind v. Wilson*, 9 Oklahoma Tribe 209 (2006).

83. See Veronica E. Velarde Tiller, ed., *Tiller's Guide to Indian Country: Economic Profiles of American Indian Reservations*, 3rd ed. (Albuquerque, NM: BowArrow Publishing Co., 2015), 610.

84. 9 Oklahoma Tribe 209 (2006).

85. Ibid.

86. Ibid., 4.

87. Ibid.

88. *Shirley v. Morgan*, No. SC-CV-02-10 (June 2, 2010).

89. Ibid., 3.

90. Ibid., 15.

91. Ibid.

92. Ibid., 17–18.

93. Ibid., 19.

94. Ibid., 29.

95. 15 American Tribal Law 55 (2018).

96. Ibid., 8.

97. https://www.saulttribe.com/newsroom/7563-sault-tribe-board-censures-tribal-chairperson

98. Ibid.

99. Ibid.

100. https://www.saulttribe.com

101. Ibid.

102. Ibid.

103. See Robert E. Kelley, "Followership," in George A. Goethals, Georgia J. Sorenson, and James MacGregor Burns, eds. *Encyclopedia of Leadership* (Thousand Oaks, CA: Sage Publications, 2004), 505.

412 NOTES

Chapter 8

1. Burt Vogel, "Who Is an Indian in Federal Indian Law," in *Studies in American Indian Law*, ed. Ralph Johnson (Pullman: Washington State University Press, 1970), 53.
2. Felix S. Cohen, *On the Drafting of Tribal Constitutions*, ed. David E. Wilkins (Norman: University of Oklahoma Press, 2006), 13.
3. See Paul Spruhan, "A Legal History of Blood Quantum in Federal Indian Law to 1935," *South Dakota Law Review* 51, no. 1 (2006): 1–2.
4. C. Matthew Snipp, *American Indians: The First of This Land* (New York: Russell Sage Foundation, 1989), 34. And see Kathleen Ratteree and Norbert Hill, eds., *The Great Vanishing Act: Blood Quantum and the Future of Native Nations* (Golden, CO: Fulcrum Publishing, 2017).
5. 35 Stat. 313.
6. 37 Stat. 518.
7. House Committee on Indian Affairs, *Controlling Indian Allottees in Respect to Education of Their Children and Liquor*, House Doc. 790, 60th Cong., 1st Sess. (1908), 2.
8. Kirsty Gover, *Tribal Constitutionalism: States, Tribes, and the Governance of Membership* (New York: Oxford University Press, 2010), 83.
9. Solicitor's Opinion, "Powers of Indian Tribes," 55 I.D. 14, October 25, 1934. George A Warren, ed., *Decisions of the Department of the Interior* (Washington, DC: Government Printing Office), 14–67.
10. Ibid., 16–17.
11. Gover, *Tribal Constitutionalism*, 83.
12. Pueblo of Laguna Constitution.
13. Ibid., 85.
14. Kim TallBear, *Native American DNA: Tribal Belonging and the False Promise of Genetic Science* (Minneapolis: University of Minnesota Press, 2013).
15. Gover, *Tribal Constitutionalism*, 112.
16. Ibid., 113.
17. Ibid., 8.
18. https://www.ncai.org/policy-research-center/research-data/prc-publications/NCAI_genetics_research_resource_guide_FINAL_2012_PDF.pdf.
19. See Kevin Taylor, "DNA Proves Kennewick Man, the Ancient One, Is Native," *Indian Country Today* (June 18, 2015). https://ictnews.org/archve/dna-proves-kenewick-man-the-ancient-one-is-natie-tribes-continue-fight-for-reburial.
20. Ibid.
21. Kim TallBear, "DNA, Blood, and Racializing the Tribe," *Wicazo Sa Review* 18, no. 1 (2003): 84.
22. Kevin Taylor, "Bitter Fight to Determine Who Is an American Indian Turns to DNA Testing," *Indian Country Today* (October 13, 2011). https://ictnews.org/archive/bitter-fight-to-determine-who-is-an-american-indian-turns-to-dna-testing.
23. 168 U.S. 218 (1897).
24. 436 U.S. 49 (1978).

NOTES 413

25. See David E. Wilkins and Shelly Hulse Wilkins, *Dismembered: Native Disenrollment and the Battle for Human Rights* (Seattle: Washington State University Press, 2017) for a detailed treatment of how and why Native nations are engaged in disenrollment practices and what can be done to address this dispiriting issue.

26. Ibid. See the four Tables on 68–77 for a list of most of these nations and the rationales they are using to disenroll, banish, or deny membership.

27. See, e.g., Lolita Buckner Inniss, "Cherokee Freedmen and the Color of Belonging," *Columbia Journal of Race and Law* 5, no. 2 (2015): 100–118.

28. 14 Stat. 799.

29. Julia Coates, "Race and Sovereignty," in The Great Vanishing Act, 115.

30. Chris Cameron and Mark Walker, "Tribes are Pressed to Confront Bias against Descendants of Enslaved People," *New York Times* (May 30, 2021), 17.

31. 267 F. Supp. 3d 86 (D.D.C. 2017).

32. Ibid., 77.

33. Mark Walker, "Cherokee Bias against Slave Descendants," *New York Times* (February 25, 2021), A15.

34. Ibid.

35. Https://theblackwallsttimes.com/2021/07/09/congresswoman-maxinewaters-warns-tribes-to-stop-discriminating-against-freedmen-descendants/.

36. Cameron and Walker, "Tribes are Pressed," 17.

37. Ibid.

38. Derek Heater, *A Brief History of Citizenship* (New York: New York University Press, 2004), 3.

39. Melissa L. Tatum, Miriam Jorgensen, Mary E. Guss, and Sarah Deer, *Structuring Sovereignty: Constitutions of Native Nations* (Los Angeles, CA: American Indian Studies Center, 2014), 41.

40. See Donald Fixico's two books, *Termination and Relocation: Federal Indian Policy, 1945–1960* (Albuquerque: University of New Mexico Press, 1986); and *The Urban Indian Experience* (Albuquerque: University of New Mexico Press, 2000) for overviews of these policies and their impact on Indigenous peoples.

41. As cited in Douglas K. Miller, *Indians on the Move: Native American Mobility and Urbanization in the Twentieth Century* (Chapel Hill: University of North Carolina Press, 2019), 194–195.

42. Coll Thrush, "Placing the City: Crafting Urban Indigenous Histories," in *Sources and Methods in Indigenous Studies*, ed. Chris Anderson and Jean M. O'Brien (New York: Routledge, 2017), 111.

43. Harvard Project on American Indian Economic Development, *The State of the Native Nations: Conditions Under U.S. Policies of Self-Determination* (New York: Oxford University Press, 2008), 355.

44. See, e.g., United Indians of All Tribes Foundation in Seattle, WA, the Minneapolis American Indian Center, the Chicago Indian Center, and the Intertribal Friendship House in Oakland, CA, which receive some of these funds.

45. Elizabeth J. D'Amico, Alina I. Palimaru, Daniel L. Dickerson, Lu Dong, Ryan A. Brown, Carrie L. Johnson, David J. Klein, and Wendy M. Troxel, "Risk and Resilience

414 NOTES

Factors in Urban American Indian and Alaska Native Youth during the Coronavirus Pandemic," *American Indian Culture and Research Journal* 44, no. 2 (2020): 21–48.

Chapter 9

1. Jan M. Shafritz, *The Dorsey Dictionary of American Government and Politics* (Chicago: The Dorsey Press, 1988), 186.

2. See, e.g., Daniel McCool, "Indian Voting," in *American Indian Policy in the Twentieth Century*, ed. Vine Deloria Jr. (Norman: University of Oklahoma Press, 1985), 105–133; Laughlin McDonald, *American Indians and the Fight for Equal Voting Rights* (Norman: University of Oklahoma Press, 2010); Jean Schroedel and Artour Aslanian, "Native American Vote Suppression: The Case of South Dakota," *Race, Gender & Class* 22, no. 1–2 (2015): 308–323; Native American Rights Fund, *Obstacles at Every Turn: Barriers to Political Participation Faced by Native American Voters* (Boulder, CO: Native American Rights Fund, 2020); Jean Reith Schroedel, *Voting in Indian Country: The View from the Trenches* (Philadelphia: University of Pennsylvania Press, 2020); and https://illuminative.org/wp-content/uploads/2022/06/indigenous_Futures_Survey_report_FINAL.pdf

3. See, e.g., Melanie McCoy and Carie Delashaw, "Tribal Elections: An Exploratory Study of the Chickasaw Nation," *Oklahoma Politics* (October 1993); David E. Wilkins, *The Navajo Political Experience*, 4th ed. (Lanham, MD: Rowman & Littlefield Publishers, 2013); Tatum, Jorgensen, Guss, and Deer, *Structuring Sovereignty* (2014); Matthew Fletcher, *American Indian Tribal Law*, 2nd ed. (New York: Wolters Kluwer, 2020), Chapter 5.

4. Thomas M. Holbrook and Raymond J. LaRaja, "Parties and Elections," in *Politics in the American States: A Comparative Analysis*, 11th ed., ed. Virginia Gray, Russell L. Hansen, and Thad Kousser (Thousand Oaks, CA: Congressional Quarterly Press, 2018), 57.

5. See, http://indigenousfutures.illluminative.org. which has compiled some useful data on contemporary voting patterns of Native individuals.

6. Glenn A. Phelps, "Mr. Gerry Goes to Arizona: Electoral Geography and Voting Rights," *American Indian Culture and Research Journal* 15, no. 2 (1991): 70.

7. Native American Rights Fund, *Obstacles at Every Turn*, 2.

8. Ibid.

9. Ibid.

10. See, Theodore J. Lowi, Benjamin Ginsberg, Kenneth A. Shepsle, and Stephen Ansolabehere, *American Government: A Brief Introduction*, 15th ed. (New York: W. W. Norton & Co., 2019): Chapter 10 for general discussion of the critical role that voting plays in democratic societies, be they Indigenous or Western.

11. www.cartercenter.org.

12. https://www.cartercenter.org/countries/united-states.html

13. Carter Center, "The Carter Center's Limited Observation Mission to the Cherokee Nation's Special Election for Principal Chief: Final Report" (unpublished report, September 2011), 3.
14. Ibid.
15. Ibid.
16. Carter Center, "Carter Center Commends Muscogee (Creek), Nation on Smooth Electoral Process" (unpublished report, December 2019), 3.
17. U.S. Department of the Interior, "Developing and Reviewing Tribal Constitutions and Amendments: A Handbook for BIA Personnel" (Washington, DC: Bureau of Indian Affairs, June 1987), 3-13-3-14.
18. 11 N.N.C. Sec. 8 (A) (4). See Fletcher, *American Indian Law*, 258–264 for any analysis of *Tsosie v. Deschene*, 12 American Tribal Law 55 (October 8, 2014).
19. Lowi et al., *American Government*, 305.
20. Mark C. Tilden, "Tribal Constitutions Handbook: A Practical Guide to Writing or Revising a Tribal Constitution" (Boulder, CO: Native American Rights Fund, 2007), 177–181.
21. Felix S. Cohen, *On the Drafting of Tribal Constitutions*, ed. David E. Wilkins (Norman: University of Oklahoma Press, 2006), 37–39.
22. Ibid., 37.
23. Ibid.
24. Ibid., 39.
25. Tilden, "Tribal Constitutions Handbook," 60.
26. Holbrook and La Raja, "Parties and Elections," 60.
27. James Dao, "'Indians' New Money Buys Lobbying Power," *New York Times*, February 9, 1998, B1.
28. David E. Wilkins and Heidi K. Stark, *American Indians and American Politics*, 4th ed. (Lanham, MD: Rowman & Littlefield Publishers, 2018), 200.
29. Allison Herrera, "Cherokee Nation Takes Steps to Protect Tribal Elections from Outside Influence, Dark Money." See https://www.kosu.org/politics-2022-05-26/cherokee-nation-takes-steps-to-protect-tribal-elections-from-outside-influence-dark-money.
30. Ibid.

Chapter 10

1. Philip S. Deloria, "Introduction," in *Indian Tribal Sovereignty and Treaty Rights* (Albuquerque, NM: La Confluencia, 1978), S23.
2. Commission on State-Tribal Relations, *Handbook: State-Tribal Relations* (Albuquerque, NM: American Indian Law Center, 1984), 35.
3. Peter A. Gourevitch, "Political Economy" in *The Oxford Companion to Politics of the World*, ed. Joel Krieger (New York: Oxford University Press, 1993), 719.

416   NOTES

4. U.S. Commission on Civil Rights, "Broken Promises: Continuing Federal Funding Shortfall for Native Americans." Briefing Report (Washington, DC: Government Printing Office, 2018), 156. See Chapter 5, "Economic Development," for a detailed analysis of the dire conditions across Native lands. Conditions grew markedly worse when the COVID-19 pandemic struck Indian Country with disastrous effects.

5. Ibid., 157.

6. Ibid., 157.

7. National Congress of American Indians, "Tribal Infrastructure: Investing in Indian Country for a Stronger America," https://www.ncai.org/NCAI-InfrastructureReport-FINAL.pdf.

8. Paul Radin, *The World of Primitive Man* (New York: Grove Press, 1953), 106.

9. Franke Wilmer, *The Indigenous Voice in World Politics: Since Time Immemorial* (Newbury Park, CA: Sage Publishers, 1993), 82.

10. Felix S. Cohen, *On the Drafting of Tribal Constitutions*, ed. David E. Wilkins (Norman: University of Oklahoma Press, 2006), 6.

11. Constitution of the Federated Indians of the Graton Rancheria, 2012.

12. Constitution of the Burns Paiute Tribe of Oregon, 1997.

13. Articles of Incorporation of the Rappahannock Tribe. Author has a copy.

14. See Marjane Ambler, *Breaking the Iron Bonds: Indian Control of Energy Development* (Lawrence: University of Kansas Press, 1990); and James R. Allison, *Sovereignty for Survival: American Energy Development and Indian Self-Determination* (New Haven, CT: Yale University Press, 2015).

15. Thomas Biolsi, "Political and Legal Status ('Lower 48' States)," in *A Companion to the Anthropology of American Indians*, ed. Thomas Biolsi (Malden, MA: Blackwell Publishing, 2004), 236.

16. Felix S. Cohen, *Handbook of Federal Indian Law* (1941; reprint, Albuquerque: University of New Mexico Press, 1972), 142, note 171.

17. See, e.g., *Crabtree v. Madden*, 54 Fed. 426 (C.C.A. 8, 1893); *Maxey v. Wright*, 3 Ind. T. 243; *Buster v. Wright*, 135 Fed. 947 (C.C.A. 8. 1905); *Morris v. Hitchcock*, 21 App. D.C. 565 (1903, aff'd 194 U.S. 384 (1904)); and see Cohen, *Handbook of Federal Indian Law*, 142–143, Chapter 13.

18. Cohen, *Handbook of Federal Indian Law*, 267, drawing upon *Talton v. Mayes*, 163 U.S. 376 (1896), and *Worcester v. Georgia*, 6 Pet. 515 (1832).

19. Vine Deloria Jr., "Land and Natural Resources," in *Minority Report: What Has Happened to Blacks, Hispanics, American Indians and Other Minorities in the 80s*, ed. Leslie W. Dunbar (New York: Pantheon Books, 1984), 174.

20. 55 I.D. 14, 46 (1934).

21. Nell Jessup Newton, ed. *Cohen's Handbook of Federal Indian Law* (Newark, NJ: LexisNexis Matthew Bender, 2005), 166.

22. U.S. Congress, American Indian Policy Review Commission, *Final Report* (Washington, DC: Government Printing Office, 1977), 179.

23. Susan M. Williams, "Preservation of Life: Guiding Principles of Indian Tribal Governments," in *The State of the Native Nations: Conditions Under U.S. Policies*

of Self-Determination, ed. The Harvard Project on American Indian Economic Development (New York: University of Oxford Press, 2008), 191.

24. 532 U.S. 645.
25. Ibid., 650.
26. See, the National Congress of American Indians website for a representative sample of Native nation Tax Codes. http://www.ncai.org.
27. 471 U.S. 195.
28. 532 U.S. 645.
29. Swinomish Indian Tribe, https://narf.org/nill/codes/swinomish/17_2.pdf.
30. Asha Glover, "Justices End South Dakota's Attempts to Tax Sales *at* Tribal Casino," *Law 360* (May 20, 2020). https://www-law360-com.ezproxy.law.umn.edu/articles/1276684/justices-end-sd-s-attempts-to-tax-sales-at-tribal-casino.
31. Brad A. Bays, "Tribal-State Tobacco Compacts and Motor-Fuel Contracts in Oklahoma," in *The Tribes and the States: Geographies of Intergovernmental Interaction*, ed. Brad A. Bays and Erin Fouberg (Lanham, MD: Rowman & Littlefield, 2002), 188.
32. Susan Johnson, Joanne Kaufman, John Dossett, Sarah Hicks, *Government to Government: Models of Cooperation between States and Tribes* (Denver, CO: National Conference of State Legislatures, April 2009), 67.
33. Bays, "Tribal-State Tobacco Compacts," 181–196.
34. https://www.taxadmin.org/assets/docs/MotorFuel/2019%20Native%20American%20Survey%Motor%20Fuel.pdf.
35. Andrea Wilkins, *Fostering the State-Tribal Collaboration: An Indian Law Primer* (Lanham, MD: Rowman & Littlefield, 2016), 59.
36. Ibid., 59–60.
37. Johnson, Kaufman, Dossett, and Hicks, *Government to Government*, 70.
38. americangaming.org
39. Reagan, with ample congressional support, cut $1 billion from the $3.5 billion budgeted for Indian affairs, terminated job-training programs, and cut funds for Indian housing.
40. Randall K. Q. Akee, Miriam R. Jorgensen, Eric C. Henson, and Joseph P. Kalt, "Letter to Steve Mnuchin, Secretary of the Treasury on 'Allocation of COVID-19 Response Funds to American Indian Nations'" (April 10, 2020). Author has a copy of this letter.
41. Randall K. Q. Akee, Katherine Spilde, and Jonathan Taylor, "The Indian Gaming Regulatory Act and Its Effects on American Indian Economic Development," *Journal of Economic Perspectives* 29, no. 3 (Summer 2015): 196.
42. Ibid.
43. Alan P. Meister, "The Economic Impact the Coronavirus Is Having on Tribal Gaming and the U.S. Economy," *Tribal Gaming & Hospitality* (April 7, 2020) https://tgandh.com/news/tribal-stories/april-7-2020-update-the-economic-impact-the-coronavirus-is-having-on-tribal-gaming-and-the-u-s-economy/.
44. Ibid.
45. 134 Stat. 281.
46. Elizabeth Warren and Debra Haaland, "The Federal Government Fiddles as COVID-19 Ravages Native Americans," *Washington Post* (May 26, 2020). https://www.was

418 NOTES

hingtonpost.com/opinions/2020/05/26/federal-government-fiddles-covid-19-rava
ges-native-americans/.

47. 594 U.S. ____ (2021).

48. 85 Stat. 688.

49. 594 U.S. ____, 26 (2021).

50. Ibid., 27.

51. 135 Stat. 4. See Subtitle M, Sec. 602, 223 (2021); and see Eric C. Henson, Megan M. Hill, Miriam R. Jorgensen, and Joseph P. Kalt, "Executive Summary: Recommendations for the Allocation and Administration of ARPA Funding for American Indian Tribal Governments" (Policy Brief No. 6, Harvard Project on American Indian Economic Development and Native Nations Institute (April 9, 2021).

52. 134 Stat. 4, 224.

53. Deron Marquez, e-mail to Tribal associates, October 13, 2015.

54. https://www.nativebusinessmag.com/waseyabek-non-gaming-diversification-empowered-tribal-economic-resilience-in-face-of-covid-19/.

55. Katherine Spilde, e-mail, August 2–3, 2021.

56. https://tribalbusinessnews.com/sections/gaming/13761-tribal-gaming-industry-faces-labor-shortage-amid-covid-19-recovery.

57. 24 Stat. 388.

58. Russel L. Barsh, "Indian Land Claims Policy in the United States," *North Dakota Law Review* 58, no. 1 (1982): 7.

59. Ibid., 7–8.

60. 48 Stat. 984.

61. Ibid.

62. Articles of Association of the Ak-Chin Community.

63. We will discuss the Settlement Act in greater detail in a later chapter. And see https://www.ncai.org/tribalnations/introduction/Indian_Country_101_Updated_February_2019.pdf.

64. 124 Stat. 3064.

65. Department of the Interior, *Interior Land Buy Back Program* (2020). See Table I Land Buy Back Program for Tribal Nations Cumulative Sales through May 20, 2020. And see https://www.doi.gov/buybackprogram/interiors-land-buy-back-program-adds-locations-its-implementation-schedule-and-makes.

66. Kristen Carpenter and Angela R. Riley, "Privatizing the Reservation?," *Stanford Law Review* 71, no. 4 (April 2019): 32.

67. 30 U.S. 1 (1831).

68. 485 U.S. 4391 (1988).

69. 131 S. Ct. 2313 (2011).

70. 555 U.S. 379 (2009).

71. 131 S. C. 2313, 2327–2328.

72. Padrosa E. McCoy, "Trust Lands," in *Encyclopedia of U.S. Indian Policy and Law*, vol. 2, ed. Paul Finkelman and Tim Alan Garrison (Washington, DC: Congressional Quarterly Press, 2009), 793.

73. 67 Stat. 588.

74. https://www.ncai.org/tribalnations/introduction/Indian_Country_101_Updated_February_2019.pdf, 27.

75. Alexandra Harmon, *Rich Indians: Native People and the Problem of Wealth in American History* (Chapel Hill: University of North Carolina Press, 2010).

76. Associated Press, "Judge Trump Administration Cannot Rescind Tribe's Reservation," *Richmond Times-Dispatch* (June 7, 2020), B13.

77. Harvard Project on American Indian Economic Development, *The State of Native Nations*, 102.

78. Carpenter and Riley, "Privatizing the Reservation?," 3–4.

79. Ibid., 4.

80. U.S. Commission on Civil Rights, "Broken Promises," 163.

81. Vine Deloria Jr. and Clifford M. Lytle, *The Nations Within: The Past and Future of American Indian Sovereignty* (Austin: University of Texas Press, 1984), 258.

82. See David E. Wilkins, ed. *Documents of Native American Political Development: 1933 to Present* (New York: Oxford University Press, 2019), 457–460.

83. Frank Bibeau and Thomas Linzey, "White Earth Files Rights of Nature Lawsuit against Minnesota DNR," *Wisconsin Citizens Media Cooperative* (August 5, 2021), 1.

84. Ibid., 2.

85. https://celdf.org/rights-of-nature/timeline/.

86. Christopher Flavelle, "U.S. to Give Tribes Millions to Escape Climate Threats," *New York Times* (December 1, 2022), A19.

87. See, e.g., Daniel R. Wildcat, *Red Alert: Saving the Planet with Indigenous Knowledge* (Golden, CO: Fulcrum Publishing, 2009); Randall S. Abate and Elizabeth Ann Kronk Warner, eds., *Climate Change and Indigenous Peoples: The Search for Legal Remedies* (Cheltenham, UK: Edward Elgar Publishing, Inc., 2013); and Zoltán Grossman and Alan Parker, eds., *Asserting Native Resilience: Pacific Rim Indigenous Nations Face the Climate Crisis* (Corvallis: Oregon State University Press, 2012).

88. Christina L. Lyons, "Native American Sovereignty," *Congressional Quarterly Researcher* 27, no. 17 (May 5, 2017): 385.

89. U.S. Commission on Civil Rights, "Broken Promises," 177.

90. Lyons, "Native American Sovereignty," 385.

91. Ambler, *Breaking the Iron Bonds*, 50. And see Tanis C. Thorne's *The World's Richest Indian: The Scandal over Jackson Barnett's Oil Fortune* (New York: Oxford University Press, 2003).

92. Ambler, *Breaking the Iron Bonds*, 50.

93. Russel L. Barsh, "Indian Resources and the National Economy: Business Cycles and Policy Cycles," in *Native American and Public Policy*, ed. Fremont J. Lyden and Lyman H. Legters (Pittsburgh: University of Pittsburgh Press, 1992), 207.

94. U.S. Congress, American Indian Policy Review Commission, *Final Report*, 339.

95. Donald L. Fixico, *The Invasion of Indian Country in the Twentieth Century: American Capitalism and Tribal Natural Resources* (Niwot: University Press of Colorado, 1998), 160.

96. Ambler, *Breaking the Iron Bonds*, 93.

420 NOTES

97. "Council of Energy Resource Tribes Enter $3 Billion Biofuels and Bioenergy Agreement," *Indian Country Media Network* (September 25, 2012) and see https://ictnews.org/archive/council-of-energy-resource-tribes-enters-3-billion-biofuels-and-bioenergy-agreement.

98. A. David Lester, "Council of Energy Resource Tribes," in Mary B. Davis, ed. *Native America in the Twentieth Century: An Encyclopedia* (New York: Garland Publishing, Inc., 1996), 144–145.

99. Lyons, "Native American Sovereignty," 387.

100. 455 U.S. 130.

101. 490 U.S. 163.

102. Stephen L. Pevar, *The Rights of Indians and Tribes* (New York: Oxford University Press, 2012), 122.

103. Matthew Frank, "Oil Bust Puts Tribes, Towns over a Barrel," *High Country News* (March 17, 2016), and see https://www.hcn.org/articles/oil-bust-puts-tribes-towns-over-a-barrel.

104. Eric Lipton, 'This Is Our Reality Now," *New York Times* (December 27, 2018), F10–11.

105. Ibid.

106. Ibid.

107. Ibid.

108. Department of Justice, "Pipeline Company to Pay $35 million in Criminal Fines and Civil Penalties for Largest Ever Inland Spill of Produced Water from Oil Drilling," Press Release Number 21-747, Office of Public Affairs (August 5, 2021).

109. See Nick Estes and Jaskiran Dhillon, eds., *Standing with Standing Rock: Voices from the NoDAPL Movement* (Minneapolis: University of Minnesota Press, 2019) for a worthy excellent collection of essays addressing this ongoing issue.

110. *Standing Rock Sioux Tribe v. U.S. Army Corps of Engineers*, 280 F. Supp. 3d 187 (D.D.C. 2017).

111. Blake Nicholson, "Tribe Challenges Dakota Access Conclusions," *Minneapolis Star Tribune* (November 6, 2018), D3.

112. Jacay Fortin and Lisa Friedman, "Dakota Access Pipeline to Shut Down Pending Review, Federal Judge Rules," *New York Times* (July 6, 2020), B5.

113. Rachel Frazin, "Court Cancels Shutdown of Dakota Access Pipeline," *The Hill* (August 5, 2020), www.thehill.com/policy/energy-environment/510748-court-cancels-shutdown-of-dakota-access-pipeline.

114. See https://www.kvrr.com/2023/04/27/sen-hoeven-pushes-for-dakota-access-pipeline-review-to-be-completed/ and https://ndncollective-org.nyc3.cdn.digitaloceanspaces.com/app/uploads/sites/3/2022/03/00099-02_NDN_DAPL_Report_BOOK_FINAL.pdf.

115. See Nicole Martin Rogers and Virginia Pendleton, "Missing and Murdered Indigenous Women Task Force: A Report to the Minnesota Legislature," *Wilder Research* (December 2020). And see www.wilderresearch.org.

116. Louise Erdrich, "Not Just Another Pipeline," *New York Times* (December 29, 2020), A19.

NOTES   421

117. Hiroka Tabucho, 'Biden Administration Backs Oil Sands Pipeline Project," *New York Times* (June 24, 2021), https://www.nytimes.com/2021/06/24/climate/line-3-pipeline-biden.html

118. Coral Davenport, "Hailed as Historic, Biden's Interior Pick Is Also Partisan Lightning Rod," *New York Times* (February 23, 2021), A18 and Carol Davenport, "Senate Vote Confirms First Native American as Cabinet Secretary," *New York Times* (March 16, 2021), A19.

119. Deloria and Lytle, *American Indian Sovereignty*, 259. See Chapter 5, note 22.

120. www.lummi-nsn.gov/Website.php?PageID=42.

121. www.nwifc.org.

122. While "bison" is the scientifically correct term for this species, the terms are used interchangeably within Native communities and, in fact, buffalo is used more often than bison.

123. See Sebastian Felix Braun's *Buffalo Inc.: American Indians and Economic Development* (Norman: University of Oklahoma Press, 2008), which is a good account of the difficulties the Cheyenne River Sioux nation faced in trying to engage with Buffalo on both a spiritual/emotional level and as a corporate enterprise.

124. Department of Justice Memorandum from Monty Wilkinson to U.S. Attorneys (October 28, 2014). According to the Centers for Disease Control (CDC), this memo was "intended to provide clarification on the Ogden Memo's pertinence to tribes; it spurred many tribes to pursue marijuana cultivation on tribal lands." This comment from the CDC is found in a CDC Public Health Law pamphlet titled "Marijuana Legalization in Indian Country: Selected Resources" (February 2, 2017), 5 note 14.

125. https://www.ncai.org/Marijuana_Policy_in_the_U.S.-_Information_for_Tribal_Leaders.pdf.

126. Jesse McKinley, "Marijuana Shops Are Blooming on Tribal Land," *New York Times*, (September 26, 2021), 28.

127. "The Ups & Downs of Insuring Tribal Cannabis," *Tribal Hemp & Cannabis Magazine* 2, no. 3: 18–19.

128. Ibid, 26–27.

129. Mary Jane Oatman, "Tribal Nations Dispensary and Farm Map," *Tribal Hemp & Cannabis Magazine* 2, no. 3 (Summer 2021): 24–25.

130. Bart Pfankuch, "Marijuana Legislation Opens New Economic Path for South Dakota Tribes," *Indian Country Today* (March 1, 2021). https://ictnews.org/news/a-potential-economic-boost-for-sd-tribes-marijuana.

131. Department of Justice, "Justice Department Issues Memo on Marijuana Enforcement," Office of Public Affairs, Press Release Number 18-8 (January 4, 2018).

132. https://osagenews/org/federal-jurisdiction-over-tribes-still-makes-marijuana-illegal-in-indian-country/.

133. See San Ildefonso Constitution, Sec. 13.40 Marijuana and Controlled Substance provision.

134. Michael G. Zimmerman and Tony G. Reames, "When the Wind Blows: Exploring Barriers and Opportunities to Renewable Energy Development on U.S.-Tribal Lands," *Energy Research and Social Science* 72 (2021): 2.

422 NOTES

135. Nicholas M. Ravotti, "Access to Energy in Indian Country: The Difficulties of Self-Determination in Renewable Energy Development," *American Indian Law Review*, 41, no. 2 (2017): 279.

136. www.campo-nsn.gov/windfarm.html.

137. Zimmerman and Reames, "When the Wind Blows," 2.

138. See https://www.energy.gov/indianenergy/maps/tribal-energy-projects-database.

139. Kalle Benallie, "It's Not Easy Being Green," *Indian Country Today* (April 22, 2021). https://ictnews.org/news/who-is-the-greenest-tribe.

140. Associated Press, "Navajo Nation Finalizes Solar Plant Leases," *Indian Country Today* (April 8, 2021). https://ictnews.org/news/navajo-nation-finalizes-solar-plant-leases.

141. Ravotti, "Access to Energy," 281.

142. Tohono O'odham Nation Constitution, 1986.

143. Ibid.

144. 126 Stat. 1150.

145. https://www.mvskokemedia.com/ok-tribal-finance-consortium-releases-findings-on-tribes-economic-impact/.

146. Kathleen Pickering, "Culture and Reservation Economies," in *A Companion to the Anthropology of American Indians*, ed. Thomas Biolsi (Malden, MA: Blackwell Publishing, 2004), 127–128.

147. Carol Anne Hilton, *Indigenomics: Taking a Seat at the Economic Table* (Gabriola Island, BC: New Society Publishers, 2021), 7–8.

Chapter 11

1. Vine Deloria Jr. and Raymond J. DeMallie, *Documents of American Indian Diplomacy: Treaties, Agreements, and Conventions, 1775–1979* (Norman: University of Oklahoma Press, 1999).

2. David H. DeJong, *American Indian Treaties: A Guide to Ratified and Unratified Colonial, U.S., State, Foreign, and Intertribal Treaties and Agreements: 1607–1911* (Salt Lake City: University of Utah Press, 2015).

3. David R. Beck, *Siege and Survival: History of the Menominee Indians, 1634–1856* (Lincoln: University of Nebraska Press, 2002), 17.

4. I learned about this treaty in a June 2021 conversation with Frank Ettawageshik (Little Traverse Bay Bands of Odawa), former Chairman of his nation. Ettawageshik shared a copy of a typescript of this short (six articles) accord that was drafted in Santa Fe, New Mexico, in December 1947, but no official copy of this treaty has thus far been located.

5. See, e.g., Tassie Hanna "Commission on State-Tribal Relations," *American Indian Newsletter* 14, no. 1 (1981); Senate Committee on Indian Affairs, *Tribal-State Compact Act*, 91st Cong., 2nd Sess. (1978), S. Report on S. 2502, Commission on

State-Tribal Relations, "State-Tribal Agreements: A Comprehensive Study" (Denver, CO: National Conference of State Legislators, 1981); and Commission on State-Tribal Relations, "Handbook: State-Tribal Relations" (Albuquerque: American Indian Law Center, 1984).

6. http://www.buffalotreaty.com.

7. DeJong, *American Indian Treaties*, 9.

8. Joseph Epes Brown, *The Sacred Pipe: Black Elk's Account of the Seven Rites of the Oglala Sioux* (Norman: University of Oklahoma Press, 1953).

9. 16 Stat. 566.

10. Deloria and DeMallie, *Documents of American Indian Diplomacy*; and DeJong, *American Indian Treaties*, both discuss agreements.

11. https://www.sudrum.com/culture/2016/06/10/ute-nation-remembers-peace-treaty/.

12. Wallace Coffey and Rebecca Tsosie, "Rethinking the Tribal Sovereignty Doctrine: Cultural Sovereignty and the Collective Future of Indian Nations," *Stanford Law & Policy Review* 12 (Spring 2001): 198.

13. Special thanks to Chairman Frank Ettawageshik for sharing several of these international accords with me and for providing context for a few of them as he was actively involved in the development of several of these documents.

14. https://lrboi-nsn.gov/government/legislative-branch-tribal-council/resolutions/2003-2/2003-1-02/03-1203-413-authorization-to-allow-reciprocity-under-the-1997-intertribal-agreement-regarding-on-reservation-hunting-fishing-and-gathering/.

15. Author has a copy of this Accord.

16. Veronia E. Velarde Tiller, *Tiller's Guide to Indian Country: Economic Profiles of American Indian Reservations*, 3rd ed. (Albuquerque, NM: BowArrow Publishing Co., 2015), 238.

17. Native American Rights Fund, "Case Updates: San Juan Southern Paiute Tribe Signs Historic Treaty," *NARF Legal Review* 25, no. 2 (Summer/Fall 2000): 13.

18. See *Masayesva v. Zah*, ongoing litigation involving the Tribes' respective claims to lands claimed by all three peoples. The Court initially found that the San Juan Southern Paiute Tribe had a joint interest with the Navajo Nation in a section of the Navajo Reservation, but refused to provide the Band with any portion of the territory. The Band appealed that decision and while it was under appeal negotiations began in earnest between the Navajo Nation and the Band that resulted in the bilateral treaty.

19. Native American Rights Fund, "Case Updates," 13; https://www.arizonahighways.com/article/i-just-want-go-home.

20. https://static1.squarespace.com/static/54ade7ebe4b07588aa079c94/t/54ea4fa3e4b06d2d72224dc0/1424641955323/Tribal-and-First-Nations-Great-Lakes-Water-Accord.pdf.

21. Ibid.

22. Author has a copy of this Accord.

424 NOTES

23. Zoltan Grossman and Alan Parker, eds. *Asserting Native Resilience: Pacific Rim Indigenous Nations Face the Climate Crisis* (Corvallis: Oregon State University Press, 2012), 18.
24. http://unpfip.blogspot.com/2012/01/united-league-of-indigenous-nations.html.
25. Telephone conversation with Frank Ettawageshik on August 6, 2021.
26. http://www.buffalotreaty.com.
27. Author has a copy of this Declaration.
28. See, Nicole Mantan Rogers and Virginia Pendleton, "Missing and Murdered Indigenous Women Task Force: A Report to the Minnesota Legislature" (Wilder Research, December 2020).
29. https://www.treatyalliance.org/.
30. Sheryl Lightfoot and David MacDonald, "Treaty Relations between Indigenous Peoples: Advancing Global Understandings of Self-Determination," *New Diversities* 19, no. 2 (2017): 25–39.
31. Ibid., 31.
32. http://www.piikaninationtreaty.com.
33. *Crow Indian Tribe v. U.S.*, 965 F.3d 662 (9th Circ. 2020).
34. https://www.globalindigenouscouncil.com/wolf-treaty.
35. Ibid., Article IV.
36. *Defenders of Wildlife* et al., *v. U.S. Fish & Wildlife Service*, et. al., (2022), no 4:21-cv-00344. U.S. District Court for the Northern District of California.
37. On July 22, 2021, Joe Byrd, the Cherokee Nation Tribal Council Speaker, traveled to the headquarters of the Navajo Nation in Window Rock, Arizona, to reignite discussions with the Navajo Nation Council that he hopes may lead to a treaty between the two largest Indigenous nations in the country. Byrd informed the Council members that similar conversations had been held twenty-five years earlier. The talks centered on land and water rights, language revitalization, commerce, and trade. In addition, as Byrd put it: "The proposed talks about what would the world think if two of the largest nations representing close to one million people came together and talked about how we could help each other out in the areas of health care, jurisdiction, law enforcement, [and] domestic violence against women," is long overdue. See Arlyssa Becenti, "Cherokee Leaders Discuss Treaty with Nation," *Navajo Times* (August 19, 2021). https://navajotimes.com/reznews/cherokee-leaders-discuss-treaty-with-nation/. To date, such an accord has not yet been crafted. And in early January 2023, the Nation of Hawaii signed a treaty with the Timbisha Shosone Tribe of California. This is the first accord between Kanaka Maoli and a federally-recognized Native nation on the continent.
38. Carolyn Kenny, "Liberating Leadership Theory," in *Living Indigenous Leadership: Native Narratives on Building Strong Communities*, ed. Carolyn Kenny and Tina Ngaroimata Fraser (Vancouver, BC: UBC Press, 2012), 3.
39. See Nicole Redvers, Yuria Celidwen, et al., "The Determinants of Planetary Health: An Indigenous Consensus Perspective," *The Lancet* 6 (February 2022): 156–163. https://pubmed.ncbi.nlm.nih.gov/35150624/.

NOTES 425

Chapter 12

1. Matthew L. M. Fletcher, *American Indian Tribal Law*, 2nd ed. (New York: Wolters Kluwer, 2020).
2. Larry Nesper, "Native Nation Building: The Long Emergence of the Oneida Nation Judiciary," *American Indian Quarterly* 42, no. 1 (2018): 88.
3. Ibid.
4. Vine Deloria Jr. and Clifford M. Lytle, *American Indians, American Justice* (Austin: University of Texas Press, 1983), 111–112.
5. Ken Traisman, "Native Law: Law and Order among Eighteenth Century Cherokee, Great Plains, Central Prairie, and Woodland Indians," *American Indian Law Review* 9 (1981): 273. And see Priscilla Buffalohead's "Warrior Images and Peacemaking Traditions: Strategies for Survival among the Southern Siouan Tribal Nations," *Great Plains Quarterly* 40 (Fall 2020): 249–256 which discusses the peacemaking traditions of the Omaha, Ponca, Osage, Kansa (Kaw), and Quapaw.
6. Ibid.
7. Deloria and Lytle, *American Indians, American Justice*, 111.
8. Vine Deloria Jr., "The Basis of Indian Law," in *Look to the Mountain Top*, ed. Charles Jones (San Jose, CA: H. M. Gousha, 1972), 76.
9. Vine Deloria Jr., "Foreword," in *The Mystic Heart of Justice: Restoring Wholeness in a Broken World*, ed. Denise Breton and Stephen Lehman (West Chester, PA: Chrysallis Books, 2001), xii.
10. Ibid., xiv–xv.
11. Deloria, "The Basis of Indian Law," 77.
12. See Francis Paul Prucha, *Documents of United States American Indian Policy*, 2nd ed. (Lincoln: University of Nebraska Press, 1990), 127.
13. Ibid., 160–162.
14. Ibid.
15. Deloria and Lytle, *American Indians, American Justice*, 115.
16. James Zion, "Harmony among the People: Torts and Indian Courts," *Montana Law Review* 45 (1984): 167.
17. 35 F. 575 (D. Or. 1888).
18. House Committee on Indian Affairs, *Reservation Courts of Indian Offenses*, 69th Cong., 1st Sess. (1926), H.R. 7826, 5.
19. www.bia.gov/CFRCourts. And see Gavin Clarkson, "Courts of Indian Offenses," in *Encyclopedia of United States Indian Policy and Law*, ed. Paul Finkelman and Tim Alan Garrison, vol. 1 (Washington, DC: CQ Press, 2009), 225–226.
20. *Denezpi v. United States*, 596 U.S. ___ (2022).
21. Frank Pommersheim, *Braid of Feathers: American Indian Law and Contemporary Tribal Life* (Berkeley: University of California Press, 1995), 65.
22. Felix S. Cohen, *On the Drafting of Tribal Constitutions*, ed. David E. Wilkins (Norman: University of Oklahoma Press, 2006), 32.
23. Ibid., 20.
24. Ibid., 114–115.

426 NOTES

25. Nell Jessup Newton, "Tribal Court Praxis: One Year in the Life of Twenty Indian Tribal Courts," *American Indian Law Review* 22 (1998): 291.

26. 127 Stat. 54.

27. Public Law No. 117–103 (March 13, 2022).

28. 1 Cranch, 137 (1803).

29. U.S. Constitution, art. 3, sec. 2.

30. U.S. Department of Justice. Bureau of Justice Statistics. *Jails in Indian Country, 2017–2018*. Bulletin (October 2020, NCJ 25 2155), 1.

31. U.S. Department of Justice. Bureau of Justice Statistics. *Tribal Crime Data Collection Activities, 2021*. Technical Report (July 2021, NCJ 301061), 3.

32. U.S. Department of Justice. *National Institute of Justice Research Report* (2016), 2.

33. Nicole Morton Rogers and Virginia Pendleton, "Missing and Murdered Indigenous Women Task Force: A Report to the Minnesota Legislature" (Wilder Research, December 2020), 1.

34. Ibid.

35. Deloria and Lytle, *American Indians, American Justice*, 120.

36. See, e.g., James W. Zion, "Traditional Indian Solutions for Victims of Crime," *Australian Journal of Law and Society* 13 (1997): 167–180 for examples of Indigenous justice systems.

37. Michelle Chen, "Restorative Justice in Indian Country," *Dissent* (April 16, 2021): 1, https://www.dissentmagazine.org/online_articles/restorative-justice-in-indian-country.

38. Raymond D. Austin, "Traditional American Indian Justice," in *Traditional, National, and International Law and Indigenous Communities*, ed. Marianne O. Nielsen and Karen Jarratt-Snider (Tucson: University of Arizona Press, 2020), 50.

39. See Marianne O. Nielsen and James W. Zion, eds., *Navajo Nation Peacemaking: Living Traditional Justice* (Tucson: University of Arizona Press, 2005).

40. 7 N.N.C. Section 204.

41. Raymond D. Austin, *Navajo Courts and Navajo Common Law: A Tradition of Tribal Self-Governance* (Minneapolis: University of Minnesota Press, 2009), xii–xiii.

42. Austin, "Traditional American Indian Justice," 52.

43. Potawatomie Constitution, art. VI, secs. 1–3 (2007).

44. See Maha Jweied, "Expert Working Group Report: Native American Traditional Justice Practices" (Washington, DC: U.S. Department of Justice, September 2014).

45. Chen, "Restorative Justice in Indian Country," 2.

46. The Memorandum of Understanding that created the multi-jurisdictional Cass County and Leech Lake Band of Ojibwe Wellness Court can be found at http://ccllwe llnesscourt.files.wordpress.com/2010/10/memorandum-of-understanding.pdf.

47. Jweied, "Expert Working Group Report," 7.

48. James W. Zion and Robert D. Yazzie, "Revisioning Traditional Indigenous Justice in Light of the United Nations Declaration on the Rights of Indigenous Peoples," in *Traditional, National, and International Law and Indigenous Communities*, ed. Marianne O. Nielsen and Karen Jarratt-Snider (Tucson: University of Arizona, 2020), 44.

49. Nielsen and Jarrat-Snider, "Conclusion," in Indigenous Environmental Justice, ed. Karen Jarratt-Snider, Marianne O. Nielsen (University of Arizona Press, Tucson, 2020), 197.

50. Deloria and Lytle, *American Indians, American Justice*, 136.

Chapter 13

1. Paul Mozur and Zia ur-Rehmon, "Taliban Employ Tweets to Push Distorted View," *New York Times* (August 21, 2021), 1, A5.

2. See the fascinating collection of editorials by William J. Lawrence, a Red Lake Anishinaabe citizen, published under the title *The Arrogance of Tribal Power*, edited by E. R. Thompson, which features many of the editorials Lawrence wrote for the *Native American Press/Ojibwe News* between 1988 and 2009. In 2003 Lawrence was the recipient of the Freedom of Information Award, given by the Society of Professional Journalists "for aggressive defense of the people's right to know and consistent support for the First Amendment."

3. Rebecca Nagle, "Muscogee (Creek) Nation Passes Bill Removing Press Freedom from Mvskoke Media," *Indian Country Today* (November 13, 2018), 2–3.

4. Peter O'Dowd, "Tribal Media Outlet Loses Free-Press Protections," *WBUR Here and Now* (January 11, 2019).

5. Nagle, "Muscogee (Creek) Nation," 3.

6. Allison Herrera, "'What's at Stake Is the Public Trust': Mvskoke Media Wins Back Free Press Protection," *KOSU: Milk Street Radio, National Public Radio* (July 24, 2020). https://www.kosu.org/local/-news/2020-07-24/whats-at-stake-is-the-public-trust-mvskoke-media-wins-back-free-press-protections.

7. Mark N. Trahant, *Pictures of Our Nobler Selves: A History of Native American Contributions to News Media* (Nashville, TN: The Freedom Forum First Amendment Center, 1995), 3.

8. Daniel F. Birchfield Jr. "Periodicals," in *Native America in the Twentieth Century: An Encyclopedia*, ed. Mary B. Davis (New York: Garland Publishing, 1996), 444.

9. Arlene Hirschfelder and Martha Kreipe de Montano, *The Native American Almanac: A Portrait of Native America Today* (New York: Prentice Hall, 1993), 193.

10. www.Indiancountrytoday.com/news/ict-at-40-we-reported-like-indians-from-the-ground-up.

11. Jodi Rave, "American Indian Media Today: Tribes Maintain Majority Ownership as Independent Journalists Seek Growth," Democracy Fund, Indigenous Media Freedom Alliance (November 2018).

12. Ibid.

13. https://www.culturalsurvival.org/publications/cultural-survival-quarterly/electronic-smoke-signals-native-american-radio-united.

14. Trahant, *Pictures of our Nobler Selves*, 21.

428 NOTES

15. U.S. Congressional Research Service Report, *Tribal Broadband: States of Deployment and Federal Funding Programs*, CRS R44416 (Washington, DC: January 9, 2019), 1.

16. John Reinan, "Fond du Lac Band Build Jobs for 21st Century," *Minneapolis Star Tribune* (September 30, 2018), B5.

17. 135 Stat. 429.

18. Matthew L. Jones, "Radio & Television," in *Native America in the Twentieth Century: An Encyclopedia*, ed. Mary B. Davis (New York: Garland Publishing, 1996), 533.

19. https://www.nativepublicmedia.org/.

20. Nick Estes and Jaskiran Dhillon, "Introduction," in *Standing with Standing Rock: Voices from the NoDAPL Movement*, ed. Nick Estes and Jaskiran Dhillon (Minneapolis: University of Minnesota Press, 2019), 1.

21. https://www.ienearth.org/wp-content/uploads/2021/09/Indigenous-Resistance-Against-Carbon-2021.pdf.

22. https://www.firstnations.org/publications/compilation-of-all-research-from-the-rec laiming-native-truth-project/.

23. Traci L. Morris and Sascha D. Meinrath, "New Media, Technology and Internet Use in Indian Country: Quantitative and Qualitative Analyses" (Flagstaff, AZ: Native Public Media, 2009). And see http://newamerica.org/oti/events/new-media-technol ogy-internet-use-in-indian-country/.

24. Ibid.

25. John Johnson, "A Navajo Newspaper Tests the Boundaries," *Los Angeles Times* (October 19, 1997), 1.

26. Osage Constitution, art. 4, sect. 3, "Declaration of Rights" (2006).

27. Karen Lincoln Michel, "Repression on the Reservation," *Columbia Journalism Review* 37, no. 4 (November/December 1998): 48.

28. Richard LaCourse, "A Native Press Primer," in Michel, "Repression on the Reservation," 51.

29. Jodi Rave, "Survey Finds a Few Tribal Governments Allow Press Freedom," *Indian Country Today* (May 23, 2019). https://ictnews.org/news/survey-finds-few-tribal-governments-allow-press-freedom.

30. Steve Russell, "A Free Press Needs More than the First Amendment," *Indian Country Today* (September 12, 2018), 4. https://ictnews.org/archive/a-free-press-needs-more-than-the-first-amendment.

31. Rave, "American Indian Media Today," 7.

32. Steve Russell, "A Free Press," 1.

33. David E. Wilkins, *The Navajo Political Experience*, 4th ed. (Lanham, MD: Rowman & Littlefield Publishers, 2013), 174.

34. Navajo Nation. "2009–2010 Comprehensive Economic Development Strategy," Division of Economic Development (Window Rock, AZ: unpublished, 2009), 33.

35. Eastern Band of Cherokee Indians. Cherokee Council Ordinance, No. 293 (August 2, 2018).

NOTES   429

36. Theodore J. Lowi, Benjamin Ginsburg, Kenneth A. Shepsle, and Stephen Ansolabehere, *American Government: A Brief Introduction*, 15th ed. (New York: W. W. Norton & Company, 2019), 280.

Chapter 14

1. See, e.g., Caroline L. Brown, "Political and Legal Status of Alaska Natives," in *A Companion to the Anthropology of American Indians*, ed. Thomas Biolsi (Malden, MA: Blackwell Publishing, 2004), 249, and Meghan Sullivan, "Can ANSCA Answer, 'Where Are You From?'," *Indian Country Today* (July 19, 2021).

2. Maria *Shaa Tláa* Williamsc, "Alaskac and Its People: An Introduction," in *The Alaska Native Reader: History, Culture, Politics*, ed. Maria *Shaa Tláa* Williams (Durham, NC: Duke University Press, 2009), 1.

3. Brown, "Political and Legal Status," 251.

4. Cari Costanza Kapur, "Native Hawaiians," in *A Companion to the Anthropology of American Indians*, ed. Thomas Biolsi (Malden, MA: Blackwell Publishing, 2004), 412–431.

5. 594 U.S. ___ 2021.

6. Lydia L. Hays, *Alaska: Native Tribes, ANCSA Corporations, and Other Organizations—Origins, Purposes, and Relationships* (Anchorage, AK: Publication Consultants, 2015), 9.

7. Brown, "Political and Legal Status," 249.

8. Hays, *Alaska: Native Tribes*, 12.

9. Colin G. Calloway, *First Peoples: A Documentary Survey of American Indian History*, 6th ed. (New York: Bedford/St. Martin's, 2019), 94.

10. Fae L. Korsmo, "The Alaskan Natives," in *Polar Peoples: Self-Determination and Development*, ed. Minority Rights Foundation (London: Minority Rights Publications, 1994), 83.

11. David H. Getches, Charles F. Wilkinson, Robert A. Williams Jr., and Matthew L. M. Fletcher, *Cases and Materials on Federal Indian Law*, 6th ed. (St. Paul, MN: West Publishing, 2011), 888.

12. David S. Case and David A. Voluck, *Alaska Natives and American Laws*, 2nd ed. (Fairbanks: University of Alaska Press, 2002), 44–45.

13. Korsmo, "The Alaskan Natives," 87.

14. 155 Stat. 539.

15. Case and Voluck, *Alaska Natives*, 46.

16. See, for example, *Tee-Hit-Ton v. U.S.* (348 U.S. 272, 279 (1955)), where Associate Justice Stanley Reed said that aboriginal title "is not a property right but amounts to a right of occupancy which the sovereign grants and protects against intrusion by third parties but which right of occupancy may be terminated and such lands disposed of by the sovereign itself without any legally enforceable obligation to compensate the Indians"; but see *U.S. v. Alcea Band of Tillamooks* (329 U.S. 40 (1946)) where the

430 NOTES

High Court went to great lengths to show that there was no clear distinction between "original Indian title" and "recognized Indian title" and *Otoe and Missouria Tribe of Indians v. U.S.* (131 Ct. Cl. 593) which held that Natives could indeed pursue claims in the Indian Claims Commission using original Indian title or aboriginal title.

17. Korsmo, "The Alaskan Natives," 87.

18. 23 Stat. 24.

19. https://akleg.gov/100years/legislature.php?id=1.

20. Roy M. Huhndorf and Shari M. Huhndorf, "Alaska Native Politics since the ANCSA," *The South Atlantic Quarterly* 110, no. 2 (Spring 2011): 389.

21. Ibid.

22. David H. DeJong, *The Commissioners of Indian Affairs: The U.S. Indian Service and the Making of Federal Indian Policy, 1824 to 2017* (Salt Lake City: University of Utah Press, 2020), 130.

23. Thomas R. Berger, *Village Journey: The Report of the Alaska Native Review Commission* (New York: Hill and Wang, 1985), 132.

24. Ibid.

25. 53 I.D. 605 (1932).

26. 48 Stat. 984.

27. Ibid., 988.

28. 49 Stat. 1250.

29. Donald Craig Mitchell, "*Alaska v. Native Village of Venetie*: Statute Construction or Judicial Usurpation? Why History Accounts?," *Alaska Law Review* 14, no. 2 (1997): 369.

30. 72 Stat. 339.

31. Ibid.

32. Ibid. Section 4.

33. Amended June 25, 1959, P.L. 86–70 Sec. 2(a), 73 Stat. 141.

34. Rosita Worl, "Indian-White Relations in Alaska," in *Encyclopedia of North American Indians: Native American History, Culture, and Life from Paleo-Indians to the Present*, ed. Frederick E. Hoxie (Boston: Houghton Mifflin, 1996), 276.

35. 85 Stat. 688.

36. Stephen Colt, "Alaska Native Regional Corporations," in *Native America in the Twentieth Century: An Encyclopedia*, ed. Mary B. Davis (New York: Garland Publishing, 1996), 13.

37. Ibid.

38. Worl, "Indian-White Relations in Alaska," 276.

39. Donald C. Mitchell, *Sold American: The Study of Alaska Natives and Their Lands, 1867–1959* (Hanover, NH: University Press of New England, 1997), 10.

40. Ibid., 136.

41. Evon Peter, "Undermining our Tribal Governments: The Stripping of Land, Resources, and Rights from Alaska Native Nations," in *The Alaska Native Reader: History, Culture, Politics*, ed. Maria Shaa Tláa Williams (Durham, NC: Duke University Press, 2009), 180.

NOTES 431

42. Stephen L. Pevar, *The Rights of Indians and Tribes*, 4th ed. (New York: Oxford University Press, 2012), 162.

43. Berger, *Village Journey*, see Chapter 7.

44. 59 Fed. Reg. 9280, 9286-87 (1994).

45. David C. Mass, "Alaska Native Claims Settlement Act," in *Native America in the Twentieth Century: An Encyclopedia*, ed. Mary B. Davis (New York: Garland Publishing Co., 1996), 10–13.

46. Willie Kasayulie, "Sovereignty in Alaska," in *The State of Native Nations: Conditions Under U.S. Policies of Self-Determination*, ed. The Harvard Project on American Indian Economic Development (New York: Oxford University Press, 2008), 336.

47. Ibid., 337.

48. U.S. Department of the Interior. *Department of the Interior Announces Final Rule for Land into Trust for Alaska Native Tribes*, News Release, Office of the Assistant Secretary-Indian Affairs (December 18, 2014); and see 25 C.F.R. Part 151.

49. *Akiachak Native Community* et al. *v. U.S. Department of the Interior*, Case No. 13.5360 (July 1, 2016). U.S. Court of Appeals.

50. Native *Village of Stevens v. Alaska Management and Planning*, 757 P.2d 32, 36 (Alaska, 1988).

51. Alaska Attorney General, Jahna Lindemuth, "Re: Legal Status of Tribal Governments in Alaska" (October 19, 2017), 10. https://law.alaska.gov/pdf/opinions/opinions_2 017/17-004_JU20172010.pdf.

52. Gina Kim, "Alaska Sues to Block U.S. from Putting Land into Trust," *Law 360*. And see *State of Alaska v. Bryan Newland*, et.al. case number 3:23-cv-00007 in the U.S. District Court for the District of Alaska. https://www-law360-com.ezproxy.law.umn. edu/articles/1566408/alaska-sues-to-block-us-from-putting-land-into-trust.

53. Case and Voluck, *Alaska Natives*, 386.

54. U.S. General Accounting Office, *Regional Alaska Native Corporations: Status Forty Years after Establishment, and Future Considerations* (Washington, DC: Government Printing Office, 2012), 1.

55. Ibid.

56. Thomas Michael Swensen, "Of Subjection and Sovereignty: Alaska Native Corporations and Tribal Governments in the Twenty-First Century," *Wicazo Sa Review* 30, no. 1 (Spring 2015): 108.

57. Ibid.

58. This definition is from the Alaska National Interest Lands Conservation Act, Title VIII, Section 803, 1980, as quoted in Lydia L. Hays, *Alaska: Native Tribes*, 25.

59. Huhndorf and Huhndorf, "Alaska Native Politics," 395.

60. Ibid., 401.

61. Ibid., 395.

62. 594 U.S. ___ (2021), 27.

63. Andrew Westney, " 'Unique' Alaska Key to Justices' Tribal COVID Funds Ruling," *Law 360* (June 28, 2021). https://www-law360-com.ezproxy.law.umn.edu/articles/ 1398294/-unique-alaska-key-to-justices-tribal-covid-funds-ruling.

432 NOTES

64. National Congress of American Indians, "A First Look *at* the 2020 Census American Indian/Alaska Native Redistricting Data," Research Policy Update, Policy Research Center (August 13, 2021).

65. Case and Voluck, *Alaska Natives*, 317.

66. Ibid., 318.

67. Felix S. Cohen, *Handbook of Federal Indian Law* (1942; reprint, Albuquerque: University of New Mexico Press, 1972), 413, note 200.

68. Ibid., 413.

69. Case and Voluck, *Alaska Natives*, 319.

70. Ibid.

71. Stephen Cornell, Jonathan Taylor, and Kenneth Grant, "Achieving Alaska Native Self-Governance: Toward Implementation of the Alaska Natives Commission Report," Final Report-AFN Version (Cambridge, MA: The Economics Resource Group, Inc., May 1999), 14.

72. See, e.g., Traditional Constitution and Bylaws of the Chignik Lake Village Council: Traditional Council of Chignik Lake. Copy in possession of author.

73. Letter from Carter to the U.S. Department of the Interior, BIA Alaska Region (April 24, 2013). Copy in possession of author.

74. Cohen, *Handbook of Federal Indian Law*, 414.

75. 49 Stat. 388.

76. Hays, *Alaska: Native Tribes*, 39.

77. 389 F.2d 778 (Ct. Cls., 1968).

78. 108 Stat. 479.

79. Case and Voluck, *Alaska Natives*, 327–328.

80. There is a Native community in British Columbia called Old Metlakatla. The community that was established later in Alaska is sometimes referred to as New Metlakatla. See John Dunn and Arnold Booth, "Tsimshian of Metlakatla, Alaska," in *Handbook of North American Indians*, vol. 7, ed. William C. Sturtevant (Washington, DC: Smithsonian Institution, 1990), 294–297 for a good overview of this community.

81. See David E. Wilkins, ed., *Documents of Native American Political Development: 1500s–1933* (New York: Oxford University Press, 2009) for a list of the rules.

82. 26 Stat. 1101.

83. Ibid.

84. 369 U.S. 552 (1962); and see Case and Voluck, *Alaska Natives*, 262.

85. Associated Press, *Anchorage Daily News*, "Some Alaska Native Tribes in Southeast Seek to Establish Tribal Courts" (December 23, 2018), 1.

86. Halley Petersen, "Banishment of non-Native's by Alaska Native Tribes: A Response to Alcoholism and Drug Addiction," *Alaska Law Review* 35, no. 2 (2019): 275.

87. *Modern Tribal Governments in Alaska*, University of Alaska/Fairbanks, https://www.uaf.edu/tribal/academics/112/unit-4/moderntribalgovernmentsinalaska.php.

88. In *John v. Baker*, 982 P.2d 738 (Alaska, 1999), the Alaska Supreme Court concluded that Alaska Native villages had the inherent power to adjudicate child custody disputes between Tribal members, even if the village was not located on a federal reservation.

89. Peterson, "Banishment of non-Native's," 275.
90. Kapur, "Native Hawaiians," 413.
91. Jonathan Goldberg-Hiller and Noenoe K. Silva, "Sharks and Pigs: Animating Hawaiian Sovereignty against the Anthropological Machine," *The South Atlantic Quarterly* 110, no. 2 (Spring 2011): 436.
92. Getches et al., *Cases and Materials*, 909.
93. Noelani Goodyear-Kaōpua, "'Now We Know': Resurgences of Hawaiian Independence," *Politics, Groups, and Identities* 6, no. 3 (2018): 454.
94. See David Keau Sai, "The American Occupation of the Hawaiian Kingdom: Beginning the Transition from Occupied to Restored State" (PhD diss., University of Hawaii, 2008) who forcefully argued that the U.S. annexation of Hawaii by joint resolution was illegal; that the U.S. does not have legal title for sovereignty over the Hawaiian Islands; and therefore the Hawaiian Kingdom's existence as an independent state remains intact, notwithstanding the U.S. prolonged occupation of the territory. See also www.hawaiiankingdom.org.
95. Gavin Clarkson, "Native Hawaiians," in *Encyclopedia of U.S. Indian Policy and Law*, vol. 2, ed. Paul Finkelman and Tim Alan Garrison (Washington, DC: CQ Press, 2009), 581.
96. 107 Stat. 1510.
97. 97 Stat. 871 (1983).
98. 100 Stat. 3207 (1986).
99. 102 Stat. 4181 (1988).
100. 108 Stat. 3518 (1994).
101. Clarkson, "Native Hawaiians," 584; and Kapur, "Native Hawaiians," 413.
102. www.worldpopulationreview.com/states/hawaii-population.
103. Kapur, "Native Hawaiians," 420.
104. Goodyear-Kaōpua, "'Now We Know'," 453.
105. 107 Stat. 1513.
106. Department of the Interior and Department of Justice, *From Mauka to Makai: The River of Justice Must Flow Freely: Report on the Reconciliation Process between the Federal Government and Native Hawaiians*, (2000) https://www.doi.gov/sites/doi.gov/files/migrated/ohr/library/upload/Mauka-to-Makai-Report-2.pdf.
107. 528 U.S. 495 (2000).
108. Melody Kapilialoha MacKenzie with Susan K. Serrano and D. Kapua'ala Sproat, eds., *Native Hawaiian Law: A Treatise* (Honolulu: Kamehameha Publishing, 2015), 312.
109. Dean E. Murphy, "Bill Giving Native Hawaiian Sovereignty Is Too Much for Some, Too Little for Others," *New York Times* (July 17, 2005), 12.
110. J. Kehaulani Kauanui, "Precarious Positions: Native Hawaiians and U.S. Federal Recognition," *The Contemporary Pacific* 17, no. 1 (2005): 2.
111. 107 Stat. 1513.
112. Matthew L. M. Fletcher, *Principles of Federal Indian Law* (St. Paul, MN: West Publishing, 2017), 358–359.
113. 81 Fed. Reg. 71,278 (October 14, 2016).
114. Ibid.

434 NOTES

115. https://www.theguardian.com/commentisfree/2021/mar/04/us-government-native-hawaiians-raw-deal.
116. Anonymous, "Aloha Āina: Native Hawaiian Land Restitution," *Harvard Law Review* 133 (2020): 2148.
117. Noelani Goodyear-Kaʻōpua, "Building Government on Flimsy Foundations: Redesigning Constitutional Creation Processes" (February 1, 2016). See https://hehiale.wordpress.com/2016/02/01/building-government-on-flimsy-foundations-redesigning-constitutional-creation-processes/.
118. Noelani Arista and Randall Akee, "Manufacturing Consent for the Living and the Dead in Hawaii," *Indian Country Today* (November 20, 2015). https://law.alaska.gov/pdf/opinions/opinions_2017/17-004_JU20172010.pdf.
119. https://www.civilbeat.org/2020/02/mauna-kea-ignited-a-new-wave-of-hawaiian-pride-where-does-it-go-from-here/.
120. Ibid.
121. Ibid.
122. Guillermo Molero, "On a Stunning Hawaiian Mountain, the Fight over the Telescope Is Nearing a Peaceful End," (2022) https://www.npr.org/2022/07/31/1114314076/hawaii-mauna-kea-telescope-space-observatory.
123. J. Kehaulani Kauanui, *Paradoxes of Hawaiian Sovereignty: Land, Sex, and the Colonial Politics of State Nationalism* (Durham, NC: Duke University Press, 2018), 200.

Conclusion

1. Laura E. Evans, *Power from Powerlessness: Tribal Governments, Institutional Niches, and American Federalism* (New York: Oxford University Press, 2011), 6.
2. 528 U.S. 495 (2000). In this case, the Court struck down state restrictions that had allowed only persons with Native Hawaiian blood to vote for the trustees of the Office of Hawaiian Affairs, a state agency created to better the lives of Hawaii's aboriginal people.
3. See *Brackeen v. Haaland*, 994 F.3d 249 (2021) where an *en banc* panel of the Fifth Circuit upheld Congress's authority to enact ICWA and ruled that ICWA's definition of "Indian Child" was not a racial definition; but also declared that parts of the law that required state child welfare agencies to perform certain acts were unconstitutional. The U.S. Supreme Court agreed to hear the case on appeal and will likely issue a ruling late in 2022 or in 2023.
4. Paul Radin, *The World of Primitive Man* (New York: Grove Press, 1960), 223.
5. Commission on State-Tribal Relations, *Handbook: State-Tribal Relations* (Albuquerque, NM: American Indian Law Center, 1984), 36.
6. Philip S. Deloria, "The Era of Indian Self-Determination: An Overview," in *Indian Self-Rule*, ed. Kenneth Philp (Salt Lake City, UT: Howe Brothers, 1986), 193.
7. 597 U.S. ___ (2022).
8. 410 U.S. 113 (1973).

NOTES 435

9. Article II, sec. 4; and see Bethany Berger, "After Pocahontas: Indian Women and the Law, 1830–1934," *American Indian Law Review* 22 (1997): 51–52.
10. *Oklahoma v. Castro-Huerta*, 597 U.S. ___ (2022), 20.
11. Bethany Berger, "Justice and the Outsider: Jurisdiction over Non-members in Tribal Legal Systems," *Arizona State Law Journal* 37 (2005): 1050.
12. Ibid., 1051.
13. Joseph Thomas Flies Away, "My Grandma, Her People, Our Constitution," in *American Indian Constitutional Reform and the Rebuilding of Native Nations*, ed. Eric D. LeMont (Austin: University of Texas Press, 2006), 153.
14. Ibid., 161.
15. Robert B. Porter, "Building a New Longhouse: The Case for Government Reform within the Six Nations of the Haudenosaunee," *Buffalo Law Review* 46 (Fall 1998): 805–945.
16. Douglas George-Kanentiio, *Iroquois on Fire: A Voice from the Mohawk Nation* (Lincoln: University of Nebraska Press, 2008).
17. Porter, "Building a New Longhouse," 850.
18. Personal interview with Ron Whitener, May 4, 2021.
19. Bylaw 2, "Procedure of the Tribal Legislature," of the Menominee of Wisconsin (1991) declares that the legislature must provide "an appropriate number of places in appropriate urban areas where such posting shall be done" for any notice, ordinance, or other document.
20. Myla Vicenti Carpio, *Indigenous Albuquerque* (Lubbock: Texas Tech University Press, 2011), 7. A number of other quality studies have been produced during the last four decades that examine the distinctive and difficult social, political, cultural, and economic situations that Indigenous citizens face when they live in urban areas. See, for example, Russell Thornton, Gary D. Sandefur and Harold G. Grasmick's *The Urbanization of American Indians: A Critical Bibliography* (Bloomington: Indiana University Press, 1982); Susan Lobo's *Urban Voices: The Bay Area American Indian Community* (Tucson: University of Arizona Press, 2002); Coll Thrush's *Native Seattle: Histories from the Crossing-Over Place*, 2nd ed. (2007; reprint, Seattle: University of Washington Press, 2017); Coll Thrush's *Indigenous London: Native Travelers at the Heart of Empire* (New Haven, CT: Yale University Press, 2016); and Douglas K. Miller, *Indians on the Move: Native American Mobility and Urbanization in the Twentieth Century* (Chapel Hill: University of North Carolina Press, 2019).
21. Angela R. Riley, "Good (Native) Governance," *Columbia Law Review* 107, no. 5 (June 2007): 1065.
22. Jennifer Weldon Felmley, "All Good Things Come from Below: The Origins of Effective Tribal Government" (PhD diss., University of California at Berkeley, 2001).
23. Ibid., 311.
24. Ibid., 61.
25. Roger Scruton, *A Dictionary of Political Thought* (New York: Hill and Wang, 1982), 89–90.
26. Ibid.

436 NOTES

27. 1 Stat. 50.

28. UN Declaration on the Rights of Indigenous Peoples, G.A. Res. 61/295, U.N. Doc. A/ RES/61/295, art. 19 (2007).

29. Dwight D. Eisenhower, *Public Papers of the Presidents of the United States, Dwight D. Eisenhower, 1953* (Washington, DC: Government Printing Office, 1960), 565. And see Carole Goldberg-Ambrose, *Planting Tail Feathers: Tribal Survival and Public Law 280* (Los Angeles: American Indian Studies Center, 1997) for a good treatment of this important law.

30. Lyndon B. Johnson, *Public Papers of the Presidents of the United States: Lyndon B. Johnson, 1968–69*, vol. 1 (Washington, DC: Government Printing Office, 1970), 336–337.

31. https://goia.wa.gov/relations/centennial-accord.

32. *Weekly Compilation of Presidential Documents*, vol. 30, no. 18 (May 9, 1994), 941.

33. Ibid.

34. Jason Searle, "Exploring Alternatives to the 'Consultation or Consent' Paradigm," *Michigan Journal of Environmental and Administrative Law* 6, no. 2 (2017): 487.

35. Robert L. Bee, "Structure, Ideology, and Tribal Governments," *Human Organization* 58, no. 3 (1999): 289.

Bibliography

Manuscripts and Archival Collections

Checote, Samuel. Collection. Western History Collections. University of Oklahoma Library. Norman.

Cohen, Felix S. Papers. Beinecke Rare Book Room and Manuscript Library. Yale University. New Haven, CT.

Foreman, Grant. Collection. Oklahoma Historical Society. Oklahoma City, Oklahoma.

Littlefield, Daniel F. Collection Projects, Great State of Sequoyah Commission, Sequoyah National Research Center. University of Arkansas. Little Rock.

Porter, Pleasant. Collection. Western History Collections. University of Oklahoma Library. Norman.

The Vindicator. Oklahoma Historical Society. Oklahoma City.

Works Progress Administration: Historic Sites and Federal Writers Project Collection. Western History Collections. University of Oklahoma Library. Norman.

Government Documents and Publications

Register of Debates in Congress. 14 vols. Washington, DC: 1824–1838.

U.S. Board of Indian Commissioners. *2nd Annual Report to the Secretary of the Interior*. Washington, DC: Government Printing Office, 1871.

U.S. Commission on Civil Rights. "Broken Promises: Continuing Federal Funding Shortfall for Native Americans." Briefing Report. Washington, DC: Government Printing Office, 2018. Online. Available: https://www.usccr.gov/pubs/2018/12-20-Bro ken-Promises.pdf.

U.S. Congress. American Indian Policy Review Commission. *Final Report*. Special Report. Washington, DC: Government Printing Office, 1977.

U.S. Congress. American Indian Policy Review Commission. *Report on Tribal Government: Task Force Two—Tribal Government*. Washington, DC: Government Printing Office, 1976.

U.S. Congress. American Indian Policy Review Commission. *Report on Federal Administration and Structure of Indian Affairs: Final Report to the AIPRC*. Washington, DC: Government Printing Office, 1976.

U.S. Congress. Congressional Globe. "Consolidation of Indian Tribes." 38th Cong., 2nd Sess., 1865.

U.S. Congress. House. *Delegate in Congress from the Indian Territory*. 45th Cong., 2nd Sess., 1878. Misc. Doc. 32.

U.S. Congress. House. *Election of Delegate from Indian Territory*. 45th Cong., 2nd Sess., 1878. H. Rept. 95.

U.S. Congress. House. *Indian Territory, West of the Mississippi*. 30th Cong., 1st Sess., 1848. H. Rept. 736.

438 BIBLIOGRAPHY

U.S. Congress. House. *Letter from Lewis Downing, Principal Chief of the Cherokee Nation.* 41st. Cong., 2nd Sess., 1870. Misc. Doc. 76.

U.S. Congress. House. *Memorial of a Council Held at Running Waters.* 23rd Cong., 2nd Sess., 1835. Doc. 91.

U.S. Congress. House. *Message from the President.* 27th Cong., 3rd Sess., 1842. Exec. Doc. 2.

U.S. Congress. House. *Objections of the Indian Delegation to a Delegate.* 45th Cong., 2nd Sess., 1878. Misc. Doc. 32.

U.S. Congress. House. *Organization of the Indian Territory.* 45th Cong., 1st Sess., 1877. Misc. Doc. 18.

U.S. Congress. House. *Organization of the Territory of Oklahoma.* 45th Cong., 3rd Sess., 1879. H. Rept. 188.

U.S. Congress. House. *Papers Relative to the Confederacy of Indian Tribes.* 41st. Cong., 3rd Sess., 1871. Misc. Doc. 49.

U.S. Congress. House. *Protest of the Cherokee Nation.* 38th Cong., 2nd Sess., 1865. Misc. Doc. 56.

U.S. Congress. House. *Protest of the General Council of the Indian Territory.* 43rd Cong., 1st Sess., 1874. Misc. Doc. 88.

U.S. Congress. House. *Regulating the Indian Department.* 23rd Cong., 1st Sess., 1834. H. Rept. 474.

U.S. Congress. House. *Remonstrance of Col. Peter Pitchlynn, Choctaw Delegate.* 30th Cong., 2nd Sess., 1849. Misc. Doc. 35.

U.S. Congress. House. *Resolutions of the Legislature of N.C. Relative to the Provision of a Permanent Home for the Indian Tribes.* 30th Cong., 2nd Sess., 1849. Misc. Doc. 39.

U.S. Congress. House. *Secretary of War to Cherokee Delegation.* 25th Cong., 2nd Sess., 1838. Doc. 376.

U.S. Congress. House. *Territory of Oklahoma.* 42nd Cong., 2nd Sess., 1872. H. Rept. 89.

U.S. Congress. House. *Western Frontier Correspondence.* 25th Cong., 2nd Sess., 1838. Doc. 276.

U.S. Congress. Senate. *A Bill to Establish Territories of Cha-lah-kee, Muscogee, and Cha-ta.* 33rd Cong., 1st Sess., 1854. Doc. 379.

U.S. Congress. Senate. *Indian Territory.* 41st Cong., 2nd Sess., 1870. H. Rept. 131.

U.S. Congress. Senate. *Letter of the Cherokee Delegation of Indians.* 41st Cong., 2nd Sess., 1870. Misc. Doc. 154.

U.S. Congress. Senate. *Memorial of the Cherokee, Creek, and Choctaw Nations of Indians.* 41st Cong., 2nd Sess., 1870. Misc. Doc. 143.

U.S. Congress. Senate. *Memorial of the Choctaw Nation of Indians Remonstrating Against Territorial Government and Railroad Construction.* 41st Cong., 2nd Sess., 1870. Misc. Doc. 90.

U.S. Congress. Senate. *Memorial of I. L. Garvin-Principal Chief of Choctaw Nation.* 45th Cong., 3rd Sess., 1879. Misc. Doc. 52.

U.S. Congress. Senate. *Message of the President of the U.S.* 41st Cong., 3rd Sess., 1871. Exec. Doc. 26.

U.S. Congress. Senate. *Proposed State of Sequoyah.* 59th Cong., 1st Sess., 1906. Doc. 143.

U.S. Congress. Senate. *Report 159.* 24th Cong., 1st Sess., 1836.

U.S. Congressional Research Service. "COVID-19 and the Indian Health Service." IN11333. May 1, 2020. Online. Available: https://crsreports.congress.gov.

BIBLIOGRAPHY 439

U.S. Congressional Research Service. "Tribal Broadband: Status of Deployment and Federal Funding Programs." R44416. January 19, 2019. Online. Available: https://crs reports.congress.gov.

U.S. Congressional Research Service. "U.S. Department of the Interior: An Overview." R45480. January 31, 2019. Online. Available: https://crsreports.congress.gov.

U.S. Department of the Interior. *Annual Report for the Commissioner of Indian Affairs, 1887 and 1888.*

U.S. Department of the Interior. "Powers of Indian Tribes." 55 I.D. 14. October 25, 1934.

U.S. Department of the Interior. "Developing and Reviewing Tribal Constitutions and Amendments: A Handbook for BIA Personnel." Washington, DC: Bureau of Indian Affairs, 1987.

U.S. Department of Justice. National Institute of Justice. *Research Report: Violence against American Indian and Alaska Native Women and Men*, by Andre B. Rosay. May 2016.

U.S. Department of Justice. Office of Justice Programs. *FY 2020 Program Summaries.* March 2019.

U.S. General Accounting Office. *Regional Alaska Native Corporations: Status Forty Years after Establishment, and Future Considerations.* GAO-13-121. Washington, DC: Government Printing Office, December 2012.

U.S. National Archives. Circular No. 3010. *Tribal Organizations.* Record Group 75, Circulars, 1904–1951. Entry 132-G, Replies to Circular 3010.

U.S. National Archives. *General Records Concerning Indian Organization, 1934–1956.* Record Group 75, Entry 1012.

Books, Articles, & Chapters

Abel, Annie H. "Proposals for an Indian State, 1778–1878." In *Annual Report of the American Historical Association*, vol. 1, 89–102. Washington, DC: Government Printing Office, 1907.

Ablavsky, Gregory. "'With the Indian Tribes': Race, Citizenship, and Original Constitutional Meaning." *Stanford Law Review* 70 (April 2018): 1025–1076.

Akee, Randall K. Q. and Katherine Spilde and Jonathan Taylor. "The Indian Gaming Regulatory Act and Its Effect on American Indian Economic Development." *Journal of Economic Perspectives* 29, no. 3 (Summer 2015): 185–208.

Akee, Randall K. Q., Miriam R. Jorgensen, Eric C. Hanson, and Joseph P. Kalt. "Letter to Steve Mnuchin, Secretary of the Treasury on 'Allocation of COVID-19 Response Funds to American Indian Nations.'" April 10, 2020.

Albers, Patricia and Beatrice Medicine, eds. *The Hidden Half: Studies of Plains Indian Women.* Lanham, MD: University Press of America, 1983.

Alden, George Henry. "The State of Franklin." *American Historical Review* 8, no. 2 (1903): 271–289.

American Civil Liberties Union. "Voting Rights in Indian Country: A Special Report of the Voting Rights Project of the ACLU." (September 2009). Atlanta, GA: ACLU.

American Indian Lawyer Training Program. *Indian Tribes as Governments.* New York: John Hay Whitney Foundation, 1975.

Applen, Allen G. "An Attempted Indian State Government: The Okmulgee Constitution in Indian Territory, 1870–1876." *Kansas Quarterly* 3 (Fall 1971): 89–99.

440 BIBLIOGRAPHY

Atleo, Cliff. "Aboriginal Capitalism: Is Resistance Futile or Fertile?" *Journal of Aboriginal Economic Development* 9, no. 2 (2015): 41–51.

Austin, Raymond D. *Navajo Courts and Navajo Common Law: A Tradition of Tribal Self-Governance*. Minneapolis: University of Minnesota Press, 2009.

Austin, Raymond D. "Traditional American Indian Justice." In *Traditional, National, and International Law and Indigenous Communities*, edited by Marianne Nielsen and Karen Jarratt-Snider, 50–70. Tucson: University of Arizona Press, 2020.

Barsh, Russel L. "The Nature and Spirit of North American Political Systems." *American Indian Quarterly* 10, no. 3 (Summer 1986): 181–198.

Barsh, Russel L. and James Youngblood Henderson. *The Road: Indian Tribes and Political Liberty*. Berkeley: University of California Press at Berkeley, 1980.

Bigler, Gregory H. "Traditional Jurisprudence and Protection of Our Society: A Jurisgenerative Tail." *American Indian Law Review* 43, no. 1 (2018): 1–74.

Biolsi, Thomas. *Organizing the Lakota: The Political Economy of the New Deal on the Pine Ridge and Rosebud Reservations*. Tucson: University of Arizona Press, 1992.

Biolsi, Thomas, ed. *A Companion to the Anthropology of American Indians*. Malden, MA: Blackwell Publishing, 2004.

Biolsi, Thomas. "'Indian Self-Government' as a Technique of Domination." *American Indian Quarterly* 15, no. 1 (Winter 1991): 23–28.

Bohannon, Paul, ed. *Law and Warfare: Studies in the Anthropology of Conflict*. Garden City, NJ: Natural History Press, 1967.

Burton, Jeffrey. *Indian Territory and the U.S., 1866–1906: Courts, Government, and the Movement for Oklahoma Statehood*. Norman: University of Oklahoma Press, 1995.

Carter Center. "The Carter Center's Limited Observation Mission to the Cherokee Nation's Special Election for Principal Chief: Final Report." September 24, 2011.

Carter Center. "October 3, 2017 Primaries and December 12, 2017 General Elections in Cheyenne and Arapaho: Final Report." May 1, 2018.

Carter Center. "Carter Center Observes Smooth Muscogee (Creek) Elections, Recommends Additional Training." November 5, 2019.

Carter Center. "Carter Center Commends Muscogee (Creek) Nation on Smooth Electoral Process." December 17, 2019.

Champagne, Duane. *Social Order and Political Change: Constitutional Governments among the Cherokee, the Choctaw, the Chickasaw, and the Creek* Stanford, CA: Stanford University Press, 1992.

Chopp, Rebecca S. and Mark Lewis Taylor, eds. *Reconstructing Christian Theology* Minneapolis, MN: Fortress Press, 1994.

Clow, Richmond L. "The Indian Reorganization Act and the Loss of Tribal Sovereignty: Constitutions on the Rosebud and Pine Ridge Reservations." *Great Plains Quarterly* 7 (1987): 1251–1334.

Cobb, Daniel M. and Loretta Fowler, eds. *Beyond Red Power: American Indian Politics and Activism since 1900*. Santa Fe, NM: School for Advanced Research, 2007.

Cohen, Felix S. *Handbook of Federal Indian Law*. Albuquerque: University of New Mexico Press, 1972. First published 1942.

Cohen, Felix S. "How Long Will Indian Constitutions Last?" In *The Legal Conscience: Selected Papers of Felix S. Cohen*, edited by Lucy Kramer Cohen, 222–229. New Haven: Yale University Press, 1960.

Cohen, Felix S. *On the Drafting of Tribal Constitutions*. Edited by David E. Wilkins. Norman: University of Oklahoma Press, 2006.

BIBLIOGRAPHY 441

Cornell, Stephen and Joseph Kalt. "Alaska Native Self-Government and Service Delivery: What Works?" Joint Occasional Papers on Native Affairs, No. 2003–01, The Harvard Project on American Indian Economic Development, 2003.

Cornell, Stephen, Jonathan Taylor, and Kenneth Grant. "Achieving Alaska Native Self-Governance: Toward Implementation of the Alaska Native Commission Report." Final Report-AFN Version. Cambridge: The Economics Resource Group, Inc., May 1999.

Crandall, Maurice. *These People Have Always Been a Republic: Indigenous Electorates in the U.S.–Mexico Borderlands, 1598–1912.* Chapel Hill: University of North Carolina Press, 2019.

Debo, Angie. *And Still the Waters Run.* Princeton: Princeton University Press, 1973.

Deer, Sarah and Mary Kathryn Nagle. "Return to *Worcester: Dollar General* and the Restoration of Tribal Jurisdiction to Protect Native Women and Children." *Harvard Journal of Law and Gender* 41 (2018): 180–238.

Deery, Phyllis Anne. "The Indigenous International Diplomacy of Indian Territory." Master's thesis, University of Arizona, 1991.

Deloria, Philip Sam. "Remarks." In *Proceedings of the Sixty-Eighth Annual Meeting of the American Society of International Law,* 276–280. Washington: Lancaster Press, Inc., 1975.

Deloria, Vine, Jr., ed. *The Indian Reorganization Act: Congresses and Bills.* Norman: University of Oklahoma Press, 2002.

Deloria, Vine, Jr. and Clifford M. Lytle. *American Indians, American Justice.* Austin: University of Texas Press, 1983.

Deloria, Vine, Jr. and Clifford M. Lytle . *The Nations Within: The Past and Future of American Indian Sovereignty.* New York: Pantheon Books, 1984.

Deloria, Vine, Jr. and David E. Wilkins. *Tribes, Treaties, and Constitutional Tribulations.* Austin: University of Texas Press, 1999.

Dennison, Jean. *Colonial Entanglement: Constituting a Twenty-First Century Osage Nation.* Chapel Hill: University Of North Carolina Press, 2012.

Dinan, John J. *The American State Constitutional Tradition.* Lawrence: University Press of Kansas, 2009.

Dowling, Christina. "The Applied Theory of First Nations Economic Development: A Critique." *Journal of Aboriginal Economic Development* 4, no. 2 (2005): 120–128.

Dozier, Edward P. "Factionalism at Santa Clara Pueblo." *Ethnology* 15, no. 2 (1966): 172–185.

Dozier, Edward P. "The Pueblos of the Southwestern United States." *The Journal of the Royal Anthropological Institute* 90 (1960): 146–160.

Dozier, Edward P. *The Pueblo Indians of North America.* New York: Holt, Rinehart and Winston, Inc., 1970.

Driver, Harold E. *Indians of North America.* 2nd ed. Chicago: University of Chicago Press, 1969.

Dye, Thomas R. and L. Harmon Ziegler. *The Irony of Democracy: An Uncommon Introduction to American Politics.* North Scituate, MA: Duxbury Press, 1978.

Eggan, Fred. *The American Indian: Perspectives for the Study of Social Change.* Cambridge: Cambridge University Press, 1966.

Ellinger, Charles Wayne. "Political Obstacles Barring Oklahoma's Admission to Statehood, 1890–1906." *Great Plains Journal* 43, no. 2 (Spring 1964): 60–83.

442 BIBLIOGRAPHY

Evans, Laura E. "Expertise and Scale of Conflict: Governments as Advocates in American Indian Politics." *American Political Science Review* 105, no. 4 (November 2011): 663–682.

Evans, Laura E. *Power from Powerlessness: Tribal Governments, Institutional Niches, and American Federalism*. New York: Oxford University Press, 2011.

Felmley, Jennifer Weldon. "All Good Things Come from Below: The Origins of Effective Tribal Government." PhD diss., University of California at Berkeley, 2001.

Fenton, William N. "Factionalism at Taos Pueblo, NM." Bureau of American Ethnology: Bulletin 164. *Anthropological Papers* 56 (1957): 297–344.

Ferguson, Kennan. "Why Does Political Science Hate American Indians?" *Perspectives on Politics* 14, no. 4 (December 2016): 1029–1038.

First Nations Development Institute and EchoHawk Consulting. "Reclaiming Native Truth and Research Findings: Compilation of All Research." (June 2018). Longmont, CA.

Fisher, Reginald G. 1939. "An Outline of Pueblo Government." In *So Live the Works of Man*, edited by Donald D. Brand and Fred Harvey, 147–157. Albuquerque, NM: University of New Mexico Press, 1939.

Flynn, Janet. *Tribal Government: Wind River Reservation* Lander, WY: Mortimore Publishing, 1998.

Fogelsen, Raymond D., ed. *Handbook of North American Indians: Southeast*. Vol. 14. Washington, DC: Smithsonian Institution, 2004.

Fowler, Loretta. *Arapahoe Politics, 1851–1978: Symbols in Crises of Authority*. Lincoln: University of Nebraska Press, 1982.

Fowler, Loretta. "Politics." In *A Companion to the Anthropology of American Indians*, edited by Thomas Biolsi, 69–94. Malden, MA: Blackwell Publishing, Co., 2004.

Fowler, Loretta. *The Columbia Guide to American Indians of the Great Plains*. New York: Columbia University Press, 2003.

Fox, Mary Jo, Eileen M. Luna-Firebaugh, and Caroline Williams. "American Indian Female Leadership." *Wicazo Sa Review* 30, no. 1 (Spring 2015): 82–99.

Gibson, Arrell. "An Indian Territory United Nations: The Creek Council of 1845." *Chronicles of Oklahoma* 39 (Winter 1961–1962): 398–413.

Gittinger, Ray. "The Separation of Nebraska and Kansas from the Indian Territory." *Mississippi Valley Historical Review* 3, no. 4 (March 1917): 442–461.

Gover, Kirsty. *Tribal Constitutionalism: States, Tribes, and the Governance of Membership*. New York: Oxford University Press, 2010.

Griffin, Stephen M. *American Constitutionalism: From Theory to Politics* Princeton, NJ: Princeton University Press, 1996.

Hargrett, Lester, ed. *A Bibliography of the Constitution and Laws of the American Indian*. Clark, NJ: The Lawbook Exchange LTD, 2003. First published 1947.

Hatheway, Glover Gillette. "The Neutral Indian Barrier State: A Project in British National American Policy, 1754–1815." PhD diss., University of Minnesota, 1957.

Hilton, Carol Anne. *Indigenomics: Taking a Seat at the Economic Table*. Gabriola Island, BC: New Society Publishers, 2021.

Hodge, Frederick Webb, ed. *Handbook of American Indians North of Mexico*. Pt. 1, Bureau of American Ethnology: Bulletin 30. Washington, DC: Government Printing Office, 1907.

Hoebel, E. Adamson. *The Law of Primitive Man: A Study in Comparative Legal Dynamics*. New York: Atheneum, 1968.

BIBLIOGRAPHY 443

Holm, Thomas. "Indian Lobbyists: Cherokee Opposition to the Allotment of Tribal Lands." *American Indian Quarterly* 5, no. 2 (May 1979): 115–134.

Horn-Miller, Kahente. "What Does Indigenous Participatory Democracy Look Like? Kahnawake's Community Decision-Making Process." *Review of Constitutional Studies* 18, no. 1 (2013): 111–130.

Hoskin, Chuck, Jr. "Five Tribes Inter-Tribal Council Critical to Oklahoma Tribes." *Native News Online* (August 14, 2020). https://www.tahlequahdailypress.com/news/five-tri bes-inter-tribal-council-critical-to-oklahoma-tribes/article_5adae957-4e30-5dde-8eb4-d52b841d42e9.html.

Hoxie, Frederick E. "Crow Leadership: Amidst Reservation Opposition." In *State & Reservation: New Perspectives on Federal Indian Policy*, edited by George Pierre Castile and Robert L. Bee, 38–60. Tucson: University of Arizona Press, 1992.

Jacobs, Wilbur. "Edmund Atkin's Plan for Imperial Indian Control." *Journal of Southern History* 19 (August 1953): 311–320.

Jorgensen, Miriam, ed. *Rebuilding Native Nations: Strategies for Governance and Development*. Tucson: University of Arizona Press, 2007.

Juan, Vivian. "Tohono O'odham Constitution in Transition." MA thesis, University of Arizona, 1992.

Kavanaugh, Thomas W. *Comanche Political History: An Ethnological Perspective, 1706–1875*. Lincoln: University of Nebraska Press, 1996.

Kenny, Carolyn. "Liberating Leadership Theory." In *Living Indigenous Leadership: Native Narratives on Building Strong Communities*, edited by Carolyn Kenny and Tina Ngaroimata Fraser, 1–14. Vancouver, BC: UBC Press, 2012.

Klein, Laura F. "Mother as Clanswoman: Rank and Gender in Tlingit Society." In *Women and Power in Native North America*, edited by Laura F. Klein and Lillian A. Ackerman, 28–45. Norman: University of Oklahoma Press, 1995.

Klein, Laura F. and Lillian A. Ackerman, eds. *Women and Power in Native North America*. Norman: University of Oklahoma Press, 1995.

Korsmo, Fae L. "The Alaska Natives." In *Polar Peoples: Self-Determination and Development*, edited by Minority Rights Group, 81–104. London: Minority Rights Publications, 1994.

Lemont, Eric., ed. *American Indian Constitutional Reform and the Rebuilding of Native Nations*. Austin: University of Texas Press, 2006.

Lerma, Michael. *Guided by the Mountains: Navajo Political Philosophy and Governance*. New York: Oxford University Press, 2017.

Lewis, Anna. Review of Amos the Maxwell's "The Sequoyah Constitutional Convention." *The Mississippi Valley Historical Review* 41, no. 2 (1954): 349–350.

Lonowski, Delmer. "A Return to Tradition: Proportional Representation in Tribal Government." *American Indian Culture and Research Journal* 18, no. 1 (1994): 147–163.

Lopach, James J., Margery Hunter Brown, and Richmond L. Clow. *Tribal Government Today: Politics on Montana Indian Reservations*. Revised ed. Niwot: University Press of Colorado, 1998.

Louisiana Coalition Against Racism and Nazism, Inc. "The Politics and Background of David Duke: Resource Packet." 5th ed. (New Orleans, 1991): 46.

Lowie, Robert H. "Some Aspects of Political Organisation among the American Aborigines." *Journal of the Royal Aboriginal Institute of Great Britain and Ireland* 78 (February 1948): 11–24.

444 BIBLIOGRAPHY

Luna-Firebaugh, Eileen. *Tribal Policing: Asserting Sovereignty, Seeking Justice*. Tucson: University of Arizona Press, 2007.

Lurie, Nancy. "The Will-o-the-Wisp of Indian Unity." In *Currents in Anthropology: Essays in Honor of Sol Tax*, edited by Robert Hinshaw. New York: Moulton Publishers, 1979.

Lyons, Oren and John Mohawk, eds. *Exiled in the Land of the Free: Democracy, Indian Nations, and the U.S. Constitution*. Santa Fe, NM: Clear Light Press, 1992.

Maxwell, Amos D. *The Sequoyah Constitutional Convention*. Boston, MA: Meador Publishing Co., 1953.

Meredith, Howard. *Modern American Tribal Governments and Politics*. Tsaile, AZ: Navajo Community College Press, 1993.

Miller, Walter B. "Two Concepts of Authority." *American Anthropologist* 57, no. 2 (April 1955): 271–289.

Miner, Craig H. *The Corporation and the Indian: Tribal Sovereignty and Industrial Civilization in Indian Territory, 1865–1907*. Norman: Oklahoma University Press, 1989.

Mitchell, Donald Craig. "*Alaska v. Native Village of Venetie*: Statutory Construction or Judicial Usurpation? Why History Counts." *Alaska Law Review* 14, no. 2 (1997): 353–441.

Moncrief, Gary and Peverill Squire. *Why States Matter: An Introduction to State Politics*. Lanham, MD: Rowman & Littlefield Publishers, 2013.

Morgan, Lewis Henry. *League of the Iroquois*. New York: Corinth Books, 1962. First published as *League of the Ho-de-no-sau-nee, or Iroquois*, Rochester, NY: Sage, 1851.

Morse, Jedediah. "A Report to the Secretary of War of the United States on Indian Affairs." New Haven, CT: Davis and Force, 1822.

Morton, Ohland. "Early History of the Creek Indians." *Chronicles of Oklahoma* 9, no. 3 (1931): 17–26.

Morton, Ohland. "The Government of the Creek Indians." *Chronicles of Oklahoma* 8, no. 1 (1930): 42–64.

Mowbray, Martin. "Localising Responsibility: The Application of the Harvard Project on American Indian Economic Development to Australia." *Australian Journal of Social Issues* 41, no. 1 (Autumn 2006): 87–103.

National Congress of American Indians. "Request That Treasury Respond to Tribal Inquiries on Economic Support Assistance under the Coronavirus Relief Fund." Letter from Kevin Allis, C.E.O. to Steve Mnuchin. May 29, 2020.

National Congress of American Indians. "Tribal Nations and the United States." 2019, Online. Available: https://www.ncai.org/tribalnations/introduction/Indian_Country_ 101_Updated_February_2019.pdf.

Native American Rights Fund. "Obstacles at Every Turn: Barriers to Political Participation Faced by Native American Voters." With contributions by James Thomas Tucker, Jacqueline DeLeon, and Daniel McCool. Boulder, CO: Native American Rights Fund, 2020.

Newton, Nell Jessup, ed. *Cohen's Handbook of Federal Indian Law*. Newark, NJ: LexisNexis Matthew Bender, 2005.

Nielsen, Marianne O. "Navajo Nation Courts, Peacemaking and Restorative Justice Issues." *Journal of Legal Pluralism and Unofficial Law* 44 (1999): 105–126.

Nielsen, Marianne O. and James W. Zion, eds. *Navajo Nation Peacemaking: Living Traditional Justice*. Tucson: University of Arizona Press, 2005.

BIBLIOGRAPHY 445

Nielsen, Marianne O. and Karen Jarratt-Snider, eds. *Traditional, National, and International Law and Indigenous Communities*. Tucson: University of Arizona Press, 2020.

Nolen, Curtis. "The Okmulgee Constitution: A Step Toward Indian Self-Determination." *Chronicles of Oklahoma* 58 (Fall 1980): 264–281.

Norcini, Marilyn. "The Political Process of Factionalism and Self-Governance at Santa Clara Pueblo, New Mexico." *Proceedings of the American Philosophical Society* 149, no. 4 (December 2005): 544–590.

O'Brien, Sharon. *American Indian Tribal Governments*. Norman: University of Oklahoma Press, 1989.

Ortiz, Alfonso. "Review of *Custer Died for Your Sins*." *American Anthropologist* 73 (1971): 953–955.

Parker, Arthur, C. *The Constitution of the Five Nations* or *The Iroquois Book of the Great Law*. Albany: New York State Museum, 1916.

Phillips, Joseph W. *Jedediah Morse and New England Congregationalism*. New Brunswick, NJ: Rutgers University Press, 1983.

Philp, Kenneth R., ed. *Indian Self-Rule: First Hand Accounts of Indian-White Relations from Roosevelt to Reagan*. Salt Lake City: Howe Brothers, 1986.

Porter, Robert B. "Building a New Longhouse: The Case for Government Reform within the Six Nations of the Haudenosaunee." *Buffalo Law Review* 46 (Fall 1998): 805–945.

Porter, Robert B. "Strengthening Tribal Sovereignty Through Government Reform: What Are the Issues?" *Kansas Journal of Law and Public Policy* 7 (Winter 1997): 72–105.

Prucha, Francis P. *The Great Father: The United States Government and the American Indians*. 2 vols. Lincoln: University of Nebraska Press, 1984.

Prucha, Francis P. *American Indian Policy in the Formative Years: The Indian Trade and Intercourse Acts, 1790–1834*. Lincoln: University of Nebraska Press, 1962.

Quarles, Charles L. *Christian Identity: The Aryan American Bloodline Religion*. Jefferson, NC: McFarland & Co., 2004.

Radin, Paul. *Primitive Man as Philosopher*. New York: Dover Publications, 1957.

Radin, Paul. *The World of Primitive Man*. New York: Grove Press, 1960.

Radosh, Daniel and Timothy Long. "Yikes! Are We the Next Bosnia-Herzegovina?" *Spy* 7, no. 6 (April 1993): 56–60.

Redfield, Robert. "Primitive Law." In *Law and Warfare: Studies in the Anthropology of Conflict*, edited by Paul Bohannon, 3–24. Garden City, NJ: Natural History Press, 1967:.

Richland, Justin B. "Hopi Sovereignty as Epistemological Limit." *Wicazo Sa Review* 24, no. 1 (Spring 2009): 89–112.

Richland, Justin B. *Arguing with Tradition: The Language of Law in Hopi Tribal Court*. Chicago: University of Chicago Press, 2008.

Riley, Angela R. "Good (Native) Governance." *Columbia Law Review* 107, no. 5 (June 2007): 1049–1125.

Rockwell, Stephen J. *Indian Affairs and the Administrative State in the Nineteenth Century*. New York: Cambridge University Press, 2010.

Roderick, Libby. *Alaska Native Cultures and Issues: Responses to Frequently Asked Questions*. Fairbanks: University of Alaska Press, 2010.

Rosser, Ezra. "The Nature of Representation: The Cherokee Right to a Congressional Delegate." *Public Interest Law Journal* 15, no. 1 (Fall 2005): 91–152.

Rusco, Elmer R. *A Fateful Time: The Background and Legislative History of the Indian Reorganization Act*. Reno: University of Nevada Press, 2000.

446 BIBLIOGRAPHY

Rusco, Elmer R. "Civil Liberties Guarantees under Tribal Law: A Survey of Civil Rights Provisions in Tribal Constitutions." *American Indian Law Review* 14 (1990): 269–299.

Russell, Steve. *Sequoyah Rising: Problems in Postcolonial Tribal Governance*. Durham, NC: Carolina Academic Press, 2010.

Sando, Joe S. *The Pueblo Indians*. San Francisco: Indian Historian Press, 1976.

Schroedel, Jean and Artour Aslanian. "Native American Vote Suppression: The Case of South Dakota." *Race, Gender & Class* 22, 1–2 (2015): 308–323.

Shultz, George. *An Indian Canaan: Isaac McCoy and the Vision of an Indian State*. Norman: University of Oklahoma Press, 1972.

Sigourney, Lydia Huntley. "The Grand June Council." *Chronicles of Oklahoma* 10 (1932): 556–559.

Simon, Michael Paul Patrick. "Indigenous Peoples in Developed Fragment Societies: A Comparative Analysis of Internal Colonialism in the U.S., CA, and Northern Ireland." PhD diss., University of Arizona, 1986.

Starna, William A. "The Repeal of Article 8: Law, Government, and Cultural Politics at Akwesasne." *American Indian Law Review* 18, no. 2 (1993): 297–311.

Strickland, Rennard. *Fire and the Spirits: Cherokee Law from Clan to Court*. Norman: University of Oklahoma Press, 1975.

Strickland, Rennard. "From Clan to Court: Development of Cherokee Law." *Tennessee Historical Quarterly* 31 (Winter 1972): 316–327.

Strickland, Rennard. *The Indians of Oklahoma*. Norman: University of Oklahoma Press, 1980.

Strickland, Rennard. "Sequoyah Statehood, The Oklahoma Centennial and Sovereignty Envy: A Personal Narrative and a Public Proposal." *American Indian Law Review* 30, no. 2 (2006): 365–372.

Strommer, Geoffrey D. and Stephen D. Osborne. "'Indian Country' and the Nature and Scope of Tribal Self-Government in Alaska." *Alaska Law Review* 22, no. 1 (2005): 1–34.

Strong, Pauline Turner and Barrik Van Winkle. "Tribe and Native American Indians and American Nationalism." *Social Analysis* 33 (September 1993): 9–26.

Sugden, John. "Early Pan-Indianism: Tecumseh's Tour of the Indian Country, 1811–1812." *American Indian Quarterly* 10, no. 4 (Fall 1986): 273–304.

Sullivan, Patrick. "Indigenous Governance: The Harvard Project on Native American Economic Development and Appropriate Principles of Governance for Aboriginal Australia." Research Discussion Paper No. 17, American Institute of Aboriginal and Torres Strait Islander Studies, February 2006.

Sullivan, Patrick. "Indigenous Governance: The Harvard Project, Australian Aboriginal Organizations and Cultural Subsidiarity." In *Against the Grain: Advances in Postcolonial Organization Studies*, edited by A. Prasad, 95–115. Copenhagen: Copenhagen Business School Press, 2012.

Swanton, John R. "Social Organization and Social Usages of the Indians of the Creek Confederacy." Bureau of American Ethnology. 42nd Annual Report: 1924–1925. Washington, DC: Government Printing Office, 1928.

Swensen, Thomas Michael. "Of Subjection and Sovereignty: Alaska Native Corporations and Tribal Governments in the Twenty-First Century." *Wicazo Sa Review* 30, no. 1 (Spring 2015): 100–117.

Tatum, Melissa L., Miriam Jorgensen, Mary E. Guss, and Sarah Deer. *Structuring Sovereignty: Constitutions of Native Nations*. Los Angeles, CA: American Indian Studies Center, 2014.

Traisman, Ken. "Native Law: Law and Order among Eighteenth Century Cherokee, Great Plains, Central Prairie, and Woodland Indians." *American Indian Law Review* 9 (1981): 273–287.

Trimble, Charles E. "Indian Country: The 51st State?" *Indian Life* 29, no. 5 (March–April 2009): 1–3.

Turner, Frederick Jackson. "The Policy of France toward the Mississippi Valley in the Period of Washington and Adams." *American Historical Review* 10, no. 2 (January 1905): 249–279.

Upham, Steadman. *Politics and Power: An Economic and Political History of the Western Pueblo.* New York: Academic Press, 1982.

Van Horn, Carl E. *The State of the States.* 2nd ed. Washington, DC: CQ Press, 1993.

Wallace, Anthony F. C. *Jefferson and the Indians: The Tragic Fate of the First Americans.* Cambridge, MA: Harvard University Press, 1999.

Wallace, Paul A. W. *The White Roots of Peace.* Philadelphia: University of Pennsylvania Press, 1946.

Warner, Linda Sue and Keith Grint, "American Indian Ways of Leading and Knowing's." *Leadership* 2, no. 2 (2006): 225–244.

Watson, Thomas D. "Strivings for Sovereignty: Alexander McGillivray, Creek Warfare, and Diplomacy, 1783–1790." *Florida Historical Quarterly* 58 (April 1980): 400–414.

Weyer, E. M. "The Structure of Social Organization among the Eskimos." In *Comparative Political Systems: Studies in the Politics of Preindustrial Societies,* edited by Ronald Cohen and John M. Middleton, 1–13. Garden City, NJ: Natural History Press, 1967.

White, David H. "The Spaniards and William Augustus Bowles in Florida, 1799–1803." *Florida Historical Quarterly* 84 (October 1975): 145–155.

Whiteley, Peter M. *Rethinking Hopi Ethnography.* Washington, DC: Smithsonian Institution, 1998.

Wilkins, Andrea. *Fostering the State-Tribal Collaboration: An Indian Law Primer.* Lanham, MD: Rowman & Littlefield Publishers, 2016.

Wilkins, David E. "Absence Does Not Make the Indigenous Political Heart Grow Fonder." *Perspectives on Politics* 14, no. 4 (December 2016): 1048–1049.

Wilkins, David E. *American Indian Sovereignty and the U.S. Supreme Court: The Masking of Justice.* Austin: University of Texas Press, 1997.

Wilkins, David E. *Documents of Native American Political Development: 1500s–1933.* New York: Oxford University Press, 2009.

Wilkins, David E. *Documents of Native American Political Development: 1933 to Present.* New York: Oxford University Press, 2019.

Wilkins, David E. "Internal Tribal Fragmentation: An Examination of a Normative Model of Democratic Decision-Making." *Akwe:kon Journal* 9, no. 3 (Fall 1992): 33–39.

Wilkins, David E. *The Navajo Political Experience.* 4th ed. Lanham, MD: Rowman & Littlefield, 2013.

Wilkins, David E. and Heidi Kiiwetinepinesiik Stark. *American Indian Politics and the American Political System.* 4th ed. Lanham, MD: Rowman & Littlefield Publishers, 2018.

Wilkins, David E. and Shelly Hulse Wilkins, "Blood Quantum: The Mathematics of Ethnocide." In *The Great Vanishing Act: Blood Quantum and the Future of Native Nations,* edited by Kathleen Ratteree and Norbert Hill, 210–227. Golden, CO: Fulcrum Publishing, 2017.

Wilkins, David E. and Sheryl Lightfoot. "Oaths of Office in Tribal Constitutions: Swearing Allegiance, but to Whom?" *American Indian Quarterly* 32, no. 4 (Fall 2008): 389–411.

448 BIBLIOGRAPHY

Williams, Robert F. *The Law of American State Constitutions*. New York: Oxford University Press, 2009.

Woods, Teri Knutsen, Karen Blaine, and Lauri Francisco. "O'odham Himdag as a Source of Strength and Wellness among the Tohono O'odham of Southern Arizona and Northern Sonora, Mexico." *Journal of Sociology and Social Welfare* 29, no. 1 (March 2002): 35–53.

Wright, J. Leitch, Jr. *Creeks and Seminoles: The Destruction and Regeneration of the Muscogulge People*. Lincoln: University of Nebraska Press, 1986.

Wright, J. Leitch, Jr. *William Augustus Bowles: Director General of the Creek Nation*. Athens: University of Georgia Press, 1967.

Wyckoff, Theodore. "The Navajo Nation Tomorrow—51st State, Commonwealth, Or ...?" *American Indian Law Review* 5, no. 2 (1977): 267–297.

Zion, James W. "The Navajo Peacemaker Court: Deference to the Old and Accommodation to the New." *American Indian Law Review* 11 (1987): 89–109.

Zion, James W. "Harmony among the People: Torts and Indian Courts." *Montana Law Review* 45 (1984): 265–279.

Zion, James W. "Traditional Indian Solutions for Victims of Crime." *Australian Journal of Law and Society* 13 (1997): 167–180.

Index

For the benefit of digital users, indexed terms that span two pages (e.g., 52–53) may, on occasion, appear on only one of those pages.
Tables and figures are indicated by *t* and *f* following the page number

AA. *See* Articles of Association (AA)
Aaniin, 334
Aaron Payment v. the Sault Ste. Marie Tribe of Chippewa Indians, 221–22
Abel, Annie H., 81, 90, 93, 94, 104–5
Ablavsky, Gregory, 25–26
aboriginal rights, 344
Aboriginal societies, 37
abortion, 157–58, 370–71
Abourezk, James, 115
Abramoff, Jack, 252
Absentee Shawnee, 62, 80*t*, 108
absentee voting, 140, 243–44
accountability
    Harvard studies and, 10–11, 14
    of leaders by oath-taking, 198–202
    Native elections and, 254
Achomawai/Pit River, 182*t*
Achomawi, 182*t*
Ackerman, Lillian A., 39
Acoma Pueblo, 75, 167*t*
acquisition, 25, 125
activism, 114, 115, 122
Adams, Hank, 82*t*, 96–97, 115, 122
Adams, John Quincy, 88
adaptations, 30, 49, 55–62
administrative, defined as type of state recognition, 161
adoption
    in clans, 36
    of constitutions, 60–61, 163, 371
    of IRA, 249, 257, 377
    of laws, 63
    of 1763 Royal Proclamation Line, 85
    of non-members, 371
adoption proceedings, 369
adultery, 40
African American Freedmen, 230–33, 368–69
African American heritage, 371
African Americans, 1, 60–61, 90, 112, 119, 230–33, 239

African American slaves, 102
African slaves, 52
Afro-Indigenous ancestry, 232–33
Afro-Indigenous persons, 230–31, 371
agreements
    biofuels and bioenergy, 285
    compacts, contracts, or, 264
    consent and, 375–76
    international, 291
    between Native courts and county courts, 327
    not by written word, 300
    oil-tax, 286
    with other Native nations, 298–99
    tax, 266
    treaties and, 53, 234–35, 274–75, 278, 295, 299, 301
    Tribal-State Tax, 266–67
agricultural resources, 284–85
agriculture, 23, 39, 47–48, 77, 107, 282–83
Aguilar, Diana, 169
AI. *See* Articles of Incorporation (AI)
AI/AN. *See* American Indian/Alaska Native (AI/AN)
AILTP. *See* American Indian Lawyer Training Program (AILTP)
Aina, defined, 359
AIPC. *See* All Indian Pueblo Council (AIPC)
air pollution and emissions, 286–87
Akaichak Native Community, 349
Akaichak Native Community et al. *v. Department of Interior*, 349–50
Akaka, Daniel K., 361–62
Akaka bill, 361–62
Akak Native Community, 305–6
Ak-Chin Indian Community, 241–42, 275
Ak-Chin Indian Community Articles of Association, 244
Akee, Randall K. Q., 267, 269–70
Akiachak Limited, 349
Akwesasne Notes, 332–33
Alabama-Coushatta, 182*t*

450 INDEX

Alaska Act, 150, 241–42
Alaska Federation of Natives, 347–48
Alaska Native Act, 163
Alaska Native Brotherhood (ANB), 356
Alaska Native Claims Settlement Act (ANCSA), 2, 270–71, 276–77, 280, 334–35, 347–48, 349, 350–52, 357–58
Alaska Native Corporations (ANCs), 270–71, 276–77, 351, 352
Alaska Native regional and village corporations (ANCs), 2–3
Alaska Natives
  ANCSA and, 347–48, 349, 350–52
  Central Council and, 356
  Collier and, 345–50
  Congress and, 345–50
  courts and, 358
  cultural groupings of, 342
  equality and human rights for, 356
  history of, 343–45
  ICRA and, 317–19
  introduction to, 342
  Kānaka Maoli vs., 342, 359
  Metlakatla and, 357
  Mnuchin and, 2
  Native governing structures in, 352–58
  Native Village of Brevig Mission, 226
  number of, 352–53
  Organic Act and, 344
  Reitmeieu and, 3
  self-determination of, 3
Alaska Native Sisterhood (ANS), 356
Alaska Native Tribes, 161, 348
Alaska Native villages, 317–19
Alaska Statehood Act, 346
Alaska Statutes, 354
Alaska Supreme Court, 350
Alaska v. Native Village of Venetie Tribal Government, 348–49
Alaska villages, 334
Alaxsxaq, defined, 342
Albuquerque Indian School Property, 315–16
Alcatraz occupation, 114
alcohol, 65, 107, 260–61, 327, 357
Aleut, 226, 342, 343
Algonquian, 55–56, 59
Alguacil, defined, 56
Alito, Samuel A., 271, 278–79, 371–72
All Indian Pueblo Council (AIPC), 56
Allegany Indian Reservation, 182t
allegiance
  federal, 202–4
  pledging, 205–6

Allen, Richard, 120
Allen, Ron, 193–95, 194f
alliances
  intergovernmental, 298
  inter-Tribal, 299, 301, 306–7
alternative dispute resolution, 367–68
Alturas Indian Rancheria Constitution, 247–48
Alutiiq, 342
American Civil War, 53, 62–63, 66–67, 102, 107, 231
American expansion, 79–80, 88. See also Euro-American expansion; Western expansion
American Gaming Association, 267
American Indian/Alaska Native (AI/AN), 352–53
American Indian Chicago Conference, 114
American Indian Constitutional Reform and the Rebuilding of Native Nations (Lemont), 6–7
American Indian Economic Development, 235
American Indian Historical Society, 332–33
American Indian Lawyer Training Program (AILTP), 5–6
American Indian Movement, 114, 122
American Indian Policy Review Commission, 114–15, 117, 261–62
American Indian Politics and the American Political System (Wilkins and Stark), 7
American Indian Relivious Freedom Act, 114–15
American Indian Treaties: A Guide to Ratified and Un-Ratified, U.S., State, Foreign, and Intertribal Treaties and Agreements: 1607–1911 (DeJong), 297
American Indian Tribal Governments (O'Brien), 6
American Indian Tribal Law (Fletcher), 7
American Indians, American Justice (Deloria, Jr. and Lytle), 6
American Indians and the Law (Duthu), 83t
American public, 23, 52, 295, 370
American Reinvestment and Recovery Act, 336–37
American Rescue Plan Act, 271–72
American Revolution, 52, 86, 90
Anarchy, 44, 46
Anaya, S. James, 118
ANB. See Alaska Native Brotherhood (ANB)
ancestral traditions, 312
ANCs. See Alaska Native Corporations (ANCs); Alaska Native regional and village corporations (ANCs)
ANCSA. See Alaska Native Claims Settlement Act (ANCSA)

INDEX   451

Anderson, H. Dewey, 44, 64
Angoon, 353–54
animals, 35, 47–48, 234, 291, 306–7, 311, 359
Anishinaabe, 182*t*, 196–98, 203, 289–90, 292, 302–3, 327
Anishinaabe Akii Protocol, 302–3, 306
Anishinaabe bands, 186, 197–98, 203, 289–90
Anishinaabe clan system, 36–37
Anishinaabe nations, 287, 335
Anishinaabe Tribes, 130
Annette Island Reservation, 176*t*, 357–58
Annual Report for 1869 (Parker), 68
Anoatubby, Bill, 232–33
ANS. *See* Alaska Native Sisterhood (ANS)
Anti-Drug Abuse Act of 1986, 359–60
Apache
    attacks by, 56–57
    Fort Sill, 227
    Jicarilla, 78, 176*t*, 335
    Kiowa-Comanche-, 132, 135, 137–38
    leader, 41
    Mescalero, 129–30, 131, 135, 136, 137–38, 139, 176*t*, 320–21, 322
    1929 business committees, 80*t*
    Pueblos *vs.*, 58
    San Carlos, 135, 190–91
    White Mountain, 76, 129, 130, 135, 140–41, 226, 335
    Yavapai-, 176*t*, 182*t*
Apache Menominee, 130
Apache Tribe of Oklahoma, 171
Apēkon Ahkihih, defined, 298–99
Arapahoe
    business committees and, 69, 70
    Cheyenne-, 129, 132, 135, 136, 137–38, 140, 216, 240
    Fowler on, 6, 70
    Northern, 176*t*, 181–85
    Shoshone and, 166, 181–85, 182*t*
Arapahoe Politics, 1851-1978: Symbols in Crisis of Authority (Fowler), 6
Archambault, Dave II, 287, 335–36
Arctic National Wildlife Refuge, 286–87, 351–52
Arctic Village and Native Village of Venetie, 182*t*
Arikara, 74, 300–1
Aristocracy, defined, 162
aristocratic governments, defined, 162
Aristotle, 158, 162, 234
armistice, 297
Armstrong, William, 68
Army Corps of Engineers, 287–88, 290

Arrow, 216
Articles, 180
Articles of Association (AA), 28–29, 164–65, 168, 179–80, 181, 241–42, 246, 257–59, 275, 338
Articles of Confederation, 89, 162
Articles of Incorporation (AI), 164, 240, 259
Arviligjuarmiut, defined, 43–44
Arviso, Tom, Jr., 339–40
Asam, Kuhio, 363
Asian Americans, 160, 360
assaults, 316, 317–19, 325
Assembly of First Nations, 305–6, 309
assimilation, 54, 58, 65, 79–80, 122–23, 124–25, 189–90, 207, 211, 224, 256, 332, 347–48, 357
Assiniboine, 182*t*, 185–86, 187
Assiniboine and Sioux Tribes, 206
Assiniboine Sioux, 71, 76–77, 149, 205–6
assistant chief, 131, 176*t*
Assistant Secretary, 129, 146–47, 349
Associate Justice, 352
Athabascan, 342, 343
Atkin, Edmund, 85
Atkinson Trading Company v. Shirley, 263, 264
Atleo, Clifford Gordon, 8–9
Atsugewi, 182*t*
Attorney General, 220–21, 228, 253, 292, 349–50
attorneys
    judges and, 358
    marijuana and, 291–92
    sovereignty and, 322
Audit, 220
Augustine Band of Cahuilla, 167*t*, 171
Austin, Raymond, 326
authority
    in *Aaron Payment vs. the Sault Ste. Marie Tribe of Chippewa Indians*, 221
    in *Alaska v. Native Village of Venetie Tribal Government*, 348–49
    in *Atkinson Trading Company v. Shirley*, 263
    canes and, 170
    citizenship and, 225, 229
    coercive, 155
    as component of government, 155
    concentrated governmental, 155
    in *Eastern Band of Cherokee v. Lambert*, 220–21
    elections and, 238
    governing, 171, 172*t*
    governmental, 161–62
    Indigenous taxing, 261

452 INDEX

authority (*cont.*)
  interest group, 190
  justice and, 315, 321
  in *Kerr McGee Corporation v. The Navajo Tribe*, 264
  law and, 37–38
  majority rule and, 159
  Mauna Kea Stewardship and Oversight, 365
  political, 26, 33, 159, 170
  Porter and, 373
  in *Shirley v. Morgan*, 217–19
  tribal organizations lack, 135
autocracy, 161–62
  defined, 162
Autonomy, 47, 164, 199, 206–7, 357

B. H., 68
Bad River, 128–29
Bad River Chippewa, 129
Baffin Islanders, 44
Baker, William, 84–85
balance
  American political system based on, 159
  justice and, 312, 326–27
  Native governments and, 159, 193–95, 208
Balmer, J. E., 77
Barbour, James, 82*t*
Bardill, Jessica, 228
Barona Band, 167*t*, 169
Barrett, Amy Coney, 271, 316, 371–72
Barrett, Citizen Potawatomi Nation Business Committee v., 215–16
Barrett, John, Jr., 211, 215
Barrett, Sharon, 220–21
Barry Creek Rancheria, 164
Barsh, Russel L., 41, 82*t*, 117, 118–19, 122, 156, 274
"Basic Memorandum on Drafting of Tribal Constitutions" (Cohen), 144, 145–48, 174–75, 249–50
BAT. *See* Business Activity Tax (BAT)
Batchewana First Nation, 304–5
Bay Mills Indian Community, 179, 266–67, 304–5
Bear, Candace, 173–74
Bear clan, 36–37
Bear River Band, 182*t*
bears, 296, 309
Beaubien, M. B., 68
Beaver Tribe, 163
Bee, Robert, 380
Begay, Manley, 10–11

Begay-Campbell, Sandra, 294
Begaye, Kelsey A., 303
Benhabib, S., 10
Berger, Bethany, 372
Berryhill, Peggy, 339
Bertrand, 68
bias, 73, 128
Bibler, Gregory, 326
Biden, Joe, 98, 271–72, 289–90, 317–19
Biden Administration, 282, 330
big government, 50, 112, 157–58
Big Lagoon Rancheria, 182*t*
Big Pine Paiute Tribe, 182*t*
Bikiss, Daagha'chii, 72
Bill of Rights, 55, 114, 159, 214, 317, 337, 338
Biloxi, 182*t*
bingo, 267
biofuels and bioenergy agreements, 285
Biolsi, Thomas, 6, 26, 141, 150, 259–60
birth, 25, 36
Bishop Paiute Tribe, 182*t*
Bitterroot Salish, 182*t*
BJS. *See* Bureau of Justice Statistics (BJS)
Black Coal (Chief), 181–85
Black Elk (holy man), 300
Black Foot (Chief), 135
Blackfeet, 39, 128–30, 131, 132, 133, 146, 175, 176*t*, 291, 306
blacksmiths, 91
Blessingway Ceremony, 43
Blight, David, 157–58
Blind v. Wilson, 216–17
blood
  Alaska Natives and, 347
  for citizenship, 225–28, 229–30, 232
  full-, 113–14, 373
  half-, 224
  lack of Native, 368–69
  mixed-, 61, 113–14, 206–7, 224, 371, 373
  Native Hawaiians and, 361
  in 1908, 224
  during nineteenth century, 224
  for political organization, 33–34, 47
blood quantum, 186, 223–24, 226, 227, 229–30, 244, 371, 372–73
blood quantum criteria, 224
blood quantum rules, 224–26, 227, 228
blood quantum systems, 371
blood requirement, 226
blood rules, 225–26
blood standard, 227
blood vengeance, 312–13
Blue Lake Rancheria, 182*t*, 294

INDEX 453

Board of Directors, 2–3, 172*t*, 174, 179, 220, 221, 222, 271, 333, 351
Board of Elections, 252–53
Board of Governors, 172*t*, 179
Board of Indian Commissioners, 66–67, 314
Board of Trade's Plan of 1764, 86
Board of Trustees, 172*t*, 179
Boards, establishing, 171–73
Boasberg, James E., 288–89
Bois Forte, 128–29, 130–31, 136, 137–38, 140, 186
Bois Forte Ojibwe, 135
Boldt decision, 378
border crossings, 306
boroughs, 20
Boudinot, Elias, 332
Boudinot, Elias Cornelius, 332
Bourassa, J. N., 68
Bowles, William Augustus, 82*t*, 84, 89, 90–91
boycotts, 114
Boyer (Chief), 91
Boys, 40
Bridgeport Paiute Indian Colon, 181, 182*t*
broadcast media, 334–35
Brown, Joseph Epes, 300
Brown, Margery Hunter, 6, 27, 185–86
Bryant, U.S. v., 328–29
budget cuts, 267
budget matters, 169
budgets, 285–86, 339
Buena Vista Rancheria of Me-Wuk, 167*t*
buffalo
  relationship with, 291, 306
  restoring, 281–82, 306–7
  slaughter of, 291, 306
  survival of, 306
buffalo ranching, 291
buffalo restoration, 291, 306–7
Buffalo Treaty, 306–7
Bulletin, 332
Bureau of Education, 344–45
Bureau of Indian Affairs (BIA)
  Alaska Natives and, 344–45, 350
  citizenship and, 223, 224–25, 235
  dismissed Native cases against, 212
  in 1834, 95–96
  elections and, 240–42
  influence of, 27
  justice and, 316
  Kānaka Maoli and, 363
  leadership and, 212, 216
  loss of land and, 274–75

  modern Native constitutionalism and, 124–25, 131–32, 141–42, 145–46, 147
  Native governments and, 373
  Native identity and, 223–24
  during Native political transitions, 71, 73, 77
  political economics and, 259–60
  renewable energy and, 295
  resources and, 285
  Shoshone and Arapahoe with, 185
  traumas inflicted by, 125
Bureau of Indian Affairs (BIA) annual list, 3
Bureau of Indian Affairs (BIA) Circular, #2565, 72, 73, 76–77
Bureau of Indian Affairs (BIA) policies, 24
Bureau of Indian Affairs (BIA) relocation program, 196
Bureau of Justice Statistics (BJS), 325
Burke, Charles, 72, 73, 78, 127–28, 131–32, 283–84
Burney, Roff v., 229
Burns, M. L., 130–31
Bush Fellowship, 196–97
Bush Jr. Administration, 361–62
Business Activity Tax (BAT), 263–64
Business Committee
  BIA Circular #2565 and, 73–75, 80*t*
  in *Blind v. Wilson*, 216–17
  of Burns Paiute Tribe, 259
  in *Citizen Potawatomi Nation Business Committee v. Barrett*, 215–16
  in Constitution of the Burns Paiute Tribe, 259
  gaming and, 273
  as governing body, 23, 280
  governing systems and, 164–65, 166, 171, 172*t*, 174, 178–79, 186, 187
  loss of land and, 280
  Menominee, 70–71
  modern Native constitutionalism and, 127–29, 140–41
  as Native governing body, 178–79
  Native political transitions and, 65–66, 68–71, 73–75, 76, 78, 79, 80*t*
  of Quapaw, 166
  on reservations, 15
  San Manuel Nation, 273
  Vizenor and, 197–98
  in *Young v. Tribal Grievance Committee*, 213, 214
Business Council, 23, 65–66, 70, 71, 73–74, 128–29, 166, 176*t*, 178–79, 186–87, 195, 262, 283–84
businesses, 2, 3, 23, 153, 255–96
But Mark, 213

454 INDEX

by blood citizens, 232
by blood language, 232
by blood quantum rules, 227
bylaws
  for Blackfeet, 146
  Circular 2565 and, 76–77
  Confederated Tribes of the Chehalis
    Reservation Constitution and, 258
  for Crow, 229
  IRA and, 125, 142, 144, 150–51
  traditional governing councils and, 354
  for women holding office, 139
Byrd, Joe, 339

Cabazon Band of Mission Indians, 164
Cachil Dehe Band of Wintun, 371
Cacique, 170, 249–50
Caddo, 80t, 106–7, 109, 227, 297
Cahto Tribe of Laytonville Rancheria, 164
Cahto Tribe of the Laytonville Rancheria,
    Articles of Association, 258–59
Cahuilla, 182t
  Augustine Band of, 167t, 171
  Los Coyotes Band of, 167t, 169, 182t
  Ramona Band of, 166–68, 167t
Cahuilla Band of Indians, 167t
Calhoun, John C., 82t, 91, 94
Cameron Solar Generation Plant, 294
campaign finance, 252–53
Campo Kumeyaay Nation, 293
canes, 170
cannabis, 292
Canoe Paddlers, 185–86
capitalism, 64–65, 73, 79–80, 189–90,
    280, 295–96
capitalistic system, 29
capitalist market, 8–9
Capitanes de la guerra, defined, 56
Capitan Grande Band of Digueno Mission
    Indians, 167t, 169
Capitan Grande Reservation, 182t
Carcieri v. Salazar, 278, 279
CARES Act. See Coronavirus Aid, Relief, and
    Economic Stimulus (CARES) Act
Caribou, 351–52
Carpenter, Kristen, 281
Carter, Jimmy, 240
Carter, Nick, 170–71, 355
Carter, Rosalynn, 240
Carter Center, 240–41
Carver, Jonathan, 46
Case, David S., 344, 353, 354, 357–58
case studies

election procedures, 241–44
focused on Native governments and
    politics, 6
Fox, 46–47
Indigenous leadership crises, 210–22
Inuit and Yupik Peoples of Alaska, 43–44
modern Native constitutionalism and, 143
Native leader, 193–98
office qualifications, 244–46
recall or removal from office, 246–49
Tohono O'odham, 45–46
traditional, 43–47
traditional offices in Native elections, 249–52
of Tribal Preambular Statements on
    economic orientation, 258–59
casino gaming, 170
casino operations, 273
casinos, 256, 267, 268, 269–70, 272–73, 292–93
Cass County Probation Department, 327
Castro-Huerta, Oklahoma v., 371–72
Catawba Nation, 228, 233, 241–42
Catawba Nation Constitution, 243–44
Catfish, Alex, 74
Catholic priests, 56–57
cattlemen, 111
Cayetano, Rice v., 361–63, 369
Cayuga Nation, 167t, 170, 182t, 298
Cayuse, 182t
CDC. See Centers for Disease Control (CDC)
celestial beings, 359
Celilo Village, 182t
censorship, 337–38, 339
Centennial Accord, 378
Center for Native American Youth, 158
Centers for Disease Control (CDC), 1
Central Algonquians, 37–38
Central Council of the Tlingit and Haida, 182t,
    204–5, 350, 356. See also Tlingit and Haida
    Central Council
ceremonial dances, 314
ceremonies, 300
CERT. See Council of Energy Resource
    Tribes (CERT)
CFR courts. See Code of Federal Regulations
    (CFR) courts
chair, 176t
  first female, 197
  Hopi Tribe, 176t
  Penobscot Nation, 176t
  Pit River Tribes, 176t
chairman
  Allen as, 193
  Archambault as, 335–36

INDEX 455

Assiniboine, 186
authority to call meeting, 131
in *Blind v. Wilson*, 216–17
in Circular No. 3010, 131
in *Citizen Potawatomi Nation Business Committee v. Barrett*, 215
Crow, 135
Faith as, 288
Julius as, 195
MacDonald as, 339
Marquez as, 272–73
Menominee, 70–71
Navajo Nation, 117
Oneida, 129
Pauma Band of Mission Indians, 164–65
Payment as, 221, 222
Ramona Band of Cahuilla Indians, 166–68
Sioux, 186
as term for majority of nations, 129–30
chairmen, 301–2
chairperson, 169, 197–98, 222, 322
chairwoman, 186, 197
Champagne, Duane, 61
Changing Woman, 40
Chapman, first name or initial or title 68, 146–47
Chapters, 73–74, 77, 117
charitable games, 267
Char-Kooska News, 332
charters, 23–24, 142, 152–53, 160, 163, 164, 165–66, 180, 181, 209–10, 240, 275
checks and balances, 150, 160, 174–75, 213, 219–20
Checote, Samuel, 108
Chehalis, 131, 132, 137–38, 140, 181, 182*t*, *See also* Confederated Tribes of the Chehalis Reservation
Chehalis Reservation, 2–3, 131, 181. *See also* Confederated Tribes of the Chehalis Reservation
Chemeheuvi, 149, 181, 182*t*, 227
Cher-ae- Heights Indian Community, 164, 182*t*
Cherokee
  African American Freedmen and, 231–33
  citizenship and, 232, 233
  content analysis and, 206–7
  creating Indigenous state, 85, 89, 90, 93, 94–95, 97–98, 102, 103, 105, 106, 107, 113, 120–21
  with divided powers of governance, 176*t*
  Eastern Band of, 165, 176*t*, 220, 228, 314–15, 340
  in *Eastern Band of Cherokee v. Lambert*, 220

  elections and, 116, 240–41, 253
  having oldest formal constitution, 131–32
  justice and, 312–13, 316
  media in, 332, 339–40
  Native political transitions, 55–56, 60–61, 76–77
  number of citizens, 119
  oaths and, 204
  political organization before contact, 33–34, 41, 42–43
  population of, 119
  separation of power arrangements, 23
  using citizenship, 233
Cherokee Constitution, 60–61
Cherokee legal system, 5–6
Cherokee Nation v. Georgia, 93, 278
Cherokee Nation v. Nash, 232
Cherokee Nation Visit Summit, 120
Cherokee National Council, 231–32
Cherokee National Government, 97
Cherokee Phoenix, The, 61, 332
Cherokee Supreme Court, 232
Cherokee Treaty, 82*t*, 97, 103, 231
Cherokee Treaty of Hopewell, 93
Chetco, 182*t*
Cheyenne, 33–34, 186, 284
Cheyenne and Arapahoe Tribes, 182*t*, 186, 292
Cheyenne-Arapahoe, 129, 132, 135, 136, 137–38, 140–41, 176*t*, 186, 216, 240, 292
Cheyenne-Arapahoe Reservation, 216
Cheyenne River Sioux, 2–3, 4–5, 76–77, 262, 335
Cheyenne River Sioux Constitution, 262
Chicago Warrior, 332
Chickaloon Native Village, 176*t*
Chickasaw, 33–34, 55–56, 60, 61, 76–77, 90, 103–4, 107, 131, 136, 140, 176*t*, 204, 206–7, 229, 232–33, 316, 323, 327, 335, 374, 376
Chickasaw Constitution, 232–33
chief
  elections and, 249–50
  in governing systems, 164
  hereditary, 70–71, 129, 140–41
  leadership and, 214–15, 220–21
  as men, 39
  in modern Native constitutionalism, 129, 135, 140–41
  Native political transitions, 61, 63, 66, 68, 70–71, 76, 78
  Penobscot Nation, 176*t*
  as term for majority of nations, 129–30
  as women, 39
chiefdoms, 312, 359

456 INDEX

Chief Executive Officer, 339–40
chief judge, 372
Chief Justice, 66, 93, 271, 278, 321, 371–72
chiefships, 37
chief system, 130–31
Chiefs Society, 141
chieftainship, 36–37
child abuse, 317–19
child custody, 358, 372
children, 21, 155, 173, 179, 224, 317–19, 369
child welfare, 312
Chimakum, 182t
Chinook, 181, 182t
Chippewa, 128–29, 302. *See also* Anishinaabe
　Bad River, 129
　Red Lake, 129
　Saginaw, 69, 266–67
　Sault-ste. Marie Tribe of, 266–67, 304–5
Chippewa Cree Indians of the Rocky Boys
　Reservation Constitution, 248–49
Choctaw, 33–34, 42–43, 55–56, 60, 61, 76–77,
　78, 82t, 90, 95, 103–4, 106, 111, 176t,
　182t, 206–7, 232–33, 316, 332, 368–69
Choctaw and Chickasaw treaty, 103–4
Choctaw Indian Agency, 78
Choctaw Nation of Oklahoma, 206
Choctaw Treaty, 82t, 97, 103–4
Christian conversion, 357
Christian converts, 59
Christian denominations, 66–67
Christian faith, 313–14
Christian Indians, 59
Christian influence, 59
Christianity, 59, 91, 203
Christianization, 91, 332
Chukchansi Band of Yokuts and
　Monache, 182t
church wardens, 56
CIA. *See* Commissioner of Indian Affairs (CIA)
cigarettes, 264
Circular No. 2565 (Burke), 72, 76–77,
　78, 127–28
Circular No. 3010 (Collier), 127–42
cities
　Alaska Natives and, 342, 353–54
　Natives in, 235–36
Citizen Band of Potawatomi, 69
Citizen Potawatomi, 80t, 210–11, 215
Citizen Potawatomi Indian Council, 215–16
*Citizen Potawatomi Nation Business Committee
　v. Barrett*, 215–16
citizenry, 25
citizens

by blood, 232
defined, 234
in electoral campaigns, 158
granted power to elect, 111
holding membership in nation, 25
justice and, 312, 315, 316, 317
Kānaka Maoli and, 360
member *vs.*, 233
Native citizen and state, 27
Navajo, 117
sharing in Native community, 33
tension between leaders and, 156
citizenship
African Americans and, 230–33
criteria for, 153, 223, 225–28, 229
extension of, 122
forced, 105
intermarriages and, 371
justice and, 317
loss or denial of, 229–30
membership *vs.*, 234, 372
in modern Native governments, 153, 186
multiple, 107
Native identity and, 223–25, 235–37
in Native political transitions, 65, 68
oaths and, 206
sine qua non and, 223
urban life and, 235–37
citizenship status, 234, 239
civilization, 91
Civilization Act of 1819, 278
civil rights, 4, 157–58, 299, 357
civil rights leaders, 198
*Claiming Turtle Mountain's Constitution: The
　History, Legacy, and Future of a Tribal
　Nation's Founding Document* (Richotte,
　Jr.), 6–7
clan-based relationships, 152
clan leader, 250
clan membership, 36, 45
clan mothers, 39, 175, 189
clans, 33–34, 35–37, 45, 47, 61, 152, 200,
　223, 343
clan structures, 60–61
clan system, 36–37, 312–13, 326–27
Clapox, United States v., 314
Clean Water Act, 287–88
Cleveland, Grover, 357
climate change, 21, 256–57, 282–90, 295–96,
　306, 307–8
Clinton, Bill, 378–79
Cloverdale Rancheria of Pomo, 167t
Clow, Richmond L., 6, 27, 185–86

coal, 111–12, 259–60, 281, 282–83, 284, 285–86, 293, 306
coal companies, 283–84
Coal industry, 293
Coalition for Fair Government II v. Lowe, 212–13
coalitions, 298, 311
coal leases, 284
Coal mine, 285–86
Coal terminal, 306
Coast Miwok, 181, 182*t*
Coates, Julia, 231–32
Cobell class action lawsuit and settlement act, 276–77
Cochiti Pueblo, 75, 167*t*
Code of Federal Regulations (CFR) courts, 314–16
codes, 160, 164, 165–66, 180, 181, 240, 263–64
coercion, 154–55
coercive authority, 155
coercive measures, 35
Coffey, Wallace, 301–2
Cohen, Felix S., 6–7, 24, 34, 63, 124–25, 127, 131–32, 141–42, 144–48, 174–75, 200, 223, 225, 249–50, 261, 316–17, 353–54, 355
cohesion, 25, 37, 210, 216–17, 312–14, 326
Cole Memorandum, 292
Collier, John, 24, 124–25, 127–28, 132, 133, 137–38, 141–42, 144, 145–46, 147, 149, 150–51, 165, 174–75, 233–34, 249, 257, 261, 274–75, 334, 345–50
Colonial Entanglement: Constituting a Twenty-First Century Osage Nation (Dennison), 6–7
colonialism, 29, 64, 70, 79–80, 189–90, 256, 313–15, 317, 343
colonial treaties, 300
colonization, 46, 92, 119–20, 210–11, 301, 343, 348
colony, as political idea, 81
Colorado River, 132, 133, 136, 139, 140, 149
Colorado River Agency, 78, 79
Colorado River Indian Reservation, 149
Colorado River Reservation, 181
Colorado River Tribes, 292
Columbus, Christopher, 50
Colville, 39, 78
Colville Indian Agency, 79
Colville Reservation, 181
Comanche, 80*t*, 109, 130, 171, 193, 204–5, 301–2, 371
comity, defined, 212
commerce, 157, 306
commerce clause, 25, 29, 206

Commission on State-Tribal Relations (CSTR), 26–27, 28, 370
Commissioner of Indian Affairs (CIA), 67, 72, 124–25, 134–35, 165, 233–34, 257, 283–84, 314, 334, 344
commissions, 171–73, 241–42, 263–64, 317
Committee on Indian Affairs, 94, 95–96, 124
committees
  business (*see* Business Committee)
  in 1929, 77
communalism, 21
communication technology, 368
communism, 156–57
communist regimes, 337
communities
  under Alaska Statutes, 354
  led by medicine men, 129
  meetings in, 131
  Morse and, 91
  as municipalities, 353–54
  Navajo, 77, 78
  as social units, 343
  using chiefs, 129–30
  without constitutions, 132
community cohesion, 25, 210
community Council, 172*t*, 187, 198
community politics, 157
compacts, 163, 264, 266–67, 277–78, 297, 298, 299
competition, 210, 266, 271, 333
Concow, 182*t*
"Condolence Matrons," 129
confederacies, 298
confederacy, defined, 162
Confederated Peoria, 108
Confederated Salish and Kootenai, 76–77, 149, 181, 182*t*, 203, 275
Confederated States of America, 102
Confederated Tribe of the Warm Springs Reservation, 251
Confederated Tribes and Bands of the Yakama Indian Nation, 182*t*
Confederated Tribes of the Chehalis Reservation, 182*t*, 271, 275–76, 305–6. *See also* Chehalis
Confederated Tribes of the Chehalis Reservation, Yellen v., 4, 270–71, 342, 352
Confederated Tribes of the Chehalis Reservation Constitution, 248
Confederated Tribes of the Chehalis Reservation Constitution and Bylaws, 258
Confederated Tribes of the Colville Reservation, 149, 178, 182*t*

458 INDEX

Confederated Tribes of the Goshute
    Reservation, 181
Confederated Tribes of the Grand Ronde
    Community, 182t, 227, 340
Confederated Tribes of the Umatilla Indian
    Reservation, 179, 182t, 378
Confederated Tribes of the Warm Springs
    Reservation, 182t
Confederated Tribes of the Warm Springs
    Tribe, 31
Confederated Tribes of Umatilla Indian
    Reservation, 182t
Confederated Tribes of Warm Springs, 182t, 378
Congress
    Alaska Natives and, 344–50, 357
    all-Native Territory and, 94, 104–5, 108–
        9, 113
    authority and, 54
    CARES Act in, 2, 3
    Choctaw and Chickasaw treaty and, 104
    consent and, 377
    crimes and, 370–71
    IRA and, 124–25
    Kānaka Maoli and, 361–62
    media and, 334
    Native political transitions in, 54, 58, 63–64,
        66–67, 70
    Organic Act and, 111
    plenary power and, 375
    political incorporation activity in, 82t
Congressional Black Caucus, 232, 371
Congressional Native American Caucus, 270
Congressional Research Service, 334
conscience, 35, 41
Consensus, 45, 47, 155–56, 187–88, 200
consent, 53, 158–59, 171, 185, 240, 283–84, 290,
    343–44, 364, 375–81
conservative
    Natives identifying as, 158
    as political ideology, 156–57
conservative ideology, 156–57
conservative Republicans, 362, 369
conservatives, 157–58, 271, 368–69
Consolidated Appropriation Act, 317–19
Consolidated Chippewa Agency, 128–29, 130–
    31, 136
Consolidated Chippewa Tribe, 186
constables, 91
constitutional sovereigns, 121–22
Constitution of the Assiniboine and Sioux
    Tribes, 205–6
Constitution of the Big Lagoon Rancheria, 262
Constitution of the Burns Paiute Tribe, 259

Constitution of the Makah Indian Tribe, 206
Constitution of the Native Hawaiian
    Nation, 363
Constitution of the Native Village of Brevig
    Mission, 258
constitutions
    adoption of, 60
    Alaska Natives and, 345–46
    amending, 23–24
    BIA Circular #2565 and, 73–74, 76–77
    in *Blind v. Wilson*, 216–17
    checks and balances in, 160
    in *Citizen Potawatomi Nation Business
        Committee v. Barrett*, 215–16
    citizenship and, 225–26, 227, 229, 233
    in *Coalition for Fair Government II v. Lowe*,
        212, 213
    elections and, 241–42
    federal, 23–24, 25, 50, 122, 159, 206, 261
    of Five Civilized Tribes, 60–62
    in government database, 179–80, 181
    Harvard Project and, 13
    Hopi, 262
    Indigenous governance and, 152–53
    Indigenous nations with, 77
    IRA (*see* Indian Reorganization Act (IRA)
        constitutions)
    justice and, 315, 316, 321
    Ka Lahui Hawaii, 164
    Kānaka Maoli, 363–64
    kinship-based, 152–53
    loss of land and, 275
    Makah, 135
    media and, 337, 338, 340
    Menominee, 70–71
    minority rights and, 159
    Native nations with formal, 163–64
    Navajo, 165
    number of Native nations with formal, 50,
        163–64, 202
    oaths of office in, 198–99, 201–2
    Osage, 134–35
    preambles of, 257–58
    Red Lake, 130–31
    to reflect distrust, 112
    shaping character, 23
    in *Shirley v. Morgan*, 217
    Sioux and Assiniboine adopting, 186
    state, 159
    study of, 6–7
    taxes and, 262
    Traditional, 163
    Tribal Council and, 23, 76

INDEX   459

for White Earth band, 198
written, 13, 60, 76–77
in *Young v. Tribal Grievance Committee*, 213
consultation, consent *vs.*, 375–76, 377–79
contracts
court systems on Native lands, 312
to raise money, 264
convention delegates, 112
Cooley, D. N., 67
Coos, 181
Coquille Indian Tribe, 323
Corbine, Sheila, 228
Cornell, Stephen, 7, 8, 9, 10–12, 14
Coronavirus, Relief, and Economic Security Act
(CARES Act), 270–71, 352
Coronavirus Aid, Relief, and Economic
Stimulus (CARES) Act, 2–3
Coronavirus (COVID-19), 1–3, 4–5, 21, 22,
166–68, 169, 185, 236, 256, 260, 267, 268–
70, 271–73
Coronavirus Relief Fund, 2, 258, 335, 352
corporate income taxes, 260–61
corporate ownership, 351–52
corporations
AA and, 164
Alaska Native, 270–71, 276–77, 351, 352
Alaska Native regional and village, 2–3
Alaska Natives and, 342, 350–51, 352
ANCSA and, 347–49, 350–52
economic profit, 353
elections and, 253
Enbridge, 282
energy, 347
Indigenous state and, 111, 112, 113–14, 145
IRA and, 125
Native, 351–52
non-profit development and service, 353
regional, 347, 351, 352
tax, 264
corruption, 13, 189, 196–97
Cosper, Sterling, 331
*Cotton Petroleum Corporation v. New
Mexico*, 286
council member, 47, 103, 133, 137–38, 169, 170,
176*t*, 195, 196–97, 198, 222, 331, 358
councilmen, 70, 129–30, 135, 169
Council of Chiefs, 172*t*, 373
Council of Energy Resource Tribes
(CERT), 285
Council of Trustees, 172*t*
Council Speaker, 330–31
counterraids, 42–43
county courts, 327

court
CFR, 314–16
county, 327
District, 214, 215–18, 288, 289–90, 327
drug, 327
High, 214, 276, 279, 286, 361, 371–72
Native, 312, 315–16, 317–19, 321, 327, 328–
29, 358, 371–72
Supreme (*see* Supreme Court)
Tribal (*see* Tribal courts)
wellness, 327
Court of Appeals, 327
court rulings, Native land lost by, 274
court systems, 312, 314–15, 316, 317, 318*f*, 328,
358, 372
Courts of Indian Offenses, 314
Covelo Indian Community, 182*t*
COVID-19. *See* Coronavirus (COVID-19)
Cow Creek Band of Umpqua, 179
Cowlitz, 181, 182*t*, 227
crab, 290–91
Crandall, Maurice, 57
Crane clan, 36–37
Crazy Horse (Lakota leader), 41, 191
Creek, 33–34, 42–43, 55–56, 60, 62, 76–77, 82*t*,
85, 89–90, 94–95, 107, 108, 111–12, 206–
7, 226, 332, 368–69. *See also* Muscogee
(Creek)
Creek Army, 90
crime rates, 308
crimes, 169, 246, 276, 286, 291–92, 316, 317–
19, 325
criminal misfeasance, 312
criminals, 107, 312–13
"Criticisms of Wisconsin Oneida Constitution"
(Cohen), 147
Cross, Ray, 286
Crow, 33–34, 41, 71, 74, 76–77, 78, 129,
132, 135, 137–38, 163, 176*t*, 226, 283,
284, 285–86
Crow Dog, Ex Parte, 50, 53
CSTR. *See* Commission on State-Tribal
Relations (CSTR)
culpability, 38
cultural advisor, 327
cultural identity
confusion in, 223
Natives from non-Natives, 281
cultural issues, 281
cultural orientation, 372–73
cultural practices, 307
cultural properties, 306
Cultural protection, 358

460 INDEX

Cultural renewal, 268–69
Cultural resources, 173, 290
Cultural systems, 25, 27, 60, 61, 210
Cultural traditions, 38, 55, 124, 170, 282–83, 311
culture
 BIA Circular #2565 and, 73
 bias against, 128
 elections and, 249
 importance of, 7, 14
 international diplomacy and, 311
 law in, 37, 38
 Native governments and, 255, 369, 370
 political/spiritual world and, 48
 political transitions and, 51
 punishment in, 38
 role of, 368
 shared, 33
 women in, 40
Cupeno, 182*t*
Curtis, Charles, 105–6
Curtis Act, 61, 62, 105–6, 111, 131–32
Custer Died for Your Sins (Deloria, Jr.), 190, 191–92
Customary law, 190
customs
 culture and, 368
 European, 39
 moieties and, 35
 Pueblo, 56–57, 75
 Radin and, 369
 traditions and, 59, 166–71, 167*t*, 210, 217, 305–6, 326, 354, 355
customs district, 344

Daiker, Fred H., 141–42, 144
Dakota, 40–41, 64
Dakota Access Pipeline (DAPL), 286–89, 305, 335–36
Dakota Access v. Standing Rock Sioux Tribe, 288–89
D'Amico, Elizabeth, 236
dances, 314
DAPL. *See* Dakota Access Pipeline (DAPL)
Dawes Rolls of 1906, 232–33
deaths, 1, 286
Declaration of Independence, 159, 160
Declaration of Peace between the Comanche Nation and the Ute Nation, 301–2
Declaration on the Exercise of Inherent Sovereignty and Cooperation, 307
Deer, Sarah, 6–7, 40, 234
Deganawida, 189

DeJong, David H., 297
Delaware, 66, 80*t*, 81–84, 82*t*, 85, 92, 93, 106, 116, 297
Deloria, Ella, 40–41
Deloria, Philip S., 115, 255, 370
Deloria, Vine, Jr., 6, 32, 34, 42, 69, 93, 115, 122, 144, 188, 190, 191–92, 193, 281, 290, 297, 313, 318*f*
DeMain, Paul, 333
DeMallie, Raymond J., 297
democracy
 consent and, 375–76
 defined, 158–59, 161–62
 elections and, 240
 governmental authority and, 161–62
 ideals of, 158–60
 indirect, 158–59
 as most viable form of government, 162
 Native nations critical of, 55
 Navajo, 190
 participatory, 219
 representative, 158–59
 sovereignty and, 55
democracy deficit, 189
democratic governments
 defined, 162
 key features of, 174, 240
Democratic Socialists, 158
Democrats, 112, 158, 238, 252, 254, 270, 368–69
Democrat Socialist, 238
demographic data, about Kānaka Maoli, 360
demonstrations, 114
Denezpi, Merle, 316
Denezpi v. United States, 316
Dennison, Jean, 6–7
Department of Agriculture, 292
Department of Commerce, 289–90
Department of Corrections, 327
Department of Energy, 285, 293, 294
Department of Health, 287
Department of Housing and Urban Development, 29
Department of Indian Affairs, 63, 95–96
Department of Interior, Akaichak Native Community et al. *v.*, 349–50
Department of Justice, 29, 287, 291–93, 318*f*, 325, 361
Department of the Interior, 3, 29, 51–52, 62, 63–64, 69, 72, 76, 124, 160–61, 163, 170, 259–60, 277, 279, 284, 345, 349, 350, 361, 362–63. *See also* Interior Department
dependent communities, 181
depopulation, 208

INDEX 461

Depp, Johnny, 371
Deputy, 82*t*, 93, 105
Deputy Chief, 240
descent
  citizenship and, 225–28
  clans and, 37
  lineal, 186–87
DiCaprio, Leonardo, 290
Dickeson, Alina, 236
dictatorship
  defined, 162
  military, 238
digital media, 340
dignity, 370–71
Diné, 1–2, 39, 40, 41, 42–43, 155, 217, 219–20,
  264, 284, 326, 372. *See also* Navajo
Dine bibee haz'anii, 218
diplomatic accords, 122, 291, 298, 299
disabilities, 370–71
discrimination, 231–32, 330, 371
discriminatory practices, 371
diseases, 21–22, 65, 79–80, 208
displacement, 65
dispute resolution, 367–68
dispute resolution processes, 8–9
Dispute Resolution System, 327
District Court, 214, 215–18, 288, 289–90, 327
diversification, 373
diversity
  in Alaska Natives, 350, 353
  as central factor, 368
  in governing bodies, 161
  governmental, 375, 380–81
  Indigenous statehood and, 119
  justice and, 319
  political, 33–35, 171
divided powers of governance, 172*t*, 174–
  78, 176*t*
DNA testing, 225–28
*Dobbs v. Jackson Women's Health
  Organization*, 370–71
doctrine of discovery, 24, 307, 343–44
*Documents of American Indian Diplomacy:
  Treaties, Agreements, and Conventions,
  1775-1979* (Deloria and DeMallie), 297
Dodge, Henry Chee, 72
Doerfler, Jill, 6–7, 186–87
*Dollar General v. Mississippi Band of
  Choctaw*, 328–29
domestic arts, 107
domestic violence, 325, 328–29, 358
Donner, William, 76
Dothliuk, 182*t*

double jeopardy, 316
Douglas Native Village of the Tlingit
  Nation, 305–6
Dowling, Christina, 8
Downing, Lewis, 102–3
Doyle, Jim, 289
Dozier, Edward P., 35–36, 56–57, 208, 209
Dragging Canoe (Chief), 121
drilling, 283–84, 286–87, 307–8, 351–52
Driver, Harold, 33–34, 43
drug courts, 327
drug-related offenses, 327
drug use and abuse, 292
Dry Creek Rancheria Articles of
  Association, 246
Dry Creek Rancheria Band of Pomo, 164
Dudas, Henry, 82*t*, 87
dues, 153
Duke, David, 119–20
Duncan, William, 357
Dunsmore (Lord), 89
Duthu, N. Bruce, 82*t*
Duwamish, 181, 182*t*

earthquakes, 282
Eastern Band of Cherokee, 165, 176*t*, 220, 228,
  314–15, 340
Eastern Band of Cherokee v. Lambert, 220–21
Eastern Shawnee, 108, 128–29, 132, 137–38
Eastern Shoshone of the Wind River
  Reservation, 176*t*, 181–85
economic environment, 39
economic issues, 157–58, 281
economic profit corporations, 353
economics
  Grant Administration and, 67
  natural, 290–93
  political (*see* political economics)
economic vitality, 2, 195, 257–58
education
  assimilation and, 224
  conservatives on, 157–58
  economic vitality and, 257
  federal programs focusing on, 345
  gaming and, 268–69
  modern Native constitutionalism and, 124
  providing, 154–55
  success and, 13
  through Native agencies, 367–68
  voting and, 241
educational attainment, 372–73
educational curriculum, 120
educational systems, 119

462 INDEX

education families, 91
Edward the Confessor (King), 200
Eells, Walter Crosby, 44
Egalitarianism, 220
Egan, Metlakatla v., 357–58
1887 General Allotment Act, 274
1851 Fort Laramie Treaty, 287
1892 Constitution, 70
1834 Non-Intercourse Act, 63
1868 Fort Laramie Treaty, 287
1867 Treaty of Cession, 344
1866 Annual Report, 67
1866 treaties, 231–32
1830 Choctaw Treaty, 97
1834 Trade and Intercourse Act, 57
Eisenhower, Dwight, 377
elders
    before contact, 45
    governance and, 176*t*, 179–87
    leadership and, 190
Elders Council, 172*t*
Elected Council, 172*t*, 179
Election Board, 215–16, 241–42
Election commissions, 241–42
election procedures, 241–44
election process, 164–65
elections
    Alaska Natives and, 353–54
    Codes and, 165
    defined, 238
    free and fair, 1
    General Councils and, 174
    IRA, 148–50
    justice and, 312, 317, 321
    media and, 339
    Native (*see* Native elections)
    in politics (*see* electoral politics)
    presidential, 124, 158, 160
    Tribal citizens controlling, 118–19, 130, 188
    2020 presidential, 158
    types of, 238
    women and, 78
electoral campaigns, 158
electoral politics
    case studies for (*see* case studies)
    election procedures in, 241–44
    introduction to, 238–40
    Native elections in (*see* Native elections)
    office qualifications for, 244–46
    recall or removal from office in, 246–49
    traditional offices in Native elections
        in, 249–52
electricity, 283, 293

Eliot, John, 59
Elk Valley Rancheria, 182*t*
Ellis, C. L., 134–35
embarrassment, to maintain order, 35
employment, 171–73
Employment Dispute Tribunal, 327
employment landscape, 256
employment opportunities, 256–57, 351
employment source, 268–69
Enbridge Corporation, 282
Enbridge Energy, 289
Enbridge Line 3, 289–90, 308, 335
Enbridge Northern Gateway, 308
encounter era, 25, 46, 50–51
Endangered Species Act, 309, 310
endangered species list, 309
endangered species protections, 309
energy
    renewable, 293–95
    solar, 283
    wind, 283, 293, 294
energy companies, 71–72, 285–86
energy contracts, 285
energy corporations, 347
energy development, 282–90
energy resources, 259–60, 283, 285
Energy Transfer Partners, 287
Engels, Friedrich, 156–57
environment, 157, 286–87
    economic, 39
    global warming gases and, 283
    Haaland and, 290
    liberals and, 157
    Native peoples' bonds with, 47–48
    sovereignty and, 48
    Trump and, 286–87
environmental degradation, 281–82, 284–85
environmental health, 169
environmental modifications, 286–87
environmental problems, 21
environmental regulations, 168, 358
equality, 25, 154–55, 159, 356, 380–81
eradication, assimilation and, 122–23
Erdrich, Louise, 289
Eskimos, 226, 345
estate and inheritance taxes, 260–61
ethical matters, 312
ethics violations, 190
ethnic groups, 1, 119, 136, 158, 181, 224, 261,
    295, 369. *See also* racial-ethnic groups;
    racial groups
ethnicity, 371–72
ethnic status, 369. *See also* racial-ethnic status

INDEX   463

ethnocentric discourse, 53
ethnocentric/racist assumptions, 52
ethnocentrism, 368–69
ethnocidal policies, 208
ethnological data, 223–24
Ettawageshik, Frank, 306
Euro-American expansion, 51–52. *See also*
    American expansion; Western expansion
European customs, 39
Evans, Laura E., 7, 29, 368
Everett, Clair, 74
excise taxes, 260–61, 263–64
Executive, defined as type of state
    recognition, 161
Executive Board, 172*t*, 179, 186
Executive Committee, 172*t*, 173–74, 179,
    186, 197–98
Executive Councils, 172*t*, 179
Executive Director, 3, 197, 222, 334
executive officers, 215–16
executive orders, 131, 161, 165–66, 274, 277,
    278, 303
Exit, defined, 122
expansion
    American, 79–80, 88
    conservatives and, 157–58
    Euro-American, 51–52
    of Native judicial systems, 6
    sovereignty and, 62–65
    states and, 51–52
    Treaty Alliance Against Tar Sands, 307–8
    of U.S., 53
    Western, 62–65, 67
Ex Parte *Crow Dog*, 50, 53
Exploring Alternatives to the "Consultation or
    Consent" Paradigm (Searle), 378–79

Facebook, 335, 337
factionalism, 135, 208–10, 211, 357, 372–73. *See*
    also factions; segmentation
factions. *See also* segmentation
    defined, 209
    existence of, 209–10
    of political and legal pluralism, 51–52
Faith, Mike, 288
families
    in citizenship and membership, 223, 229–30
    communities composed of, 343, 373
family law, 312
family unit, 39, 43–44, 47
Farm Chapters, 73–74, 77
farmers, 91, 310
farm improvement associations, 77

farming, 77
Farver, Peru, 129
FCT. *See* Five Civilized Tribes (FCT)
feasts, 314
federal allegiance, 202–4
federal coercion, 314–16
federal constitution, 23–24, 25, 50, 122, 159,
    206, 261
federal contexts, for international diplomacy,
    298–300
federal government
    Alaska Natives and, 345, 346, 347, 354, 356
    amendments and, 337–38
    Article VI of Constitution and, 53
    assimilation by, 332
    business committee concept and, 68
    citizenship and, 223–24, 228, 230–31, 236–
        37, 239
    communication networks and, 337
    consent and, 375–76
    consultation and, 376, 378, 379
    COVID-19 and, 1
    1834 Non-Intercourse Act and, 63
    fossil fuel pollution and, 290
    governing authority and, 71–72
    Indian reservation program and, 54
    Indigenous land taken by, 274
    justice and, 316
    Kānaka Maoli and, 359–60, 361–63, 368
    loss of land and, 277, 278, 279, 280
    media and, 337
    Native government and, 368
    Native nations, state, and, 20–30, 367, 368
    political economics and, 257–58
    Pueblos and, 57, 58
    renewable energy and, 294
    sovereignty and, 51, 61
    taxes and, 260–61, 262–63, 270
    treaty federalism and, 117
federal Indian policy, 124, 223, 235–36, 378–79
federalism, 52, 53, 54–55, 84, 117, 121–22, 145
federalism paradigm, 52, 53, 54–55
Federalist Papers, The (Hamilton, Madison,
    Jay), 209
federal land confiscations, 274
federal plenary power, 24, 114, 207
federal/state deference, 205–6
Federated Indians of the Graton Rancheria, 182*t*
Federated Indians of the Graton
    Reservation, 181
Federated Tribes of Graton, 233
fees, 153
Felmley, Jennifer Weldon, 29, 374

464 INDEX

female inmates, 325
Fenton, William N., 209
Field, Michael B., 318f
Fifth Amendment, 346
Finance Director, 197
financial status, 372–73
Fire and the Spirits: Cherokee Law from Clan to Court (Strickland), 5–6
Fire Keeper Casino, 273
1st Amendment, 333–34, 337. *See also* free press
fiscales, defined, 56
fish and wildlife management, 367–68
fish clan, 36–37
Fish Wars, 378
Fisher, Reginald, 58–59
fisheries, 282–83
fishing, 288, 302, 344, 346, 357–58
fishing rights, 114, 275–76, 347, 350–51
Five Civilized Tribes (FCT), 55–56, 60–62, 64, 76–77, 82t, 102, 103–4, 105–7, 108, 109, 111–12, 120, 131–32, 189, 224, 231–32, 280, 298–99, 314–15, 371
Flandreau Santee Sioux Tribe, 264
Flandreau Santee Sioux Tribe, Noem v., 264
Flathead, 71, 74, 149, 203
Flathead Indian Reservation, 182t, 275
Flathead Reservation, 203
Fletcher, Matthew L. M., 7
Flies Away, John Thomas, 372
Floyd, George, 230–31
Floyd, James, 331
followers, leaders and, 48
followership, defined, 222
Fond du Lac, 130–31, 135, 137–38, 140, 186, 289, 334
Fonda, Jane, 290
food production, 35
foreign businesses, 153
Fort Apache Indian Agency, 76
Fort Belknap, 149, 182t, 187
Fort Belknap Indian Community, 292
Fort Belknap Reservation, 149, 187
Fort Berthold, 74, 78, 80t
Fort Berthold Indian Reservation, 182t
Fort Berthold Reservation, 227
Fort Bidwell, 78, 130, 131, 135, 136, 139, 140
Fort Hall, 76, 78, 131, 132, 133, 136, 137–38, 140
Fort Independence Indian Community, 164, 182t
Fort McDermitt, 130, 135, 182t
Fort McDermitt Paiute and Shoshone Tribe, 320
Fort McDermitt Paiute and Shoshone Tribe Constitution, 245
Fort McDermitt Paiute-Shoshone, 374

Fort McDowell, 130
Fort McDowell Yavapai Nation, 324
Fort Peck Reservation, 182t, 185–86, 206
Fort Sill Apache, 227
Fort Sumner, 71–72
Fort Totten, 135, 136, 137–38, 139
Fort Totten Agency, 77
fossil fuel companies, 308
fossil fuel industry, 370–71
fossil fuel pipeline, 305
fossil fuel pollution, 290
Fowler, Loretta, 6, 70, 140–41, 181–85
Fox, 33–34, 37–38, 41, 42–43, 46–47, 80t, 109, 130
fracking, 286–87, 307–8
fracking processes, 282
Frazier, Harold, 5
free press, 330–31, 333–34, 337–41
Free Republic of Frankland, 89
Freedmen of the Cherokee Nation, 232
Freedmen of the FCT, 371
Freedom of Information Act, 338
French Revolution, 156
Friends of the American Indian, 64–65
fuel excise tax, 263–64
full-blood, 113–14, 373
fundamental law, 218, 219–20

Gadsden Purchase, 62–63
gambling, 210, 267, 357
gambling operations, 260
gaming, 170, 171–73, 264, 267–73, 312, 317, 340–41
gaming enterprises, 268
gaming facilities, 256
gaming jurisdiction, 361–62
gaming operations, 2, 165, 260, 273, 368
gaming revenues, 252, 267, 268f, 268–69, 269f, 274–75, 277, 340–41
Gandhi, Mahatma, 198
GAO. *See* General Accounting Office (GAO)
Garden River First Nation, 304–5
Gardner, Booth, 378
gas, 111–12, 259–60, 282–83, 284, 286
gas companies, 72, 111, 283–84
gas reserves, 285
gathering, 302
Gayanashagowa, 170, 298. *See also* Great Law of Peace
GCPC. *See* General Council Planning Committee (GCPC)
gender
    as challenge in government, 372–73
    women and, 48

INDEX 465

gender dynamics, 78
gender roles, 39–40
General Accounting Office (GAO), 351
General Allotment Act, 69, 280
General Council
  Assiniboine and Sioux, 186
  Business Council and, 166
  Capitan Grande Band of Digueno Mission
    Indians, 169
  Choctaw and Chickasaw treaty and, 104
  Crow, 71, 176t
  as data in Indian Country, 73–74
  defined, 23, 173–74
  FCT, 82t, 103–4
  as governing body, 164–65
  Ho-Chunk, 212–13, 282
  Kiowa Tribe, 186
  leadership and, 190, 212–13, 282
  Los Coyotes Band of Cahuilla and Cupeno
    Indians, 169
  in Muskogee County, 108
  as Native governing arrangement, 65–66
  Native nations with, 129, 158
  Navajo, 71–72
  number of, 172t
  Okmulgee Constitution and, 109
  Pauma Band of Mission Indians, 164–65
  Penobscot Nation, 176t
  Seminole, 176t
  Skull Valley Band of Goshute, 173–74
  Tribal Council and, 229
  Western Territory Bill and, 96, 103
  Wilton Rancheria, 176t
General Council arrangement, 23
General Council meeting, 327
General Council Planning Committee
  (GCPC), 213
General Council Resolutions, 173–74
genocidal policies, 208
George III (King), 85–86
George-Kanentiio, Douglas, 373
Georgia, Cherokee Nation v., 93, 278
Georgia, Worcester v., 53
Geronimo (Apache leader), 191
Giago, Tim, 333
Gila River, 76, 176t
Gila River Indian Community
  Constitution, 244–45
Girls, 40, 325, 330, 370–71
Glenn, James L., 129
Glover, Danny, 290
Goldberg-Hiller, Jonathan, 359
Goldtooth, Dallas, 336

Gomez, John, Jr., 166–68
Goodnews Bay Village, 163
Goodyear-Ka'ōpua, Noelani, 360
Gorsuch, Neil, 271, 276
Gourevitch, Peter A., 255
Gover, Kirsty, 224–26, 227, 228
governance
  divided powers of, 174–78, 176t
  dual system of, 380
governing authority, 71–72, 171, 172t,
  186, 367–68
Governing Board, 172t
governing bodies, 2, 14, 20, 30, 111, 129, 130–
  31, 153, 161, 165–66, 259–60, 368. *See also*
  Native governing bodies
governing committee, 132, 172t
Governing Council, 132, 172t, 179, 213–15, 298,
  342, 354–55
Governing documents
  AA as, 164–65
  charters as, 165–66
  codes as, 165–66
  customs as, 166–71
  governing resolutions as, 165–66
  other governing bodies as, 166
  traditions as, 166–71
governing officials, 238, 284–85, 370
Governing Resolutions, 164, 165–66, 240, 338
governing systems
  consensus in, 187–88
  democracy in, 158–60
  elders in, 179–87
  governance in, 179–87
  governing bodies in (*see* governing bodies)
  Indigenous governing organizations
    in, 160–61
  introduction to, 152–53
  modern Native governments as, 153–54
  multinational Native communities in, 181–
    87, 182t
  Native governing bodies in (*see* Native
    governing bodies)
  Native governments with other forms of
    governing documents in (*see* governing
    documents)
  Native nations with formal constitutions
    in, 163–64
  nature of government in, 154–56
  political organizations in, 161–62
  Robert's Rules of Order in, 187–88
  role of ideology in, 156–58
  role of politics in, 156–58
governing units, 20–21

466 INDEX

government
  Alaska Natives and, 353–54
  aristocracy as, 162
  aristocratic, 162
  authority and, 161–62
  autocracy as, 162
  BIA Circular #2565 and, 73–74
  bias against, 128
  big, 50, 112, 157–58
  categories of, 162
  citizenship and, 223
  components of, 155
  confederacy as, 162
  conservatives view of, 157–58
  consultation and, 379
  defined, 20, 154–55
  democracy as (*see* democracy)
  democratic (*see* democratic governments)
  dictatorship as, 162
  difference betweeen people and, 155
  establishment of, 109
  federal (*see* Federal government)
  functions of, 161
  gender roles in, 39–40
  Hawaiian, 359
  Indigenous (*see* Indigenous/Native governments)
  individualism and, 159–60
  IRA, 342, 354, 355
  law in, 38
  local, 2, 4–5, 77, 117, 153, 268, 270, 271–72, 279–80, 299, 353–54, 376
  media and (*see* media)
  military regimes as, 162
  modern Native political systems and, 153
  monarchical, 162
  monarchy as, 162
  Native (*see* Indigenous/Native governments)
  nature of, 154–56
  Navajo, 165
  number of, 20
  oligarchy as, 162
  power and, 155, 156
  purposes of, 154–55
  self-, 115–16, 125, 144, 145, 212, 223, 258, 299, 350–51
  special district, 20
  state (*see* state government)
  structure of, 161
  territorial, 82t, 84, 103–4, 108–9
  theocracy as, 162
  T.O., 45
  town, 62
governmental diversity, 375
governmental traditions, 51
Governor
  among Tewa people, 56
  Anoatubby as, 232–33
  Board of, 172t, 179
  Chickasaw salary for, 131
  in 1848, 82t
  in 1866 treaties, 108–9
  Gardner as, 378
  Haskell as, 113
  Keating as, 120
  Lieutenant, 56, 170, 176t
  Locke as, 378
  Noem as, 264
  Organic Act and, 111
  Passamaquoddy Tribe, 176t
  Pueblo, 170, 176t
  removing, 246
  Smith as, 120
  State of Frankland and, 89
  Walker as, 349–50
  Western Territory Bill and, 96
Grand Council, 82t, 107, 170, 220–21
Grand June Council of 1843, 107
Grand Portage Band, 130–31, 186
Grand Ronde, 128–29, 133, 135, 136
Grand Ronde Community, 181
Grand Ronde Indian Legislature, 135
Grand Traverse Band of Ottawa and Chippewa, 182t, 266–67, 302
granite, 111–12
Grant, Ulysses S., 66–67, 82t, 104–5, 314
Great Lakes Indian Fish and Wildlife Service Commission, 302
Great Lakes Tribes, 302
Great Law of Peace, 164n, 170, 189, 201, 206–7, 298
Great Pueblo Revolt, 170
Great Society and War on Poverty programs, 332–33
Great State of Sequoyah Commission, 120
greenhouse emissions, 293
Green New Deal, 290
Grievance Committee, 213, 214, 215–16
Grindstone Indian Rancheria of Wintun-Wailaki Indians, 182t
Grint, Keith, 40–41, 192, 193, 222
grizzly bear population, 281–82
grizzly bears, 296, 309
grizzly Treaty, 309, 310
gross gaming revenue (GGR), 268f, 268

INDEX 467

Gros Ventre, 74, 76–77, 149, 182*t*, 187
Guss, Mary E., 6–7, 234
Gwich'in Athabascans, 351–52

H. R. 2687, 105
H. R. 3435, 105
H. R. 7922, 105
Haaland, Deb, 232–33, 270, 290, 370–71
Habematolel Pomo of Upper Lake, 228
Halbritter, Ray, 167*f*, 170
Haldimand, Frederick, 82*t*, 87
half-blood, 224
halibut, 290–91
Hamilton, Alexander, 209
Hamilton, Joseph D., 166–68
Handbook of Federal Indian Law (Cohen), 174
Hannah, 353–54
Hannahville Indian Community, 266–67
Harvaqtôrmiut, 43–44
Harvard Project on American Indian Economic
    Development (HPAIED), 7–14, 235, 267
harvesting, 368–69
Haskell, Charles N., 113
hatchery, 290–91
Hathaway, Glover Gillette, 86, 88
Haudenosaunee, 162, 170, 290–91, 298
Haudenosaunee Confederacy, 373
Haudenosaunee (Iroquois), 33–34
Haudenosaunee (Iroquois) Confederacy, 122
Havasupai, 140–41
Hawai'i v. Office of Hawaiian Affairs, 362
Hawaiian Government, 359
Hawaiian Native community, 14
Hawaiian natives, 359–60, 361, 362–63,
    364–65. *See also* Kānaka Maoli; Native
    Hawaiians
Hawkins, Benjamin, 90–91
Hayehwatha, 189
headmen, 129, 135, 140, 141, 192, 200, 249–50
healers, 39
healthcare, 1, 23, 138, 157, 193, 236, 268–69,
    270, 367–68, 373
Health Department, 330–31
Healy Lake Village, 187
HEARTH Act. *See* Helping Expedite and
    Advance Responsible Tribal Home
    Ownership (HEARTH) Act
Heirship rights, 276–77
Helping Expedite and Advance Responsible
    Tribal Home Ownership (HEARTH)
    Act, 295
Hembree, Todd, 253
hemp, 291, 292, 293

Henderson, James Youngblood, 82*t*, 117, 118–
    19, 122
Henson, Eric C., 267
hereditary chiefs, 70–71, 129, 140–41
hereditary system, 130
HEREDITY, 238
herring, 290–91
High Court, 214, 276, 279, 286, 361, 371–72
Hill, W. W., 42–43
Hilton, Carol Anne, 295–96
Himdag, defined, 45
historic traditions, 290–91
Hitatsu, 227
Hitchcock, Ethan, 76
Hitchcock, Lone Wolf v., 375
Hitler, Adolph, 162
Hobbes, Thomas, 32
Ho-Chunk, 130, 131, 132, 137–38, 140, 212,
    213, 228, 282
Hodge, Frederick, 37
Hoebel, E. Adamson, 326
Hogan, Thomas, 232
Hoh, 181, 182*t*, 305–6
Hohokam Indians, 45
Holm, Tom, 113–14, 120, 179–80
homeland, spiritual connection to, 47–48
homesteaders, 111
homesteading, 274
Hoonah Indian Association Tribal
    Administrator, 358
Hoopa Valley, 163, 204–5
Hoover, Herbert, 105–6
Hopi, 117, 131, 132, 136, 137–38, 140–41, 149,
    162, 166, 176*t*, 181, 182*t*, 191–92, 262,
    284, 303
Hopi Agency, 77, 78
Hopi Constitution, 262
Hoskin, Chuck, Jr., 98
Hotel occupancy tax, 263–64
House Caucus, 118
House Committee on Financial Services, 232
House Committee on Indian Affairs, 95–96
House of Kings, 62
House of Representatives, 94, 105, 111, 118
House of Warriors, 62
House Report 474, 94–95
housing, 21–22, 23, 171–73, 196, 368, 370–71
housing and education specialists, 327
Housing and Urban Development
    funds, 330–31
Housing and Urban Development program, 196
Houska, Tara, 290
Hozho, defined, 326–27

468 INDEX

HPAIED. *See* Harvard Project on American
    Indian Economic Development (HPAIED)
Hualapai, 128–29, 130, 132, 136, 140, 372
Huhndorf, Roy M., 352
Huhndorf, Shari M., 352
human behavior, 13, 50–51, 210–11
human rights, 4, 52, 157, 240, 299, 356
human trafficking, 370–71
Hunkapi, 300
Hunkpapa and Sihasapa of Lakota Oyate, 182*t*
Hunkpatina Dakota, 182*t*
Hunter, John G., 77
hunters, 310
hunting, 44, 288, 302, 344, 346, 368–69
hunting permits, 310
hunting rights, 275–76, 347, 350–51
Hupa, 182*t*
Hydaburg, 353–54

Ickes, Harold, 146, 147
ICRA. *See* Indian Civil Rights Act (ICRA)
ICT. See Indian Country Today (ICT)
ICWA. *See* Indian Child Welfare Act (ICWA)
identity
    cultural, 223
    elections and, 249
    Native, 223–25, 235–37
    Tribal, 223, 371
ideology
    conservative, 156–57
    defined, 156
    in governing systems, 156–58
    liberal, 156–57
Ihunktuwona and Pabaska of Dakota
    Oyate, 182*t*
Iipay Nation, 292
Illuminative (nonprofit initiative), 158
illustrations, 300
"Immediate Program for Organization of
    Indian Tribes" memorandum, 142
imprisonment rate, 325
Inaja and Cosmit Band of Indians, 167*t*
incarceration, 38, 71–72, 325, 329
income taxes, 260–61
Independent Press Act, 339
Indian, defined, 224–25
Indian agents, 206–7
Indian Appropriation Act, 64
Indian Board of Representatives or
    Commissioners, 116
"Indian Canaan," 91–92
Indian Center News, 332
Indian Child Welfare Act (ICWA), 114–15, 369

Indian Civil Rights Act (ICRA), 5–6, 114, 214,
    317–19, 328–29, 338, 377
Indian Claims Commission award, 166
Indian colonies, 82*t*, 98
Indian Country Today (ICT), 333
Indian Education Act of 1973, 114–15
Indian Health Service, 3, 216, 235, 236, 270
Indian Mineral Development Act, 286
Indian Peace Commission, 66–67
Indian Removal Act (1830), 62–63, 94, 220
Indian removal campaign, 332
Indian Removal era, 113–14
Indian Reorganization Act (IRA) constitutions
    Alaska Natives and, 354
    justice and, 316
    leadership and, 191, 198–99, 202, 203,
        204, 206–7
    "Powers of Indian Tribes" and, 144
    TGCs and, 354
Indian Reorganization Act (IRA) governments,
    342, 354, 355
Indian Reorganization Act (IRA) of 1934
    Alaska Natives and, 345, 349
    Business Committee and, 140–41
    citizenship and, 224–25
    Deloria Jr. and Lytle on, 6
    divided powers of governance and, 174–75
    elections and, 241–42, 249
    Fort Belknap and, 187
    justice and, 315, 316–17
    leadership and, 191, 197–98, 209–10
    Los Coyotes Band and, 169
    loss of Indigenous land, 274–75, 276–77,
        279, 280
    modern Native constitutionalism and, 124–
        25, 127, 130–32, 133, 141–51
    Native constitutions adopted before, 4
    Native political transitions and, 50, 62, 73, 77
    Navajo and, 165
    oaths of office and, 198–200
    objectives of, 125
    organizing under, 141–51
    political economics and, 257, 261, 262, 274–
        75, 276–77, 279
    Pueblos adopting, 209
    Quapaw and, 166
    taxes and, 261, 262
    written constitutions before, 163
Indian Reorganization Act (IRA) of 1934
    constiutions, 144, 191, 198–99, 202, 203,
        204, 206–7, 275, 316, 354
Indian Reorganization Act (IRA) system, 317
Indian reservation program, 54

Indian reservations, 63, 124–25, 187, 348
Indian Self-Determination Act (ISDA), 3, 114–15, 270–71
Indian Self-Determination and Education Assistance Act, 2–3, 352
Indian Self-Determination era, 199, 206
Indian Self-Determination period, 367–68
Indian State, 82t, 84, 86, 87, 88, 91–92, 105. *See also* Indigenous state
Indian Territory
  after American Civil War, 102
  bill calling for, 82t
  Choctaw and Chickasaw treaty and, 104
  confederacy in, 82t
  creation of, 82t
  Curtis Act and, 105–6
  1866 treaties and, 108–9
  establishing boundaries for, 95–96
  FCT and, 103
  forming Indigenous state, 84
  Grant establishing, 104
  ideas of, 98
  with Indian Removal Act of 1830, 94
  Jefferson establishing, 93–94
  meeting requirements for statehood, 111–12
  Monroe establishing, 94
Indian Territory Act, 353–54
Indian tribe, defined, 2–3, 4, 270–71, 352
Indian Tribes as Governments (Strickland), 5–6
Indigenomics Institute, 295–96
Indigenous diplomacy
  for Anishinaabe Akii Protocol, 302–3, 306
  for Buffalo Treaty, 306–7
  for Comanche and Ute, 301–2
  contemporary, 301–10
  for Declaration on the Exercise of Inherent Sovereignty and Cooperation, 307
  for Grizzly Treaty, 309, 310
  for hunting, fishing, gathering, 302
  as model for future, 311
  for San Juan Southern Paiute and Navajo Nation Settlement Treaty, 303–4
  for Treaty Alliance Against Tar Sands Expansion, 307–8
  for United League of Indigenous Nations Treaty, 305–6
  for water protection treaties, 304–5
  for Wolf Treaty, 310
Indigenous Environmental Network, 336
Indigenous Futures Project, 158
Indigenous governance, effective, 374
Indigenous governing organizations, 160–61
Indigenous judicial systems, 326

Indigenous leadership crises, 210–22
Indigenous leadership perspectives, 190–93, 194f
Indigenous nations. *See also* Native nations
  defined, 5
  IRA and, 142
  modern Native political systems and, 153
  number of, 160–61, 352
  population of, 108, 111–12
  into the United States, 63
  with written constitutions, 77
Indigenous/Native governments
  CARES Act and, 270
  challenges facing, 368–73
  culture and, 255
  differences to other governments, 25–28
  economic footing of, 262–63
  elections and, 238
  evolving, 4–5
  free press and, 338, 339, 340–41
  Importance of, 367–68
  improving, 375
  IRA and, 145
  modern, 153–54
  Native corporations *vs.*, 351–52
  Native identity and, 223–24
  number with radio stations, 335
  obstacles of, 256
  recommendations for consideration, 375–81
  respect for, 20
  revenue for, 259–60
  role of, 21
  similarities to other governments, 22–24
  state and federal governments and, 20–30, 367, 368
  taxes and, 261–62, 264, 266
  termination of, 24, 26
  treaties between, 298
  treaty paradigm and, 55
Indigenous People in International Law (Anaya), 118
Indigenous peoples
  defined, 152
  extinction of, 91–92
  inhabiting United States, 152
  rights of, 114
Indigenous political adaptations, 55–62
Indigenous political incorporation activity, 81–84, 82t
Indigenous political leadership, 190
Indigenous state. *See also* Indian State
  European plans for, 84–88
  federal efforts to establish, 92–106

470 INDEX

Indigenous state (*cont.*)
    first serious discussion of forming, 92
    implications for sovereignty, 121–23
    Indigenous efforts to form, 106–14
    introduction, 81–84
    private and religious attempts to
      create, 89–92
    State of Sequoyah, 120–21
    Twentieth-Century attempts at, 114–20
Indigenous taxing authority, 261
Indigenous treaty-making, 97
IndiJ Public Media, 333
indirect democracy, 158–59
individualism, 21, 47, 70, 159–60
infrastructure and planning, 286–87
Infrastructure Investment and Jobs Act, 334
inheritance, 153
inmates, 325
Inouye, Daniel K., 361–62
Instagram, 335
Institute of Government Research, 124
"institutional niches," defined, 368
institutions
    elections and, 249
    importance of, 7
integration, 189–90
Inter-Tribal Council of Michigan, 221
Inter-Tribal Marijuana Enforcement
    Commission, 292
interest group authority, 190
Interim Chairman, 216
Interim Treasurer, 216
Interior Department, 68, 72, 145–46, 147, 153,
    160–61, 163, 283–85, 349, 362–63. *See also*
    Department of the Interior
Interior Secretary, 76, 149–50, 279, 290, 314,
    362–63. *See also* Secretary of the Interior
intermarriages, 113–14, 371
international agreement, 291
International Compact, 82*t*
international diplomacy
    diplomatic relations prior to European
      contact, 300–1
    Indigenous diplomacy in (*see* Indigenous
      diplomacy)
    introduction to, 297–98
    national federal contexts for, 298–300
International Indian Treaty Council, 115
International organizations, 353
international treaties, 297
Internet, 330, 335–37
InterTribal Bison Cooperative (ITBC),
    291, 306–7

Intertribal Reciprocal Agreement Regarding
    Hunting Fishing and Gathering on the
    Tribes' Reservations, 302
Inuit, 43–44, 45
Inupiaq, 342, 343
Inupiat, 351–52
Inupiat Community of Arctic Slope, 182*t*
Iowa Tribe, 80*t*, 227
IRA. *See* Indian Reorganization Act (IRA)
    of 1934
Iroquois, 33–34, 37, 39, 85, 170
Iroquois Confederacy, 85, 201
Irrigation, 124
Isabella Indian Reservation, 69
ISDA. *See* Indian Self-Determination
    Act (ISDA)
Isleta Pueblo, 75, 209, 210–11, 226
ITBC. *See* InterTribal Bison
    Cooperative (ITBC)

*Jackson Women's Health Organization, Dobbs
    v.,* 370–71
jails, 38, 325. *See also* prisons
Jamestown S'Klallam, 233
Jamul Indian Village, 226
Jarrat-Snider, Karen, 328
Jay, John, 209
Jefferson, Thomas, 93–94, 160
Jemez Pueblo, 75, 167*t*, 209
Jennings, Jane, 146
Jewell, Sally, 362–63
Jicarilla Apache, 78, 79, 176*t*, 335
Jicarilla Apache Indian Tribe, Merrion v., 286
Jicarilla Apache v. U.S., 278–79
job creation, 157, 268–69
jobs, 267–68, 283, 292, 294, 295
Johnson, Horace J., 71
Johnson, Lyndon, 332–33, 378
Johnson, R. W., 82*t*
Johnson, William, 85
Joint Council, 176*t*
Jones, William A., 76
Jorgensen, Miriam, 6–7, 9, 10–11, 234, 267
Joseph, United States v., 57
Joseph (Chief), 191
judge
    Alaska Natives and, 358
    appointment procedures of, 322–24
    Barrett as, 220–21
    Butterfield as, 213
    as formalized position of power, 222
    justice and, 314, 317, 322–24, 327, 328
    leadership friction and, 212

Morse and, 91
Organic Act and, 111
Pueblo, 170
judicial review, 190, 218, 321
judicial systems
Alaska Natives, 358
contemporary Native, 316–19
Indigenous, 326
leadership struggles and, 190
Native, 6, 312, 316–19, 328, 329
Native nations building support for, 205
Native nations subsituting, 328
Natives creating, 316–19, 318*f*
Navajo, 326–27
Julius, Jay, 195–96
junk food tax, 263–64
justice
CFR courts and, 314–16
contemporary Native judicial systems and, 316–19, 318*f*
federal coercion and, 314–16
introduction to, 312
judges and, 317, 322–24
judicial review and, 321
modern Native governments and, 153
in nation's identity and values, 205
Native judiciaries and, 319–21
peacemaking as, 326
reparative, 326
restorative, 326, 327, 363–64
traditional, 312–14
Justice Department, 290, 292
Justice practice systems, 325–29
justices
in leadership, 222
life tenure to, 322
removing, 323
juvenile deliquency, 358
juvenile inmates, 325

Kabapikotawangag Resources Council, 302
Kagama, U.S. v., 375
Kagan, Elena, 271
Kaibab Paiute, 374
Kakwahiv, 192
Ka Lāhui Hawaii, 164
Kalispel Tribe, 179, 378
Kalt, Joseph P., 7, 8, 9, 10, 11–12, 267
Kamehameha I (King), 359
Kanahole, Dennis, 364–65
Kānaka Maoli
constitution-making in, 363–64
demographic data about, 360

diversity and, 368, 369
governing systems and, 160–61, 164
introduction to, 342, 359–60
political dynamics among, 360–65
Thirty Meter Telescope and, 364–65
Kânaka Maoli Constitution, 363
Kānaka Oiwi, 160–61
Kansas Indians, The, 53
Kansas Treaty of 1825, 376
Karuk, 182*t*
Karuk Tribe, 171, 182*t*
Kasayulie, Willie, 349
Kasigluk Traditional Elders Council, 176*t*, 180
Kauanui, J. Kehaulani, 362, 365
Kavanaugh, Brett M., 271, 371–72
Kaw, 78, 80*t*, 105–6, 128–29, 130, 132, 135, 136, 137–38, 233
K'e, 218, 326–27
Keating, Francis Anthony, 120
Keechi, 182*t*
K'ei, 326–27
Kelly, Lawrence, 71–72, 209
Kelly, Melville, 71
Kenny, Carolyn, 192–93, 311
Kerr McGee Corporation v. The Navajo Tribe, 264
Kewa Pueblo, 167*t*
Khashgii, 44
Kickapoo, 37–38, 80*t*, 106–7, 297
Kidwell, Clara Sue, 108–9, 113
Kilkitat, 182*t*
Kinder Morgan's Trans Mountain, 308
King, Martin Luther, 198
Kingsbury, G. P., 82*t*
kinship, 5, 22, 25, 33, 38, 40–41, 47, 153, 155–56, 189–90, 192–93, 196, 209, 222, 254, 310, 313–14
kinship alliances, 209
kinship-based constitutions, 152–53
kinship bond, 300, 311
kinship connections, 45
kinship institutions, 4, 152
kinship principles, 190
kinship relations, 273–74, 300–1, 359
kinship systems, 40–41, 152, 175, 223, 257, 313, 326–27
kinship traditions, 298
Kiowa, 80*t*, 106–7, 109, 130, 175–78, 176*t*
Kiowa-Comanche-Apache, 132, 135, 137–38
Kitdlinermiut, 43–44
Klallam, 182*t*
Klamath, 76, 182*t*
Klawock, 353–54

472 INDEX

Klein, Laura F., 39
Koi Nation Constitution, 173
Kootenai, 149, 182t, 203
Korsmo, Fae L., 343–44
Kracke, Waud H., 40–41, 192–93
Kramer Cohen, Lucy, 6–7, 144–45
Ku Klux Klan, 119
Kuyuidokado, 182t
Kymlicka, W., 10

La Jolla Band of Luiseno Indians, 292
Lac du Flambeau, 226
Lac du Flambeau Agency, 79
LaDuke, Winona, 290
LaFlesche, Susan, 41
Laguna Pueblo, 75, 209, 232, 370–71, 374
Laguna Pueblo Constitution, 225–26
Lake Miwok, 182t
Lakota, 41, 138–39, 141, 150, 175, 187, 287,
    300–1, 376
Lakota lands, 181–85
Lakota of Pine Ridge and Rosebud Tribe,
    6, 76–77
Lakota of Pine Ridge Reservation, 76–77
Lakota Times, 333
Lambert, Eastern Band of Cherokee v., 220–21
Lambert, Patrick, 220–21
LaMotte, Peter, 70
land allotment, 109
land boundaries, 47
Land Buy Back program, 276–77
land ownership, 111
land rights, 88, 138–39, 347, 350–51, 375
land rushes, 120
lands
    of Alaska Natives, 346–47
    cizenship and, 223
    Kānaka Maoli and, 359, 362
    loss of, 274–75
    Native (see Native lands)
    ownership of, 303
    political economics and, 273–82
    resources and, 283
    shared, 33
    trust, 261, 276–77, 279, 373
    ULIN Treaty and, 306
land use matters, 169
languages
    Alaska Natives, 342
    citizenship and, 223
    elections and, 249
    loss of, 210
    Natives from non-Natives, 281

for political organization, 47
    protection of, 307
    shared, 33
Latinos, 239
Latinx, 160
Lauger, Amy D., 318f
law
    authority and, 37–38
    blood quantum formula into, 224
    Cherokee first to publish, 61
    customary, 190
    defined, 37, 50
    family, 312
    federalism and, 53
    in government, 154–55
    lack of Indigenous voice in, 51
    Native governments and, 368–69
    native political transitions and, 50–55
    nature of, 50
    race-based, 369
    treaties as basis of, 63
    treaty paradigm and, 53, 55
law enforcement officers, 317–19
lawlessness, 153
leader positions, 140
leaders
    consultation and, 379
    followers and, 48
    of Hualapai, 130
    for international diplomacy, 299, 300, 301–2
    of Morongo, 130
    peace, 33–34, 42–43, 175
    of Sac and Fox, 130
    of Santa Rosa, 130
    of Seminole, 130
    spiritual, 170
    war, 33–34, 42–43
    of White Mountain Apache, 130
leadership
    accountability by oath-taking (see oaths)
    of ANB, 356
    by ballot, 158–59
    BIA Circular #2565 and, 74–75
    case studies, 193–98, 210–22
    changes in Native government, 189–90
    conflict and, 210
    corruption in, 189
    defined, 40–41, 48, 192, 222
    elections and, 250
    factionalism in, 208–10
    Harvard studies and, 10–11
    importance of, 7
    of Indigenous people, 156, 311

INDEX 473

in Native societies, 40–43, 44, 45–46, 48, 60
Native *vs.* Western, 190
of Navajo, 218
oaths of office in (*see* oaths of office)
segmantation in, 208–10
tainted, 208
in 21st Century, 194*f*
women in, 39, 40
leadership crises, 210–22
leadership perspectives, Indigenous, 190–93, 194*f*
leadership style, 195, 196, 198
leadership traditions, 193
Leech Lake, 130–31, 135, 136, 186, 289, 327
Leech Lake Band Tribal Court, 327
legal systems
elections and, 249
factors influencing, 61
legal traditions, 51
legislative, defined as type of state recognition, 161
legitimacy, 14
Lehi, Johnny, 303
Lemont, Eric, 6–7
Lester, David, 285
Leupp Agency, 77
LGBTQI, 39, 160, 370–71
liability, 38
liberal
Natives identifying as, 158
as political ideology, 156–57
liberal ideology, 156–57
liberals, 157
libertarianism, 156–57
liberty, defined, 160
Lieutenant Governor, 56, 170, 176*t*
Lieutenant War-Chief, 169, 170
life expectancy, 1, 191, 360
life-tenure, 136
Lindemuth, Jahna, 349–50
lineal descent, 228, 244
liquor, 63, 136
liquor tax, 263–64
Littlefield, Daniel, 120
Littlefield, Daniel, Jr., 120–21
Little Lake Pomo, 182*t*
Little River Band of Ottawa, 176*t*, 266–67, 302
Little Shell Tribe of Chippewa Indians, 179
Little Traverse Bay Bands, 176*t*, 266–67, 302, 321
livestock, 77
livestock improvement associations, 73–74, 77
Llewellyn, Karl N., 326

local governments, 2, 4–5, 77, 117, 153, 268, 270, 271–72, 279–80, 299, 353–54, 376
Locke, Gary, 378
Locke, John, 32, 313
logging, 70–71
Lone Pine Paiute-Shoshone Tribe, 182*t*
Lone Wolf v. Hitchcock, 375
Loon clan, 36–37
Lopach, James J., 6, 27, 185–86, 187
Los Coyotes Band of Cahuilla and Cupeno, 167*t*, 169, 182*t*
lotteries, 267
Louis XIV (King), 31–32
Lowe, Coalition for Fair Government II v, 212–13
Lower Brule, 74
Lower Brule Sioux Tribe, 327
Lower Creek, 90–91
Lower Skagit, 182*t*
Lower Umpqua, 181
Lowi, Robert, 42
Lowry, Henry Barry, 41
Lozan (Apache), 41
Luiseno, 182*t*
Lujan, Tillett v., 212
Lumbee, 41, 290–91
lumber, 111–12
Lummi, 163, 195–96, 283, 290–91, 305–6
Lurie, Nancy, 209–10
Lyng v. Northwest Indian Cemetery Protective Association, 278
Lytle, Clifford M., 6, 32, 34, 69, 188, 281, 290, 313, 318*f*

MacDonald, Peter, 339
Madison, James, 160, 209
Madison, Marbury v., 217, 321
magazines, 333
Maidu, 182*t*
Maine, H. S., 200
Maine Land Claims Settlement Act, 114–15
Majoritarianism, 155–56
majority rule, defined, 159
Makah, 128–29, 135, 136, 140, 206, 305–6
Makah Constitution, 23
Making of Relatives Ceremony, 300–1
malfeasance, 190
"man camps," 370–71
Mana, defined, 46
Mandan, 74, 149
Mandan, Hidatsa, and Arikara (MHA), 182*t*, 227, 286, 287
Manifest Destiny, 62–63, 301

474 INDEX

Manitu
   defined, 46
   function of, 47
Mankiller, Wilma, 120
Manoomin, 282
Manuelito (Chief), 41
Manzanita Band of Digueno, 227
Maori, 46
Marbury v. Madison, 217, 321
Marchard, Sehay, 90
marches, 114
Margold, Nathan, 144, 145, 146–47, 153, 225, 249, 261
Maricopa, 76, 182*t*
marijuana, 291–93
Marquez, Deron, 272–73
marriage, 45
marriage partners, 45
Marsden, Edward, 357
Marshal, 111
Marshall, John, 93, 145, 217, 278, 321
Martin, 11
Martinez, Santa Clara Pueblo v., 229
Marx, Karl, 156–57
Marxist theory, 156–57
Mashpee Wampanoag, 175, 176*t*, 228, 280–81
Massachusett, 59
massacres, 211, 330
Match-E-Be-Nash-She-Wish Band of Pottawatomi, 266–67
maternal line, 36
Mattaponi, 161
Mattole, 182*t*
Mauna Kea Stewardship and Oversight Authority, 365
Mayes, Talton v., 50
Mazhue, 68
McCormick, Mary, 213, 214
McCormick, T. F., 75
McCoy, Isaac, 81–84, 82*t*, 89, 91–92
McGillivray, Alexander, 82*t*, 84, 89, 90
McGirt v. Oklahoma, 276, 371–72
McIlvane, Abraham Robinson, 82*t*
McIntosh, Rory, 107
Mckeel, Scudder, 141
McLaughlin, James, 376
MCT. *See* Minnesota Chippewa Tribe (MCT)
media
   broadcast, 334–35
   digital, 340
   free press in, 330–31, 337–41
   as institution, 331–35
   Internet as, 335–37

introduction to, 330–31
   Muscogee (Creek), 331
   news, 370
   oral transmission for, 331–32
   print, 332–34, 340
   in Russia and Ukraine, 330, 331
   social, 330, 336
   Taliban, 330, 331
Medicare, 157
Medicine Lodge Treaty, 216
medicine men, 129, 131
medicine people, 314
meditation, 36–37
Mehta, Amit P., 2–3
member
   Alaska Natives and, 354
   citizen *vs.*, 233
   defined, 233–34
   justice and, 317
membership. *See also* citizenship
   African Americans and, 232
   Alask Natives and, 354
   authority on, 63
   Chemeheuvi Tribe and, 227
   Cherokee and, 232
   citizenship *vs.*, 234, 372
   clan, 36, 45
   criteria for, 25, 153, 164–65
   determining, 223–24, 229–30
   Harvard studies and, 10–11
   Jamul Indian Village and, 226
   justice and, 312, 317, 321
   Khashgii and, 44
   Laguna Pueblo Constitution and, 225–26
   loss of, 229, 231–32, 234–35
   Mandan, Hidatsa, Arikara and, 227
   Native Village of Brevig Mission and, 226
   Pueblo and, 35–36
   self-determination and, 236–37
   sine qua non and, 223
   as term for Native individuals, 233, 234
membership criteria, 164–65, 317, 354
membership issues, 228
membership policies, 225–26
membership rules, 229
membership status, 223–24, 234
Memorandum of Understanding, 327
"Memorandum on Government-to-Government Relations with Native American Tribal Governments" (Clinton), 378–79
men, 39, 40–41, 43, 44, 65, 78, 129, 131, 317–19, 370–71

Menominee, 37–38, 70–71, 76–77, 80*t*, 114–15, 130, 135, 176*t*, 204–5, 282, 298–99
Mentasta Traditional Council, 180
Meredith, Howard, 6–7
Merrion v. Jicarilla Apache Indian Tribe, 286
Mesa Grande Band of Digueno, 164, 227
Mescalero, 131, 135, 136
Mescalero Apache, 129–30, 131, 136, 137–38, 139, 176*t*, 320–21, 322
Meshkwakihug, 47
Meskwaki, 46. *See also* Fox
metallurgy, 47–48
Metcalf, Richard P., 47
Metlakatla, 176*t*, 348, 354, 357–58
Metlakatla v. Egan, 357–58
Mexican Kickapoo, 80*t*, 131
MHA. *See* Mandan, Hidatsa, and Arikara (MHA)
Mianco, 68
Middletown Rancheria of Pomo Indians, 182*t*
Midwest Alliance of Sovereign Tribes, 221
military regimes, defined, 162
Mille Lacs, 130–31, 186, 287, 289
Miller, Edgar, 78
Miller, Walter B., 38, 42
Miner, Craig, 113–14
mineral deposits, 284
mineral resources, 284–85
minerals, 283
mining, 284, 286
ministers, 91
Minnesota Chippewa Tribe (MCT), 179, 182*t*, 186–87, 197–98, 203
Minnesota Department of Commerce, 289–90
Minnesota Department of Corrections, 327
Minnesota State Legislature, 325
Minnesota Supreme Court, 289–90
minority groups, 261, 359–60
minority rights, 157, 159
misfeasance, 190
Missing and Murdered Indigenous Women (MMIW), 325, 370–71
missionaries, 37–38, 61, 199, 206–7
missionary groups, 124–25
Mission Indian Cooperative, 138–39
Mission Indian Federation, 138–39
missions, 181
Mississippi Band of Choctaw, 226, 327
Mississippi Band of Choctaw, Dollar General v., 328–29
mistreatment, 371
Mitchell, Charlie, 72
Mitchell, Deidra, 273

Mitchell, Donald C., 347–48
Miwok, 181, 182*t*
mixed-blood, 61, 113–14, 206–7, 224, 371, 373
MMIW. *See* missing and murdered indigenous women (MMIW)
MMO. *See* Mvskoke Media Outlet (MMO)
Mnuchin, Steven, 2, 267
model community, 91
Modern American Tribal Governments and Politics (Meredith), 6–7
Modoc, 179, 182*t*
Mohave, 149, 181
Mohawk, 298, 373
Mohawk Reservation, 332–33, 373
Mohegan, 180
moieties, 35–37, 45
moiety membership, 45
Monacan, 176*t*, 241–42
Monacan Nation Constitution, 242–43
monarchical governments, defined, 162
monarchs, 31–32
monarchy, defined, 162
Mono, 181, 182*t*
Monroe, James, 82*t*, 91, 94
Montesquieu, Charles de, 32
Mooretown Rancheria of Maidu Indians, 182*t*
moral equality, 25
Morales, Evo, 118, 282
Morgan, Shirley v., 217–20
Morongo, 130, 138–39, 140
Morongo Band of Mission Indians, 182*t*
Morongo Reservation, 315
Morse, Jedediah, 81–84, 82*t*, 89, 91–92, 94
Mossman, E. D., 74
motor fuels, 264, 266
Mountain Maidu, 182*t*
Mowbray, Martin, 11–12, 13, 14
Muckleshoot, 130, 136, 138, 140–41, 182*t*
Mullin, Markwayne, 98
Multinational Native communities, 181–87, 182*t*
multiple citizenship, 107
multi-regional political organizations, 353
Municipal Incorporation Law, 353–54
municipalities, 20, 59, 342, 353–54
Muscogee (Creek), 62, 85, 108, 176*t*, 232–33, 240, 241, 276, 316, 331, 340. *See also* Creek
Muscogee National Council, 330–31
museum, 120
Muskhogean, 37
Mvskoke Media Outlet (MMO), 330–31

Naataanii, 42–43

476 INDEX

NAJA. *See* Native American Journalist
    Association (NAJA)
Nakinek Native Village, 179
Nambe Pueblo, 75, 167t, 176t
NARF. *See* Native American Rights
    Fund (NARF)
Narragansett, 59, 167t, 279
Nash, Cherokee Nation v., 232
Nation Council, 165, 172t, 219, 283–84,
    303, 339
*Nation Within: Navajo Land and Economic
    Development, A* (Rosser), 6
National Commercial Convention, 82t
National Congress of American Indians
    (NCAI), 3, 6, 115, 154, 221, 256–57, 266–
    67, 299, 305–6, 332, 333
National Environmental Policy Act, 287–88
National Indian Justice Center, 322
National Policy Toward Gambling, 267
national security, 298
*Nations Within: The Past and Future of
    American Indian Sovereignty, The* (Deloria,
    Jr. and Lytle), 6
*Native American and Political Participation: A
    Reference Handbook* (Stubben), 7
Native American Endangered Species Act, 310
Native American Indian Court Judges
    Association, 322
Native American Journalist Association
    (NAJA), 331–32, 334, 338–39, 340
Native American Natural Resource
    Development Federation, 284–85
Native American Rights Fund (NARF), 239, 303
native constitutionalism
    BIA in, 124–25
    Circular No. 3010 in, 127–41
    Cohen's statement in, 125–27
    hereditary chiefs in, 140–41
    Institute of Government Research in, 124
    IRA in, 124–25, 127, 141–51
    New Deal in, 124
    Roberts and, 133
    Shephard's statement in, 127
    Snyder Act in, 124
    women and, 139–40
Native corporations, Native governments
    vs., 351–52
Native courts, 312, 315–16, 317–19, 321, 327,
    328–29, 358, 371–72. *See also* Tribal courts
Native court systems, 148, 372
Native elected bodies, 116
Native elections
    accountability and, 254

campaign finance and, 252–53
conducting, 240–41
recall or removal in, 246–49
traditional offices in, 249–52
native governing arrangements, 65–72
native governing bodies. *See also*
    governing bodies
    Business Committees as, 178–79
    Business Councils as, 178–79
    citizenship and, 235
    divide powers of governance in, 174–78, 176t
    General Council as, 173–74
    Indigenous governing authority in, 172t
    introduction to, 171
    Kānaka Maoli and, 361
    miscellaneous entities as, 179
    Tribal Council as, 171–73
Native governing officials, 284–85
Native governing structures, 352–58
Native governments. *See* Indigenous/Native
    governments
Native groups, number of, 161
Native Hawaiian Education Act, 359–60
Native Hawaiian governing entity, 364
Native Hawaiian government, 363
Native Hawaiian Health Care Act of
    1988, 359–60
Native Hawaiian Study Commission
    Act, 359–60
Native Hawaiians, 160–61, 361–63, 364. *See also*
    Hawaiian Natives; Kānaka Maoli
Native identity, 223–25, 235–37. *See also* Tribal
    identity
Native judicial systems, 6, 312, 316–19, 328, 329
Native judiciaries, 319–21
Native lands
    court systems on, 312
    Indigenous statehood and, 118–19
Native nationalism, 21
Native nations. *See also* Indigenous nations
    African Americans and, 230–33
    ANCs and, 2–3
    death rate of, 1
    in diplomatic affairs, 152
    economic collapse of, 256
    with formal constitutions, 163–64
    harsh realities surrounding, 152
    income for, 256–57
    issues and developments confronting, 21
    life expectancy of, 1
    monies distributed to, 63
    number of sovereign, 1, 14, 20, 160–61, 181,
    256, 368

INDEX 477

as political and racial-ethnic bodies, 233–35
population count of, 21, 108, 111–12
as sovereigns, 154
state and federal governments and, 20–30
with taxation authority, 262
Native Nations Institute (NNI), 7, 8, 9, 13
Native Nations of the Great Plains, 312–13
Native Organizers Alliance, 158
Native political transitions
diminishing or destroying rights, 52
during the encounter era, 50–51
from 1492-1930s, 50
Indigenous political adaptations as, 55–62
lack of Indigenous voice in law and
politics, 51
native governing arrangements in, 65–72
pluralism and, 51–52
from 1600s-1800s, 50
since early 1800s, 51
sovereignty and expansion in, 62–65
superiority negatively affected, 51
survey in 1929, 72–80t
treaty paradigm and, 52–55
Native priests, 56–57
Native Public Media (NPM), 335, 336–37
Native Village of Brevig Mission, 226, 258–59
Native Village of Eek, 167t, 170–71, 355
Native Village of Egegik, 262
Native Village of Georgetown, 251
Native Village of Hooper Bay, 176t
Native Village of Kipnuk, 176t
Native Village of Venetie Tribal Government,
Alaska v., 348–49
Native women, 21, 286, 317–19, 325, 371
natural economics, 290–93
natural gas, 281, 293
natural gas industry, 293
natural gas supply, 285–86
naturalization, 25
natural resource problems, 21
natural resources, 23, 256–57, 282–83, 284–
86, 312
Natural Resources Board, 310
Navajo. See also Diné
Atkinson Trading Company v. Shirley and, 263
chapter organizations in, 77–78
Codes and, 165–66
court system of, 372
courts and jurists of, 326
COVID-19 in, 1–2
Denezpi v. United States and, 316
diplomacy for, 303–4
with divided powers of governance, 176t

elections and, 116, 244, 253
ethnic groups in, 181
governing systems in, 155
governing units, 20–21
Hopi and, 131
IRA and, 149
judges and, 322
media and, 335
as multi-national Native community, 182t
Northern, 76
number of citizens, 1–2, 119, 148–49
philosophical concepts, 326–27
political incorporation activity, 82t
political transition of, 56–57, 58, 71–72, 74,
76, 77–78
population of, 119
requirements for office, 244
resources and, 283–84, 294
San Juan Southern Paiute and Navajo Nation
Settlement Treaty, 303–4
in Shirley v. Morgan, 217–20
Southern, 76
taxes and, 263–64
Tribal Council and, 171
Western, 76
Wyckoff and, 117
Navajo Agency, 77
Navajo Nation Code, 165–66, 252–53, 326
Navajo Nation Council, 165, 219, 283–84,
303, 339
Navajo Nation Reservation, 276, 284, 303
Navajo Nation Supreme Court, 217, 326
"Navajo Nation Tomorrow—51st State,
Commonwealth, Or, The" (Wyckoff), 117
Navajo Nation's judicial system, 326–27
Navajo Political Experience, The (Wilkins), 6
Navajo Times, The, 332, 339
Navajo Times Publishing Company, 339–40
Navajo Tribal Code, 165–66
Navajo Tribe, Kerr McGee Corporation v., 264
NCAI. See National Congress of American
Indians (NCAI)
Nelson v. Shirley, 217–18
Neolin (Prophet), 85
Neosho, 82t
"Ne-shy-chut," defined, 31
Nesper, Larry, 312
Neutral Indian State, 82t
New Deal, 51–52, 124
New Mexico, Cotton Petroleum Corporation
v., 286
New York Times, 286–87, 289, 330
News from Indian Country (NFIC), 333

478 INDEX

newsletter, 332–33
news media, 370
newspaper, 61, 332–33, 339
Newtok Traditional Council, 163
Nez Perce, 76–77, 80t, 179, 182t, 282, 301, 378
NFIC. See News from Indian Country (NFIC)
Ngarrindjeri, 305–6
Nielsen, Marianne O., 326, 328
1987 Northwest Ordinance, 376
1915 Village Act, 353–54
1947 Treaty of Peace, Friendship and Mutual
    Assistance, 299, 301
1908 water law case, 187
Nineteenth Amendment, 78
Nixon, Richard, 114–15
NNI. See Native Nations Institute (NNI)
Noem, Kristi, 4–5, 264
Noem v. Flandreau Santee Sioux Tribe, 264
Nomlaki, 182t
non-Indian lawyers, 206–7
non-native governing units, number of, 20
non-profit development and service
    corporations, 353
nonrenewable resources, 283–84
Norcini, Marilyn, 209
Norgren, Jill, 64–65
Northern Arapahoe, 176t, 181–85
Northern Cheyenne, 80t, 136, 137–38, 139, 140,
    191, 226, 283, 321
Northern Cheyenne Reservation, 284
Northern Navajo, 76
Northern Paiute/Shoshone, 129, 182t
Northern Pueblo Agency, 75
Northern Tribes Buffalo Treaty, 306–7
Northern Ute, 301
North Fork Rancheria, 233
Northway Village, 187
Northwest Federation of American Indians, 138
Northwest Indian Cemetery Protective
    Association, Lyng v., 278
Northwest Indian Fisheries
    Commission, 290–91
Northwest Ordinance of 1787, 53
Nottawaseppi Huron Band of Potawatomi, 273
NPM. See Native Public Media (NPM)

Oaths of office
    accountability and, 198–202
    categories for, 202–8
    in contemporary Native constitutions, 201–2
    history of, 199–201
    hypotheses pertaining to, 196, 206–7
    introduction to, 198–99

    number of, 202–3, 204–5
Obama, Barack, 288, 291–92, 309
O'Brien, Sharon, 6
off-reservation members, 136
office
    in Native elections, 249–52
    qualifying for, 244–46
    recall or removal from, 246–49
    serving, 130
Office of Hawaiian Affairs, 361
Office of Hawaiian Affairs, Hawai'i v., 362
Office of Indian Affairs (OIA), 150, 344–45
office qualifications, 244–46
officers
    Barrett and, 215–16
    BIA, 143
    Eastern Band of Cherokee, 165
    election of, 135
    law enforcement, 317–19
    Los Coyotes Band of Cahuilla and Cupeno
        Indians, 169
    police, 327
    Pueblo, 56
    of Spanish civil government, 56–57
    terms for, 130
Ogee, L. H., 68
Oglala Lakota, 4–5, 333
Ohkay Owingeh Pueblo, 167t, 169
OIA. See Office of Indian Affairs (OIA)
oil, 111–12, 259–60, 282–83, 284, 286, 287, 288
oil and gas severance tax, 263–64
oil companies, 72, 111, 283–84
oil drilling, 351–52
oil embargo, 283
oil extraction, 351–52
oil industry, 293
oil pipeline conflicts, 335
oil pipelines, 281, 282, 286–87, 288–89, 335
oil production, 286
oil reserves, 285
oil sands, 307–8. See also tar sands
oil spill, 288, 290
oil-tax agreements, 286
Ojibwe, 130–31, 132, 135, 136, 182t, 196, 302,
    333. See also Anishinaabe
Oklahoma, McGirt v., 276, 371–72
Oklahoma Centennial Commemorative
    Commission, 120
Oklahoma Indian Welfare Act, 150, 166,
    216, 241–42
Oklahoma Tribal Finance Consortium, 295
Oklahoma v. Castro-Huerta, 371–72
Oklahoma Welfare Act, 163

INDEX 479

Okmulgee Constitution, 108–9
Okmulgee Council, 82*t*
oligarchy, defined, 162
Oliphant ruling, 317–19
On the Drafting of Tribal Constitutions
(Cohen), 6–7
Onate, Juan de, 56
Oneida, 129, 135, 136, 147, 167*t*, 170, 298, 333
Onondaga, 167*t*, 170, 298
ONPD. *See* Osage Nation's Police
Department (ONPD)
OPEC. *See* Organization of the Petroleum
Exporting Countries (OPEC)
oral histories, 300
oral recollections, 31
oral tradition, 301, 331–32, 334
oral transmission, 331–32
Organic Act, 111, 344
Organization of the Petroleum Exporting
Countries (OPEC), 283, 284–85
Organized Village of Kake, 327
Organizing the Lakota: The Political Economy of
the New Deal on Pine Ridge and Rosebud
Reservations (Biolsi), 6
origin account, 39
Orr, Raymond I., 7, 210–11, 215
Ortiz, Alfonso, 191–92
Orutsaramuit Traditional Native Council, 250
Orutsararmuit Native Council, 164
Osage, 76, 106–7, 108, 128–29, 131, 132, 134–
35, 137–38, 176*t*, 204–5, 280, 284, 292–93,
314–15, 332, 338, 340
Osage Constitution, 205
Osage Indian Agency, 134–35
Osage Nation's Police Department
(ONPD), 292–93
Osage resources, 284
Oshkenaniew, Mitchell, 70
Otoe, 80*t*, 109, 135, 136, 137–38, 140
Otoe-Missouria, 182*t*
Ottawa, 66, 80*t*, 85, 108, 135
Oumet-zi- ou- hou (Chief), 91
Ouray, 80*t*
Owen, Robert L., 105
Oxford English Dictionary, 233, 234, 375–76
Oysters, 290–91

paintings, 300
Paiute, 78, 181, 182*t*
Paiute-Shoshone Tribe of the Fallon
Reservation, 182*t*
Pala Band of Mission Indians, 227
Palus, 182*t*

Pamunkey, 39, 161, 371
Pari-mutuel wagering, 267
Parker, Alan, 5–6
Parker, Ely S., 68, 314
Pascua Yaqui Tribe, 176*t*, 319–20, 322–23
Passamaquoddy, 204–5, 335
Passamaquoddy Tribe of the Pleasant Point
Reservation, 176*t*
paternalism, 52, 53, 54–55, 58, 73
paternalism paradigm, 52, 53, 54–55
Patrick, Oma, 214–15
Pauma Band of Mission Indians, 164–65
Pawnee, 80*t*, 106–7, 130, 135, 136
Pawtucket, 59
Payment, Aaron, 221, 222
peace leaders, 33–34, 42–43, 175
Peacemakers Circle, 327
peacemaking, 326
Peace Naataanii, 43
Peace Policy, 66–67
Pelosi, Nancy, 98
Pend d'Oreilles, 182*t*
Penobscot, 28–29, 176*t*, 327
Perry, Steven W., 318*f*
Perryman, J. M., 105
personal income taxes, 260–61
Peter, Evon, 348
petroglyphs, 300
Phelps, Glenn A., 239
Picayune Rancheria of Chukchansi Indians, 228
Pickering, Kathleen, 295–96
Picuris Pueblo, 75, 167*t*
Pima, 62, 76, 135, 140, 182*t*, 191–92
Pimain, 44
Pine Ridge, 129, 132, 138–39, 140–41
Pine Ridge Reservation, 129, 333
Pine Ridge Sioux, 80*t*, 136
Pinoleville Pomo, 233, 234
pipelines, 281, 282, 305, 308, 335–36
PIT. *See* Possessory Interest Tax (PIT)
Pit River, 78, 119, 176*t*, 180, 182*t*
P.L. 153, 70
Place, defined, 42
plants, 359
plenary power, 277, 278–79, 360, 375–81
plenary power doctrine, 236–37
Plenty Coups (Chief), 41
pluralism, 51–52, 55
Poarch Band of Creek, 335
Pojoaque Pueblo, 75, 167*t*
Pokagon Band of Potawatomi, 180
police, 138, 264, 339
police force, 36–37

480 INDEX

police officers, 327
political authority, 26, 33, 159, 170
political dynamics, among Kānaka
    Maoli, 360–65
political economics
    case studies, 258–59
    climate change in, 282–90
    conclusion, 295–96
    defined, 255
    economic vitality in, 257–58
    energy development in, 282–90
    introduction to, 255–57
    natural economics in, 290–93
    opportunities and challenges, 259–95
    renewable energy in, 293–95
political entities, defined, 25–26
political equality, defined, 159
political experience, 136
political ideology, defined, 156
political organization B.C. (Before Contract)
    authority in, 37–38
    case studies for, 43–47
    categories of, 43
    clans in, 31–33, 37, 45
    conclusion, 47–49
    defined, 33
    diversity in, 31–33
    gender roles in, 39–40
    introduction to, 31–33
    law in, 37–38
    leadership in, 40–43, 44, 45–46, 48
    moieties in, 31–33, 37, 45
    organizational structures in, 31–33
political organizations, types of, 161–62
political orientation, 158
political party
    defined, 209
    established in Indian Country, 210
    image of, 209–10
political systems
    balance and, 159
    customs as, 166
    democracy and, 158
    factors influencing, 61
    functions of, 153
    ideology in, 156
    leadership struggles and, 190
    traditions as, 166
political traditions, 143, 192
political transitions, Native. *See* Native political
    transitions
politics
    community, 157

defined, 153
economics and, 255
ideology and, 156–58
lack of Indigenous voice in, 51
political transitions and, 51
Vizenor and, 196
pollution, 282, 286
polygamy, 314
Pomo, 182t
Ponca, 80t, 179, 282
Pontiac (Chief), 85, 121
popular consent, defined, 159
popular sovereignty, defined, 159
population
    of Alaska Natives, 352–53
    of Hawaii, 360
    of Kānaka Maoli, 360
    of Native nations, 21, 108, 111–12
    of Native women, 325
    prison, 360
population size, 372–73
Porter, Robert, 210, 373
Port Madison, 130, 138
Possessory Interest Tax (PIT), 263–64
Potawatomi, 37–38, 66, 68–69, 140, 211–12
poverty, 21–22, 152, 283, 327, 334
poverty rate, 256–57, 360
power
    citizenship and, 229, 236–37
    defined, 42, 192
    democracy and, 161–62
    dictatorship and, 162
    of federal government, 223
    federal plenary, 24, 114, 207
    of governments, 155, 156, 159
    of judicial review, 321
    leadership and, 211–12
    plenary, 277, 278–79, 360, 375–81
    solar, 293–95
    taxes and, 261
    Tribal civil leaders and, 42
    wind, 293–95
Power from Powerlessness: Tribal Governments,
    Institutional Niches, and American
    Federalism (Evans), 7, 29, 368
"Powers of Indian Tribes" (Margold), 144, 153,
    225, 261
Pownall, Thomas, 82t, 84–85
Prairie and Woodland Native peoples, 312–13
Prairie Band of Potawatomi, 78
Prairie Band Potawatomi, 327
praying towns, 59–60
preambles, 257–58

INDEX 481

Preambular Statements, 258–59
President
Asam as, 363–64
Begaye as, 303
in Circular No. 3010, 131
Congress power to, 51–52
Fort Totten Agency, 77
of Hawaiian Nation, 363–64
Ho-Chunk, 213
Kasayulie as, 349
Lehi as, 303
Leupp Agency, 77
meetings and, 131
Mitchell as, 273
Morales as, 282
Organic Act and, 111
recall and, 246
Shirley as, 218–19
as term for majority of nations, 129–30
for Tribal nations' issues, 63–64
U.S., 246
Western Territory Bill and, 96
Zelenskyy as, 330
Preston-Engle Irrigation Report, 124
Price, Hiram, 314
priests, 56–57
principal chief, 213, 240, 241, 253, 331
print media, 332–34, 340
prison population, 360
prisons, 38. *See also* jails
Problem of Indian Administration, The (Institute
of Government Research), 124
"progressive," 373
"Project for Proper Separation of the British and
French Dominions in North America, A"
(Baker), 84–85
Promyshleniki, 343
property, 40, 153, 209
property damage, 358
property rights, 225, 314–15
prosecutor, 327
Protestantism, 64–65
Provisional Treaty, 87
Pruden, Harlan, 39
psychological aggression, 325
public defender, 327
public law 83-280, 377
public Law 280, 279, 291
public safety, 23, 292, 368
public safety services, 268–69
public school districts, 20
Pueblo Bonito Agency, 77
Pueblo factionalism, 209

Pueblo Nations, 298–99
Pueblo of Cochiti, 176*t*
Pueblo of Isleta, 176*t*
Pueblo of Jemez, 176*t*
Pueblo of San Felipe, 171
Pueblo of San Ildefonso, 176*t*, 293, 324
Pueblo of Sandia, 170
Pueblo Revolt, 56–57
Pueblos, 35–36, 48, 55–59, 75, 124–25, 160–61,
162, 166, 169, 170, 175, 181, 191–92, 208,
209, 238, 256, 314–15
punishment, 38, 326
Puritanism, 59
Putin, Vladimir, 162, 330
Puyallup Tribe, 76
Pyramid Lake Indian Reservation, 182*t*

Qualla Housing Authority (QHA), 220
Quapaw, 80*t*, 106–7, 108, 129–30, 165, 166
Quartz Valley Indian Community, 182*t*
Questionnaire on Tribal Organization
(Government), 127–33
Quileute, 130, 135, 181, 182*t*, 226
Quinault, 78, 80*t*, 181, 182*t*, 282, 321

race, 13, 119, 352–53, 360, 371–72
race-based law, 369
racetrack betting, 267
racial entities, defined, 25–26
racial-ethnic groups, 360
racial-ethnic status, 368–69. *See also* ethnic
status; racial status
racial groups, 1, 158, 224, 261. *See also* ethnic
groups; racial-ethnic groups
racial status, 26
racism, 1, 13, 73, 152, 230–31, 232–33,
368–69
Radin, Paul, 35, 36–37, 257, 369
radio, 253, 331–32, 333–35
radio ads, 120
radio stations, 335
raids, 42–43
railroad interests, 111
railroads, 67, 104, 111, 308
Ramona Band of Cahuilla, 166–68, 167*t*
Rancherias, 160–61, 181, 256
rape, 325
Rappahannock Tribe, 164, 259
Rave, Jodi, 333, 339
Raven moiety, 35
Rawls, John, 313
Reagan, Ronald, 267
real property taxes, 260–61

482 INDEX

Rebuilding Native Nations: Strategies for Governance and Development (Jorgensen), 7
recalls, 164–65, 246–49
reciprocity, 189–90
recognized tribes, 125, 378
records of proceedings, 368–69
Red Bottom, 185–86
Red Cloud (Oglala Lakota leader), 191
Redding Rancheria, 182*t*, 228
Red Lake, 128–29, 130–31, 132, 135, 139, 140–41, 186, 252, 289, 292
Red Lake Anishinaabe, 62
Red Lake Band of Anishinaabe, 287
Red Lake Chippewa, 129
Red Lake Council, 130–31
Red Mesa Tapaha Solar Generation Plant, 294
Reeves, J. R. T., 141–42
referendum, 112, 178–79, 186–87, 198, 217, 262, 292–93
Regguinti, Gordon, 334
regional corporations, 347, 351, 352
regional tribal council, 172*t*, 182*t*
rehabilitation, 327
Rehnquist, William, 371–72
reindeer industry, 345
Reitmeieu, Kim, 3
religion, 60–61, 200, 249, 338, 342
religious differences, 372–73
religious factionalism, 357
religious instruction, 357
religious leaders, 99, 166, 250
religious persuasion, 371–72
religious traditions, 46, 233–34
relocation, 106–7, 211, 235, 282, 332
relocation policy, 235–36
relocation process, 220
relocation program, 196, 280
remoteness, 334, 342, 359
removal from office, 246–49
removal treaties, 94, 95, 111
removal treaty of 1834, 376
renewable energy, 293–95
Reno-Sparks Indian Colony, 182*t*
reparative justice, 326
representative democracy, 158–59
Republic of Watauga, 89
republicanism, 158–59
Republicans, 112, 158, 238, 252, 254, 362, 368–69
Reservation Politics: Historical Trauma, Economic Development, and Intra-Tribal Conflict (Orr), 7

reservations
    in Alaska, 345, 347, 348, 357–58
    BIA and, 71
    chiefs on, 140–41
    consent and, 377
    court systems on, 314–15, 316
    defined, 125
    establishment of, 63, 345
    lock down on, 4–5, 77
    media and, 333–34
    missionary groups on, 124–25
    Natives weakened on, 65
    number of acres on, 276–77
    political life on, 73
    recognized tribes and, 125
    resources on, 285
    Shoshone and Arapahoe on, 185
resource endowments, 283
resources
    agricultural, 284–85
    of Alaska Natives, 346–47
    cultural, 173, 290
    development of, 283–84
    energy, 259–60, 283, 285
    justice and, 315–16
    mineral, 284–85
    native political transitions and, 52, 55
    natural, 23, 256–57, 282–83, 284–86, 312
    nonrenewable, 283–84
    Osage, 284
    water, 284–85
responsibilities, rights *vs.*, 313–14
restorative justice, 326, 327, 363–64
restorative justice systems, 312
Revolutionary War, 92
Rice v. Cayetano, 361–63, 369
Richland, Justin, 326
Richotte, Keith, Jr., 6–7
Ridge, John Rollin, 332
Ridge, Major, 97
ridicule, to maintain order, 35
rifts, 210
rights
    aboriginal, 344
    of Alaska Natives, 347
    citizenship and, 236–37
    civil, 4, 157–58, 299, 357
    consent and, 377
    fishing, 114, 275–76, 347, 350–51
    heirship, 276–77
    human, 4, 52, 157, 240, 299, 356
    hunting, 275–76, 347, 350–51
    of Indigenous peoples, 114, 121, 138

individualism and, 159–60
land, 88, 138–39, 347, 350–51, 375
minority, 157, 159
of Native Hawaiians, 362
native political transitions and, 50, 51, 52, 53
of people, 370–71
property, 225, 314–15
responsibilities *vs.*, 313–14
to rivers, 282
sine qua non and, 223
Supreme Court and, 371–72
territorial, 92, 118, 122, 275–76
treaty, 21, 109, 138, 232–33, 290, 378
voting, 118–19, 180, 344
water, 124–25, 138–39, 303–4
Riley, Angela R., 281, 374
Rincon Band of Luiseno, 164
Rio Grande Pueblo, 35–36
rivers, rights to, 282
Rivers and Harbors Act, 287–88
Road: Indian Tribes and Political Liberty, The
(Barsh and Henderson), 117
Roberts, John G., 271, 371–72
Roberts, W. O., 133
Robert's Rules of Order, 187–88
Rockwell, Stephen J., 50
Rocky Boys, 136
Roe v. Wade, 370–71
Roff v. Burney, 229
Rogers, Will, 113
Roosevelt, Franklin D., 124
Roosevelt, Theodore, 113
Rosebud, 137, 138–39, 141, 150
Rosebud Reservation, 133
Rosebud Sioux, 76–77, 129, 133, 136, 137–38,
171, 210–11
Rosebud Sioux Tribe, 294
Rosen, Deborah, 38
Ross, John, 41, 97, 102, 107
Rosser, Ezra, 6, 97
Round Valley Indian Tribes, 182*t*
Rousseau, Jean-Jacques, 32
royal absolutism, 31–32
Royal Proclamation Line, 82*t*, 85–86
Royal River Casino, 264
royalties, 284
royalty rates, 284–85
rule of law, defined, 160
"Rules for the Navajo Tribal Council"
(Collier), 165
"Rules of Metlakatla" (Duncan), 357
Rusco, Elmer, 73, 204
Russell, Steve, 7, 121, 189, 338–39, 379–80

Sa/a Naaghai Bik'e Hozhoo (SNBH), 155
Sac and Fox, 71, 80*t*, 108, 109, 130, 131, 135,
179, 182*t*, 204–5, 213, 214, 292
Sac and Fox Bill of Rights, 214
Sac and Fox Supreme Court, 213
Sachems, 298. *See also* chiefs
Sacred Heart Citizen Potawatomi, 211, 215
sacredness, 25, 309
Sacred Pipe, The (Brown), 300
sacred sites, 303–4, 307, 363
Sacristan, defined, 56
safety, 23, 154–55, 292, 368, 371
Saginaw Chippewa, 69
Saginaw Chippewa Indian Tribe, 266–67
Saint Regis Mohawk Tribal Council, 373
Salazar, Carcieri v., 278, 279
sales tax, 263–64
Salish, 149, 203
salmon, 290–91
salmon operations, 345
Salt River Pima, 136
Salt River Pima-Maricopa Indian
Community, 182*t*
Samish, 181, 182*t*
San Carlos Apache, 135, 190–91
Sandia Pueblo, 75, 167*t*
Sandoval, United States v., 58
San Felipe Pueblo, 75, 167*t*
San Ildefonso Pueblo, 75, 167*t*
San Juan Agency, 77
San Juan Pueblo, 75
San Juan Southern Paiute, 303–4
San Juan Southern Paiute and Navajo Nation
Settlement Treaty, 303–4
San Juan Southern Paiute Tribe, 276
San Manuel Band of Mission Indian, 165
San Manuel Nation, 272–73
sanitation, 154–55
Santa Ana Pueblo, 75
Santa Clara Pueblo, 75, 167*t*, 209
Santa Clara Pueblo v. Martinez, 229
Santa Fe Indian School Property, 315–16
Santa Rosa, 130, 138–39, 140
Santa Rosa Band of Pueblo, 167*t*
Santa Ysabel Reservation, 149
Santo Domingo Pueblo, 75
Sargent, Aaron A., 68
Sault-ste. Marie Tribe of Chippewa, 266–
67, 304–5
*Sault Ste. Marie Tribe of Chippewa Indians,
Aaron Payment v.*, 221–22
sawmills, 345
Scalp Dance, 314

484 INDEX

Scanlon, Michael, 252
Schoolcraft, Henry Rowe, 82t, 89, 92
Schumpeter, Joseph, 158–59
Scruton, Roger, 376
Searle, Jason, 378–79
Second Chief, 240
secretary, 111, 129, 169, 195, 214–15, 222
   Crow, 135
   Julius as, 195
Secretary of the Interior, 2, 24, 66–67, 72, 105,
   124, 146, 150–51, 165, 213, 232, 274–75,
   277, 279–80, 283–84, 290, 309, 314,
   345–46, 357–58, 370–71. *See also* Interior
   Secretary
Secretary of the Nation, 213
Secretary of the National Congress of American
   Indians, 221
Secretary of War, 82t, 91, 94
Secretary-Treasurer, 164–65
segmentation, 208–10, 372–73. *See also*
   factionalism; factions
self-administration, 133
self-determination
   Alaska Natives and, 350–51
   BIA and, 24
   citizenship and, 236–37
   consent and, 375
   consultation and, 377, 378
   electoral politics and, 280, 284–85
   Indigenous state and, 114–15, 138–39
   international diplomacy and, 299, 301,
      308, 311
   justice and, 326
   media and, 332–33
   modern Native constitutionalism and, 198–
      99, 201–2, 203, 204–5, 206, 207, 208
Self-Determination Act of 1975, 270–71
Self-Determination era, 206
self-development, 378
self-governance, 20, 144, 147–48, 150–51, 154,
   199, 203, 207, 280, 316
self-government, 115–16, 125, 144, 145, 212,
   223, 258, 299, 350–51
self-help, 378
self-rule, 128, 141–42, 150–51, 317
Seminole, 33–34, 55–56, 60, 62, 76–77, 90, 129,
   130, 131, 132, 136, 140–41, 176t, 232–
   33, 368–69
Seminole Freedmen, 232–33
Senate
   as Indigenous governing authority, 172t
   Institute of Government Research and, 124
   Modoc, 179

   Preston-Eagle Irrigation Report and, 124
   reorganization of, 124
   Swinomish and, 179
Senate Caucus, 118
Senate Committee on Indian Affairs, 124
Seneca, 62, 68, 76, 108, 128–29, 176t, 182t, 210,
   298, 314, 373
Seneca-Cayuga Nation, 182t
separation of powers, 174–75, 190, 219–20
Sequoyah Commission, 120–21
Sequoyah Constitution, 121
Sequoyah Constitutional Convention, 111–12
Sequoyah Movement, 112, 120
*Sequoyah Rising: Problems in Postcolonial Tribal
   Governance* (Russell), 7, 121, 189, 379–80
Sequoyah movement, 120
Serano, 182t
Sessions, Jeffrey, 292–93
1785 Cherokee Treaty, 97, 105
Treaty of Canandaigua, 66
1778 Delaware Treaty, 97
severance taxes, 286
Seward, William H., 343–44
sex trafficking, 286, 317–19
sexual assault, 317–19, 325
sexual assault charges, 316
sexual crimes, 325
sexual freedom, 40
sexual harassment, 330–31
Sexual violence, 325
Sexually violent crimes, 317–19
Shafritz, J. M., 209
Shagwe, (Chief), 68
Shakopee Mdewakanton, 368
Shakopee Mdewakonton Sioux, 228
Shasta, 182t
Shattuck, Petra, 64–65
Shawnee, 33–34, 41, 66, 74, 88, 106–7,
   204, 297
Shephard, Ward, 127
sheriff, 56, 91, 170
Shingle Springs Band of Miwok, 164
Shingle Springs Band of Miwok Indians, 182t
Shinnecock Nation, 292
Shirley, Atkinson Trading Company v., 263, 264
Shirley, Joe, Jr., 217–19
Shirley, Nelson v., 217–18
Shirley, William, 84–85
Shirley v. Morgan, 217–20
Shivwits (Paiute), 136
Shoalwater Bay Tribe, 204–5
Shoshone, 76, 166, 181–85, 182t
Shoshone-Bannock, 333

Shoshone-Bannock Tribes of the Fort Hall Reservation, 182*t*
Shoshone-Paiute Tribes of the Duck Valley Reservation, 182*t*
Shoshone reservation, 181–85
Sicade, Henry, 76
Sigourney, Lydia Huntley, 107
Siletz Confederated Tribe, 74, 78
Siletz Indians, 181
Silva, Noenoe K., 359
sine qua non, 223
Sioux, 182*t*, 185–86
Sipayik, 205
Sisseton, 185–86
Sisseton-Wahpeton, 62, 135, 204
Sisseton-Wahpeton Oyate of Laker Traverse Reservation, 182*t*
Sisseton-Wahpeton Sioux, 136
Sisseton-Wahpeton Tribe, 204
Sitka Tribe, 233
Sitting Bull, 41
Siuslaw, 181
Six Chippewa Bands, 182*t*
Six Nations, 170
Six Nations Confederacy, 298
1607 Powhatan Confederacy treaty, 301
Skagit, 181, 182*t*
Skokomish, 131, 136, 138, 182*t*, 204–5
Skull Valley Band of Goshute, 173–74
slavery, 231–32
smallpox epidemic, 59, 187
smartphones, 340
Smith, Chad, 120
Smith, E., 141–42
Smith River Rancheria, 204–5
SNBH. See Sa/a Naaghai Bik'e Hozhoo (SNBH)
Snohomish, 78, 80*t*, 181, 182*t*
Snoqualmie, 80*t*, 181, 182*t*
Snyder Act, 124, 278
Social contract theory, defined, 32
socialism, 156–57
social issues, 157–58
social media, 330, 336
social media platforms, 335
social networks, 335
social order, 37
social Security, 157
social services, 367–68
social traditions, 143
solar energy, 283
solar power, 293–95
soldiers, 37–38
Songhees Nation, 305–6

Sotomayor, Sonia, 270–71, 352
Southern Navajo, 76
Southern Paiute, 132, 136, 303
Southern Pomo, 181, 182*t*
Southern Pueblo Agency, 75
Southern Ute, 283, 285–86, 301, 335
sovereign immunity, 4, 153, 212, 222, 362
sovereigns
  comparison of three, 20–22
  conclusion, 28–30
  constitutional, 121–22
  governing differences, 25–28
  governing similarities, 22–24
  Native nations as, 154
  in *Shirley v. Morgan*, 217
  Shoshone and Arapahoe as, 185
sovereign state, 359
sovereign status, 5, 50, 51, 64, 235–36, 277–78, 301, 368–69
sovereignty
  Alaska Natives and, 349–50
  of Cherokee Nation, 61, 120, 131–32
  consent and, 375, 377
  consultation and, 377, 379
  defined, 48
  importance of, 7
  Indigenous state and, 81, 114, 116, 121–23
  international diplomacy and, 301, 305–6
  IRA and, 145
  justice and, 312, 322, 326
  Kānaka Maoli and, 164, 360, 362–63, 365
  media and, 332–33
  nationalism rooted in, 21
  native political transitions and, 50, 51, 52, 55, 62–65
  oaths of office and, 199–200, 202, 204, 206, 207
  plenary power and, 375
  political economics and, 273–82, 286
  popular, 159, 190
  taxes and, 262–63, 264
  treaty paradigm and, 55
  Vizenor and, 198
  Western expansion and, 62–65
sovereignty accords, 299
speaker, 186
Speaker of the Council, 218
special district governments, 20
Special Master, 214
species, 273–74
Spilde, Katherine, 269–70, 273
Spirit Lake, 163
spirituality, 189–90

486 INDEX

spiritual energy, 46
spiritual leaders, 170
spiritual values, 223
Spokane, 78
Squaxin Island, 131, 373
St. Regis Mohawk Tribe, 176t
Stalin, Joseph, 162
stalking, 317–19
Stamp Act of 1765, 86
Stand Watie, 102
Standing Rock Reservation, 182t
Standing Rock Sioux, 74, 76–77, 80t, 287, 294, 305, 335–36
    DAPL and, 287–89
Standing Rock Sioux Tribe, Dakota Access v., 288–89
Starbard, Robert, 358
Stark, Heidi K., 7
starvation, 330
state constitutions, 159
state government
    altering Indigenous diplomatic affairs, 152
    amendments and, 337–38
    balance and, 159
    communication networks and, 337
    consultation and, 376, 379
    COVID-19 and, 2, 4–5
    diplomatic accords and, 299
    Indigenous, 84
    leadership and, 199, 206, 207, 212
    marijuana and, 291
    Native nations, federal, and, 20–30, 367, 368
    oil industry and, 348
    Pueblo and, 56
    recognition of Indigenous communities by, 161
    taxes and, 260–61, 262–63, 268, 270
    treaty federalism and, 117
state law, defined, 161
state lotteries, 267
State of Frankland, 89
State of Muscogee, 82t, 90–91
State of Sequoyah, 82t, 112, 114, 120–21, 298–99
State of the Native Nations, The (Evans), 7, 235
statehood, 58, 60
states, 153
stereotypes, 53
Sterritt, Neil, 10–11
Stewart, John, 85
Stewart, William, 67
Stillaguamish Tribe, 179, 181, 182t
Stilliguamish, 227
Stockbridge-Munsee Tribe, 327

Stoeckl, Edward de, 343–44
Strickland, Rennard, 5–6, 61, 113, 120, 326
Strong, Duncan, 141–42
Strong, Pauline, 29–30
Structuring Sovereignty: Constitutions of Native Nations (Tatum, Jorgensen, Guss, Deer), 6–7
Stubben, Jerry D., 7
sub-chiefs, 76, 78
subchiefships, 37
subordinate, 38
subsistence, defined, 351–52
substance abuse, 327
substance abuse counselor, 327
Sucker Creek, 305–6
Suiattle, 181, 182t
Sullivan, Patrick, 9, 11
Summer (Hajeb), 35–36
Summit Lake Paiute, 164
Summit Midstream Partners, LLC, 287
Sun Dance, 314
superintendent
    authority to call meeting, 131
    Circular No. 3010 to, 127
    constitution and bylaws and, 132
    Crow, 135
    governing body and, 130–31
    hereditary chiefs and, 140–41
    Indigenous state and, 85, 108–9
    issues handled and, 132, 133
    issues handled by committees or councils and, 135
    meetings and, 131
    Native political transitions and, 71–79
    organization on reservation and, 128–29
    political affairs and, 137–38
    responding to Circular No. 3010, 128
    tribal organization and, 133, 135
    tribal organization weaknesses and, 135–37
    voting and, 140
    women, 139–40
Superintendent of Indian Affairs, 108–9
superior, 38
superiority, 51
Supremacy Clause, 206
Supreme Court
    Alaska, 350
    Alaska Natives and, 346, 361–62
    authority and, 54
    Cherokee, 232
    denial of treaty rights, 54
    Hawaiian Natives and, 362–63
    justice and, 317–19

leadership and, 213, 214–16, 217, 218, 220–21
Minnesota, 289–90
Navajo Nation, 217, 326
political economics and, 256, 276, 278, 286, 288–90
Pueblo and, 58
Sac and Fox, 213
U.S. (*see* U.S. Supreme Court)
Suquamish Tribe, 228
Susanville Indian Rancheria, 182*t*
Sutton, 11
Swenson, Thomas, 351
Swinomish, 80*t*, 130, 136, 138, 179, 182*t*
Swinomish Indian Tribal Community, 264
Swinomish Indians of the Swinomish Reservation, 182*t*
Sycuan Band of Kumeyaay, 335
Sycuan Band of Mission Indians, 164

Table Mountain Rancheria, 182*t*
Taliban, 330, 331
TallBear, Kim, 228
Talton v. Mayes, 50
Talwa, defined, 62
tankers, 308
Taos Pueblo, 57, 75, 114–15, 167*t*, 169
tariffs, 260–61
tar sands, 281–82, 307–8
Tasiget tuviwarai, 182*t*
Tatum, Melissa L., 6–7, 175, 234
Tawakonie, 182*t*
tax agreements, 266
taxation, 25, 260–67, 286, 348
taxation clause, 346–47
tax codes, 263–64
tax commissions, 263–64
taxes, 134–35, 153, 157–58, 173, 239, 260–62, 263–64, 266, 270, 274–75, 286, 346–47
tax revenue, 268, 292, 294
tax revenue collections, 265*t*
Taylor, J. B., 9, 10–11
Tazlina Village, 163
Te Runanga O Ngati Qwa Tribe, 305–6
teachers, 91, 156
technology, 23, 331–32, 336–37, 368
Tecumseh, (Chief), 41, 82*t*, 88, 121, 298–99
"Tee-cha-meengsh-meesin-with na-me aw-wa-ta-man-wit," 31
Teehee, Kimberly, 98
Tee-Hit- Ton v. United States, 346, 347
telescope, 363, 364–65
television, 253, 330, 334–35

television ads, 120
television stations, 331–32, 335
Teller, Henry M., 314
Temporary Assistance for Needy Families, 157
temporary housing, 370–71
Tennessee Valley Authority, 145, 157
Tenskwatawa (Shawnee Prophet), 298–99
tenure, 74–75, 129, 130, 180, 190, 191, 193, 197–98, 236–37, 322
termination, 121, 229–30, 235
termination era, 114
termination policies, 114–15, 228, 332, 378
termination program, 280
territorial government, 82*t*, 84, 103–4, 108–9
territorial rights, 92, 118, 122, 275–76
territory, as political idea, 81
Tesuque Pueblo, 75, 167*t*
Teton Hunkpapa, 185–86
Tewa, 56
TGCs. *See* Traditional Governing Councils (TGCs)
theocracy, defined, 162, 166
theory of an irreducible minimum, 35
Thirty Meter Telescope, 363, 364–65
Thom, Laurie, 292
Thomas, Clarence, 29, 271, 279, 371–72
Thornton, Russell, 120
Throckmorton, J. W., 105
Thunderbird Project, 285
Tibbet, Jonathan, 138–39
Tigua Tribe, 170. *See also* Ysleta de Sur Pueblo
TikTok, 335
Tilden, Mark C., 250
Tillett v. Lujan, 212
timber, 282–83
timber harvesting, 351–52
Timbisha, 182*t*
Timbisha Shoshone Tribe, 319
Tkwakwamish, 182*t*
Tlingit, 35, 36
Tlingit and Haida Central Council, 354. *See also* Central Council of the Tlingit and Haida
Tlingit and Haida Indian Tribes, 182*t*, 204–5, 342, 350, 356
Tlingit and Haida Indians v. U.S., 356
T.O. *See* Tohono O'odham (T.O.)
tobacco, 260–61, 266
tobacco products tax, 263–64
TOC. *See* Tribal Organization Committee (TOC)
Tocqueville, Alexis de, 52
Tohono O'odham (T.O.), 45–46, 176*t*, 307
Tohono O'odham (T.O.) 1986 Constitution, 294

488 INDEX

Tolowa, 182t
Tonawanda Band of Seneca, 167t, 170
Tongass National Forest, 351–52
Tonkawa, 132, 135, 136
totalitarian regimes, 337
Towers, Lem A., 75
town governments, 62
townships, 20
toxic substances and safety, 286–87
trade and commerce, 306
Trade and Intercourse Act, 95–96
Trade and Intercourse laws, 95–96
traders, 37–38, 63, 85, 229, 343
Traditional Constitutions, 163
Traditional Councils, 172t, 176t
Traditional Governing Councils (TGCs), 354–55
"traditionalist," 373
traditions
    ancestral, 312
    Cohen and, 148
    cultural, 38, 55, 124, 170, 282–83, 311
    customs and, 59, 166–71, 167t, 210, 217, 305–
        6, 326, 354, 355
    governmental, 51
    historic, 290–91
    identity and, 223
    kinship, 298
    leadership, 193
    legal, 51
    lost, 148
    oral, 301, 331–32, 334
    oral histories and, 300
    political, 143, 192
    protecting, 349
    Pueblo, 57
    religious, 46, 233–34
    social, 143
    Western, 329
    White Christian influence and, 59
traffic, 312
traffic deaths, 286
Trahant, Mark, 333, 339
Trail of Broken Treaties, 114
Trail of Tears, 97
TransCanada's Energy East, 308
TransCanada's Keystone XL, 308
transparency, 10–11, 14
treasurer, 77, 129, 169, 215, 216–17
Treasury Department, 270
Treasury Secretary, 2, 267
treaties
    agreements and, 53, 234–35, 274–75, 278,
        295, 299, 301

colonial, 300
of Confederate-aligned nations, 102
consent and, 375–76
from 1872-1911, 301
end of, 104
with foreign nations, 298
to form indigenous state, 94, 95, 102, 104, 106
for Great Lakes Tribes, 302
international, 297
for international diplomacy, 297–98, 299,
    300, 301, 302, 304–5, 306, 311
Kānaka Maoli and, 359
leadership and, 196
Native governments and, 368–69
Native political transitions and, 52, 54–55,
    63–65, 66–67
number ratified by U.S. government, 376
with other Native nations, 298
political economics and, 274, 277–78,
    296, 342
removal, 94, 95, 111
water protection, 304–5
treaties paradigm, 24, 52, 54–55
Treaty Alliance Against Tar Sands
    Expansion, 307–8
Treaty Clause, 206
Treaty Council, 115, 141
treaty era, 298
treaty federalism, 117
treaty-making
    centuries of, 299
    leading scholar on, 297
    termination of, 297
Treaty of Dancing Rabbit Creek, 94–95
Treaty of Doak's Stand, 95
Treaty of 1867, 343–44
Treaty of Fort Pitt, 81–84, 92
Treaty of Ghent, 88
Treaty of Guadalupe Hidalgo, 62–63
Treaty of Hopewell, 93
Treaty of New Echota, 94–95, 97
Treaty of Paris, 85–86
Treaty of 1783, 86
treaty paradigm, 53–55
treaty provisions, 106, 154, 261, 298, 321, 377
treaty rights, 21, 109, 138, 232–33, 290, 378
Treaty with the Six Nations, 66
Tribal Administrator, 215–16, 355
Tribal and First Nation Joint Commission, 305
Tribal and First Nations Great Lakes Water
    Accord, 304
Tribal Assembly, 172t
Tribal Caucus, 118

INDEX 489

Tribal Chair, 166–68, 173–74, 176*t*
Tribal Chairman, 70–71, 193, 216
Tribal chairman, 70–71, 193, 216
Tribal Chairperson, 172*t*
tribal codes, 164, 217
Tribal Council
  Alaska Natives and, 358
  duty of, 23
  elected, 23
  General Council and, 229
  governing systems and, 165, 169, 170, 171–73, 172*t*, 174, 186
  Howard on, 6–7
  international diplomacy and, 303, 304
  justice and, 322
  leadership and, 220–21
  media and, 339
  modern Native constitutionalism and, 128–29, 133
  Native political transitions and, 61, 64, 73–74, 76
  Navajo Nation, 117
  Penobscot Nation, 176*t*
  political economics and, 262, 283–84
Tribal Council arrangements, 23
Tribal court structures, 358
Tribal court systems, 318*f*, 329
Tribal courts. *See also* Native courts
  bias and, 371–72
  Curtis Act and, 105–6
  establishing, 173
  growth and diversification of, 317
  Leech Lake Band, 327
  as paradoxical concept, 312
  power of, 321
  women and, 317–19, 325, 370–71
Tribal Executive Board, 186
Tribal Government Today: Politics on Montana Indian Reservations (Lopach, Brown, Clow), 6
Tribal Governments Today (Lopach, Brown, Clow), 27
Tribal Grievance Committee, Young v., 213–15
Tribal House Caucus, 118
Tribal identity, 223, 371. *See also* Native identity
Tribal Judicial Systems, 5–6
Tribal Law and Order Act of 2010, 328–29
Tribal meetings, 131
Tribal nationalism, 21
"Tribal Nations and the US: An Introduction" (NCAI), 154
tribal officials, 199
tribal organization

blood quantum issues of, 136
confidence, 136
conflict, 135
education, 136
emotional members of, 136
ethnic groups, 136
factionalism, 135
funding, 136
jealousies and selfishness, 136
lacks legal status and authority, 135
leadership, 136
life-tenure, 136
liquor of, 136
meeting times of, 136
members appointed or elected for, 136
off-reservation members of, 136
physical space of, 136
political experience of leaders, 136
population, 136
size of, 136
trivial and personal matters of, 136
Tribal Organization Committee (TOC), 141–43, 146
Tribal resolution, 166–68
Tribal Senate Caucus, 118
Tribal-State compacts, 299
Tribal-State relations, 266
Tribal-State Tax Agreements, 266–67
tribes, defined, 125
Trimble, Charles, 117
Trump, Donald, 157–58, 160, 280–81, 286–87, 288, 309, 310, 364
Trump Administration, 270, 280–81, 310
Trumpism, 157–58
trust, defined, 277
trust doctrine, 277, 278
trust lands, 261, 276–77, 279, 373
Tsimshian Native community, 357
Tubatulabal, 182*t*
Tu-gu, 44
Tulalip Tribes, 2–3, 76, 179, 181, 182*t*, 292, 335
Tule River, 135, 136, 137–38, 139
Tule River Indian Tribe of the Tule River Reservation, 182*t*
Tunica, 182*t*
Tunica-Biloxi Indian Tribe, 182*t*
Tuolumne Band of Me-Wuk Indians, 182*t*
Turner, Dale, 189–90
Turner, Frederick Jackson, 66, 85
Turtle Mountain, 131, 137–38
Turtle Mountain Ojibwe, 136
Tuscarora Nation, 167*t*, 189, 298
Twana, 182*t*

490 INDEX

Twenty-Nine Palms Band of Mission Indians, 164
2020 presidential election, 158
Twitter, 330, 335
Two Spirit, 39, 40
Two Spirit people, 370–71
2004 Out-of-State Accord, 378
2007 United Nations Declaration on the Rights of Indigenous Peoples, 377

Uintah, 80t
Uintah and Ouray Reservation, 206
Uintah Ouray, 135, 139, 140–41
ULIN Treaty. See United League of Indigenous Nations (ULIN) Treaty
Umatilla, 182t
Umatilla Reservation, 181
unemployment, 22, 327, 360
unemployment rate, 256–57
Union Agency, 105
Union of Indian Nations, 116
United League of Indigenous Nations (ULIN) Treaty, 305–6
United Nations, 122
United States, Denezpi v., 316
United States, Tee-Hit-Ton v., 346, 347
United States, Winters v., 187
United States v. Clapox, 314
United States v. Joseph, 57
United States v. Sandoval, 58
United Tribes of Michigan, 221
Universal Service Fund, 336–37
Unrau, William, 106
Upham, Steadman, 36
Upper Puyallup, 182t
Upper Skagit, 182t
uranium, 282–83, 284
uranium reserves, 285
Urban life, Native identity and, 235–37
U.S. Bill of Rights, 55, 114, 159, 317, 337, 338
U.S. Census data, 352–53
U.S. Commission on Civil Rights (USCCR), 21–22, 236, 256, 281
U.S. Constitution, 25–26, 29, 53, 55, 62, 82t, 117, 118, 157, 160, 175, 178, 200, 202, 203, 204–6, 209–10, 231–32, 234–35, 277, 316, 321, 333–34, 337, 368–69
U.S. economy, 270, 273
U.S. Fish and Wildlife Service, 309, 310
U.S. Indian Inspector, 376
U.S., Jicarilla Apache v., 278–79
U.S. Louisiana Purchase, 93–94
U.S. Supreme Court

abortion and, 370–71
Alaska Natives and, 342, 348–49, 352, 358, 361
CARES Act and, 3, 4
justice and, 316, 321, 328–29
political economics and, 263, 264, 270–71, 288–89
Pueblo and, 57
sovereignty and, 50
U.S., Tlingit and Haida Indians v., 356
U.S. v. Bryant, 328–29
U.S. v. Kagama, 375
U.S. v. Wheeler, 26
USCCR. See U.S. Commission on Civil Rights (USCCR)
Ute, 301–2
Ute Bulletin, 332
Ute Indian Tribe of the Uintah and Ouray Reservation, 182t, 271
Ute Mountain Ute, 301
Ute Mountain Ute Reservation, 316
Ute Tribe, 206, 316
utilities, 256–57
Utility Business Activity Tax Code, 264

vacancies, 73, 132, 164–65
vaccinations, 1
vaccine distribution, 3
Van Winkle, Barrik, 29–30
Vann, Marilyn, 232
Vaughan, Alden T., 38
Vega, Danae Hamilton, 166–68
Vice-Chair, 176t
Vice-Chairman, 117, 129, 168, 186, 215
vice-chairperson, 169
Vice-Chief, 176t
Vice-German, 164–65
vice-president, 66, 77, 105–6, 363–64
Viejas Band, 167t, 169
village councils, 164, 172t
Village of Platinum, 354
village representatives, 176t
villages, 2–3, 33–34, 43–44, 45, 61, 160–61, 176t, 181, 182t, 276–77, 317–19, 334, 342, 343, 345–46, 348–49, 353–54, 355
violence, 22, 40, 115–16, 191–92, 289, 291–92, 317–19, 325, 327, 328–29, 358, 370–71, 372–73
Violence Against Native Women Act Reauthorization, 317–19
violent offenses, 325
Vizenor, Erma, 186–87, 196–98, 235
Vizenor, Gerald, 6–7, 186, 198

INDEX   491

Voluck, David A., 344, 353, 354, 357–58
voter suppression efforts, 160
voting, 140, 159, 169, 198, 239–40, 243–44, 317
voting behavior, 238
voting choices, 254
voting rights, 118–19, 180, 344
voting slant, 149

Waban, 59
Waco, 182t
Wade, Roe v., 370–71
wage gap, 256–57
wage rates, 157–58
Wahee, John, 364
Wahpeton, 185–86
Wahwassuck, Korey, 327
Wailaki, 182t
Walker, Bill, 349–50
Walker, Francis, 344
Walker River Agency, 79
Walkingstick, David, 253
Walla Walla, 182t
Wampanoag, 59
Wampanoag Tribe of Gay Head
    (Aquinaah), 251
wampum belts, 300
Wanapam, 182t
Wappo, 182t
War Captains, 56, 170
War-Chief, 42, 169, 170
War Chief complex, 191–92
War Department, 51–52, 63–64, 91
war leader, 33–34, 42–43
War Naataanii, 42–43
War of 1812, 88
Warm Springs Reservation, 181
Warm Springs Tribe, 31, 32, 76, 80t
Warner, Linda Sue, 193
Warren, Elizabeth, 270
Warrior Societies, 312–13
warriors, 39, 48, 66, 85
wars, 65, 67, 157–58, 208
War Ways, 42–43
Waséyabek Development Co., LLC, 273
Washburn, Kevin, 349
Washington Post, 270
Washoe, 181, 182t
Wassaja, 332–33
Watauga Association, 89
water, 173, 187, 195, 256–57, 258, 264, 272,
    273–74, 278, 281–83, 284–85, 287, 305,
    306, 346–47, 359
water developments, 124

water matters, 23
water pollution regulations, 286–87
water projects, 268–69
water protection treaties, 304–5
water quality, 367–68
water resources, 284–85
water rights, 124–25, 138–39, 303–4
Watergate scandal, 252
Waters, Maxine, 232
water systems, 264
Watie, Buck, 97
Watie, Charles, 332
websites, 337
Wellness courts, 327
Welpley, 144
Wenatchi, 182t
Western expansion, 62–65, 67. *See also*
    American expansion; Euro-American
    expansion
Western Mono, 182t
Western Navajo, 76
Western Navajo Agency, 77
Western Shoshone, 76, 182t
Western Territory Bill, 95–97
Western traditions, 329
Westmoreland Coal Company, 285–86
wetlands, 290
We Wai Kai Nation, 305–6
whales, 368–69
Wheeler, U.S. v., 26
Wheeler-Howard Act, 124, 138–39. *See also*
    Indian Reorganization Act (IRA) of 1934
White, Jeffrey, 310
White Americans, 256–57
white ascendancy, defined, 61
White Christian nationalism, 369
white colonists, 89
White Earth Band, 130–31, 186, 198, 289
White Earth Band of Anishinaabe, 282, 287, 292
White Earth Nation, 196, 197, 198
*White Earth Nation: Ratification of a Native
    Democratic Constitution, The* (Vizenor and
    Doerfler), 6–7
White Earth Reservation, 186
white encroachment, 90
White Mountain Apache, 76, 129–30, 135, 137–
    38, 140–41, 226, 335
White Mountain Apache Tribe
    Constitution, 247
white people, death rate of, 1
white reform groups, 79–80
White River Valley Tribes, 182t
white settlers, 59, 89, 111, 274

492 INDEX

white supremacists, 119–20
Whitener, Ron, 373
whites, 58, 90, 111, 112, 119, 229, 313–14
Wichita, 80t, 106–7, 182t
Wichita and Affiliated Tribes, 182t
wild rice, 282, 290
Wilkins, David E., 6, 7, 93, 204
Williams, Robert, 23
Williams, Susan M., 262–63
Wilmer, Frankie, 257
Wilson, Blind v., 216–17
Wilton Rancheria, 175–78, 176t, 180
wind energy, 283, 293, 294
wind power, 293–95
Wind River Inter-Tribal Council, 166, 185
Wind River Reservation, 69, 166, 182t
Winnebago, 76–77, 80t, 266, 294
Winnemucca Indian Colony, 182t, 292
Winter (Kwaereh), 35–36
Winters v. United States, 187
Wintu, 182t
Wintun, 182t
Wisconsin Winnebago Nation, 212
Wishram, 182t
Wiyot, 182t
Wiyot Tribe, 233
Woehlke, Walter, 141–42, 144
Wolf moiety, 35
wolf population, 281–82
Wolf Treaty, 310
wolves, 296, 310
women
    adultery and, 40
    assimilation of, 65
    Cherokee and, 60–61
    in early-twentieth-century government, 78
    Indigenous, 370–71
    land and, 40
    as leaders, 39, 40, 129
    Missing and Murdered Indigenous,
        325, 370–71
    Naataanii and, 43
    Native, 21, 286, 317–19, 325, 371
    Native constitutionalism and, 139–40
    Potawatomi, 68
    rights of, 52
    roles of, 39
    status of, 39

Taliban and, 330
    violence against, 40
Worcester v. Georgia, 53
World War I, 185–86
World War II, 332
Wounded Knee, 114
written constitutions, 13, 60, 76–77
written language, 61
Wukchumnis, 182t
Wyandotte, 80t, 108, 171
Wyandotte Nation, 262
Wyckoff, Theodore, 117

Yahooskin, 182t
Yakama, 182t
Yakama Nation, 181, 182t, 378
Yakima, 76
Yana, 182t
Yanktonais, 185–86
Yankton Sioux, 76–77, 80t, 136, 206
Yavapai-Apache, 176t, 182t
Yavapai-Apache Tribe Constitution, 245–46
Yavapai-Prescott Community, 164
Yazzie, Robert D., 328
Yellen v. Confederated Tribes of the Chehalis
    Reservation, 4, 270–71, 342, 352
Yilalkoamish, 182t
Yokut, 182t
Young, Dora S., 213
Young (Chief), 214
Young v. Tribal Grievance Committee, 213–15
YouTube, 335
Yowlumne, 182t
Ysleta de Sur Pueblo, 167t, 169, 170
Yuhaaviatam of San Manuel Nation, 165, 368
Yuki, 182t
Yupik, 43–44, 45, 342, 343
Yupik Village of Bill Moore's Slough, 180
Yurok, 182t, 282, 292

Zah, Peterson, 82t, 339
Zelenskyy, Volodymyr, 330
Zia Pueblo, 75, 167t
Zinke, Ryan, 309
Zion, James, 325, 326, 328
zone, as political idea, 81
zoning, 312
Zuni Tribe, 176t

The manufacturer's authorised representative in the EU for product safety is Oxford
University Press España S.A. of El Parque Empresarial San Fernando de Henares,
Avenida de Castilla, 2 – 28830 Madrid (www.oup.es/en or product.safety@oup.com).
OUP España S.A. also acts as importer into Spain of products made by the manufacturer.

Printed in the USA/Agawam, MA
August 8, 2025

891696.008